Labour Law in the USA

Labour Law in the USA

Fifth Edition

Alvin L. Goldman
Roberto L. Corrada

This book was originally published as a monograph in the International Encyclopaedia of Laws/Labour Law and Industrial Relations.

Founding Editor: Roger Blanpain
General Editor: Frank Hendrickx
Volume Editor: Frank Hendrickx

Wolters Kluwer

Published by:
Kluwer Law International B.V.
PO Box 316
2400 AH Alphen aan den Rijn
The Netherlands
E-mail: international-sales@wolterskluwer.com
Website: lrus.wolterskluwer.com

Sold and distributed in North, Central and South America by:
Wolters Kluwer Legal & Regulatory U.S.
7201 McKinney Circle
Frederick, MD 21704
United States of America
Email: customer.service@wolterskluwer.com

Sold and distributed in all other countries by:
Air Business Subscriptions
Rockwood House
Haywards Heath
West Sussex
RH16 3DH
United Kingdom
Email: international-customerservice@wolterskluwer.com

Printed on acid-free paper

ISBN 978-94-035-0013-3

e-Book: ISBN 978-94-035-0014-0
web-PDF: ISBN 978-94-035-0015-7

Printed in the United Kingdom.

The Authors

Alvin L. Goldman received his AB from Columbia University in 1959 and his LLB from New York University in 1962. After practicing law in New York City, specializing in labor relations, he began full-time teaching at the University of Kentucky in 1965 and was granted emeritus status in 2008.

Prof. Goldman served as Professor in Residence to National Labor Relations Board Member Sam Zagoria during the 1967–68 academic year, was a visiting scholar at the Institute for Labor Law, Catholic University, Leuven, Belgium, in 1973, and was Visiting Professor at the School of Law, University of California-Davis, in the 1976–1977 academic year. In addition, he is a labor arbitrator.

Professor Goldman is a member and a former Chair of the Labor Law Group Trust for which he prepared *Processes for Conflict Resolution* (BNA 1972) and coauthored *Legislation Protecting the Individual Employee* (BNA 1982 with R. Covington), and *Legal Protection for the Individual Employee* (West 1989, 1996, 2002 with M. Finkin, C. Summers and K. Dau-Schmidt). He also authored *Settling for More: Mastering Negotiating Strategies and Techniques* (BNA 1991) and *The Supreme Court and Labor–Management Relations Law* (D.C. Heath 1976), coauthored *Negotiation: Theory and Practice* (Kluwer Law International, 2003 with J. Rojot), and has written chapters for several books including *Comparative Labour Law and Industrial Relations in Industrialized Market Economies* (Kluwer). He is US co-reporter for *International Labour Law Reports* (Martinus Nijhoff) and is past Chair of the US Branch, International Society for Labor Law and Social Security.

Roberto L. Corrada, co-author of the last full edition, is Professor of Law and Mulligan Burleson Chair in Modern Learning at the University of Denver Sturm College of Law, where he teaches employment and labor law, contracts, administrative law, and race and the law. He is author of articles in the field of labor, civil rights, and employment discrimination law, particularly in the areas of religious discrimination and employment arbitration. Professor Corrada has published articles in numerous law reviews, including the *Wake Forest* and *Villanova Law Reviews,* and the *University of Cincinnati, Houston, Denver*, and *Miami Law Reviews*, the *La Raza Law Review*, the *Journal of Legal Education,* and the *Berkeley Journal of Employment and Labor Law*. He is a member of the Labor Law Group and has casebooks in *Employment Discrimination Law* and *Labor Law*, in addition to a casebook in *Administrative Law*.

Prior to joining the law faculty, Professor Corrada was a labor attorney with the Washington, DC office of Akin, Gump, Strauss, Hauer & Feld where he worked on matters involving Continental Air Lines, Burlington & Northern Railroad, Purolator Courier, GTE, and Albertson's, among others. Professor Corrada has served in a variety of administrative roles, including as Associate Dean of the University of Denver College of Law (2005), chair of the board of the ACLU of Colorado (1998) and chair of the Association of American Law Schools' Section on Labor and Employment Law (2002).

Professor Corrada was named Mulligan Burleson Chair in Modern Learning in 2013. Professor Corrada has won various additional honors and awards, including the University of Denver Law Stars Award (2009), the University of Denver Legal Research Professorship (2008–09), the University Distinguished Teaching Award (2006), the University of Denver Donald & Susan Sturm Professorship for Excellence in Teaching (2003–2005), the Edward Sherman Award (presented by the American Civil Liberties Union of Colorado to the Outstanding Cooperating Attorney of the Year, in 1997), the Colorado Hispanic Bar Association Community Service Award (1997), and the University of Denver College of Law Hughes Research Professorship (1996). Professor Corrada graduated from the Catholic University of America Columbus School of Law in 1985, where he served as editor-in-chief of the law review.

Table of Contents

Table of Contents

List of Abbreviations

ADEA	Age Discrimination in Employment Act
ADA	Americans with Disabilities Act
AFL	American Federation of Labor
AFL–CIO	American Federation of Labor–Congress of Industrial Organizations
ALJ	administrative law judge
BFOQ	bona fide occupational qualification
BLS	Bureau of Labor Statistics
CIO	Congress of Industrial Organizations
COBRA	Consolidated Omnibus Budget Reconciliation Act (important amended portions of ERISA)
Code Fed. Reg.	Code of Federal Regulations (also CFR)
DOL	Department of Labor
EEOC	Equal Employment Opportunity Commission
ERISA	Employee Retirement Income Security Act
ESOP	employee stock ownership plan
FELA	Federal Employers' Liability Act
FLRA	Federal Labor Relations Authority
FLSA	Fair Labor Standards Act
FMCS	Federal Mediation and Conciliation Service
FMLA	Family and Medical Leave Act
HIPPA	Health Insurance Portability and Accountability Act
HMO	Health Maintenance Organization
ILO	International Labor Office/Organization
IRA	individual retirement account
IRCA	Immigration Reform and Control Act
LMRA	Labor Management Relations Act (Taft–Hartley Act)

List of Abbreviations

LMRDA	Labor Management Reporting and Disclosure Act (Landrum– Griffin Act)
LSHWCA	Longshoremen's and Harbor Workers' Compensation Act
MNSHA	Mine Safety and Health Act
NIRA	National Industrial Recovery Act
NLRA	National Labor Relations Act (Wagner Act)
NLRB	National Labor Relations Board
NMB	National Mediation Board
NRAB	National Railroad Adjustment Board
OFCCP	Office of Federal Contract Compliance Programs
OPM	Office of Personnel Management
OSHA	Occupational Safety and Health Act or Occupational Safety and Health Administration
OSHRC	Occupational and Safety and Health Review Commission
PAC	political action committee
PBGC	Pension Benefit Guaranty Corporation
PHI	protected health information
PPO	preferred provider organization
RICO	Racketeer Influenced and Corrupt Organizations Act
RLA	Railway Labor Act
SOX	Sarbanes–Oxley Act
US Code	United States Code (also USC)
WARN	Worker Adjustment and Retraining Notification Act (Plant Closing Act)

General Introduction

Chapter 1. General Observations

1. Labor[1] and employment law in the United States of America differs in many significant ways from its counterparts in other industrially developed nations. For example, unlike most other labor and employment law systems, although subject to some later discussed exceptions, employment in the US is presumed to be an 'at will' arrangement in which the worker can quit for any reason at any time, or the employer can dismiss the worker for any reason at any time, without any resulting liability.

Also, to a much greater extent than most other labor relations systems, in the US if employees have a recognized collective bargaining agent, the terms and conditions of employment are established with considerable specificity by collective bargaining (most often conducted at the plant or enterprise level). As a result, collectively bargained agreements in the United States are long, detailed documents encompassing almost every aspect of labor–management relations; they are more detailed and comprehensive than collective agreements generally found in other systems. Additionally, the contractual rights of union represented workers normally are protected through enforcement of the collective agreement, not through enforcement of the individual employment contract.

Another, and related, special characteristic of labor–management relations in the US is the separate body of quasi-legal rules that have been developed through a private system of grievance arbitration established by collective bargaining. These rules constitute a formal recognition of normal labor-management practices, the customs of the particular work place ('law of the shop'), and the special characteristics of the collective bargaining process as important reference points for interpreting collective agreements.

Still another special characteristic of American labor relations is that unionized American workers are represented by a single union selected by majority choice. The selected union is the sole representative of all workers in the bargaining unit, regardless of whether they are members of the union (this is known as the 'exclusivity principle').[2] On the other hand, no bargaining representative is present in the

1. This work uses American spelling conventions.
2. Prof. Charles Morris, joined by some other scholars argues that in the absence of a majority representative, members-only collective bargaining is both lawful and required under the National Labor Relations Act (NLRA). *See The Blue Eagle at Work*, ILR Press (2005). One of the co-authors of this monograph joined in a statement supporting that thesis, the other rejects it.

vast majority of employing units in the United States. Thus, one might say that where present, union representation is more intrusive and inclusive in the United States than in most other industrial nations, but, overall, collective representation plays a smaller role in the United States than it does in most other advanced economies.

An additional special characteristic of labor relations in the US is the fact that American unions rely upon political action to achieve their goals less often than do their counterparts in most other advanced economies. Similarly, although the government supervises and assists the collective bargaining process, it rarely intrudes into the actual adjustment of the parties' respective interests resolved through collective bargaining. In contrast, to a greater extent than in other nations with a freely elected representative political system, American labor law imposes rules upon the conduct of internal union affairs so as to ensure democratic processes and to protect against abuses of trust.

Perhaps most unique to labor relations in the United States is the very active role lawyers play throughout the labor–management and employment relations system. Lawyers constantly provide guidance for managers and union representatives respecting the bureaucratic mazes through which the laws are administered, staff the government agencies that regulate employment relations, represent the parties in the frequently used public and private adjudicative processes, and assist in the policy planning and execution of contract negotiations, writing and interpretation. As a result, popular mystique has evolved that regards the labor lawyer as an almost magical master of the arts of conflict creation and conflict resolution.

2. American labor law undoubtedly owes its unique characteristics to its historical experience which combined industrial development with territorial expansion and conquest that almost annihilated the indigenous population and was accomplished by the partial blending of culturally diverse peoples arriving in large waves of immigration. Extraordinary upward social, economic and political mobility, the initial dependence on and later destruction of a caste-based slave system, and the widespread adoption of the ideals of individual liberty and of the virtues of free market competition were additional key aspects of that historical experience.

Despite the general prosperity enjoyed in the United States, until recent decades large portions of the working population lived in poverty. Historically, efforts to modify the distribution of wealth and broaden the distribution of economic power in the United States concentrated on marshaling economic power and negotiating any adjustments between the respective interest groups. Often, however, the economic power of employers overwhelmed that of workers and commonly was used to prevent workers from maximizing their bargaining strength by preventing them from engaging in concerted activity.

A turning point came in the mid-1930s when the nation was in the midst of the Great Depression. Government intervention in the form of laws designed to facilitate the collectivization of worker bargaining power, and to compel employers to bargain in good faith, enabled the representatives of labor, through the process of collective bargaining, to achieve dramatic economic and social gains. Those gains generated considerable political confidence in the viability of the collective bargaining system, a confidence that began to decline in the 1980s, however, with the severe reduction in the portion of the workforce that is union represented.

The 1930s also was a time of adoption of fundamental worker protective legislation such as minimum wage and overtime pay laws, workers' compensation laws, child labor laws, and retirement security insurance laws; laws similar to legislation that largely had been adopted one to three decades earlier by most other industrial nations.

3. Today, the American economy is largely a management led system with a moderate degree of governmental oversight. Labor–management relations law in the United States continues to emphasize private dispute resolution and adjustment of interests between the representatives of collectivized capital (management) and the representatives of those employed to make that capital productive (labor organizations). Reliance on private dispute resolution mechanisms has expanded into a significant portion of individual employment arrangements as a result of widespread employer imposition of arbitration provisions for resolution of all disputes arising out of employment contracts.

Where the parties engage in collective bargaining, on both sides the representatives are chosen by a scheme of majority rule[3] and have the exclusive authority to represent their respective interest groups. However, most American workers remain unorganized and only a few segments are predominantly organized. Although the size of the strata of greatly disadvantaged workers has shrunken considerably since the 1930s, many still are impoverished. In addition, large numbers of persons are unemployed or unemployable and have no legal access to many of the necessities or basic amenities that Americans regard as constituting the minimum standard for decent living. Moreover, the perception of what one needs to live a healthy, comfortable life and attain recognized status in the community has expanded with increased prosperity for the wealthier third of the population, mass media merchandising of new and more luxurious sources of physical gratification, and the development of additional material symbols of achievement. Public welfare programs and some private welfare funds meet the basic material needs of most people who are on the low end of the economic fringes. Nevertheless, since the early 1980s there has been little if any reduction in the number of those whose needs are not met, while at the same time welfare programs for the poor have been significantly curtailed. Moreover, as a result of the Great Recession that began in 2007, there was marked growth in the number of impoverished and near impoverished Americans.

Many impoverished, but far from all, Americans improve their income by engaging in criminal activities or employment in the underground economy. Some mitigate their needs through illegal manipulation of welfare benefits programs. People dependent on such income sources constitute a stigmatized and alienated subculture whose children have great difficulty adjusting to and joining the social structures

---

3. On the management side, theoretically the majority is determined by the portion of total ownership (most often, shares of corporate stock); on the union side it is determined by the portion of total participants. Observers long have recognized that in widely owned enterprises, actual control resides with the top members of management or with one or a small group of shareholders.

that dominate the American economy. The persistence and growth of such economic dislocation is aggravated by the fact that a few ethnic minorities are over-represented among this segment of the population, creating an almost de facto quasi-caste system.

Some argue that to a large degree collective bargaining is responsible for the inequities, inefficiencies, and structural dislocations that continue to frustrate America's achievement of its widely shared ideals. On one side of the political spectrum are those critics who would displace the present labor–management relations system with more comprehensive government programs of resource management, wealth distribution and social and cultural improvement. On the other side of the spectrum are those who would displace collective bargaining with a wholly free market for labor and would rely upon the individual employee to self-select more lucrative employment opportunities and private insurance contracts so as to provide personal financial security – if any is desired.

Nevertheless, political power in the United States belongs to the vast group in the middle. Although this group, too, finds fault with the economic and social consequences of the system of labor–management relations in the United States, it is a relatively mild discontent that seldom alters the results of political elections. In recent decades, concerns respecting inadequacies of labor and employment laws, standards, and practices have been neither sufficiently intense nor widespread to promote or support sharp departures from the status quo. Accordingly, to study existing employment and labor–management relations law in the United States is to gain an understanding of procedures and principles that are likely to characterize American labor and employment law and practices for a considerable time to come.

Chapter 2. General Background

§1. Geography

I. Size

4. When the United States of America declared its independence from the British crown on 4 July 1776, it was a collection of 13 states occupying the central portion of the eastern coastal region of the North American continent. It expanded north, south and west to the point where it now occupies all of the central portion of the continent plus the large northwestern corner of the continent (Alaska) and a chain of islands in the central Pacific Ocean (Hawaii). In addition, it has territorial or trusteeship jurisdiction over an assortment of islands in the Caribbean Sea and in the Pacific Ocean. Finally, by treaty, executive agreement, or international trusteeship, the United States globally occupies and administers a variety of small territorial portions of other nations. The total land mass covered by the United States exceeds 3.5 million square miles (9.1 million sq km). The land mass of its territories and possessions totals an estimated 5,138 square miles (13,307 sq km).

II. Boundaries

5. Canada lies on the northernmost boundary of the contiguous portion of the continental United States. On the east, the United States is bounded by over 2,000 miles (over 3,300 km) of Atlantic Ocean coastline and, in a small portion of the northeast, by Canada. The southern boundary consists of over 1,600 miles (over 2,600 km) of coastline on the Gulf of Mexico and an additional boundary of over 1,300 miles with Mexico (over 2,400 km). The Pacific Ocean, with almost 1,300 miles (2,400 km) of contiguous coastline, forms the western boundary of the continental portion of the nation. The state of Alaska has an additional 5,580 miles (8,978 km) of Pacific Ocean and 1,060 miles (1,706 km) of Arctic Ocean coastline.

§2. Industrial Resources

I. Transportation

6. The United States has an extensive river system providing considerable north–south and substantial east–west transportation by navigable waters. In the 19th century, and occasionally in the 20th century, canals and locks were built to expand and enhance this transportation internet. Although utilization of these waterways has dwindled substantially since the mid-20th century, many still are used. The US also has an extensive, though inefficiently designed, railroad network, most of which is privately owned. While the nation's highway, pipeline and air transportation systems are highly developed, in the last third of the 20th century a significant portion of bridges and local roads and streets began to suffer from decay, a situation that is slowly being remedied. In addition, the United States has numerous deep water harbors on all coasts as well as deep water ports on the Great Lakes to which ocean-going vessels using the St. Lawrence Seaway can link commerce between the central portion of the nation and the Atlantic Ocean.

II. Physical Resources

7. The geophysical characteristics of the United States include just about every possible variation – sandy beaches, rock strewn coasts, desert, fertile valleys and plains, semi-tropics, glaciers, high mountains, rolling hills, dense rain forests, eroded wastes, huge lakes, swamps, and long rivers. A large portion of the land mass consists of fertile to very fertile soil with either ample rainfall or adequate irrigation that supports all forms of farming and forestry. As a result, the United States exports vast amounts of most foods and forestry products. The United States also enjoys substantial supplies of most mineral resources needed by an industrial nation, including enormous coal reserves and considerable natural gas and petroleum pools. In addition, it has large tapped and untapped hydroelectric resources, some readily accessible geo-thermal pools, and vast expanses of territory that are available to utilize any major advances in tidal, wind, solar, and bio-mass energy technology.

On the other hand, there has been considerable pollution of ground water, streams and rivers from chemical, animal and human wastes. Virgin forests have diminished to the point that extinction is a realistic threat. In some regions, reforestation is inadequate to maintain either continued lumber supplies or protect soil from erosion. Agricultural and human wastes have destroyed much fresh and salt water fisheries as well as posing a danger to human health. Although government efforts have had moderate success in stemming these dangers, strong economic interests wielding considerable political power are constantly trying to reduce such government intervention.

§3. Governmental Structure

I. Formal Federal Structure

8. Since 1781, the United States has been governed under a quasi-federal system authorized by a written Constitution. The initial constitutional document, the Articles of Confederation, created a federation joined together by a weak central government. It was displaced in 1788 with the present structure established by the Constitution of the United States of America.

The central, or federal government, consists of the executive, legislative, and judicial branches. These are supplemented by administrative agencies; some are independent and others are appended to one of the government's three basic branches. Most principal offices of the federal government are located in the District of Columbia (Washington, DC), a constitutionally established enclave near the central east coast. The federal government has full jurisdiction over the District of

Columbia and over the nation's territories, possessions and trusteeships. It has more limited jurisdiction over the fifty states that compose the federation.

A. Executive Branch

9. The President of the United States heads the executive branch of the federal government and sometimes is referred to as the Chief Executive. The President is elected indirectly by a state-based electoral system that only partially reflects the popular vote (as demonstrated in the elections of George W. Bush in 2000 and Donald Trump in 2016). All citizens of the United States, 18 years or older, can participate in electing the presidential electors from their state who, in turn, elect the President and Vice President. The President serves a four-year term and can be reelected once. The President, directly or through his appointed secretaries (ministers) and ambassadors, represents the United States in the conduct of foreign affairs. In addition, he is Commander-in-Chief of the federal military forces. The President can propose legislation and veto laws subject to being overridden by a two-thirds vote of both chambers of the legislative branch. The President ultimately presides over most of the administrative machinery of the federal government[4] and is charged with the responsibility of enforcing the laws of the United States. Under various laws, including legislation dealing with the emergencies arising out of labor relations conflicts, the President in many instances is given discretionary authority to invoke or withhold government action or intervention.

Because the Chief Executive is the single nationally elected official and is entrusted with very considerable governmental authority, the President of the United States is in a unique position to wield substantial political and personal influence and has often provided broad social and even cultural leadership to the American people. At times this influence has been used to promote, other times to discourage, unionization, and to shape the parties' approach in major collective bargaining situations.

B. Legislative Branch

10. The legislative branch (Congress) has two chambers: the House of Representatives and the Senate. The members of the House of Representatives are popularly elected from geographically structured, but population based, districts established within each of the states of the United States. The citizens of each state elect at least one Representative. Beyond that the number of additional Representatives is determined by the state's population. Representatives serve a two-year term and can be reelected.

The Speaker of the House of Representatives is elected by its membership and is its presiding officer. The House uses a committee system in which an informal seniority structure, plus the voting power of the majority political party, generally

---

4. The judicial and legislative branches have separate administrative bodies that assist in managing the affairs of their branch.

determines who chairs the committees and their respective subcommittees. The person chairing a committee or subcommittee often wields determinative influence over its actions and inactions.

The House has sole authority to initiate federal tax laws. Every law adopted by the United States must receive approval of a majority of the members of the House present and voting. Similar approval is required from the other legislative chamber, the Senate.

11. The Senate's membership is elected for six-year terms and can be reelected. Each state, regardless of how large or small in territory or population, elects two senators by popular vote.

All laws of the United States must receive majority Senate approval. In addition to its legislative functions, the Senate must approve all treaties by a two-thirds vote, and by a majority vote it must approve all appointments to high office in the executive branch (including administrative agencies) and to the federal judiciary.

Although the Senate is technically presided over by the Vice President of the United States, the true center of power in that branch is the Majority Leader who is elected by a caucus of those senators whose political party is in a majority. In part because party discipline is relatively lax in the American system, the leader of the minority party, too, can often wield considerable influence. The Senate, like the House, uses a committee system, generally abides by seniority (and party voting power) in selecting committee and subcommittee chairs, and its actions often are greatly influenced by the various committee and subcommittee chairpersons who largely control committee and subcommittee agendas.

12. The authority of the Congress of the United States is limited to those powers enumerated in the Constitution. The scheme of enumeration was designed to limit the national legislative power to those issues that require national, as contrasted with local, action. Included is the power to expend money for the general welfare of the United States and to regulate commerce with foreign nations and among the several states. Because of expanded national and international interdependence in economic and monetary activities, in the 20th century Congress's powers to regulate commerce were interpreted very broadly and form the main basis for federal efforts to deal with employment related problems.

Laws enacted by Congress and signed by the President, or adopted despite the President's veto, are compiled by chapter title number and section in the United States Code. Federal laws, federal administrative actions, and decisions of federal courts, are given constitutional preference over conflicting state laws, actions or decrees, and are binding on all federal and state officials.

C. Judicial Branch

13. The judiciary is the third branch of the federal government. Its members, at all levels, are nominated for life terms by the President of the United States and are appointed upon approval of a majority of the Senate. They can be removed by impeachment for violation of the standard of 'good behavior'. The charge of violating that standard is issued by a majority vote of the House of Representatives. The impeachment trial is conducted by the Senate and conviction requires a vote by at least two-thirds of the Senators present.

The highest court is the Supreme Court of the United States which is presided over by the Chief Justice of the United States. Presently there are eight Associate Justices of the Supreme Court plus the Chief Justice. (Fewer if there are unfilled vacancies.) The number is established by Congress but has remained stable since the 1870s.

Decisions of the Supreme Court are determined by majority vote. Dissenting opinions, however, are common and occasionally the doctrines advocated in the dissent become the majority position in a later case. The custom of the Supreme Court is for a single justice to prepare the Opinion of the Court for the majority. Occasionally, decisions are issued *per curiam* or with an announcement of the result accompanied by a series of opinions, none of which has majority support. In the event of a tied vote, the decision of the highest court below remains in force.

The American legal system adheres to the principle that the Supreme Court of the United States has the final authority to interpret and apply the Constitution, and the laws and treaties of the United States. That is, the judiciary can nullify the actions of the other branches of government by finding them to be in conflict with the nation's laws, treaties or Constitution. It can also frustrate the intent of federal law makers by placing unanticipated interpretive glosses upon enactments. Because the Constitution provides that federal law prevails over any conflicting state or local laws, the Supreme Court additionally can nullify any state or local law it finds to be in conflict with the Constitution of the United States of America, a treaty or with the letter or even the scheme of federal legislation or with a lawful act of the federal executive branch. In this manner, the federal judiciary wields very considerable power over law-making and enforcement. This power is heightened by the fact that a basic juridical concept guiding American judges is that lower courts must apply the law as interpreted by higher level courts.

14. In addition to the Supreme Court, the federal judiciary consists of a system of trial and appellate courts, as well as some courts of highly specialized jurisdiction. The basic federal trial level court is the district court. Each state has at least one United States District Court. Normally, a single district court judge presides over a trial or hearing. The number of district judges assigned to a district varies depending on the normal case volume in that district.

District courts have the authority to appoint magistrates who are assigned the responsibility of hearing and deciding a variety of routine pre-trial issues subject to appeal to a district court judge. Additionally they can be assigned to conduct trials and prepare decisions which then must be approved by a district court judge. If all parties agree, magistrates can conduct trials and decide cases with the same authority as a district court judge. Magistrates are appointed for a specified number of years and during that time are subject to removal for misconduct.

The Courts of Appeals constitute the basic federal appellate courts. These are divided into 12 geographically based circuits, each circuit having appellate authority over specific district courts and over appeals from certain administrative agencies. Eleven of these courts are identified by a circuit number (1–11) and the twelfth by the title US Court of Appeals for the District of Columbia. A thirteenth circuit, the Court of Appeals for the Federal Circuit, specializes in certain types of appeals from or by various federal administrative agencies. The number of judges assigned to a circuit varies depending upon the normal case volume in that circuit. Most cases in the Courts of Appeals are heard and decided by three judge panels. Occasionally a case is decided *en banc*, that is, by all of the judges in that circuit. Because the Supreme Court grants review in only a very small percentage of appealed cases, and because of the expense and delay of judicial review, the federal appeals courts for all practical purposes often are the parties' court of last resort in applying and interpreting the Constitution and the laws and treaties of the United States.

D. Administrative Agencies

15. In addition to the constitutionally established three branches of the central government, Congress has created what often is called a fourth branch. This consists of administrative agencies that are substantially independent of the other branches. These agencies normally are delegated quasi-legislative, quasi-executive and quasi-judicial power to regulate or police particular industries or deal with specific types of problems. Included among these agencies are the National Labor Relations Board, Federal Mediation and Conciliation Service, Federal Labor Relations Authority, and National Mediation Board, all of which play vital roles in the American labor–management relations system. Although these agencies are referred to as 'independent', their authority is not final and they are subject to considerable influence or control from the three constitutional branches of government.

Some administrative agencies are part of an executive department and, therefore, are not separated from political policy influence. For example, the Secretary of Labor promulgates standards and regulations adopted under the Occupational Safety and Health Act and a subordinate agency, the Occupational Safety and Health Administration, investigates possible violations of that Act and orders remedies when violations are found. On the other hand, an independent agency (not directly subject to the authority of an executive branch officer such as the Secretary of Labor), the Occupational Safety and Health Review Commission, conducts trials and issues decisions in those cases in which an employer appeals from an order issued by the Occupational Safety and Health Administration.

16. Federal administrative agencies are headed by persons nominated by the President and appointed upon the approval of the Senate. Those who head independent administrative agencies serve for a fixed term of years and can be reappointed. The duration of the term of office and the number of agency heads (variously called 'Commissioner', 'Member', 'Director', etc., depending upon the agency) varies with the agency. The use of the varying agency titles, such as 'Agency', 'Board', 'Commission', 'Service', 'Authority', etc., is of no legal or political significance. If the agency has several persons in its top-level decisional position, the President of the United States designates one to be the presiding officer or 'chairman'. (Despite the title, some of the agency heads, of course, are women.)

Requests for budget appropriations for all administrative agencies are forwarded to Congress through the executive branch which can offer its own recommendations. Congress, by passage of a law (subject to presidential veto), determines the amount appropriated. In addition, Congress, by passage of a law (subject to presidential veto), can change the structure, procedures and responsibilities of the administrative agencies, or can eliminate them. Accordingly, agency heads typically try to avoid arousing the wrath of the executive or legislative branches because of the desire of the officials to be reappointed to another term in office, fear of possible budget reductions, or even the threat to terminate the law that established the agency. Furthermore, a substantial portion of the determinations of these agencies are subject to review by the courts. Hence, as noted above, none of these agencies is 'independent' in an absolute sense of the term.

II. Formal State Governmental Structures

17. Whereas the federal government is theoretically charged with dealing with those problems requiring a national solution, all other governmental power in the United States is supposed to reside in the state governments and their subdivisions. In fact, the policies shaping much of what was once thought to be local in nature are now substantially influenced either by the expansion of federal regulatory power, or by the impact of monies granted by the federal government to local governments subject to various federally established conditions and supervisory authority respecting the expenditure of that money. The expansion of the impact of federal law has been justified as necessitated by the increased inter-relationships and interdependencies of economic activity. Nevertheless, local government power has far from disappeared in the United States and, in recent years, there has been growth in the scope and nature of such governmental activities.

Territorial governments also are assigned varying degrees of local authority. For example, the government of Puerto Rico, an 'insular' territory possessing special and unique status, has considerable local authority – arguably at least as much local authority as the states.

Limited local governmental authority is also given by treaty or statute to the surviving tribal nations of the indigenous population – the American Indians or Native Americans – whose ancestors possessed the land when European colonizers first invaded the North American continent. By the time most of the surviving indigenous population[5] had agreed to peace terms with the US government in 1881, about 156 million acres were held in trust for their use and benefit. Nevertheless by

5. A significant portion of the indigenous population was killed in the wars of conquest and resistance but far more died from starvation resulting from being driven from their lands or the destruction of bison herds and other game on which many were dependent for food. The greatest devastation of the indigenous population resulted from dietary changes (alcoholism and increased diabetes and cardiovascular disease) and exposure to European diseases (including smallpox, measles, influenza, and diphtheria) to which they had not acquired resistance.

2017, the Bureau of Indian Affairs reported that its trust holdings had diminished to about 56.2 million surface acres and 57 million acres of subsurface minerals administered for the benefit of the surviving generations of the indigenous population. Much of that acreage, moreover, is barren wasteland or land with marginal agricultural value. Native Americans individually and through tribal arrangements own additional lands but data respecting the extent of that ownership are not compiled. Some American Indian groups retain special hunting and fishing privileges that have significant commercial value and in recent years have been permitted to operate gambling casinos on tribal lands, businesses that often bring considerable income to small segments of the Native American population.

The 2010 census reported 5.2 million people who identified themselves as Native American or Alaska Native of which 2.9 million reported that they had no other ancestry. Even though some 24 percent currently live on tribal lands or villages, assimilation into American culture has become the overwhelming trait as is evidenced by the fact that overall, Native Americans report that they speak only English at home and for most tribal groups the English-only speakers represented over 90 percent of those questioned. On the other hand, starting in the 1960s, many Native Americans initiated renewed interest and pride in the customs, traditions and languages of their ancestors with the result that despite the high level of assimilation, there is increased awareness and practice of ancient customs and activities.

18. The state is the dominant local governmental unit in the United States. There are 50 states, each with a three-branched government similar to that of the central government. Every state has a bicameral legislative structure except Nebraska which has a unicameral legislature. Each state has its own written constitution. The terminology designating the high governmental officials varies from state to state as does the scope of their authority. The chief executive officer in every state, however, carries the title 'Governor'. States are further divided into counties ('parishes' in the state of Louisiana). Villages, towns and cities provide additional local governmental jurisdictions and their structure and scope of authority vary widely based on state statutes or the state constitution.

Unlike the federal judiciary, with a few exceptions, state court judges are elected for a specific term of years but can seek reelection. The concept of judicial review (that is, the final authority of courts to interpret the laws and to nullify laws or decrees that violate the state or federal constitutions) is followed in the states just as in the federal government. The federal Constitution requires all state courts and officials to abide by federal law when it is applicable. However, in the absence of a conflict with federal law (including the nation's Constitution and treaties), state governments have the full scope of governmental power to levy taxes, spend public funds and regulate economic and social activities.

III. Constitutionally Protected Liberties

19. The Constitution of the United States places various restrictions upon the exercise of governmental power – local as well as federal. Most of these restrictions are designed to protect individual liberty. Included either expressly or by interpretation is protection of free expression; academic freedom; freedom of association; freedom of assembly; freedom of religion and conscience; separation of religious institutions from the government; freedom of movement; freedom from arbitrary or invidious treatment; recognition of the right of privacy; freedom from unreasonable arrest or unreasonable searches of one's home or person; the right to be treated equally by the government without distinction based on race, religion, national origin or ethnic identity; the right not to have property taken by the government without a public purpose; the right to just compensation for any governmental taking of property; the right to counsel and to a trial by jury in criminal and certain civil cases; the right to a fair trial by an impartial tribunal; and others. Probably, America's proudest achievement is that in most instances and in most times since the early 20th century, these liberties exist in fact and not merely in the law books. Constitutional protections have been the focal point for deciding some leading cases involving the labor–management relations area, most especially those disputes concerning organizational rights and the right to publicize labor disputes.

§4. Political Structure

20. The American political system long has been dominated by two parties, the Republican Party and the Democratic Party. In very broad terms, the Republican Party gives greater emphasis to protection of property rights, is more reluctant to finance social welfare programs, favors minimal governmental regulation of business activities, seeks lower rates of taxation of income and property, and prefers local rather than national solutions to social and economic problems. The Democratic Party, generally, is more supportive of governmental solutions for social welfare problems, is more willing to raise taxes on income and property to support wealth redistribution programs, is more inclined to look upon governmental intervention into business activities as a necessary evil, and is more inclined to seek national, rather than local, solutions to social and economic problems. Both parties identify themselves as seeking to perpetuate a capitalist market economy. Although the foregoing general statements can be substantiated, the rhetoric used by leaders of the two parties is highly interchangeable. Moreover, because the party hierarchies do not control who may seek elected office, one cannot predict the political behavior of an elected official merely by knowing that person's party affiliation.

21. Union leadership generally supports Democratic Party candidates and prominent business leaders most often support Republican Party candidates. But there have been important exceptions to both patterns.

Congress has prohibited unions and businesses from making direct contributions to political candidates or political parties. A comprehensive system for requiring disclosure of the identity of large campaign contributors is, in part, designed to reduce the evasion of laws prohibiting certain groups from making such contributions. Under the statutes adopted by Congress, individual union leaders and members can, however, make their own campaign contributions and can do so through a voluntary fund-raising effort that keeps these funds separate from union dues. Similarly, individual management personnel can make their own voluntary campaign contributions and funnel them through solicitors recruited by business leaders. Thus, labor and management organizations solicit and distribute individual political contributions in ways that make clear the interests groups that are the source of the financial support. Such direct contributions are subject to dollar limits in federal elections and many states impose similar restrictions.

In a decision discussed at paragraphs 535, 537–38 and 554, below, the Supreme Court struck down portions of Congress's legislation respecting the financing of political campaigns. This ruling has greatly enhanced the ability of those who control large business and financial entities to select and influence America's elected officials.

Even under the statutes adopted by Congress, prior to the Supreme Court's limitation on their enforcement, labor and management organizations have been free to provide relatively unconstrained indirect political support for candidates by engaging in 'independent' political advertising that endorses programs, slogans and themes identified with their candidates of choice so long as these efforts are not directly coordinated with the political campaign.

22. At the national level there long has been very little political party discipline. In most decades, various liberal Republicans voted consistently with moderate and even with liberal Democrats on key issues. Similarly, conservative Democrats voted in the same column as moderate and even with conservative Republicans with great frequency. Often the President of the United States has been able to wield a modest degree of party discipline over his own party's members of Congress, especially if he has enjoyed a high popularity rating making him a potential valuable ally for raising election campaign funds and providing campaign endorsements. However, even this source of political leadership has been weak in comparison with European norms of partisan behavior. Thus, regional self-interest, personal political philosophies, and the influence wielded by various special interest lobbies long have been more important in shaping national legislative policy in the United States than the political leadership or supposed political philosophies of the Democratic and Republican Parties.

In recent years there has been some change in the pattern described above, especially with respect to the Republican Party. Party discipline wielded by Republican leaders has been strengthened through increased influence with large campaign contributors. In addition, the leadership has largely adhered to the program of a more radical fringe group, the Tea Party, that has received considerable financial support from a small group of billionaires enabling it to create fear among more moderate Republicans office holders of losing their office by being defeated in a primary for the party candidacy for the elected office. Since 2010 this has resulted in strict party-line voting in both the House and Senate on numerous major legislative issues.

23. Political discipline long has been a more important factor on the state and local government level. However, there the political leadership frequently is nothing more than the force of personal loyalties. It is not uncommon for the principal focus of such leadership to involve sharp factions within the same party, and such factions represent at least as much adversity as is found across party lines. Because the state judiciary generally is elected and most often must run under a political party's label,[6] local political leadership sometimes has an impact upon the prevailing judicial philosophies as well as on legislative and executive behavior.

24. There has always been a variety of minor political parties in the United States. A few have been principally concerned with the labor–management relations system. The influence of minor political parties, however, has mainly been through their potential ability to drain enough votes from a sympathetic mainstream candidate to cause that candidate to lose the election. Minority party movements, therefore, have been most influential through their impact upon particular Democrats and Republicans who modify their own stands in an effort to avoid losing the support of voters who may momentarily shift their attention to a particular reform effort.

§5. The Bureaucracy

25. The bureaucracy is an important, though sometimes overlooked, source of influence in the policy choices made by government officials. There are two groups in the American bureaucracy: those hired without regard to political affiliation (and who usually have employment security), and those hired to assist a particular elected or appointed official (and who usually have no job security).

26. It often has been observed that elected officials in the United States expend a very considerable portion of their daily efforts laying the groundwork for reelection in ways that do not involve exemplary performance but instead involve effective public relations activities and campaign fund raising. Both to the extent of the truth of this observation, and to the extent of the vast breadth of responsibility imposed upon high elected officials in a country as large as the United States, these officers are very dependent upon the fact-finding, analysis, legislative drafting, and advice of their staff subordinates. The elected official is often so dependent upon the staff's efforts that, in reality, the staff frequently determine the shape of the elected official's decision.

Appointed officials, too, can be highly dependent upon their staffs to gather information and suggest solutions. Moreover, staffs tend to develop their own styles and their own normative behaviors and values. Thus, students of government have noted that, through the process of acculturation, a new staff member's values often go through a transition moving in the direction of greater compatibility with the staff

---

6. Some states bar judicial candidates from identifying their political party affiliation on the ballot. In *Republican Party of Minnesota* v. *White*, 536 US 765 (2002), the Supreme Court ruled that a prohibition against a judicial candidate announcing views on disputed legal or political issues was an unconstitutionally vague and overly broad restriction of free expression.

norm. Therefore, it is often as important to know which staff has authority to deal with a particular issue as it is to be familiar with the legal precedents or political ideology that presumably guide the decision.

§6. The People

I. Generally

27. Because the US does not have a national identity card or other resident registration system, population estimates have a considerable margin of error. It is estimated that as of mid 2017 the total resident American population was about 325.719 million including about 3.337 million living in Puerto Rico (a decline from 2010) plus about 106,000 residing in the US Virgin Islands. (Those born in Puerto Rico and the US Virgin Islands are US citizens by birth.) More than 2 million additional Americans reside in other countries. Additionally, the population of United States possessions and territories (American Samoa, Guam, Wake Island and the Northern Mariana Islands) is about 320,000.

As of the 2010 census, population density in the US was 87.4 persons per square mile. The most densely populated section of the US is the middle to north-middle Atlantic coastal area from Massachusetts to Washington, DC.

Over 80 percent of the American population resides in urbanized areas occupying about 2 percent of the land area. About 57 percent of the nation's population resides in cities of a million or more people. In the year 2010, the US had nine cities with over a million population and 49 metropolitan statistical areas with populations of over one million. Many are considerably larger.

At the time of the census 1.4 million US residents were on active duty status in the armed forces. Of this group, 339,000 lived in military housing and 1.08 million lived in the United States. Another 2.26 million US residents lived in adult correctional facilities. Of that population, 91 percent were male. The largest age component (33 percent) was 25–34 years of age.

Invidious discrimination based on perceptions of a person's ancestry, religion, gender, sexual life style, disability, appearance, and age has been a persistent social and economic problem in the US. For this reason, it is of some significance to note the extent to which the population appears to fit within some of these divisions.

US Census data rely on self-identification and do not an attempt to define race biologically, anthropologically, or genetically. Based on the 2010 census, about 72.4 percent of US residents identified themselves as white and another 2.4 percent as white in combination with another race. American residents who identified themselves as Hispanic or Latino (in addition to Spain, this includes most whose families come from the Western Hemisphere south of the US and includes Puerto Rico) represented 16.3 percent of the total. Another 12.6 percent of Americans identified themselves as black alone and 1 percent identified themselves as black plus another race.[7] The remaining residents identified themselves as of Asian, Pacific Island, or Native American ancestry.[8]

28. The 14th Amendment to the Constitution of the United States says that any person born in the US is a citizen of the US. (There is a minor exception for family members of foreign diplomats and their staff.) By statute, children of US citizens are citizens even if born abroad so long as they comply with required citizenship registration procedures. Immigrants gain citizenship through a naturalization procedure.

A very large portion of the American population is less than three generations removed from immigrant parentage. In the 19th century, immigration was restricted for Africans and Asians, but quotas on European, Australian, and Latin American entry were not imposed until 1921. From the mid-1920s until the mid-1960s, immigration was sharply curtailed with most of the new entrants coming from northwestern Europe. The Immigration Act of 1965, and later legislation, increased the annual immigration level with a larger percentage of entrants being permitted from the eastern hemisphere than from the western hemisphere. The 1965 Act established world-wide quotas and limited to 7 percent of the quotas the total number of immigration visas that can be issued to persons born in the same foreign state. There are several categories of special quotas (for example, reuniting family members or persons who have special employment skills) and special provisions for political refugees and other humanitarian concerns. As of 2012 there were 13.3 million legal permanent alien residents living in the US. Some aliens enter the US by unlawfully crossing the borders; others enter under student, travel or work visas and fail to return to their homeland after the visa expires. At the end of 2016 it was estimated that about 11.1 million persons residing in the US were not lawfully in the country, a figure that has been fairly stable since 2009. Persons engaged in political discourse have claimed the number as being as high as 14-50 million.

The Immigration and Naturalization Reform and Control Act of 1986 established an amnesty period during which several million aliens transferred from illegal to legal status. Renewing that or a similar amnesty currently is a hotly debated political issue.

In California, in 2010 the foreign born portion of the population was 27 percent, in New York 22 percent, New Jersey 21 percent and Illinois 14 percent. In eight states less than 5 percent of the population was foreign born. Over 80 percent of

---

7. Nouns used for racial and ethnic identification are culturally and politically sensitive and have changed over time. Nouns that the target group generally regards as acceptable to identify them in one generation sometimes are regarded as derogatory in another generation. For example, 'black' is a term that was not acceptable at a time when 'Negro' and 'colored' were acceptable. Over time, this has been reversed. 'African American' is now generally accepted by the target group as a polite synonym for 'black' even though it encompasses many people who are of European (for example, whites born in South Africa) or Semitic (for example, Libyans) ancestry and are not part of the intended identity group.
8. The indigenous population at the time of the European conquest is also known as American Indians. At the time of conquest, they were socially and culturally organized into tribal groups. The federal Department of Interior registers members by their tribal affiliation and often includes people who have little or no known genetic ancestry in common with the overall group.

immigrants who were in the US for more than 30 years had become American citizens. Because undocumented aliens generally evade participating in the census, these estimates likely exclude most people in that category.

29. In 2012, it was estimated that the median age of the US population was 37.3 years (36.1 years for men, 38.5 years for women). Of the total population, 26.7 percent was under age 20, 20.5 percent was 20 through 34, 27.1 percent was 35–54, 12.3 percent was 55 through 64 and 13.5 percent was 65 years or older. In 2015, the birth rate per 1,000 persons in the total population was 12.5 and the death rate was 7.3.

30. Americans are highly mobile. Although many reside in the same locale as did their parents and grandparents, many others move to other locations. As a result, most Americans have family ties with diverse national regions. For example, in 2010 it was estimated that 27 percent of American residents were born in a state other than the state of their current residence. It was estimated that between 2012 and 2013, almost 7 million American residents moved to a different city in the same state, over 2 million moved to a different state in the same region of the country, almost 2.5 million moved to a different region of the nation, and over a million move to a different country. The cumulative impact of such changes over two or three decades results in a steady modification of regional differences in speech, dress, manners, food, and similar cultural characteristics. Mass communications media have also had an important impact in reducing cultural differences among the nation's states and regions.

31. An important cultural change in the US in recent decades has been the increased age at marrying and the shorter duration of marriages among the younger segment of the adult population.

As of 2009, it was estimated that 33 percent of the population age 15 and older had never been married. Almost 76 percent of men who were ever married had been married only once. The percentage of the population 15 years and older who had been married once and were still married was 42.5. (Widowhood and divorce without remarriage account for those no longer married.) Of those men who had ever married, 52.8 percent of those who had married only once had been married for 20 or more years. Of those men who had married twice, 36.7 percent had been married for 20 or more years and of those married three or more times, 24.8 percent had been married 20 or more years. The data for women was almost identical … Estimates for 2009 are that the median age for a first marriage for men was 28.4 years; for women it was 26.5 years.[9]

The majority of Americans live in households. As of the 2012 there were 2.6 people per household on average and it was estimated that married family households were 66 percent of the total. Households of married couples with children

9. For additional details, *see* US Census Bureau, *Number, Timing and Duration of Marriages and Divorces*, 2009.

were 20 percent of the total and 53 percent of children under age 18 lived in a married couple family group. However, 55 percent of black children, 31 percent of Hispanic children, 21 percent of white children and 13 percent of Asian children lived in single parent households.

Overall there is a correlation between academic and economic success and household arrangements. For example, in 2012 the household income was at least 200 percent above poverty level in 70 percent of all households in which children lived with both married parents. In contrast, the household income was below poverty level in almost half of the households in which children lived with their mother only, with two unmarried parents, or with no parent.

In 2012 it was estimated that 15.2 percent of women and 12.3 percent of men lived alone and 17.8 percent of the population lived in households in which there was no married couple.

32. Because of the principle of separation of religion and government in the US, census questionnaires do not ask for religious identity. Other studies, however, estimate that 85 different religious organizations in the US have memberships exceeding 50,000. Based on a survey, it was estimated in 2008 that 76 percent of American adults identified themselves as Christian. A different survey more recently reported that 78.5 percent identified themselves as Christian. Depending on the survey source, between 25 and 28 percent of the adult population identified themselves as members of the Roman Catholic church and one survey found that collectively over 26 percent of adults identified themselves as members of an evangelically oriented church. The next largest groups were the several Baptist and Methodist churches. Jews, variously estimated as 1.2 to 1.7 percent of the population, are the largest non-Christian religious group in the US. Adults identifying themselves as Muslims, Buddhists, or Hindus each compose roughly half that percentage, though their relative numbers vary considerably depending on the survey. The portion reporting attending religious services at least weekly in the US has been variously estimated as between 40 and 43 percent.

33. Formal educational attainments in the US are high. Of the population 25 years and above in 2012, almost 88 percent had successfully completed at least 12 years of schooling (high school) and almost 31 percent completed at least a first university level degree. Moreover, over 11 percent of the 25 years or older population had a second level university degree or higher.

The principal underprivileged minority groups in the US, persons identifying as being of black or Hispanic ancestry, have lower average levels of formal schooling whereas those identifying as being of Asian ancestry have the highest levels. Based on self-identification of ancestry, in 2012, in the population that was 25 years or older, a high school diploma (12 years of education) was the highest level of education achieved for 30.8 percent of blacks, 26.7 percent of Hispanics, 27.5 percent of non-Hispanic whites, and 19.9 percent of Asians. The highest level of education achieved was a bachelor's degree for 9.2 percent of blacks, 7.8 percent of Hispanics, 15.5 percent of non-Hispanic whites, and 24.5 percent of Asians. The highest educational level achieved was a masters degree for 5.7 percent of blacks, 3.2 percent of Hispanics, 9.1 percent of non-Hispanic whites and 13.8 percent of Asians.

Finally, the highest level achieved was a doctorate or professional degree for 1.8 percent of blacks, 1 percent of Hispanics, 3.5 percent of non-Hispanic whites, and 5.9 percent of Asians.[10]

Measuring the meaning of educational attainment in the US is a matter of considerable controversy. Despite the high portion of persons with substantial formal education, lax graduation standards often mask serious deficiencies in the attainment of basic academic skills. The OECD's *Skills Outlook 2013* ranked the US in the 'significantly lower' category in testing of literacy, numeracy, and problem solving in a technology-rich environment. Although there is a lack of agreement respecting the appropriate criteria and testing tools for making such estimates, there is general agreement that a high proportion of Americans learn too little during their first twelve years in school and, perhaps, beyond. Higher education in the US is provided both by government sponsored colleges and universities and by private institutions. The latter often receive some government financing through research and other program supporting grants. However, government financial support for higher education has been declining. Even in publicly sponsored institutions of higher education, student tuition normally helps finance educational activities. Institutions of higher learning also receive considerable private donations.

Most university students in the US are enrolled in full-time programs. Nevertheless, studies indicate that a substantial portion of them work while attending school because, unlike many other countries with advanced economies, most university students in the US do not receive government stipends to assist them in meeting tuition or living expenses while in school.

A significant portion of college students in the US work full-time and attend school part-time. A Census Bureau sponsored study reported in 2011 that 20 percent of college level students worked full-time and 52 percent worked part-time. About 15 percent of all college students who worked part-time worked more than 20 hours a week for more than 26 weeks in the year.

Government and private loan programs help students finance their higher education and many students compile considerable debts by the time they graduate. According to the Federal Reserve Bank of New York, by mid-2017 the outstanding balance for student loans was about $1,440,000,000, an amount that was greater than the nation's credit card debt ($780,000,000) and the total indebtedness for auto purchases ($1,119,000,000). The average student graduated in 2016 with $37,172 in student debt and over 44 million Americans had some student debt from current or past borrowing. A 2011 study showed that for over 11 percent of students who had educational indebtedness, the amount exceeded $50,000 and an estimated 27 percent of the borrowers had past due balances that resulted in 21 percent of the outstanding loans being in delinquent status. Thus, there is growing concern that young people from lower to middle income families are beginning to question the wisdom of acquiring debt in order to obtain higher education.

---

10. Not reflected in these figures are those who achieved less than a high school diploma or whose education went beyond high school but either did not result in being awarded a degree or resulted in a less academically prestigious degree such as a technical or associate degree.

As a group, because of the length and cost of their education, medical students accrue the largest student indebtedness. According to the American Medical Association, the average educational indebtedness of medical students who graduated in 2012 was $166,750. Eighty-six percent of the graduates had some education loan indebtedness and 62 percent had education loan indebtedness of $150,000 or more.

The 2010 census found that 22 percent of high school students were employed or seeking employment. Those with jobs constituted 16 percent of all high school students. Normally, these are part-time jobs and a large portion of the students use their earnings to pay for personal luxuries, entertainment, and social activities. A related study found that almost 30 percent of high school students age 16 and older worked 20 or more hours a week during the school year in 2011. This data is significant because several studies indicate that students who work fewer than 12 hours a week generally have similar or better grades than those who do not work. However, there is a noticeable drop in grades after about 12 hours of work per week suggesting that excessive work may hinder student learning.[11]

II. The Work Force

34. At the end of 2016 the total non-institutionalized population over the age of 16 in the United States was approximately 253.5 million. For this same period, the total labor force (that is, persons who are employed or who are unemployed but seeking employment) was about 159.2 million of whom almost 151.4 million were employed in civilian jobs.[12] In 2016 there were 131.0 million non-institutionalized females age 16 and over. Of that population segment, 74.4 million were in the civilian work force and over 70.9 million females were employed.

In the US, employees are counted as part-time if normally they are scheduled to work fewer than 35 hours a week. (A few statutes define part-time as fewer hours. See paragraph 663, below.) Almost 25.9 million people (about 17 percent of all civilian employees) were employed part-time in 2016. Of those employed part-time, a little over 5.8 million (22 percent of the part-time workers) reported they would prefer full-time employment.

35. In early 2017, a time of moderately low unemployment, the average unemployment rate for all males 16 years or older was 4.1 percent; for females it was the same. However, the unemployment rate for black male workers age 16 or over was 8.0 percent and for black females it was 6.8 percent; for those of Hispanic ancestry (includes all from Latin American countries) it was 4.9 percent for males and 5.5 percent for females; but for those of Asian ancestry it was only 3.2 percent for males and 3.0 percent for females.

---

11. K. Quirk, T. Keith and J. Quirk, 'Employment During High School and Student Achievement: Longitudinal Analysis of National Data', 95 *J. Educ. Research* 7 (2001).
12. The US Bureau of Labor Statistics counts as 'employed' all persons who did any paid work or who worked for a family operated enterprise for 15 or more paid hours in a week or who had a job but did not work due to illness, family or personal crisis, vacation, severe weather, a labor dispute, or the like.

Unemployment for the youth component was considerably higher. The unemployment rate for all persons in the civilian labor force ages 16 through 24 was 11.5 percent in mid-2016. The unemployment rate for all black workers in that age group was 20.6 percent, for those of Hispanic ancestry it was 11.3 percent, and for Asian workers ages 16 through 24 it was 10.0 percent.

The seasonally adjusted average duration of unemployment for all persons in the first quarter of 2017 was 24.9 weeks while the median duration of unemployment was 10.4 weeks. The comparable duration of unemployment during times of high unemployment are substantially longer (generally approaching double those figures).

In December 2016 the seasonally adjusted average number of work hours per week for production and non-supervisory workers (including part-time workers) was 33.6 hours.

'Contingent workers' are employees who are regarded by their employer as casual or temporary and not part of the employer's regular work force. Generally, such workers do not receive benefits provided to the 'regular' work force such as paid sick leave, paid vacation, or health insurance. The US Bureau of Labor Statistics uses three alternative methods of measuring contingent workers. The variations, among other things, either include or exclude self-employed contractors, and include or exclude those at the job for more than a year but who do not expect the job to continue for more than another year. Depending on the measurement method, a special Bureau of Labor Statistics study estimated that contingent work constituted between 1.8 to 4.1 percent of total employment in February 2005. For that period, independent contractors constituted 7.4 percent of total employment, on-call workers were 1.8 percent of all employees, temporary help agency workers provided 0.9 percent of total employment, and 0.6 all workers were provided by contract firms.[13] For the period of the study, contingent workers were twice as likely as non-contingent workers to be under age 25 and were less likely to be white than non-contingent workers. Fifty-five percent of contingent workers reported they would have preferred a 'permanent' job. In contrast, 82 percent of independent contractors preferred their work arrangement to a traditional job but only 32 percent of temporary help agency workers preferred that arrangement.

The Great Recession that began toward the end of 2007 caused a significant increase in unemployment that peaked at 10 percent in late 2009.

13. A mid-2007 survey by the American Staffing Association estimated that over 3 million workers were employed by firms that assign their own employees to temporary jobs at other establishments.

Table 1 Employment and unemployment – selected years

	Total non-institutional population 16 years and older	*Percent of population in labor force*	*Total civilian labor force*	*Percent civilian labor force unemployed*
1950	106,645,000	59.9	62,208,000	5.3
1960	119,759,000	60.2	69,628,000	5.5
1970	140,182,000	61.3	82,715,000	4.9
1975	153,449,000	61.8	92,613,000	8.5
1980	169,848,000	64.2	106,940,000	7.1
1985	179,912,000	64.8	115,461,000	7.2
1990	189,686,000	66.4	124,787,000	5.5
1995	198,584,000	66.6	132,304,000	5.6
2000	209,699,000	67.2	140,863,000	4.0
2005	226,082,000	66.0	149,320,000	5.1
2010	237,830,000	64.3	153,639,000	9.4
2016	254,742,000	62.9	159,640,000	4.8

36. In early 2017, for all occupations the average hourly wage was $26.10 and the average weekly earnings was $895.23. The median weekly earnings for all full-time workers in the first quarter of 2017 was $865. The following examples, though broad, indicate with some greater precision the range of wages and distribution of occupations.

It was estimated that in 2016, close to 2.2 million were employed in general managerial jobs. The median hourly wage for those in such jobs was $47.74. Over 332,000 were employed in computer and information system jobs Their median hourly wage was $65.29. Over 8.6 million were employed in education, training and library service occupations. The median hourly wage in such jobs was $23.08. More than 793,000 were employed in food preparation jobs and had a median hourly wage of $12.64. More than 22 million were employed in office and administrative support occupations and had a median hourly wage of $16.37. Farming, fishing and forestry occupations employed over 463,000. The median hourly wage for such jobs was $11.30. Over 4.2 million worked in construction or extraction occupations where the median hourly wage was $20.34. And, over 2.8 million were employed as registered nurses and had a median hourly wage of $32.91.

The Bureau of Labor Statistics estimated that in 2015 53 percent of all workers employed in management, professional, and related occupations were women. The share of women in specific occupations varied. For example, 18 percent of software developers, 28 percent of chief executives, and 35 percent of lawyers were women, while women occupied 89 percent of the registered nurse positions, 81 percent of the elementary and middle school teacher jobs, and 60 percent of the accounting and auditing positions. In contrast, less than 1 percent of employed women worked in natural resource and construction occupations compared with 17.1 percent of employed men, and 6.1 percent of employed women were in production, transportation and materials moving occupations compared with 19 percent of employed men. For the same year, the Bureau estimated that median weekly earnings of women was 81.1 percent of that of men. Although this disparity is indicative of continued gender based employment discrimination favoring males, the median earnings figures are somewhat misleading because a higher percentage of women than men are employed part-time and such jobs typically pay less than their full-time equivalents. Another factor affecting the relative median earnings is that career employment of women often is disrupted by child birth and child rearing with accompanying disruption of longevity pay increases and cumulative experience needed in competing for promotions.

37. At the end of 2016 it was estimated that a little over 2.8 million persons were employed by the federal government in civilian capacities plus 0.6 million were employed by the postal service, that state government had over 5 million employees of which 2.4 million were employed by state operated educational institutions and over 0.3 million by state operated hospitals. Local government employed over 14.4 million of which 8 million worked for local government operated schools and almost 0.7 million worked for local government operated hospitals.

III. Income Distribution

38. In the first quarter of 2017, about 62.8 percent of personal income in the US was received in the form of wages, salaries, and related direct and indirect compensation such as contributions to employee benefit funds. In the same period, proprietors' income from businesses (including farming) was about 8.9 percent of all personal income, rental income was 4.5 percent, corporate dividends and interest receipts 14.1 percent and the remainder was social insurance receipts from non-government contributions.

Measures of income vary based on differences in methodology and definitions of the group being measured. According to the Federal Reserve Bank of St. Louis the per capita disposable income in 2009 dollars was $39,729 in mid 2017.

Whatever data source is used, it is apparent that there is considerable income disparity. For example, the Bureau of the Census reported that in 2015 approximately 13.5 percent of the American population, or 43.1 million people, lived in poverty. In the US poverty is defined as the inability to pay for basic living needs. It is measured by the number of people in a household who share income sources and in some measures takes into account their ages. The proportion of persons living in poverty in 2015 ranged from a low of 8.2 percent for New Hampshire to a high of 24.22 percent for Mississippi and 46.1 percent for Puerto Rico.

Income disparities in the US are evident based on such factors as race and other ethnic identity. For example, a Census Bureau report found that in 2015 median household income was $60,109 for white households the mean was $82,216, for Asian and Pacific Island households was the median was $77,166 and the mean

$105,417, the median was $45,148 and the mean $63,612 for Hispanic households, and for black households the median was $36,898 and the mean was $54,352.

39. The pattern of changes in income distribution in the United States is reflected in the chart below. As can be seen, there was a major income distribution shift from the very wealthy toward middle and lower income groups between the mid-1930s and the end of the World War II post-war period. Most of that change took place during the war. By the mid-1970s, a reversal of that trend started to emerge and largely resulted in a decline in the relative position of the poorer two fifths of the nation. At the same time, the portion of national income received by the wealthiest two fifths began to increase. Since the 1980s, however, using aggregate income as a gauge, overall there has been a decline in the relative position of all segments except the wealthiest fifth and the wealthiest 5 percent. The Great Recession of 2008–2011 slightly interrupted this trend. With aggregate income reduced, income security and welfare programs resulted in the poorest section of the nation receiving a slight increase in the distribution of aggregate wealth. Similarly, with investment returns and bonuses often down, the aggregate portion of income going to the wealthiest 5 percent also declined. Additionally, the recession resulted in the loss of many upper income jobs as well as lower and middle income jobs. The earlier trend of increasing wealth concentration at the top returned at the end of the Great Recession.

Table 2 Percent of aggregate annual income received by each fifth and highest 5 percent of families in the United States

Item and income rank	*1935–1936*	*1955*	*1975*	*1985*	*1995*	*2000*	*2005*	*2010*	*2015*
Lowest fifth	4.1	4.8	5.4	4.7	3.7	3.6	3.4	3.3	3.1
Second fifth	9.2	12.2	11.8	10.9	9.1	8.9	8.6	8.5	8.2
Middle fifth	14.1	17.7	17.6	16.8	15.2	14.8	14.5	14.6	14.3
Fourth fifth	20.9	23.4	24.1	24.1	23.3	23.0	23.0	23.4	23.2
Highest fifth	51.7	41.8	41.1	43.5	48.7	49.6	50.4	50.3	51.1
Highest 5%	26.5	16.8	15.5	16.7	21.0	21.9	22.2	21.3	22.1

In terms of total income, overall all segments of the population gained over the past forty years when measured in real dollar terms, but as shown in the following table, the gains have not been proportionate. Data for the highest 1 percent of income earners is more difficult to obtain but a 2013 study by Prof. Emmanuel Saez found that the highest 1 percent of families enjoyed 95 percent of the total gain in family income for the first three years of recovery after the Great Recession.

Table 3 Mean annual household income received by each fifth and highest 5 percent of families in the United States in year 2015 dollars

Item and income rank	*1975*	*1985*	*1995*	*2000*	*2005*	*2010*	*2015*
Lowest fifth	$11,656	$11,797	$12,897	$13,979	$12,932	$11,844	$12,457
Second fifth	28,633	29,896	31,523	34,904	33,202	31,017	32,631
Middle fifth	46,977	49,624	52,711	58,125	56,194	53,450	56,832
Fourth fifth	68,262	74,646	81,029	90,357	88,385	85,748	92,031
Highest fifth	120,520	139,433	169,094	195,412	193,680	184,146	202,360
Highest 5%	182,891	215,085	291,833	348,687	341,228	312,218	350,870

Examining the distribution of aggregate household income has shortcomings as a method of measuring wealth distribution because it does not include non cash transfer payments, such as health insurance and social services, nor does it account for the net impact of income taxation. A study of the change in after tax household income from 1977 to 1999, however, showed a 9 percent decline for the fifth of the households with the lowest annual income, a 1 percent increase for the next fifth, 8 percent increase for the middle group, 14 percent increase for the next to highest fifth, 43 percent increase for the fifth receiving the highest incomes, and 115 percent increase for the 1 percent of the households with the very largest incomes. In significant part this change was due to changes in income tax laws that substantially reduced the burden on those receiving large and very large incomes but only modest or marginal changes for those below them on the annual income scale. A Congressional Budget Office study showed that this trend continued through 2010 but subsequent tax law changes linked to financing efforts to expand health care insurance coverage may have slightly reversed the pattern at the highest income levels.

Another distortion of the portrayal of income distribution that may occur when aggregate household income is examined, results from its failure to measure in-kind income such as personal use of a family's own home, car or other property, a family's consumption of home grown produce or consumption benefits often given executives such as travel to attractive conference sites, chauffeured transportation, elegant meals, company vacation retreats, country club membership, and the like. Whether these measurement inaccuracies or gaps have a greater distorting affect on one income quintile than on another is difficult to say. For example, not accounting for the benefits of a school lunch program for poor children results in understating the income of the fifth of the population with the lowest family income; not accounting for the benefits of publicly maintained or subsidized golf courses, tennis courts, airports, postal services, and opera houses, results in understating the income of the fifth to three-fifths of the population with the highest income.

Thus, as a general proposition it appears that beginning in the mid-1970s, there has been growing, unfavorable disparity between family incomes of the middle and poorest two thirds of the population in the US as contrasted with that of the wealthiest third. Even more dramatic, however, is the pattern of marked growth in the portion of aggregate income received by the wealthiest 5 percent of the population and still more so, the wealthiest 1 percent. In part, at least, the growth in disparity is due to the shift for a large group of workers away from employment in higher paid manufacturing occupations to lower paid service jobs. It is also partly due to the increase in the overall portion of the elderly, retired population, and the dramatic increase in one parent family households.

A study of wealth concentration in the US between 1913 and 2013 reported: '[W]ealth concentration was high in the beginning of the twentieth century, fell from 1929 to 1978, and has continuously increased since then.'[14] It is estimated that in 2012 the wealthiest 1 percent owned about 22 percent of all wealth owned by US

14. E. Saez and G. Zucman, 'Wealth Inequality in the United States Since 1913: Evidence from Capitalized Income Tax Data', 131 *Q.J. Eco* 519 (2016).

households.[15] Measuring such holdings has its complications inasmuch as asset values fluctuate and until sold can only be estimated. Additionally, wealthy households often own bonds, equities, real estate, jewels, bullion, art treasures, and the like held in a third party's name or an anonymous account by offshore banks and others. Further, some of the wealthiest families control corporations and non-profit foundations whose wealth may not directly generate income or cannot be liquidated in their name but nevertheless can be expended or wielded to enhance the value of their income producing assets or to influence social and economic policies favored by those who control these institutions.

40. Measuring the portion of a population that lives in poverty is more complicated than merely measuring income disparity. Income in kind and other unreported income such as maintaining a food garden, receipt of charitable gifts, the surrounding physical environment, health status, and the like, can make substantial differences in the impact of a particular income level on the standard of living. In the 1960s the federal government developed a measurement of poverty based on the cost of achieving minimum standards for decent living. The definition of minimum standards for decent living is, of course, subject to differing perceptions. In addition, applying the standards to aggregate population data is a complex task because there is controversy respecting the proper way to account for such factors as taxes, insurance supplements, welfare payments and services, subsidized housing, and the imputed value of living in one's own house. Thus, depending on the methods used for making those measurements, the estimated portion of the population living in poverty has significant variations.

Government efforts to refine the measurement of poverty have continued. The official definition of poverty in the US looks to household money income which includes all money income received by individuals who are 15 years or older before deductions for taxes and other expenses and does not include lump-sum payments or capital gains. It also does not include the value of non-cash benefits such as food stamps. In determining what household income is below the poverty level, the measure varies that level based on the household's size and place of residence. For example, in 2017 it was estimated that the poverty level income for a single person household was $12,060 or below if that person was living in the contiguous 48 states or the District of Columbia. If living in Alaska, the threshold was $15,060 and in Hawaii $13,860. Similarly, for that year, a household with four persons was designated as living in poverty unless its income exceeded $24,600 if living in the contiguous 48 states or the District of Columbia, $30,750 if living in Alaska, and $28,290 if living in Hawaii.

In 2015, using the official income definition, the overall poverty estimate for the United States was 13.5 percent. Poverty is more common for some groups than for others. For example, for white households the official estimate of the portion living in poverty in 2015 was 9.1 percent (this excluded those of Hispanic ancestry), for blacks it was 24.1 percent, for all persons of Hispanic ancestry it was 21.4 percent, and for persons of Asian ancestry the rate was 11.4 percent.

15. Saez and Zucman, above at 573.

A high portion of those living in poverty are unemployed, most often because they are disabled, too young or too old to work, are in school, or are caring for other household members. Nevertheless, the Bureau of Labor Statistics estimated that 9.5 million workers in 2014 lived at or below the poverty level. The greatest portion lived in households in which those who were employed worked part-time. Nevertheless, 4.1 percent of those employed at least half the year as full-time workers lived at or below poverty standards. Earlier surveys revealed that the highest concentration of impoverished persons live in the central sections of urban areas (inner city) but that the relatively rural states of Mississippi and New Mexico had the highest poverty rates. The lowest rates were in New Hampshire and Alaska, also relatively rural states.

41. Earned income distribution in the US generally is affected by a combination of status identity factors. Education is one such variable. For example, in 2012, the median weekly earned income of all workers whose highest academic achievement was a high school diploma (normally 12 years of schooling) was $652. For those with a bachelor's degree it was $1,066; with a masters degree it was $1,300; with a doctorate it was $1,624; and with a professional degree it was $1,735. Significant disparities also can be shown based on gender, race and national origin.

IV. Union Membership

42. In 1954 an estimated 34.7 percent of the American workforce belonged to a labor union. By 1980, union representation had declined to 23.1 percent of employed workers. The decline has continued and by 2016 only 10.7 percent of all employed wage and salary workers were union members. Because in the US a union has a legal duty to represent non-members if it is the recognized bargaining representative, 12.0 percent of all workers had union representation in 2016. The total number of union members was 14.6 million. The union membership rate for all government workers in 2016 was 34.4 percent. The highest concentration of union members among government workers was at the local level (40.3 percent). In contrast, only 6.4 percent of non-government civilian employees were union members.

Among all occupations, education, training, library staff, and protective service occupations had the highest unionization rate (34.6 percent). Among major private industries the highest rate of unionization was in utilities (21.5 percent), transportation and warehousing (18.4 percent), telecommunications (14.6 percent), and construction (13.9 percent). The lowest rate of unionization in the private sector was in food preparation and serving (3.9 percent).

Union membership for employed workers was higher in 2016 among men (11.2 percent) than for women (10.2 percent). Black workers were more likely to be union members (13.0 percent) than were whites (11.0 percent), Asians (9.0 percent), or Hispanics (8.8 percent). Union membership rates were highest among workers 55 to 64 years old (13.3 percent) and lowest for those ages 16 to 24 (4.4 percent). Full-time workers were more than twice as likely as part-time workers to be union members.

There also are significant regional differences in the degree of union membership. Thus, in 2016 over half of the nation's union members lived in seven states that together had about a third of the nation's employees. Those states were California (2.5 million); New York (1.9 million); Illinois (0.8 million); Pennsylvania (almost 0.7 million); and Michigan, New Jersey, and Ohio which each had a little over 0.6 million union members.

Not all American workers have a protected right to organize and obtain union representation. A 2002 study by the Government Accounting Office estimated that 22 percent of private sector workers and 34 percent of government sector workers do not have such rights. Private sector workers whose right to organize is not protected include supervisors and managers, household employees, independent contractors, most employees of very small businesses, and most agricultural workers. Some states do not recognize the right of their government sector workers to engage in collective bargaining, others limit such rights to only small segments of the government work force, and many states and the federal government exclude from collective bargaining some categories of government workers such as the military and other security branches (broadly defined), and managerial employees. (See, also, paragraph 496, below.)

43. Collective bargaining representation in the US can operate on any of several levels. Often it is at the plant or even departmental level; sometimes it is multi-plant or enterprise wide and occasionally even industry wide. Since the early 1980s the government has discontinued its systematic compilation of collective agreements making it very difficult to estimate the number of agreements now in force and the scope of their coverage.

Wages paid under collective agreements generally exceed those paid unrepresented workers. It was estimated by the Bureau of Labor Statistics that in 2016, the median weekly earnings of full time wage and salary employees in the private sector who were union represented was $1,004 compared with the median of $802 for those who were not represented by a union. The extent of the differential varied considerably by industry and occupation. For example the median weekly earnings for union represented workers in the construction industry was $1,142, for non-represented it was $719; in production occupations the median for union represented workers was $837, for the unrepresented it was $641. Overall, data indicates that the proportionate wage advantage of union represented workers is greatest for lower paid workers.[16]

16. J. Schmitt, *The Union Wage Advantage for Low-Wage Workers*, May 2008, p. 4, paper published by Center for Economic and Policy Research.

Chapter 3. Special Definitions and Concepts

§1. Degree of Government Intervention

44. Most American leaders proclaim, as a self-evident principle, the thesis that private sector initiative in resolving social as well as economic problems is superior to governmental intervention. Accordingly, government programs dealing with social and economic problems in the United States frequently are given political justification as helping the parties to help themselves or to ensure that competition is conducted in a fair, honest manner.

Private sector innovation and experimentation has in fact played an important role in American labor law. For example, many facets of the collective bargaining process now incorporated into law in the United States, were first privately developed by the parties. Thus, the Railway Labor Act represented an approach to regulating labor–management relations that evolved out of the bargaining experiences of World War I and the post-war era. The exclusivity concept – that is, the principle that the union selected by a majority of employees in a bargaining unit is the sole and exclusive representative of all employees in that unit – emerged from the dominant approach to collective bargaining that evolved in the United States prior to the adoption of the National Labor Relations Act, the legislation regulating such relationships. Indeed, due to a philosophical split within the Roosevelt Administration, some early governmental efforts at intervention under the predecessor National Industrial Recovery Act rejected the exclusivity doctrine. However, since exclusivity was the general practice in established labor–management relations in the 1930s it became the statutory standard under the Wagner Act. (For discussion of a contrary view see paragraph 424, below.) In like regard, the nature and stature of arbitration as a process for resolving disputes concerning the interpretation and application of collective agreements was an established, mature characteristic of American labor–management relations years before it was fully recognized and incorporated into the American system of labor law.

Although, since the second half of the 20th century, government has been playing an expanding role in shaping labor–management relations and the terms and conditions of employment in the United States, privately shaped accommodations continue to be the method preferred by the parties and by the legislative and executive branches as reflected in official statements of policy and in national political platforms.

§2. Income Policy

45. With the exception of wartime and post war wage and price stabilization measures, the United States has never adopted an ‘incomes policy’. From time to time, however, initiatives have been taken in that direction. In a general sense, the Federal Reserve Board, the American counterpart to a central bank, uses its authority over monetary policy in an effort to accomplish much of the economic stabilization sought by an incomes policy.

46. Early in 1946, Congress established the Council of Economic Advisers to the President whose duty it is to assist the President in preparing an annual economic report to Congress, and to assist him in carrying out the declared policy of governmental responsibility in coordinating efforts to maximize employment opportunities, production, and purchasing power. At the same time, Congress established a Joint Economic Committee of Congress charged with similar responsibilities in providing leadership and coordination in legislative efforts to foster economic growth, maintain full employment and encourage equitable distribution of national wealth. But while the Council and the Joint Committee have produced a great deal of useful data and analysis, they have not generated an incomes policy.

47. From time to time, the executive branch attempts to use the persuasive powers of its leadership position in an effort to stabilize or stimulate the economy through mediatory activities, or by the President or some other high officials cajoling the parties. Such efforts have been characterized as 'jawboning'. Although effective in some individual cases, jawboning has failed to provide the sort of comprehensive direction that constitutes an incomes policy.

Much closer to a true incomes policy approach was the power exercised under the Economic Stabilization Act of 1970. This law, as later amended, gave the President broad power to stabilize prices, wages, salaries, interest rates, dividends and rents for the purpose of reducing inflation, minimizing unemployment, improving America's balance of trade, or assuring the availability of essential goods and services – all necessitated by the economic dislocations caused by the substantial costs in manpower and materials to carry on the nation's unsuccessful efforts to preserve South Vietnam as a non-Communist nation. The effectiveness of the resulting efforts are less than clear and Congress's eventual lack of enthusiasm for those efforts led it to terminate the Act by early 1974. Whether that particular episode in American economic life can be classified as an incomes policy is subject to debate since largely it was a wartime and post war stabilization program.

From time to time states adopt business regulations that involve aspects of incomes policy, such as standards of conduct for businesses involving such matters as carrying on industrial relations or financial responsibilities toward workers when closing or relocating facilities. However, the judiciary sometimes thwarts such efforts on the ground that federal statutes implicitly exclude state regulation of such matters.[17]

§3. Labor Law

48. The scope of labor law in the United States can be variously defined. A relatively narrow definition of 'labor law' in the US describes it as constituting that body of rules governing collective bargaining representation, collective bargaining and the use of stoppages and other industrial warfare techniques, the enforcement of collective agreements and the law regulating the relationship between unions and

17. *Compare*, *Wisconsin Dept. of Industry* v. *Gould Inc.*, 475 US 282 (1986) with *Fort Halifax Packing Co.* v. *Coyne*, 482 US 1 (1987) and *Malone* v. *White Motor Corp.*, 435 US 497 (1978).

their members. A much broader definition of labor law encompasses all those areas of law that constitute the problems handled by the American lawyer who is a specialist in labor law. This definition reaches such additional matters as the regulation of employer financed pension and medical insurance plans that benefit workers and their families. It includes laws regulating internal union affairs, the law governing federal old age pension benefits, workers' compensation and other disability claims, minimum wage laws, health and safety laws, equal employment opportunity laws, and issues involving the individual employment contract. Many of the latter subjects are now taught in law schools under the course heading 'Employment Law'. Thus, one might more accurately refer to the labor lawyer's sphere of expertise as the law of work.

In order to provide a meaningful overview of the American law of work, this monograph provides a basic familiarity with the concerns of the American labor law specialist while giving particular emphasis to those aspects of the law of work that most distinguish it from other bodies of law – especially the collective bargaining relationship, the collective bargaining process, and the machinery for enforcing benefits workers gain through collective representation.

§4. Jurisdiction

49. The term 'jurisdiction' has a broader meaning in American law than it has in many other legal systems. It includes the concept of competence to resolve particular disputes as well as the scope of authority to impose rules on particular groups of people or to regulate specific forms of activity.

Because of the federal structure of American government, one jurisdictional issue in any area of social or economic regulation is the determination of which governmental entity, federal or state, has authority to establish and enforce legal policies. A related problem is which entity should prevail in the event that more than one governmental body has established a policy.

American law is based on the principle that the people are sovereign and have granted limited power to government through the federal and state constitutions. A resulting jurisdictional issue is whether a governmental entity has constitutional power to act in a particular situation. Another way of putting it is that the issue of jurisdiction sometimes involves the problem of whether a particular rule can be imposed upon particular people or particular events. In addition, to the extent that a governmental entity has jurisdiction, it may choose to exercise some but not all of its power. Accordingly, another problem encountered under the legal heading of 'jurisdiction', as that term is used in the US, is determining the extent to which a particular principle was intended to govern particular people or particular events.

50. American labor law encounters all varieties of jurisdictional issues. For example, the federal government has jurisdiction to establish safety laws concerning the operations of interstate roads and such rules affect the manner in which state government workers carry on their job activities. Yet, in the not very distant past, the Supreme Court took the position that the federal government does not have jurisdiction to fix minimum wage standards for state government workers. It later overruled that decision but later still, under the thesis that the federal Constitution implicitly immunizes states from monetary remedies asserted by private persons (in accordance with its perception of the concept of sovereign immunity), imposed limits on the remedies available for enforcing such federal regulations.[18]

Further complicating the judicial perception of state sovereign immunity, under another constitutional doctrine the Supreme Court has held that the federal legislature can by-pass the constitutional restrictions imposed by state sovereign immunity by offering financial grants to the states on the condition that they submit to the remedial regimens attached to those grants.

In addition to the Constitutional uncertainties respecting federal regulatory power, the federal legislature does not follow consistent rules in exercising that power. For example, Congress has established principles regulating collective bargaining relationships in the food distribution and food manufacturing industries and subjects those industries to its minimum wage and overtime pay standards. Yet, although it regulates the minimum wages and overtime pay of many, but not all farm laborers, it has not exercised its jurisdiction over union activities in the food growing industry. In contrast, although federal legislation regulates collective bargaining relationships of professional workers whose employment has a direct or indirect affect on interstate commerce, federal minimum wage and overtime pay standards exempt most such employees from those standards. Similarly, Congress has adopted a different set of rules and procedures for the regulation of union–management relations for that part of the transportation industry that involves carriage by air and rail than is imposed on carriage by motor vehicles or maritime vessels.

Thus, there is no easily discerned or explained pattern in the legislative or constitutional lines drawn when jurisdictional issues are raised. Often the legislative decisions reflect historical circumstances, idiosyncratic political alliances, lack of decisional foresight, or the personal philosophic predilections of the decision makers respecting the proper functions of government. Nevertheless, understanding jurisdictional authority is the starting point in understanding what source of legal authority governs a particular aspect of the law of work in the United States. Accordingly, throughout this work references are found concerning the jurisdictional boundaries that apply regarding the various bodies of controlling laws.

§5. Employee

51. Discussions of American labor law written by American lawyers most often use the word ‘employee’ in referring to workers even though use of the word ‘worker’ poses less danger that a typographical or reading error will cause confusion with the word ‘employer’. The habit of using ‘employee’ is probably a result of the selection of that noun in the principal statutes where the word ‘employee’ is defined in such a way as to set some of the jurisdictional limits on the statute. In

18. *Kimel* v. *Florida Board of Regents*, 528 US 62 (2000). *See*, especially, Justice Souter’s dissent beginning at p. 93. The Court has further complicated the issue of federal power by holding that local governments (cities, counties, school districts, and the like) are not protected by sovereign immunity.

common usage, some persons perceive of the word 'employee' as indicating someone holding a higher social or operational status than a 'worker'. In general discussion, however, the words worker and employee are used interchangeably in the US and are so used in this work.

52. Because the statutory definition of 'employee' is a means of limiting the scope of regulation established by the particular law, the meaning of the word is not uniform from statute to statute. American labor law often, but not always, separates those who manage business assets (managers or executives) and those who direct the work of others (supervisors) from other workers and treat the latter group as the 'employees' whose rights and benefits require legal protection. Those in a confidential relationship with the managers and those who have close family ties with the owners are also commonly, but not always, excluded from the protected class of 'employees'. In addition, some labor laws impose greater responsibilities on employers and provide workers with greater benefits if the employing unit involves a larger number of workers or handles a larger volume of business. In other words, very small businesses are excluded from much of the coverage of the laws regulating employment in the United States. Often, too, special categories of treatment are established for government, agricultural, casual (occasional), and temporary workers, trainees, and seafarers. Generally, American labor and employment laws also exempt independent contractors from statutory protections provided for employees.

§6. Exclusivity and Majoritarian Principles

53. To at least some degree, American labor law adopts the premise that collective bargaining imports democratic institutions into the work place. As a result, the concept of majority rule, and its counterpart of minority rights, prevails in the selection of the bargaining representative or bargaining agent (the terms agent and representative are used interchangeably). The representative, selected by a majority of workers, moreover, is the sole and exclusive collective representative of the workers irrespective of their union membership or non-membership. Because of the exclusive right of collective representation, the bargaining agent is also charged with duties to equally protect the interests of all workers in the bargaining unit, including any who actively seek to remove the representative from its bargaining status.[19]

§7. Bargaining Units

54. Collective bargaining units established in the private sector (non-government) in the United States come in a variety of sizes and shapes. Under

19. Technically, under American labor law a bargaining representative can be a single individual rather than a labor organization. Nevertheless, in most instances workers are represented collectively by a labor organization. Accordingly, because the bargaining representative most often is an entity, the impersonal pronoun 'it' is used throughout this work in referring to that representative.

NLRB doctrine, the structure of the bargaining unit must reflect a shared community of employee interests. A few special statutory rules affect the structure of bargaining units containing security personnel, craft workers and professional employees. Beyond that, the shape of the bargaining unit is influenced mainly by the manner in which the work is organized and directed, bargaining unit customs in the industry, past bargaining history of the establishment, the structure of the employing enterprises' ownership and management, the ambitiousness or caution of those who led the activities of organizing the workers, and the mutual preferences of union leaders and management. Thus, some bargaining units include all employees employed by any of the major employers in an entire industry, others include all employed by a single enterprise, while still others are confined to a particular work site or even a particular job category or work group at the work site.

Bargaining units in government employment follow different patterns than in the private sector and tend to be larger. Often they are defined by the state's collective bargaining law.

§8. Public and Private Sector Employment

55. American labor law treats public employment – that is, government employment – differently from employment in the private (non-government) sector. In part, this distinction relates to the more limited authority of the federal government to regulate state and local government employment than to regulate private employment. In part, the difference in approach results from historic differences in the nature and level of benefits provided public, as contrasted with private, employees during the periods when unionizing was at its peak. Additionally, it reflects recognition that government employees have the alternative of resorting to the political processes as a method for improving work benefits.

56. Sometimes it is difficult to determine whether employment is in the public or in the private sector. Private employers that contract to perform work for the government may employ people to work side by side with workers who are on the public payroll. Sometimes private contractors are engaged to employ people to do work that otherwise would be done by public employees. On occasion, public entities and private entities undertake joint ventures such as the construction and operation of a civic center with an arena, concert auditorium, restaurants, shops, meeting rooms, and the like. Public funds also are sometimes awarded to private entities as grants to encourage research and development that serves the public interest. In all such situations, fine lines must be drawn to determine whether the workers in question are protected by laws enacted to regulate private sector employment or by those enacted to regulate government employment.

57. The distinction made in American labor law between public sector and private sector employment can lead to functionally irrational results. Thus, in one municipality the bus transportation system may be privately owned and operated and, therefore, labor–management disputes of a collective nature will come under the jurisdiction of the NLRA. But that law will not govern an identical dispute in a nearby municipality that owns and operates its own bus transportation system. As a result, the entire structure, procedure and substantive rights can be strikingly different for the bargaining relationship in these two otherwise almost identical situations.

§9. Collective Agreements and Contracts of Hire

58. Whereas an employment contract, or contract of hire,[20] is an undertaking between the worker and the employer concerning the employment of that individual, a collective agreement is an undertaking between the employer and the collective bargaining representative selected by a group of workers. The collective agreement covers the wages, hours and other terms and conditions for the employment of all persons represented by the bargaining agent in the collective bargaining unit. Unlike an employment contract, or contract of hire, which need not be a formalized agreement in the United States, collective agreements are committed to writing.

59. When non-government workers are covered by a collective agreement, that instrument is the paramount contractual undertaking regulating the relationship between the employer and the worker. In addition, most collectively bargained agreements in the US contain dispute resolution provisions establishing the procedure for settling or deciding disputes respecting the proper application of the agreement. These provisions normally designate the collective bargaining agent as the party to enforce employee claims arising under the collective agreement. Thus, enforcement of any terms or conditions of employment established by the collective agreement, whether that alleged breach or failure of performance involved collective interests or an individual's personal interests, normally requires the labor organization to decide to pursue the grievance. That enforcement may take the form of economic pressure or resort to an arbitral forum provided for by the agreement (or by statute if under the Railway Labor Act (RLA) or some public employee bargaining laws), or by resort to a judicial forum. Whatever the method of enforcement or forum, however, the action is based on the collective agreement and not on the employment contract.[21] For the most part, if employment is in a unit that has a collective bargaining representative, the contract of hire between a worker and employer does little more than establish that the employee will work for the enterprise and, perhaps, will also designate the initial job classification and wage rate assigned to the worker. All other terms and conditions of employment normally are governed by the collective agreement. An exception to this practice is found in professional sports and other areas of the entertainment industry where the compensation of those with extraordinary talents is individually negotiated, though often in accordance with a procedure prescribed by the collective agreement.

---

20. The terms 'employment contract' and 'contract of hire' are used interchangeably.
21. *Smith* v. *Evening News Ass'n*, 371 US 195 (1962).

60. In addition to supplanting the employment contract by establishing most, if not all, terms and conditions of employment, the collective bargaining representative can, at least to some degree, modify the individual's work rights and privileges, even to the worker's detriment, so long as in doing so it is not violating its duty of fair representation.[22] Thus, it has long been recognized that the collective representative can sacrifice the interests of the individual worker for the collective good.[23]

Less clear is whether the union can sacrifice a vested right of an individual employee for the collective good. In at least one setting the Supreme Court held that the union, in settlement of a strike, could bargain away the claimed seniority rights of strikers to bid into job vacancies in exchange for a settlement that left some strikers without any benefits to offset the loss of their seniority rights as job bidders. The Court observed that even though the settlement may have been an unwise agreement, the union's action was permissible because there was no showing that the allocation of interests agreed to by the union was either irrational or designed to serve an invidious purpose.[24] In addition, the Court's decision particularly noted that when the union entered into the settlement there was some uncertainty as to whether the sacrificed seniority claims in fact would be enforced by the courts. Accordingly, it is possible that the Court will not reach the same result in a situation in which a union purports to waive the right of individual workers to wages or vacation benefits, or the like, where those benefits indisputably have already been earned by the employees.

22. *Vaca* v. *Sipes*, 386 US 171, 191–192, 194 (1967); *Hines* v. *Anchor Motor Freight, Inc.*, 424 US 554, 567 (1976). In *14 Penn Plaza LLC* v. *Pyett*, 556 U.S. 247, 269–72 (2009) the Court held that a broad arbitration provision can preclude an employee from bringing a statutory suit for age discrimination. It noted that this was not tantamount to waiving the substantive claim but merely substituted the arbitration process as the means of determining the dispute regarding the statutory claim.

23. *J.I. Case Co.* v. *NLRB*, 321 US 332 (1944).

24. *Air Line Pilots Association* v. *O'Neill*, 499 US 65 (1991).

Chapter 4. Historic Background

§1. Growth of Constitutional Government

61. The present system of government in the United States is constituted under a charter promulgated in 1787. At that time the United States of America occupied about one-third of that part of the central section of the North American continent that borders on the Atlantic Ocean. The population consisted of three basic groups: (a) the indigenous population, the American Indians, who were being steadily challenged by European colonizers for possession of the land and for the survival of their culture and population; (b) the European colonizers and their descendants who looked upon this new land as a place to make one's fortune and establish oneself under a new social-political order; and (c) slaves and indentured servants (the former, and larger group, being imported from Africa, but occasionally including members of the indigenous population whose ancestors had arrived thousands of years earlier from Asia).

At the time of its declared independence from British rule, a small industrial and mercantile system was beginning to form in several of the prospering port cities such as Boston, New York, Baltimore, Philadelphia, Charleston, and Savannah. But most persons in the new nation were employed in agriculture either on the small farms of the middle and northern states or the large plantations of the southern region (which also had small farms, especially in its more mountainous sections).

62. Legal doctrine in the United States, at the time of its founding, followed the common law approach and was predominantly influenced by British doctrines and procedures. In the case of slaves, the employment relationship was based upon the law of property. In the case of indentured servants and free workers, it was based upon principles of the developing law of contract and upon the master–servant status relationship.

63. The Constitution of the United States, written in 1787, reflected the political clash over the institution of slavery. The Constitution established a federated union of sovereign states with limited, enumerated powers entrusted to the central government. Among those powers, however, was the authority to regulate commerce within the federation and with foreign nations. That power potentially could be used to halt trade in slaves. A compromise was reached that included a commitment that for a specific number of years Congress would not be able to ban the importation of slaves and the extent to which slaves could be counted in allocating congressional representation. During that time a constitutional limit was also placed upon the tariff that could be levied for importation of slaves.

The conflict over the slavery issue, as well as related economic and social pressures, eventually led a group of the southern states to attempt to secede from the federated union of states. This crisis resulted in a civil war fought between 1861 and 1865. The federal forces prevailed and constitutional amendments eliminated property rights to slaves. Constitutional changes were also adopted for the purpose of ensuring that state and local governments would be required to treat all persons equally and with full respect for their individual rights as free persons. The implementation of these guaranties was largely neglected for close to one hundred years but increasingly occupied legislative and judicial attention beginning in the early part of the 20th Century. It should be noted that implementation of other basic liberties was also largely neglected until the early part of the 20th century.

The implementation of constitutional guaranties of basic liberties has played a significant role in the development of labor–management relations law in the United States.

§2. Growth of the Labor Movement

I. Development

64. The development of labor unions in the United States was slow and fitful. It began in a very small way as early as the mid-1790s. The earliest unions in many ways imitated trade guilds. They operated as fraternal organizations that pledged their members to work only under standards of pay and working conditions established by the labor organization and only side-by-side with fellow association members. Some early labor organizations concentrated on political action to gain improvements in working conditions through legislative reform; others concentrated on obtaining immediate improvements by collectively bargaining with employers, a technique for establishing improved working conditions that by the end of the 19th century had largely superseded unilaterally imposed union work rules.

In some trades, viable unions had moderate success in the early 19th century. By 1881 a federation of unions was formed and a few years later it adopted the name 'the American Federation of Labor' (AFL). Throughout most of its first forty years, this organization was led by Samuel Gompers who believed that workers could best achieve their goals by pressing employers for improvements through the process of collective bargaining. Gompers' influence was sufficiently great so that collective bargaining has continued to be the principal tool through which the American labor movement pursues its goals.

65. Most unionization successes in the early years of the American labor movement came in the skilled trades. Thus, the terms 'trade union' and 'labor union' came to be used interchangeably. With the growth of mass production industries, however, some influential union leaders urged that the focus for unionizing be broadened to include all persons, skilled and unskilled, employed by the same employer or even by the same industry.

After much internal struggle, in the 1930s several member unions of the AFL established a task force to achieve major unionizing gains in key industries. This task force soon came into conflict with the rest of the AFL leadership. As a result, several influential unions were ejected from the AFL and formed a new federation of unions called the Congress of Industrial Organizations (CIO). This group had significant success in organizing workers in such major industries as automotive manufacturing and steel production. A bitter rivalry developed between the industrially oriented CIO unions and the trade skills oriented AFL unions, and this conflict continued until 1955 when the two federations merged (AFL–CIO). With merger came adoption of rules of conduct designed to reduce such inter-union competitive practices as enticing members from each other to gain status as the recognized bargaining agent in units represented by another union. The AFL–CIO has been largely successful in eliminating such internecine competition.

A few unions were expelled from the CIO in the late 1940s on charges of being Communist-dominated and several were expelled from the AFL–CIO in the mid-1950s for violating the AFL–CIO Code of Ethical Practices. The largest such union outside the AFL–CIO for many years was the Teamsters union which was the largest union in the country. Another major union, the United Automobile Workers Union, left the AFL–CIO in 1968 over an ideological conflict that involved, as well, substantial elements of internal political rivalry between the leadership of the federation and the Auto Workers' leadership. It returned to the AFL–CIO in 1981 and the Teamsters returned in 1987.

II. Unions Today

66. As of 2016, total union membership was estimated to be 14.6 million. In addition, collective agreements negotiated by unions protect an estimated 1.7 million non-members. (See paragraph 42, above, and paragraphs 497–500, below, for further membership details.)

The AFL–CIO continued to suffer from breakaways. The most significant recent one came in mid-2005 when several major unions, asserting that AFL–CIO leadership was placing too much of its resources on unproductive political activities and too little on organizing new workers, formed the Change to Win coalition leaving the AFL–CIO with fewer than 10 million members. Several later returned to the AFL–CIO and one, the United Food and Commercial Workers remained in Change to Win but also resumed its AFL–CIO membership.

By 2017, four major and one minor national union are affiliated with the Change to Win coalition. Their total memberships are 5.5 million workers in industries such as hospitality, retail, food processing, healthcare, needle trades, communications, and transportation. To date, the split has not returned the labor movement to the level of the former hostile AFL rivalries with the CIO inasmuch as the two groups have cooperated on some national political lobbying efforts and many of the local organizations of the Change to Win coalition unions continue to participate in AFL–CIO sponsored state and local union councils.

67. In recent years, the major growth in labor organizations has been in those unions that represent government workers. There has also been considerable organizing success among health care workers and innovative efforts to organize the lowest paid service employees.

The shift in the American economy away from manufacturing industries has adversely affected union growth due to the greater resistance to unionization encountered in most white collar industries. Decline in private sector union membership also has been influenced by increased employer use of threats and coercion to dissuade workers from supporting unions, interpretations of the National Labor Relations Act that have reduced its protection of union activities, the tactic of unionized companies outsourcing or threatening to outsource work to companies (sometimes under the same ownership) whose workers are not unionized, the exporting of jobs (and threat thereof) to overseas operations, and the increased employment of workers who are not legally in the US and who, therefore, fear deportation if they engage in activity that challenges management.

§3. DEVELOPMENT OF FEDERAL LABOR LEGISLATION

68. Although labor organizations and other reform groups were largely unsuccessful at obtaining worker protective legislation in the 19th century, they made some progress. Some states adopted laws imposing a maximum number of daily work hours (usually 10), and in 1868 the federal government adopted a law limiting to an eight-hour work day those employed by the federal government as mechanics and laborers. Statutes facilitating suits for job related injuries were adopted in a few states, but probably the most important legislative impact unions had in the 19th century was their influence in getting the states to establish a system of universal public school education.

While European nations were busy experimenting in the late 19th century with legislative programs to provide workers with compulsory health insurance, work injury compensation programs and pension benefits, American courts often struck down as unconstitutional such elementary reforms as minimum wage and maximum hour limitations for factory work. The constitutional doctrine by which the courts justified their actions was that a statute limiting the terms and conditions under which employees sell and employers buy their services constitutes an impairment of the guaranty of freedom of contract and a taking, without due process and without just compensation, of the property interest in one's work output. Thus, the courts perversely struck down reforms in aid of workers under the guise of protecting the workers' constitutional rights.

I. Early Constitutional Struggle

69. The modern constitutional approach to legislation regulating the terms and conditions of employment emerged in the decision of the Supreme Court of the United States in *Holden* v. *Hardy*, 169 US 366 (1898), where it held that the federal constitution is not violated when a state limits the maximum number of hours per day that can be worked in underground mines. But the broad potential impact of the decision was delayed inasmuch as the holding soon was narrowly interpreted to emphasize the state's special concern for protecting against the extraordinary health and safety hazards involved in mining operations. Thus, although a state law limiting the hours of employment for women was upheld in *Muller* v. *Oregon*, 208 US 412 (1908), on the ground that it directly served to protect the health of women and especially safeguarded them as society's child bearers, a state law limiting the number of hours per day that a person could be employed as a baker was declared void by the Supreme Court on the ground that it subjected to an unreasonable restraint the liberty of selling one's labor.[25] Several years later, the Supreme Court also held void a federal law that prohibited interstate commerce in goods produced at plants which employed children below age 14 or which employed children ages 14–16 beyond specified hours. Such regulation, explained the majority of the Court, was a matter of local concern and, therefore, beyond the scope of federal power.[26] Moreover, although the Court had sustained the authority of the states to impose maximum hours of work for women, in *Adkins* v. *Children's Hospital*, 261 US 525 (1923), it held that a statutory minimum wage for women was constitutionally barred on the ground that the price paid for labor, when set by broadly applied standards, has no direct relationship to preserving health or the public welfare and, therefore, unduly restricts freedom to contract for the sale of one's work efforts.

70. Initially, the Supreme Court had similarly placed a number of specific constitutional roadblocks in front of legislative efforts to protect, promote and regulate unionization and collective bargaining. As a result of a highly publicized violent strike in the railroad industry, in 1898 Congress adopted the Erdman Act which required the Interstate Commerce Commission to mediate labor controversies in that industry and encouraged the arbitration of such disputes and provided a means for enforcing any resulting arbitration awards. In addition, the Erdman Act prohibited railroads from engaging in various forms of conduct designed to coerce or discourage workers from joining unions. In *Adair* v. *United States*, 208 US 161 (1908), the Supreme Court held that Congress could not prohibit anti-union discrimination by the railroads. The Court justified its decision on the ground that, in its view, the common good was not adequately served by this restriction on employer prerogatives and, therefore, did not justify interfering with the freedom to choose the terms and conditions under which parties enter into an employment contract.

71. In a decision known as the *Danbury Hatters* case, 208 US 274 (1908), issued a week after *Adair*, the Supreme Court affirmed a civil suit for treble damages against a union. The suit was based on the theory that the union had violated the Sherman Antitrust Act by promoting a boycott against a hat manufacturer that refused to recognize the union as its employees' collective bargaining representative. A few years later, in the course of modifying the Sherman Antitrust Act, Congress adopted language in the Clayton Act which declared that 'the labor of a human being is not an article of commerce'. Most union supporters assumed that this change freed future union organizing efforts from the threat of federal antitrust suits. But in 1921, in *Duplex Co.* v. *Deering*, 254 US 443, the majority of the Supreme Court narrowly interpreted the Clayton Act exclusion of labor disputes as covering only those conflicts in which the disputing employer and the disputing workers are affected by the economic pressure being exerted. Since *Duplex* involved a union request to potential customers not to buy the employer's product, and a request to workers not to install or repair that product, the pressure affected employers that were only indirectly involved in the dispute. Therefore, the Supreme Court ruled

25. *Lochner* v. *New York*, 198 US 45 (1905).
26. *Hammer* v. *Dagenhart*, 247 US 251 (1918).

that an action was properly brought under the Sherman and Clayton Acts to enjoin the union's activity as an unlawful restraint of trade.

72. It was not until the mid-1930s, when the nation was in the midst of the Great Depression, that the Supreme Court withdrew the constitutional barriers to social-economic legislation. In 1937, deciding *West Coast Hotel Co.* v. *Parrish*, 300 US 379, the majority of the Supreme Court overruled the *Adkins* decision and announced that the federal legislature can introduce greater equity into the marketplace by establishing minimum wages designed to counteract the unequal bargaining position of workers. Similarly, in 1937 the Supreme Court: (a) upheld the NLRA; (b) recognized the authority of Congress to adopt the Social Security Act, which created a national old age retirement insurance system and induced the states to adopt unemployment insurance programs; and approved the constitutionality of federal laws that established minimum wages and overtime pay requirements for most employees whose work directly and indirectly affects interstate commerce.[27]

II. Development of Modern Labor Legislation

A. *Railway Labor Act*

73. During World War I, the labor movement enjoyed substantial membership growth. From about 2.5 million members in 1914, total union membership had reached about 5 million by 1920. This growth was aided by the policy adopted by the National War Labor Board, co-chaired by former President, and later Chief Justice of the Supreme Court, William Howard Taft, which used its persuasive authority to promote labor peace by getting employers to recognize the 'right of workers to organize in trade unions and to bargain collectively through chosen representatives'.

The railroad industry was under direct government regulation during the First World War and the federal regulatory bodies accepted the principle that railroad workers had a right to unionize and bargain. Government mediation was used to facilitate bargaining and promote labor peace. When control of the railroads was returned to private hands in 1920, Congress adopted laws to continue much of the labor–management relations system developed during the war. The initial legislative attempt failed, however, because it lacked adequate methods for enforcing the resolution of conflicts among the parties.

Under pressure from President Coolidge, the railroad employers' association and the heads of the railroad unions reached a compromise regarding how to best structure their dispute resolution mechanisms and Congress adopted their jointly sponsored proposal under the title the 'Railway Labor Act of 1926'. The 1926 law has

27. *NLRB* v. *Jones & Laughlin Steel Corp.*, 301 US 1 (1937); *Helvering* v. *Davis*, 301 US 619 (1937); *Steward Mach. Co.* v. *Davis*, 301 US 548 (1937). *See also United States* v. *Darby*, 312 US 100 (1941).

been amended several times and, in 1936, was extended to cover the airline industry. It continues to regulate labor–management relations in the railroad and airline industries. Among other things, it protects the right of workers to organize in these two industries and provides governmental machinery for determining which union, if any, has majority support of the workers. The Act also requires the majority union and management to negotiate prior to making changes in the terms and conditions of employment.

In 1930, when a challenge to the constitutionality of the RLA reached the Supreme Court, it upheld the statute on the ground that protecting the right to unionize and to bargain collectively was a reasonable effort by Congress to find an equitable, stabilizing method for settling labor–management disputes in an industry carrying goods in interstate commerce.[28]

B. Norris–LaGuardia Act

74. In the latter part of the 19th century and the first third of the 20th century, the injunction became a major legal tool used by employers to combat unions. Under American law, disobedience of an injunctive order is treated as a contempt of court. Traditionally it is punished, after a hearing by the judge whose order was disobeyed, by fine or imprisonment or both. The imprisonment can be punitive or it can be conditioned upon the respondent purging himself of his wrong by taking the required corrective action.

Some authors have suggested that the reason the injunction became a management tool in combating unions in the latter part of the 19th century was that, at the time, many railroads were operating in receivership because investment speculation and fraud had caused their financial failure. When the railroad workers made collective demands under threat of a walkout, the court that supervised the receivership would issue an injunction against such action in order to protect the assets from further depletion. Whether from the example of the effectiveness of injunctions against union activities in the railroad industry, or from judicial inventiveness and antagonism toward the labor movement, employers frequently found the courts to be receptive in permitting the injunctive remedy to come to the aid of the 'employer's freedom of contract'.

Adding to the problems that injunctive relief posed for unions, under American legal traditions a temporary restraining order can be issued upon an *ex parte* presentation of the facts, and a temporary injunction can be issued with less than a full-fledged adversary hearing. Therefore, these remedies often were granted to petitioning employers without giving the union an opportunity to present its version of the facts or its arguments concerning the respective equities of each side's claims. Not surprisingly, some judges issued labor injunctions in situations that, under all of the facts and normal standards of equity, probably did not qualify for this form of relief.

---

28. *Texas & New Orleans Railroad Co.* v. *Brotherhood of Railway & Steamship Clerks*, 281 US 548 (1930).

75. Obtaining injunctive relief was facilitated if the employer and worker had executed what unions called a 'yellow-dog contract'. This was a contract in which the worker agreed that, as a condition of continued employment, he would not join a union or assist in union activities. (Union leaders often said only a 'dirty yellow dog' – a symbol of an untrustworthy coward – would sign such a contract.) Employers that had yellow-dog contracts with their workers sought injunctions against union activity to protect the sanctity of those contracts against the threat of union interference.

76. In 1894, when workers walked out to protest a wage reduction by the Pullman company, the manufacturer and operator of railroad sleeping cars. Eugene Debs, president of the American Railway Union, called for a sympathy boycott asking workers to refuse to operate trains that carried the sleeping cars rented by the struck company. The boycott became widespread and, when Pullman began hiring strikebreakers, violence in the form of extensive property damage and personal injury followed. On the theory that the resulting interruption to rail transportation was interfering with the delivery of mail by federal employees, the Attorney General of the United States received a federal court injunction against Debs and other union officials and 'all other persons combining and conspiring with them, and to all other persons, whosoever, to desist and refrain from, in any way or manner, interfering with, hindering, obstructing, or stopping any of the business of any' of the named railroads. Within a few days, federal troops arrested Debs, who was charged with violating the order. He was tried by the judge who issued the order and was sentenced to six months' imprisonment. His conviction was upheld by the Supreme Court of the United States.[29] This event focused political attention on the use of the injunction as an anti-labor weapon, and eventually the labor movement was successful in curbing its availability in labor–management disputes.

77. The Norris–LaGuardia Act, adopted in 1932, announced a national policy recognizing the benefits of collective bargaining, outlawed the yellow-dog contract (see paragraph 75, above), removed labor–management conflicts from laws prohibiting restraints of trade, and insulated labor–management disputes from the threat of federal court injunctions. Among other things, the Act placed rigorous limitations upon the availability of injunctions in labor disputes and required that any person charged with contempt of such an injunction is entitled to a jury trial conducted by a judge other than the one who issued the order.

C. National Labor Relations Act

78. Franklin D. Roosevelt, with the help of labor union efforts, was elected President of the United States in 1933, a few years after the United States became enmeshed with the Great Depression that had enveloped the economies of the industrial world. The Roosevelt administration proposed a series of programs designed to promote national economic recovery. Included was the National Industrial

29. *In re Debs*, 158 US 564 (1895).

Recovery Act which was designed to stabilize business activities and encourage members of various industries to propose codes of fair conduct to regulate business in their industry. Upon the President's approval of these codes, they were to have the force of law and be exempt from antitrust law restrictions. In order to qualify for approval, the codes were required to deal with specified problems and to adopt certain policies. One of these policies was the guarantee of the right of employees to unionize without employer interference.

In 1935, in *Schechter Poultry Corp.* v. *US*, 295 US 495 (1935), the United States Supreme Court unanimously held the NIRA unconstitutional on the grounds that it delegated too much legislative authority to the executive branch and to private parties and that it permitted federal regulation of what the Court characterized as purely local (and, therefore, not federal) issues. During the brief life of the Act, however, unions were provided with a modest degree of protection and a considerable degree of encouragement in their organizing campaigns.

79. The National Industrial Recovery Act was scheduled to expire in 1935 unless renewed by Congress and many doubted whether it would be renewed. As the end drew near for the National Industrial Recovery Act, Senator Robert F. Wagner proposed and fought for the adoption of a new statute designed solely to regulate unionization and labor–management relations. His efforts were successful and the resulting law, the National Labor Relations Act of 1935, is often referred to as the Wagner Act.

80. The constitutional validity of the NLRA of 1935 was upheld by a closely divided Supreme Court in a series of decisions on the same day. The principal, and most often cited, of these cases was *National Labor Relations Board* v. *Jones & Laughlin Steel Corp.*, 301 US 1 (1937). The Court held that federal authority to regulate interstate commerce includes the power to regulate both transactions that are directed at utilizing the interstate market place and those that, when combined with similar transactions, cumulatively have a substantial impact upon the flow of interstate commerce regardless of whether that impact is direct or indirect. These decisions also rejected the concept that freedom of contract and property interests are infringed when the government provides rules that require an employer to establish the terms and conditions for employment by bargaining collectively with the representative chosen by a majority of its[30] workers.

81. The NLRA of 1935 remains at the core of that body of federal legislation that regulates union organizing activity and the collective bargaining process. The Act was substantially revised in 1947 by the Labor Management Relations Act (LMRA), otherwise known as the Taft–Hartley Act. The latter designation is based on the names of its two principal congressional sponsors. Another significant revision of the NLRA came in 1959 with the adoption of the Labor–Management

30. Although many employing units in the United States are owned and managed by individual proprietors, most workers are employed by corporate enterprises, or other limited liability entities, in which ownership is at least structurally separate from management. Because most employment is by a legal entity, the impersonal pronoun 'it' is used throughout this work to refer to the employer.

Reporting and Disclosure Act (LMRDA) which is popularly known by the names of its congressional sponsors – the Landrum–Griffin Act. Although their names are not attached to the 1959 legislation, four US Senators who played important roles in shaping that legislation were John F. Kennedy, who was soon to be elected President of the United States; Richard Nixon, who lost the presidential election to Kennedy but was later elected President; Hubert Humphrey, who later became a Vice President of the United States; and Barry Goldwater, who later was an unsuccessful candidate for the Presidency. In addition to the 1947 and 1959 amendments there have been a few less extensive modifications of the NLRA.

Because the NLRA when revised in 1947 was enacted as Title I of the Labor Management Relations Act, it is also often referred to by the latter name. Either reference title – NLRA or LMRA – is correct. The NLRA is codified in the federal statutes at 29 US Code §§141–169.

82. The revisions of the original Wagner Act largely involved some reorganization of the National Labor Relations Board, the administrative agency established to enforce that law, plus efforts to place controls over union activities deemed by Congress to be improper. Accompanying these modifications were efforts to deal with specific problems – protecting the right of members to control their unions, protecting the rights of dissident union members, discouraging corrupt practices in labor–management relations, providing machinery for enforcing collective agreements, and devising a method for resolving those work stoppages that can cripple the entire economy. These accompanying modifications of American labor law were adopted in those sections of the Taft–Hartley and Landrum–Griffin Acts which did not involve amendment of the NLRA.

Although initial union reaction to both the Taft–Hartley Act and the Landrum–Griffin Act was marked by fury and charges of being designed to destroy unions, the labor movement in time adjusted to living with these modifications. As a result, labor's own legislative reform plans no longer include major repeal of the 1947 or 1959 changes. Rather, they largely are aimed at reversing a number of Supreme Court decisions that interpreted vague, broad principles of the NLRA in ways that hinder union organizing and bargaining activities.

III. Other Labor Legislation

83. While the NLRA is the core of federal legislation regulating labor–management relations in the United States, several other statutes have a considerable impact upon the terms and conditions of employment and some impact on the collective bargaining process.

A. Fair Labor Standards Act

84. The Fair Labor Standards Act of 1938 (FLSA), 29 US Code §201 *et seq.,* as now amended, covers most wage earners in the private and public sectors of employment in the United States. The Department of Labor estimated in 2017 that 130 million workers, over 85 percent of the labor force, are protected by the Act. Together with the Portal-to-Portal Act of 1947, it established a minimum hourly wage, which has been amended upward and has been $7.25 since 24 July 2009. The FLSA also limits the types of deductions that may be taken which reduce wages below the minimum, and requires that for employment beyond 40 hours per week an added premium be paid equal to one-half of the regular wage rate.

Changes in the minimum wage are made by the Congress. Therefore, the issue of when and by how much the minimum should be changed is a highly politicized issue. Although the minimum was about 50 percent of the national mean wage rate for hourly workers during the first four decades of the Act, the ratio declined considerably and by mid-2017, the minimum wage was not quite 28 percent of the mean hourly wage for such workers.

At $7.25 an hour, a worker who is employed 40 hours a week for 52 weeks will annually earn $15,080. Under the Census Bureau's poverty threshold definitions, that is sufficient income to keep a single person household above the 2017 poverty level ($12,060) but not a household of two persons (poverty level $16,240). In 2015, an estimated 4 percent of female hourly workers and 3 percent of male hourly workers were paid at or below the federal minimum wage. (This included workers in jobs not covered by the federal minimum or whose circumstances permit payment at reduced minimum rates. See paragraph 85, below.) The portion of all wage workers earning at or below the minimum was 15.1 percent in 1980, 9.9 percent in 1985, 5.1 percent in 1990, 5.3 percent in 1995, and 3.6 percent in 2000 and 3.3 percent in 2015. State minimum wage laws and market pressures increased the functional national minimum in the absence of Congressional action. Nevertheless, in 2015, 9.5 percent of women and 5.4 percent of men below age 25 were paid at or below the federal minimum wage.

85. There are numerous exemptions to the FLSA minimum wage and overtime pay requirements. These include exemptions for executive personnel and for administrative and professional employees who are paid a weekly salary that is at least as high as a minimum amount designated by Department of Labor regulations. As of the preparation of this work, it was $455 per week as contrasted with a weekly wage of $290 if paid for 40 hours at the minimum of $7.25. (On an annual basis, the threshold salary is $23,660 which is below the $24,600 poverty level guide for a family of two adults and two children under age 18.) Additionally, although under amended regulations adopted in 2004 the employee must primarily perform an administrative, executive or professional function, the exempt employee may perform a significant amount of production work. Further, the executive exemption is applicable to an employee who has supervisory responsibilities over as few as two full-time employees. In 2016 the Department of Labor increased the annual exemption threshold earnings for these groups to $47,476 ($913 a week), which at the time was 40 percent of the national average annual earnings, and provided for adjustments every three years based on the same 40 percent criteria. However, a federal district court enjoined enforcement of the rule and the Trump administration has asked the court to stay proceedings while it engages in new rule making that is expected to eliminate the exemption's minimum earnings requirement. In addition, the Department of Labor can certify employers to lawfully pay a reduced minimum wage to certain categories of employees if the employment satisfies administratively established criteria. The categories for such reduced minimum standards include employment of learners, apprentices, messengers, full-time students and the handicapped. 'Student-learners', for example, can be paid as little as 85 percent of the minimum. A similar reduction is available for the initial few months of employing new entrants to the labor market, subject to restrictions on the percent of the employer's work force that is so employed and prohibitions against hiring workers at the sub-minimum rate to replace current employees.

86. Federal law does not require that the entire wage 'payment' be in monetary form. Some 'in kind' payments, such as employer provided lodging and meals, are permitted but the credited value cannot exceed the employer's actual cost and, in any event, cannot exceed fair value. In addition, provision of such accommodations cannot be credited against the minimum wage if they are provided for the employer's convenience.

Gratuities given to employees by customers cannot be counted toward more than half of the required minimum wage.

87. Businesses with less than $500,000 annual gross sales or activity are excluded from the FLSA. Some types of businesses, such as small agricultural operations, commercial fishing, and certain seasonal recreational or educational enterprises, are exempted from the federal standards. However, often such businesses are governed by the minimum wage laws of the state in which they are situated.

88. Many state minimum wage standards are now higher than the FLSA minimum and, in that event, the state standard prevails even though the employment is covered by the federal law. Twenty-nine states and the District of Columbia had higher minimum hourly pay rates than the federal minimum by late 2017. The District of Columbia had the highest hourly minimum ($12.50); in Washington and Massachusetts it was $11.00 an hour. A few municipalities have an even higher minimum wage standard.

89. Work performed in American Samoa is subject to separate wage–hour regulation under the FLSA. Some businesses in Puerto Rico were covered by lower FLSA rates until 1996. At one time there were similar special provisions covering the Virgin Islands.

90. The FLSA prohibits most employment of children under age 14 and restricts the types of employment and hours and conditions of employment of those under age 18. The latter restrictions are designed to ensure that the children have time available to attend school and study, and that they are not exposed to dangerous machinery or equipment.

91. The FLSA did not apply to government employees until the 1960s. The Supreme Court of the United States initially ruled the extension to be constitutionally valid. A few years later it reversed itself but in *Garcia* v. *San Antonio Metro. Trans. Auth.*, 469 US 528 (1985), it again reversed itself and ruled that the FLSA can set minimum pay standards for state and local government employees. Thereafter, Congress modified the extension of the Act so as to allow local governments to substitute mandatory extra time off in lieu of having to pay an overtime premium to some categories of workers who often are called-in for emergency duty or who have rotating shift schedules that combine long hour and short hour work weeks.

As explained in numbered paragraph 50, above, because the Supreme Court has construed the Constitution as containing an implicit protection of state sovereign immunity from monetary remedies, although the Fair Labor Standards Act is enforceable against local governments in the same manner as against non-governmental employers, only the Department of Labor can seek the Act's monetary remedies if the state government is the employer.

B. Other Federal Wage-Hour Laws

92. Employment under contracts to sell goods or services to the federal government is subject to additional wage and hour legislation designed to discourage convict labor and child labor and to ensure that people employed to do the work paid for by the federal government are paid not less than the prevailing wage standards for such work. The principal statutes are popularly known as the Walsh–Healey, Service Contract, and Davis–Bacon Acts. These laws are found at sections 35 to 45 and 351 to 358 of Title 41 and sections 276a to 276a–5 of Title 40 of the US Code. The precise regulations that are applicable depends on the nature of the goods or services being provided.

The Walsh–Healey Act, which applies to those who sell the federal government manufactured or assembled goods, requires, at the minimum, wages for that work equal to the wage that prevails for similar work in the locality where the goods are manufactured or assembled. However, as a result of a federal court of appeals decision issued in 1963,[31] the Department of Labor has found it impractical to establish up-dated prevailing wage rate regulations under that Act. Over the intervening years, increases in the FLSA minimum wage and general inflationary trends have rendered the Walsh–Healey prevailing wage rates irrelevant. The Davis–Bacon and Service Contract Acts require that benefits such as paid vacations, health care insurance, and retirement insurance, be included as part of the prevailing compensation that constitutes the minimum that must be paid those doing work for which the federal government pays by contract or grant where the work respectively involves construction or repair of permanent attachments to land, or services provided to the government of the United States. The Davis–Bacon Act also regulates the ratio of apprentices to journeymen allowed in performing skilled trade work. Each of these laws has cumbersome administrative enforcement mechanisms to determine the precise minimum required under the standard. In addition, many close questions arise

31. *Wirtz* v. *Baldor Electric Co.*, 337 F.2d 518 (DC Cir. 1963).

respecting whether the Act is applicable to a particular contract or aspect of a contract.

Special regulations of employment under federally sponsored contracts or grants are also found in legislation such as the National Foundation on Arts and Humanities Act (20 US Code §952(m))§§, the Antikickback Act (41 US Code §51 *et seq.*), and the Contract Work Hours Standards Act (40 US Code §3702). In addition, many states have laws regulating minimum employment conditions for workers engaged in performing contracts paid by the state government or its local subdivisions (counties and municipalities).

C. Protection from Job Injury

93. For most workers, a state workers' compensation law provides income protection for losses resulting from job related disease or injury. State workers' compensation laws require employers to finance, through insurance or direct payment, the cost of medical treatment, rehabilitation devices and treatment, and a portion of lost earnings. As a general principle, workers' compensation laws protect the worker regardless of the fault of the claimant or fellow employees in causing the injury or illness. In many states, however, the income replacement benefit may be respectively increased or decreased if the injury was caused by the employer or the injured worker failing to abide by established safety practices or regulations.

Permanently injured workers who are partially disabled receive partial compensation for their disability either based on a scheduled definition of the extent of the particular type of loss (for example, a lost toe equals so many weeks of disability pay, a lost foot equals so many more weeks of such pay) or by estimating the lost earning capacity. Typically, the benefit payment is two-thirds of the worker's normal weekly earnings for the specified number of benefit weeks. However, benefits for partial and total disability are subject to a maximum weekly amount – normally, two-thirds of the average earnings of all employees covered by such benefits in the state – and in most states additional limits are placed upon the duration of such benefit payments. Some states also provide a minimum amount for weekly benefit payments. Thus, in relation to normal earnings, higher paid workers receive proportionally less income substitution than do lower wage workers when suffering the same disability.

In many states, workers' compensation coverage is administered through a government operated insurance fund. In other states coverage is solely through private insurance or self-insurance, and still other states allow employers to choose between private and government operated insurance funds. Generally, a worker is barred from suing her or his employer for damages from an injury or illness that is covered by workers' compensation benefits, and in most states cannot sue fellow workers, even if that party's negligence caused the injury or illness. On the other hand, workers' compensation laws do not bar suits against those who deliberately inflicted an injury or illness and workers can sue third parties who negligently caused on-the-job injuries. In the latter situation, the provider of workers' compensation benefits has a right to subrogate from the recovery any payments it made to the victim.

Federal government employees are provided with workers' compensation benefits under a separate federal law. Federal legislation also provides a workers' compensation program for the benefit of those employed in loading and unloading maritime vessels or in building or repairing such vessels. This law, popularly known as the Longshore and Harbor Workers' Compensation Act, also protects Americans employed in foreign countries by defense contractors and some other categories of government contractors.

In addition, employees who have made a minimum number of contributions to the federal Social Security program are entitled to receive disability benefits if they are permanently and totally disabled from performing any 'substantial gainful work' and are not eligible to receive any benefits or any further benefits under a workers' compensation program. Social Security disability benefits are small but are available regardless of whether the injury or illness was work related.

94. Instead of a workers' compensation insurance system, seafarers who suffer a job caused injury or illness can bring a damages suit under the Jones Act (46 US Code App. §688) or the Federal Employers' Liability Act (45 US Code §51 *et seq.*), or both. The Jones Act preserves a seafarer's maritime actions for injuries due to unseaworthiness of a vessel and for a seafarer's right to maintenance and cure when ill or injured. The Federal Employer's Liability Act eliminates certain common law defenses when an employee is injured due to the employer's or fellow servant's fault. It provides for apportionment of damages when the injured worker is partially at fault, but a full recovery if the employer's violation of safety rules contributed to the injury or illness.

Railroad workers who suffer job related illness or injury must seek their recovery by bringing suit under the above described Federal Employers Liability Act. In addition, railroads are required by federal law to provide disability insurance benefits for their workers.

95. The 1977 Mine Safety and Health Act (30 US Code §801 *et seq.*), provides both a system for federal regulation and inspection of this especially hazardous industry and a system for compensating the victims of some of those work hazards.

96. The Occupational Safety and Health Act (29 US Code §251 *et seq.*), adopted in 1970, provides a broad preventive program for reducing injuries and illnesses caused by work hazards to health and safety.

D. Social Security Act and Retirement Benefits

97. The Social Security laws, adopted in the mid-1930s, establish a compulsory federal system of old age retirement benefits and induce states to adopt unemployment insurance programs. Later amendments provided federal benefits as well for disabled workers and the dependents of disabled and deceased workers.

The pension portion of the Social Security program is financed by a payroll tax paid by both workers and employers. Self-employed persons also participate. In

2007 it was estimated that over 96 percent of the workforce was covered by the Social Security System.

Those not covered by the Social Security System largely work in jobs that are subject to alternative mandatory government retirement programs. For example, railway workers (see 45 US Code §231 *et seq.*) and many state and local government workers receive similar protection under separate laws.

Until 2000, the Social Security retirement benefit was based on the assumption that the normal retirement age is 65. Beginning in that year the presumed normal retirement age increases two months each year until it reaches age 67 in the year 2022. Although a person who is covered by Social Security can begin receiving retirement benefits at age 62, the monthly benefit is actuarially reduced so as to result, on average, in the person receiving the same lifetime benefit that would be received if the beneficiary began receiving benefits at the presumed normal retirement age. Similarly, adjustments that increase the monthly benefit are made for those delaying their receipt of retirement benefits up to age 70. A beneficiary's spouse is entitled to an additional benefit and former spouses from marriages of long duration additionally are entitled to benefits. The Social Security benefit level varies depending on the level of contributions made to the system by the beneficiary who is the source of the benefit and benefits are automatically adjusted to reflect changes in the cost of living. Social Security retirement beneficiaries need not be fully retired. There is a partial benefits reduction for earned income. However, persons age 65 and above can receive Social Security benefits without any deduction for employment income. (For more details see paragraphs 261–263 below.)

In 2008, persons 65 and older in aggregate received 39.8 percent of their income from Social Security benefits, 19.7 percent from private and other government pensions and annuities, 13 percent from personal asset income, and 25.6 percent from earnings. In the same period, Social Security benefits were paid to almost 90 percent of persons 65 years and older, whereas only 55.3 percent of this population received some income from pensions or annuities, only 35.4 percent received some income from personal assets, and only 20.4 percent received income from current earnings. Thus, for most elderly people, Social Security benefits were their principal or only source of income. It has been estimated by the Center on Budget and Policy Priorities that in 2012, without Social Security retirement benefits, 44.4 percent of the elderly would live in poverty whereas with those benefits, the portion of elderly living at poverty income levels was 9.1 percent.

98. Additional legislation, most recently the Employee Retirement Income Security Act of 19 74 (29 US Code §1001 *et seq.*), and the Multi-Employer Pension Plan Amendments Act of 1980 (29 US Code §1322a *et seq.*), were adopted to encourage and to regulate the fiscal soundness and financial and social integrity of privately funded employee retirement programs. Similar earlier legislative efforts, such as portions of the LMRA and the LMRDA, are designed to assure the financial and social integrity of those privately financed collectively bargained programs that provide health insurance and other welfare benefits to workers and their families.

According to the Investment Company Institute, Americans held a total of $26.1 trillion in all forms of retirement assets at the end of the first quarter of 2017. A little over half was in individual retirement funds or individual defined contribution accounts over which the retiree or future retiree controls at least some aspects of the investment decisions. The potential financial power resulting from control of the investment of retirement funds has not gone unnoticed. Unions in particular have urged that investment of these assets be directed toward improving work opportunities and increased worker participation in management. However, efforts in this direction have not been extensive and some categories of funds such as defined benefit funds (about $3 trillion in assets) face legal constraints in the form of the Employee Retirement Income Security Act's requirements for prudent, diversified investment solely in the interests of the fund beneficiaries.[32]

99. Medicare, a partial medical insurance program for elderly former workers and their spouses, is a separate federal program funded by a payroll tax.

E. Unemployment Insurance

100. Generally, unemployment compensation is provided on a state-by-state basis. Three states, Alabama, Alaska and New Jersey, finance these benefits through taxes imposed on workers as well as on employers. The others finance their program solely by taxing employers.

The state unemployment insurance programs have been encouraged and shaped by a special federal tax upon employer payrolls. Employers receive a credit against all but a very small part of the federal tax based on their responsibility to pay into a state unemployment insurance program. As of 2005, about 97 percent of non-farm workers were covered by these programs.

Unemployment insurance programs use experience ratings to reduce the premium charged to those enterprises that seldom layoff or dismiss workers. Although state plans must satisfy some general federally established standards, the amount of individual benefits and structure for financing these programs varies from state to state.

Generally, benefits are designed to pay about one-half of the unemployed worker's normal earnings for a maximum benefit period of 26 weeks. However, benefits are subject to minimum and maximum benefit amounts that most often are based upon statewide average earnings. About one fourth of the states provide small additional allowances based on the number of the recipient's dependents. Weekly benefits from unemployment insurance also vary because of the substantial state to state differences in the minimum and maximum weekly benefits. The benefit ceiling imposed by the maximum amount that can be paid substantially reduces the benefit's relationship to normal wages for higher paid workers. Partly for this reason and partly because lower paid workers have higher unemployment rates, in 2013 the average unemployed worker was paid a benefit equal to about 33 percent of average weekly earnings when measured nationally.

---

32. J. Zanglein, 'High Performance Investing: Harnessing the Power of Pension Funds to Promote Economic Growth and Workplace Integrity', 11 *The Lab. Lawyer*, 59 (1995).

The federal government provides an extension of the benefit payment period for an added 13 weeks in times of high unemployment and it has given additional extensions during periods of weak economic conditions. Also, extended benefits are provided by the federal government to those whose job loss is attributable to particular problems such as adverse foreign competition. Separate unemployment compensation programs protect federal government workers and railroad workers.

In order to qualify for unemployment benefits, some states require that the applicant had a minimum amount of employment (usually 14–20 weeks) during the previous twelve months. A few states base eligibility on the employee having had a minimum level of earnings (varying from $1,000 to $2,000) during the qualifying base period, while many other states require the applicant to have earned, at the minimum, a specified multiple (for example, 30) of the weekly benefit during the qualification period.

Two other standard eligibility requirements are that the applicant did not lose the most recent job due to the worker's wrongdoing and is able and willing to accept a suitable job. A number of states also deny benefits to seasonal workers during their non-work seasons.

Only two states, Rhode Island and New York, make unemployment benefits available to strikers. Most states, however, allow strikers to draw unemployment compensation benefits if the employer has hired others to take their jobs.[33]

In recent decades 55–65 percent of unemployed workers were not receiving unemployment insurance benefits either because they had insufficient prior employment to qualify, the conditions under which they lost their most recent employment disqualified them, they never applied for benefits, or they had exhausted the benefits to which they were entitled. On the other hand, some part-time or casual workers are able to receive unemployment insurance benefits based on their recent loss of qualifying full-time employment.

Differences in payment policies and benefits levels largely are responsible for the considerable differences in the average employer contribution rate for unemployment insurance as a percentage of payroll. In 2016 it ranged from an average rate of 0.24 percent in Tennessee to an average rate of 1.45 percent in Rhode Island. Comparisons of the rates can be misleading, however, because states vary in the amount of an employee's annual pay that is subject to the tax. In a number of states the tax is assessed on only the first $7,000 of pay, as in California, while the base is much higher in other states. For example, in 2016 it was $39,700 in Alaska and $42,200 in Hawaii.

F. Employment Discrimination

101. Few, if any, national populations approach the racial, religious, and cultural diversity of the American people. Employment discrimination based upon such differences has been a major social and economic problem in the United States since the earliest colonization by Europeans which displaced and partially annihilated the indigenous 'Indian' population. The importation of black slaves and Asian

33. *See N.Y. Tel. Co.* v. *N.Y. State Dep't of Labor*, 440 US 519 (1979).

indentured labor introduced two other segments of the population under conditions of sub human treatment. With that legacy, employment discrimination based upon race, alienage, religion, sex, sexual orientation, national origin, age and non job-related physical or mental disability, have too often characterized work force decisions in the United States. Federal legislation known as the Civil Rights Acts, passed shortly after the Civil War, initially accomplished almost nothing to combat such employment discrimination even though these laws required that all persons shall have rights to make and enforce contracts equal to those enjoyed by the dominant white citizenry. In the second half of the 20th century, a combination of pressures, including race riots and new techniques for political utilization of the mass media, provided the momentum for change – a momentum reinforced by public indignation at the assassinations of popular leaders (first President John F. Kennedy and a few years later Martin Luther King, Jr. and President Kennedy's brother, Senator Robert Kennedy) who were identified with the civil rights movement. In the 1960s and 1970s, new legislative and executive initiatives were adopted to prohibit job discrimination based upon race, religion, national origin, sex, age (40 and older), and mental or physical handicap. A variety of governmental agencies, new remedies, and private causes of action were introduced by these laws to enforce the legal standards of equal employment opportunity. In the second decade of the 21st century, legal and social barriers to those with non-conventional sexual orientation and those choosing transsexual modification began to fall.

G. Family and Medical Leave Act (FMLA)

102. Although American culture purports to place great emphasis on the central role of the family, customary terms and conditions of employment have not been very accommodating to employee family responsibilities. Moreover, the government has been very slow to intervene for the purpose of facilitating an employee's ability to meet those responsibilities. The FMLA (29 US Code §§2611–2619), adopted in 1993, offers some protection for longer term employees by requiring all but very small employers to provide a minimum amount of unpaid leave during a 12-month period for the purpose of allowing the employee to attend to serious personal or family medical needs.

Chapter 5. The Role of Government in Shaping and Administering Employment Law and Labor Relations Policy

103. The dominant characteristic of government intervention in private sector labor and employment relations in the United States is to officially recognize the status relationships and regulate and facilitate much of the procedure by which the parties themselves resolve their differences and administer their resulting agreements. Generally, during peacetime, American law has intervened in setting the terms and conditions of employment only to the extent of establishing minimum standards and trying to ensure that work opportunities are based on merit rather than on status differences.

Nevertheless, government agencies regularly investigate and remedy violations of individual and collective employee rights. Because the statutory standards respecting these rights often are vaguely or even ambiguously worded, administrative agencies and courts must interpret the intent of legislative policy as applied to specific facts. Similarly, many of the statutory standards are broad and intentionally give the administrative authorities the power to shape more specific rules for carrying out the legislative policies. When these factors are combined with a national characteristic of readily resorting to litigation in resolving conflicts, and of involving lawyers in all levels of enterprise decision making, it can be seen why the governmental entities charged with enforcing American labor laws require (but generally do not receive) large staffs and have heavy case loads.

104. Individuals who are appointed by elected officials for short terms of office preside over the key administrative agencies responsible for enforcing collective and individual employment law in the United States. Although they are supposed to enforce the law with an even hand and without regard for their own policy preferences, the wide breadth of discretion entrusted to these officials, plus their short terms of office, result in their being more politically sensitive than would be expected of life-tenured judges. This characteristic is not, however, necessarily a deficiency in the enforcement structure. Labor relations policy is a vital dimension of the nation's economy. Sound policy choices in this field cannot be based on scientifically ascertained truths or irrefutable logic. Rather, they inevitably reflect changing social and political values as well as imperfect knowledge. In addition, they require at least some flexibility to adjust rules based on wisdom gained from experience and to keep pace with financial and technological changes as well as to reflect the nation's changing political preferences and social norms. The structure chosen by Congress for enforcing labor relations policy offers that flexibility.

105. Because of the large number of cases administered by the key agencies responsible for enforcing labor and employment laws in the United States, the manner in which these agencies are staffed and the processes for handling cases can have a substantial influence upon the results. Because of differences in skill and integrity in investigating facts and researching and arguing law, the composition and dedication of the agency staff can alter the effectiveness with which the pronounced law of the land becomes the enforced law of the land.

106. American lawyers tend to be skilled adjudicative tacticians. Manipulation of procedural rules frequently shapes the substantive result. Thus, the procedural structure for enforcing labor and employment law, to the extent that it is susceptible to tactical manipulation, has an important influence upon the effectiveness with which the underlying legislative policies are translated into practical results.

107. To summarize the above four paragraphs, individual and collective employment law in the US is administered by a large bureaucracy whose staff, structure and procedures have a very real impact on the nature of that law as enforced. Accordingly, Part III of this work is devoted to a closer examination of the key agencies that administer labor relations law and employment law and the procedures for the enforcement of those laws. Without an understanding of these staffs, structures and procedures, one cannot accurately appreciation the nature and content of American labor and employment law as it is known by American legal specialists.

Chapter 6. Sources of Labor and Employment Law

§1. Judicial Authority and Case Precedent

108. There are two principal sources of labor law in the United States: (a) governmental policy as specified in statutes, regulations and judicial precedents, and (b) the law of the shop as recognized, modified and made enforceable through collectively bargained agreements. The application of norms established by both sources relies on the adjudicative process and uses the case method of decision-making guided by respect for case precedent.[34] The applicable norms often can be altered by legislative action, quasi-legislative rule making,[35] adjudicative rule making, or negotiated contract modification. However, ultimately the determination of the competency of the legislature, the administrative agency, the lower courts, or the parties, to make such changes is a matter for judicial review. And, despite the fact that the judiciary is the weakest branch of government, for well over 200 years the American constitutional system has abided by the doctrine of judicial supremacy in interpreting the law, including the Constitution.

109. The theoretical role of the judiciary in its capacity as the ultimate source for interpreting statutory, regulatory, or constitutional law is to determine the true intent of the promulgators of the law and to shape the decision so as to reach the result, in the circumstances at issue, that most closely reflects the intentions of the law makers. However, as legal realists note, those who make the law are unable to foresee all contingencies for its application, deliberate with complete thoroughness, nor write with sufficient precision to always make clear all aspects of their intentions. Therefore, the concept of the lawmakers' intent often is nothing more than a convenient or expedient fiction. Accordingly, adjudicative decision makers often must make their own policy choices. In addition, adjudicative decision makers are often in a position to substitute their own preferences for those of the lawmakers – even when the intent of those lawmakers can be discerned. The temptation to impose one's own strongly held convictions, moreover, is heightened to the extent that the doctrine of judicial supremacy increases the prospects that the adjudicative decision makers' policies will have a lasting impact. Although such decisions can be over-ruled by the legislature modifying its statute, or by contracting parties rewriting their agreement, inertia and the unwillingness of the party benefiting from the erroneous adjudicated choice can pose substantial barriers to re-instating that original intent. For these reasons, the study of American labor law focuses largely on the policies announced in the course of adjudication.

---

34. This means that in making their own decisions, lower courts and administrative agencies are expected to abide by the principles of law announced by higher courts in prior decisions. In addition, higher courts are reluctant to modify previously announced legal principles (doctrine of *stare decisis*).
35. The announcement of a governing legal standard when issued by an administrative agency or department of government other than the legislature or the judiciary is interchangeably referred to as a 'rule' or 'regulation'.

§2. CONSTITUTION

110. A basic American legal doctrine is that the authority of government is limited to that which has been delegated by the people through the constitution by which they have created the government. In addition, the federal constitution imposes many restrictions upon state governmental authority. Therefore, no area of American law can ignore the Constitution of the United States. It is the paramount law. In the case of employment law, constitutional doctrines play an especially important role both in limiting and assigning the governmental bodies that are competent to adopt policies respecting worker rights, privileges and interests, and in restricting the ability of government to interfere with personal liberties in the course of regulating collective labor–management and individual employment relations. For example, the constitutional division of authority between state and federal governments permits the federal government to pronounce whether its statutes shall be the sole source for regulating particular conduct or whether the conduct shall be additionally regulated by state laws that do not conflict with the federal regulations. In addition, whatever the source of the law, it cannot violate constitutionally preserved individual liberties. To illustrate, the constitutional regulation of governmental searches limits the conditions under which a government inspector may enter an employer's premises without the owner's consent and limits, as well, the conditions under which a court may issue a warrant authorizing such a search.

§3. COMMON LAW

111. The law of individual contracts of hire in large measure is common law developed by judicial decisions. Common law – that is, the behavioral norms that reasonable, law abiding people are expected to follow – also largely governs internal union affairs. A federal common law of collective agreements has been shaped by the judiciary since the late 1950s pursuant to the Supreme Court's determination that it has received a statutory mandate to develop such rules. And, a common law of the shop is enforced by labor arbitrators in the course of deciding disputes submitted to them under collective agreements.

§4. LEGISLATION

112. Most principles of labor–management relations law in the United States are based on legislation. Although federal legislative policy dominates the field, state statutes, too, are important respecting issues over which federal law has preserved substantive state jurisdiction. Federal legislation is less pervasive respecting standards governing the individual employment relationship.

§5. Administrative Processes

113. Most federal legislation both in the collective labor relations area, and in the area of regulating individual employment relations, pronounce basic regulatory principles and establish an administrative agency which receives delegated authority to promulgate detailed rules for carrying out those principles. The administrative agency often has responsibility, as well, for prosecution and hearing level adjudication of violations.

The scope and type of authority delegated to administrative agencies varies. The National Labor Relations Board, for example, has the authority to promulgate substantive rules or regulations (a power it rarely uses), to investigate violations of the National Labor Relations Act, to prosecute and hear cases involving allegations of such violations, to remedy such violations, and to seek judicial enforcement of its remedies. It also has authority to conduct elections to ascertain employee wishes respecting collective representation in appropriate bargaining units. The Federal Mediation and Conciliation Service, in contrast, has little authority that could be classified as investigatory, no significant rule-making authority, no prosecutorial authority and no adjudicative authority. Part III of this monograph examines the structure and authority of the key administrative agencies that establish and enforce labor and employment relations law in the United States.

§6. Executive Fiat

114. Those employed by government in non judicial or non legislative capacities technically serve under the chief executive officer of the governmental authority that establishes the employing entity. In the absence of legislative enactments regulating the rights and responsibilities of public servants, the chief executive officer can issue orders governing their terms of employment. For many public employees, therefore, executive fiat often is an important source of law.

115. Absent controlling legislative enactments, the executive branch is responsible for entering into contracts that are necessary for carrying out the business of government. Occasionally, executive fiat has been used to impose terms that affect the employment practices of those who contract with the government. For example, this authority has been used in the United States to promote greater equality of employment opportunities.

§7. Collective Bargaining

116. The principal function of collective bargaining is to regulate the law of the shop, including the conditions of employment and the levels and forms of remuneration. In the United States, collectively bargained agreements establish most of the specific terms and conditions of employment and normally establish, as well, the decisional machinery for administering the collective agreement. Collective bargaining is also used for adjusting individual grievances and resolving disputes arising under the interpretation and application of the collective agreement. Collective agreements are legally enforceable contracts in the US.

§8. ARBITRATION AWARDS

117. Most collectively bargained agreements in the United States require resort to private arbitration tribunals for resolving those grievances and disputes concerning the interpretation and application of the agreement that are not resolved through grievance negotiations. Under the Railway Labor Act, resort to tribunals of this sort is mandatory. Normally, grievance arbitration decisions are final and binding and, if necessary, are enforced by the courts.[36]

Not only are arbitration awards the governing law in the individual cases, but labor arbitration decisions often are published and form a body of persuasive precedent that guides future decisions by being treated as the common law of the shop.

118. Occasionally in the private employment sector, and with significant frequency in the public employment sector, arbitration awards resolve interests conflicts between labor and management. That is, the arbitrator is called upon to establish the terms and conditions of employment that will govern the parties during the designated period.

36. In some instances, such as federal civil service, arbitration awards concerning government employee grievances are subject to administrative review.

Part I. The Individual Employment Relationship

Chapter 1. Concepts

§1. Law of Master–Servant

119. The relationship between the employer and the worker is governed by a mixture of legal doctrines in the United States. To a considerable extent it is treated as an area of the law of contracts; in other respects, it is treated as an area of the law of status. In addition to the influence of these two basic doctrinal divisions is the overriding impact of legislatively enacted rules that often ignore traditional legal concepts and, therefore, defy classification based on the traditional modes of legal analysis.

120. One traditional classification that continues to provide some guidance respecting the legal ties between the worker and employer is the area most often referred to as the law of master and servant – a label that itself reveals the outmoded conceptual framework of much of the included doctrine. Nevertheless, the common law principles of master and servant (or, employer–worker) law continue to provide a starting point for analysis and some guiding principles that govern the employer–worker relationship under American laws.

I. The Status of Master–Servant

121. Under the law of master and servant, a servant is defined as one who places himself under the right of a master to control and direct the performance of work, the product of which work is the property of the master. It is the right of control, not actual control, that is important. Thus, one is treated as a servant even though the worker's knowledge or skill respecting the work is beyond the employer's competence.

122. The generally accepted master–servant definition, however, also describes other relationships that are distinguished from master–servant for a variety of legal purposes. Although under the law of agency, a principal–agent relationship always exists between an employer and an employee, many principal–agent relationships do not constitute a master–servant relationship. In a sense, though, an agent is a special type of servant. And, some relationships combine the elements of employment for some purposes with the elements of principal–agent for others. To illustrate, a corporate officer is an employee for some purposes and an agent for other purposes. Some aspects of the parent–child relationship satisfy the definition for master– servant. Yet, the parent–child relationship is governed by a different set of rules, often enforced by a special court using different types of remedies based upon different public policy concerns than those giving rise to the law of master–servant. The same can be said of some aspects of the employment relationship in comparison with such special relationships as those between the government and a prisoner, a student and teacher, a religious order and its novices, or among partners.

II. Employee Status Contrasted with Other Relationships

123. A frequently disputed distinction is the one between the employer–worker relationship and the relationship between an independent contractor and one contracting for that person's or entity's services. This distinction is particularly important in American labor law because independent contractors are excluded from the coverage of many statutes that govern employment relationships or collective bargaining.

Generally, the common law distinction between employee and independent contractor focuses upon whether the employing entity has the right to control how the work is to be performed. An independent contractor retains substantial autonomy over the mode and means of execution of the work, whereas an employee does not. This distinction, however, must be applied in light of the customs of the particular vocation being performed. For example, an attorney employed by a large corporation or by a partnership of lawyers, although legally classified as an employee, typically exercises great autonomy over the mode of execution. At common law, the employee-independent contractor distinction is made primarily to determine whether the employing entity will be responsible, through the doctrine of *respondeat superior*, for acts committed by the worker. Thus, the employer's retention of the right to control how the work is performed justifies holding the employer liable for wrongdoing committed by the employee within the scope of the employment.

In addition to the right of control, other factors considered at common law in distinguishing between an employee and an independent contractor include the length of the engagement, whether the engagement is terminable at will or automatically terminates at the end of the contract term, the method and measure of compensation, whether others are simultaneously engaged to perform the same tasks, whether the tasks performed are part of the principal operations of the enterprise, whether the worker operates his or her own business separate from the principal's business, whether the worker has the opportunity to earn extra profit or suffer losses based on performance efficiency, and the extent to which the principal provides or pays for tools, materials, equipment and other capital goods and expenses needed or expended in carrying out the assigned tasks.

This same analysis is sometimes used in determining whether an individual is an employee or independent contractor for purposes of a particular statutory scheme.[37] But other times statutory distinctions between employees and independent contractors are applied with some recognition given to the policy goals of the legislation, goals that may call for an analysis not so heavily dependent upon the employer's right of control. For example, employee status under the Fair Labor Standards Act and under state legislation providing benefits for unemployed workers is less concerned with the employer's right of control and places more emphasis on whether the worker is economically dependent upon the employing entity.[38] Thus, an individual retained to perform work may qualify as an employee under some statutes, even if he would be classified as an independent contractor under the common law.

III. Who is the Employer?

124. Another difficulty in determining whether a relationship belongs in the employer–worker category is encountered when a worker is subject to the directions of two or more principals who benefit from the worker's output. Who, for example, is the employer of the typist temporarily assigned from a company that specializes in providing temporary help? Is it the insurance company whose work the typist is performing, or is it the company that assigned the typist to work at the insurance company for a day, a week, or a month? As with the problem of independent contractors, in American law the critical factors shaping this decision shift depending on the purpose for which the distinction is being made. Thus, the individual may be treated as the insurance company's employee for occupational safety purposes but as the employee of the company making the work assignments for minimum wage purposes. That result can be justified on the grounds that the owner of the work site can best protect the worker's safety but the company providing temporary workers is in a position to ensure that minimum wage standards are satisfied. Sometimes the issue is resolved by treating both entities as the joint employers of the worker.

125. The NLRA excludes 'independent contractors' from its protections. In *NLRB* v. *United Ins. Co.*, 390 US 254 (1968), based on legislative discussions respecting that term when it was added to the Act in the Taft–Hartley amendments, the Court explained: 'The obvious purpose of this amendment was to have the Board and the courts apply general agency principles in distinguishing between employees and independent contractors under the Act.' However, the Court

37. *Nationwide Mutual Insurance Co.* v. *Darden*, 503 US 318, 323–324 (1992). This decision, which arose under the Employee Retirement Income Security Act (ERISA), stated that unless otherwise specified by federal legislation, courts interpreting federal statutes should use the common law of agency to determine employee status. In describing the common law, however, the Court drew attention to 20 factors that are used under that test and observed: 'Since the common-law test contains "no shorthand formula or magic phrase that can be applied to find the answer … all of the incidents of the relationship must be assessed and weighed with no one factor being decisive"'. *NLRB* v. *United Ins. Co. of America*, 390 US at 258.

38. *Goldberg* v. *Whitaker House Cooperative*, 366 US 28 (1961).

did not attempt to recite those principles. The NLRB, on the other hand, has turned to the *Restatement of Agency (Second)*, §220(2), for guidance as to the common law.[39] That summation of legal principles states that the following facts are to be weighed in deciding whether a relationship is employment or an independent contract:

(a) the extent of control which, by the agreement, the principal may exercise over the details of the work;
(b) whether or not the one employed is engaged in a distinct occupation or business;
(c) the kind of occupation, with reference to whether, in the locality, the work is usually done under the direction of the employer or by a specialist without supervision;
(d) the skill required in the particular occupation;
(e) whether the employer or the worker supplies the instrumentalities, tools, and the place of work for the person doing the work;
(f) the length of time for which the person is employed;
(g) the method of payment, whether by the time or by the job;
(h) whether the work is part of the regular business of the employer;
(i) whether the parties believe they are creating the relation of master and servant; and
(j) whether the principal is or is not in the business.

This statement of principles does not require that all of the listed factors point in the same direction for a particular result, nor does the statement establish the relative weight to be given each factor. Thus, considerable discretion is left to the fact finder's judgment.

The variations of results under the NLRA provide some illustrations of the almost case-by-case resolution of whether a person is an employee and, if so, whose employee. For example, the NLRB has held that dancers who perform as guest artists with a symphony orchestra are independent contractors and not employees of the orchestra. On the other hand, it has held that a band leader who employs musicians for a night club engagement is not an independent contractor but rather is himself an employee of the night club.[40] Taxi cab drivers who own their vehicles, but operate solely under the name of a company that provides rules of operation and that regulates who can drive the cabs on second and third shifts, have been held to be employees of that company and not independent contractors.[41] However, the courts reviewing more recent decisions have tended to find taxi drivers to be independent contractors when they have significant autonomy over the vehicle's use and

---

39. *First Legal Support Services*, 342 NLRB 350 (2004); *Roadway Package System, Inc.*, 326 NLRB 842 (1998). *See also Community for Creative Nonviolence* v. *Reid*, 490 US 730 (1989) (applying general common law of agency to the meaning of employee). *The Restatement of Agency (Third)* generally follows the *Restatement (Second)* approach. *See Restatement of Agency (Third)* §7.07(3) (2006).
40. *Musical Artists*, 157 NLRB 735 (1966) and *Musicians Local 368*, 170 NLRB 271 (1968).
41. *Yellow Cab Co.*, 229 NLRB 1329 (1977), reversed on the facts, 603 F.2d 862 (DC Cir. 1978); *Trade Wind Transp. Co.*, 168 NLRB 860 (1967).

fare receipts increase.[42] Similarly, a court set aside a decision finding an employment relationship even though a truck owner who distributed snack food products was required to get the manufacturer's approval in hiring a driver's helper.[43] On the other hand, a company in the business of supplying temporary drivers to other companies was held by the NLRB to be the joint employer of those drivers together with the companies whose driving work was being performed.[44]

126. The joint employment relationship sometimes is divided into the general employer and the special employer with legal responsibility being delegated based on the respective employer's authority to control the worker's conduct. Thus, the general and special employer may in the same situation share legal responsibility under a minimum wage law but only the general employer is liable as employer when enforcing occupational health and safety regulations and only the special employer is liable in the event of an unfair labor practice. Yet, in some other work situations, both general and special employers may jointly be liable for all three purposes.[45]

§2. Basic Characteristics of Employment Contracts

I. Generally

127. Although, as noted above, there are non-contractual elements of the employer–worker relationship, generally the engagement to employ and to be employed is most often treated as a contractual undertaking. A contract of hire, or employment contract, can be an express or an implied contract and normally need not be in writing or be evidenced by any other formalities. An exception is in the employment of seafarers where, by statute, a written employment contract (called 'shipping articles') is required for vessels of commercial size. By law, too, a seafarer's employment contract must contain statutorily specified provisions (46 US Code §574).

128. Contracts of employment normally are governed by the laws of the place where most of the work will be done, although some written employment agreements specify that they are to be governed by the law of another state. Some aspects

---

42. *Yellow Taxi Co.* v. *NLRB*, 721 F.2d 366 (DC Cir. 1983); *City Cab Co. of Orlando*, 285 NLRB 1191 (1987).
43. *Frito-Lay, Inc.* v. *NLRB*, 385 F.2d 180 (7th Cir. 1967)(emphasizing the driver's autonomy in generating business and retaining profits); *accord NLRB* v. *Associated Diamond Cabs, Inc.*, 702 F.2d 912 (11th Cir. 1983).
44. *Manpower, Inc.*, 164 NLRB 287 (1967); *Troupe Leasing Co.*, 174 NLRB 200 (1969).
45. For a discussion of the criteria for establishing joint employment status, *see NLRB* v. *Browning Ferris Indus.*, 691 F.2d 1117 (3d Cir. 1982). *See also Restatement of Agency (Third)*, §7.03, comment (d)(2) (2006) (liability should be allocated to both the general and the special employer on the basis that 'both exercised control over the employee and both benefitted to some degree from the employee's work').

of the employment agreement may be governed by federal law which, at least theoretically is uniform throughout the states. Differences in the statutory interpretations of lower federal courts, however, can make that uniformity illusory.

129. Absent an express agreement for the engagement to be for a specified period of time, an employment contract is presumed to be 'at will'. This means that either party is free to terminate the contract without prior notice or justification. However, a few jurisdictions (Montana, Puerto Rico and the Virgin Islands) impose statutory restrictions upon employment termination that effectively alter most employment contracts so as to eliminate the 'at will' presumption. Accordingly, in the typical employment arrangement in the United States, there is no need to attempt to spell out all of the terms and conditions of the engagement in writing. Employment terms such as the amount of vacation, job responsibilities, holidays, and the like are often explained in a set of written employment policies drafted by the employer. These policies can be established, clarified, or modified as issues arise with either side being free to choose between accepting the implied employment contract in accordance with the policy changes or terminating the contract. However, since the early 1980s a growing number of state courts restrict an employer's authority to unilaterally modify employment contracts without reasonable prior notice of the intended change.[46] Using theories of promissory and equitable estoppel, these courts require the employer to present longer term workers with a reasonable opportunity to decide whether to continue working under the new terms of employment or seek alternative employment. At least one court permits modification only if new consideration (either some benefit to the employee, detriment to the employer, or a bargained for exchange) has been given for the modification.[47] In addition, federal laws such as the ERISA impose prior information and notice requirements respecting changes in some types of benefits.

In the absence of agreed terms of employment, courts sometimes find those terms by implication based upon custom and practice. In like regard, the rule of definiteness, imposed as a test of the enforceability of many other forms of contract, is greatly relaxed with respect to the contract of employment. Similarly, the rule of mutuality of obligation often is avoided in employment contract situations. Thus, an employer's undertaking to employ someone for a specific period of time does not lack mutuality of obligation simply because the worker is free to quit at will, or because the worker undertakes to perform the service only 'if physically able'.[48]

---

46. *See*, for example, *Hathaway* v. *General Mills, Inc.*, 711 S.W.2d 227 (Tx. 1986) and *National Rifle Ass'n* v. *Ailes*, 428 A.2d 816 (DC Ct. App. 1981).
47. *Brodie* v. *General Chem. Corp.*, 934 P.2d 1263 (Wy. 1997).
48. The phrase 'mutuality of obligation' is interchangeable with the requirement of American law that there be an exchange of consideration for a contract to be enforceable. However, that requirement does not apply to a contract formed when the obligee performs what was asked by an obligor who made a unilateral offer. *See*, for example, *State* v. *Lex Assocs*. 730 A.2d 38 (Conn. 1999). *See also* M. Pettit, Jr., 'Modern Unilateral Contracts', 63 *B.U.L. Rev*. 551 (1983).

II. Capacity to Enter into an Employment Contract

130. Legal capacity to contract generally begins at age 18 in the United States. The usual rule is that a contract for labor or personal services asserted against a minor (normally defined as under 18 years) is voidable at the minor's election but is enforceable by the minor. In some jurisdictions (such as New York and California), statutory provisions allow courts to supervise employment contracts entered into with minors. In such situations, the contracts are enforceable against the child as well as by the child. These provisions are particularly significant in the entertainment industry where the services of uniquely talented minors can be in great demand and can command high wages.

A person who is legally incompetent due to mental deficiency or insanity has a right to rescind or to enforce a contract.

Under some circumstances aliens lack legal competence to enter into an employment contract. The Immigration Reform and Control Act of 1986 (IRCA) prohibits the knowing employment of aliens unauthorized to work in the United States. An unauthorized alien can be in the country illegally or in the country legally but not authorized to work. The IRCA requires employers to obtain from all workers (citizens and non-citizens alike) documentation (such as passport, certificate of US citizenship, green card,[49] or driver's license plus social security card) documenting authorization to work in the United States.

In the wake of the IRCA, there is some uncertainty regarding what protection, if any, unauthorized aliens may receive under various employment statutes. Prior to the passage of the IRCA, the US Supreme Court held the unauthorized aliens were employees for purposes of the National Labor Relations Act.[50] However, there has been less agreement over what remedy an unauthorized alien may recover for a statutory violation. That reinstatement is not an available remedy has been well accepted. But disagreement existed on the issue of back-pay until the Supreme Court's decision in *Hoffman Plastics, Inc.* v. *NLRB*, 535 US 137 (2002). There, the Court held unequivocally that the award of back-pay to unauthorized aliens 'would unduly trench upon explicit statutory prohibitions critical to federal immigration policy, as expressed in IRCA'. However, an appellate court has held that the *Hoffman* decision does not prevent recovery by an unauthorized worker for injuries suffered while on the job and numerous lower courts have held that the decision does not preclude recovery of wages earned while employed.[51]

131. Child labor laws, enacted both at the federal and state levels, place additional restraints upon employment contracts entered into with a child. These laws make it illegal, and punishable by a penalty, to employ children except in limited circumstances. The federal child labor laws prohibit almost all employment of children under age 14 where the employing enterprise ships goods in interstate commerce. It also prohibits the employment of children ages 14 and 15 in manufacturing

---

49. This document certifies that the holder has a visa that permits the non-citizen to be employed.
50. *Sure-Tan, Inc.* v. *NLRB*, 467 US 883 (1984).
51. *Affordable Housing Found., Inc.* v. *Silva*, 469 F.3 219 (2d Cir. 2006); *Jin Ming Lin* v. *Chinatown Restaurant Corp.*, 771 F. Supp. 2d 185, 186 (D. MA 2012).

and mining establishments and in certain other enterprises that ship goods in interstate commerce and limits the employment of children ages 16 and 17 in various industries.

The federal FLSA assigns to the Secretary of Labor responsibility to designate additional prohibited employments for children age 14–17. The Secretary has exercised this authority by limiting the number of hours, times of day and number of days children can work under any circumstances. Various occupations, such as truck driving, handling of explosives, meat packing, wrecking, demolition, working with power-driven saws and shears, and the like, are prohibited by the Secretary as being particularly hazardous to child labor.

132. State laws regulating child labor also often limit the hours of work, time of work and number of days of work. Certification procedures, including work permits, often are used as a policing device. Generally, however, child labor laws make exceptions for employment by the child's parent or legal guardian. This is consistent with the principle that parents have a right to an unemancipated child's services and earnings.[52] Where, however, a child's earnings are a result of a court supervised exception to minimum age laws, provision normally is made for earnings in excess of maintenance costs to be treated as the child's property and be held in custody or trust until the child reaches majority.

Child labor laws in the United States also often contain exceptions that permit activities considered non-commercial employment (such as mowing a neighbor's lawn or baby sitting) and for activities that in American culture have traditionally been considered appropriate for minors (such as delivering the morning or evening newspaper to residences or delivery of groceries from the shop to the customer).

III. Void, Illegal and Unenforceable Employment Contracts

133. Generally, it is illegal to enter into a contract to engage in an unlawful employment. Such contracts are void and unenforceable.

A. *Peonage and Slavery*

134. An agreement to work for an employer in order to pay off a debt, an arrangement known as peonage, is made unenforceable by a federal law enacted in 1867. This law was adopted pursuant to the 13th Amendment to the US Constitution which prohibits slavery and involuntary servitude. Criminal penalties are imposed on the employer. In the past, these penalties were authorized only if the employer used or threatened to use physical force or engage in coercive use of the law to hold the employee in peonage,[53] but in 2000 the US enacted the Trafficking

52. J. Barnett and D. Spradlin, 'Enslavement in the Twentieth Century: The Right of Parents to Retain their Child's Earnings', 5 *Pepperdine L. Rev.* 673 (1978).
53. *United States* v. *Kozminski*, 487 US 931 (1988). (An example of coercive use of the law would be threatening to report the worker for committing a crime.)

Victims Protection Act which explicitly expanded the actionable conditions under which an employer might hold an employee in peonage.[54] Thus, if a worker voluntarily assigns his wages to pay off a debt owed the employer, the federal Act may well be violated. In addition, such deductions might violate state laws restricting the deductions that can be made from wages. Also, a federal regulation, 16 Code Fed. Reg. §444.2(a), places substantial restraints on such assignments resulting from a loan or retail sale.

B. Unlawful Occupations

135. Employment in an illegal occupation and employing someone in an illegal occupation are crimes. Employment at the trade of prostitution, for example, is illegal in most jurisdictions in the United States. Thus, a contract to engage in such employment is unenforceable in most parts of the US.

C. Licensed Trades and Professions

136. A contract of employment is void if the employment involves a licensed or certified trade or profession and the worker does not possess the requisite license or certificate. In some licensed trades or professions, a licensed individual can only be employed by another holder of that form of license if the employment involves providing those services to third parties. This rule is based on the assumptions that the goals of a business enterprise are inconsistent with the fiduciary responsibilities a professional has toward her or his clients and that one who has the authority to direct professional work should at minimum have the same qualifications and professional responsibilities as those whose work is being directed. Although the prohibition against a non professionally owned and managed enterprise providing professional services has been applied at various times to real estate and securities brokers, physicians, lawyers and certified public accountants,[55] in recent years this restriction has begun to disintegrate.[56]

D. Apprenticeship

137. The traditional form of apprenticeship is illegal under the child labor law prohibitions and under minimum wage legislation. However, modern forms of

54. Public Law (PL) 106–386 (2000), 22 US Code §§7101 *et seq. See United States* v. *Marcus*, 487 F. Supp. 2d 289 (2007). (The Trafficking Victims Protection Act was a response to the Supreme Court's narrow interpretation in *Kozminski*); *United States* v. *Kaufman,* 546 F.3d 1242 (10th Cir. 2008).
55. For example, *Arizona State Bar* v. *Arizona Land Title and Trust Co*., 366 P.2d 1 (AZ 1961). *See also* M. Asimov, 'Embodiment of Evil: Law Firms in the Movies', 48 *UCLA L. Rev*. 1339 (2001) for indications of the extent to which some of the ethical problems presented when non-professionals manage the services provided by professionals are encountered as well when professional enterprises become very large and operate with substantial overhead expenses.
56. For example, *Cincinnati Insurance Co.* v. *Wills*, 717 N.E.2d 151 (Ind. 1999).

apprenticeship are permitted so long as they meet standards established by the agencies that regulate minimum wages and child labor. Thus, the federal Fair Labor Standards Act authorizes the Secretary of Labor to issue certificates to apprenticeship programs permitting the payment to apprentices of wages below the minimum wage standards. These certificated apprenticeship programs are, additionally, subject to the Secretary's regulations respecting the number of apprentices, the length of the apprenticeship, the instructional content of the program, and the ratio of apprenticed to non-apprenticed workers in the enterprise.

E. *Yellow Dog Agreements*

138. The Norris–LaGuardia Act prohibits so-called yellow dog contracts. (See paragraph 75, above.) The Norris–LaGuardia Act made yellow dog contracts, or such provisions in employment contracts, void and unenforceable in the federal courts. In addition, such contracts now constitute an unfair labor practice under the NLRA. A majority of the states have adopted separate laws invalidating such contracts or making them illegal and unenforceable.

F. *Statutes of Frauds*

139. As a result of what is referred to as the 'statute of frauds', under limited circumstances employment contracts are unenforceable unless committed to a signed writing. Typically, the statute of frauds requires that if a contract is not to be fully performed within one year of its making, it is unenforceable unless is in writing and signed by the person against whom it is being enforced. Accordingly, if an employment contract is for a specified duration of more than one year, it is unenforceable unless it is in writing and signed by the person against whom it is being asserted.

Most employment contracts in the United States are terminable at will, and, therefore, are outside the statute of frauds and thus need not be in writing. An at-will employment contract, which is terminable at any time for any reason, may be fully performed within one year of its making. This holds true even though many at-will employment relationships in fact continue well in excess of one year. This same analysis generally holds true for 'lifetime' employment contracts; because the contract by its terms will be fully performed within one year if the employee dies within one year of its making it need not be in writing to be enforceable. Although this is the clear majority rule, there are states that find lifetime contracts to be within the statute of frauds (because such contracts clearly envision a long-term employment relationship) and thus unenforceable unless supported by a signed, written contract.

The one-year period within which the contract must be susceptible of performance dates from the making of the contract, not from the beginning of performance.[57]

57. *See generally*, R. Bales, J. Hirsch and P. Secunda, *Understanding Employment Law*, §4.01(C) (2013).

140. An employment contract that is not terminable at will but that lacks a specific duration generally is not considered to be within the statute of frauds, and a signed writing is thus unnecessary for enforcement. For example, an oral contract not to fire the employee without just cause can be fully performed by its terms within one year if there no longer is a business need for the employee's services, even if it is more likely than not that the employment relationship will continue for more than one year.

A few jurisdictions follow the minority rule of treating all service contracts as outside the statute of frauds on the grounds that the possibility of the employee's death always makes an employment contract susceptible of performance within a year. On the other hand, other jurisdictions require a signed writing to enforce a contract of "permanent" employment.[58] However, if the contract of hire has been fully performed, most jurisdictions treat the writing requirement as inapplicable.[59]

141. Even if a contract is not enforceable because it is within the statute of frauds and is not evidenced by a signed writing, the worker is entitled to recover for the fair and reasonable value of any services rendered in that employment. Moreover, by invoking doctrines such as estoppel and unjust enrichment, courts occasionally enforce oral employment contracts that come within the statute of frauds in order to prevent unconscionable enrichment of an employer or unconscionable injury to a worker. For example, some courts have upheld oral employment contracts that came within the statute of frauds where an employee was induced by that contract to give up another job and to move to a distant location.[60]

IV. Renewal of the Employment Contract

142. If an employment contract is for a definite period of time, the rule in a majority of American jurisdictions is that the continuation of the employment at the end of the stated period is prima facie evidence that the parties entered into a new contract for a renewed period of the same duration. However, that presumption can be rebutted. Moreover, if the initial duration necessitated a signed writing, a new writing will be required to enforce the contract for the new period unless the original signed, written contract contained an automatic renewal or continuation clause.

In some jurisdictions, the continuation of employment at the end of a period of employment under a contract with a specified duration is merely evidence of an agreement to renew the contract on the same terms and conditions as the previous contract, including its duration. However, the renewal is not proven in these jurisdictions without additional evidence of the parties' intention to renew for that specific duration.[61]

---

58. For a detailed survey of cases, *see* H. Specter and M. Finkin, *Individual Employment Law and Litigation*, Charlottesville, VA, §1.18 (1989, 1991 Supp.); *see also* R. Bales, J. Hirsch and P. Secunda, *Understanding Employment Law*, §4.01(C) (2013).
59. Specter and Finkin, above, at §1.19.
60. *Alaska Airlines* v. *Stephenson*, 217 F.2d 295 (9th Cir. 1954); *Rowe* v. *Noren Pattern & Foundry*, 283 N.W.2d 713 (Mich. 1979). *See* cases collected at 54 *ALR3d* 715, 736 (1973) and Supp. (May 2008).
61. *See generally*, Specter and Finkin, at §2.15.

V. Misrepresentation

143. Many states have laws prohibiting employers and employment agencies from misrepresenting work opportunities. These laws are aimed at preventing such agencies from using false claims about available jobs in order to lure clients into their office. Often, too, state law requires an employer or employment agency to inform a job applicant of any existing work stoppage due to a labor dispute at the place of intended hiring. The Wagner–Peyser Act (29 US Code §49j) imposes this requirement on federally funded state employment offices and administrative regulations have expanded this prohibition to bar making job referrals that will fill a vacancy created by a work stoppage that was caused by a labor dispute.

A worker's material misrepresentation in a job application or at a job application interview, upon later discovery by the employer, generally is considered just cause for discharge.

VI. Termination of Employment

A. *Breach of Contract or Exercise of the Right to Rescind*

144. Since the late 19th century, American courts have treated employment as a contractual relationship that either side has the power to terminate without explanation or justification unless the parties have placed specific restrictions on that power. This is referred to as an 'at will' contract which means that it continues only at the will of both sides. Treating employment contracts as terminable at will has been characterized as an evidentiary presumption and a formal contract is unnecessary for the courts to recognize that the relationship has this status. Thus, the party asserting limitations upon the power to terminate the relationship has the burden of overcoming the presumption and proving that the contract's duration is terminable only under specified conditions.[62] Accordingly, if an employment contract expressly provides that it is terminable only upon 'good cause' or 'just cause', courts have enforced such limitations.[63]

Contractual provisions limiting the power to terminate employment only upon showing good cause for dismissal are recognized as an enforceable term of the individual employment contract when that protection is provided through a collectively bargained agreement. Moreover, such protection of job security is commonly specified in collective agreements. (In the case of employment covered by a collective agreement, most often the agreement also provides for an arbitral procedure for enforcing this contractual right.) (See Part III, Chapter 7, below, for further details.)

Under general practices in the US, either by statute, contract or, possibly, by custom, full-time teachers similarly acquire such job protection after a probationary

62. For example, *see Murphy* v. *American Home Products Corp.*, 448 N.E.2d 86 (NY 1983); *Wal-Mart Stores, Inc.* v. *Coward*, 829 S.W.2d 340 (Tex. App. 1992).
63. For example, *Sanders* v. *May Broadcasting Co.*, 336 N.W.2d 92 (Neb. 1983).

period of several years.[64] This job security practice is referred to as 'tenure'. At least in the field of higher education, the protection of academic freedom long has been regarded as a principal justification for granting teachers such job security. Government employees, other than those who work in policy-making positions, or who work in close support of those in such positions, generally (but not always) are provided with comparable job security under civil service laws.

However, most American workers are employed without a formal contract being executed; even when one is executed, normally it does not contain an explicit job security provision. Thus, such employment falls within the employment at will concept.

Termination of employment is the most extreme form of disciplinary power normally possessed by American employers. Warnings, demotions, suspensions from work, denial of wage increases, and cancellations of privileges are examples of less extreme methods by which employers are able to maintain work force discipline. Just as employment at will permits arbitrary dismissal, it also insulates the less severe disciplinary measures from judicial or administrative scrutiny.

There are limits upon the disciplinary discretion of even an at will employer. Civil law protection of freedom of movement and prohibitions against physical abuse protect employees from penal type punishment. Similarly, minimum wage and wage payment laws (sometimes referred to as 'truck' laws) restrict or prohibit the use of fines as a form of work place punishment. (The only industry in which fines customarily are used is professional sports.) However, by law, at the ship's master's judgment seafarers who engage in disciplinary infractions are subject to partial deprivations of food and comfort and to confinement. Additionally, under admiralty law the ship's master's disciplinary authority is supplemented by judicially imposed penalties for those forms disobedience that constitute crimes at sea.

145. Although employment at will remains the default rule in almost every state (resulting in most Americans being employed at will), employment at will has been largely eliminated by the legislatures of Montana, Puerto Rico and the Virgin Islands. Montana provides an employee dismissed without good cause a statutory action for up to four years' lost pay and benefits. It also provides punitive damages upon clear and convincing proof of the employer's actual fraud or malice when an employee has been discharged in violation of public policy. The Montana statute encourages (but does not require) submission of such actions to a final determination through impartial arbitration. Puerto Rican law gives to workers dismissed without good cause mandatory severance pay based on their length of service. The Virgin Islands statute is ambiguous in that arguably it is limited to situations in which a resident worker dismissed without good cause is replaced by a non-resident. The remedy is reinstatement with backpay.

State legislatures often adopt laws recommended by the National Conference of Commissioners of Uniform State Laws. A Model Employment Termination Act was approved by the Commissioners in 1991, and that act, if adopted, would largely do away with employment at will. Although the Act was the product of sustained

64. Compare, *Bowen* v. *Calallen Indep. School Dist.*, 603 S.W.2d 229, 233–234 (Tex. App. 1980) with *People ex rel. Davidson* v. *Bradley*, 47 N.E.2d 93 (Ill. 1943).

efforts by the Commissioners to produce a balanced piece of legislation that would be fair to employers and employees alike, the Model Employment Termination Act has yet to be adopted by any state and thus has proved far less influential than its sponsors had hoped.

146. Employees sometimes are engaged for a specific period of time in the US. In such situations, in contrast with employment 'at will', the courts find an implied restriction on the right to terminate and hold that either party may rescind the contract only for good cause. Logic and normal rules of contract law suggest that the party that has exercised the right to terminate the contract should have the burden of proving good cause for invoking that power. That is, the party that terminated the relationship initiated the change in the *status quo* and, therefore, should have the burden of providing a satisfactory explanation for that change. To put it another way, as a general principle, termination of a contract prior to its completion is justified only if the other side is guilty of a substantial failure of performance and the party asserting that there has been a substantial failure should have the burden of proving that fact. This is the approach normally taken by labor arbitrators when enforcing job security provisions of collective agreements. Nevertheless, some courts have been unclear respecting the distribution of the burden of proof in cases involving termination of an individual employment contract that is for a specified duration.[65] Other courts have expressly required the former employee, as the complaining party seeking redress for termination, prove that the employer lacked good cause to terminate the relationship.[66] And still other courts have applied what would appear to be the better view and place on the employer the burden of proving just cause for dismissal of a worker employed for a specified duration.[67]

Even when the parties have agreed that employment shall be 'permanent', or for the life of the employee, or so long as the employee wants the job, or have used similar language suggesting job security, American courts traditionally refuse to treat such language as restricting the employer's power to rescind the contract. Generally, such restrictions are found only if the contract is for a specified period or the parties have stated that it is terminable only for good cause. However, a just cause restriction on the employer's right to terminate has been implied by a number of courts where 'separate consideration' has been given to the employer in exchange for the promise of lifetime, permanent, or similar indeterminate but long-term employment. Many case decisions have been reported in which such separate consideration consisted of the employee's waiver or surrender of a valuable claim against the employer (such as a tort claim arising out of an injury to the worker), or the conveyance of some property to the employer (such as the sale of a business with the understanding that the prior owner will continue as a lifetime employee), or the purchase of property from the employer (such as shares in the employing enterprise). On the other hand, the courts are divided as to whether implied or

65. For example, *Rudman* v. *Cowles Communications*, 280 N.E.2d 867 (NY 1972). In *Stiles* v. *Skylark Meats, Inc.*, 438 N.W.2d 494 (Neb. 1989), the court imposed on the dismissed employee the burden of making out a prima facie case that dismissal was without cause and ruled that once that was established the burden of proof shifted to the employer to justify the dismissal.

66. For example, *Kass* v. *Brown Boveri Corp.*, 488 A.2d 242 (NJ App. Div. 1985).

67. For example, *Turner* v. *Allstate Ins. Co.*, 902 F.2d 1208 (6th Cir. 1990).

expressed promises of job security are enforceable based on the employee's sacrifice of alternative job or business opportunities or based on the employee bearing the burdens and costs of undertaking the employment (such as moving from a distant residence, selling a home, and the like). The modern trend appears to be to treat such relinquishment of a prior source of income, or undertaking substantial expenses or family inconvenience in order to take a job, as constituting the required separate consideration to support an implied job security commitment if the employer actively encouraged the sacrifice.[68]

When expressed or implied contractual provisions limit the ability to terminate employment at the will of either side, courts generally provide a contractual remedy for dismissal unless it is proved that the employee was guilty of substantial misconduct that injured or threatened injury to the enterprise or to persons encountered in the course of employment. The same standard applies when an employee is forced to quit because the employer has made job conditions intolerable. The courts will, however, honor contractually specified reasons justifying dismissal or contractually specified dismissal procedures.

A few state courts have upheld a dismissal from employment based on the employer's good faith belief, supported by substantial evidence, that the employee was guilty of significant misconduct and leave to the employer's unreviewable discretion the question of whether particular conduct justified dismissal. In such jurisdictions, even if it is shown that in fact the worker was not guilty of the suspected misconduct, the employer's action will not be set aside since the test is the employer's good faith, reasonable belief and not the actual merits of the dismissal decision.[69]

Other courts review the substantiality of the employer's justification and delegate to the jury the weighing of close questions concerning the reasonableness of the employer's action as well as the determination of the underlying facts. Assessing the substantiality of the employee's misconduct includes taking into account customary expectations respecting work performance including faithfulness, honesty, diligence, competence, and responsiveness to managerial directions. It also takes into account mitigating factors such as the employee's prior work record; motivation for the disputed conduct; the adequacy of the training, direction and information provided; and the extent of injury to the employer. There is considerable division of authority respecting whether and when the employee's conduct away from the job (for example, intoxication, crimes, social relationships, political activity, public statements) can be treated as just cause for dismissal,[70] and several states have laws prohibiting employers from terminating employees based on their legal conduct outside the workplace.[71]

---

68. Cases dealing with the issue of separate consideration as support for job security under a 'permanent' contract of hire can be found at 60 ALR 3d 226.
69. For example, *Baldwin* v. *Sisters of Providence*, 769 P.2d 298 (Wash. 1989).
70. *See generally*, Specter and Finkin.
71. *See generally*, R. Bales, J. Hirsch and P. Secunda, *Understanding Employment Law*, §8.03(B) (2013). The states with such statutes include: California, Colorado, New York, and North Dakota. Connecticut has a limited law that protects employee off-duty free speech and association. The

147. In theory, an employee is liable for damages upon quitting employment without just cause prior to the expiration of the specified term for its duration.[72] Nevertheless, suits seldom are brought to enforce this responsibility. One reason is that normally the employer can substantially mitigate or eliminate any damages by hiring a competent replacement. Another explanation is that in most cases the employer's cost of bringing such an action will exceed the former employee's financial ability to satisfy any resulting judgment, thus making the suit financially impractical. However, with the growth in economic activity involving high priced, highly trained specialists, future years may witness more frequent resort to this potential employer remedy.

B. Enforcement of Employment Handbooks

148. American employers, especially larger employers, often provide workers with informational publications describing the enterprise, employee benefits, and employee obligations. (Among other things, these publications in part can be used as a means of satisfying statutory requirements that employers provide employees with summaries of benefits plans regulated by the Employee Retirement Income Security Act.) These publications are variously referred to as company policy manuals, employee handbooks, and the like. When hired, employees typically are told they should be familiar with and are required to sign a receipt for the handbook or manual. The same process is repeated when supplements or new editions of the documents are distributed. Often such handbooks describe the employer's disciplinary policies and any probationary standards and procedures, and gives express or implied assurance that the employer will protect the worker's welfare and will treat the worker fairly, and that the employer expects that the employment relationship will be of long duration.

During the 1980s a substantial number of state courts began treating the representations in such handbooks as establishing enforceable contracts, and ruled that employees can rely on commitments in handbooks as a basis for legal redress if dismissed from employment in violation of such commitments. Moreover, many courts enforce handbook provisions regardless of whether at the time the grieved employer conduct occurred, the worker knew that the protection was provided in the handbook.[73] However, most courts decline to enforce an employee handbook provision if the document contains a clear, prominently displayed disclaimer announcing that the policies contained in the book do not constitute a contractual commitment. A few courts weigh the seeming inconsistency between the specific assurances in the

NLRA also protects both union and nonunion employees from employer action on the basis of speech respecting the merits or lack of merits of union organizing. *See* below Part II, Chapter 2, §1.

72. *Wilmington Coal Mining & Mfg.* v. *Lamb,* 90 Ill. 465 (1878)(dicta).

73. For example, *Woolley* v. *Hoffman-LaRoche, Inc.*, 491 A.2d 1257 (NJ 1985).

handbook and a general disclaimer of liability, and permit the jury to determine the reasonable meaning of the document taken as a whole.[74]

A related issue is whether an employer can unilaterally modify a contract of employment that is not for a specific duration. While there are court decisions that reject such unilateral modification of the original terms of hire[75] and court decisions that permit such modification without restriction, a number of courts take a middle position that allows such modification but only where it is not motivated by bad faith and the employee has sufficient notice before the change becomes effective so that the employee has an opportunity to decide whether to seek and take alternative employment.[76]

C. Good Faith and Fair Dealing

149. The law of contracts in the US has much of its foundation in a philosophical preference for the private arrangement of affairs. Indeed, an influential school of current legal commentators is devoted to fitting all policy issues into a framework of the economic free market model and denounces or supports legal doctrines based on what it deems inconsistent or consistent with the proper functioning of free market arrangements of social and economic conduct. Although these market determinists have influenced many members of the judiciary, generally when balancing the demands of justice, American courts continue to be responsive to competing value systems that reflect an understanding that human behavior is more complex than free market economists assume it to be.

150. A widely accepted doctrine in American law is that contracting parties have a duty to avoid impairing the other side's opportunity to receive the fruits of the agreement. Most often this concept is implemented by requiring that parties perform their agreements in accordance with principles of good faith and fair dealing. Thus, in the context of terminating an employment contract, the standard would be violated by a failure to make a reasonable effort to ensure that the facts were accurately determined before a decision was made or by a failure to base the decision on an assessment of the employee's merits rather than on bias or some ulterior motive. Some courts, though, use a narrow approach in enforcing this responsibility by intervening only if a party has intentionally interfered with the other's ability to carry out its contractual obligations or receive its contractual benefits. As one court explains, the principle of good faith and fair dealing is breached only if a party acts for the purpose of violating, impairing, or significantly nullifying any benefit of the employment relationship. Under that approach, termination of the relationship does not breach the duty of good faith and fair dealing where it is based on a mistaken

74. *Compare Dore* v. *Arnold Worldwide, Inc.*, 139 P.3d 56 (Cal. 2006) with *Worley* v. *Wyoming Bottling Co.*, 1 P.3d 615 (Wyo. 2000). For a state-by-state survey, *see* Specter and Finkin, §§1.28–1.71. *Also*, Befort, 'Employee Handbooks and the Legal Effect of Disclaimers', 13 *Indus. Rel. L.J.* 326 (1992).

75. *DeMasse* v. *ITT*, 984 P.2d 1138 (AZ 1999)(continued employment is not sufficient consideration for a unilateral modification).

76. *Compare Robinson* v. *Ada S. McKinley Community Svcs*, 19 F.3d 359 (7th Cir. 1994) *with Asmus* v. *Pacific Bell*, 999 P.2d 71 (Cal. 2000).

or overly hasty judgment of misconduct or an unsound assessment that its continuation is no longer beneficial.[77]

Even among those commentators who follow a philosophical preference for arrangements freely arrived at in a wholly competitive market, there are some who find merit in the good faith and fair dealing concept because it reduces the risk of not gaining the benefits of a bargain and, thereby, removes the need to include in each side's costs a premium charge for that risk. Thus, the legal duty to not interfere with the other's ability to perform decreases the cost of participating in the market with the result that such participation is encouraged.

The good faith and fair dealing rule, similarly, finds support from those whose concept of justice is based on the law's duty to protect weaker parties. For this group the rule is justified by the proposition that only dominant parties dare ignore norms of good faith and fair dealing. Others normally will avoid such misconduct for fear of market retribution by their victims and the friends and associates of those victims.

Additionally, the rule requiring contracting parties to act in good faith and deal fairly finds support from those who view the law's function as requiring people to live up to their commitments so as to foster social and economic stability.

In the US, the legal requirement of good faith and fair dealing most often has been imposed through the law of torts. The law of torts protects people from interfering with the reasonable expectations and well being of others. Thus, many courts have reasoned that the 'duty' of good faith and fair dealing enforces a social obligation toward those with whom one has a contractual relationship, especially if the other party is not readily able to protect itself from unfair dealing. Others argue that it is more appropriate to enforce this obligation as an implied contractual covenant and, appropriately, refer to it as an implied 'covenant' of good faith and fair dealing. The measure of recoverable damages is quite different depending on which approach is taken. Under the norms of American law, contract remedies are compensatory only and include a potential offset based on the claimant's duty to mitigate damages. In contrast, tort remedies are 'make-whole', can include emotional injury, do not always include a duty to mitigate damages and, if malice is shown, may include exemplary damages.

Despite the general acceptance of the doctrine of good faith and fair dealing in other types of contractual obligations, only a few courts have found it applicable to 'at will' employment contracts and those courts that have accepted the applicability of the doctrine to such contracts generally treat it as an implied covenant.[78]

151. Courts that support the applicability of the good faith and fair dealing standard to at will employment contracts point out that the 'at will' doctrine is an evidentiary rule, not a substantive standard defining the employment relationship. They

77. *Metcalf* v. *Intermountain Gas Co.*, 778 P.2d 744 (Idaho 1989).

78. *See* discussion in *Foley* v. *Interactive Data Corp.*, 765 P.2d 373 (Cal. 1988), but compare *Foley* with *Guz* v. *Bechtel National, Inc.*, 8 P.3d 1089 (Cal. 2000). Also see *Huong Que, Inc.* v. *Luu,*150 Cal. App. 400, 412 (Ct. App. 6th Dist. 2007) (duties that are implied covenants of the employment relationship need not be specified in the contract but can be expressly modified by agreement).

reason that while it is appropriate to assume, in the absence of specific contract language, the parties understand that either can walk away from the relationship without having to prove the wisdom of its decision or the accuracy of the information underlying the determination to sever the relationship, it is unreasonable to assume that they mutually understand that they are free to deal in a manner that completely disregards the interests of the other, that seeks to harm the other, or that is designed to undermine the purpose of the established relationship.

A few courts have limited the application of the standard of good faith and fair dealing to cases in which the employee produces evidence showing a reasonable basis for expecting fair treatment by the employer or where society requires fair treatment because the employer occupies a clearly dominant bargaining position.[79]

Some courts and commentators reject the judicial application of the good faith–fair dealing concept to employment relations not because it lacks merit or is logically inconsistent with broad principles of contract law, but because its adoption is a substantial alteration of the traditional at will concept and, in a democratic system of government, a major policy change of this sort should come from the legislature, not the judiciary.

Others argue that any erosion of the at will doctrine is unsound judicial policy because it conflicts with the notion that in such relationships each party should be entitled to end the arrangement arbitrarily; even in bad faith or through unfair dealing. In support of this position is the argument that the employment relationship is too intimate and complex to compel its continuation unless both sides are willing participants. Another justification for rigorously adhering to the rule that the courts should not review terminations of at will employment is that society benefits when managers are allowed to exercise judgments without having to reveal confidential sources of information underlying their determinations and that society benefits, as well, if managers are allowed to make choices based on intuitive and subjective foundations that cannot be articulated, substantiated or scrutinized by principles of logic.

152. The equity-based concept of fiduciary responsibility arguably is applicable to the employer's exercise of authority over the worker, including the authority to terminate employment, and is related to the duty of good faith and fair dealing. Standards of fiduciary conduct are imposed by law upon a party that substantially dominates a relationship as a result of its superior legal privileges, bargaining power, or special knowledge, or as a result of the high degree of trust that the other party reposes in the dominant side. Although typically an employer possesses the characteristics that give rise to fiduciary responsibility, American courts have not used that theory as a basis for remedying wrongfully dismissed workers. On the other hand, much of the explanation for applying the theory of good faith and fair dealing and for applying what has come to be called the public policy tort exception (see paragraphs 154–157, below), closely resembles the doctrine of fiduciary responsibility. Courts may not be willing to use the fiduciary doctrine in these situations because it is highly protective of the dependent party and fiduciary remedies

79. *See* discussion in *Murphy* v. *American Home Products Corp.*, 448 N.E.2d 86 (NY 1983). *See also First Security Bank of Idaho* v. *Gaige*, 765 P.2d 683 (Idaho 1988).

are especially severe and can be punitive regardless of whether the fiduciary's misconduct resulted from improper motive or from mere neglect or error.[80]

153. Logic suggests that if the obligation of good faith and fair dealing is an implied contractual covenant, it should not be applicable in those situations in which an employer has communicated to the employee, whether through an employee handbook or by other means, that it does not undertake a legal obligation to treat the workers fairly or in good faith. (Most employers, of course, would be reluctant to say this to their employees.)

When it is applied to employment contracts, the covenant of good faith and fair dealing should hold the employer to something less rigorous than good cause justification required for terminating those employed for a specific duration. For example, if after making a reasonable inquiry the employer dismissed the worker based on an honest but mistaken belief that the worker was guilty of misconduct, the good cause standard generally would provide relief for the worker. Under the same circumstances, however, the good faith and fair dealing standard may not offer relief.

The Alaska Supreme Court has explained that under the good faith and fair dealing standard, the jury must decide whether the employer judged the dismissed worker under the same rules that it applied to other workers, whether the employer acted in good faith, in a reasonable manner, and without violating any notions of fairness that the law regards as fundamental public policy. Using that criterion, the Alaska court held that an encroachment on a worker's personal privacy, such as subjecting a worker's urine sample to drug testing without prior notification to the worker, can constitute a violation of the good faith and fair dealing standard.[81]

D. *Interference with a Fundamental Individual Privilege or Responsibility Recognized by Public Policy*

154. A growing number of state high courts have declared in words or substance that 'the employment at will doctrine does not insulate an employer from liability where an employee is fired in a manner or for a reason that contravenes a clear and substantial public policy'.[82] The earliest case decisions along this line of authority imposed tort liability without presenting a clearly enunciated doctrinal foundation. Some later cases explored several justifications for employer liability and different labels have been used to identify the action or its subcategories (for example, abusive discharge, wrongful discharge, malicious discharge, retaliatory dismissal). A majority of jurisdictions now allow tort recovery by an employee dismissed in violation of a substantial public policy. The cause of action generally has been labeled as 'dismissal in violation of public policy' or simply 'public policy

---

80. M. O'Connor, 'Restructuring the Corporation's Nexus of Contracts: Recognizing a Fiduciary Duty to Protect Displaced Workers', 69 *N.C. L. Rev.* 1189 (1991); T. Frankel, 'Fiduciary Law', 71 *Cal. L. Rev.* 795 (1983).
81. *Luedtke* v. *Nabors Alaska Drilling, Inc.*, 834 P.2d 1220 (Alas. 1992).
82. *Peterson* v. *Browning*, 832 P.2d 1280, 1281 (Utah 1992).

tort'. However, a more descriptive definition would be 'tortious interference with the exercise of a fundamental public responsibility or with a fundamental legal privilege'.

Many courts limit recovery in a public policy suit to situations involving violation of a specific statute or constitutional provision while some also permit recovery if the dismissal violated a fundamental public policy reflected in statutes, constitutional provisions, administrative regulations, or professional rules of ethics, even though the conduct has not explicitly been made unlawful. A few courts also extend this theory of relief to employment dismissal that violates judicially recognized fundamental policies regardless of whether reflected in a specific constitutional provision, statute or regulation. Thus, there is disagreement respecting the availability of relief to employees dismissed for such reasons as reporting misconduct to higher corporate officials or to public authorities, refusing to perform work hazardous to public health or in violation of ethical standards, refusing to falsify reports or promotional material, engaging in controversial social activities, and the like.[83]

In applying the concept that an employer must remedy a dismissal if the employment termination violated a fundamental legal policy, some courts have looked not only to the law of their own jurisdiction but also the law of any other jurisdiction whose law regulates or protects the conduct that gave rise to the dismissal. Thus, under this doctrine a state court might grant recovery where the employer violated a public policy of federal law even though the federal law does not specify such a remedy.[84]

Another type of dismissal in violation of public policy occurs when the employer dismisses an employee for performing a public duty, such as serving on a jury, or for exercising an important job-related right or privilege, such as applying for worker's compensation benefits. The idea underlying the claim is that an employer should not be allowed to discharge an employee for reasons that would negatively affect society at large rather than just purely the personal interests of the particular employer or employee involved.[85]

155. An array of federal and state statutes provides remedies for employees who are dismissed under specified circumstances. One category of such laws is designed to stabilize the worker's financial security by encouraging advance notice of a protracted layoff or dismissal due to changes in technology or business activity. The most significant law of this sort is the federal Worker Adjustment and Retraining Notification Act (WARN), also popularly known as the Plant Closing Act (29 US Code §§2101–2109). This law applies to enterprises with at least 100 full-time employees and to situations either involving a plant closing affecting at least 50 full-time employees at an employment site, or a layoff for at least 30 days affecting 500

83. *See*, for example, the discussion in *Gantt* v. *Sentry Insurance*, 824 P.2d 680 (Calif. 1992). Case developments are gathered in 'Modern Status of Rule that Employer May Discharge At-Will Employee for Any Reason', 12 ALR 4th 544. Some courts continue to treat the at-will doctrine as sacrosanct.
84. *Rickman* v. *Premera Blue Cross,* 358 P.3d 1153 (WA 2015).
85. See *ibid.*; *Roberts* v. *Atlantic Richfield Co.*, 88 Wash.2d 887, 568 P.2d 764, 770 (1977); *Crawford Rehab. Servs., Inc.* v. *Weissman*, 938 P.2d 540, 552 (Colo. 1997).

or more employees, or affecting 50 or more employees if they constitute at least a third of the employees at the site.

The basic scheme of the Plant Closing Act is to compel the employer to give at least 60 days' advance notice to the employees affected by a mass dismissal or extended mass layoff by requiring the employer to pay wages for any of the 60 days for which advance notice was not given. However, the Act makes no provision for paid or unpaid time off from work to find other employment nor for specific employer assistance in such job searches during the notice period. In addition, the employer is excused from its notice obligation if it provides reasonably accessible alternative work opportunities at another facility. The employer is also excused to the extent that the work force reduction was compelled by unpredictable business changes or natural disaster. Further, the notice requirement is excused to the extent that good faith efforts to avert the reduction compelled the employer to withhold from publicizing its adverse financial or business situation. Finally, the notice requirement does not apply to reductions caused by labor disputes or where, when hired, employees were told that the duration of the work project was for a specific limited period.

The law of the state in which the suit is brought controls the time period in which suits to enforce the WARN Act must be filed. Because state laws use different time limits for different types of claims, the period applied to WARN Act suits must be based on the type of state action most analogous to the federal remedy.[86]

In addition to providing 60 days advance notice to the employees, the Act also requires the employer to give notice to the local government. Plant closing notification requirements for smaller establishments are imposed by state law in a few jurisdictions.

156. Another category of public policy restriction on the employment at will doctrine is the statutory right given to employees to communicate with particular government agencies, to apply for particular public benefits or to engage in specially protected activities. Thus, laws protecting special rights of workers, such as the NLRA (right to engage in concerted worker activities), OSHA (safe and healthy work environment), FLSA (minimum wage and overtime pay), Title VII of the 1964 Civil Rights Act (freedom from employment discrimination based on sex, race, national origin, religion), the Americans with Disabilities Act (freedom from disability based employment discrimination), the Motor Carrier Act (employee and public safety), other federal laws, similar state laws, and workers' compensation laws, generally provide explicit remedies for employees who are dismissed or disciplined for seeking the protection of those statutes or for participating in enforcement procedures under the statutes. Most often the special statutory remedies protecting access to these processes provide for both reinstatement of the dismissed employee to his or her former job and backpay. Some statutes also allow for compensatory (emotional distress) and punitive damages against the wrongdoer.

---

86. *North Star Steel Co.* v. *Thomas*, 515 US 29 (1995).

157. One of the more unique public policy job protections is provided by Title III of the Consumer Protection Act of 1970 (15 US Code §§1673–1674) which prohibits employers from dismissing a worker because a lien has been placed on the worker's wages (wage garnishment) as a result of indebtedness unless the wages have been subjected to more than one such executed lien. Employers are also prohibited by Bankruptcy Code sec. 525 (11 US Code §525) from discriminating against employees or job applicants who file for or receive relief under that statute.

E. Whistleblower Protection

158. Still another form of public policy restricting an at will employer's ability to terminate employment of a worker is referred to as 'whistleblower' protection. (The name is based on the police patrol officer's blowing a whistle to demand that a fleeing felon stop, calling attention to the targeted criminal who is to be apprehended, or receiving aid in carrying out the apprehension.) Whistleblower laws prohibit retaliation against the employee who reports wrongdoing on the part of an employer or a high ranking official of the establishment. The federal government has adopted several very specific whistleblower protection laws. For example, one that applies to employees of companies that sell goods or services to the military branches prohibits employer retaliation if the workers report to the government their employer's violation of laws, regulations or contract provisions. The remedy, however, requires Defense Department initiation of a proceeding on the employee's behalf.

Similar federal statutory protections are provided for workers in the energy generation industry when they report their employer's misconduct. Other federal laws designed to protect against environmental pollution and to ensure various types of public safety give workers the same sort of protection. These include the Occupational Safety and Health Act, the Pipeline Safety Improvement Act, the International Safe Container Act, the Energy Reorganization Act, and the Surface Transportation Act.

Whistleblower protection is also provided for those seeking to vindicate their rights or assist in vindicating the rights of others under most basic federal labor–management and labor standards laws such as the FLSA, the FMLA and the NLRA. In addition, the Sarbanes–Oxley Act, designed to uncover corporate and securities fraud, provides whistleblower protection for employees who provide to appropriate authorities information they reasonably believe is evidence of violations of that law. This statute and many other such federal whistleblower protection laws delegate enforcement authority to the Department of Labor.

Government officials charged with the responsibility of initiating protection against retaliation sometimes appear to give low priority to investigating and prosecuting such cases. Hence, some commentators assert that a private right to sue is essential for effective protection of the employee. The Sarbanes–Oxley Act of 2002 provides protection and a claim for relief for those employees who report financial wrongdoing. Section 806 of the Act protects whistleblowers who provide information or who initiate or assist in investigation or who participate in proceedings that the employee reasonably believes constitute a violation of federal fraud statutes or Securities and Exchange Commission (SEC) rules.[87] Protection extends also to employees reporting alleged violations to corporate managers. Civil remedies provided by the law include reinstatement. The law also imposes criminal penalties on any employer that interferes with an employee who raises concerns regarding violations of any federal criminal law.[88] The law is enforced by the Department of Labor through OSHA, whose traditional statute of limitations has been reduced to 90 days for Sarbanes–Oxley claims. In addition to Sarbanes–Oxley, the Notification and Federal Employee Anti-discrimination and Retaliation Act (No FEAR), also signed into law in 2002, gives new whistleblower protection to federal employees.[89]

159. The False Claims Act (31 US Code §§3729–3733) is a distinctive form of federal whistleblower law. It provides a significant financial incentive to individuals to report and sue to recover funds wrongfully obtained from the federal government by 'persons' who submitted false or fraudulent information. Employees of employers receiving federal government grants or contracts sometimes discover misuses of those funds, and by initiating a successful recovery of the funds receive a portion of the recovered amount. The statute thus serves as a substantial incentive to discover and to report such misappropriations, as the bounty awarded to the employee can be substantial.[90] In *Vermont Agency of Natural Resources* v. *United States ex rel. Stevens*, 529 US 765 (2000), the Supreme Court upheld the standing of individuals to bring these actions, known as *qui tam* suits. However, the Court also held that states are not 'persons' within the meaning of the False Claims Act and thus may not be subject to *qui tam* liability. The Act requires notice to the US Justice Department prior to bringing suit and seals any complaint for 60 days while the Justice Department decides whether to itself bring the action. If the Department chooses to pursue an action, the whistleblower's (relator's) recovery is reduced but is still substantial. However, in recent years courts have allowed the Justice Department to keep cases under seal for extended periods while 'studying' the file, a procedure that encumbers the process and allows for politically motivated delays.

Employees who initiate these *qui tam* proceedings can obtain damages and reinstatement in the event of any retaliation.

160. The federal Whistleblower Protection Act of 1989 (5 US Code §1211-1213) protects the federal government's own employees who report wrongdoing within their agency or department when the wrongdoing is in the form of violation

87. 18 US Code §1514A (2007). For a more detailed description of Sarbanes–Oxley's employee protections and their potential shortcomings, *see* R. Moberly, 'Sarbanes Oxley's Structural Model to Encourage Corporate Whistleblowers', 2006 *B.Y.U. L. Rev*. 1107.
88. 18 US Code §1513(e) (2007).
89. Public Law (PL) 107–174 (2002).
90. For a discussion of the *qui tam* bounty as an economic incentive, *see generally* G. Rapp, 'Beyond Protection: Invigorating Incentives for Sarbanes Oxley Corporate and Securities Whistleblowers', 87 *Boston U.L. Rev*. 91 (2007).

of laws or regulations or gross mismanagement, abuses of authority, dangers to public health, or gross waste of public funds. The Act also established an Office of Special Counsel (OSC) and procedures for investigating alleged reprisals against government employees who report such misconduct. Presidential Policy Directive 19 (PPD-19), issued on 12 October 2012, also prohibits retaliation for protected whistleblowing by federal employees involved in national security and intelligence. Where retaliation is substantiated, remedies such as reinstatement, compensatory damages and attorneys' fees are available to the federal employee.

161. One source states that three-fourths of the states have statutes that protect employee whistleblowers in one form or another, and others that do not have statutes provide protection through a judicially developed public policy exception to the at will doctrine.[91] The scope of the exception varies considerably from state to state. Some state whistleblower laws take a broad approach to what constitutes protected employee disclosures while other states' approaches are more narrow, such as requiring that the disclosed misconduct threatened public health or safety. Some state laws require the employee to first report the alleged misconduct internally before reporting it to the government enforcement agency, while others only protect those who report externally, without regard to whether any internal reporting has occurred. States also vary in whether the employee's allegation must be correct in order for protection to exist or whether instead a good faith belief will suffice. Some states do not permit an employee who was himself involved in the wrongdoing to receive whistleblower protection.[92]

F. Collateral Sources of Relief for Wrongfully Dismissed Workers

162. Sometimes workers have a right to recover from their former employer for damages arising out of the manner in which the employer carried out the dismissal or to recover from persons other than the employer as a result of efforts to bring about the worker's dismissal. Recovery in such situations is not concerned with whether the employer had a right to terminate the employment; rather relief is available if termination was initiated or carried out for a wrongful purpose.

The concept of defamation protects against a person's reputation being injured by false statements. Thus, truth is a defense to such an action. Expressions of opinion that criticize or condemn a person but that are not presented as statements of fact (for example, 'I do not trust Jones' as contrasted with 'Jones is untrustworthy') are excluded from the class of communications that give rise to an action for defamation unless the statement of opinion carries a clear implication of specific defamatory facts.[93]

91. M. Rothstein, *et al.*, *Employment Law*, 2004 at §8.10. *See also generally* R. Bales, J. Hirsch and P. Secunda, *Understanding Employment Law*, §5.02(B)(4), (2013).
92. Rothstein, *et al.* §8.10.
93. R. Smolla and M. Nimmer, *Freedom of Speech* §23.11 (2017). In any event, the falsity of the statement must be proven even when it is an explicit of implied statement of fact.

There is danger that allowing defamation recoveries will discourage lawful expression on the part of those who fear being sued for defamation if their level of criticism of others becomes harsh. In order not to unduly chill free expression, therefore, the constitutional protection of freedom of speech limits the extent and conditions under which courts can protect reputation from defamatory statements.

The most basic constitutional restriction is that to recover for defamation there must be a showing of actual fault on the part of the person being sued. Secondly, if the defamatory statement was part of a discussion that involved a matter of public interest (such as a labor dispute), the injured party must show some actual damage. Thus, hurt feelings is not a sufficient basis for recovery if the defamation arose in the context of discussing a matter of public interest. In addition, if the defamation arose in the course of a discussion concerning a matter of public interest, recovery is dependent upon proving that the defendant was negligent or acted willfully. Also, in such a situation the recovery can include presumed damages (such as damages for presumed lost earning ability if the defamation injured the person's reputation as a worker) or punitive damages but only if it is also proven that the defendant knew that the statement was false or acted with reckless disregard for whether the statement was true or false. Finally, if the person bringing the defamation suit is a public figure (a government official or someone, such as an entertainer, who regularly thrusts himself into the public's attention), then recovery for defamation is conditioned upon proving by 'clear and convincing evidence' (a standard of proof requiring something substantially more than the greater weight of the evidence) both that the defamatory statement was published with actual knowledge of its falsehood or with reckless disregard for its truth and that the defamation caused actual damage to the public person bringing the suit.[94] Although the Supreme Court has not specifically ruled on the question, the logical extension of the rationale for its decisions in this area would prohibit public persons from recovering punitive damages in a defamation suit.[95]

163. Some special rules apply when a defamatory statement arose out of an employment relationship. One is that the mere information that a person was terminated or demoted is not enough to constitute defamation. Also, the traditional rule is that defamatory statements about an employee or former employee are privileged if they are conveyed to someone, such as a prospective employer, who has a special need to be informed about the subject's work conduct or characteristics. If the false statement is privileged, under established principles of the law of defamation, it does not constitute actionable defamation unless it was made with 'malice'. Malice, in this context, is defined as knowledge of the statement's falsity, or gross disregard for whether the statement was true or false. Similarly, statements made to fellow employees for the purpose of explaining the employer's action in terminating the worker and warning the others against engaging in similar misconduct are privileged.[96]

---

94. *See generally*, *Dun & Bradstreet, Inc.* v. *Greenmoss Bldrs.*, 472 US 749 (1985); *Gertz* v. *Robert Welch, Inc.*, 418 US 323 (1974).
95. J. Nowak and R. Rotunda, *Constitutional Law*, 7th ed., 2004 at §16.33(e).
96. For example, *Ponticelli* v. *Mine Safety Appliance Co.*, 247 A.2d 303 (RI 1968).

On the other hand, some courts have moved away from treating such communications as privileged or, alternatively, allow the privilege to be a defense only in situations in which the defendant, in addition to confining the communication to those with a business need to know, took reasonable precautions to ascertain the truth prior to making the defamatory statement. In jurisdictions in which an employer's communication concerning an employee or former employee is deemed privileged due to the business need to learn about the worker or the worker's misconduct, generally recovery is dependent not only on showing that the employer's false communication resulted from more than mere negligence, but also on showing that it caused specific financial damage to the defamed employee.[97]

If a falsely accused employee has been dismissed from employment and then, when applying for a new job, has had to explain the reason for dismissal, a few courts have held that the former employee's own compelled statement of the reason given to him for dismissal itself constitutes defamation by the former employer to the prospective employer. However, the former employer can still assert that the communication was privileged if it would have been privileged had the prospective employer made the inquiry directly to it and the facts would otherwise support allowing the employer to be protected by the privilege.[98]

164. Employers often learn information about a worker or a worker's private life that the worker would want to be kept confidential. This can arise out of activities such as employer sponsored medical examinations (for example, learning that the worker has a sexually communicated disease, uses illegal drugs, or has been diagnosed as being psychologically abnormal), intercepted or overheard communications such as telephone calls, or investigations into the worker's honesty. A growing number of state courts have ruled that an employee can recover damages if the employer discloses such private information unless there was a business justification such as the protection of workplace health or safety and the disclosure did not go beyond those with a compelling need to know.[99] Unlike defamation suits, actions for breach of privacy are not subject to the defense that the disclosed information was true. In addition, the federal Health Insurance Portability and Accountability Act (HIPAA),[100] gives some protection respecting the dissemination of employee medical information, and OSHA Reg. 29 CFR 1910.20 gives employees access to their own medical records.

165. State courts generally recognize the right of tort recovery for intentional infliction of severe emotional distress. To prove the tort it must be shown that the conduct was so outrageous as to shock the community's conscience. Mere insult is not enough. Moreover, the tort is tied to the community's standards of bad manners – what might be considered merely insensitive or in poor taste in one community might be considered outrageous in another. Thus, in a few cases employees have

---

97. For example, *Babb* v. *Minder*, 806 F.2d 749 (7th Cir. 1986).
98. For example, *McKinney* v. *County of Santa Clara*, 110 Cal. App. 3d 787 (1st Dist. 1980); *Theisen* v. *Covenant Medical Center, Inc.*, 636 N.W.2d 74 (Iowa 2001); *Churchey* v. *Adolph Coors Co.*, 759 P.2d 1336 (Colo. 1988).
99. *See* examples in R. Covington and K. Decker, *Employment Law*, 2d ed., 2002 at pp. 134–140.
100. 42 US Code §300gg *et seq.*

recovered under this theory of action based on the humiliating manner in which the employee was interrogated in a disciplinary investigation or was escorted from the premises and his personal effects were deposited on the ground outside the place of employment. But cases have been dismissed in other jurisdictions even though they involved similarly cruel disregard of the dismissed worker's feelings and sense of dignity.[101]

166. The manner in which the employer conducted a disciplinary investigation can also lead to a claim for relief. Employers sometimes rely on an intimidating environment in an effort to coerce an employee confession of wrongdoing. If sufficiently coercive, the employee may have a right of action under a theory of false imprisonment. In some jurisdictions the injury in such a situation would be deemed work related and as such a separate suit might be barred by the workers' compensation statute with the result that the only remedy would be a claim for the very limited benefits available under that law. Other jurisdictions, however, treat a coercive interrogation as serious and willful misconduct by the employer. Since workers' compensation statutes do not insulate employers from tort liability if guilty of willful infliction of injury, a separate suit for false imprisonment or assault may be available if there has been a coercive interrogation. Another explanation for allowing a separate suit in such circumstances is that the workers' compensation program is designed as the sole remedy for injuries arising out of the normal scope of employment and that coercive interrogation goes beyond the employer's proper relationship with the employee.[102]

167. Occasionally, newly employed or newly transferred workers have recovered damages when dismissed due to the termination of a job or business activity under circumstances in which they were induced to accept the position based on misleading or false information that created an expectation of long-term employment. Similarly, in a few cases, recovery of damages has been allowed where the employer failed to disclose critical information about the job or business situation that would have dissuaded the employee from accepting the job or transfer.[103]

168. Another collateral source of relief for a dismissed worker is a suit against a third party who caused the employer to terminate the employment. Such claims often are referred to as claims for tortious interference with contract or tortious interference with business relations. Not all interference, however, is actionable. Only improper interference gives rise to a claim. The conduct is improper if it involves some form of wrongdoing, such as defamation or fraud. When the employment contract is for a fixed duration, a third party's improper interference that

---

101. *Compare*, for example, *Archer* v. *Farmer Bros. Co.*, 70 P.3d 495 (Colo. App. 2002) with *Murphy* v. *American Home Products Corp.*, 448 N.E.2d 86 (NY 1983).
102. *See*, for example, *Fermino* v. *Fedco, Inc.*, 872 P.2d 559 (Calif. 1994).
103. For example, *compare Walsh* v. *Ingersoll Rand Co.*, 656 F.2d 367 (8th Cir. 1986) and *Berger* v. *Security Pacific Information Systems, Inc.*, 795 P.2d 1380 (Colo. App. 1990) *with Mackenzie* v. *Miller Brewing Co.*, 623 N.W.2d 739 (Wis. 2001). *See also* R. Perna, 'Deceitful Employers: Intentional Misrepresentation in Hiring and the Employment-at-Will Doctrine', 54 *Kansas L. Rev.* 587 (2006).

causes an employee to leave his employment during the contract term or causes an employer to terminate the employee during the contract term will support a tortious interference claim. A number of states permit this claim to proceed even when the employment relationship is at will, reasoning that the fact that the employer and the employee are free to terminate the relationship at will does not mean that an outsider should be allowed to improperly interfere with the relationship. Thus, even when the employment is at will, some courts hold that a third party's interference with employment is actionable if the interference is for a malicious purpose or is inconsistent with community mores or ethical standards or is without legal justification or excuse.[104]

G. Limits on the Right to Quit

169. Normally, the law does not compel an employee to work even if the employment is for a specified period of time. The 13th amendment to the US Constitution prohibits involuntary servitude, and has been used to explain judicial unwillingness to order specific performance of employment contracts by employees. However, an employer may sue an employee for damages occasioned by the employee's breach of contract.

In some circumstances, a licensed or certified employee's ethical responsibilities require the completion of the services undertaken unless excused by the employer. Disciplinary proceedings might be brought by the licensing agency against the employee who violates this ethical requirement, and a violation of the standard might provide the employer with a civil cause of action for damages.

Employment in the military service and as a merchant seafarer carries penal sanctions for quitting prior to completion of the term of service.

H. Illness or Injury

170. The common law doctrine of employment at will offers the worker no redress against unfair or arbitrary termination of employment. Accordingly, it entitles an employer to dismiss an employee for any illness or injury. However, under the Americans With Disabilities Act, discussed below at paragraphs 352–359, an employer is prohibited from dismissing a person who has (or is perceived to have) a physical or mental impairment that substantially limits a major life activity of the individual unless the accommodations that would enable the individual to perform the essential functions of the job (such as process changes, assignment changes, equipment changes or schedule changes) would amount to an undue hardship on the employer. This law applies to employers that regularly employ at least 15 workers.

---

104. *Hunter* v. *Board of Trustees of Broadlawns Med. Ctr.*, 481 N.W.2d 510 (Iowa 1992); *Valdez* v. *Power Industry Consultants, Inc.*, 451 S.E.2d 87 (Ga. App. 1994). *See also* A. Long, 'Tortious Interference with Business Relations: The "Other White Meat" of Employment Law', 84 *Minnesota L. Rev.* 863 (2000).

171. Workers employed under a contract for a specific durational period or under a contract expressly protecting against termination without just cause may be terminated for illness or other disability only if the incapacity will last a substantial period of time. Short-term illness or injury generally is not just cause for termination. Only in the unique situation in which the particular employee's constant services are essential is a short-term illness or injury considered just cause for discharge. Many employees now, moreover, are protected by the FMLA, discussed in Chapter 13, which entitles covered employees to up to 12 weeks of unpaid leave in a 12-month period for a serious health condition. Thus, even if the contract permits dismissal, federal law may protect an employee's short-term absence caused by illness or injury. Recovery in such cases, however, is under the statute and not under the contract.

Generally, it is held that an employer's right to terminate the employment contract due to illness or disability is independent of both the worker's and the employer's ability to avoid the suffered illness or injury.

I. Impossibility of Performance

172. Death of the employer or employee is the ultimate cause of impossibility of performance and automatically terminates the employment contract. The law, for this purpose, assumes that an implied condition of every employment contract is the continued existence of both parties.

173. Imprisonment of a worker for a substantial period of time is treated as making the performance of an employment contract impossible and thereby terminates that contract. Other changed conditions have also been held to terminate the employment contract due to impossibility of performance. However, an employer's voluntary cessation of business or discontinuance of a job position, even though caused by financial or business disaster, does not relieve the employer of liability for the employment contract of one engaged for a specific duration. Discontinuance of a business or its transfer pursuant to the bankruptcy laws, in contrast, results in the termination of any employment contracts at the election of the court-appointed trustee of the bankrupt employer's assets, subject, however, to the dismissed employee's claim for damages. (In bankruptcy reorganizations, American courts normally designate the owner or principal manager of the bankrupt business as the trustee.)

VII. Notice of Termination

174. Absent a contractual provision to the contrary, there is no prescribed procedure for terminating an employment contract. Termination can be accomplished by a written or oral communication ('You are fired', 'You are canned', 'You are sacked', 'You are finished', 'You are discharged', etc.). Frequently, American employers use a special written form notifying the worker of the discharge. Because that form traditionally (though not invariably) has been on pink colored paper, the phrase 'being handed a pink slip' has come to mean that one was discharged from employment.

Termination can also be accomplished by the worker's offer of resignation and the employer's acceptance or simply the worker's declaration that he or she is quitting the job. The offer and acceptance of severance pay accomplishes the same purpose. Leaving work during work hours without explanation is sometimes treated as a voluntary quit, as is the failure to appear for work for several days without notice or explanation.

175. At least one state has a statutory requirement that within a specified period of time after termination, at the terminated worker's request the employer must provide the employee with a 'service letter' specifying the period of employment and job assignments. The service letter requirement is limited to specified categories of employees and requires that the letter specify the reason for termination. Courts have held that the reasons listed in the service letter are the only ones the employer can rely on in any subsequent challenge to the lawfulness of the dismissal or the employee's right to unemployment benefits.[105]

176. Unlike some labor relations systems, in the United States an employment contract is terminated immediately upon either party communicating by word or deed his election to terminate, unless there is an explicit contractual or statutory requirement (see paragraph 155, above) of prior notice. Failure to give the required prior notice is remedied by payment of damages.

VIII. Remedies for Breach of Employment Contracts

A. Damages

177. A worker whose contract of employment was at will is entitled to be paid for services performed up until the time of termination. If the contract was for a specific term, and was terminated by the employee, the common law rule in the US is that the employee is entitled to unpaid compensation at the time of termination only if he had good cause to quit. Absent such good cause, the employee has no right to recover unpaid compensation. Some courts, however, allowed the employee to recover the fair value of his services (not to exceed the contractual rate) up to the time he quit on the theory that there is an implied contract to pay the reasonable value for services requested and received.[106] (Also, see below.)

---

105. *See generally, Thompson* v. *Skelgas, Inc.*, 896 S.W.2d 645 (Mo. 1995). For a discussion of Missouri's approach and some of its limitations, *see* C. Shainblatt, Comment: 'The New Missouri Employer Immunity Statute: Are Missouri Employers Still Damned if they Do, and Damned if they Don't?', 44 *St. Louis Law J.* 693 (2000).

106. *See generally*, M. Rothstein *et al.*, *Employment Law*, 2004, at §§1.6–1.7; *Ramsey* v. *Ellis*, 484 N.W.2d 331 (Wisc. 1992).

178. State statutes establishing the minimum frequency for the payment of wages or salary have in large measure abrogated the common law rule of damages for breach of employment contracts. Such state laws require the payment of wages for the hours worked and do not provide for exceptions based on the employee's unjustified quit. Many of these state laws also require the immediate payment of wages upon the termination of employment or require that such payment be made within a stated short interval thereafter. A few state statutes expressly prohibit an employer from refusing to pay because of a breach of the employment contract. In addition, most states expressly limit the purposes for which deductions can be made from wages owed for work performed. Offsets for the employee's contractual breach are not among the permitted deductions. Some municipalities have passed laws, called 'Living Wage Laws' that provide minimum wages higher than federal and state law and other protections as well.[107]

179. In addition, the federal and state minimum wage laws provide an absolute minimum level of compensation for work performed even though an employee quit without good cause and even though the fair value of the work was worthless. And, to the extent that overtime hours were worked, the federal wage-hour law, the FLSA, applies without regard to the common law rule and requires that the employee be paid for those overtime hours at the regular wage paid to the employee plus a 50 percent premium.

180. A wrongfully discharged worker employed under a contract for a specific duration is entitled to recover damages for the breach of contract. Such damages are measured by what the worker would have earned over the life of the contract (including such items as gratuities and profit sharing) less any wages or salary the worker earned from replacement employment during the contract period, or wages or salary the worker would have earned if he made diligent efforts to find such work. In most jurisdictions the employee can sue for damages for the entire contract period without waiting for the expiration date.

181. A worker whose employment contract was not for a specific duration, but whose termination violated other contractual commitments made by the employer will usually recover, as a component of damages, lost earnings and related compensation losses. The worker's duty to make reasonable efforts to find alternative employment and, thereby mitigate damages, is taken into account in measuring that loss.

Contract damages do not include recovery for accompanying psychic injuries such as hurt feelings, emotional distress or humiliation. Nor can punitive damages (also known as exemplary damages) be added to the recovery.

Courts add interest to the contract damages for the period from the time the earnings would have been received until the time payment is made pursuant to the judgment. However, the cost of hiring an attorney and other litigation costs are not

107. *See* William Quigley, 'Full-Time Workers Should Not Be Poor: The Living Wage Movement', 70 *Mississippi Law J.* 889 (2001).

charged to the losing party in a contract suit unless the contract explicitly provided for such additional recovery.

Courts are divided over the question of the period for which contract damages can be recovered by an employee whose employment contract was not for a specific duration. Such an issue arise, for example, if an employer dismissed an 'at will' worker without following the procedures set out in the employee handbook. Some argue that since the employer could terminate the worker at any time, at most the worker should be able to recover for the amount of time the employment would have continued had the employer followed the correct procedures. Others argue that since the employer may have been persuaded to not terminate the worker had it followed the correct procedures, damages should be based on the assumption that the employment would have continued indefinitely. This latter approach has been taken, for example, where the contract action is based on the breach of the duty of good faith and fair dealing.[108]

182. A worker's legal damages, if based on a tort theory of recovery, include the past and prospective financial losses resulting from the wrong (backpay and reduced future earnings capacity) and accompanying psychic injuries such as pain, suffering, emotional distress, humiliation and reputational damage. If the fact-finder determines that the wrong was malicious or with gross disregard for the injured party's rights, punitive damages additionally can be assessed.[109] Normally, however, there is no right to recover attorney's fees and other litigation costs.

B. Reinstatement

183. Suits based on a statutory right of action often combine contract, tort and equitable remedies. Reinstatement, a remedy generally unavailable in a tort or contract cause of action, often is available for breach of a statutory protection of worker interests. Statutory remedies also often include reasonable attorney's fees and costs.

184. Federal income taxes levied on earned income constitute the major form of tax burden imposed on most workers. Until 1996, income taxes were imposed on recoveries for contract-based claims but not for tort injuries. Because both contract and tort-based claims may grow out of the facts and circumstances surrounding an employee's termination, allocation of damages among such claims had a considerable impact on the net income for the employee and thus had an influence on settlement negotiations. In 1996, Congress amended the Internal Revenue Code to exclude from gross income only 'the amount of damages (other than punitive damages) received (whether by suit or agreement …) on account of personal physical injuries or physical sickness'.[110] The amendment further clarified that emotional distress shall not be considered a physical injury or sickness but recovery for medical

108. *Compare Grouse* v. *Group Health Plan*, 306 N.W.2d 114 (Minn. 1981) with *Foley* v. *Interactive Data Corp.*, 765 P.2d 373 (Calif. 1988).
109. For example, *Thompson* v. *Better-Bilt Aluminum Prods. Co.*, 832 P.2d 203 (Ariz. 1992).
110. Section 104(a)(2) of the Internal Revenue Code, 26 US Code §104(a)(2).

care attributable to emotional distress is excluded from income. The end result is that only damages from an underlying physical injury may be excluded from gross income. Punitive damages, as was true before the amendments, are taxable, whether or not they are awarded as a result of a physical injury (except in some wrongful death cases). Because it is the unusual situation in which an employee's termination results in physical injuries or sickness, recovery in employment litigation is almost always included in gross income for tax purposes.

185. In the exercise of traditional equity powers, courts generally do not order an employee to perform an employment contract. The reasons for this rule include the reluctance of courts to issue orders requiring long-term judicial supervision of compliance with the order. Moreover, the US Constitution's 13th Amendment prohibition against involuntary servitude provides an additional reason for not ordering the performance of an employment contract.

However, courts may order specific performance of a contract of forbearance; that is, a court may enjoin an employee from taking action inconsistent with the employment contract's terms. In deciding whether to grant these injunctions, a court possesses considerable discretion and will not grant an injunction if it is being sought as an indirect means of enforcing a duty to render personal service or will leave the employee without the means of subsistence, or the employer can readily find others to perform the employee's duties.[111]

186. Although courts do not order workers to perform employment contracts, in a number of circumstances American courts order that an employee be reinstated to his job position. Generally, reinstatement is ordered by labor arbitrators where a worker has been discharged in breach of the collective agreement and courts enforce such orders. Similarly, reinstatement is commonly part of the remedy that may be imposed where a worker has been discharged in violation of rights under laws such as the NLRA, the Age Discrimination in Employment Act, the FMLA, the FLSA, the Americans with Disabilities Act, Title VII of the 1964 Civil Rights Act, and the OSHA. In these cases, reinstatement is not provided as a remedy for the breach of an individual employment contract. Rather, it remedies the breach of a collectively bargained agreement or the violation of a constitutional liberty or statutory right or privilege.

Because reinstatement is commonplace in the United States, one might expect courts to order reinstatement of a worker who was discharged in violation of an individual contract of employment. However, in such cases, the courts continue to limit the remedy for the successful employee to a monetary recovery. There are two apparent reasons for this. First, in individual employment contracts, unlike with statutory claims, there is no labor organization or government agency to oversee or actively police enforcement of the reinstatement order. Secondly, suits to vindicate rights of individual employees normally are pursued on what American lawyers call

111. *Restatement of Contracts (Second)*, §§357, 367. See *Ticor Title Ins. Co.* v. *Cohen*, 173 F.3d 63 (2d Cir. 1999) for a comprehensive exploration of factors weighed in exercising discretion in such cases.

a contingency fee basis. The employee's lawyer receives a fee only if successful; but if successful, the fee is a substantial portion of the monetary recovery. Under such fee arrangements, the lawyer is less likely to press the court to order reinstatement in lieu of recovering for future lost wages.

§3. Special Employment Relations

I. Seafarers

187. The law governing the rights and duties of seafarers draws upon traditions that date back to a time when voyages generally were hazardous and often extremely long. The uncertainties of the sailor's return to a jurisdiction presented a multitude of problems respecting the service of legal process and the presentation of evidence in cases involving both the protection of the rights of the seafarer and his dependents as well as those involving claims against him. Many of these difficulties were eliminated or reduced by treating seamen as wards of the admiralty courts. This tradition received statutory sanction from Congress and continues to influence the special relationship between a sailor and the ship's owners and master.

By statute, a seafarer's right to future wages for the remainder of the contract is barred if he unlawfully failed to work when required or was lawfully imprisoned. Similarly, the sailor's right to future wages for the remainder of the contract terminates upon the loss or wreck of his vessel. However, if the seafarers save freight from a wrecked vessel, they are entitled to wages for the time spent caring for the salvaged goods. In addition, the general rule is that a sailor who, without giving at least 24 hours prior notice of disability, fails to report at the time designated before a ship's departure is subject to statutory forfeiture of a half day's wages for every hour of delay in reporting aboard. And, a sailor forfeits all wages earned if he abandons a vessel prior to the end of the journey for which he has signed on.[112]

188. On the other hand, if a seafarer is discharged without fault prior to the commencement of an overseas voyage or before earning one month's wages, he is entitled to a month's wages in addition to any wages he may have earned. The Admiralty statutes similarly require that payment of wages due be made to the seaman within a specified period of hours or days after the termination of the employment period or the seaman's discharge. Statutory damages are fixed for each day of delay in paying the seaman. The law also entitles the seaman to be paid, with specified limitations, half of his balance of wages earned each time the vessel arrives in a new port.

A seafarer who is dismissed in a foreign port is entitled to a month's wages or employment aboard a returning vessel meeting his approval. If discharged for cause, the seafarer is entitled to passage back to the US unless the misconduct was aggravated.

112. 42 US Code §§10313, 10317.

189. The Supreme Court has held that a seafarer's statutory right to wages and damages for nonpayment of wages is an independent cause of action that cannot be displaced by the terms of a collective agreement.[113]

II. Government Employees

A. *Constitutional Rights*

190. The grounds and procedures for hiring and terminating government employees (also referred to as 'public employees' and sometimes as 'civil servants') often are statutorily prescribed by civil service laws. In addition, the 5th and 14th Amendments to the US Constitution prohibit the government from taking liberty and property without due process of law and the courts have held that a reasonable expectation of continued employment is a property interest. Accordingly, courts impose some substantive and procedural constitutional restraints upon the termination of government workers.

191. As a general proposition, government employees retain their constitutional rights and liberties both on and off the job. Thus, a public employee cannot be disciplined or dismissed from employment to curtail or penalize the employee's exercise of the right of free expression, freedom of association, or freedom of religion, unless the employee's conduct functionally interferes with the employee's ability to carry out duties effectively or unless the employee's conduct significantly disrupts the workplace or work relationships.[114] When a government employee claims that disciplinary action was taken in violation of constitutionally protected liberty, the court must also weigh whether the disciplinary decision was based on findings reached in good faith and in a manner that was consistent with a reasonable manager's efforts to learn the truth about a disciplinary situation.[115]

On the other hand, in a number of instances and by divided decisions, the Supreme Court has refused to grant constitutional protection to government employees under circumstances in which the employee's conduct did not clearly interfere with work performance. Freedom of speech exercised by government workers has been particularly controversial. The Supreme Court has held that government employee speech is not protected unless it relates to a matter of public concern.[116] Also, even if the speech relates to a matter of public concern it is unprotected speech if it nonetheless deals with an issue that falls within the scope

113. *US Bulk Carriers, Inc.* v. *Arguelles*, 400 US 351 (1971).
114. For example, in *US* v. *National Treasury Employees Union*, 513 US 454 (1995), it was held that the government cannot impose an ethics rule prohibiting a non-policy-making government worker from accepting fees or royalties for giving or writing speeches or articles that do not directly involve the employee's job responsibilities.
115. *Waters* v. *Churchill*, 511 US 661 (1994).
116. *Connick* v. *Myers*, 461 US 138 (1983); *Rankin* v. *McPherson*, 483 US 378 (1987). *See also* Cynthia L. Estlund, 'Speech on Matters of Public Concern: The Perils of an Emerging First Amendment Category', 59 *George Washington L. Rev.* 1 (1990).

of an employee's official duties.[117] Beyond freedom of speech, a majority of the Court has ruled that government employees may be prohibited from taking an active part in political campaigns or the management of political parties, even though the activity is during non-work hours and does not identify the person as a government worker.[118] The Court has also held that a government employee whose services are needed in emergency situations may be required to live in the employing governmental district even if there has not been a specific showing that excessive time would be involved in reporting for work from an adjoining residential area.[119] In another case, the Court decided that a police department can constitutionally regulate the length and style of a male officer's hair and prohibit such employees from having beards. The Court justified its decision by asserting that a police department has a functional need for appearance standards that allow the public to more readily recognize officers and that such standards promote an improved *esprit de corps*.[120] A decision of an intermediate level federal court went further and held that a male police officer can be prohibited from wearing a small gold stud in his ear lobe during non-work hours. The court noted that officers were subject to being recalled to work except when on vacation, that the conservative standards of the community did not accept the idea of men wearing earrings, and that the community was sufficiently small so that the officers were generally known and recognized by the populace.[121]

192. Government employment, absent a contrary statutory, contractual or customary undertaking, is at will. As a result, the majority of the Supreme Court has held that so long as a government employee is not discharged for unlawful reasons, the Constitution places no procedural or substantive restraints upon the power of the government to terminate the worker. Thus, a divided Supreme Court has held that a public employee whose employment contract is at will has no right to any procedural safeguards respecting a decision to terminate that employment. Moreover, the Court held that the Constitution does not protect such an employee from termination based on false information or unsound reasons.[122]

193. If by statute, contract or custom, a public employee has been awarded job tenure, that employee is constitutionally protected from discharge except for good cause shown after a fair and impartial hearing.[123] That hearing, however, need not precede the discharge, and the decision maker can be the same governing body that charged the employee with wrongdoing.[124] However, some minimal, informal process must precede termination. This includes the right to receive a statement of the

---

117. *Garcetti* v. *Ceballos*, 547 US 410 (2006).
118. *US Civil Service Commission* v. *National Association of Letter Carriers*, 413 US 548 (1973); *Broadrick* v. *Oklahoma*, 413 US 601 (1973).
119. *McCarthy* v. *Philadelphia Civil Service Commission*, 424 US 645 (1976) (*per curiam*).
120. *Kelley* v. *Johnson*, 425 US 238 (1976).
121. *Rathert* v. *Village of Peotone*, 903 F.2d 510 (7th Cir. 1990).
122. *Bishop* v. *Wood*, 426 US 341 (1976).
123. *Board of Regents* v. *Roth*, 408 US 564 (1972); *Perry* v. *Sindermann*, 408 US 593 (1972).
124. *Arnett* v. *Kennedy*, 416 US 134 (1974); *Hortonville Dist.* v. *Hortonville Educ. Ass'n*, 426 US 482 (1976).

grounds for dismissal, an explanation of the evidence in support of the action, and a meaningful opportunity to respond.[125]

194. The Supreme Court has not provided clear or consistent guidance respecting what representations concerning the permanency of public employment are necessary to qualify that employment as constitutionally entitled to protected job tenure. Nor has the Court provided much guidance respecting what constitutes good cause for the discharge of such a tenured government employee.[126] Often, however, a statute or contract regulating the employment relationship, or a collective agreement, provides substantive and procedural safeguards for public workers that exceed those constitutionally imposed when a government worker's job status is constitutionally recognized as tenured.

B. *Civil Service Laws*

195. Protection of government worker job rights often, though not always, is part of a comprehensive statutory structure for regulating government personnel policies. These laws are generally referred to as civil service laws.

196. Government employment was initially regarded in the United States as an item of political patronage available to the rulers of the prevailing political party for the reward of their followers. By the mid-19th century, various groups were protesting against the evils of this spoils system and demanded that the role and power of political patronage be drastically curtailed by basing government employment decisions upon merit. Reformers especially wanted civil service personnel decisions to be insulated from political influence.

In 1871 Congress authorized the President to establish a system for appointing civil servants on the basis of merit and President Ulysses Grant appointed a board to carry out this responsibility. The board later became known as the Civil Service Commission. Within a few years, however, Congress ceased funding this new process for weighing the job candidate's merit. But, the call for reform did not subside and these demands were given dramatic reinforcement on 2 July 1881 when President James A. Garfield was shot by a man whose request to be appointed United

---

125. *Cleveland Board of Education* v. *Loudermill*, 470 US 532 (1985). So long as there was a sufficiently prompt post-suspension hearing, a police officer charged with a felony was not entitled to pay while on suspension pending the hearing. *Gilbert* v. *Homar*, 520 US 924 (1997).

126. Some decisions indicate that lack of personal confidence on the part of the person to whom the worker reports, or a personality conflict with that person, might satisfy the good cause standard. *Rankin* v. *McPherson*, 483 US 378 (1987); *Connick* v. *Myers*, 461 US 138 (1983); *Branti* v. *Finkel*, 445 US 507 at n.14 (1980); *Givhan* v. *Western Line Consol. School Dist.*, 439 US 410 at n.4 (1979). Although a personality conflict or lack of personal confidence may have merit to the extent that the subordinate worker holds a position involving a close working relationship with an elected official, its appropriateness in other situations is questionable. Otherwise, the personal bias of one government employee can succeed in repressing the constitutional due process and equal protection rights of some other government worker.

States Consul in Paris had been denied. Public resentment against the patronage system was greatly aroused by Garfield's death and support for reform of the civil service system swelled.

The Pendleton Act, a civil service reform law, adopted early in 1883, dealt mainly with hiring and discharge. It called for the President to establish a list of federal jobs for which employment would be based upon the applicant's score on a competitive examination. These jobs were called 'classified' or 'competitive' positions. The Act also prohibited discharge because of a worker's refusal to contribute to or work in a political campaign.

Under the Pendleton Act, a three-member Civil Service Commission was established. No more than two members could be from the same political party and all were to be appointed by the President with the advice and consent of the Senate.

An additional civil service policy reform was adopted by President William McKinley who, in 1897, acting under his authority as Chief Executive of the United States, announced that no person was to be removed from a classified position except for just cause. McKinley's policy also required that the intended dischargee be given a written copy of the charges against him and an opportunity to present his defense to the responsible official. That reform was codified, and slightly expanded, with the adoption of the Lloyd–LaFollette Act in 1912.

The Civil Service Retirement Act of 1920, as amended, established statutory pension benefits for those in federal employment; the Classification Act of 1923, as amended, provided for a more detailed system of testing, classifying and regulating the policies under which federal government employees are employed. The Hatch Act of 1939, as amended, added prohibitions against classified government workers engaging in various types of political activities. The Veterans' Preference Act of 1944, as amended, as its title suggests, introduced a major modification of the merit principle by offering veterans of military service privileged treatment in the competition for civil service positions. The Federal Employees Pay Act of 1945, as amended, established the forty-hour week and overtime pay benefits; and the Annual and Sick Leave Act of 1951, as amended, established a schedule of paid vacation and holiday benefits and the policies for granting leaves of absence. A major restructuring of the federal civil service system was adopted with the enactment of the Civil Service Reform Act of 1978. This Law replaced the Civil Service Commission with the Office of Personnel Management and with the Merit Systems Protection Board. (See, generally, 5 US Code §3301 *et seq.* and 5 US Code §1201 *et seq.*)

197. At first the classified civil service encompassed but a small portion of all federal employees. A dramatic increase in its coverage resulted from Theodore Roosevelt's terms of office in the early part of the Twentieth Century. Roosevelt was a former member of the United States Civil Service Commission and believed in the merit system. By the time he left office, close to 64 percent of all federal jobs were subject to the classified system. By the beginning of the Great Depression, the classified system had been expanded by various Presidential orders and directives to the point that over 80 percent of federal employment was covered. But with the onset of the Great Depression in 1929, the growth of government jobs, designed to create work for the unemployed, reversed the trend and reduced the portion employed in the classified civil service. As the Depression eased, the trend toward expansion of civil service coverage was resumed once more but that growth has not been steady. Currently the merit system protects almost two-thirds of federal employees. Historic comparisons respecting reliance on the merit principle are complicated by the fact that sound competitive examinations often are unavailable and extremely difficult to design for the purpose of hiring employees with specific technical or professional qualifications and experience. As of 1992, for example, 32 percent of federal civil servants worked in positions under what is called the 'comparable' appointment system which relies on interviews, recommendations and assessment of background credentials and prior performance made by impartial, non-political evaluators. Further, some protections against the spoils system, such as the Hatch Act's (see paragraph 196, above) prohibitions insulating most federal employment from political activities, apply to thousands of federal employees who are outside the merit system.

198. Both those holding classified civil service positions and those eligible for veterans' preferences are entitled to substantive and procedural job security protections under the federal civil service laws. These protections include a right to appeal to the Merit Systems Protection Board in the event of an adverse personnel decision and may involve a hearing within the employing agency and another before a board appointed Administrative Law Judge. As an example of the resulting protection, it has been held that the off-duty immoral conduct of a federal worker, such as sexual abuse of children, cannot be grounds for dismissal unless the government proves that the conduct impairs the worker's job performance or the agency's operations.[127]

199. The substitution of a merit based civil service system in place of a spoils system came later to state and local government employment than to federal employment. By the end of World War I, only nine states had adopted such systems. The pace of reform in the direction of adopting the merit principle for state employment increased rapidly in the late 1930s and by the mid-1950s every state had adopted the merit principle for at least some of its employees. One important impetus in this direction was a provision in the Social Security Act permitting federal grants-in-aid to go only to those state and local government workers who are subject to a merit system.

The scope of coverage and systems of job protection varies greatly under the existing state versions of the civil service classification system. Even more varied, and less universal, are civil service systems that impose the merit principle on local government employers.

200. A civil service merit system is also intended to adjust the level of remuneration to reflect the skills, knowledge and responsibilities of the job and the capabilities and performance of the worker. Civil service systems assign job positions to

127. *Bonet* v. *US Postal Serv.*, 661 F.2d 1071 (5th Cir. 1981); *D.E.* v. *Department of the Navy*, 721 F.2d 1165 (9th Cir. 1983).

an established schedule of broad grade classifications. Each classification has additional pay levels and individual employee pay is adjusted to reflect the job holder's responsibilities, credentials and assessed performance. Since 1990, the federal civil service system, in order to reduce the impact of regional variations in the cost-of-living, additionally has adjusted pay rates by the work situs (*see*, 5 US Code §5304).

201. Since the 1960s the merit principle of hiring, promotion and termination of government employees has been complicated by the affirmative action principle adopted in connection with equal employment opportunity programs. To the extent that sex-based or minority group-based goals are used to alter the sexual or ethnic profile of the work force, the merit principle may be sacrificed. On the other hand, affirmative action programs have forced public, as well as private, employers to reassess the standards and procedures long relied on for merit evaluation. Charges from various minority groups that the use of particular tests have an adverse impact upon them have resulted in more careful assessment of the reliability of such tests and standards as predictors of actual job performance. Greater attention has also been given to the possible availability of alternative merit evaluation procedures.

Without question, many of the tests used in the past as a means for establishing the 'merit' of job or promotion candidates, such as written examinations of vocabulary and reading speed, often had little or no relevancy to actual job performance. As a result, a major challenge to the continuation of the merit principle in the civil service system is whether more effective, more accurate tests can be developed for ranking the relative merit of job candidates.

202. Another challenge to the merit principle of hiring, promotion and termination of government employees has been the adoption of laws giving public employment job preference to war veterans. In the federal civil service, for example, the percentage of veterans employed and the percentage of veterans employed in upper-level positions far exceeds the percentage of veterans in the total work force. Because most veterans are men, the veterans' preference discriminates both against merit and against women. The emotional justification for the preference, however, is a powerful political force.

203. A special challenge to the civil service system has been the growth of public sector collective bargaining with its alternative model for protecting public employee interests. Although the merit principle and public sector collective representation are not inherently incompatible, the introduction of unions has raised some issues respecting the proper definition of merit.

For example, to what extent should job seniority be treated as a legitimate factor to be weighed in assessing the relative merit of two candidates for a promotion? Generally, American unions place greater weight on seniority than has been traditional under a civil service system.

Similarly, the introduction of collective bargaining representation has challenged the wisdom of continuing the civil service system for reviewing employee grievances regarding adverse personnel actions. Most labor unions prefer the private sector's approach of using contractual grievance arbitration machinery for dealing with such matters. Also, the collective bargaining representative is likely to insist upon a role in representing the employee in any appeal regarding an adverse action. Such participation introduces a new level of adversariness that often modifies the civil service system's methods for reviewing such problems.

Finally, there is considerable tension between the status of the collective agreement and the status of civil service laws or regulations when they conflict with respect to an issue of employee rights.

Chapter 2. Rights and Duties of the Parties under Individual Employment Contracts

§1. Express and Implied Terms

204. The parties may regulate their respective rights and duties by expressly adopting particular terms and conditions of employment. Such self-regulation is limited, however, to those terms and conditions that do not conflict with public policy, statutory restrictions and requirements, or administrative regulations of the employment relationship. If the employment is also regulated by a collectively bargained agreement, the latter engagement prevails over terms established by the individual employment contract.

205. Issues that arise under the employment agreement are resolved by the judicial interpretation of the express, implied or constructive terms and conditions of the contract, as well as rules imposed by statute or administrative regulation.

The following sections discuss basic rules courts apply in the absence of express contractual provisions. A few of the rules are statutory requirements that control regardless of the parties' agreement. Because enforcement of employment contracts generally is governed by state law, unless otherwise stated, the doctrines discussed below represent the principles applied by a majority of state courts, but not necessarily by all of them.

§2. The Employer's Right to the Employee's Work Product

I. Earnings Generated by the Worker

206. Products, profits and earnings produced by an employee's activities during work time are the property of the employer. In addition, absent the employer's permission or acquiescence, an employee has a duty to avoid engaging, at any time, in undertakings that compete with or conflict with the employer's interests. This is known as the employee's duty of loyalty to the employer. If the worker breaches this duty, any resulting profits belong to the employer. Thus, in *United States* v. *Drumm*, 329 F.2d 109 (1st Cir. 1964), it was held that a government health inspector is liable to the government for monies received as a consultant for work performed on his own time where that consulting work is done for a company that the inspector is assigned to police. The conflict of interest created by the consulting job necessitated imposing this liability regardless of whether there is any proof that the inspector was lax in his inspection duties. The court ruled that the mere appearance of possible impropriety constitutes a conflict with the government's interests in maintaining public confidence in the integrity of its actions and its employees.

Workers who breach their duty of loyalty generally forfeit their wages, as well as any gains from the improper conduct. In some circumstances, a worker has been held liable for the gross, rather than the net, profits derived from conduct in breach of the duty of loyalty owed the employer.[128]

207. Unless the parties agree otherwise, a worker is entitled to work for other employers during non-work time, provided the work does not create a conflict of interest. A second job in the United States is referred to as 'moonlighting'. As of 2014, 4.9 percent of all employed workers held more than one job.[129] Those employed in professional specialties have even higher rates of multiple jobs. Studies have shown that single women and married men are more likely to hold two jobs than are married women or single men.

II. Interference with the Worker's Devotion to the Employer's Well-being

208. Many states make it a crime to bribe a worker to breach the duty of loyalty owed to his employer. In addition to penal sanctions, violation of this prohibition gives the employer a damages or restitution cause of action against the briber as well as against the bribe taker.[130]

III. Property in Dispute between Employer and Worker

A. Property Found by the Worker

209. If a worker, during work time, finds lost or abandoned property, the American rule is that, as between the employer and the worker, the worker has a superior claim to the property irrespective of where it was found. There is an exception to this rule for the worker engaged in a job, such as security guard or housecleaner, with duties that include looking for lost or misplaced articles or turning such items over to the employer.[131]

B. Worker Inventions

210. A worker is entitled to keep his own discoveries (inventions) even though made during the course of employment unless the employment contract specifically provides otherwise or unless the worker is employed specifically for the purpose of applying his inventive capacity to produce an invention of the sort that is in dispute. The fact that the employer paid the expenses of developing the invention and that the creative activity was performed during work time does not itself defeat the worker's property right in the invention. However, if the employer substantially

128. American Law Institute, *Restatement of the Law of Agency (Second)*, §403 at comment (c) (1958). *Kaye* v. *Rosefielde*, 121 A.3d 862 (NJ 2015).
129. Bureau of Labor Statistics (http://www.bls.gov).
130. *Wall Sys.* v. *Pompa*, 154 A.3d 989 (CN 2017).
131. See 1 *Am. Jur.* 2d, 'Abandoned, Lost and Unclaimed Property' §30.

contributed to the worker's ability to produce the invention, by doing such things as paying the expenses of development and allowing the inventive work to be done during work time, the employer receives an implied, irrevocable, but nonexclusive right to thereafter use that invention without paying anything further to the worker for the privilege of use. This implied right is an equitable claim called the employer's 'shop right'.[132] A shop right cannot be assigned by the employer, but it is passed along to an employer's corporate successor. An employer can by express agreement or by conduct surrender its 'shop right' claim. An employer may not have a 'shop right' in an invention developed by an employee soon after employment is terminated despite the employer's negotiation of a 'holdover clause' that contractually preserves the employer's rights in inventions developed after termination of employment.[133]

211. A worker does not have rights to an invention if it is but an improvement upon a basic design or principle owned by the employer and if it is consistent with the concepts inherent in the employer's invention. But, if the worker's improvements involve significant departures in principle from the employer's invention, then the property rights in the invention belong to the worker and not to the employer.[134] A few states, such as California, expressly prohibit unpaid assignment of inventions to the employer unless the employer made a substantial contribution to the employee's ability or opportunity to develop the invention.[135]

C. Worker Creations

212. Although the presumption is that an inventing worker owns the right to the patent to the invention, if the intellectual property created by the worker is of the sort that is subject to copyright law, the opposite presumption applies. Under the Copyright Act, an employer is entitled to the copyright if the work was created within the scope of employment. The concept of 'within the scope of employment' is sufficiently broad to include creative activity engaged in while the worker is away from the employer's premises, including while the worker is at home. Moreover, the employer's property in the copyright for its worker's creations extends to all works based on the existing work, including adaptation rights. For example, if a television script writer's video play is transformed into a novel or film, the employing broadcaster owns the right to control, transfer, and benefit from the modified form of the work. The presumption of employer ownership of the copyright can, however, be altered by contract.[136]

The Copyright Act provides different rules for works depending on whether the copyright is held by the creator or by an employer of the creator. Thus, while the

---

132. R. Bales, J. Hirsch and P. Secunda, *Understanding Employment Law*, §11.05 (2013).
133. *See Ingersoll-Rand Co.* v. *Ciavatta*, 542 A.2d 879 (NJ 1988) (holdover clause unreasonable and unenforceable); R. Mergens, 'The Law and Economics of Employee Inventions', 13 *Harv.J. L. & Tech.* 1 (1999).
134. *See generally*, R. Moy, *Walker on Patents*, §10:14 (4th ed. 2007).
135. *See* California Labor Code §2870; Bales, Hirsch and Secunda, §11.05 (2013).
136. *See, generally,* 1 *Nimmer on Copyright* § 5.03.

creator has lifetime ownership in the right and can transfer it for an added seventy years beyond, an employer's ownership is limited to 95 years from publication or a maximum of 120 years from the date of creation.

The Supreme Court has held that general common law standards control whether an employment relationship exists for purposes of the Copyright Act. This requires weighing a variety of factors including the right to control the manner, means, duration and schedule of the work activity; the skill required; the source of the needed tools, materials and assistants; the location of the work activity; the duration of the relationship; the method, frequency and scope of remuneration; the normal business activities of both sides; and the right to assign additional projects to the creator.[137]

213. Treatises and some case law long supported the proposition that the teacher, and not the employing institution, owns the copyright to the teacher's writings, prepared lectures and other creations. This exception to the general rule was a product both of custom and of concern for the preservation of academic freedom. It is uncertain whether under more recent legislation the courts will continue to recognize for teachers, or at least for university professors, this academic exception to the general rule regarding the respective copyright claims of employers and employees inasmuch as the exception is not mentioned in the copyright statute.

One argument supporting American tradition of treating the copyright as the teacher's property reflects a concern for insulating the institution from liability for defamation, copyright infringement and the like. If the copyright automatically goes to the academic institution, that institution will be liable for any infringements of other works or for any defamatory statements in the work product. Accordingly, if it receives the copyright, the employing institution has a need to supervise and control the content and form of the creation. Hence, the desired independence of academic commentary and creativity is better served if the teacher's creations are his own responsibility and property.

Moreover, there is a constitutional argument in support of the traditional rule excluding teachers from the normal presumption that the employer owns the copyright. The guaranty of academic freedom is implicit in the US Constitution's guaranty of freedom of speech. A core element of academic freedom is the teacher's right to explore and to comment – to profess – free from institutional control and free from institutionalized orthodoxy. Arguably, therefore, the teacher must be given copyright to creations in order to insulate the teacher-creator from institutional efforts to regulate those creations.

Although a literal reading of the most recent Copyright Act would appear to favor the institution's copyright claim to the professor's work products over that of the professor, the legislative history reveals that Congress did not examine this question. Therefore, the judiciary has a basis for interpreting the legislative intent in a manner that is consistent with constitutional needs and traditional assumptions. Accordingly, several commentators and judges have suggested that ultimately the

137. *Community for Creative Non-Violence* v. *Reid*, 490 US 730 (1989).

law will be interpreted in favor of preserving the tradition of presuming ownership by the individual academic creator and not by the university or school.[138]

214. Although the employer owns the intellectual property of one who is employed to produce copyrightable material, the employer does not have property rights in such material when produced by someone employed for other purposes even though the creative work draws upon the creator's work experience or work environment. Nor is broad employment contract language making the employee responsible for devoting his entire efforts to the employer adequate to give the employer the copyright in creative works produced during the employee's leisure time. However, generally, if the employment contract specifically states that the employer is the owner of all intellectual work products produced during the period of the employment agreement, the employer owns the copyright for all works created by the worker irrespective of when, where and how produced. In some states, there are statutory restrictions on the enforceability of these broad agreements. See above at paragraph 211.

IV. Worker's Duty to Not Misappropriate a Former Employer's Property

A. Protection of Trade Secrets

215. Generally, an employee's duty of loyalty to his employer ceases when the employment ends. One dimension of a worker's duty of loyalty, however, survives the term of employment. Although an employee is entitled to take with him, and use for his own or for a succeeding employer's benefit, any general knowledge, information, experience and skill gained in employment, a worker is not entitled to profit from or to give a successor employer the benefit of the trade secrets or confidential information entrusted to him by a previous employer. Breach of that confidence gives rise to a cause of action for damages, possibly including punitive damages, and injunctive relief against the former employee and any employer seeking to benefit from the breach of confidence.[139]

---

138. *Shaul* v. *Cherry-Valley-Springfield Central School District*, 363 F.3d 177 (2d Cir. 2004); *Hays* v. *Sony Corporation of America*, 847 F.2d 412, 416 (7th Cir. 1988) (*dicta*); *contra*, *Weinstein* v. *University of Illinois*, 811 F.2d 1091-1093-94 (7th Cir. 1987) (*dicta*); *Pavlica* v. *Behr*, 397 F. Supp. 2d 519 (SDNY 2005) (distinguishing high school teachers and university professors); G. Gertz, 'Copyrights in Faculty-Created Works', 88 *Wash. L. Rev.* 1465 (2013); M. Nimmer and D. Nimmer, *Nimmer on Copyright*, §5.03(B)(1)(b)(i) (2008); E. Townsend, 'Legal and Policy Responses to the Disappearing Teacher Exception, Or Copyright Ownership in the 21st Century', 4 *Minn. Intellectual Prop. Rev.* 209 (2003); G. Holmes and D. Levin, 'Who Owns Course Materials Prepared by a Teacher or Professor? The Application of Copyright Laws to Teaching Materials in the Internet Age', 2000 *BYU Educ. & L.J.* 165 (2000).

139. The Uniform Trade Secrets Act, codified now in some form in every state, provides for the payment of royalties by the new employer as well as payment of the former employer's reasonable attorneys' fees in bringing the challenge. *See* Bales, Hirsch and Secunda, *Understanding Employment Law*, §11.03 (2013); *see also* e.g. California Civil Code §§3426– 3426.10 (2013); North Dakota Cent. Code §9-08-06 (2013).

216. The cause of action for misappropriation of a previous employer's trade secrets is sometimes conceptualized as an action for the protection of property rights. More often it is conceptualized as an action based on breach of a trust. If an employee has been induced to bring away a former employer's trade secrets, the action may be framed in terms of a conspiracy to engage in unfair competition or a tortious interference with contractual relations.

217. If injunctive relief is granted based on the disclosure of a former employer's trade secrets, it is usually designed to bar the new employer from using the secret process, technique, device or information until such time as the new employer would probably have been able to discover the secret through its own lawful investigations and research.

218. In some jurisdictions, disclosure of a former employer's trade secrets and the inducement of such a disclosure, is treated as a form of the crime of larceny and subjects the wrongdoer to penal sanctions as well as to civil remedies. In a few jurisdictions, the disclosure of a former employer's trade secrets is a crime only if it is accomplished by means of the transfer of tangible items such as drawings, written formulas, or maps. The Economic Espionage Act of 1996, has made misappropriation of trade secrets a federal criminal offense and the statute is extra-territorial in its reach.[140]

219. Drawing the lines between trade secrets and general knowledge acquired in employment poses considerable difficulty. A trade secret has been described as information or knowledge that is not readily accessible to others in the trade. But a trade secret need not be so unique as to be patentable or copyrightable in order to be entitled to protection. On the other hand, to be protected, the trade secret must involve sufficient novelty to merit trying to maintain secrecy. In addition, to be protected from a former employee's appropriation, the employer must have impressed upon the worker the confidential nature of the information, knowledge, device or technique, and must have made reasonable efforts to maintain secrecy.[141] In most jurisdictions, absent the above factors, the information used by the former employee will be treated as general knowledge over which the previous employer has no continuing claim.

220. Employers sometimes claim that information about customers or prospective customers is a 'trade secret' in order to prevent a former employee from competing by soliciting its customers. Although the names and addresses of customers and prospective customers may be generally known or available, specific facts about the customers may not be generally or widely known and may give a particular business a competitive advantage. As a result, under limited conditions, American courts are willing to treat lists of customers and potential customers as trade secrets.

---

140. 18 US Code §§ 1831–1839; *see also United States* v. *Martin*, 228 F.3d 1 (1st Cir. 2000).

141. *See*, for example, *K-2 Ski Co.* v. *Head Ski Co. Inc.*, 506 F.2d 471 (9th Cir. 1974); *Delta Filter Corp.* v. *Morin*, 485 N.Y.S.2d 143 (NY 1985); Epstein and Levi, 'Protecting Trade Secret Information', 43 *Bus. Law* 887 (1988).

On the other hand, employers cannot simply claim customers as 'trade secrets' in order to prevent lawful competition. Not all customer lists are trade secrets. Unless there is an enforceable agreement to the contrary, a former employee is entitled to compete with the previous employer. The fact that a customer list containing specific information was kept confidential by the employer and was secretly copied or removed by the employee, or that it was made or removed in violation of the previous employer's work rules, is treated as evidence of its protected status.[142] On the other hand, an employer cannot transform into a trade secret that information which is readily obtainable by others.[143]

221. In determining whether to give a prior employer relief from a former employee's use of its customer or potential customer lists, courts look at several factors including: the extent of the employer's special efforts and investment in gathering and developing the list, the degree of confidentiality in the particular employer-employee relationship, the extent to which the employer sought to safeguard the information, the role played by the employee in gathering the information, the presence or absence of malice as a factor motivating the former employee's conduct, the extent to which deception was practiced by the former employee, and the ability of the former employee to practice his trade or profession while foregoing solicitation of the listed customers or potential customers. In weighing these factors, courts consider two basic competing concerns: (a) the employer's right to retain investments in know-how entrusted to employees; and(b) the worker's right to remain employed in a position in which he can utilize knowledge and skill gained by past diligent performance of his work.

Many courts cut short this analysis in certain cases by adhering to the rule that a former employee can always use lists carried away solely through his powers of memory.[144]

222. An employee is permitted to inform customers that he is leaving his employment and going into business for himself or taking a job with another enterprise. But the employee may not try to solicit business away from his current employer while he is still employed there. Absent an agreement to the contrary, such solicitation is, of course, permissible once there has been a change of employment so that the solicitation is of former customers.

B. Covenants not to Compete with a Former Employer

223. Employers sometimes enter into express agreements with their workers barring them from competing with the employer after termination of the employment. These covenants are most often found in the employment contracts of

142. *See generally*, American Law Institute, *Restatement of the Law of Agency*, 2d §396 (1958); R. Milgrim, 'Trade Secrets', vol. 12 of *Business Organizations* (1981).
143. *See Guy Carpenter & Co.* v. *Provenzale*, 334 F.3d 459 (5th Cir. 2003).
144. For example, *Carl A. Colteryahn Dairy Inc.* v. *Schneider Dairy*, 203 A.2d 469 (Pa. 1964); *Ikon Office Solutions, Inc.* v. *Am. Office Prods.*, 178 F. Supp. 2d 1154 (D. Ore. 2001). But *contra*, *MAI Systems Corp.* v. *Peak Computer, Inc.*, 991 F.2d 511 (9th Cir. 1993).

sales, managerial and technical personnel. In entering into such a covenant, an employer may be seeking to preserve the value of the worker's employment activities or to reduce the prospects for the worker's misappropriation of trade secrets. However, American courts will not enforce such covenants if they unduly restrain a worker's opportunities to be gainfully employed or unduly deprive society of a worker's special knowledge, skill or experience. In more general terms, courts often regard such provisions with great suspicion since they are restraints of trade that detract from the virtues of a competitive market.[145]

224. The general rule respecting enforcement of a former employee's covenant not to compete is that the employer bears the burden of justifying the covenant. It is enforceable only if:

(a) the restriction is no greater than is necessary for the protection of some legitimate interest of the former employer;
(b) the restriction does not impose undue hardship on the worker; and
(c) the restriction is not injurious to the public.[146]

The variables that courts most often look to in determining whether a non-competition clause is excessive are:

(a) the duration of the restraint;
(b) the geographic area covered by the restraint;
(c) the scope of the prohibited activities;
(d) the employer's contribution to the worker's special knowledge and skill; and
(e) the extent to which the former employer in fact suffers hardship as a result of the former employee's activities.[147]

Some states have adopted statutory limitations on the enforceability and duration of these restrictions. Courts generally look, too, to the nature of the business interest being protected in determining whether the restraint of a non-competition clause is excessive. Thus, a one year noncompetition clause against a salesperson employed in a shop likely will not be enforced if it prohibits future employment as a sales clerk within a radius of 50 miles of that shop, but a one year noncompetition covenant against a research and development project director for a pharmaceutical company may be enforceable even though it applies to employment in a similar capacity with any direct competitor anywhere in the world.

---

145. *See generally*, P. Rubin and P. Shedd, 'Human Capital and Covenants Not to Compete', 10 *J. Legal Studies* 93 (1981); C. Fisk, 'Working Knowledge: Trade Secrets, Restrictive Covenants in Employment, and the Rise of Corporate Intellectual Property: 1800–1920', 52 *Hastings L.J.* 441 (2001); R. Arnow-Richman, 'Noncompetes, Human Capital, and Contract Formation: What Employment Law Can Learn From Family Law', 10 *Texas Wesleyan L. Rev.* 155 (2003).
146. *See Restatement of Contracts (Second)*, §188.
147. *See* Bales, Hirsch and Secunda, §11.04; *see*, e.g. *Harris* v. *Primus*, 450 N.E.2d 80 (Ind. 1983). Note that the geographic scope limitation is not treated as definitive with respect to internet businesses, where competition tends to be global. *See* e.g. *Earth Web, Inc.* v. *Schlack*, 71 F. Supp. 2d 299 (SDNY 1999).

225. Some courts enforce restrictive covenants only to the extent that the provisions are reasonable and are severable from any unreasonable provisions found in the same covenant.[148] Such courts will strike the unreasonable provisions (a procedure known as 'blue-penciling') and enforce the remainder of the agreement. If the unreasonable provisions are not severable, the entire agreement is void. In determining whether a provision is severable, some courts appear to give weight to the overall reasonableness of the restrictive covenant – finding the provision not severable if the covenant's overall impact is unconscionable. An alternative approach, taken by a significant number of courts, is to reformulate the covenant into one that is reasonable, thereby reforming the parties' agreement in a way that protects the employer's protectable interests while avoiding unreasonable restrictions on the employee.[149] Yet other jurisdictions evaluate the covenant as written and if any provision, whether or not severable, is unenforceable, the entire covenant falls.[150]

226. Another possible barrier to the enforcement of a noncompetition clause is the presence or absence of consideration[151] for that undertaking. If the covenant not to compete is entered into after the commencement of employment, several courts have held that it must be supported by separate consideration other than the continuation of employment; otherwise, it is not enforceable. Such separate consideration might consist of an increase in wages or other benefits, or an alteration of an at will duration of employment to one for a specific period of time.[152] Other courts hold that the continuation of employment is sufficient consideration for the noncompetition covenant.[153]

§3. The Employer's Responsibility for the Worker's Health, Safety and Property

I. Protection of the Worker

A. Common Law

227. Historically, an employer was liable for those injuries to an employee that resulted from failure to provide a work environment, tools, equipment and procedures that were free from foreseeable and unnecessary danger. Under the

148. *See generally*, R. Bales, J. Hirsch and P. Secunda, *Understanding Employment Law*, §11.04 (B)(2)(2013); *see* e.g. *Timenterial, Inc.* v. *Dagata*, 277 A.2d 512 (Conn. Sup. Ct. 1971).
149. *See* e.g. *Dean Van Horn Consulting Assocs.* v. *Wold*, 395 N.W.2d 405 (Minn. Ct. App. 1986).
150. *See* cases collected in 61 A.L.R.3d 397, 407B19 (1975) and (2007 Supp.).
151. Consideration in American law is a bargained-for exchange, typically involving a benefit given to the promisor or a detriment suffered by the promisee in exchange for the agreed obligation or privilege. *See Restatement of Contracts (Second)*, §71.
152. For example, *Burroughs Corp.* v. *Cimakasky*, 346 F. Supp. 1398 (E.D. Pa. 1972). *See generally* T. Staidl, 'Enforceability of Non-competition Agreements When Employment Is At-Will: Reformulating the Analysis', 2 *Employee Rights & Employment Pol. J.* 95 (1998).
153. *See Lucht's Concrete Pumping, Inc.* v. *Horner*, 255 P.3d 1058, 1060 (Colo. 2011).

common law in the United States, four doctrines were appended to this principle that made it extremely difficult for a worker to ever recover from his employer for job-related injury by bringing a personal injury lawsuit based on the negligence of the employer or another worker.[154]

One doctrine limiting the availability of the common law right of the worker to recover for job-caused injury or illness was the requirement that the worker prove that the injury was proximately caused by the employer's breach of its duty of good care. According to some early decisions, the reasonableness of the employer's precautions (good care) was to be judged by customary practices. Thus, the worker's recovery was in part dependent on the level of protection generally afforded by the health and safety practices in the industry. Additional impediments to meeting this requirement were that most employee witnesses to an injury were reluctant to testify against the employer's interests either because of loyalty or because of fear and that, often, the employer had close ties with those who possessed the expertise to ascertain what mishaps were foreseeable and what precautions were available.

The second doctrinal impediment to common law recovery for a job-related illness or injury was that recovery was not available if the illness or injury was caused by a risk knowingly and willingly assumed by the worker. Known as the 'assumption of the risk' doctrine, this barrier also excluded from liability those injuries caused by risks inherent in the type of employment.

The third common law hurdle for the injured or ill worker was the contributory fault doctrine, holding that the worker was totally barred from recovering for an injury if his own negligence was a contributing cause.

Finally, the common law right of recovery was lost if the injury or illness was caused by the negligence or misconduct of a fellow employee engaged in the same general employment as the claimant. This defense, known as the fellow servant doctrine, in actuality was a special dimension of the assumption of the risk defense.

228. By the early twentieth century a few courts rejected the assumption of the risk defense where a worker had placed himself in danger in order to avoid endangering others or to safeguard the employer's property. American courts also gradually transformed the contributory negligence defense from a total barrier to recovery into a defense of 'comparative' responsibility under which recovery was reduced in proportion to the worker's contribution to the causes of the loss. (Prior to the general judicial modification of this defense, some jurisdictions imposed the change by statute for cases involving employee suits for recovery against their employers.) Finally, the fellow servant defense was limited by some courts to those workers who habitually worked with the injured employee and, under what was called the 'vice principal' doctrine, some courts rejected the defense if the injury or illness was caused by the negligence of supervisory or managerial personnel.

---

154. The case decision that provided the foundations for these defenses to employer liability was *Farwell* v. *Boston & Worcester R.R.*, 4 Metc. 49 (Mass. 1842).

B. Statutory Modifications of the Common Law

229. The common law respecting an employer's responsibility for the protection of a worker's health and safety has been displaced by federal legislation, including the Occupational Safety and Health Act, the Federal Employers' Liability Act, the Jones Act, and by state and federal workers' compensation laws. Such legislation greatly improves the injured or ill worker's prospects for recovery of damages from the employer when the injury or illness arises out of employment. Thus, the Occupational Safety and Health Act has established a basis for employees to be able to prove employer *per se* responsibility when injuries have resulted from violations of established safety and health standards. In addition, in situations in which an employee must still prove employer fault, generally so-called employer liability statutes have eliminated the fellow servant defense, and in many jurisdictions the assumption of the risk defense also has been eliminated or, at least, greatly modified. More broadly, workers' compensation statutes eliminate the claimant's need to prove fault, and the defense of contributory negligence has either been eliminated or modified in most jurisdictions by a workers' compensation law or by an employers' liability statute.

230. The Federal Employers' Liability Act (45 US Code § 51) protects persons employed by railroads operating in interstate commerce. It eliminates the defense of contributory negligence if the injury was caused at least in part by the railroad's violation of a safety statute. In all other situations, the Act provides that the worker's contributory negligence reduces liability in proportion to the worker's own fault in causing the injury. The Act also eliminates the assumption of risk and the fellow servant defenses.

231. State law governs the worker's right to recover for job related injuries or illness for most forms of employment in the United States. Workers' compensation statutes in the US establish an insurance program that normally provides benefits for work-related injuries or illnesses without regard to fault or assumption of the risk. These benefits pay for medical care, including rehabilitation, and offset at least part of the worker's loss of income due to temporary or permanent disability. Disability benefits are subject to maximum weekly payments. In some states extra payments are provided based upon the number of dependents supported by the disabled worker. Permanent disability benefits often are determined by fixed schedules that relate the precise nature of the disability to a particular level of benefit. The maximum benefit amount most typically is two thirds of the injured worker's average weekly pay over a specified period with an absolute maximum based on the statewide average weekly pay.

Disability from a work-related injury or illness can be total or partial. A partially disabled worker receives proportionally reduced benefits while continuing to work. The measure of benefits is sometimes based on the overall functional reduction of the worker's ability to engage in all aspects of his life. However, most jurisdictions now measure disability only by the extent to which there has been a reduction in the worker's earning ability.

Most workers' compensation statutes in the US also have a maximum period of benefit with the result that 'permanent disability' does not mean that the benefit is paid for the remainder of the worker's life. In the event of the worker's death, the worker's dependents receive death benefits unless the maximum permanent disability benefit has already been paid to the worker.

Recovery is barred in most jurisdictions if the disability resulted from the worker's intentional self-injury. In many states, recovery is barred for injuries resulting from the worker's intoxication.

232. If a worker has been employed for a minimum qualifying period in a job covered by the national Social Security program and is totally disabled for a period expected to last for at least one year, upon the exhaustion of workers' compensation benefits the Social Security program provides a monthly disability benefit to the worker. The Social Security benefits are available even if the disability was not work-related.

233. Workers' compensation statutes provide that the benefit under the program is the sole and exclusive claim the worker has against the employer for the suffered injury. That is, the insurance program provided by workers' compensation bars the employee from bringing a negligence suit against the employer. Based on the Supreme Court's interpretation of federal legislation respecting farm labor, some agricultural workers for a time were exempt from this exclusivity rule.[155] However, Congress amended the Migrant and Seasonal Agricultural Worker Protection Act in 1995, effectively overruling the Court's decision.[156] Thus, workers' compensation is the exclusive remedy for farm workers, as well, if the state's workers' compensation law applies to them.

Most workers' compensation statutes also prohibit the injured worker from bringing suit against a negligent fellow employee who caused the injury or illness. However, the employee is free to sue a third party who caused a work-related illness or injury, and the employer has a right of indemnity to share in the recovery from the third party to the extent of benefits paid to or on behalf of the injured or ill worker.

Where the injury was maliciously inflicted by the employer or fellow worker, most statutes provide an exception to the rule that workers' compensation recovery is the employee's only remedy. Many states also provide for an increased disability payment if the injury resulted from the employer's failure to obey government safety regulations, and some states reduce the disability benefit if the worker was injured as a result of violating a work-safety rule.

234. In 2011 workers' compensation covered an estimated 125.8 million workers. Workers in smaller enterprises, railroad, maritime and agricultural workers, and

155. *Adams Fruit Co.* v. *Barrett*, 494 US 638 (1990) (holding that workers covered by the Migrant and Seasonal Agricultural Worker Protection Act, 29 US Code §§1801, 1854, were entitled to sue for injuries resulting from violations of regulations under that act even though they also recovered workers' compensation benefits for their illnesses or injuries).

156. 29 US Code §1854(d).

casual workers are among the groups most often excluded from workers' compensation law coverage. As a result of rising insurance costs in the last several decades, some states have acted to limit workers' compensation benefits.[157]

235. The Jones Act (46 US Code App. §688), adopted in 1920, extended to seafarers the same benefits provided to railroad workers by the Federal Employers' Liability Act. In a series of cases, the Supreme Court of the United States held that because general maritime law often is more protective of the seafarer's right to a remedy than is the Federal Employers' Liability Act, and because the Jones Act was intended to be remedial, a seafarer is entitled to recover under whichever principle (the Jones Act's incorporation of the Federal Employers' Liability Act or general maritime law) is more protective of the seafarer's interests.

Thus, because the Supreme Court has held that under general maritime law a ship owner warrants the seaworthiness of the vessel at all times, the seafarer can recover for injuries or illnesses caused by unseaworthiness without having to prove that the unseaworthiness was due to the ship owner's negligence. Similarly, the Court has held that the assumption of the risk defense is not available in a seaman's action brought under the Jones Act. And, under the Jones Act, even where the success of the action depends on proving that the ship owner was negligent, that negligence need be established only by the maritime standard of a scintilla of supporting evidence rather than by the civil law standard of a preponderance of the evidence. Jones Act recoveries are not limited by the maximum benefit restrictions of workers' compensation statutes and provide damages for pain and suffering as well as for lost wages and wage earning ability. Thus, Jones Act recoveries are significantly greater than workers' compensation benefits for the same injury or illness.[158]

Only seafarers, however, are covered by the Jones Act. The Supreme Court regards as seafarers those who regularly face 'exposure to the perils of the sea', and thus a plaintiff must establish a substantial connection to a vessel or fleet of vessels while in navigation.[159] A land-based employee who happens to be injured while on a ship is not covered, whereas a seafarer who is injured while off the ship will not lose coverage because of the place of injury. In deciding whether an employee is a seafarer courts consider the nature of the employee's service, his status as a member of the vessel, and his relationship to the vessel while it is in navigation.[160]

C. Tribunal for Determining Liability and Damages

236. As a general rule, if the worker's right of recovery is conditioned upon proving the employer's negligence, the worker has a right to a jury trial and the jury decides both liability and the amount of damages. If the worker's right of recovery

157. *See* Martha T. McCluskey, 'The Illusion of Efficiency in Workers' Compensation Reform', 50 *Rutgers L. Rev.* 657 (1998).
158. *See generally*, 1B Gelpi, Sullivan, Carroll & Gibbens, *Benedict on Admiralty*, Chs. I, IV; 2 Martin J. Norris, *The Law of Seamen*, ch. 26 (4th ed. 1985 & Supp. 1999).
159. *Harbor Tug and Barge Co.* v. *Papai*, 520 US 548 (1997).
160. *Chandris, Inc.* v. *Latsis*, 515 US 347 (1995).

does not depend on proof of fault, as in the situation under workers' compensation laws, an administrative agency most often determines liability and determines what benefits the employee is entitled to under the applicable statute. In an action by a seafarer based on the alleged unseaworthiness of the vessel, questions of liability and damages are resolved by the judge acting as a court of admiralty.

D. Scope of the Employer's Liability

237. An employer's workers' compensation liability for injury or illness suffered by a worker extends not only to events occurring during work time or while discharging duties for the employer, regardless of where the worker is located, but also while the worker is on the premises preparing to go to work or preparing to leave work. The employer's liability similarly extends during lunch and break periods if the worker remains on the premises. If the cause of injury or illness is food or drink sold by someone other than the employer, but on the employer's premises, some courts confine the worker's recovery to an action against the vendor. If the worker lives on the employer's premises because of the remoteness of the job to other residential facilities, as in a logging camp or on an offshore oil drilling rig, the employer's liability generally is held to continue during all times while the worker is on the employer's premises regardless of whether engaged in work. Similarly, workers' compensation generally covers traveling employees during the entire time they are engaged in work or normal life sustaining activities, such as eating and lodging.

238. In most jurisdictions, the employer's duty of good care includes providing medical assistance to an employee who, on the job, is too ill or injured to be able to care for himself. Failure to provide such aid renders the employer liable for damages resulting from that lack of assistance. If an employer provides a worker with medical assistance or requires the worker to submit to a medical examination, the employer's duty of good care requires the employer to disclose to the worker any dangerous or potentially dangerous condition discovered by the medical examination or treatment.[161] The injury resulting from failure to make such disclosure has been held by some courts to itself constitute a work-related injury covered by workmen's compensation insurance, even though the dangerous condition was not itself job-related. Other courts have allowed a separate suit for failure to disclose on the ground that the resulting injury is not work-related.[162]

239. Ship owners traditionally have been held to an especially high duty of good care for the well being of seafarers. Thus, a sailor who becomes ill or is injured

---

161. Employees have the right to access their own medical information under other laws as well. *See*, e.g. OSHA Reg. 29 Code Fed. Reg. §1910.20. *See also*, the federal Health Insurance Portability and Accountability Act of 1996 (HIPAA), which requires privacy for 'protected health information' (PHI), defined as individually identifiable health information. 42 US Code §201 (2006).
162. *See*, for example, *Millison* v. *E.I. DuPont de Nemours & Co.*, 501 A.2d 505 (NJ 1985).

while in the service of a vessel is, at the ship owner's expense, entitled to maintenance and medical treatment to the point of maximum cure. If the disease or injury is declared permanent, the ship owner's duty of maintenance and cure terminates and the sailor is left with whatever Jones Act claim he might have against the ship owner based on the job-related nature of the disability. However, the right to maintenance and cure exists even though the injury or illness was not job-related and even though the seaman suffered from the malady when he boarded the ship – unless he knowingly concealed it when hired.

A ship owner's duty of maintenance and cure applies to all employed on vessels flying the flag of the United States, including those employed on vessels traveling on navigable waterways within the United States and those who sleep ashore. Workers aboard offshore oil rigs are covered by this protection if the rig is moved into its position as a floating platform. A seafarer is covered while on shore leave and while traveling to and from the vessel, as well as while aboard the ship. Only a seafarer's gross misconduct in causing the illness or injury can bar his right to cure and maintenance. (Venereal disease is not covered due to this exception, nor are injuries suffered from brawls or extreme drunkenness.)

240. Although the duty of maintenance includes paying the seafarer a daily allowance for the reasonable costs of housing, clothing and food when ashore, for many years admiralty courts automatically assessed a per diem of $8 without further inquiry. Maritime unions, in exchange for other collective bargaining benefits, negotiated the $8 per diem as a contractual standard. In recent years, some courts have been responsive to petitions for a higher maintenance per diem based on a showing that actual costs are now three or more times the standard established through collective bargaining. Nevertheless, a number of courts have ruled that a seafarer covered by a collective bargaining agreement is limited to the negotiated amount. The rationale is that the right to maintenance is based on the contractual relationship established by the shipping papers and that, therefore, the parties can contractually modify the level of benefit, at least when the seafarer has comparable bargaining power as a result of collective representation. The minority position is that the right to maintenance was established by admiralty law and that collective bargaining cannot reduce that benefit below a minimum standard of reasonable sustenance, just as a collective bargaining agreement cannot reduce wages below the statutory minimum.[163]

In the past, an ill or injured seafarer had to accept care and treatment at a hospital maintained by the US Public Health Service when available. Refusal of such care and treatment, if adequate to meet the seafarer's needs, terminated the claim for maintenance and cure. This requirement substantially reduced the ship owner's financial liability for maintenance and cure inasmuch as the Public Health Service

---

163. *Gardiner* v. *Sea Land Service, Inc.*, 786 F.2d 943 (9th Cir. 1986) (holding $8 is all seaman is due if that is what collective bargaining agreement provides); *Ammar* v. *United States*, 342 F.3d 133 (2d Cir. 2003) (following *Gardiner*). But *see, Hall* v. *Noble Drilling (US) Inc.*, 242 F.3d 582, 589 (5th Cir. 2001) ('A seaman is entitled to the reasonable cost of food and lodging in his locality, provided that he actually spends that amount on his upkeep') and *Barnes* v. *Andover Co., L.P.*, 900 F.2d 630 (3d Cir. 1990).

is financed from general tax revenues and was provided to seafarers free of charge. The Public Health Service hospitals and clinics were phased out in the 1980s.

The failure to provide maintenance and cure has been held to provide a separate claim for relief in which the seafarer can recover compensatory damages for resulting pain and suffering, lost wages and medical expenses.[164] The courts differ regarding whether punitive damages may be recovered.

241. Some jurisdictions hold that an employer becomes the absolute insurer against injury of a child employed in violation of minimum age laws. Thus, in such situations, the child's contributory negligence would not be a defense against liability for job-caused injury.[165]

II. Protection of the Worker's Property, Dignity and Privacy

242. In a few cases, employers have been held liable for loss of a worker's property (such as tools, coats or money) stolen from the employer's premises during work time. The worker's chances for recovery are enhanced if the employer is required by statute to provide lockers or if the employer requires employees to store their belongings in a particular place. But where the employer has merely provided a place of convenience to store personal goods, and has not undertaken to secure those areas, several courts have held that the worker bears the risk of loss.[166] Generally, the courts have analyzed these cases not in terms of the duties owed by an employer to safeguard an employee, but rather in terms of the law of bailments. Accordingly, the key question is whether the employer has taken custody of the items and, if so, whether it is a gratuitous bailment or one for consideration with the resulting difference in the degree of care owed to the bailee. Most often, courts find that the employer undertook a gratuitous bailment only.

If the employment is governed by a collectively bargained agreement, the employee's right of recovery may be confined to the grievance process established by the collective agreement. For example, where an employer dismissed a worker for failure to report for work and dumped the contents of the worker's locker in the garbage, a closely divided federal court ruled that because it was necessary to interpret the collective agreement in order to decide whether the employer had a contractual right to dispose of the locker contents in this manner, federal law required that the employee's claim be confined to the procedures for enforcing the collective agreement.[167]

243. If an employer lacks confidence in the integrity of its employees, it must take precautions, often expensive precautions, to minimize the potential losses that

164. *Vincent* v. *Riggi & Sons Inc.*, 285 N.E.2d 689 (NY Ct. App. 1972).
165. For example, *Vincent* v. *Riggi & Sons Inc.*, 30 N.Y.2d 406 (1972). Compare, *Devin* v. *Jones*, 426 P.2d 343 (Okla. 1967).
166. For example, *Collins* v. *Boeing Co.*, 483 P.2d 1282 (Wash. App. 1971).
167. *McCormick* v. *AT&T Technologies, Inc.*, 934 F.2d 531 (4th Cir. 1991) (*en banc*), *cert.* denied 502 US 1048 (1992).

can result from employee dishonesty. American employers often resort to tests and investigations in an effort to determine whether a job applicant is an honest person.

Some efforts to detect employee dishonesty probe the employee's values, thoughts and non-work conduct. From the worker's perspective, probing thoughts, values or non-work conduct invades privacy, freedom of conscience, and, depending on the content and manner of the probe, additionally may affront the worker's dignity. If the employer's inquiry results in a conclusion that the worker is guilty of dishonesty, not only can the worker expect to lose his job, but also his reputation may be injured. Hence, those who act to advance employee interests often support legislation to restrict the scope and manner of employer probes of employee honesty and to ensure the reliability of those probes that are permitted.

Tests to detect dishonesty generally rely either on: (a) correlating particular personality characteristics with the propensity to be deceptive or (b) ascertaining whether the suspected person is displaying elements of stress that are presumed to be associated with engaging in dishonest conduct. The first approach typically uses questionnaires designed by psychologists to analyze the subject's personality profile. Questions posed by such instruments often inquire into intimate family relationships, sexual preferences and conduct, personal habits, and the like. For example, one 'psychscreen test' used by a discount retail store chain for about four years (until discontinued in 1991 during the course of a law suit challenging its use) asked the employees to answer whether the following statements, among others, were true or false: 'I feel sure there is only one true religion' 'I am very strongly attracted by members of my own sex' 'I have had no difficulty starting or holding my bowel movement' 'I am fascinated by fire'.[168]

Requiring employees or job applicants to complete such questionnaires is treated by some states as an interference with the worker's right of privacy. For example, the high court in Massachusetts has observed that if a threat of dismissal coerces an employee to complete a questionnaire that intrudes into the employee's private affairs, the worker has a right to relief unless the inquiry is justified by the nature of the employment responsibilities.[169]

244. The best known approach that purports to detect dishonesty is the 'lie detector' or polygraph test which, in its prevalent format, records changes in a person's respiration, perspiration, and pulse. Additional physical responses, such as voice pattern and eye pupil size changes, are measured by some types of polygraph equipment. The examiner asks questions and then observes the patterns of the recorded physiological changes to evaluate whether the answer was accompanied by alterations indicating the stress that is presumed to accompany lying.

There has been considerable debate respecting the reliability of polygraphs and similar tests and the manner in which they sometimes have been administered. (For example, questions that are expected to arouse the subject's indignation, anger,

168. Generally, questionnaires of this type rely, directly or indirectly, on questions and data derived from the Minnesota Multiphasic Personality Inventory (MMPI), an instrument long used by psychologists and developed for diagnosis and categorizing of personality disorders and psychosis. Normally, psychologists and psychiatrists use this instrument in a clinical setting and in conjunction with other testing instruments, a detailed medical-emotional history, and clinical observations.

169. *Cort* v. *Bristol-Myers Co.*, 431 N.E.2d 908 (Mass. 1982).

embarrassment, and the like are often used to establish the subject's response patterns.) Protests against the widespread use of the polygraph and similar tests to screen job applicants, check on employee conduct, and detect wrongdoers, have led most states to adopt a broad array of restrictions on employer use of such tests as well as regulations respecting the qualifications and conduct of those who administer the tests.[170]

Some state courts, relying on constitutional protections of privacy, have prohibited employers from requiring workers to take polygraph and related types of tests in certain circumstances even absent specific statutory prohibitions.[171]

The federal Employee Polygraph Protection Act of 1988 (29 US Code §§2001–2009) imposes minimal national restrictions on employer uses of polygraph examinations and other mechanical or electronic devices for analyzing psychological stress to evaluate honesty. Several different types of employment are excluded from the federal statute's restrictions. Excluded are all government employees, nongovernment employees working on contracts with the federal defense and energy departments or providing security services for federal government national security and criminal investigation agencies, security contractors protecting any vital government services or functions, and employees of companies that manufacture or distribute particular categories of drugs.

The federal Employee Polygraph Protection Act prohibits use of such tests for prospective employees as well as for current employees. It does allow an employer to use a polygraph test to supplement its investigation of employees reasonably suspected of causing a loss or injury to the employer's business or property. The suspected employee cannot be compelled to take the test and cannot be dismissed either for refusing to be tested or solely based on the test results. (An employee who refuses to take the test can, of course, be dismissed based on other evidence of wrongdoing.) It should be noted that although an employee working under an 'at will' employment arrangement cannot require the employer to demonstrate a good cause for dismissal, the federal law in effect grants the employee such a right if the employer requests or requires the suspected worker to take a polygraph test prior to terminating the employment.

In situations where a polygraph test is permitted, the employee must be given advance written notification of the test method, location, setting, questions, and the right to refuse to be tested. In addition, the questions cannot be designed to embarrass the employee or needlessly intrude on the worker's privacy, or inquire into opinions or affiliations respecting such things as race, religion, politics, union activity, or sexual behavior. Finally, the employee must be given an opportunity to consult a lawyer or employee representative before deciding whether to take the test. Among the other requirements of the federal law are that the employee receive a copy of the test results and analysis and the results not be disclosed except to the employer and employee, or to a court, arbitrator, mediator, or government agency pursuant to a court order. In addition to any state law remedies that might be available to the employee, violation of the federal restrictions on polygraph examination

---

170. *See*, Bales, Hirsch and Secunda, §9.05(2013).

171. *See*, for example, *Long Beach City Employees Association* v. *City of Long Beach*, 719 P.2d 660 (Calif. 1986).

of workers can result in a civil penalty of up to $10,000, a court order prohibiting further violations (violation of such court orders are punishable as a contempt of court and can result in imprisonment), and a private civil action to recover any losses and require hiring the wronged prospective employee or reinstating the wronged dismissed employee.

245. State privacy law governs the limitations imposed on employer investigations of employee conduct both at and away from the workplace. Generally, employees have a right to a remedy (normally monetary damages) if: (a) the employee has a reasonable expectation of privacy respecting the particular conduct, communication or possession, and (b) the intrusion is 'highly offensive' and is not out-weighed by any social interests that motivate the employer's conduct. For example, it has been held that an employee may recover damages where she was greatly embarrassed when personal letters kept in a plant locker were disseminated to other workers by the plant security staff, who broke open her lock in the course of investigating a suspected theft by another worker.[172] On the other hand, filming an employee working outside his home in order to demonstrate the invalidity of the employee's disability claim, is held by some courts not to invade the employee's privacy, especially if done in an unobtrusive manner. In contrast, peering into the windows of an employee's home in order to establish the same information concerning the employee's true physical capacity, or placing a listening device on the door of the employee's abode to gain access to incriminating conversations, is more likely to constitute invasion of the employee's privacy.[173]

If the worker is employed by a government entity, an additional source for protection is the restriction upon unreasonable searches imposed by the Fourth Amendment to the Constitution of the United States. In *O'Connor* v. *Ortega*, 480 US 709 (1987), it was held that a government employee's possessions stored at work in a desk, file cabinet, or the like, cannot be unreasonably searched by management. The majority of the Court ruled, however, that the constitutional protection does not prevent a search to the extent that management seeks documents or other items needed to carry on work activities or seeks evidence of the employee's wrongdoing if management reasonably suspects that the search will produce the desired evidence and limits the scope of the search to finding such evidence. Four of the nine members of the Court dissented on the ground that, in order to adhere to the stated language of the Fourth Amendment, searches for evidence of a government employee's wrongdoing normally should be limited to enforcing a judicially issued warrant based on a showing of probable cause to suspect that the evidence will be found. Such a warrant would specify the place to be searched and type of evidence to be seized. The dissenting Justices observed that they would not require a warrant if there is a substantial threat that the evidence will disappear or that other serious harm will occur before a warrant can be obtained and executed.

172. *K-Mart Corp.* v. *Trotti*, 677 S.W.2d 632 (Ct. App. Tx. 1984).

173. *Compare, McClain* v. *Boise Cascade Corp.*, 533 P.2d 343 (Ore. 1975) with *Pemberton* v. *Bethlehem Steel Corp.*, 502 A.2d 1101 (Md. App. Ct.) *cert.* denied 479 US 984 (1986). *See generally* M. Selmi, 'Privacy for the Working Class: Public Work and Private Lives', 66 *Louisiana L. Rev.* 1035 (2006) (suggesting a line should be drawn between the workplace and outside of it in defining the employer's interests versus the employee's).

246. Another form of employer search for evidence of wrongdoing is secretly listening to employee conversations. Generally, the previously discussed state law standards control the extent to which an employee has a right to relief from such intrusions on privacy. The Omnibus Crime Control and Safe Streets Act, known as the Wiretap Act (18 US Code §§2510–2520) prohibits the intentional interception or disclosure of the contents of an interception of a wire or electronic communication. An interception occurs when the contents of the communication are obtained 'through the use of any electronic, mechanical or other device'. This prohibition includes workplace interceptions, such as secret listening on an extension telephone at work. However, two important exceptions exist. First, the interception is permitted if it is made in the ordinary course of business, such as to determine if employees are speaking to customers politely or are improperly using business phones for private calls. To take advantage of this exception, an employer should notify employees that the monitoring may occur (if that is feasible under the circumstances), and the monitoring should not exceed that needed to fulfill the business purpose. Secondly, if a party to the communication, such as an employee, gives prior consent to the interception, the law is not violated. In some jurisdictions, implied consent is sufficient for this exception.

A victim of a Wiretap Act violation can recover the greater of (a) actual damages plus any resulting profits received by the violator, or (b) the greater of $10,000 or $100 per day for each day of the violation. In addition, the victim may recover punitive damages if malice is shown and may recover reasonable attorney's fees and expenses. (Except where provided by statute, American courts generally do not provide a recovery of attorney's fees or other litigation expenses.)[174]

The federal Electronic Communications Privacy Act amended the Wiretap Act to protect oral communications from interception when the speaker has a reasonable expectation that a non-electronic communication will not be intercepted through an electrical, mechanical or other device. And, the federal Stored Communications Act further amends the Wiretap Act by defining the extent to which communications that are electronically stored are secure from unauthorized prying. The latter statute is of particular concern respecting employer monitoring of e-mail and voice mail.[175] Although intercepting such communications while in process, including while temporarily stored awaiting transfer or receipt, appears to be subject to the same rules as telephonic communications, accessing the communications once placed in 'permanent' electronic storage may be outside the scope of the federal statutory restrictions.[176]

247. Employers often compile a broad range of information about an individual worker's prior experience, education, work performance, financial problems, legal problems, marital status, health history, and the like. Most workers prefer that such information be treated as confidential. Several states have laws both restricting

174. For illustrative cases *see Deal* v. *Spears*, 980 F.2d 1153 (8th Cir. 1992) and *Briggs* v. *American Filter Co.*, 630 F.2d 414 (5th Cir. 1980).

175. For a discussion of issues related to e-mail and employee websites in particular, *see Konop* v. *Hawaiian Airlines, Inc.*, 302 F.3d 868 (9th Cir. 2002).

176. *Fraser* v. *Nationwide Mutual Ins. Co.*, 135 F. Supp. 2d 623 (E.D. Pa. 2001); *Smyth* v. *Pillsbury Co.*, 914 F. Supp. 97 (E.D. Pa. 1996).

access to such information and providing the worker with an opportunity to review and, if necessary, correct it.[177] In recent years, some states have restricted an employer's ability to collect consumer credit information and other private information about employees or prospective employees, and have prohibited employers from requiring employees to grant the employer access to the employee's social media accounts.[178] Even if a state statute does not limit an employer's dissemination and use of information about employees, the judicially developed concept of the right to privacy may provide some protection for the worker. To illustrate, in one case an employer was held subject to liability for damages when it revealed to co-workers that an employee's extended absences were for the purpose of receiving reconstructive surgery following a mastectomy. The insensitive reaction of the co-workers allegedly created such a hostile work environment that the returning employee felt compelled to quit her job. In addition, the federal Health Insurance Portability and Accountability Act of 1996 (HIPAA) requires privacy for 'protected health information' (PHI), which is defined as individually identifiable health information.[179]

248. Chemicals entering a person's body through food or drugs can alter work performance and behavior in both constructive and detrimental ways. For example, medication that eliminates a fever may permit a clerical employee to work competently but reduce the equilibrium or reaction time necessary to safely drive to and from the job. Similarly, the caffeine in a cup of coffee may provide a worker who has high blood pressure with the stimulation to stay awake on the job but increase the prospects of stroke. Such aspects of food and drug intake present rational functional employment concerns respecting the impact of food and drugs on a worker's job performance and worker safety and health, and have led to some functional reforms such as the rapidly growing prohibition of smoking in the work place and the occasional modifications of plant cafeteria menus to reduce fat and sugar intake. However, most attention on the part of American employers focuses on enforcing moral objections to, and legal bans on, recreational drug use regardless of the impact on employee health, safety or job performance.

With the exceptions of alcohol, nicotine and caffeine, recreational drugs generally are unlawful in the US and are the subject of constant attention in the news media. For decades the federal government has led largely ineffective efforts to eradicate the distribution and use of illegal recreational drugs; the most common of which are marijuana and cocaine. Ironically, neither of these drugs has been shown to have anything close to the adverse health or safety impact on American society

177. *See*, for example, Conn. Gen. Stat. §§31–128a *et seq.* (2006).

178. *See*, for example, Colo. Rev. Stat. § 8-2-126, 127 (2013).

179. *See Miller* v. *Motorola, Inc.*, 560 N.E.2d 900 (Ill. App. 1990). Some common law exceptions to disclosure of medical information, including the concept of the 'circle of confidentiality' that immunizes entities from disclosure to other entities that also have a duty of confidentiality to the employee, have been superseded by HIPAA (1996) which has generally tighter restrictions on disclosure. State privacy law, on the other hand, sometimes is more restrictive than the federal HIPAA respecting access to confidential medical information. *Pac. Radiation Oncology* v. *Queens Med. Center*, 375 P.3d 1252 (HA 2016). *See generally*, M. Maddigan, *Medical Records Privacy under HIPAA*, 2d ed. (Matthew Bender, 2 vols.)

as does the legal drug alcohol, or the adverse health impact of the legal drug nicotine and its accompanying carcinogens.

In the last several years, there has been a trend toward abandoning efforts to eradicate the use of marijuana. As of 2017, seven states and the District of Columbia have legalized recreational marijuana use by persons age 21 and older and 19 states legalize the use of marijuana for medicinal purposes. During the Obama presidency, the Department of Justice instructed federal prosecutors across the country not to focus federal law enforcement resources on individuals who were complying with state laws regarding the use of marijuana. Early in the Trump administration the Department of Justice announced that it would resume rigorous enforcement of federal drug laws which continue to list marijuana as an illegal controlled substance. As of the latest revision of this text, it is unclear how rigorously the federal Justice Department will pursue its announced policy. Even in the states that allow medicinal or recreational use of marijuana by adults, the laws make it clear that employers are not required to permit or accommodate the use, consumption, possession, transfer, display, transportation, sale or growing of marijuana in the workplace or to affect the ability of employers to have policies restricting the use of marijuana by employees.[180]

Among the efforts to combat illegal drug use has been government encouragement of employer drug screening to reject job applicants and dismiss workers who are illegal drug users. Often, these programs provide a brief opportunity to discontinue such drug use ('drug abuse' is the value laden term typically used to describe such conduct) and offer counseling assistance as an alternative to immediate dismissal. The pressure for employer scrutiny of employee drug use is reinforced by various civic and business groups that assert that the withholding of employment from users of illegal drugs is a powerful means of motivating users to abandon such activity. The policy of using the job as the place to identify drug users also has been encouraged by promotional campaigns financed by companies in what probably is now more than a one-billion-dollar ($1,000,000,000) business of testing for exposure to illegal drugs.

A key instrument in what has been referred to as the 'War on Drugs', is the urinalysis test. Drugs that react with the body leave tell-tale chemical by-products (metabolites) that eventually are eliminated in the urine flow. A variety of chemical analysis techniques detect the presence of such metabolites in urine. These test results, when accurate, report that the person's body has been exposed to the particular type of drug. However, the test often cannot determine the exact metabolite source. For example, some foods, such as poppy seeds, produce metabolites used to detect exposure to opiate based drugs, and some legal medications, such as ibuprofen, do likewise. The test also does not determine the nature of the exposure. For example, being in the presence of marijuana smoke can cause production of the tell-tale metabolites days and even weeks earlier even though the tested individual did not actively smoke the marijuana.

Although there are data demonstrating correlations between various levels of blood alcohol and loss of various motor and cognitive skills, metabolite testing for other drugs does not show whether the subject is currently under, or ever was under,

180. *See*, for example, Colo. Const. art. XVIII, § 16.

the influence of the drug or whether the drug exposure caused or is causing any performance impairment or enhancement. One complication in testing for drugs other than alcohol, which is detected while being used by the body, is that urine metabolites appear after the body has utilized the substance and many remain for days after exposure. In the case of marijuana, for example, the urine continues to contain the tell-tale metabolites for several weeks after exposure.

Another characteristic of urinalysis is the variation in reliability depending on the particular analytic method and equipment used, the training, skill and diligence of those who do the testing, and the parameters established for distinguishing positive (significant presence of the incriminating metabolites) from negative results. No test procedure or method has been demonstrated to have total reliability and even 2 or 3 percent unreliability can result in many false accusations when dealing with a large population.

249. The effort to use the place of employment as a primary battleground in the 'War on Drugs' was initiated by President Ronald Reagan who issued Executive Order 12564 which required that federal employment be 'drug-free'. This Order directed federal agencies to establish regulations prohibiting possession and use of drugs on and off the job and establishing drug testing of job applicants, employees involved in accidents or unsafe practices, and employees reasonably suspected of drug use. The Order also provided for government counseling and assistance for workers who voluntarily are tested and found to have been exposed to the designated illegal drugs. Those who resume use or who are found guilty of use as a result of mandatory testing are subject to dismissal. The Executive Order establishes the safeguard of a confirmatory, second analysis of the urine sample and allows for rebuttal of positive test results through the presentation of other evidence. Among the expressed justifications for the program are the assertions that drug users are less reliable, less productive, less safe employees; are prone to irresponsible actions; and are subject to undue influences by those who would use the threat of revealing the illegality of the conduct as a means of coercing desired actions by the drug using federal employee. The accuracy of these portrayals of drug users and the appropriateness of current legal and employment policies toward drug use have been challenged by serious scholars.[181]

Congress later imposed some restrictions on the implementation of the Executive Order including certification of the testing laboratories, specification of and justification for the categories of employees subject to testing, and confidential treatment of test results.

Congress itself has adopted laws requiring employers to discourage employee use of drugs off as well as on the job. The Drug-Free Workplace Act of 1988 (41 US Code § 8102) requires all employers that contract with the federal government to certify that use, possession and distribution of illegal drugs are prohibited at the contractor's workplace and that employees convicted of drug related crimes be dismissed unless they participate satisfactorily in a rehabilitation program. Although

181. For reasoned assessments critiquing policies for dealing with recreational drug use, *see*, e.g. F. Zimring and G. Hawkins, *The Search for Rational Drug Control*, 1992 and C. Mitchell, *The Drug Solution*, 1990.

the Drug-Free Workplace Act does not mandate drug testing, a variety of federal laws or regulations require employee drug testing for specific industries. For example, 42 US Code § 2473c requires contractors doing business with the National Aeronautics and Space Administration to engage in such testing of job applicants, employees reasonably suspected of using illegal drugs, employees involved in accidents, and a program of random testing for all covered employees in safety and security sensitive jobs. That law additionally prescribes basic procedures for such tests. Similarly, preemployment, reasonable suspicion, random, and post-accident testing is required for all railroad employees responsible for safety-sensitive functions (49 US Code §20140), and for employees responsible for safety-sensitive functions of federally assisted public transportation operations (49 US Code §5331). These federal laws typically provide for reinstatement of employees who are successfully 'rehabilitated' and protect employee privacy to the extent of requiring that the collection of urine specimens 'to the maximum extent practicable' respect individual privacy. Test reliability is improved by requiring that testing is done by certified laboratories, that discipline be confined to situations in which there is a second, confirmatory analysis of the specimen, that the most advanced analytic methods are used, and that a portion of the specimen is preserved to give the employee an opportunity to have it tested by an independent laboratory in an effort to challenge an adverse analytic report.

250. Whenever the government directs an employee to do something or orders an employer to direct its employees to do something, that governmental requirement is subject to challenge under the US Constitution as an attempted exercise of power in excess of the limits imposed by some provision of the Constitution. Federal directives mandating drug testing using urinalysis have been challenged as violating the Constitution's Fourth Amendment protection against unreasonable searches and seizures and the Amendment's requirement that even reasonable searches and seizures be pursuant to a court issued warrant based on probable cause to believe that the search or seizure will produce evidence of wrongdoing. Mandatory drug testing imposed by states and local governments have similarly been challenged under the Due Process Clause of the Fourteenth Amendment to the US Constitution which has been held to incorporate the Fourth Amendment's restraints upon searches and seizures.

The Supreme Court has held that government ordered urinalysis, as a means of drug testing, is subject to the restrictions imposed against unreasonable searches and seizures. The Court reasoned that the privacy rights protected by the 4th and 14th Amendments are affronted because in American society passing urine is regarded as an activity normally done in privacy and because the analysis of a urine specimen can reveal a wide range of information about the source of the specimen, including many matters that normally are expected to be treated as confidential and of no legitimate employer concern. These include whether the person has particular noncontagious diseases, whether the person had recent sexual activity, whether a woman is pregnant, whether the person takes particular medications used to modify neurosis or depression, and the like.

Although the literal protection given by the Fourth Amendment allows reasonable searches and seizures only upon judicial issuance of a warrant based on probable cause, the majority of the Court has relaxed that requirement in many types of situations, and it did so when confronted with the need to determine when the government may order employees to submit urine samples for drug analysis. The Court ruled that the protection of privacy interests provided by the warrant as well as the probable cause provision of the Fourth Amendment are outweighed by the impracticality of obtaining a warrant when the tests are used for employment decisions (as contrasted with use for criminal prosecution) and the employment involves a substantial safety or national security risk.[182] Federal appellate courts have construed the Supreme Court's decision as permitting random urinalysis of employees in safety and national security sensitive positions so long as there are reasonable efforts to ensure reliable, confidential testing methods and reports. The federal courts typically decide these cases based on an implicit acceptance of the unproven proposition that any use of illegal drugs at any time impairs safe and reliable employee job performance. Thus, the tests may be mandated and adverse employment action may be taken for refusing to take the test or for test results indicating drug exposure, even in the absence of proof that the purported drug exposure impairs job performance.[183]

If the government does not direct that a category of employees or job applicants be subjected to urinalysis tests (that is, if a private employer imposes such testing on its own initiative), objecting employees have no recourse to federal constitutional protections. However, since this is a changed working condition, the employees have recourse to contractual protections if the terms of employment are established by a contract for a specific duration or are established by collective bargaining. In the latter case, any introduction of drug testing procedures must be accomplished through collective bargaining.[184]

A number of states have statutes requiring drug testing of state or local government employees involved in safety sensitive jobs when the employee has been involved in a serious accident or where there is cause for suspicion.[185] Other states provide statutory regulation of the methods and situations in which drug testing of

182. *Skinner* v. *Railway Labor Executives*, 489 US 602 and *Treasury Employees* v. *Von Raab*, 489 US 656 (1989). But *see Chandler* v. *Miller*, 520 US 305 (1997) (state statute requiring random drug testing of candidates for political office is a constitutional violation where issues of public safety are not involved).

183. *See*, for example, *Dimeo* v. *Griffin*, 943 F.2d 679 (7th Cir. 1991) (*en banc*).

184. *Niagara Hooker Employees Union* v. *Occidental Chemical Corp.*, 935 F.2d 1370 (2d Cir. 1991). However, the court ruled that as a result of the balancing of equities, an employer's unilateral introduction of random drug testing will not be enjoined even though under challenge in arbitration as a contract violation. The court emphasized the potentially great dangers of explosions and other mishaps due to employee error in the chemical industry.

185. For example, Arizona requires drug testing of applicants for school bus drivers and for school transportation workers involved in an accident. Florida requires drug testing of government workers under circumstances similar to those imposed by federal law on federal employees. Kentucky allows public school teachers to be drug tested randomly or based on suspicion. *See Knox County Educ. Ass'n* v. *Knox County Board of Education*, 158 F.3d 361 (6th Cir. 1998).

employees is allowed.[186] Finally, some state courts limit the use of urinalysis tests for drugs based on the common law or on state constitutional protections of privacy. Nevertheless, those courts that have provided this added source of protection from drug testing also allow testing for employees in safety sensitive job functions, especially if there has been evidence of on-the-job drug use threatening to cause injuries or damage and it is not practical to rely on alternative means of oversight (for example, supervisory observation of inept performance or the employee's deficiency in completing physical and mental reaction tests).[187]

III. Employer Provided Income Protection when an Employee is Unavailable for Work

251. In the early industrial period in America, employees and their dependents relied on customary, voluntary contributions from their employer and their coworkers to provide some income when ill health or injury prevented an employee from earning wages. In the 20th century, the federal government adopted a number of income tax incentives and mandatory benefits programs that replaced the uncertainties of such charity with predictable schedules of benefits financed and administered through government or private insurance. On occasion, state governments led the way in developing incentives for employer financed benefit programs or mandatory employer financed protections.

During the latter part of the 19th and first half of the 20th centuries, labor organizations often offered members a program for the systematic pooling of members' periodic contributions to meet financial needs caused by ill health, injury, and death. These union-sponsored insurance programs helped attract new members since workers seldom had alternative means of obtaining such income security for themselves or their dependents. As union strength grew, collective bargaining often included demands for employer contributions to these funds in lieu of, or to supplement, the members' contributions. In time, collective bargaining agreements increased the amount and added new categories of such benefits. In addition, federal regulations, such as the Labor Management Relations Act and the Labor Management Reporting and Disclosure Act, eventually were adopted to curb corrupt extractions of employer contributions to, or misuse of, these funds.

Because employment is the source for most people's ability to meet financial demands, employees, unions and government in the US typically look to the employment relationship to pay for programs designed to provide care and sustenance accompanying poor health or injury, regardless of whether this is the most rational or efficient method for financing a common need shared by all in a national society including those who are unemployed or unemployable as well as those who are employed. Moreover, in looking to the employment relationship to finance such

186. For example, Maryland and North Carolina regulate the procedures to be followed, the laboratory certification needed, and the information to be provided by employers that test employees for exposure to drugs.

187. *See*, for example, *Hennessey* v. *Coastal Eagle Point Oil Co.*, 609 A.2d 11 (NJ 1992) and *Twigg* v. *Hercules Corp.*, 406 S.E.2d 52 (W.Va. 1990).

needs, there are a number of options, including placing the direct burden solely on the employer, solely on the employees, sharing all or part of the cost among them, or sharing all or part of the cost with the government's general revenue sources. All of these combinations are found in the various employee welfare benefits programs adopted in the US. No rational pattern can be discerned to explain the variations in approach to the distribution of financing burdens for these programs. Rather, the particular structure for each program is best explained as a product of political and historical accident.

Rather than require employers to finance employee benefits, the federal government sometimes uses income tax incentives to encourage employers to provide certain benefits. The principal mechanism for doing this is to allow the employer to treat as a business expense (and, therefore a deductible cost in calculating income tax liability) the cost of financing particular types of employee benefits (sometimes limited to a specified level of benefit) while at the same time not treating the value of the benefit received by the employee as part of the employee's taxable income. Because federal income tax rates are substantial, such tax treatment enables the employer to provide a higher level of benefits for the employees than they could purchase themselves with their earnings if the employer instead paid the money directly to them as wages. (The reason for this is that income taxes would be deducted from the employees' wages before the money would be available to pay their benefit program premiums.) In addition, the tax laws often require that most employees be included in the benefits program in order for the company to receive the favorable tax treatment. Therefore, if higher paid executives want the income security of such benefits provided through the company's income tax exempt program, they must structure the program to provide these benefits for lower level employees as well as for themselves.

252. In addition to laws that require compensation for job-related calamities, most employers provide a wide range of non mandatory employee welfare benefits as part of a compensation package. Collectively bargained agreements normally specify some benefits of this sort, but even in the absence of collective bargaining, most American employers, especially those with 100 or more workers, provide full-time employees with welfare benefits beyond those required by law. Some employers contribute a set amount of money per employee to pay for non mandatory employee welfare benefits selected by the individual employee from a list of available benefits. Generally referred to as a 'cafeteria plan', this approach allows the worker to customize coverage to suit the worker's priorities respecting the benefits that can be purchased with a fixed amount of employer contribution to premiums. For example, an employee with no dependents may choose to have no life insurance coverage in favor of having more generous financial protection from disability or in favor of a larger number of paid sick leave days. On the other hand, an employee whose spouse's job provides family medical insurance coverage may choose to apply the available cafeteria plan premiums to provide more life insurance coverage for both of them in lieu of a contribution to medical insurance premiums.

253. Most American employees are covered by income security programs established by the Social Security Act that are financed by payroll taxes paid both by the employer and the employee. Benefits are provided for the employee and certain categories of the employee's dependents if the employee meets the coverage qualifications. Qualification is based on the employee having worked a sufficient length of time in employment for which Social Security taxes are payable. The amount of that time can vary depending on the employee's age. Most self-employed persons are now included in the Social Security program. Excluded are federal employees hired prior to 1984, railroad workers who are covered by a separate retirement program, some state and local government workers who are covered by separate local retirement programs, some persons employed in households or on small farms, and persons with very low annual earnings. (These workers are covered, however, to the extent that they had prior covered employment for at least the qualifying period or may have a benefit claim as a spouse of an employee covered by Social Security.) In all, those engaged in about 95 percent of all jobs contribute to the fund that provides Social Security benefits.

254. The Social Security program provides income maintenance and vocational rehabilitation benefits for qualified persons, and their dependents, regardless of whether the disability preventing employment was work-related. Several tests are used to determine when Social Security disability insurance benefits are available for a disabled person. These tests generally require an employee to have been employed and paying into Social Security for the better part of the period prior to disability. However, an employee who has had ten years of work in employment for which the taxes were payable is thereafter qualified regardless of recent employment experience. In addition, the qualifying standards are adjusted to make it possible for most younger workers to be covered by the disability protections. Also, the requirements are more lenient for blind workers than for others.

Social Security disability benefits are available only if the worker has been physically or mentally impaired from engaging in any gainful activity for pay or profit for at least five months and that impairment can be expected to continue for at least twelve months or until the worker dies. The level of benefits is based on the amount of Social Security retirement payment the worker would receive if the worker was 62 years of age and retired. The Social Security disability payment is reduced by any workers' compensation disability benefits paid to the disabled worker. However, payments under private insurance programs do not affect the Social Security benefit. The Social Security disability payments end, and Social Security retirement benefits are substituted, when the disabled worker reaches age 65 and can shift to retirement benefits.

In 2015, approximately 10.8 million workers and dependents received Social Security disability payments. The average monthly benefit for a disabled worker was $1166. The Social Security disability program also finances vocational rehabilitation services for the disabled beneficiaries. In 2015 the United States ranked 29th among 34 developed countries in the percentage of a median worker's earnings that the public-pension system replaces.

255. As of 2017, the United States had agreements with 26 countries (Australia, Austria, Belgium, Canada, Chile, Czech Republic, Denmark, Finland, France, Germany, Greece, Hungary, Ireland, Italy, Japan, South Korea, Luxembourg, Netherlands, Norway, Poland, Portugal, Slovak Republic, Spain, Sweden, Switzerland, and United Kingdom) to provide for coordination of their respective social security programs and negotiations were currently underway with a number of other countries to obtain similar treaties. When a person has worked in the United States and one or more of these other countries, the treaties prevent duplication of social security taxes and benefits and also protect against reduction of benefits by giving credit for periods of work in the other signatory country if that other country is not providing benefits for that term of work.

256. Since World War II, tax incentives, collective bargaining demands, market efforts to attract and keep a good work force, a sense of social responsibility, and other factors, have resulted in widespread inclusion of insurance benefits as part of the employee compensation package. Occasionally, employers require workers to share in the cost of funding income security benefits or require the worker to pay the full insurance premium for the benefit. Even in the latter situation, employees usually are in a better financial position than they would be if the employer did not provide the benefit program inasmuch as insurance costs typically are lower when insurance coverage is purchased for a large group than when purchased individually.

Although, as discussed below, by law most American workers and their dependents have medical care and income loss protection in the event of a work related injury or illness, often American workers and their dependents do not have comparable protection if the injury or illness is unrelated to their job.[188]

For the most part, paid sick leave is contractual in the United States. Either it is a benefit unilaterally provided by the employer or it is provided under the terms of an individual contract or a collectively bargained agreement. A paid sick leave benefit in effect supplements an employer's statutory obligations when the leave is the result of a job caused injury or illness. Normally, in such cases the employee is entitled to receive the greater benefit; the benefits are not added together. In 2017, some 19 percent of nongovernmental full-time workers had no paid sick leave benefit. (Many more of those in full time professional, technical and white collar jobs, receive paid sick leave as compared to the number of full-time blue collar workers who receive this form of benefit.) Only a very small percentage (about 36 percent) of all part-time employees receive paid sick leave.[189] Although the federal government does not require paid sick leave, several cities, such as Washington DC, Seattle, and New York City, have passed laws requiring paid sick leave as have the states of California, Connecticut, Massachusetts, Oregon, and Vermont.

---

188. California, Hawaii, New Jersey, New York, Rhode Island and Puerto Rico require employers to provide non-work-related short-term disability benefits for employees. As discussed above, the Social Security Act requires employers and workers to jointly finance a program of employee welfare insurance that provides benefits for permanently and totally disabled employees after an extended waiting period.
189. Data reporting employee benefits is gathered by the Bureau of Labor Statistics and updated, more detailed reports can be found at its web site: http://www.bls.gov.

American employers have a wide variety of paid sick leave programs. Most programs provide a specified number of such days per year with the number of days increasing slightly for employees with longer terms of service. A 2009, survey showed that a majority of full-time private industry workers, regardless of length of service, annually received five to nine days of sick leave.

Earlier studies showed that although paid sick leave normally is available regardless of whether inability to work is caused by an injury or by illness, some employers treat claims differently depending on the cause of absence. Also, a majority of employers allow employees to use sick leave for medical check-ups or to care for an ill or disabled dependent. In 2011 about 44 percent of workers in private industry were permitted to accumulate unused annual sick leave days but earlier studies show that about four fifths of such employees were subject to a maximum number of accumulated days. Although currently there are no federal legal requirements for paid sick leave, The FMLA (29 US Code §2601 *et seq.*), discussed in more detail below, mandates up to 12 weeks of unpaid leave be granted to employees who need to attend to urgent personal and family medical matters. If the employer provides paid sick leave, the paid leave may be substituted for unpaid FMLA leave. In 2016, 13 percent of all private sector workers had access to paid family leave including paid maternity and paternity leave. Twenty-four percent of workers in management, professional, and related occupations had access to such leave. Additionally, partial paid maternity leave benefits sometimes are provided as part of a disability insurance plan.

257. Paid disability leave is distinguished from paid sick leave in that paid disability leave typically is of longer duration. In 2016, about 37 percent of full-time civilian workers were provided with at least partial earnings replacement in the event of non-work-related short-term disability that prevented the employee from working. This was a decline from about 45 percent in 2003. About 33 percent of civilian employees received long-term disability insurance benefits that gave them at least partial income replacement. Earlier studies show that in a significant minority of such insurance plans, the employee helps pay the premium cost.

Disability insurance typically covers about 60 percent of the employee's normal earnings and most often is subject to a maximum benefit amount. Also, disability insurance plans typically do not begin paying benefits until the worker has missed a specified number of weeks of work, but most waive the waiting period if there is immediate hospitalization. Most of the short-term programs continue benefits for at least three months, while long-term disability programs normally do not begin paying benefits until the worker has been disabled for at least three months. (Many withhold benefits until the disability has continued for six months.)

258. Social, civic, religious, family and personal needs can interfere with an employee's availability for work. Legislation requires that absence from work be excused to allow employees to fulfill some of these obligations. In a few situations the law additionally directs the employer to pay the worker during such periods. A little over half of the states and Puerto Rico require employers to give employees time off, usually two or three hours, to vote in elections of government officers.

Twelve states require that employees be paid for time needed to vote. The right to pay varies from one to three hours.

Jury trials, which draw jurors from the general citizenry, are constitutionally guaranteed for crimes subject to significant penalties and for many categories of civil cases. Therefore, employees can expect to be summoned for jury duty once every half dozen or so years. Persons called for jury duty normally receive nominal compensation from the government while performing this service. Federal law makes it a crime for an employer to interfere with an employee's fulfillment of jury duty in a federal court. It does not, however, require the employer to provide any compensation for the employee while performing that duty. Excused absence for jury duty is a statutory requirement in almost every state, and a few states mandate that the employer pay normal wages to employees called to jury duty, less a deduction for the jury fee paid by the government to the worker.[190] In 2015, 65 percent of all employees were entitled to paid leave for jury duty. For full-time employees the figure was 75 percent.

The Uniformed Services Employment and Reemployment Rights Act of 1994 (38 US Code §4301 *et seq.*) generally entitles a person inducted into the Armed Forces to return to employment if application for reinstatement is made within 90 days after being honorably discharged from military service. (Shorter periods for reemployment application are provided for those who serve less than 180 days. These shorter periods cover most situations in which reservists are called to active duty for training or activation to provide domestic emergency services.) If the period of military service was for less than 90 days, the employee must be returned to the previously held position; if it was for a longer duration, reinstatement may be to a position of like seniority, status, and pay. An employee who is reinstated under this law is protected from dismissal without cause for one year regardless of whether the previous employment included such job security. Similar reinstatement rights are given to those who enlist for military service and remain in the military for not more than five years. In addition, employees are granted a right to a leave of absence for reserve military training. Employers are excused from reinstatement if the employee was discharged from military service under less than honorable conditions, if the employee is unable to perform the work or if the work is no longer available to the enterprise.

State law often supplements these requirements, especially with respect to reserve service through the state military arm. Called the National Guard, these volunteer units, which can be called to service by the state governor, or by the President of the United States, are largely federally financed and are integrated into the national military forces. Thus, state and local government employees are sometimes given paid leave time for their annual National Guard service. Moreover, the overwhelming majority of government employees, a little over half of those employed by medium and large size employers, and about one fifth of those employed by small

190. For a variation, *see* Colo. Rev. Stat. §13-71-126. (Employer pays wages up to first $50 per day for first three days of jury service, thereafter the state pays juror $50/day. Unemployed jurors are compensated by the state for the first three days. A juror can be excused for financial hardship; the employer's obligation can be excused for the same reason. The daily compensation is less than the federal minimum wage for eight hours of work.)

employers (under 100 employees), are given paid leave time for reserve military service. Generally, employers pay the difference between the worker's military pay and the worker's normal wage. Except for government employers, this is a negotiated benefit or one the employer voluntarily provides.

259. State and federal law declare certain days as holidays on which government offices are closed, and prohibit some types of businesses from operating on such days. Generally, however, non-government workers do not have a statutory right to paid leave for such days or to receive premium pay if they work on legally declared holidays. Nevertheless, the overwhelming majority of full time workers receive at least several paid holidays each year and get holiday pay plus premium rate wages if they must work on the holiday. (Only a substantial minority of part-time workers receive this benefit.) On average, non-government employees whose employers have 100 or more workers receive 9 annual paid holidays, those who work for smaller employers receive 7–8 such days; government workers on average receive over 13 such annual paid leave days. New Year's Day, President's Day, Memorial Day, Independence Day (July 4), Labor Day, Thanksgiving Day and Christmas Day are the holidays for which paid leave is most commonly given. In addition to paid holiday leave, some employers allow employees to take two or three paid personal leave days per year to attend to personal affairs or celebrate a special occasion such as a birthday, wedding anniversary, child's birth, religious holiday, or the like.

Paid funeral leave is received by a majority of full time workers employed by establishments with fewer than 100 employees and by over 80 percent of those employed by larger employers. Generally, funeral or bereavement leave is limited to the occasion of the death of a close family member and most often is limited to a maximum of three days.

Most full-time American workers are allowed two paid rest breaks a day; usually for 10 or 15 minutes each. Often state law requires such breaks. Meal periods of a half hour (often an hour for white collar workers) are a normal part of most full-time work schedules but only a small percentage of workers who are paid on an hourly basis are paid during their meal break.

260. Prior to 1993, most American workers did not have a legal right to take a leave of absence to deal with personal illness or serious family related matters such as child birth, family illness or to assist family members in a time of crisis. Although employees often can deal with problems of a shorter duration by using paid sick leave, personal leave, and the like, as discussed above, many workers do not have such contractual benefits; even when the employee has a contractual right to such leaves of absence, often the duration of the leave is inadequate to enable the worker to cope with the particular situation. President Bush's veto of legislation to entitle employees to take a leave of absence in time of medical or family crisis received considerable political attention during the 1992 Presidential election campaign. Early in its next term, Congress adopted a new bill addressing this issue and newly elected President Clinton signed it into law as the FMLA of 1993.

The FMLA, 29 US Code §§2601–2654, applies to employees who: (a) have worked for their employer at least 12 months, (b) have worked for at least 1250 hours during the previous 12 months, and (c) are employed by an enterprise that employs at least 50 people at work sites within a 75 mile radius of the claimant's place of employment and has employed at least 50 employees during each work day for at least 20 workweeks of the current or preceding calendar year. The Act also applies to most government workers. The FMLA entitles the covered employee to take an unpaid leave of absence for up to 12 workweeks in any 12 month period if taken because of: (a) the need to care for a newly born, adopted or foster child, (b) the need to care for the employee's child, spouse, or parent whose health condition requires inpatient medical care or continuing oversight by a physician, or (c) the employee's own incapacitating medical condition. The employer can require the worker to apply to this 12-week period, and the worker has a right to apply to this period, any applicable paid family leave, personal leave, medical leave, or vacation leave provided by the employer. When feasible, the employee is required to give at least 30 days' advance notice respecting expected birth, adoption, foster care, or parental care. The right to a leave of absence under this statute entitles the employee to return to the previous position of employment or an equivalent one, without loss of pay, benefits or other terms and conditions of employment. However, the employer is not required to credit the employee with seniority or longevity during the period of absence. Under some conditions, the Act excludes salaried employees who are among the employer's 10 percent highest paid employees working within a 75 mile radius of the claimant. Violation of the Act subjects the employer to civil suit by the employee or by the Secretary of Labor for remedies similar to those provided under the FLSA. In addition, an employee who was unlawfully prevented from taking a leave may sue for the cost of providing substitute care, up to a maximum amount that is equal to the employee's compensation for 12 weeks. An employee on leave must continue to receive any group health care protection otherwise provided by the employer.

Amendments to the FMLA grant a spouse, child, parent or next of kin a right to take up to 26 weeks of unpaid leave in a 12-month period to care for a military service member who, as a result of a serious injury or illness incurred in the line of duty while deployed to a foreign country, is undergoing medical treatment, recuperation, or therapy.

Another amendment specifies the amount of annual work required for airline flight crews to qualify for FMLA benefits.

IV. Retirement Benefits

261. Eventually, all employees leave or are removed from their job or the job market by death or retirement. In the case of the employee's death, an income security problem materializes for any dependents of the employee; in the case of retirement, an income security problem arises for the employee as well as any dependents. Federal legislation, principally the Social Security Act, provides a safety net of income security for most Americans and their dependents in the event of retirement or death. Most workers not eligible for Social Security retirement and death benefits have comparable protection under either a state or federal government employees' retirement program or under the Railroad Retirement Act. The basic eligibility rules for Social Security benefits and international agreements to coordinate with similar programs in other countries, are described in paragraphs 253-255.

Social security retirement benefits were first established in 1935. Amendments to the Social Security Act later extended protection to dependents and to disabled workers. Over the years, there has been a progression both in the amount of earned income subject to Social Security taxes and in the tax rate. As of 2017, the first $127,200 of annual earned income was subject to the tax with the employer and employee each paying the tax at the rate of 6.2 percent of earned income for retirement and disability insurance. (Self-employed persons paid a tax rate of 12.4 percent.) Additional payroll taxes of 1.45 percent are paid on all earned income both by the employer and employee to finance the Social Security related Medicare program that provides health insurance protection for older and certain disabled persons. (A tax rate of 2.9 percent is levied for the self-employed.) Furthermore, an added 0.9 percent is taxed on annual earned income over $200,000 for individuals and on annual earned income over $250,000 for married coupled filing jointly. The Social Security taxes collected are placed in trust funds for each program and are maintained as independent accounts, separate from the federal government's general revenues. As of 2017, and for at least a decade, these trust funds are adequate to meet the full projected liabilities of these programs. Until 1999, Social Security retirement benefits assumed a normal retirement age of 65. Starting in the year 2000, the presumed normal retirement age increases by two months per year to 67 by the year 2022. Eligible persons can begin drawing retirement benefits as early as age 62, but the amount of benefit is permanently reduced to reflect the early retirement. As of 2000, the benefit of those drawing at age 62 was reduced to about 87 percent of the full benefit the retiree would receive if benefits did not begin until age 65. The percentage paid to early retirees will decrease to about 70 percent when the statutory normal retirement age increases to 67. In contrast, the amount of benefits is increased for each year retirement is postponed beyond the normal retirement age but no increase is given for postponements beyond age 70. (In 2017, the maximum monthly benefit for an individual retiring at age 62 was $2,153; retiring at age 65, it was $2,687; and retiring at age 70, it was $3,538.) The benefit amount is also affected, under complex computation formulas, by the year in which the worker retired and the average amount of taxable earnings received during the 35 years of highest earnings. Spouses, former spouses (if married a sufficient period of time), and dependent children receive, as an addition to benefits paid to the retiree, a benefit equal to one half of that paid the qualified retiree. However, there is a maximum amount that a family (not including divorced spouses) may receive in benefits. This limit is imposed even if both spouses are eligible for full retirement benefits based upon their own earnings histories. Upon the death of the eligible worker or retiree, the worker's spouse in effect qualifies as a substitute beneficiary, and dependent children and parents receive benefits of 70 to 82.5 percent of the retirement benefit that would have been paid to the eligible person, the exact percentage being affected by several variables. It is estimated that the average monthly Social Security retirement benefit awarded in mid-2017 was $1,314.

As of 2017, anyone receiving benefits who was under full retirement age during the entire calendar year lost $1 in benefits for every $2 earned over $16,920. During the calendar year in which the individual reaches full retirement age, $1 is deducted from benefits for each $3 earned over $44,880 up to the month in which full retirement age is reached. Thereafter, there are no benefit reductions for earning any amount of money.

Social Security benefits for a person filing an individual tax return are exempt from income taxes if one half of the annual benefit plus the individual's annual modified gross income is under $25,000. Income taxes are paid on up to one half of the retirement benefit if the combined annual income is between $25,000 and $34,000 (between $32,000 and $44,000 for those filing joint tax returns). Above those thresholds, up to 85 percent of social security benefits are subject to income tax..

At the start of 2016, an estimated 168 million workers and their employers were contributing to the Social Security system and over 60 million Americans annually received $886 billion in Social Security benefits.

Social Security is the major source of income for the elderly. It contributes 90 percent or more of income for 21 percent of married couples and 43 percent of unmarried persons aged 65 or older and is the major source of income (providing at least 50 percent of total income) for 48 percent of married couples and 71 percent of unmarried persons aged 65 or older. Savings, pensions and continued earnings constitute the rest of the income for the elderly. Social Security also provides benefits for the disabled and their dependents, which accounted for 19 percent of total benefits paid. Even though it is estimated that 1 in 4 of today's 20 year-olds will become disabled before age 67, 65 percent of the private sector workforce has no long-term disability insurance. In 2011, about 91 percent of workers age 21–64 had Social Security protection in the event of a long-term disability. Social Security also provides for survivors of deceased workers, which accounts for about 11 percent of total benefits paid. About one in eight of today's 20-year-olds will die before reaching age 67. About 96 percent of persons aged 20–49 who worked in covered employment in 2011 have survivors' insurance protection for their young children and the surviving spouse caring for the children.[191]

262. Overall, 55 percent of private sector employing units and 80 percent of state and local government employing units provide employees with access to group life insurance. Such group insurance policies generally have lower premium costs than if individually purchased. Access to employer sponsored group life insurance is less common among smaller employing units. Thus, in the private sector, only 40 percent of those employed in units with fewer than 100 employees have access to such insurance.[192]

191. The information in these paragraphs was obtained from *Social Security Basic Facts* (26 July 2013) Social Security Administration's Official website, http://www.ssa.gov/pressoffice/basicfact.htm.
192. March 2016 data found at: https://www.bls.gov/ncs/ebs/benefits/2016/benefits_life.htm.

263. Upon retirement, an American worker can receive income from occasional or partial employment or self-employment; from interest, dividends or rents produced by the employee's own assets; from gifts given by relatives and friends; from Social Security benefits; from retirement insurance or investments directly purchased or funded by the employee; or from employer sponsored retirement income programs. The latter can be funded by employee as well as employer contributions. The federal income tax laws encourage the purchase and funding of private retirement income maintenance plans by exempting from taxation income that is directly or indirectly contributed to fund investment accounts that generally are not available for withdrawal until retirement. There are limits to the amount of annual income that can be insulated in this manner from income taxation and exemption from income taxation requires compliance with a variety of regulations. Included in the requirements for employer contributions to qualify for favorable income tax treatment is the prohibition against funding or benefit formulas that give higher paid employees larger percentage contributions. Thus, to provide such benefits for themselves, corporate executives must provide similar retirement income benefits formulas for the rest of the work force.

There are two main types of retirement benefit plans: defined benefit, and defined contribution. In defined benefit plans, companies promise to pay workers a specified amount in retirement benefits. In defined contribution plans, companies promise to contribute a specified amount to a retirement fund. According to the Bureau of Labor Statistics, the trend is away from defined benefit plans and toward defined contribution plans. The percentage of workers covered by defined benefit plans has decreased, while the percentage covered by defined contribution plans has increased. This means that risk – in terms of steady retirement income – has been transferred from the employer to the eventual retiree.[193] For recent data on privately funded retirement income plans, see paragraphs 97-98.

V. Employer-financed Health Care Benefits

264. Traditionally, medical care in the US was privately paid for by the patient or the patient's family or was a charitable gift to the poor. One exception was that from 1798 to the mid-1980s the federal government provided free medical care for merchant seafarers. A similar program was established in the 20th century for the benefit of low-income veterans of active duty military service and veterans with extensive service related disabilities. Other active duty veterans can participate in the government provided medical care program by paying modest co-payments for the benefits received.

The concept of privately financed medical care insurance is said to have begun in the US in 1929 with the development of an insurance system under which employers paid the insurance premium. Soon thereafter the city of Los Angeles established a program of paying hospitals and physicians to provide health care services for city workers, a program that evolved into what is now known as a Health Maintenance

193. *See* http://www.bls.gov/spotlight/2008/older_workers.

Organization (HMO) program. But by 1940, less than 10 percent of American workers still had any form of health care insurance. A significant change came during World War II when, due to its labor shortage, wartime regulations restricted wage increases. These restrictions, however, did not prevent an employer from offering supplemental or 'fringe' benefits. Health care insurance became a popular benefit with which to attract new workers. Over the next several decades, the growth of employer provided medical care insurance was encouraged by provisions in the income tax laws that allow employers to deduct premiums as a business expense but do not tax the value of the insurance to the worker as income.

Employer sponsored medical care insurance normally does not cover all types of medical care or procedures or all expenses. The employee must pay some of the costs for covered care and all of the cost for other types of care. In addition, the employee often pays part of the premium, especially if the insurance covers other family members.

265. HMO protection generally is more comprehensive in coverage than is medical insurance because the plan itself provides health care services, facilities, medication and devices for the beneficiaries. The Health Maintenance Act of 1973 provided additional impetus for the growth of HMO-type medical care insurance. The Act requires that an HMO plan be offered as an alternative insurance program by an employer of 25 or more employees if such a plan is available in the area. The employer, however, is not required to contribute any more toward the HMO premium than it pays for the standard health insurance plan it provides its employees. By 2008 it was estimated that over 88 million Americans were covered by HMO plans.

266. Another form of medical insurance, known as a Preferred Provider Organization (PPO), became widespread beginning in the 1980s. This approach differs from the traditional fee-for-services type insurance in that users must select their physicians and medical care facilities from designated providers that have agreed to accept fees based on the insurance policy's predetermined rates.

267. Although the bulk of the cost of health, life and disability insurance is borne by employers, and those costs are continuing to comprise an increasingly large share of an employer's wage and benefit tab, employees are often required to pay a portion of these costs. In 2016, employer-provided health insurance was available to 88 percent of full-time private industry workers in the United States. By contrast, only 20 percent of part-time workers had access to employer sponsored medical care insurance. Access, or availability, also varied by employment size: 56 percent for all workers in small establishments with fewer than 100 employees, compared with 85 percent in medium and large establishments with 100 employees or more.[194]

Dependence on employment as the primary source for obtaining individual and family health care insurance poses a variety of problems both when employment is terminated and when an insured child reaches adulthood. One part of the Employee

194. Bureau of Labor Statistics, bls.gov/ncs/ebs/benefits/2016/ownership/civilian/table09a.htm

Retirement Insurance Security Act (ERISA), known by the acronym COBRA (Congressional Omnibus Reconciliation Act) (29 US Code §§1161–1167), provides some continued access to such health care insurance. Under that provision, group health benefits plans sponsored by employers of 20 or more workers must allow workers and their dependents to continue their participation in the medical benefits up to ager 26, at their own expense (plus up to a 2 percent administrative fee), after the worker's employment is terminated, when an employee's work hours are reduced below the plan's threshold for participation, or after the relationship qualifying the dependent as a plan beneficiary has ended. This statutory right to continuation of benefits is not available to an employee who was dismissed for 'gross misconduct'. The duration for which the employee or dependents must be allowed to continue to participate is 18 months if the covered worker was dismissed from employment; in other situations the available duration of continued participation is 36 months. A deceased worker's spouse or a divorced spouse is entitled to make the same election.

The COBRA provisions do not require an employer to continue the group health plan itself. Thus, if the plan is terminated, all participants – current workers, former workers and their dependents – lose their medical insurance protection.[195]

268. Despite the widespread provision of medical care insurance for employees, in 2012, 45.5 million persons of all ages (14.7 percent) were uninsured.[196]

The reason for non-coverage was basically twofold: (a) smaller employers often did not provide this benefit, and (b) for the unemployed, coverage either was unavailable or unaffordable. The elderly and the poor, however, were covered by various government financed programs such as Medicare (a Social Security tax financed program for retired persons), and Medicaid, a program for impoverished persons that is financed by general revenues. Uninsured persons also had a right to treatment at emergency care facilities. Payment for those services is absorbed by the facilities and passed along as increased fees for other patients. Uninsured persons depending on emergency care facilities generally do not receive preventive care or early diagnosis with the result that their treatment is complicated by dealing with advance stages of ailments. Additionally, because the nature of such facilities requires expensive equipment not needed for more routine medical examinations and treatment, the added use by uninsured persons requires more or larger and, therefore, more expensive facilities. In 2010, Congress enacted the Affordable Care Act (ACA),[197] which is designed to improve the quality and affordability of health insurance by reducing the cost of health care and expanding insurance coverage, especially for individuals who had limited access to health insurance coverage previously, either because of exorbitant cost or because of denials of private coverage

195. *Local 217, Hotel & Restaurant Employees Union* v. *MHM, Inc.*, 976 F.2d 805 (2d Cir. 1992).

196. 'Health Insurance Coverage: Early Release of Estimates From the National Health Interview Survey, 2012', Centers for Disease Control, http://www.cdc.gov/nchs/data/nhis/earlyrelease/Insur201306.pdf.

197. Pub.L. 111–148, 124 Stat. 119, codified as amended in various sections of the Internal Revenue Code and in Title 42, USC.

based on pre-existing health conditions. Among other things, the Act requires insurance companies to offer all applicants minimum standards of coverage and offer the same rates regardless of pre-existing conditions or sex.

Republican legislators condemned the ACA as 'socialized medicine' and an overreach of federal power. It was a focus of their efforts to defeat the re-election of President Obama in 2012. He was re-elected but Republicans gained a majority in the House of Representatives. In the 2014 election, Republicans also gained a majority in the Senate. Throughout this period, Republicans in Congress repeatedly voted for bills to repeal the ACA but did not have sufficient votes to override President Obama's veto. A more serious problem for the ACA's supporters was that most states with Republican governors failed to adopt programs designed to provide expanded federally subsidized health insurance for their poorer constituents. This reduced the premium flow to insurance companies. In the 2016 Presidential election, Republican candidate Donald Trump variously proclaimed he would repeal or repeal and replace the ACA. Although the popular vote favored the Democratic candidate, Hillary Clinton, Trump was elected President as a result of receiving the majority of Electoral College votes (see paragraph 9, above) and Republicans continued to hold a majority of seats in both houses of Congress. By early 2017 the number of Americans not covered by healthcare insurance had been reduced to about half of what it had been when the ACA was adopted. However, a large portion of the uninsured were younger, healthy persons for whom insurance outlays could be expected to be a good bit less than the premiums. Partly as a result of the reduced premium flow, partly as a result of the uncertainties as to what changes would be made in the law, and partly as a result of incomplete reforms intended to provide greater efficiencies in medical services, premiums were increasing.

Despite Republican pledges to repeal the ACA, that effort failed in mid-2017 by a one vote margin in the Senate, a result attributed to public outcry against making such changes without simultaneously adopting a replacement that provides at least as much healthcare protection as the public has experienced under the ACA.

The ACA originally mandated that individuals obtain health insurance coverage, but provides subsidies to low-income individuals. (Those not purchasing the mandated insurance, largely young, healthy persons, were subject to a tax penalty to help pay for the program's costs.) The goal of mandatory coverage was to generate premiums from younger healthier people and, thereby, reduce overall per capita costs. At the end of 2017, Congress partially fulfilled the Trump campaign promise by eliminating the mandatory requirement, a change that is projected to increase premiums for the insured and to leave 10-14 million more people uninsured and, therefore, dependent on emergency treatment or their own financial resources.

The Affordable Care Act also creates insurance exchanges designed to increase the availability of coverage and affordability to individuals. At the same time, the Act discourages employers from dropping health insurance benefits to their employees by penalizing employers with more than 50 employees that do not offer health insurance to their full-time workers.[198]

198. 26 USC §4980H(a).

A series of suits challenging the ACA or parts thereof followed after its adoption. In closely divided decisions, its constitutional validity was upheld as was the Internal Revenue Service's interpretation of a key provision concerning access to tax credits if health insurance is purchased through a state or federal exchange in which various carriers participate.[199] However, a provision attempting to mandate state expansion of Medicaid coverage for poorer citizens was struck down.[200]

VI. Regulation of Employer Benefit Plans

269. The Employee Retirement Income Security Act of 1974 (ERISA), 29 US Code §1001 *et seq.*, established a national system that regulates employer sponsored employee retirement and welfare benefit plans and partially insures some types of employer sponsored retirement plans. Although ERISA requires that retirement benefits vest after a certain amount of time, it does not require vesting of welfare benefits. A welfare benefit plan includes employer provided benefits such as health insurance, life insurance, severance pay programs, vacation pay, assistance to disabled or laid off workers, prepaid legal services and education allowances. Excluded from all aspects of the Act, are statutorily mandated payments for disability and government operated benefits programs such as unemployment insurance.

ERISA establishes standards and procedures for resolving claims related to covered programs. Those standards and procedures ensure that employees are notified respecting their benefit rights and require that retirement and welfare benefit programs be administered in a fair and prudent manner. Because retirement benefits become vested, ERISA's regulation of retirement programs is considerably greater than is its regulation of welfare benefit programs.

Retirement programs distribute income in two ways. One is to pay periodically a specified amount of benefits. The benefit can be a specific amount of money, or it can be an amount that is determined by an established formula. An example of the latter would be a plan that promises to pay each month 60 percent of the average monthly wage earned during the last five years of employment, plus a cost of living adjustment. Such plans are called 'defined benefit' plans. Defined benefit plans are funded either by purchasing annuity insurance or by making contributions to the fund based on actuarial and financial projections of how much capital must be accumulated to provide the income necessary to make such periodic benefit payments after retirement. ERISA requires that for each potential retiree with a claim on the fund, a defined benefit plan financed by an individual employer pay to a government entity, the Pension Benefit Guaranty Corporation (PBGC), an annual premium (as of 2017) of $69 for single-employer plans. As of 2014, a little under 10 percent of all employed persons were covered by single-employer retirement benefit plans.

Some defined benefits plans are established by collectively bargained agreements that pool the contributions of two or more employers. As of 2014, a little over 3 percent of all employed persons were covered by a multi-employer retirement benefit

199. *Nat'l Fed. of Independent Businesses* v. *Sebelius*, 567 US 519 (2012); *King* v. *Burwell*, 135 S. Ct. 2480 (2015).
200. *Nat'l Fed. of Independent Businesses* v. *Sebelius*, 567 US 519, 576-84 (2012).

plan. (Some employees have accrued benefits under more than one retirement benefit plan whether single or multi-employer plans.) Such multi-employer defined benefit plans are treated as a separate plan category under ERISA and for 2017 are required to pay only $28 per participant per year as a PBGC premium. The lower premium is due to the fact that historically multi-employer plans generally were adequately funded. However, the shrinking of many key industries in the US has made the future of multi-employer funds more uncertain inasmuch as the premiums that are paid per employee now involve fewer active workers than in the past whereas there is a growing number of retirees whose benefit claims must be paid by the plans.

As a result both of reduced employment in many companies with defined benefit plans and past overly optimistic expectations respecting income from investments, a significant percentage of single-employer defined benefit plans are underfunded. Some very large companies, in industries such as steel, automotives, tires and airlines, are among the sponsors of underfunded retirement plans. The Pension Protection Act of 2006 and subsequent amendments addressed some of the underfunding issues and both increased minimum funding requirements for defined benefit plans and, using a complex formula, increased the annual premium amounts employers with underfunded plans must contribute to the PBGC. In 2017 the additional premium paid by underfunded plans varied from $34 to $517 per $1,000 of underfunding. (See 29 US Code §1306.) Because the adequacy of funding depends on the value of fund investments, declines in market values, such as those experienced in recent economic recessions, inevitably increased the amount of underfunding and number of underfunded plans. Improvements in market values a few years later, of course, bolstered the funding profile for many of the covered retirement funds. The insurance provided by the PBGC does not protect all defined benefit retirement plans nor fully protect those defined benefit retirement plans that are covered by the insurance. Benefits are not insured by PBGC until the plan and benefit level has been operative for at least five years and the benefit is protected only to the extent of a coverage formula. Once a plan is terminated and the PBGC takes over payments, the guaranteed benefit amount does not change and is determined by, among other factors, the age at retirement. The maximum amount guaranteed differs somewhat for beneficiaries of multi-employer defined benefit plans.

The PBGC has the responsibility of monitoring the financial affairs of retirement plans, including the responsibility to seek fines and recoup deficiencies in the event of underfunding. In addition, it participates in the liquidation or reorganization of plans with funding deficiencies.[201]

The second type of retirement plan is a 'defined contribution' plan. These are funded by periodically contributing a specified amount into an account that is accumulated for the employee. Upon retirement, the accumulated capital in the employee's account, plus income earned by that capital, can be: (a) used to purchase an annuity; (b) paid to the employee as a lump sum; or (c) placed in another type of investment program for periodic retirement distribution. Although about twice as many workers were in defined benefit programs as were in defined contribution

201. Detailed data is found in the *Annual Report* of the Pension Benefit Guaranty Corporation and on PBGC fact sheets found at the PBGC website, www.pbgc.gov.

plans when ERISA was enacted, that no longer is true. A majority of employees covered by employer sponsored retirement programs now are in defined contribution plans. Among reasons employers favor selection of defined contribution plans are the lack of a PBGC insurance premium, less complex regulation, and the ability to link annual contributions with profitability and thereby create an incentive for productivity improvement.

270. ERISA also protects employees by requiring that retirement benefit rights vest within specified periods of employment. To the extent that the employee makes direct contributions of funds to the retirement plan, the employee's interest is not subject to forfeiture – it vests completely when the contribution is made. However, the employer can delay the employee's right to participate in a retirement plan until the employee reaches age 21 and has had a year of service with the employer. After that, the employee must be credited with benefits financed by the employer though, as explained below, for a period of time these benefits can be subject to forfeiture. Alternatively, an employer can delay crediting the employee's service toward determining benefits for three years if after the three years the employee's interest is 100 percent vested without being subject to forfeiture.

In no event can the employee's benefits in a plan financed by a single employer be subject to forfeiture after five years of service unless the plan provides for a gradual increase in the fully vested benefits claim under which, starting after three years of service, for each added year of service an additional one fifth of the benefit is protected from forfeiture. Accordingly, by the end of seven years of service the benefit is 100 percent vested and not subject to forfeiture. In the case of retirement plans in which more than one employer participates (multi-employer plans), the employee's claim need not become non forfeitable until the completion of 10 years of service.

A maximum of 10 percent of the assets of a defined benefit or defined contribution plan can be invested in the employer's business. An alternative program that can serve to provide retirement benefits is an employee stock ownership plan (ESOP—26 US Code §§ 409(a), 4975(e)(7)). An ESOP involves contributing shares in the employer corporation into a special trust fund with the shares then being allocated to individual employee accounts. Within limits, the employer can even borrow money to 'purchase' these shares for the employees. An ESOP arrangement offers income tax benefits for both the employer and employees and, among other things, is a financing method that can be used when employees acquire the ownership of their employing enterprise. The employee's right to sell or otherwise transfer shares in the ESOP fund may delayed until a year after the employee leaves employment. Hence, if the employee remains until retirement, the ESOP account can serve as a retirement fund. As of 2017, an estimated 28 million employees were participating in an ESOP.

Congress has adopted a variety of methods for both self-employed persons and employees to establish their own retirement savings programs using either contributions that are untaxed (up to a specified amount) or after-tax contributions whose distributions will be untaxed. Among those available to employees are Individual Retirement Accounts (IRAs), of which there are two categories, section 401(k) accounts, section 403(b) plans for federal employees, and section 457 plans for state and local government employees. Some of these individual programs, such as 401(k) accounts, allow the employer to make limited supplemental contributions to the employee's account. This latter approach simplifies and limits the employer's involvement in providing retirement benefits and provides 'portability' for the employee. That is, the account is the same whether the worker remains with the same employer or gets a different job. Increasing numbers of employers are opting for the 401(k) approach to retirement benefits. In all of these programs, as with employer sponsored retirement plans, a primary incentive for setting aside the funds is that their earnings are untaxed.

271. The portion of ERISA which is known as COBRA, discussed above in paragraph 267, additionally addresses issues of the effect of family status changes upon benefits in retirement and employee stock ownership plans. Together with other statutes, COBRA makes the currently vested claim to benefits in such plans the joint property of the employee and his or her spouse. COBRA does this by prohibiting the employee or retiree from encumbering or transferring the right to benefits or from designating a surviving beneficiary to such benefits, without the spouse's informed consent. It also requires that annuity benefits be for the joint lives of the employee and spouse unless informed consent is given to measure the annuity in another manner or to designate other beneficiaries. The benefit provided by the joint annuity can be based on the surviving spouse receiving payments at a level that is as low as 50 percent of that paid while both are living. Moreover, a spouse's claim to retirement benefits of an ERISA regulated retirement plan is not altered by divorce unless it is expressly modified by the divorce decree.[202]

272. Employee benefits financed by direct payments from an employer's general operating accounts, such as paid vacation, sick leave, jury duty, military service, overtime pay, and statutorily required severance pay, are excluded from ERISA regulation.[203] Other types of benefits that involve special administrative structures or which are financed by setting aside funds in special accounts are deemed employee welfare plans and unless they fall within a specific ERISA exemption, their administration, and resolution of disputes concerning the plans and benefits arising under them, are covered solely by ERISA. ERISA coverage of such covered plans excludes state regulation.

Federal law expressly permits state law to govern the operation of insurance companies and the content of insurance plans. Often employers pay the premium for an insurance policy that provides employee welfare benefits, such as disability pay or medical care. Federal law permits state law to regulate the financial soundness of an insurance company and the content of its policies.[204] However, disputes respecting an employee's right to benefits under such a policy, when financed in whole or part

202. 29 US Code §1056(d); *Boggs* v. *Boggs*, 520 US 833 (1997).

203. *See* 29 CFR § 2510.3-1; *Massachusetts* v. *Morash*, 490 US 107 (1989); *Fort Halifax Packing Co.* v. *Coyne*, 482 US 1 (1987).

204. *Kentucky Ass'n of Health Plans, Inc.* v. *Miller*, 538 US 329 (2003); *Metropolitan Life Insurance Co.* v. *Massachusetts*, 471 US 724 (1985).

as an employment benefit, must be resolved solely under ERISA procedures and standards.[205]

ERISA regulations and standards are not always as protective of the employee as is comparable state law. For example, although in many states an employee who was dismissed to prevent vesting of retirement benefits would be able to bring a tort suit that could be heard by a jury and could result in collecting punitive as well as compensatory damages, ERISA provides a more narrow opportunity for obtaining relief.[206] In such a situation, the exclusive ERISA remedy is a civil suit for equitable relief that is tried by a judge in federal court; the state claim for relief is barred by the availability of that ERISA remedy.[207] Thus, neither a jury nor punitive damages would be available. On the other hand, the federal judge can order reinstatement of the employee, a remedy rarely if ever provided in state court suits.

Among ERISA's requirements are those designed to ensure adequate information for employees respecting their benefits and available protective procedures. The information requirements apply if a plan of employee welfare benefits exists, even if it was established for an improperly limited group of employees and even if the employer has never publicized the existence of the benefit to its employees.[208]

If an employer, plan trustee, or the designated plan administrator rejects an employee's claim to an ERISA regulated benefit, the federal court construes the contractual rights of the parties without regard to state law. When construing contractual language to resolve an ERISA dispute, federal courts apply the ordinary meaning that the language would convey to people of reasonable intelligence, not the special meaning it carries among people who are trained in fields such as law, insurance or welfare benefits administration. If the language is ambiguous or unclear, the uncertainties are resolved against the interests of the party that prepared the contract and in favor of the beneficiary.[209] However, the federal courts defer to the plan administrator's, trustee's, or employer's interpretation if the plan expressly

205. *Aetna Health, Inc.* v. *Davila*, 542 US 200 (2004); *Rush Prudential HMO, Inc.* v. *Moran*, 536 US 355 (2002); *Pegram* v. *Herdrich*, 530 US 211 (2000); *Pilot Life Ins. Co.* v. *Dedeaux*, 481 US 41 (1987). But *see, Wurtz* v. *Rawlings Co.*, 761 F3d 232 (2d Cir. 2014) (ERISA does not preempt state law that bars employer and its insurer from adopting an insurance provision requiring reimbursement of medical expenses paid to employee as part of judgment for tort damages suffered by the insured employee).

206. *Aetna Health, Inc.* v. *Davila*, 542 US 200 (2004); C. Medill, 'Resolving the Judicial Paradox of "Equitable Relief" under ERISA section 502(a)(3)', 39 *John Marshall L. Rev.* 827 (2006). Claims for fiduciary breaches under 502(a)(2) are likewise limited. *See Massachusetts Mutual Life Insur. Co.* v. *Russell*, 473 US 134 (1985). Claims for equitable relief under section 502(a)(3) are distinct from legal relief and require the identification of funds in the possession of the defendant to be recoverable. *See Great West Life & Annuity Insurance Co.* v. *Knudson*, 534 US 204 (2002); *Sereboff* v. *MidAtlantic Medical Services*, 547 US 356 (2006). But *see Wurtz* decision in the previous footnote where state law barred insurers from treating medical expense recoveries in tort claims as funds to be reimbursed to the insurer or those paying the insurance premium. *See also* Bales, Hirsch and Secunda, at §14.05(C).

207. *New York State Conference of Blue Cross & Blue Shield Plans* v. *Travelers Insurance Co.*, 514 US 645 (1995); *Ingersoll-Rand Co.* v. *McClendon*, 498 US 133 (1990); *Pilot Life Insurance* v. *Dedaux*, 481 US 41 (1987).

208. *Firestone Tire and Rubber Co.* v. *Bruch*, 489 US 101 (1989); *Varity Corp.* v. *Howe*, 516 US 489 (1996).

209. *Pegram* v. *Herdrich*, 530 US 211 (2000); *Phillips* v. *Lincoln Nat'l Life Ins. Co.*, 978 F.2d 302 (7th Cir. 1992).

gives that person the right of final authority or discretion to resolve such uncertainties and if there is no conflict between that person's interests and those of the beneficiary. If there is such a conflict, it must be weighed by the court in deciding whether the interpretation given by the party whose interpretive discretion is reserved by the contract was so unreasonable as to be an abuse of that discretion.[210] A different rule applies to welfare benefit plans created by collectively bargained agreements where the Labor Management Relations Act establishes a system of joint employer-union trusteeship and conflicts between the two sides are resolved by an impartial third party.

273. ERISA expressly requires that those who invest funds used for the payment of employee welfare benefits adhere to fiduciary standards of conduct.[211] Many, including the AFL–CIO, argue that such investment should be guided not only by the desire for reasonable investment returns and financial security, but also by moral and social considerations such as not helping to finance companies that transfer employment out of the country, that resist unionization of the work force, that operate facilities in countries with repressive regimes, and the like. An unresolved question is whether weighing social and moral concerns in making investment decisions violates ERISA's fiduciary standards. Moreover, even if such concerns can properly be weighed when they reflect employment-related interests of the fund beneficiaries, such as increased employment opportunities or expansion of union bargaining power, must they be discarded if they go beyond such interests? For example, if some of the beneficiaries are no longer in the work force, can investment of the funds used to pay their benefits take into consideration whether the investment will promote US employment opportunities? Or, if a significant number of the beneficiaries object to birth control, can the fund managers consciously avoid investing in companies that produce birth control devices?[212]

The financial impact of employer sponsored retirement plans (private and government defined benefit and defined contribution plans), IRAs (individual retirement accounts, including rollovers from other retirement accounts), and annuities, is substantial. Such retirement assets totaled $24.9 trillion at mid 2015. The largest components of retirement assets were IRAs and employer-sponsored defined contribution plans, holding $7.6 trillion and $6.8 trillion, respectively. Private sector defined benefit plans held $3.2 trillion and $5.1 trillion was invested by government sponsored defined benefit plans..

210. *Firestone Tire & Rubber Co.* v. *Bruch*, 489 US 101 (1989).

211. In *Varity Corp.* v. *Howe*, 516 US 489 (1996), the Supreme Court discussed the sources for determining the rules applicable when applying that duty under this statute. *See also Harte* v. *Bethlehem Steel Corp.*, 214 F.3d 446 (3rd Cir. 2000); *Krohn* v. *Huron Mem. Hosp.*, 173 F.3d 542 (6th Cir. 1999); Bales, Hirsch and Secunda, at §14.05(A).

212. See *Board of Trustees of the Employees' Retirement Fund* v. *Mayor and City Council of Baltimore*, 562 A.2d 720 (Md. 1989), *cert. denied* 493 US 1093 (1990) holding that banning investment in corporations doing business in or with South Africa, as a means of protesting apartheid, did not interfere with the duty to provide a secure, reasonable investment return. *See also*, J. Zanglein, 'High Performance Investing: Harnessing the Power of Pension Funds to Promote Economic Growth and Workplace Integrity', 11 *The Lab. Lawyer* 59 (1995); R. Vishkai, 'Pension Plans Explore the Potential of International Investment', 30 *Pension World*, No. 4, p. 6 (1994); W. Tucker, 'Investing Overseas', 10 *Insight*, No. 15, p. 16 (1994).

VII. Safety and Health Standards

274. Worker safety and health are protected by general safety and health regulations adopted under state or local authority including building codes, motor vehicle traffic codes, food handling regulations, and the like. Similarly, federal regulation of general safety and health matters; such as transportation laws governing interstate highways, airlines, shipping, and railways; federal food, drug and other consumer health and safety laws; and some very specialized federal safety and health regulations, such as those dealing with radioactive materials or employee safety and health at federally funded construction sites; provide a considerable degree of worker health and safety protection. However, two federal statutes, the Occupational Safety and Health Act (29 US Code §651 *et seq.*), normally referred to as OSHA, and the Mine Safety and Health Act (30 US Code §801 *et seq.*), often referred to as MNSHA, are particularly designed to improve the health and safety of the work environment and the methods by which people work. Both laws encourage comparable state regulation and enforcement procedures if the state standards are at least as protective of the work force as the federal statute.

The Occupational Safety and Health Act applies to any non government employer whose business affects interstate commerce. The Supreme Court has given a very expansive reading to the concept of 'activity affecting interstate commerce'. Its approach to applying that term includes looking at the cumulative impact of similar enterprises that use, sell, compete, or work with goods or services that are transported or transferred in interstate commerce. Accordingly, most non government American employers fall within the Act's potential reach. MNSHA's safety and health regulations are more particularized inasmuch as they govern only work directly related to extraction of non liquid minerals from the ground. The potential conflict of authority is resolved by a provision in OSHA (29 US Code §653(b)(1)) that excludes from OSHA regulation those activities controlled by state health and safety regulation involving handling radioactive substances or by federal agencies specifically authorized to protect employee safety and health. Similarly excluded from OSHA are various aspects of maritime employment that are governed by Coast Guard regulations and other employment whose safety and health is regulated by other statutorily designated federal agencies. Also, through appropriations legislation (laws providing annual funding of government agencies), Congress has given partial OSHA exemption to very small businesses (10 or fewer employees) in industries w(th less than the average per employee annual number of days lost through work related injury or illness.

Although they differ in a number of respects, both OSHA and MNSHA are enforced through abatement orders requiring the removal or reduction of a hazardous condition and through the assessment of civil and criminal penalties.

On rare occasions, state criminal laws prohibiting conduct as 'wanton endangerment' have been invoked to punish managers who have knowingly and callously exposed workers to serious health or safety hazards.[213]

---

213. For example, *People* v. *Pymm*, 546 NYS2d 871 (App. Div. 1989). State criminal prosecutions for wanton exposure of employees to grave danger have been held permitted by OSHA, *see People* v. *Chicago Magnet Wire Corp.*, 534 N.E.2d 962 (Ill. 1989) and *State* v. *Far West Water & Sewer Inc.*,

275. The OSHA requires employers to maintain safety data and report work related deaths. It also mandates that employers furnish each employee with work and a work environment 'free from recognized hazards that are causing or likely to cause death or serious physical harm'. (29 US Code §654, also referred to as OSHA §5). This requirement, characterized as the general duty clause, can be read to refer to the likelihood that the hazard will cause harm or the prospect that any resulting harm, even if its occurrence is but a remote possibility, will cause serious injury, or both. Case decisions have resolved this issue by emphasizing the phrase 'recognized hazard' and hold the employer responsible either if the employer knew the condition posed a hazard of serious injury or if safety experts aware of the condition would consider it a serious hazard.[214]

The Occupational Safety and Health Review Commission (OSHRC), which is the agency charged with reviewing determinations that OSHA has been violated, also requires proof that it is feasible to materially reduce or eliminate the hazard to which the employees have been exposed.[215] Thus, workers can be employed to perform a very hazardous task so long as there is no feasible means of reducing or eliminating the hazard. Clearly, the most protective approach to employee health and safety would totally prohibit employing people to undertake high-risk activities. The interpretation of OSHA's requirements does not go that far; the enforcing agency has held that the statutory requirement that proof of a violation include demonstrating that there is a feasible method of material reduction or elimination of the hazard is consistent with Congress' stated purpose of assuring safe working conditions 'so far as possible'.

On occasion, OSHA enforcement has relieved employers of responsibility for violations based on the employer's inability to provide a safe work environment where: (a) that work environment is controlled by another entity, (b) the employees' employer made reasonable but unsuccessful efforts to get the controlling party to remove those safety or health hazards, and (c) alternative means of protection are unavailable.[216]

OSHA's general duty clause is expressly directed at the employer's duty to its employees. It does not address the safety and health of customers, visitors or the employees of other employers. However, the Act normally has the effect of protecting most people exposed to a hazard under an employer's control because a hazardous condition that principally threatens customers, passers-by, or others, violates OSHA so long as the employer's workers, too, may be subject to the dangerous condition or process. In addition, there is some authority supporting the proposition that if an employer controls the work environment or process, its responsibility extends

---

228 P.3d 909 (AZ 2010) In contrast, state imposition of criminal penalties for noncompliance with a state administrative safety program is preempted by OSHA if the state scheme has not been approved by the US Secretary of Labor. *Gade* v. *National Solid Waste Management Ass'n*, 505 US 88 (1992).

214. *Kelly Springfield Tire Co., Inc.* v. *Donovan*, 729 F.2d 317 (5th Cir. 1984); *Pratt & Whitney Aircraft* v. *Secretary of Labor*, 649 F.2d 96 (2d Cir. 1981).

215. *Pelron Corp.*, 12 BNA OSHC 1835 (1986).

216. *See*, e.g. *Dun-Par Engineered Form Co.* v. *Marshall*, 676 F.2d 1333 (10th Cir. 1982) and the discussion of that decision in *A/C Elec. Co.* v. *OSHRC*, 956 F.2d 530 (6th Cir. 1991).

to those who work for another employer that is engaged with it in a common undertaking.[217]

276. The OSHA also gives the Secretary of Labor authority to adopt mandatory employment health and safety standards and procedures. Standards and procedures are adopted after an opportunity has been given for interested persons to submit objections to the proposal. Court decisions hold that to be valid, OSHA standards and procedures must be responsive to significant risks recognized by a substantial body of reputable experts. In addition, precautions prescribed by the standards and procedures must be technologically feasible, and the costs must have a reasonable relationship to the achieved protection.[218] Accordingly, appellate courts have indicated that an OSHA standard requiring expensive precautions may be valid for an industry in which the risk of injury or illness that is being combated is frequently encountered while the same standard would be invalid if applied to an industry in which the risk of that injury or illness is very remote.[219]

Once a specific safety or health standard has been adopted by the Secretary, an employer that has not complied with the standard has the burden of proving that compliance is impossible or infeasible.[220]

The Secretary of Labor's authority under OSHA includes the power to prescribe labeling requirements to warn employees respecting hazards to which they are exposed, precautions to be observed to avoid exposure, and the best responses and treatment if accidentally exposed. Additionally, the Secretary of Labor can require employers to provide medical examinations and other tests to monitor exposure to hazards and training to avoid exposure.

OSHA states that employees have a duty to abide by OSHA standards but there are no government remedies for employee violations.

§4. Employer's Responsibility for the Worker's Wrongdoing

277. Under the doctrine of *respondeat superior*, the employer is responsible to third parties for a worker's torts committed within the scope of the worker's employment. In such situations, the employer is deemed to be constructively present. The justification for this policy is also based on the equitable concept that just as the employer is entitled to reap the benefits of the employee's conduct, so too must the employer bear the responsibilities of that conduct. Thus, if a worker acting within the scope of his employment injures a third party, the employer is

---

217. *Brennan* v. *OSHRC (Underhill Construction)*, 513 F.2d 1032 (2d Cir. 1975).

218. *American Textile Manufacturing Inst.* v. *Donovan*, 452 US 490 (1981).

219. *UAW* v. *OSHA*, 938 F.2d 1310 (DC Cir. 1991). For an example of the administrative burdens of satisfying these criteria for justification of a new standard, *see AFL–CIO* v. *OSHA*, 965 F.2d 962 (11th Cir. 1992).

220. *Harry C. Crooker & Sons, Inc.* v. *OSHRC*, 537 F.3d 79 (1st Cir. 2008).

liable for that injury even though the worker's conduct was contrary to the employer's express instructions and even though the worker's conduct was wanton and malicious.[221]

278. The doctrine of respondeat superior does not apply if the worker is acting solely in his own behalf, and in a manner that would not be reasonably foreseeable, even if the worker is using the employer's property or is acting while on paid work time. However, conduct engaged in for the worker's comfort that is a normal aspect of the work day (keeping warm, using a toilet, etc.) is not a deviation from normal worker activity and, therefore, does not remove the activity from the scope of employment.[222] Violent, emotional conduct of an employee is sometimes treated as abnormal activity that is solely designed to satisfy the worker's own needs and, therefore, does not fall within the scope of the employer's liability unless the conduct was foreseeable or, however misguided, had the purpose, at least in part, of furthering the employer's interests.[223]

279. An alternative basis for holding an employer liable for its worker's misconduct is an action based on the employer's negligent selection or training of the employee. To prove such an action, it must be shown that the employer's negligence was the proximate cause of the injury in question. This cause of action is sometimes available in situations in which liability cannot be fixed based on the doctrine of *respondeat superior* because the worker's misconduct occurred at a time when he was not acting in the course of his employment. A cause of action against an employer because of a worker's misconduct has, for example, been recognized under the negligence theory where the employer entrusted the worker with an unusually dangerous instrumentality.[224]

280. In the area of government employment, the doctrine of sovereign immunity sometimes poses a barrier to holding the employer liable for its worker's misconduct. The doctrine has been partly relaxed by statute and judicial modification with respect to federal employees and has been partly or fully abrogated by many state legislatures and some state courts. Often, even when the doctrine is not applicable, an action to recover against a government employer requires special notice (often within a short period of time after the claim accrues) and sometimes must be brought in a court of special jurisdiction. The procedures and time limitations may vary considerably from those applicable if the same case was brought against a private employer. Such variations invariably impose a shorter time limit for initiating suit. In addition, monetary limits often are imposed upon such recoveries.[225]

---

221. Prosser and Keeton, *Torts* (5th ed. 1984) pp. 502–503.
222. *Ibid.*, pp. 503–505.
223. *Ibid.*, pp. 505–507.
224. *Ibid.*, pp. 507–508.
225. *Ibid.*, pp. 1032–1055.

§5. Worker's Liability for Wrongs Committed in the Course of Employment

281. An employee is liable at common law for his own misconduct, even though he was acting while in the course of his employment and at the specific directions of his employer.[226] An employee is not liable to a third party at common law, however, for failure to perform a duty owed by the employer to that third party even though the employee has been directed by the employer to do so.[227]

Whether supervisory employees will be personally liable for violations of statutory rights depends on the statute in question. Most courts, for example, have held that supervisors may not be held individually liable for violations of employment discrimination statutes, such as Title VII, the ADEA or the ADA.

282. An interesting problem is posed where the worker's wrongdoing results in an injury to the employer. The traditional rule in most American jurisdictions prevents a party from recovering for an injury if his own misconduct to any degree was a contributing, proximate cause of that injury. Under the doctrine of respondeat superior, many courts have taken the position that an employer, therefore, cannot recover against a negligent third party if the negligence of the employer's worker was a contributing, proximate cause of the injury.[228] A few courts have held that this reasoning also prevents an employer from recovering against its own employee if the employer was injured in whole or in part due to the employee's negligence.[229]

§6. Work Schedules

283. Many states have laws regulating the number of consecutive hours a worker can be employed without a rest or meal period or without a prolonged interval away from the job. Some also have laws prohibiting various forms of work from being performed on Sunday. The Federal Aviation Administration regulates the maximum duty hours that can be worked by flight personnel and the Department of Transportation sets various limits upon the continuous work hours of long distance train, bus and truck operators.

---

226. *Wood* v. *Miller*, 76 P.2d 963 (Ore. 1938).
227. *Knight* v. *Atlantic Coast Line R.R.*, 73 F.2d 76 (5th Cir. 1934).
228. American Law Institute, *Restatement of the Law of Torts (Second)*, 486 (1964); *Nagele–Kelly Mfg. Co.* v. *Hannak*, 164 N.W.2d 540 (Mich. App. 1968). *Contra, Walker* v. *Stokely-Van Camp Inc.*, 144 N.W.2d 540 (Minn. 1966).
229. *Capitola* v. *Minneapolis, St. Paul & S.S.M. R. R.*, 103 N.W.2d 867 (Minn. 1960).

Chapter 3. Remuneration and Benefits

§1. Basic Concepts

I. Usage of Terms 'Salary' and 'Wage'

284. Although the terms 'wage' and 'salary' are often used interchangeably in American law and labor relations, distinctions have been drawn. In common usage, 'wage' refers to money paid for time spent working during a specific period, whereas 'salary' refers to payment given by an employer to an employee for the engagement of employment during a time period regardless of the amount of time actually spent working during that period. Another variant in the usage of these terms relates them to job status. Payment for performance of work in a job carrying lower social status is generally spoken of as a 'wage'; payment for the performance of work in jobs carrying higher social status is generally spoken of as a 'salary'. A related but still different distinction in usage is to apply the term 'salary' to remuneration and benefits given to those whose jobs entail responsibilities that will command the employee's attention during seemingly leisure time. In contrast, 'wage' refers to the remuneration and benefits given to those whose job responsibilities have clearly marked starting and stopping times.

II. Rate of Compensation

285. A minimum level of pay often is fixed by law. Minimum levels of compensation occasionally are also established by state or federal law with respect to some benefits other than pay, such as disability insurance, unemployment benefits, and the like. Beyond such minimum standards, the level of compensation normally is a matter of express agreement. If a collective agreement covers the employment in question, any provisions in that collective agreement which set the level of compensation prevail over a conflicting term of an individual employment contract between the employer and worker.[230] A statutory provision, on the other hand, prevails over both the individual employment agreement and the collective agreement.

286. Occasionally, even though the law does not require that a particular type of benefit be given to workers, the law affects how the benefit is administered and various characteristics of the benefit if in fact the benefit is given by the employer. This occurs, for example, with respect to retirement benefits.

287. Unless there is an agreed level of compensation, courts require an employer to pay the reasonable or customary rate of compensation for the work performed. Generally, however, this remedy is limited to pay, including commissions and reimbursable expenses, but does not include other benefits such as medical insurance.

---

230. *J. I. Case Co.* v. *NLRB*, 321 US 332 (1944).

§2. Pay

I. Time When Wage is Due

288. State laws, the federal minimum wage and overtime laws, and even some state constitutions, contain various provisions governing the frequency and form of payment of wages. For example, in the state of Arizona, employees must be paid on designated, fixed paydays twice each month. Paydays may not be more than 16 days apart. However, Arizona permits out-of-state employers to designate a single monthly payday for executive, administrative, professional and supervisory personnel.

Deductions from wages may only be those required or allowed by state or federal law for such things as federal and state income taxes or Social Security or mandatory health insurance premiums or as authorized in writing by the worker for purposes allowed by law. State laws vary but typically allow wage withholding for such things as employee designated charitable contributions, voluntary retirement or other employee benefit insurance or funds, union dues, domestic relations support payments, or court ordered wage assignments. Further, state laws often specify that wages be paid in US currency, by negotiable bank check payable on demand, or direct deposit into an employee designated bank account.

Some state laws expressly prohibit the taking of money from the worker by the employer for a loss or shortage resulting from a customer's wrongdoing or the employee's unintentional negligence. Also expressly prohibited in some states are wage deductions for the employer's or a manager's benefit. (Such extractions, commonly known as kickbacks, have occasionally been imposed during periods of high unemployment by those in a position to hire or to assign work.)

Finally, state statutes or regulations specify written information that must be given to employees when wage payments are made.

II. Compensation in the Form of a Commission

289. Sometimes employees are compensated in whole or in part on the basis of the profits or sales produced by their work effort – generally called a 'commission'. In such situations, the worker often is entitled each week or month to draw an advance payment to be deducted from future commissions.

A majority of US jurisdictions presume that the parties do not intend to obligate the worker to repay advances should they exceed the commissions actually earned. This presumption can be overcome either by express agreement or by the parties' conduct giving rise to an implied employee undertaking to reimburse the employer should advances exceed earnings.[231]

231. *Insurance Mngmt. of Wash. Inc.* v. *Guthrie*, 310 A.2d 61 (DC Ct. App. 1973); *Farr Insurance Inc.* v. *Rogers*, 510 P.2d 470 (Colo. Ct. App. 1973).

Unless there is a contrary agreement, commissions are earned when the sales agreement or service agreement is made even if the right to the commission is revocable if the agreement is not performed. In many jurisdictions, the right to a commission is based on procuring the contract and accrues so long as all acts of procurement have been completed even if the formal agreement has not yet been executed.[232]

III. Parents' Compensation of Child for Work Performed

290. Minimum wage and child labor laws often exempt from their coverage situations in which a child works for his parent. The services of a child for a parent generally are presumed to be gratuitous in American law regardless of the child's age. Some courts confine that presumption to minor children and to adult children living in the parent's household. By proof of a contrary agreement, this presumption can be overcome.[233]

IV. Gratuities

291. In many service industries in the United States, it is customary for satisfied patrons to provide employees with a gratuity (a tip). Despite the general rule that the profits of employment are the property of the employer, it is normally held that, absent an explicit agreement to the contrary, tips belong to the worker who receives them if employed in an industry in which the giving of gratuities is customary.[234] Statutes in some states expressly prohibit an employer from requiring that customary gratuities be given to the employer. On the other hand, laws prohibiting commercial bribes make it a crime to give or receive something of value with the intention of causing or rewarding a worker for violating the worker's duty of loyalty to the employer. Customary gratuities are excluded from that prohibition on the theory that they reflect enhanced performance that benefits the employer.

Under the Fair Labor Standards Act, if a tipped employee regularly receives at least in tips, the employer is only required to pay $2.13 per hour in direct wages if that amount combined with the tips received at least equals the federal minimum wage. If the employee's tips combined with the employer's direct wages of at least $2.13 per hour does not equal the federal minimum hourly wage, the employer must make up the difference. Many states, however, require higher direct wage amounts for tipped employees.[235]

---

232. *Furth* v. *Inc. Publishing Corp.*, 823 F.2d 1178, 1180 (7th Cir. 1987).

233. J. Long, *Domestic Relations*, §270 (3d ed. 1923); J. Barnett and D. Spradlin. 'Enslavement in the Twentieth Century!', 5 *Pepperdine L. Rev.* 673, 675–676 n. 7 (1978).

234. *Williams* v. *Jacksonville Term. Co.*, 315 US 386 (1942); *Sheaffer* v. *Industrial Comm'n.*, 139 N.W.2d 106 (Wisc. 1966). *See also*, e.g. Colo. Rev. Stat. §8-4-103(2) (2006).

235. 29 Code of Fed. Reg. § 531.56.

V. Reimbursement of Expenses

292. Workers may incur many different forms of expense in the course of performing their assigned duties. These range from the purchase of special clothing or safety equipment, to extraordinary costs of maintaining the cleanliness of one's person, clothing or equipment, to the cost of travel, food and lodging while away from home. When items of expense are statutorily required for the protection of health or safety, it is normal for legislation or regulation to expressly impose such expenses on the employer. In some cases, courts have found an implied understanding that the employer will pay for any expenses, such as traveling expenses, reasonably incurred in worker's carrying out assigned responsibilities.[236] An employee's entitlement to reimbursement for travel expenses has been held by at least one court to include the depreciation in the value of the worker's motor vehicle.[237]

The Internal Revenue Service annually calculates the average cost per mile of operating a motor vehicle and allows income tax deductions for business use of vehicles based on that calculation. The calculation includes vehicle depreciation and employers often use that figure when reimbursing employees for the use of their own vehicles for business travel.

293. Normal living expenses are reimbursable only when they are expressly included in the employment agreement or are customarily covered by the employer in the particular line of work. Thus, in an interesting older case a court held that because the employer had not entered into an express undertaking to pay the hotel expenses of a strikebreaker brought in from a distant town, those expenses were the worker's own responsibility.[238] An employer may deduct the reasonable cost to it of necessities, such as food and lodging provided to a worker, when calculating the minimum wage owed under the FLSA. However, a deduction is not permitted if the item was provided for the employer's rather than the worker's convenience.[239]

294. By statute, most US merchant vessels must satisfy various standards respecting the crew's free accommodations and provisions. Details vary according to the vessel size and the type and duration of voyage. At one time this included specific clothing and bedding requirements. Current law specifies that the seafarer must be served three meals a day with a total of at least 3,100 calories including a balance of needed vitamins and minerals. The crew must also be housed in an area that is clean and sanitary with proper ventilation and proper working plumbing. Special procedures are established by which the crew can challenge the adequacy of these provisions and obtain an inspection and determination by government officials if they claim that these standards have not been met.

---

236. For example, *Bernstein* v. *Sirotta*, 1 P.2d 8 (Calif. 1931).
237. *Safway Steel Scaffolds* v. *Coulter*, 94 S.E.2d 541 (Va. 1956).
238. *Dell* v. *Lancaster*, 285 S.W. 685 (Ct. Civ. App. Tex. 1926).
239. *Caro-Galvan* v. *Curtis Richardson, Inc.*, 993 F.2d 1500 (11th Cir. 1993).

VI. Paid Vacations

295. Although state statutes often require an employer to give workers brief periods of time off from work every given number of hours or days of work, entitlement to paid vacations or holidays generally is a matter of contract. Almost all long-term undertakings of employment in the United States carry with them some agreed period of paid vacation and some paid holidays. The word 'vacation' in the United States is distinguished from 'holiday'. If a place of employment regards a day as a paid holiday, all employees generally are entitled to a paid day off on that day. The length of an employee's vacation, however, typically is greater for those with longer service.

Nearly all full-time employees are given some annual paid vacation. The average and median number of annual paid vacation days for full-time workers in the private sector is 10 after a year of service and 15 days after five years of service. However, less than 40 percent of part-time private sector workers receive paid vacation. Moreover, in 2017 only 67 percent of full-time workers employed by small employers (fewer than 50 employees) received paid vacation. (Many such workers are employed in seasonal businesses.)

Often an employee has some choice respecting when to take vacation and where that choice is available, priority normally is given to the preferences of longer-term employees. However, in some businesses all employees take vacation for the same amount of time and at the same time inasmuch as the entire industry or the entire enterprise closes for the vacation period.

Whether the worker will be entitled to pay for his unused vacation depends on the law of the particular state or the terms of the particular employment contract. Some jurisdictions have ruled that a worker who has earned a vacation is entitled to vacation pay upon termination if termination precedes the vacation. And, some jurisdictions treat vacation pay as a form of deferred compensation and, therefore, an integral part of a worker's wages.[240]

Vacation benefits are sometimes conditioned upon the employee's being employed in good standing as of the first day of vacation and returning to work at the end of the vacation.

296. Employment contracts sometimes permit workers to accumulate unused vacation benefits over a series of years. On the other hand, some case decisions hold that, unless the employment contract provides otherwise, an employee who terminates his employment, or who is terminated, is not entitled to collect vacation pay for previous years, even though the vacations were not taken – a result that conflicts with the concept that vacation pay is an integral part of a worker's wages.[241] In explaining the decisions, the courts have asserted that vacation pay is similar to overtime pay except that the employee is not working. Thus, it is argued, the benefit is not accrued until the time for taking it has arrived. An alternative explanation

240. *Jones* v. *District Parking Mgmt.*, 268 A.2d 860 (D.C. Ct. App. 1970); *Chapman* v. *Southeast Region, ILGWU Health & Welfare Recreation Fund*, 280 F. Supp. 766 (DSC 1968).

241. *Chester* v. *Jones*, 386 S.W.2d 544 (Ct. Civ. App. Tex. 1965); *Lim* v. *Motor Supply, Ltd.*, 364 P.2d 38 (Hawaii 1961).

could analogize vacation leave to sick pay benefits or health insurance benefits on the ground that vacation pay is a conditional form of deferred compensation whose payment is due if the employee takes off from work during the appropriate period. If the employee has not elected to take the time off during the vacation year, the condition for payment has never occurred. This latter rationale takes strength from the recognition that vacation leave benefits the employer as well as the worker. The employer can anticipate that the worker will return from vacation refreshed and, therefore, able to perform better. According to this approach, the principles governing vacation pay benefits should reflect the parties' mutual interest in encouraging workers to take vacations rather than bank the pay while working without break.[242]

Other courts have held that absent an express agreement to the contrary, vacation benefits accrue when earned and upon termination of employment the employer must pay for all earned vacation, regardless of when earned, that was not taken by the worker.[243] This is the modern trend evident in many wage statutes. Implicit in this rule is an understanding that although contractually provided, paid annual vacation is a social benefit that should be enjoyed by the employee, at one point in time or another, regardless of whether the employer receives any return.

VII. Bonuses and Awards

297. Employers variously offer pay bonuses either as an incentive to accept a job, to remain in the job, or as an extra inducement to perform efficiently. American courts often find an implied, enforceable agreement to pay a promised bonus. Generally, courts imply such an undertaking if:

(a) the worker has complied with all of the conditions motivating the bonus offer;
(b) the bonus has been given on a regular and customary basis; and
(c) there is a reliable method for calculating the probable size of the bonus.[244]

298. Some employers offer workers a bonus as an award for valuable employee suggestions. Many courts treat such suggestion plans as an offer to enter into a contract accepted by the worker's submission of a suggestion. Any recovery to which the worker is entitled is then governed by the terms of the suggestion plan and the worker has a right of action on a breach of contract theory if the employer's committee that reviews suggestions rejects a suggestion in a manner that does not conform with the employer's rules for operating the suggestion system or if the committee has made a gross or palpable mistake.[245]

---

242. T. Mohn 'Vacation Deprivation: Americans Have Twice as Many Unused Days off as Last Year, New Survey Finds', *Forbes* 30 November 2013.
243. *National Rifle Ass'n* v. *Ailes*, 428 A.2d 816 (DC 1981).
244. *Schwieger* v. *Iowa Beef Processors, Inc.*, 802 F.2d 1032 (8th Cir. 1986); *Thatchter* v. *Wasatch Chem. Co.*, 507 P.2d 365 (Utah 1973); *Hildenberg* v. *Iowa Beef Packers Inc.*, 175 N.W.2d 353 (Ia. 1970); *Simon* v. *Riblet Tramway Co.*, 505 P.2d 1291 (Wash. Ct. App. 1973).
245. *Joyce* v. *GMC*, 551 N.E.2d 172 (Oh. 1990); *Carlini* v. *US Rubber*, 154 N.W.2d 595 (Mich. App. Ct. 1967).

If the employer rejects the worker's suggestion but uses it anyway, the employee is entitled to recover either under a theory of breach of contract or under a theory of unjust enrichment. In some cases, however, the employee's claim has been rejected on the ground that the employer's suggestion plan contained an illusory promise because it left the decision to make an award and the determination of the amount of such an award wholly within the employer's discretion.[246]

299. Federal employees are paid incentive awards for suggestions that improve the efficiency of government operations or that constitute superior accomplishments.[247] Recommendations for these awards are submitted by the employing agency or department to the Office of Personnel Management which makes the final decision respecting the grant of an incentive award that normally is under $10,000. Highly exceptional suggestions or accomplishments are rewarded with cash awards between $10,000 and $25,000. Each year several thousand federal employees share several million dollars of such awards.

A more dramatic federal government incentive for employee innovations is the Federal Technology Transfer Act (15 US Code §§3710c, 3710d) which allows government employees to patent inventions the government has decided it will not use, awards to them cash incentives for those inventions it uses, and for those inventions which the government licenses, gives the employee inventor the first $2,000 of royalties plus at least 15 percent of additional royalties up to an annual maximum of $150,000 unless the President of the United States approves a larger award.

VIII. Priority Rights to Wages in Insolvency Proceedings

300. American bankruptcy law gives some priority consideration to the payment of wages owed by a party undergoing a bankruptcy proceeding. Under the bankruptcy law's system of priorities claims given statutory priority are paid from the unencumbered assets of the bankrupt estate in the order of the designated priorities. Debts owed general creditors not given a priority are not paid until all priority claims have been satisfied. Under section 507 of the Bankruptcy Code (11 US Code §507), first priority of distribution of the bankrupt's general assets is given to administrative expenses including wages, salaries, and commissions earned while the bankruptcy proceedings are pending. Wages, salaries, commissions, earned vacation and sick leave pay for up to 180 days prior to the filing of the bankruptcy petition or termination of the business (whichever was first) are given fourth priority up to $12,850 per employee. This includes vacation, severance and sick leave pay.

If the wages were earned in a state that gives a statutory lien for wages, that lien is a security interest in the bankrupt's assets. As a result, a worker with such a lien has the right to collect against the assets of the estate ahead of general creditors, including those assigned priority status.

246. *Calkins* v. *Boeing Co.*, 506 P.2d 329 (Wash. Ct. App. 1973).
247. 5 US Code §4501 *et seq.*

Protection provided by the Bankruptcy Code's priority preferences for earnings owed to employees can be illusory. Typically, it takes months or years to resolve the bankruptcy proceeding. Generally, payments are not made for fourth priority claims until the administrative process is nearing completion. And, more disastrous for employees is the possibility that there are insufficient unsecured assets to pay even part of the fourth priority claims.

301. The fifth priority in distribution of the general assets of a bankrupt is given to contributions owed to benefit plans (medical insurance, pension and the like) during the period up to 180 days prior to the filing of the bankruptcy petition or termination of the business (whichever was first) but is limited in amount to the number of employees times $12,850 less the amount paid to satisfy fourth priority debts. However, unlike wage and similar 'pay' claims, claims for employee benefit plan contributions are not necessarily entitled to first priority even when based upon work provided while the employing entity is under the Bankruptcy Court's jurisdiction. This is because contributions to employee benefits have been held to be distinguishable from wages, salaries and commissions, under bankruptcy law, and the first priority is statutorily specified only for the latter type of claim.[248]

In contrast, claims for payment of monies scheduled to be deducted from a worker's pay as the worker's contribution to such employee benefits plans may be entitled to the same treatment as claims to wages, salaries and commissions for purposes of establishing the priority of rights to the bankrupt's general assets.[249]

248. *Joint Indus. Bd.* v. *US*, 391 US 224 (1968); *US* v. *Embassy Restaurant*, 359 US 29 (1959). The cited case decisions rejected the contention that benefit plan contributions are the functional equivalent of wages paid and, therefore, are entitled to the same priority as wage claims. Senate Report No. 95–989, accompanying the Bankruptcy Act's 1978 amendments that granted fourth priority to claims for employee benefit contributions (later amended to fifth priority status) asserted that this change overruled the *Embassy Restaurant* decision because the new provision recognized that 'fringe benefits may be substituted for wage demands'. However, the House Report did not make the same assertion. Moreover, 11 US Code 503(b)(1)(A), which defines what is included in administrative expenses, speaks only of 'wages, salaries, and commissions for services rendered after the commencement of the case' with the exception of also including 'benefits awarded pursuant to a judicial proceeding or a proceeding of the NLRB as back pay attributable to any period of time occurring after commencement of the' bankruptcy proceeding. Even in that situation, the judicial award is not to be given first priority if it would substantially increase the likelihood that current employees will be laid off or terminated. This explicit exception respecting first priority payment of employee benefits pursuant to an adjudicative order suggests that Congress did not intend such first priority payments in any other benefit situations. *See also, Howard Delivery Service, Inc.* v. *Zurich American Insurance Co.*, 547 US 651 (2006) (holding that claims based on an employer's liability for workers' compensation benefits are not entitled to fifth priority status as an employee benefit plan claim).

249. *In re Carl R. Korte, Inc.*, 95 LRRM 3353 (USDC OH 1977).

Chapter 4. Equal Employment Opportunity

§1. Concept

302. The notion that employment decisions will be based on an individual's merit, and not on characteristics or traits unrelated to job performance, is an ideal embraced by most American workers.

303. However, it is important to understand that US law in fact does not require that all employees be treated equally or fairly. Most US employees (particularly in the private sector) are employees at will, who can be hired or fired for a good reason, a bad reason or no reason at all, so long as that reason is not one the law prohibits. Perhaps the most important prohibitions contained in US employment law are those that prohibit employers from making employment decisions on the basis of race, sex, color, religion, nationality, age or disability. These laws govern the actions of most US employers, public and private, and have led many Americans to believe they have a general right to fair and equal treatment, even though often no such right exists. Rather, employees covered by these laws have a right not to be discriminated against within the meaning of these statutes. However, because inequality in treatment between members of different races, or between the sexes, and the like, can be powerful evidence that an action was taken because of the prohibited motive, the spillover effect of US anti-discrimination laws has resulted in a measure of more equitable treatment for employees across the board. That is, the best way for an employer to avoid violating laws against specific prohibited forms of employment discrimination is to follow a policy of fair treatment for all employees.

304. American law has not always promoted the policy of equal employment opportunity. At times in its history, American law has tolerated or even encouraged or required the practice of some discrimination in employment opportunities. The most prominent victims of such policies have been persons of African descent, other racial minorities, women, religious minorities, immigrants, older workers and the disabled. In particular, the discriminatory treatment of African Americans, in employment as well as in other aspects of life, led the US Congress to consider legislation that would prohibit on-the-job discrimination because of race. This legislative initiative was quickly expanded to prohibit discrimination because of sex, religion and national origin as well. Legislation prohibiting discrimination against individuals age 40 or older because of their age and, most recently, against individuals with disabilities followed.

305. Many states have their own laws outlawing discrimination in employment on the basis of race, sex, age, religion, national origin or disability. The substantive protection of these laws closely mirror that provided in the federal legislation. Some states (and/or local governments), however, extend their anti-discrimination laws to protect groups who are not protected by federal legislation. A prominent example is state or local legislation that prohibits discrimination based on sexual orientation.

Often, moreover, state laws cover actions by small employers who are not covered by federal laws. An employer with fewer than 15 employees is not covered by most federal anti-discrimination statutes but may be covered by state anti-discrimination laws.

When an employer is covered by both federal and state anti-discrimination law, it must comply with both so long as the state law is consistent with the aims and objectives of the federal statute. State law that is more employee protective than federal law is not preempted by federal law.[250]

306. Because most state and local statutes are closely patterned after federal laws, and because the federal laws obviously apply nationwide, only the principal federal laws are described here. In any situation, it is important, however, to determine whether state or local laws provide additional protection.

§2. The Reconstruction Era Civil Rights Acts

I. Generally

307. After the Civil War, 1861–1865, and pursuant to the authority granted to Congress by the Thirteenth and Fourteenth amendments to the Constitution, a number of laws were adopted to undo the institution of slavery, to rectify its damage, and to prevent its resurgence. These laws, adopted in 1866, 1870 and 1871, are known as the Reconstruction Civil Rights Acts. For employment discrimination purposes, the most important are the statutes known as sections 1981 and 1983 (42 US Code §§1981, 1983). These statutes went largely unnoticed until the 1960s, when they became widely used to combat discrimination. They today remain important tools for combating discrimination in employment.[251]

---

250. *California Savings & Loan Assoc.* v. *Guerra*, 479 US 272 (1987).

251. Section 1985(3) [42 US Code §1985(3)] has also sometimes been used as a separate tool to combat discrimination, particularly in the state workplace. Like section 1983, section 1985(3) is a purely remedial statute that provides no substantive right in itself. Although section 1985(3) is not available to a person who can proceed under Title VII, a terminated employee who can otherwise prove the elements of a section 1985(3) claim may find protection from the statute. To be successful under section 1985(3), a plaintiff must prove: (1) a conspiracy, (2) for the purpose of depriving any person or class of persons of the equal protection of the laws, or of equal privileges and immunities under the laws, (3) an act in furtherance of the conspiracy, (4) where a person is injured in his person or property or deprived of any right or privilege of a citizen of the United States. *See Griffin* v. *Breckenridge*, 403 US 88 (1971); *Great American Federal Savings & Loan Ass'n* v. *Novotny*, 442 US 366 (1979). While termination of employment can satisfy the fourth prong, most claimants face an enormous challenge with the second prong, which requires proof of an identifiable class as well as proof of invidious discrimination to deny equal protection. *See*, for example, *Farber* v. *City of Paterson*, 440 F.3d 131 (3d Cir. 2006). Nonetheless, the section has been successfully used to challenge employment discrimination. *See Dickerson* v. *Alachua County Comm'n*, 200 F.3d 761 (11th Cir. 2000).

II. Section 1981

308. Section 1981, originally enacted in 1866 after ratification of the Thirteenth Amendment and reenacted in 1870 after ratification of the Fourteenth Amendment, is designed to ensure that all persons in the United States will have equal rights to make and enforce contracts without regard to race. Because the employment relationship is contractual, section 1981 provides a cause of action for race discrimination in the workplace. It is not limited to workplace discrimination, however, but applies to all contractual relationships. Thus, one need not be an employee to take advantage of section 1981. An independent contractor, for example, who was denied a contract because of his race could have a claim under section 1981.

The Supreme Court of the United States construed the words 'make and enforce contracts' narrowly by finding that those terms applied only to the initial formation or to the enforcement of a contract and not to discriminatory conduct that occurred after hiring.[252] Congress, however, in response to the Court's decision amended section 1981 to specify that the phrase 'make and enforce contracts includes the making, performance, modification, and termination of contracts, and the enjoyment of all benefits, privileges, terms and conditions of the contractual relationship'.[253] The statute, accordingly, now reaches post-hiring racial discrimination, including termination.

309. Section 1981 confers a substantive right to be free of race-based discrimination in the making and enforcement of contracts. It reaches only race discrimination; it does not apply to discrimination based on any other grounds, such as sex. The Supreme Court of the United States, however, has held that the statute protects all persons from race discrimination, not simply those who are racial minorities. Accordingly, Caucasians who have been discriminated against because of their race may bring a section 1981 claim.[254]

The Supreme Court, moreover, has construed the concept of race broadly for purposes of section 1981. In deciding what constitutes 'race' under section 1981, the Court looked to the common understanding of that term in the 19th century, when the statute was enacted. It thus found that race under section 1981 sweeps more broadly than the term 'race' is understood today and encompasses discrimination based on ancestry or ethnicity as well as anthropological categories.[255] Thus, section 1981 provides a remedy, for example, to Arabs, Jews, Hispanics, Greeks, Germans, and gypsies, if discriminated against because of their ancestry or ethnicity. It does not, however, provide a remedy for discrimination based solely on place of birth.

310. By its terms, section 1981 applies to race discrimination by both private and public employers. However, it is unclear whether a suit against a state or local governmental entity under section 1981 must confront the immunities and defenses

---

252. *Patterson* v. *McClean Credit Union*, 491 US 164 (1989).
253. 42 US Code §1981.
254. *McDonald* v. *Santa Fe Trail Transp. Co.*, 427 US 273 (1976).
255. *St. Francis College* v. *Al-Khazraji*, 481 US 604 (1987).

provided such employers under section 1983, discussed below. Moreover, federal employees may not use section 1981 to combat race discrimination by their federal government employers; they instead must look to Title VII alone.[256]

311. With the exception of federal employees, workers may bring suit under both section 1981 and Title VII.[257] The Supreme Court has held that enactment of Title VII, a statute aimed specifically at discrimination in employment, does not displace section 1981; both statutes are available to victims of racial discrimination in the workplace.[258]

Although both claims may be pursued simultaneously, a section 1981 claim has many advantages over a Title VII claim. It has a longer statute of limitations than does a Title VII claim. It does not require a plaintiff to pursue administrative proceedings before filing suit, as does Title VII. It does not require that an employer have 15 or more employees before coverage exists, as does Title VII. It does not depend upon a finding of employee (as opposed to independent contractor) status, as does Title VII. And it does not contain caps on the compensatory or punitive damages that may be awarded, as does Title VII. However, a plaintiff who sues under both statutes may not obtain a double recovery.

Unlike Title VII, which reaches discrimination based on sex, religion, color and national origin, except as explained in paragraph 309, above, section 1981 reaches only race-based discrimination. Importantly, moreover, section 1981 has been interpreted by the Supreme Court only to reach intentional discrimination based on race. The disparate impact theory of discrimination, explained below, is unavailable under section 1981.[259] Finally, while the claims may be pursued simultaneously, filing a charge with the Equal Employment Opportunity Commission (EEOC) under Title VII does not toll the running of the statute of limitations under section 1981.

III. Section 1983

312. Section 1983, enacted by Congress in 1871, provides a cause of action to persons who are deprived, under color of state law, of any right, privilege or immunity secured by the Constitution and laws of the United States.[260] Unlike section 1981, section 1983 creates no substantive rights but instead provides the means for obtaining a remedy in court for violations of constitutional and other federal rights.

In order for a section 1983 claim to exist, the deprivation must occur under color of state (or local) law. Unlike under section 1981 and modern employment discrimination statutes, section 1983 applies only to governmental acts. Purely private conduct is not actionable under section 1983. But when an employer is a governmental entity, section 1983 can be an important vehicle for remedying a government employer's violation of its employee's constitutional rights.

256. *Brown* v. *General Services Admin.*, 425 US 820 (1976). *See* paragraph 318, below.
257. *See* paragraph 318, below.
258. *Johnson* v. *Railway Express Agency*, 421 US 454 (1975).
259. *General Bldg. Contractors* v. *Pennsylvania*, 458 US 375 (1982).
260. 42 US Code §1983.

Section 1983, however, is a complex statute. To successfully bring a section 1983 claim, the defendant must be a 'person', who is acting under color of state law, and causes a person to be injured or deprived of rights secured by the constitution or laws of the United States.

313. For a section 1983 claim to exist, the plaintiff must allege a violation of the US constitution or of federal law. For purposes of a discussion concerning employment discrimination, the most important constitutional provision is the equal protection clause of the fourteenth amendment, which provides that 'no State shall ... deny to any person within its jurisdiction equal protection of the laws'. When a government employer discriminates on the basis of a 'suspect classification', its action is unconstitutional unless the government has a compelling interest for engaging in the discrimination. Race is a suspect class for purposes of the equal protection clause, and governmental actions based on race are subject to strict scrutiny by the courts.[261] Alienage classifications usually are also subject to strict scrutiny, unless the job involves direct participation 'in the formation, execution, or review of broad public policy'.[262]

In *Rutan* v. *Republican Party*, 497 US 62 (1990), the Supreme Court held, 5-4, that, with the exception of those employees who hold policy making positions, the First Amendment's constitutional protections of beliefs and association are violated when a government agency discriminates in the hiring or treatment of employees based on political belief or affiliation. Gender-based classifications, however, are subject to a less exacting standard, known as intermediate scrutiny, but that, too, is a rigorous test for a government to meet. A gender-based classification 'must serve important governmental objectives and must be substantially related to achievement of those objectives'.[263] Other classifications, such as those based on age, need only be rationally related to a legitimate government purpose, a far less stringent standard for the government to meet.[264]

314. Because public employers are constrained by employment discrimination statutes, as well as by the constitution, there is considerable overlap between section 1983 and these federal laws. For example, if a state or local government employee is denied a promotion because of her sex, she can allege that her rights under Title VII and under the equal protection clause have been violated, with the latter claim being brought under section 1983. Neither claim preempts the other; a plaintiff often may bring both a statutory and a constitutional claim. Advantages of

261. *City of Richmond* v. *J.A. Croson Co.*, 488 US 469 (1989) (all race-based classifications by state or local government subject to strict scrutiny).

262. *In re Griffiths*, 413 US 717 (1973) (state may not require applicants for admission to the bar to be US citizens); *Ambach* v. *Norwick*, 441 US 68 (1979) (state law forbidding aliens who would not apply for citizenship from serving as elementary and secondary school teachers was rationally related to promoting civic values).

263. *United States* v. *Virginia*, 515 US 518 (1996) (invalidating Virginia Military Institute's males-only policy).

264. *Massachusetts Board of Retirement* v. *Murgia*, 427 US 307 (1976) (state did not violate equal protection clause when it required state police officers to retire at age 50 because the law rationally related to the state's interest in having physically fit police officers).

bringing the section 1983 claim to remedy on-the-job discrimination include a longer statute of limitations, no need to exhaust administrative procedures, and exemption from the damages limitations often applicable to statutory claims.

The Supreme Court, however, has held the equal protection clause only prohibits intentional discrimination. The disparate impact theory, discussed below, is not available when pursuing an action based on the equal protection clause.[265] Although the disparate impact of a classification may be evidence it was adopted for an improper purpose, there is no constitutional violation unless the classification was adopted because of, not merely in spite of, its adverse effect on a protected group.[266] In deciding whether an act was motivated by the prohibited purpose, the analysis developed under Title VII of the Civil Rights Act of 1964 has been followed by the courts.

315. Section 1983 provides a cause of action against a 'person' who deprives another of constitutional rights under color of state law. Any flesh and blood person sued in her individual capacity is a person for purposes of section 1983. However, that person may have immunity from suit, as described in the next paragraph, below. Importantly, a state is not a person for section 1983 purposes, and thus a state (and its officers in their official capacities) may not be sued under section 1983.[267] There is one exception to this rule; a state official may be sued in his official capacity for prospective injunctive relief, as such actions are not regarded as actions against the state.[268]

Political subdivisions of the state (such as local governmental entities and their officials in their official capacities) are persons for purposes of section 1983. Thus, they may be sued under section 1983, although they may not be held liable for punitive damages in a section 1983 action. Moreover, the concept of *respondeat superior* does not apply in section 1983 actions, and local governments (and their officials sued in their official capacity) accordingly are liable only for actions taken pursuant to an official government policy or custom, not for wrongdoing by subordinate employees.[269] An act by an official with final policymaking authority can constitute an official government policy for section 1983 purposes.[270]

316. Often, a constitutional violation, such as a decision to dismiss someone because of her race, will occur at the hands of an individual supervisor in violation of his governmental employer's official policy. A section 1983 claim may be brought against any individual, whether the employee of a state or local government, when he is sued in his individual, as opposed to his official, capacity. All individuals are persons for purposes of section 1983 when sued in their individual capacities. But some persons may be entitled to immunity from suit.

Individuals acting in a legislative capacity are absolutely immune from suit in their individual capacity. Moreover, individuals sued in their individual capacity are

265. *Washington* v. *Davis*, 426 US 229 (1976).
266. *Personnel Administrator* v. *Feeney*, 442 US 256 (1979).
267. *Will* v. *Michigan Department of State Police*, 491 US 58 (1989).
268. *Ex Parte Young*, 209 US 123 (1908).
269. *Monell* v. *Department of Social Services*, 436 US 658 (1978).
270. *Pembaur* v. *City of Cincinnati*, 475 US 469 (1986).

entitled to qualified immunity from suit when their conduct did not violate a 'clearly established constitutional right of which a reasonable person would have known'.[271] In many employment discrimination cases this immunity is unavailable because a reasonable individual should know that dismissing government workers because of their race, sex, etc., violates the Fourteenth Amendment's equal protection clause.

317. The absence of *respondeat superior* liability and the presence of various immunities from suit can make section 1983 litigation complex. For example, it presently is unclear whether these requisites of section 1983, and its period of limitations for bringing suit, apply to section 1981 claims brought against state or local governmental entities.[272] But it is clear that such limitations do not apply to other statutory employment discrimination claims, such as Title VII, the Age Discrimination in Employment Act and the Americans with Disabilities Act. Accordingly, the statutory claims, that may be asserted directly against the governmental entity (unless Eleventh Amendment immunity attaches, as explained in the next numbered paragraph), often are viewed as a more attractive remedy, despite the advantages of section 1983, outlined above. Moreover, because these statutory claims apply to both private and public employers, they are the most common vehicles used to police employment discrimination.

§3. Title VII of the Civil Rights Act of 1964

318. Title VII of the Civil Rights Act of 1964 (42 US Code §2000e, *et seq.*) prohibits employers whose business affects interstate commerce and who employ 15 or more persons for each work day of at least 20 weeks a year from discriminating against any employee or applicant for employment on the basis of race, color, sex, religion or national origin. An employee is counted for coverage purposes for each day on the employer's payroll, whether or not the employee is actually working each of those days.[273] The law also applies to unions and to employment agencies.

The statutory definition of employer includes the agents of that employer. Accordingly, an employer may be held vicariously liable for the discriminatory actions of its supervisory employees and others acting in an agency capacity. The agents themselves cannot be held personally liable for violations of Title VII.

---

271. *Harlow* v. *Fitzgerald*, 457 US 800 (1982).
272. A separate statute, 28 US Code § 1658, establishes a four year period of limitations for federal claims. Several US Courts of Appeals have ruled that the period of limitations in § 1983 suits is based on the period for bringing a tort suit under the law of the state where the action arose and that a discrimination claim against a government entity, rather than against a government employee, is available under § 1983 but not under §1981. *See*, for example, *McGovern* v. *City of Philadelphia,* 554 F.3d 114 (3d Cir. 2009) and *Campbell* v. *Forest Preserve Dist.*, 752 F.3d 665 (7th Cir. 2014). Contra, *Federation of African American Contractors* v. *City of Oakland,* 93 F.3d 1204 (9th Cir. 1996) (holding that 1990 amendments to §1981 created an implied separate discrimination claim against state entities).
273. *Walters* v. *Metropolitan Educ. Enter., Inc.*, 519 US 202 (1997).

State and local governments are included in the definition of 'employer' under the Act and, therefore, are subject to the Act's general enforcement structure. The Act separately prohibits employment discrimination by the federal government, but it does so in a manner that excludes the federal government from the Act's normal enforcement procedures. Federal employees have separate administrative processes for enforcement of the Act.

States (as opposed to political subdivisions of the state or government officials wielding authority under color of state law) enjoy Eleventh Amendment immunity from damages suits by individuals, unless that immunity has been waived by the state itself or by Congress. Congress may waive states' 11th amendment immunity only when enacting legislation pursuant to a later amendment such as the Fourteenth Amendment. The Supreme Court has held that Congress validly enacted Title VII pursuant to the Fourteenth Amendment and validly waived the states' immunity from suit under that statute.[274] Accordingly, individuals may sue states in either federal or state court for violation of their Title VII rights.

Title VII's prohibitions against discrimination are enforced by a federal administrative agency, the Equal Employment Opportunity Commission. If the EEOC decides not to bring an enforcement action, a private enforcement suit is available in state or federal court. The EEOC and the enforcement procedures for Title VII claims are described in Part III, below.

319. Title VII applies to discrimination in the terms, conditions and privileges of employment. Even if an employer is not contractually required to provide a benefit, it may not dispense benefits in a discriminatory manner.[275] Presently, the lower courts disagree on how significant an employment action must be for Title VII liability to attach. While some find that any employment action that is wrongfully motivated may violate the statute, even if the action is not particularly harmful, others require a materially adverse employment action before a Title VII claim may be stated. The Supreme Court, however, has ruled that an employment action must be materially adverse in order to support a claim of retaliation under Title VII, but it remains unclear how its decision will apply to non-retaliatory liability under Title VII.[276]

320. Two theories of discrimination are available under Title VII: disparate treatment and disparate impact. In order for a disparate treatment claim to exist, there must be an intent to discriminate on the part of the employer. Intent is not the same thing as animus, hatred or ill will, although animus may well be present when an employer discriminates. Instead, the intent requirement is satisfied if the challenged action was taken because of the employee's race, sex or other protected characteristic, whether or not animus motivated the action.[277] For example, an employer that

274. *Fitzpatrick* v. *Bitzer*, 427 US 445 (1976).
275. *Hishon* v. *King & Spalding*, 467 US 69 (1984).
276. *Burlington Northern & Santa Fe Railway* v. *White*, 548 US 53 (2006).
277. *Los Angeles Dept. of Water & Power* v. *Manhart*, 435 US 702 (1978).

does not harbor animus against women nevertheless is guilty of intentional discrimination if it refuses to hire a woman for a position because of a business concern that its customers would rather interact with a man.

A disparate impact claim, in contrast, does not depend on the presence of an intent to discriminate. Instead, a facially neutral practice, adopted and applied without any intent to discriminate, may violate the statute if it more harshly impacts a protected group and if the practice is not job-related and consistent with business necessity.[278]

As a result of amendments to Title VII in 1991, disparate treatment claims now may be tried to a jury if either party so desires. There is no jury trial available for disparate impact claims which, instead, are tried by the court.

I. Disparate Treatment Theory

321. Most Title VII claims are individual claims of disparate treatment. An individual worker claims that (s)he was not hired, or was dismissed, or otherwise adversely treated, because of race, sex or other protected characteristic. The key to a disparate treatment claim is the existence of discriminatory intent or motive, and it is the plaintiff who has the burden of proving that the prohibited intent actually motivated the challenged action. Much of the law surrounding Title VII has been dedicated to determining how unlawful intent may be proved, as it is the unusual case in which an employer admits it acted because of an employee's race, sex, religion or national origin. Accordingly, unlawful motive most often is proved through circumstantial evidence.

322. In most circumstantial evidence cases, a plaintiff can create an inference of unlawful intent by establishing what is referred to as a *McDonnell Douglas* prima facie case.[279] A *McDonnell Douglas* prima facie case generally is stated when a plaintiff establishes (1) that he is a member of a protected class, (2) that he was qualified for the position at issue, (3) that he was not hired, was fired or suffered some other adverse action, and (4) that persons outside his protected class were treated differently. Proof of these four factors creates a mandatory, rebuttable presumption that the challenged action was impermissibly motivated.

Establishment of the prima facie case transfers to the defendant the burden of production to articulate a legitimate, nondiscriminatory reason for its action.[280] Once the defendant articulates its legitimate, nondiscriminatory reason, the mandatory presumption of unlawful motive drops from the case. The reason put forward by the defendant need not be fair, sensible, or even the actual reason for the action; it need only be a nondiscriminatory reason. As a practical matter, however, a reason that appears flimsy, unreasonable or false is less likely to be credited by the factfinder.

If the defendant articulates a nondiscriminatory reason for its action, the plaintiff must prove that the real reason for the challenged action was the prohibited one. The

278. *Griggs* v. *Duke Power Co.*, 401 US 424 (1971).
279. *McDonnell Douglas Corp.* v. *Green*, 411 US 792 (1973).
280. *Texas Dep't of Community Affairs* v. *Burdine*, 450 US 248 (1981).

factfinder's disbelief of the reason put forward by the defendant does not entitle the plaintiff to judgment as a matter of law,[281] but disbelief of the proffered reason, coupled with the evidence underlying the prima facie case, may support decision in favor of the plaintiff.[282]

Sometimes, the judge or jury will believe that multiple reasons motivated a challenged action. For example, the jury may find that a woman was denied a promotion at least in part because of her sex, while also believing that performance problems motivated the employer's decision. Such cases are referred to as 'mixed motive' cases. In *Price-Waterhouse* v. *Hopkins*, the Supreme Court held that when the plaintiff proves that the unlawful motive was a substantial motivating factor for the challenged decision, the burden of persuasion passes to the defendant to prove that it would have made the same decision even if it had not taken the protected characteristic into account.[283]

However, Congress responded to the *Price-Waterhouse* decision by amending Title VII to provide that liability is established when the plaintiff proves that the unlawful factor was a motivating one. The plaintiff may prove that the unlawful factor was a motivating factor by direct evidence or by strong circumstantial evidence.[284] The defendant's proof that it would have made the same decision anyway goes only to remedies, not to liability. A defendant that proves it would have made the same decision anyway will not be ordered to instate or reinstate the plaintiff or to provide backpay or other monetary relief. The plaintiff, however, may receive declaratory relief and be awarded attorneys' fees even if the employer establishes its remedial defense. Congress amended Title VII only with respect to status-based discrimination--that is, discrimination on the basis of race, color, religion, sex, or national origin, in hiring, firing, salary structure, promotion and the like. The Supreme Court has held that the amendment was not intended to apply to the anti-retaliation provisions of Title VII. Thus, to prove a claim that the employer violated the anti-retaliation provisions of Title VII (discussed further in paragraph 345 below), the plaintiff must prove that his or her protected conduct was the but-for cause of the adverse employment action--that is, that the challenged employment action would not have occurred but for the employer's desire to retaliate.[285]

Likewise, the Supreme Court has refused to extend the 'motivating factor' standard of causation (for status-based discrimination claims under Title VII) to claims under other anti-discrimination statutes. For example, the Court has held that claims under the Age Discrimination in Employment Act of 1967 (ADEA)(discussed in paragraph 346, below) require proof that the prohibited criterion was the but-for cause of the prohibited conduct.[286]

323. Claims against an employer charged with engaging in a pattern or practice of unlawful discrimination are referred to as systemic claims of disparate treatment. The focus in these cases is on whether such a discriminatory practice exists, rather

281. *St. Mary's Honor Ctr.* v. *Hicks*, 509 US 502 (1993).
282. *Reeves* v. *Sanderson Plumbing*, 530 US 133 (2000).
283. *Price Waterhouse* v. *Hopkins*, 490 US 228 (1989).
284. *Desert Palace, Inc.* v. *Costa*, 539 US 90 (2003).
285. *Univ. of Texas Sw. Med. Ctr.* v. *Nassar*, 133 S. Ct. 2517, 2528, 186 L. Ed. 2d 503 (2013).
286. *Gross* v. *FBL Financial Services, Inc.*, 557 US 167 (2009).

than on the treatment of particular individuals. Occasionally, the challenged practice is facially discriminatory; an employer, for example, may announce that it is only hiring males or females for a particular job. In those cases, no search for intent need occur. Instead, the question in such cases is whether a defense, such as a bona fide occupational qualification, as discussed in the next numbered paragraph, is proven.

More often, there is no announced intent to discriminate, and the focus, as in individual disparate treatment claims, is on whether the employer's actions are being taken for a discriminatory purpose. Usually evidence of unlawful motive is statistical in nature; a statistically significant disparity between the employer's workforce and the relevant labor pool from which it is drawn may supply an inference of unlawful motive.[287] For example, if a school district has virtually no black teachers despite a significant number of black teachers working in the geographical area, an inference of race discrimination may be drawn from the disparity between the active number of black teachers working for the school district and the number of black teachers available for hire. The statistical evidence is usually bolstered by anecdotal evidence of individual instances of discrimination.[288]

If the plaintiffs establish the existence of a pattern or practice of discrimination, the burden of proof will be on the employer to prove that individuals within the class were not in fact victims of the unlawful practice.

II. Bona Fide Occupational Qualifications

324. An employer does not violate Title VII when it discriminates on the basis of sex, religion, or national origin if sex, religion or national origin is a bona fide occupational qualification (commonly referred to as a BFOQ) for the job. There is no BFOQ for race. A BFOQ is one in which the protected characteristic is reasonably necessary for the normal operation of the business. It is the employer's burden to prove that a BFOQ.

325. The Supreme Court has taken a very narrow approach to what may constitute a BFOQ. The aspect of the job for which sex, religion or national origin is alleged to be necessary must go to the essence of the employer's business. For example, an employer's concerns about the welfare of its employees' unborn children or about possible future tort liability for fetal harm were insufficient to permit the employer to insist that fertile women (but not fertile men) be excluded from lead exposure jobs in a battery making plant. The essence of the employer's business was making batteries. Because fertile women were as capable of assembling batteries as other workers, the employer could not exclude them from its battery making operations without violating Title VII.[289]

---

287. *International Brotherhood of Teamsters* v. *United States*, 431 US 324 (1977).
288. *Hazelwood School District* v. *United States*, 433 US 299 (1977).
289. *International Union, UAW* v. *Johnson Controls*, 499 US 187 (1991).

326. Although the BFOQ defense is a narrow one, it can be satisfied. Lower courts, for example, have found that concerns over privacy may entitle an employer to insist that certain positions, such as restroom attendants, be of a particular sex.

III. Affirmative Action

327. Although the term 'affirmative action' has been applied in differing contexts, it generally is used to refer to the practice of employers giving a preference to minorities and women in employment. Opponents of affirmative action often refer to the concept as 'reverse discrimination'.

Because Title VII prohibits discrimination on the basis of race and sex, and because Caucasians and men are both protected by Title VII, the question becomes whether an employer's decision to prefer minority and/or female applicants for positions because of their race or sex violates Title VII by discriminating against white males. Also, because the equal protection clause generally prohibits public employers from discriminating on the basis of race or sex, affirmative action by public employers may run afoul of the Constitution. Finally, under Executive Order 11246, many federal contractors are required to adopt an affirmative action program as a condition of doing business with the federal government.

328. The Supreme Court has upheld affirmative action under Title VII when plans are adopted for remedial purposes. Despite statutory language that may be read as categorically prohibiting any discrimination on the basis of race or sex, benign or otherwise, the Supreme Court held that affirmative action, so long as carefully limited, is within the spirit of Title VII and thus is not unlawful.[290] The Court found that Congress did not intend to prohibit voluntary race conscious decision making by an employer designed to overcome an historical lack of minority workers in the employer's workforce. The Court has extended its rationale to encompass affirmative action programs that favor women.[291]

However, in upholding the use of a remedial affirmative action plan in both of these Title VII cases, the Court explained that such plans must satisfy a two-prong test. First, the plans must be aimed at correcting 'a manifest imbalance in a traditionally segregated job category'. Such an imbalance will exist when there is a disparity between the minorities or women in the employer's workforce and those in the relevant labor pool from which the workforce is drawn. For example, in *Johnson* v. *Transportation Agency of Santa Clara County*, a comparison between the number of women holding skilled trades positions for Santa Clara County (0 percent) and the number of women working in skilled trades jobs in the local area (5 percent) was enough to justify giving women a preference for such positions. The Court, however, did not specify how great a disparity must exist, other than to hold that it need not be great enough to support a prima facie case of discrimination by the employer. In other words, societal discrimination, as reflected by the manifest imbalance in a traditionally segregated job category, will justify an employer's use

290. *United Steelworkers of America* v. *Weber*, 443 US 193 (1979).
291. *Johnson* v. *Transportation Agency of Santa Clara County*, 480 US 616 (1987).

of voluntary affirmative action under Title VII. Second, the plan must not 'unnecessarily trammel' the interests of majority group members. For example, while an affirmative action plan may be used to decide among similarly qualified applicants for a position, none of whom has any entitlement to the job, it does not necessarily follow that an employer could lay off employees out of seniority order in order to retain less senior minority and female workers. Moreover, an affirmative action plan may be used only to attain, and not to maintain, a racially balanced workforce.

To date, the Supreme Court has considered the lawfulness of affirmative action plans under Title VII only when a remedial purpose was put forward to justify the plan. The Supreme Court has not decided whether a remedial purpose is the only one that will satisfy Title VII or whether a non-remedial purpose may support affirmative action under Title VII.[292]

329. Public employers, state and federal, must comply not only with the commands of Title VII but also must satisfy constitutional requirements when taking race or sex into account. The Supreme Court has held that race-based classifications must satisfy strict scrutiny analysis, even if the classification is made pursuant to an affirmative action program.[293] Accordingly, race-based classifications, even those that are benign, are permitted only if there is a compelling state interest for race conscious decision making by public employers. Importantly, the Court has held that remedying the effects of societal discrimination is not a compelling enough interest to support a race-based classification; only prima facie proof of an employer's own prior discrimination is a compelling enough state interest to support an affirmative action program adopted for a remedial purpose. The standard for justifying considering race in making a selection among candidates requires a showing that all factors relevant to accomplishing the government's legitimate goals are weighed and that the goals cannot be achieved without weighing race as a decisional factor.[294] As a result, Title VII allows employers more latitude to engage in affirmative action on behalf of racial minorities than does the US Constitution. Thus, private employers have more leeway to engage in affirmative action than do public employers. Because sex-based classifications are subject to less demanding scrutiny under the equal protection clause than are race-based classifications, arguably public employers have more freedom to engage in affirmative action in favor of women than for racial minorities. On the other hand, an affirmative action remedy imposed on a private employer by a court or administrative agency would constitute government action and be subject to the same strict standard for a government entity's consideration of race as a selection factor.

330. The government of the United States is the nation's, and probably the world's, largest single consumer of goods and services. Its business dealings include such diverse activities as financing privately or institutionally performed contracts to do research, construct buildings, purchase military materials, procure paper, fuel,

292. *Fisher* v. *Univ. of Texas*, 570 US 297 (2013).

293. *Richmond* v. *J.A. Croson Co.*, 488 US 469 (1989); *Adarand Constructors, Inc.* v. *Pena*, 515 US 200 (1995).

294. *Fisher* v. *Univ. of Texas*, 570 US 297 (2013).

computers, food, books, etc. As a result, there are few large employers in the United States that do not do business with the federal government. In addition, many small and medium sized businesses, and a few large ones, rely on the federal government as the sole or predominant purchaser of their services or products.

American Presidents, starting with Franklin Roosevelt, have issued or maintained executive orders conditioning the ability of businesses to contract with the federal government upon their taking steps to end employment discrimination. Currently, Executive Order 11246, subject to a few exceptions, prohibits any contractor or subcontractor doing at least $10,000 in annual business with the federal government from engaging in employment discrimination based on race, color, religion, national origin, sex, sexual orientation, or gender identity. It also requires non-construction contractors that have contracts or subcontracts with the federal government worth $50,000 or more, and that have 50 or more employees, to adopt a written affirmative action program. Many aspects of these programs, such as the need to publicize job openings and to recruit minority and female applicants, are relatively noncontroversial. However, Executive Order 11246 also requires non-construction contractors subject to its commands to implement an eight-factor 'utilization analysis' to determine whether minorities and women are 'underutilized' in the employer's workforce, and if so, to set goals and timetables for ending such underutilization. The employer then must make a good faith effort to meet the goals within the established time frame. Construction contractors must also have affirmative action plans, but their regulation is more tightly controlled by the Office of Federal Contract Compliance Programs (OFCCP). Construction contractors must validate section criteria and offer on-the-job training and apprenticeships for minorities and women. The OFCCP issues goals and timetables for minority employment by region for construction contractors.

The Executive Order does not mandate that women or minorities be given a preference for job openings, but questions nonetheless have been raised about the constitutionality of the Executive Order. As of this writing, its dictates are being enforced..

IV. Disparate Impact

331. Although disparate treatment claims depend upon a finding of unlawful intent or motive, Title VII also prohibits practices that are 'fair in form but discriminatory in operation'. An employment practice adopted and applied without any discriminatory intent may still violate Title VII if it has a disparate impact on a protected group.

The Supreme Court recognized the concept of disparate impact in the early days of Title VII. In *Griggs* v. *Duke Power Co.*, the Court found a violation of Title VII when an employer required new hires and those transferring within the company to have a high school diploma and to achieve a certain score on a standardized test. These practices screened out disproportionately more blacks than whites. Although the requirements were adopted without any intent to discriminate on the basis of race, and although the requirements were applied across the board to all employees regardless of race, their disparate impact on black applicants and employees violated the statute because the requirements were not necessary for successful job performance.[295]

In 1991, after Supreme Court decisions signaling a retreat from *Griggs*, Congress amended Title VII to codify the disparate impact theory. Under the statute, it is the plaintiff's burden to prove that a facially neutral practice adversely impacts on a protected group. Generally speaking, the plaintiff must identify the particular practice or practices that are causing the impact; (s)he may not simply point to a disparity between the racial make-up of the employer's workforce and that of the relevant labor pool but instead must demonstrate that a particular policy or practice of the employer is falling more harshly on the protected group. Only if the elements of the employer's selection process are incapable of separation may the plaintiff rely on the 'bottom line' results of an employer's practices to support an impact claim. Conversely, even when there is no disparity between the racial make-up of the employer's workforce and the labor pool from which it is drawn, an impact claim may still exist if the employer uses a particular practice that impacts a protected group more harshly than others. A racially balanced bottom line will not preclude the existence of an impact claim.[296]

Once a plaintiff establishes that a particular practice or practices adversely impacts a protected group, the burden of persuasion passes to the employer to prove that the challenged practice is 'job-related for the position in question and consistent with business necessity'. The precise meaning to be given this defense is unclear. Certainly, it is a less demanding burden than the showing required to support a bona fide occupational qualification, discussed in paragraph 324, above, but at the same time, the defense requires considerably more from an employer than simply identifying a legitimate business goal served by the challenged practice. Even if the employer is able to prove a business necessity defense, a plaintiff may still prevail on a disparate impact claim if the employer refused to adopt a proposed alternative business practice shown to meet the employer's business objectives but with less impact on a protected class of employees.

332. The Supreme Court has not determined the quantum of impact needed to support a disparate impact claim. A measure often used, however, is what is known as the '4/5ths' rule. Under this rule, if the success rate for a group is less than 80 percent of the success rate of the group with the highest success rate, then the necessary quantum of impact will likely be found. For example, if 1,000 men take a test and 900 pass, then males have a 90 percent success rate on the test; if 500 women take the same test and only 250 pass, then women have a 50 percent success rate on the test. Because the women's 50 percent pass rate is less than 80 percent of the male pass rate, the test would have an adverse impact on women under the 4/5ths rule. Of course, more sophisticated statistical techniques are also often used to establish the existence of actionable impact.

---

295. *Griggs* v. *Duke Power Co.*, 401 US 424 (1971).
296. *Connecticut* v. *Teal*, 457 US 440 (1982).

333. One practice that is immune from disparate impact attack is seniority. It is not uncommon for an employer's use of a seniority system to have an impact on minorities and women because in many workplaces these workers will have less seniority than white males. Title VII, however, expressly shelters seniority systems from disparate impact claims. On the other hand, a seniority system adopted or maintained for a discriminatory purpose may be challenged using disparate treatment theory.

V. Pregnancy Discrimination

334. Title VII prohibits discrimination because of sex. However, the statute does not define the term. At the time of Title VII's enactment, congressional focus was on race, not sex, discrimination. The prohibition against sex discrimination was added shortly before the bill was passed, with no meaningful debate or attention given to the term's meaning.

When the Supreme Court first confronted the scope of the prohibition against sex discrimination in a case involving pregnancy discrimination, it reasoned that a pregnancy-based classification was not a sex-based classification, because the class of non-pregnant workers included both men and women. Congress reacted to the Court's decision by enacting the Pregnancy Discrimination Act (the PDA), which amended Title VII to clarify that 'because of sex' includes because of 'pregnancy, childbirth and related medical conditions'. The statute provides that 'women affected by pregnancy, childbirth and related medical conditions shall be treated the same for all employment-related programs, including receipt of benefits under fringe benefit programs, as other persons not so affected but similar in their ability or inability to work'.[297] Accordingly, Title VII now considers discrimination because of pregnancy to be sex-based discrimination. The contrary approach pursued by the Supreme Court, however, still controls in constitutional claims. A pregnancy-based classification is not a sex-based classification for equal protection clause purposes.[298]

335. Although Title VII now protects women from pregnancy-based discrimination, it is important to understand the limits of that protection, particularly as compared to the protections extended pregnant women by many other industrialized countries. By its terms, Title VII does not compel an employer to provide an employee any leave for childbirth or to provide health insurance coverage for childbirth. It only requires that pregnancy be treated the same as other similar conditions. Thus, if an employer offers health insurance coverage to its employees, it may not exclude pregnancy from coverage. And if an employer provides its employees with a leave of absence (paid or unpaid) for health conditions that render them unable to work, pregnant women must be offered the same leaves. Title VII does not require an employer to provide any maternity or child rearing leaves, and if an

297. 42 US Code §2000e(k).
298. *Geduldig* v. *Aiello*, 417 US 484 (1974).

employer does not provide a leave of absence for individuals who are able to work, then the refusal to provide women with maternity leave does not violate Title VII.

The Supreme Court has ruled that if a state chooses to require an employer to provide a maternity leave, even though the state does not mandate leaves for other purposes, that state law is not preempted by Title VII. The Court rejected arguments that a California statute mandating allowing four months of unpaid leave to women following the birth of a child discriminated against men.[299] The Court found that the PDA was intended by Congress to be 'a floor, not a ceiling', thus allowing states to mandate preferential treatment of pregnancy. This reasoning likely would extend to an employer's voluntary decision to provide maternity leave, but not other forms of unpaid leave, to its workers.

The Court, however, will allow such preferential treatment only for the time the woman is unable to work due to childbirth. Thus, an employer that allowed women, but not men, childrearing leaves presumably would be in violation of Title VII. While only women give birth, and are thus medically incapacitated by the birth of a child, both men and women can care for a child. Thus, an employer must permit both men and women, or neither, to enjoy childrearing leaves. This reasoning serves to invalidate so-called 'female protective laws' adopted by many states before Title VII's enactment. These female protective laws, which often limited the hours women could work, imposed limits on heavy lifting or limited night time work, conflict with Title VII's equal treatment mandate. Such laws are therefore preempted by Title VII.

Although Title VII does not require an employer to provide a leave of absence for pregnancy, childbirth or child rearing, that requirement is contained in another federal law, the FMLA. However, the FMLA, described, above, in paragraph 260, only applies to employers with 50 or more employees and only to those employees who have worked for the employer a stated minimum number of hours during the previous 12 months and who have not exhausted the FMLA maximum annual leave entitlement, so its coverage is less extensive than that of Title VII.

VI. Sexual Harassment

336. The Supreme Court has determined that discrimination because of sex encompasses a prohibition against sexual harassment. Since the mid-1980s, there has been considerable focus on sexual harassment in the courts, in the media, and in the American workplace. Many companies have policies against sexual harassment and often provide training to educate the workforce on the do's and don'ts of appropriate workplace behavior in order to avoid sexual harassment claims.

Both men and women can assert sexual harassment claims, and the claim also encompasses same sex harassment. If the victim is the target of the harassment because of his/her sex, then the causation element is satisfied. When the conduct is

299. *California Savings and Loan Assoc.* v. *Guerra*, 479 US 272 (1987).

sexual in nature and occurs between the sexes, it is generally inferred that the harassment was directed at the victim because of her sex. Determining whether harassment was motivated by the victim's sex becomes more difficult in same sex harassment cases or when the harassment, even when occurring between men and women, was not sexual in nature. Nonetheless, that causation element must be satisfied before a sexual harassment claim exists.

337. If an employee's rejection of a sexual advance results in a tangible job detriment, the employer is liable for sexual harassment. For example, if a supervisor fires an employee who refuses his sexual advances, the employer is liable for sexual harassment. This form of sexual harassment is often referred to as *quid pro quo* sexual harassment. The controverted issues in most cases of *quid pro quo* sexual harassment are whether the alleged conduct in fact occurred and, if so, whether the employee's rejection of the supervisor's sexual advance was the cause of the adverse employment action suffered.

338. A sexual harassment claim also may be based on a hostile work environment theory. In these cases, unlike in *quid pro quo* claims, the employee need not point to any tangible job detriment suffered as a result of the harassment.

In order for an employee to prevail on a claim that she was the victim of sexual harassment resulting in a hostile work environment, she must show that she was the victim of sexual conduct that was unwelcome and that was sufficiently severe or pervasive so as to alter the conditions of employment and create an abusive work environment.[300] Thus, while no tangible job detriment need be shown, the conduct complained of must be relatively egregious. No bright-line test exists for making this determination. All of the circumstances surrounding the harassment, including its frequency, severity and form, will be considered in deciding whether it is severe or pervasive enough to state a claim.

When a supervisor creates the hostile work environment, the employer is liable for the supervisor's actions unless it can establish an affirmative defense. If an employer can show it 'exercised reasonable care to prevent and correct promptly any sexually harassing behavior' and that 'the plaintiff employee unreasonably failed to take advantage of any preventive or corrective opportunities provided by the employer or to avoid harm otherwise', it will not be liable for a hostile work environment created by its supervisory personnel.[301] This affirmative defense is available only in hostile work environment cases; the defense does not apply to *quid pro quo* claims. An employer lacking any policy prohibiting sexual harassment would find it difficult to establish the affirmative defense. Thus, the defense gives employers a powerful incentive to adopt and to enforce effective policies against sexual harassment. The Supreme Court has upheld the theory of constructive discharge under Title VII, holding that employees may have a Title VII claim if they quit because of 'unendurable' working conditions (a 'constructive' discharge), but

300. *Meritor Savings Bank* v. *Vinson*, 477 US 57 (1986).
301. *Faragher* v. *City of Boca Raton*, 524 US 775 (1998).

the Court also found that the above-stated affirmative defenses may be applicable in constructive discharge cases as well.[302]

While only supervisory personnel can engage in *quid pro quo* harassment, co-workers and even customers may engage in actions that create a hostile working environment. Although the Supreme Court has not confronted such a case, the lower courts have imposed liability on employers for hostile work environments created by co-workers or customers when the employer knew or should have known of the harassment and failed to take steps to correct it.[303]

339. Although most harassment cases involve sexual harassment, harassment cases can be based on racial or national origin harassment as well. An employee who is the target of offensive conduct that is racially motivated, for example, may bring a claim for a racially hostile work environment. The requirements that the conduct be sufficiently severe or pervasive apply in these cases as well, as do the employer liability principles established in the sexual harassment context.

VII. Sexual Orientation

340. Although the Supreme Court has not confronted the issue, the lower courts are in agreement that Title VII's prohibition against discrimination 'because of sex' does not encompass discrimination because of sexual orientation. Numerous attempts have failed in the effort to amend Title VII to provide protection against discrimination because of sexual orientation.[304] President Obama, however, expanded the Executive Orders prohibiting employment discrimination in federal employment and by those contracting with the federal government so as to include discrimination based on sexual orientation. Many states and localities, moreover, provide such protection. Close to half the states, the District of Columbia, Puerto Rico and Guam have laws protecting all employees from discrimination based on sexual orientation and many of these laws also specify protection based on gender identity. Additional states by statute or executive order provide such protection for their government employees. Many of these laws exclude employers that are religious organizations. Hundreds of companies also have employment policies protecting their lesbian, gay, bisexual and transgender employees.[305]

In 2013, the Supreme Court struck down the Defense of Marriage Act, a federal law designed to deprive same sex married couples of the rights and privileges enjoyed by married heterosexual couples, holding that the law violated the equal protection clause of the Fifth Amendment of the US Constitution.[306] This decision did much to further equality for gays and lesbians, at least under federal law.

302. *Pennsylvania State Police* v. *Suders*, 542 US 129 (2006).
303. *See*, for example, *Summa* v. *Hofstra Univ.*, 708 F.3d 115 (2d Cir. 2013).
304. HR 1755; S. 815 was the most recent effort.
305. *See*, *United States* v. *Windsor*, 133 S. Ct. 2675, 2693 (2013).
306. *United States* v. *Windsor*, above.

VIII. National Origin Claims

341. Title VII's prohibition against discrimination because of national origin protects individuals from discrimination based on their country of birth or the country from which their ancestors came. Discrimination against someone because of his or her ethnicity would fall within this prohibition. Title VII, however, does not protect against discrimination based on citizenship.

Over the years, a number of cases have arisen involving an individual's foreign accent or inability to speak English. While the courts have had little difficulty upholding job requirements that require employees to be able to understand and to speak English, if such requirements are legitimately job-related, claims involving discrimination based on accent have proved difficult for the courts. Generally speaking, the courts have permitted an employer to discriminate against an employee because of his foreign accent only when the accent interferes with the ability to do the job. For example, if an individual's heavy accent makes his English difficult to understand, and the job at issue requires oral communication with the public, the employer may rely on the accent in denying the applicant the position.[307]

342. Although Title VII does not protect individuals from discrimination based on citizenship, the Immigration Reform and Control Act (IRCA), 8 USCS §§1101 *et seq.*, makes it unlawful for employers to hire an unauthorized alien. An unauthorized alien is one in the United States illegally or who is not authorized to work. The IRCA, additionally, makes it unlawful to discriminate on the basis of citizenship status against US citizens or those who are intending to become citizens. An employer remains free to discriminate on the basis of citizenship against authorized aliens who are not intending to become citizens.

The IRCA requires employers to verify that every individual seeking employment is not an undocumented alien. Various documents may be used to satisfy this requirement, including a passport, birth certificate, 'green card' (work visa issued by the Immigration and Naturalization Service), certificate of US citizenship, drivers' license and social security card.

IX. Religious Discrimination

343. Title VII prohibits discrimination on the basis of religion, and the statute defines religion to encompass religious observances and practices, as well as religious beliefs. While organized or established religions obviously are encompassed within the definition of religion, the term is understood to apply more broadly, reaching an individual's sincerely held moral or ethical beliefs, even if those beliefs are not embraced by an established religion.

In addition to prohibiting discrimination on the basis of religion, Title VII also imposes a duty on employers to reasonably accommodate their employees' religious beliefs, observances and practices, unless the accommodation would pose an undue hardship on the employer. Most of the religion cases brought under Title VII

307. *Fragante* v. *City and County of Honolulu*, 888 F.2d 591 (1989).

deal with the question of reasonable accommodation. An employee, for example, may request exemption from work on Sunday because of his religious beliefs or an employee may seek permission to wear religious garb that conflicts with a company's dress code.

The duty of reasonable accommodation of religion imposed by Title VII is not onerous. The Supreme Court has held that an accommodation that would pose more than a *de minimis* cost on employers is an undue hardship and thus not a reasonable one.[308] For example, paying another employee overtime to make up for a co-worker's Sunday absence would be more than a *de minimis* cost and thus would be an undue hardship. Additionally, the Court has determined that an employer is not required to provide the accommodation preferred by an employee. So long as the employer offers a reasonable accommodation, it has met its duty under Title VII, even if a different accommodation preferred by the employee and rejected by the employer would not pose an undue hardship.[309]

344. Title VII provides three exceptions to its prohibitions against religious discrimination. First, the statute permits a religious institution or corporation to discriminate on the basis of religion. This exemption is a very narrow one and generally has been recognized only when the employer is wholly or partially owned by a church. When recognized, however, the exemption extends to all of the institution's positions, not only its clergy positions, at least so long as the positions involve the institution's nonprofit activities. It is unclear whether the religious institution exemption applies to a religious institution's for-profit activities. The Catholic Church, for example, could insist that not only its priests and nuns, but also its lay teachers and clerical staff, be Catholic.

This exemption for religious institutions, on its face, exempts these entities only from claims of religious discrimination and not from other forms of discrimination. However, because of first amendment concerns, the courts have extended the exemption to other forms of discrimination when a clergy position is involved. Thus, a church may insist that its priests or ministers not only be of the church's religious faith but that they be male. When a clergy or clergy-like position is not involved, however, Title VII's prohibitions against race, sex, color and national origin discrimination have been applied to religious institutions.

Second, section 703(e)(2) of Title VII allows educational institutions to employ persons of a particular religion if the institution is in whole or in substantial part owned, supported, controlled or managed by a particular religion or when its curriculum is directed toward the propagation of a particular religion. Such educational institutions may not qualify as religious institutions but nonetheless may insist on hiring persons of a particular faith. This, too, is a difficult burden to meet for an employer asserting the exemption.

Third, an employer may be able to establish that religion is a bona fide occupational qualification for a position. (The BFOQ defense is discussed above in paragraphs 324–326.) There are very few religious BFOQ cases, however, because the

308. *Trans World Airlines, Inc.* v. *Hardison*, 432 US 63 (1977).
309. *Ansonia Board of Education* v. *Philbrook*, 479 US 60 (1986).

employers who likely could assert a religious BFOQ are usually religious institutions which are exempt from the prohibition against religious discrimination.

Courts have ruled that the federal government's ability to excuse burdening its employees' religious practices or beliefs is limited by the Religious Freedom Restoration Act (42 US Code §2000bb *et seq.*). That statute requires the government to establish a compelling need to burden religious beliefs or practices and to adopt only the least restrictive means of protecting those needs.[310]

X. Retaliation

345. In addition to prohibiting discrimination on the basis of race, color, sex, religion and national origin, Title VII also prohibits discrimination against an employee because of his/her opposition to an employer's violations of Title VII or because (s)he has made a charge, assisted or participated in a Title VII investigation or hearing.[311] The first prohibition is referred to as the 'opposition clause' and the latter as the 'free access clause'. The protections extended by these two clauses differ.

Protection under the free access clause is practically absolute. Employer retaliation against an employee who has filed a charge with the EEOC or who has testified in a Title VII proceeding is unlawful, even if the charge was made in bad faith. Because enforcement of Title VII depends largely on plaintiffs' willingness to file charges and to bring lawsuits to enforce their Title VII rights, permitting employers to discipline employees for making use of the statute's remedial procedures would unduly deter employees from coming forward.

The statute's protections extend beyond an employee's involvement in the statute's remedial procedures. The opposition clause protects other activity of employees aimed at protesting or objecting to what the employee reasonably and in good faith believes is unlawful conduct by his employer. An employee who complains internally about perceived discrimination, for example, generally is protected by the statute. However, protection under the opposition clause is not absolute. Rather, a job applicant, employee or former employee claiming to be a victim of retaliation for exercising rights protected by Title VII must establish that but for engaging in the protected activity, the employer would not have taken the adverse action against the claimant.[312]

Although the wording of the statute extends its protections only to applicants and employees, the Supreme Court has interpreted the statute as protecting former employees from retaliation as well.[313] Thus, an employer violates the statute if it provides a negative reference concerning a former employee because the employee had filed a charge of discrimination. Such post-employment retaliation could easily dissuade employees from bringing discrimination complaints and, thus, is within the scope of the statutorily established wrong. The Supreme Court has ruled that the Act

310. *E.g.*, *Tagore* v. *US*, 735 F.3d 324 (5th Cir. 2013).
311. 42 US Code §2000e–3(a).
312. *Univ. of Tex. Southwestern Med. Ctr.* v. *Nassar*, 133 S. Ct. 2517 (2013).
313. *Robinson* v. *Shell Oil*, 519 US 337 (1997).

covers those employer actions that would have been "materially adverse" to a reasonable employee or applicant and defined 'materially adverse' as actions that are harmful enough to dissuade a reasonable employee from making or supporting a charge of discrimination.[314]

§4. The Age Discrimination in Employment Act

346. Three years after Title VII was enacted, Congress passed the Age Discrimination in Employment Act (ADEA), 29 US Code §§621 *et seq.* As originally enacted, it prohibited on-the-job discrimination against individuals aged 40 through 65. The statute was amended to raise the protected class age limit to 70 and eventually was amended to eliminate the upper age cap altogether. Accordingly, the statute now protects individuals age 40 and above from discrimination because of age. It does not, however, protect those below 40 from age discrimination and permits mandatory retirement after age 64 of persons who for at least two years prior held an executive or high policymaking position and whose employer sponsored a nonforfeitable retirement benefit of at least $44,000 a year. It similarly permits state and local governments to mandatorily retire police officers and firefighters at or after reaching age 55.

The ADEA applies to employers, public and private, whose business affects interstate commerce and who employ 20 or more persons for each work day of at least 20 weeks a year. This threshold for coverage is higher than Title VII's 15 employee threshold. However, like Title VII, the ADEA also applies to the actions of unions and employment agencies. Moreover, as is true with Title VII, the statutory definition of employer includes the agents of that employer. Accordingly, employers have been held vicariously liable for the discriminatory actions of supervisors and others acting in an agency capacity. Agents are not personally liable for violations of the ADEA.

State and local governments are included in the definition of 'employer' under the ADEA, and the substantive requirements of the law apply to those employers. The ADEA also prohibits age discrimination by the federal government but provides a separate enforcement procedure, as does Title VII, for claims by federal employees.

Although the ADEA by its terms applies to the states, the Supreme Court has held that Congress lacks authority to override the Eleventh Amendment's implied grant of state immunity from monetary suits by individuals.[315] Congress may disregard state immunity from suit by individuals only when Congress adopts legislation pursuant to a later amendment, such as the 14th amendment. In *Kimel* v. *Florida Board of Regents*, the Court held that Congress can bar state discrimination based on age only when there is no rational relation between that classification and a legitimate governmental interest. The Court found that age is a rational proxy for legitimate state concerns such as physical or mental capacity to perform a job and, therefore, Congress' authority under the Fourteenth Amendment does not include abrogating a state's Eleventh Amendment immunity from monetary suits. (This immunity does

314. *Burlington Northern & Santa Fe Railway* v. *White*, 548 US 53 (2006).
315. *Kimel* v. *Florida Board of Regents*, 528 US 62 (2000).

not extend to local governments.) This means that individual suits for damages may not be brought against states under the ADEA unless the state has waived its immunity from suit. (Injunctive relief requiring reinstatement or other prospective relief is still available in an individual's suit against a state.)[316] Moreover, the Department of Justice, as opposed to individuals, are not barred by the Eleventh Amendment from bringing a damages suit to enforce the ADEA against state employers.

There is a right to a jury trial for ADEA damages claims, and such claims may be brought in either state or federal court.

I. Disparate Treatment Theory

347. As is true for Title VII, most claims under the ADEA are individual claims of disparate treatment. To prevail in such a case, the plaintiff must prove that (s)he suffered the adverse action complained of because of age and that there was intent to discriminate because of age, with the plaintiff bearing the burden of persuasion on the issue of unlawful intent. Moreover, the plaintiff must prove it was age, and not something highly correlated with but analytically distinct from age that motivated the decision.[317] For example, a decision to terminate all persons with 20 or more years of service is not facially discriminatory under the ADEA. Although such a decision likely would impact more older workers than younger workers, counting years of service is analytically distinct from age. However, if the employer adopted the policy for the purpose of getting rid of older workers, unlawful intent would exist.

Analysis of disparate treatment claims under the ADEA largely parallels the analysis developed under Title VII. The lower courts often use the *McDonnell-Douglas* prima facie case, discussed above in numbered paragraph 322 to establish an inference of unlawful intent when direct evidence of motive is lacking. The Supreme Court has held that the plaintiff satisfies the fourth element of the *McDonnell-Douglas* prima facie case by proving that someone 'substantially younger' received the position plaintiff sought or from which plaintiff was removed, even if the individual is also over 40 and therefore within the protected class.[318] Establishment of the prima facie case transfers to the defendant the burden of articulating a legitimate nondiscriminatory reason for its action that is unrelated to age. Once a defendant satisfies that burden, the plaintiff has the ultimate burden of proving that age motivated the challenged action. The Supreme Court has also held that an employer may favor older workers over younger workers, even those over 40, without violating the Act. According to the Court, 'the ADEA was concerned to protect a relatively older worker from discrimination that works to the advantage of the relatively young'.[319]

Although Congress amended Title VII to address 'mixed motive' cases (i.e., cases where a plaintiff may prove unlawful discrimination even though both lawful and

316. *See*, e.g., *Va. Office for Prot. & Advocacy* v. *Stewart*, 563 US 247, 255-57 (2011).
317. *Hazen Paper Co.* v. *Biggins*, 507 US 604 (1993).
318. *O'Connor* v. *Consolidated Coin Caterers Corp.*, 517 US 308 (1996).
319. *General Dynamics Land Systems. Inc.* v. *Cline*, 540 US 581, 590-91 (2004).

unlawful reasons motivated the decision), the ADEA was not so amended. Consequently, a plaintiff is required to show that her age was the but-for cause of the challenged decision.[320]

348. Systemic disparate treatment cases also may be brought under the ADEA. The analysis of such claims is similar to the analysis of systemic disparate treatment claims under Title VII, as described in paragraph 321, above.

Additionally, as is true under Title VII for sex, religion and national origin claims, defendants may claim that age is a bona fide occupational qualification (BFOQ). The BFOQ analysis is the same under the ADEA as it is under Title VII. To prevail, the defendant must prove that the aspect of the job for which age is necessary goes to the essence of the employer's business and that all or substantially all persons in the protected class cannot perform the job or that it is impractical to determine which ones can. For example, an airline's defense of BFOQ was rejected for flight engineer positions. Although the aspect of the job for which the airline claimed that persons under 60 were needed (safe transportation of passengers) did go to the essence of the employer's business, many persons over 60 could safely perform as flight engineers, and it was neither impossible nor impractical to figure out, through physical examinations, those who were healthy enough to serve as flight engineers.[321]

II. Disparate Impact

349. In *Smith* v. *City of Jackson*[322] the Court found that a disparate impact claim could be brought by several senior police officers who alleged they were adversely impacted by a new pay plan granting proportionately higher raises to officers with less than five years of seniority on the job. The Court, however, distinguished the ADEA and Title VII, indicating that the ADEA disparate impact theory is narrower than Title VII for two reasons. First, the ADEA contains a defense not found in Title VII. An employer may defend an ADEA claim by showing that Reasonable Factors Other than Age (RFOA) were the basis for the employment action in question. Second, the ADEA was not amended by the Civil Rights Act of 1991which added the provision allowing a claimant to override the business interest defense by showing that the employer declined to adopt an alternative that is less burdensome to the affected class. Accordingly, ADEA disparate impact claims are governed by the more employer-friendly standards adopted by the Supreme Court in *Wards Cove Packing* v. *Atonio*[323] than by the more plaintiff friendly standards adopted by Congress in its amendments to Title VII. Under *Wards Cove*, once the plaintiff establishes that a particular practice has an impact on a protected group, the burden of

320. *Gross* v. *FBL Financial Services, Inc.*, 557 US 167 (2009).
321. *Western Airlines* v. *Criswell*, 472 US 400 (1985).
322. *Smith v. City of Jackson*, 544 US 228 (2005).
323. 490 US 642 (1989).

production of evidence, not persuasion, passes to the defendant. That burden is satisfied, moreover, if the employer produces evidence showing the challenged practice significantly serves a legitimate business goal.

In *Smith* v. *City of Jackson*, though the Court found that senior police officers could bring an impact claim, it denied relief because the plaintiffs had not identified the particular part of the pay plan that resulted in the alleged adverse impact. Further, the employer had satisfied the defense of Reasonable Factors Other than Age because the reason for giving junior officers a greater percentage raise was to make their positions competitive with comparable positions in the market. The Court explained that there is no need under the ADEA, unlike Title VII, for an employer to adopt a less harmful alternative.

III. Retirement Incentives

350. Many employers offer their employees early retirement incentives. Setting a minimum age for receipt of these incentives does not violate the ADEA. Moreover, so long as the employee's decision to accept or to reject the early retirement incentive is completely voluntary, offering such incentives does not run afoul of the ADEA.

IV. Waiver

351. It is usual for employers to couple early retirement incentives with a release and waiver of all claims. The Older Workers Benefit Protection Act amended the ADEA to regulate these waivers. The ADEA, unlike other employment discrimination statutes, establishes minimum criteria that must be met before an employee's waiver of his rights will be effective, whether or not an early retirement option is involved. Seven criteria are listed in the statute and include written reference to the ADEA, additional consideration for the release, written notification that the employee should consult an attorney, a 21-day period to consider the agreement, and a 7-day period to revoke it. If the waiver is part of an early retirement program or other reduction in force, additional requirements apply, including information on the ages of others affected by the reduction in force and 45 days in which to weigh whether to sign the release.

§5. Americans with Disabilities Act

352. The Americans with Disabilities Act (42 US Code §12101 *et seq.*), adopted in 1990, applies to employers with 15 or more workers. The ADA broadly protects individuals with disabilities from discrimination in a wide spectrum of situations, including employment. The ADA's employment provisions are found in Title I which protects qualified individuals with a disability from on-the-job discrimination and entitles them to reasonable accommodation. Despite its name, one need not be an American to be protected by the ADA.

Unlike Title VII and the ADEA, the ADA goes beyond a prohibition against discrimination and imposes the obligation to reasonably accommodate qualified individuals with disabilities. Although the ADA does not require an employer to prefer a disabled applicant over the non- disabled or set quotas for hiring the disabled, it does require that employers engage in some forms of preferential treatment of disabled employees when that preferential treatment will enable the disabled employee to perform her job.

The ADA incorporates the enforcement provisions of Title VII of the Civil Rights Act of 1964, but its substantive provisions are modeled after the Rehabilitation Act of 1973 (29 US Code §701, 794 *et seq.*), a less sweeping federal law that applies to federal agencies and to employers receiving federally funded grants and contracts. Title I of the ADA applies to private sector employers, and to state and local government employers with 15 or more employees, and to employment agencies and labor unions. It does not apply to the United States government.

The statutory definition of employer under the ADA is similar to the definition under Title VII and includes the agents of the employer. Accordingly, vicarious liability principles developed and applied under Title VII apply to the ADA as well.

The Supreme Court has held that states (as opposed to political subdivisions of the states) are entitled to Eleventh Amendment immunity from individual suits for money damages brought under the ADA.[324] Nevertheless, ADA enforcement suits can still be brought against states in federal court by the US Attorney General. As a practical matter, due to the burdens of other responsibilities and the limited resources of the Department of Justice, such enforcement actions are theoretical.

I. Definition of Disability

353. In order to be protected by the ADA, one must be an individual with a disability. Under the ADA, an individual with a disability is someone: (1) who has a physical or mental impairment that substantially limits one or more of his or her major life activities, (2) who has a record of such an impairment, or (3) who is regarded as having such an impairment.[325] As this definition reveals, a person who has no actual disability can qualify as an individual with a disability within the meaning of the statute if regarded as disabled. Conversely, a person with a serious impairment may not be an individual with a disability if the impairment does not substantially limit any major life activity.

354. The original statute did not define the terms ‘impairment’, ‘substantially limits’, or ‘major life activity’. As a result, the EEOC, which has administrative responsibility for enforcing the ADA, and the courts, wrestled with the meaning of each of these terms.

In 2008, the ADA was amended by the ADA Amendments Act of 2008, 42 US Code §12101, (‘ADAAA’) to correct Supreme Court interpretations and EEOC regulations that were too restrictive, narrowing the scope of the Act’s protections.

---

324. *Board of Trustees* v. *Garrett*, 531 US 356 (2001). *See* paragraph 346, above, for fuller discussion.
325. 42 US Code §12102.

The ADAAA expressly rejects these Court decisions and directs the EEOC to promulgate new regulations consistent with the findings and the broadened definitions in the ADAAA. Among other things, the ADAAA directs that the definition of disability 'be construed in favor of broad coverage of individuals … to the maximum extent permitted by the terms of' the Act. It also clarified that 'an impairment that substantially limits one major life activity need not limit other major life activities in order to be considered a disability' and that 'an impairment that is episodic or in remission is a disability if it would substantially limit a major life activity when active'. The ADAAA additionally settled questions raised by the Supreme Court, specifying that 'major life activities include, but are not limited to, caring for oneself, performing manual tasks, seeing, hearing, eating, sleeping, walking, standing, lifting, bending, speaking, breathing, learning, reading, concentrating, thinking, communicating, and working' and covers 'the operation of a major bodily function, including but not limited to, functions of the immune system, normal cell growth, digestive, bowel, bladder, neurological, brain, respiratory, circulatory, endocrine, and reproductive functions'. Moreover, the ADAAA directed that:

> the determination of whether an impairment substantially limits a major life activity shall be made without regard to the ameliorative effects of mitigating measures such as – medication, medical supplies, equipment, or appliances, low-vision devices (which do not include ordinary eyeglasses or contact lenses), prosthetics including limbs and devices, hearing aids and cochlear implants or other implantable hearing devices, mobility devices, or oxygen therapy equipment and supplies; use of assistive technology; reasonable accommodations or auxiliary aids or services; or learned behavioral or adaptive neurological modifications.

Nevertheless, the amendment expressly permits consideration of the ameliorative effects of the mitigating measures of ordinary eyeglasses or contact lenses intended to fully correct visual acuity or eliminate refractive error.

Even if an individual does not presently have an impairment that substantially limits a major life activity, she falls within the statutory definition if she has a record of such an impairment. Thus, an individual who years earlier was hospitalized for an extended period of time to treat her mental illness would have a record of such an impairment, even if she presently is of sound mental health.

Finally, an individual may meet the statutory definition of disability, even though perfectly healthy, if she is regarded as having such an impairment. For example, if an employer mistakenly believes that an employee is suffering from AIDS and fires her because of that belief, but the employee in fact does not have AIDS, the individual would be within the protected class. An individual meets the requirement of 'being regarded as having such an impairment' if the individual establishes that he or she has been subjected to discrimination because of an actual or perceived physical or mental impairment, whether or not the impairment limits or is perceived to limit a major life activity. 42 US Code § 12102 (3)(A). An individual is 'regarded as' having a disability if he or she: '(1) Has a physical or mental impairment that does not substantially limit a major life activity, but is treated by the employer as having such a limitation; (2) Has a physical or mental impairment that is substantially limiting only because of the attitudes of others towards the impairment; or (3) Does not have an impairment at all but is regarded by the employer as having such a substantially limiting impairment.' Since a plaintiff does not have to prove that the perceived impairment substantially limits a major activity, in most cases it is much easier for the plaintiff to prove the employer 'regarded' her as disabled than to prove that she actually was 'disabled'.

The ADAAA expressly states that the 'regarded as' coverage does not apply to impairments that are transitory and minor. There is no definition of 'minor'. A 'transitory impairment' is an impairment 'with an actual or expected duration of six months or less'.

355. Alcoholism is a disability for purposes of the ADA, but the statute provides that an employer may prohibit the use of alcohol in the workplace and may hold an alcoholic to the same job standards that apply to other workers, even if the alcoholic's inability to meet those standards is a result of the addiction.

Drug addicts who have successfully completed rehabilitation are individuals with a disability. However, the statute provides that employees and applicants who are engaged in the current illegal use of drugs are not protected by the ADA when an employer takes action based on that drug use. The ADA neither prohibits nor advocates drug or alcohol testing of employees.

The following conditions are statutorily excluded from the definition of disability: 'transvestism, transsexualism, pedophilia, exhibitionism, voyeurism, gender identity disorders not resulting from physical impairments, or other sexual behavior disorders'. Also excluded are compulsive gambling, kleptomania and pyromania. Finally, the statute states that homosexuality and bisexuality are not impairments, and thus not disabilities, under the ADA (42 US Code §§ 12208, 12211).

II. Qualified Individual with a Disability

356. The protections of Title I of the ADA are limited to 'qualified individuals with a disability', which the statute defines as those individuals who, 'with or without reasonable accommodation, can perform the essential functions of the employment position that such individual holds or desires'.[326] Thus, the essential functions of the job must be determined, and if the individual cannot perform those functions without accommodation, it must be determined whether there is a reasonable accommodation available that would enable the individual with a disability to perform those essential functions.

The essential functions of the job generally are those the job is designed to perform. Although the employer's judgment about which functions are essential are given weight, it is not determinative. Factors considered include how often the task is performed and how much time is spent performing the task. Tasks that are merely marginal are not essential job functions.

326. 42 US Code §12111(8).

The statute does not define what constitutes a 'reasonable accommodation' but instead states the term may include '(A) making existing facilities used by employees readily accessible to and usable by individuals with disabilities; and (B) job restructuring, part-time or modified work schedule, reassignment to a vacant position, acquisition or modification of equipment or devices, appropriate adjustment or modifications of examinations, training materials or policies, the provision of qualified readers or interpreters, and other similar accommodations for individuals with disabilities'.[327] Thus, the concept of reasonable accommodation under the ADA is significantly more demanding than that imposed under Title VII in religious discrimination cases (see paragraph 343). Also, the duty to reasonably accommodate an employee's disability requires that employers extend special or preferential treatment to workers in order to enable them to perform their jobs.

An accommodation that would pose an undue hardship on an employer is not a reasonable accommodation and need not be provided. Any accommodation that would require 'significant difficulty or expense' is an undue hardship, and the resources of the particular employer are taken into account in making this determination. The Supreme Court has decided that the reasonable accommodation mandate of the ADA does not supersede the requirements of a bona fide and established seniority system, meaning that another employee's seniority rights to a particular position outweigh an ADA claimant's rights to the same position under the reasonable accommodation requirement.[328]

357. It is the plaintiff's burden to prove he is an individual with a disability, but the issue becomes less clear in assessing whether the plaintiff is a qualified individual with a disability. For example, if the parties dispute whether a job function is essential, it is unclear who bears the burden of persuasion on that issue. Lower courts also disagree on who bears the burden of proving whether an accommodation is reasonable. However, courts appear to regard the issue of undue hardship as a defense concerning which the employer bears the burden of persuasion.

358. An employer may discriminate against an individual with a disability when the individual poses a direct threat to the health and safety of others or to himself.[329] The statute defines a 'direct threat' as one posing a 'significant risk to the health or safety of others that cannot be eliminated by reasonable accommodation'. This determination is made on the basis of objective evidence from qualified professionals and should consider the type of risk, its duration and its severity..

III. Medical Examinations

359. An important provision of the regulations adopted pursuant to the ADA restricts how medical information concerning applicants and employees may be

327. 42 US Code §12111(9).
328. *US Airways, Inc.* v. *Barnett*, 535 US 391 (2002).
329. *Chevron USA, Inc.* v. *Echazabal*, 536 US 73 (2002).

gathered and maintained (29 Code Fed. Reg. §1630.14). The ADA generally prohibits pre-offer medical examinations for job applicants and inquiries concerning the applicant's medical history. The employer may describe the job to the applicant and ask if the applicant can perform it but may not ask the applicant whether she or he has any disabilities. However, once an employment offer has been extended, the employer may condition the offer on the applicant's satisfactory completion of a medical examination. Such post-offer examinations must be given to all new employees in the job classification, and the job offer may be withdrawn only if the refusal to hire is based on adverse test results that are job-related. Moreover, the confidentiality of test results must be maintained.

An employer may offer its employees voluntary medical examinations. It also may require medical examinations when there is a job-related basis for doing so. These examination results also must be kept confidential. In addition, the federal Health Insurance Portability and Accountability Act of 1996 (HIPAA) requires privacy for 'protected health information' (PHI), which is defined as individually identifiable health information.[330] Under HIPAA rules, the person whose health information is being transferred by a health care provider (is generally required to give permission for use or disclosure of health care data.[331]

The Genetic Information Nondiscrimination Act (42 US Code §§ 2000ff, 2000ff-1 to 2000ff-10) prohibits employers, labor organizations, and work referral agencies from discriminating based on an employee's genetic information. It also prohibits acquiring such information except when it is needed for health or genetic services offered by the employer, or is needed to comply with certification laws respecting medical leaves, or to protect against laboratory DNA identification contamination or when, with employee informed consent, it is used for monitoring workplace toxic exposure.

§6. Equal Pay Act

360. The Equal Pay Act, adopted by Congress in 1963, preceded enactment of Title VII by one year. The Equal Pay Act, which amended the FLSA, was and is limited in its scope; the statute is aimed solely at the elimination of pay differentials based on sex. Title VII, in contrast, prohibits sex discrimination in employment in all terms, conditions and privileges of employment. As the broader statute, Title VII receives the most attention in discussions of sex-based discrimination in the workplace. The Equal Pay Act, however, remains important because its protections are not dependent on the 15 employee requirement of Title VII but instead reaches all employees covered by the FLSA, as described in paragraph 84.

Proposals for equal pay legislation had been offered by federal study commissions in 1898 and again in 1915. For many years, some collective bargaining agreements incorporated the principle of equal pay for equal work regardless of sex, but other collective agreements provided for separate pay scales for men and women,

330. 42 US Code §201.
331. 42 Code Fed. Reg. §164.102.

with female workers invariably receiving lower pay than their male counterparts. Such separate pay scales for men and women were not uncommon in the non-union sector as well. The Equal Pay Act, by prohibiting such practices, not only precludes underpayment of women but also prevents men from having to compete with a lower paid female workforce.

361. The Equal Pay Act applies to executive, administrative and professional employees (who are generally exempt from the FLSA's minimum wage and overtime provisions). When a pay disparity exists, the Equal Pay Act requires that equality be achieved by increasing the lower wage rather than by lowering the higher one. Although referred to as a separate statute, the Equal Pay Act in fact is incorporated into the FLSA. Thus, enforcement of the Equal Pay Act initially was the responsibility of the Secretary of Labor, who delegated that duty to the Wage-Hour Division. Enforcement responsibility was transferred to the EEOC in 1979.

362. A prima facie violation of the Equal Pay Act is established by proof of: (1) unequal pay (2) for equal work (3) at the same establishment (4) because of sex. Unequal pay is not limited to wages but includes fringe benefits as well. The pay inequality must exist within the same establishment, which generally means a physically separate place of business, unless personnel for various physical locations are centrally hired. That the unequal pay within an establishment has occurred because of sex is established, for prima facie case purposes, by pointing to one other person of the opposite sex who is receiving unequal pay for equal work.

The most difficult element of the prima face case is the equal work requirement. The statute provides that equal work consists of jobs requiring equal skill, effort and responsibility and that are performed under similar working conditions. Although the jobs need not be identical, they must be substantially equal before the comparison may be used to support a prima facie case. As for the requirement that the jobs be performed under similar working conditions, the Supreme Court has held that working conditions refers only to surroundings and hazards.[332] Accordingly, the Court has held that night shift and day shift jobs are similar working conditions under the Equal Pay Act.

Accordingly, without equal work, there is no Equal Pay Act violation, even if a woman is being paid less because she is a woman. An employer who pays a female administrator less than a male secretary because the administrator is a woman may be liable for sex discrimination under Title VII but not liable under the Equal Pay Act unless the jobs involved equal work.

From time to time, plaintiffs have attempted to argue that pay practices are unlawful if they undervalue women's work, even when the work is not 'substantially equal' within the meaning of the Equal Pay Act. Many job categories within the United States remain effectively segregated by sex, and many times job categories that are predominately filled by women are paid less than are job categories predominately filled by men, even when those jobs are of 'comparable worth' to society. The 'comparable worth' theory, however, has met with little success. If the jobs do not involve 'equal work', there is no Equal Pay Act violation. Nor is reliance

332. *Corning Glass Works* v. *Brennan*, 417 US 188 (1974).

upon the marketplace to set wage rates the equivalent of intentional discrimination under Title VII.

363. Once a prima facie case of wage discrimination has been shown, the burden passes to the defendant to establish one or more of the statutorily identified affirmative defenses. This is a burden of persuasion, not of production. Unequal pay between men and women for equal work does not violate the Equal Pay Act if the pay is based on (1) a seniority system, (2) a merit pay system, (3) a piece-work rate system or other system measuring earnings by quality or quantity or (4) any other factor other than sex. The last defense is the one most frequently relied upon by employers. A factor that is sex-based, such as an actuarial distinction based on life expectancy, does not qualify as 'any other factor other than sex', and therefore does not relieve the employer of liability.[333]

364. Because both Title VII and the Equal Pay Act address on-the-job sex discrimination, there is an overlap between the two statutes when sex-based wage disparities are at issue. Claims may be brought under both statutes, although double recovery is not permitted. Moreover, when a pay practice is permissible under one of the Equal Pay Act's affirmative defenses, it is also immunized under Title VII because the so-called Bennett Amendment, as interpreted by the Supreme Court, incorporates into Title VII the Equal Pay Act's affirmative defenses when an employer's compensation practices are attacked under Title VII as sex-based discrimination. The Supreme Court has suggested that at least in cases where pay discrimination has been ongoing, the EPA may be a better route to recovery than Title VII[334] because: (1) the EPA does not require that an administrative charge be filed as a prerequisite to court litigation, and (2) the EPA does not require proof of intent in order to establish a violation.

In a highly publicized case, Lilly Ledbetter filed an employment discrimination charge with the EEOC, asserting that the paychecks that she had received during the charging period, although not discriminatory acts in and of themselves, gave present effect to past discrimination. In 2007, the United States Supreme Court held that Ledbetter's discrimination charge did not meet the applicable filing deadline because the discriminatory act that triggered the time limit for filing an EEOC charge was the discriminatory pay decision, not the ongoing paychecks that resulted from the discriminatory decision. Because the later effects of past discrimination did not restart the clock for filing an EEOC charge, Ledbetter's claim was untimely.[335]

In 2009, Congress enacted the Lilly Ledbetter Fair Pay Act (FPA), codified in scattered sections of Titles 29 and 42 of the United States Code. The FPA amended Title VII and also the Age Discrimination in Employment Act, the Americans with Disabilities Act, and the Rehabilitation Act. Under the FPA, an unlawful employment practice occurs with respect to discrimination in compensation, when: (1) a discriminatory compensation decision or other practice is adopted; (2) an individual

333. *City of Los Angeles* v. *Manhart*, 435 US 702 (1978).
334. *County of Washington* v. *Gunther*, 452 US 161 (1981).
335. *Ledbetter* v. *Goodyear Tire & Rubber Co.*, 550 U.S. 618 (2007), overturned due to legislative action, in Pub. L. No. 111-2 (Jan. 29, 2009). See next paragraph in the text.

becomes subject to a discriminatory compensation decision or other practice; or (3) an individual is affected by application of a discriminatory compensation decision or other practice, including each time that wages, benefits, or other compensation is paid, resulting in whole or in part from such a decision or other practice.[336]

The FPA also allows an aggrieved person to recover backpay for up to two years preceding the filing of the charge where the discriminatory acts that occurred during the charge-filing period are similar or related to discriminatory acts that occurred outside the time for filing a charge.[337]

Under the FPA, the issuance of each paycheck influenced by a discriminatory compensation decision, no matter how long ago it occurred, is deemed an independent employment action that renews the time period for filing a charge of discrimination.

§7. Protection of Military Reservists and Veterans

365. Military reservists sometimes are required to engage in prolonged active duty, as was the case during the Gulf War, the Iraq and Afghanistan wars, and US participation in various UN sponsored peace keeping actions. Currently, employment protection is afforded by the Uniformed Services Employment and Reemployment Rights Act which, among other things, protects reemployment rights of those returning from regular or reserve military service if their cumulative length of the absence and of all previous absences from a position of employment with that employer by reason of service in the uniformed services has not exceeded five years. The Act also prohibits treating the absence for military service as a break in longevity for purposes of determining the employee's entitlement to employment benefits. Reemployment rights under this law are dependent upon the employee making a prompt request to return to the previous employment with the maximum time for making that request being determined by the duration of the uniformed service. The right is not available if the employer's business circumstances have changed so as to make re-employment impossible or unreasonable or would impose an undue hardship on the employer (38 US Code §4312).

An employer is not required to give the reservist preferential treatment. Thus, it has been held that an employer is not obligated to schedule work so as to assure an opportunity to make-up the pay lost while on reserve duty.[338]

The Family and Medical Leave Act was amended in 2008[339] to cover employees who are active service members or who have immediate family members serving in

336. 42 USCA §2000e-5(e)(3)(A).
337. 42 USCA §2000e-5(e)(3)(B).
338. *Monroe* v. *Standard Oil Co.*, 452 US 549 (1981). But *see Gummo* v. *City of Depew*, 75 F.3d 98 (2d Cir.), *cert. denied* 517 US 1190 (1996), held that legislation known as the Veterans' Employment and Reemployment Rights Act, which in 1994 recodified and updated the Vietnam Era Veterans' Readjustment Assistance Act (*see* 38 US Code §4301 *et seq.*), a predecessor to the current law, modified the *Monroe* decision by giving protection against adverse employment actions even when those actions are motivated only in part by the worker's performance of military or reserve duties.
339. 29 USCA §§2601–2654, as amended by Pub. L. No. 110-181, effective 28 January 2008; *see also* 29 CFR Pt. 825.

the military. Employers with 50 or more employees must grant the following unpaid leaves to employees with a spouse, child, parent, or 'next of kin' on active duty or call to active duty status with the National Guard or military reserves in support of a contingency operation:

- up to 12 weeks of FMLA leave in a single 12-month period for certain qualifying exigencies[340] arising out of a covered military member's active duty status, or notification of an impending call or order to active duty status, in support of a contingency operation, and
- up to 26 weeks of FMLA leave in a single 12-month period to care for a covered servicemember recovering from a serious injury or illness incurred in the line of duty on active duty.

Eligible employees may take up to 26 total weeks of all types of FMLA leave combined during the applicable 12-month period. FMLA leave is unpaid.

340. 'Qualifying exigencies' include: short-notice deployment for seven days following the notice; attending certain military events and related activities such as official ceremonies, programs, or briefings; certain childcare and related activities arising from active duty or a call to active duty status such as arranging alternative childcare or transferring children to a new school; addressing certain financial and legal arrangements to address a covered military member's absence; attending certain counseling sessions the need for which arises from the active duty or call to active duty; taking up to five days to spend time with a covered military member who is on temporary leave for rest and recuperation during deployment; attending post-development ceremonies or reintegration briefings or addressing issues arising from the death of a covered military member; and any other event the Company and employee agree is a qualifying exigency. 29 USCA §2612(a)(1)(E).

Part II. Collective Labor Relations

Chapter 1. The Impact of Collective Bargaining on Worker Benefits

§1. The Paramount Role of Collective Bargaining

366. If a person is employed in a bargaining unit for which a collective bargaining agent has been certified or recognized as the representative chosen by a majority of those employees, no terms or conditions of that person's employment may be modified except in conformity with the collective bargaining agreement or as otherwise agreed to by the bargaining agent. If there is no collective agreement in effect, changes in the conditions or terms of employment may be implemented only if they have been proposed to the bargaining agent and either: (a) the employer and collective representative have bargained to impasse over those proposals, or (b) the bargaining agent has consented to the changes. Thus, when there is a duty of collective bargaining, the collective bargaining process is all-important to the employment relationship.

§2. Compensation Comparison between Organized and Unorganized Workers

367. In light of the elaborate system for regulating collective bargaining relationships in the United States, and the central role collective bargaining plays in fixing the terms and conditions of employment for those employees who by majority choice have designated a collective bargaining agent, it is reasonable to ask whether the process makes any difference. Social scientists have made some comparative measurements between the employment terms and conditions of organized and unorganized workers and these provide at least a degree of insight into the impact of collective bargaining on worker benefits in the United States.

368. Studies concerning the impact of collective bargaining have examined wage differentials between comparable organized and unorganized workers. Techniques for conducting these studies differ considerably as do the data sources. Not surprisingly, the results, too, are widely varied. Nevertheless, past findings almost uniformly support the proposition that the union represented American worker is better paid than is his unorganized counterpart.[341] Studies support a finding that generally there is a 20 percent earnings differential favoring union represented workers.[342] Moreover, union wage and benefit gains have been shown to drive up the wages and benefits of non-union workers and its affect increases with increases in the portion of union represented workers.[343]

369. Estimates of the favorable wage differential enjoyed by union represented workers over their unrepresented counterparts in the United States range from about 8–25 percent and even higher. One study found that the wage differential is significantly affected by such variables as the worker's sex, race, and occupation. For example, for white males in craft related occupations, the union workers studied earned about 26 percent more than non-union workers. In service occupations, unionized white workers received still more than their non-union counterparts, but the difference for this occupational category were considerably less – about 16 percent. Black male workers who were union represented in service occupations earned about 30 percent more than their unorganized counterparts and unionized black males in craft occupations earned about 20 percent more than black males in the same occupations who were not union represented. In laborer occupations, the pay differential enjoyed by union represented workers was 34 percent for white males, 28 percent for black males, 8 percent for white females and 22 percent for black females.[344] Another study found that 'the unadjusted union wage gap for low-skilled workers overstates the true union wage effect … while the unadjusted gap for high-skilled workers actually understates the true union wage effect'.[345] Another study indicates that although unionized workers enjoy higher wages, in times of economic downturn they are more prone to lay off than are their unrepresented counterparts. This is particularly true for middle-aged craft workers. (It is possible that the cause for this is related to the respective sensitivities to recessions of industries with high union representation compared with those with low representation.) The data gathered by those studying the subject indicate that young minority group workers, on the other hand, enjoy greater employment security, as well as higher wages, if they are union represented.[346]

341. D. Belman and P. Voos, 'Union Wages and Union Decline: Evidence from the Construction Industry', 60 *Ind. and Lab. Rel. Rev*. 67 (2006); H. Farber, 'Nonunion Wage Rates and the Threat of Unionization', 58 *Ind. and Lab. Rel. Rev*. 335 (2005); C. Robinson and N. Tomes, 'Union Wage Differentials in the Public and Private Sectors', 2 *J. Lab. Eco.* 106 (1984).
342. S. Raphael, 'Estimating the Union Earnings Effect Using a Sample of Displaced Workers', 53 *Indus. and Lab. Rel. Rev.* 503, 514 (2000).
343. J. Rosenfeld, P. Denice and J. Laird, 'Union Decline Lowers Wages of Nonunion Workers' (Report of Eco. Pol. Inst., 30 August 2016).
344. P. Ryscarage, 'Measuring Union-non Earnings Differences', 97 *Monthly Lab. Rev.*, December 1974, pp. 3, 7.
345. D. Card, 'Unions and Labor Markets: The Effect of Unions on Wage Inequality in the US Labor Market', 54 *Indus. & Lab. Rel. Rev.* 296, 306 (2001).
346. M. Baldwin and W. Johnson, 'The Employment Effects of Wage Discrimination Against Black Men', 49 *Indus. and Lab. Rel. Rev*. 302, 310 (1996); P. Andrisani and A. Kohen, 'The Effects of Collective Bargaining as Measured for Men in Blue-Collar Jobs', 100 *Monthly Lab. Rev*. Apr. 1977, p. 46.

Government employees who have union representation have been found to enjoy about a 7 percent compensation advantage over their counterparts who are unrepresented. The bulk of the advantage, however, is in the form of benefits other than pay.[347]

370. The impact of union representation upon the level of remuneration is affected by structural characteristics of the employing enterprise and the level at which bargaining takes place. For example, one study estimated that all else being equal, negotiating at the enterprise level or on a multi-employer basis rewards employees with 5–9 percent greater benefits than when the collective agreement is negotiated at the plant level.[348] Not surprisingly, the extent to which competitors are union-organized also affects negotiated benefits. Thus, an examination of wages in the supermarket industry concluded that a 10 percentage point increase in the union represented portion of supermarket employees in urban areas results in a 2.2 to 2.3 percent improvement in the wage differential enjoyed by union represented workers.[349] Also, a relationship has been found between the size of the employing establishment and the impact of collective bargaining on the overall pattern of earnings. For example, large establishments on average pay newly hired workers 10 percent more than do smaller establishments in the same industry when only union organized enterprises are compared. In contrast, when the comparison is made only among unorganized establishments, the differential paid by large establishments to new hires is negligible. On the other hand, the pattern is reversed when examining comparable pay for long term employees. Longer term workers in larger unorganized enterprises receive about 15 percent more than their counterparts at small and medium size unorganized establishments. However, if only union organized enterprises are compared, there is a negligible pay difference between long-term employees of large establishments and their counterparts at small and medium size enterprises.[350]

Several non-wage benefits generally enjoyed by union members are not normally available to their unorganized counterparts. Formal grievance procedures and protection from arbitrary or invidious disciplinary actions are almost always available to union represented workers but normally are not available to the unorganized employee. Rest periods and clean-up periods are more likely to be religiously guarded in the union organized establishment than in an unorganized shop.

347. J. Antos, 'Union Effects on White Collar Compensation', 36 *Indus. & Lab. Rel. Rev.* 461 (1983). *See also*, D. Belmon, J. Haywood and J. Lund, 'Public Sector Earnings and the Extent of Unionization', 50 *Indus. and Lab. Rel. Rev.* 610, 624 (1997).

348. L. Mishel, 'The Structural Determinants of Union Bargaining Power', 40 *Indus. and Lab. Rel. Rev.* 90, 100 (1986).

349. D. Belman and P. Voos, 'Wage Effects of Increased Union Coverage', 46 *Indus. and Lab. Rel. Rev.* 368, 392 (1993).

350. J. Pearce, 'Tenure, Unions, and the Relationship between Employer Size and Wages', 8 *J. Lab. Eco.*, 251 (1990).

Similarly, union members are more likely than their non union counterparts to collect benefits when injured or unemployed.[351]

A competing consideration is that union sponsored seniority systems may inhibit the opportunities of some individuals for rapid advancement, and pay schedules published in collective agreements may reduce the prospects of management paying a higher wage rate to more valued workers.

It has been argued that the decline of union representation in the US is an outcome of the success unions have had in achieving higher benefits and thereby making non-union labor more attractive to employers. A study of whether this has happened in the construction industry led to the conclusion that 'actually existing wage differentials did not set off a chain of events that reduced union membership'.[352]

351. B. Hirsch, D. MacPherson and J. Dumond, 'Workers' Compensation Recipiency in Union and Non Union Workplaces', 50 *Indus. and Lab. Rel. Rev.* 213 (1997); W. Budd and B. McCall, 'The Effect of Unions on the Receipt of Unemployment Insurance Benefits', 50 *Indus. and Lab. Rel. Rev.*, 478 (1997).

352. D. Belman and P. Voos, 'Union Wages and Union Decline: Evidence from the Construction Industry', 60 *Indus. & Lab. Rel. Rev.* 67, 86 (2006).

Chapter 2. Freedom to Organize and Obtain Mutual Aid

§1. The Right to Engage in or Refrain from Concerted Activity

I. The Basic Policy of the National Labor Relations Act

371. Section 7 of the NLRA states the basic policy governing the rights of workers with respect to concerted activities. It reads:

> Employees shall have the right to self-organization, to form, join, or assist labor organizations, to bargain collectively through representatives of their own choosing, and to engage in other mutual aid or protection, and shall also have the right to refrain from any or all of such activities except to the extent that such right may be affected by an agreement requiring membership in a labor organization as a condition of employment as authorized in section 8(a)(3).

One consequence of this statement is that the Act does not protect purely individual activities of a worker who seeks to improve the terms and conditions of his or her employment. To be protected, the worker's activity must in some way be in concert with the efforts or interests of at least one other worker or be based on a right provided by a collectively bargained agreement.[353] Another consequence of section 7 is that concerted employee activity is protected whether or not it is designed to support a labor organization or the demands of such an organization.[354] Section 7 protects all concerted activity for mutual aid and protection, extending to nonunion as well as union workers. This protection has recently been invoked to safeguard employees from employer action based on employee use of social media,[355] employer promulgation of policies demanding employee courtesy and

353. *NLRB* v. *City Disposal Systems, Inc.*, 465 US 822 (1984). The legislative history of section 7 indicates it was intended to protect all employee actions in service of employment interests whether or not pursued mutually with others. R. Gorman and M. Finkin, 'The Individual and the Requirement of "Concert" Under the National Labor Relations Act', 130 *U. Pa. L. Rev.* 286 (1981).

354. *NLRB* v. *Washington Aluminum Co.*, 370 US 9 (1962). In *NLRB* v. *J. Weingarten, Inc.*, 420 US 251 (1974), it was held to be an unfair labor practice for an employer to deny a worker's request for a union representative at an interview that can result in disciplinary action. At times the NLRB has ruled that only employees in union represented workplaces have a right to such representation while at other times it has protected the right to obtain the aid of a fellow employee when working in an unorganized workplace. Most recently the Board reverted to the rule that the *Weingarten* right applies only in situations in which a union is the collective bargaining representative. *IBM Corporation*, 341 NLRB 1288 (2004).

355. *See Hispanics United of Buffalo*, 359 NLRB No. 37(2012)(finding section 7 protection for criticism of coworker through Facebook posting); *Purple Communications, Inc.*, 361 NLRB No. 126 (2014)(if the employer gives access to its email system and has not limited its use for work activities only, employees are protected in using it for matters of mutual concern); Christine Neylon O'Brien, 'The First Facebook Firing Case under Section 7 of the National Labor Relations Act: Exploring the Limits of Labor Law Protection for Concerted Communication on Social Media', 45 *Suffolk U. L. Rev.* 29(2011).

confidentiality in the workplace,[356] and even employer agreements mandating employee waiver of class action rights in arbitration or litigation.[357]

372. Section 7 of the NLRA, quoted at paragraph 371 above, does not by itself regulate employer or union conduct. Those regulations are found, instead, in sections 8 and 9 of the Act. Section 8 is divided into lettered subsections, the first two of which are the source for most unfair labor practice charges. Section 8(a) prohibits employers from engaging in various forms of conduct that interfere with the protected right of workers to act or refrain from acting in concert. Section 8(b) prohibits labor organizations from engaging in various forms of conduct that interfere with the protected right of workers to act or refrain from acting in concert or that interfere with the protected right of employers not to be subjected to coercive pressures concerning labor disputes in which they are not directly involved. In general, section 9 of the Act prescribes the procedures for determining whether a demand for collective representation involves an appropriate unit for collective bargaining, whether a majority of employees have elected or selected a bargaining representative, and whether a majority of bargaining unit employees wish to withhold certain bargaining authority from their representative.

373. The essence of the underlying policy of the NLRA is group self-determination by majority rule of the workers in a unit appropriate for bargaining, and recognition of collective bargaining as a legal and beneficial process. Neither employers nor labor organizations are permitted to interfere with that employee collective self-determination and both must facilitate established collective bargaining relations.

II. Prohibition against Interference with the Right to Organize

374. Section 8(a) of the NLRA contains five paragraphs, the first of which is so broad that it encompasses the other four. It prohibits employers from interfering with, restraining or coercing employee exercise of section 7 rights. (Those rights are quoted in paragraph 371, above.) As a result, the official NLRB form for filing unfair labor practice charges against an employer has printed on it the allegation that the named respondent violated section 8(a)(1). The form then has a space in which the charging party can specify any additional paragraph designations that might be relevant to the charged misconduct.

356. *See Directtv US Directtv Holdings, LLC.*, 359 NLRB No. 54 (2013); *Karl Knauz Motors, Inc.*, 358 NLRB No. 164 (2012); *COSTCO Wholesale Corp.*, 358 NLRB No. 106 (2012).

357. *See D.R. Horton, Inc.* 357 NLRB No. 184(2012)(holding employer violated section 7 by maintaining a mandatory arbitration agreement prohibiting employees from filing joint, class, or collective employment-related claims in any arbitral or judicial forum), *aff'd in part, rev'd in part, D.R. Horton* v. *NLRB,* 2013 WL 6231617 (5th Cir. 3 December 2013)(holding Federal Arbitration Act is not superseded by the National Labor Relations Act, but striking employer waiver agreement void for vagueness). This issue is currently under review by the US Supreme Court.

375. Some employer unfair labor practices fit only within the prohibitions of 8(a)(1). These are referred to as independent 8(a)(1) charges. Other types of employer unfair labor practices are more specifically prohibited by one or more of the other four paragraphs as well as prohibited by the broad language of section 8(a)(1). In such situations, the 8(a)(1) charge is referred to as a 'derivative 8(a)(1) violation'.

376. Just as section 8(a)(1) of the NLRA prohibits employer coercion that interferes with the section 7 rights of employees, at section 8(b)(1)(A) the Act prohibits unions from restraining or coercing workers in the exercise of those rights.

A. *Coercion to Engage in or Refrain from Engaging in Concerted Activity*

377. Employer conduct that tends to coerce a reasonable person against engaging in concerted activity violates section 8(a)(1) of the NLRA. This prohibition reaches not only physical violence, or the threat thereof, but more subtle means of coercion as well. Thus, actions such as intrusive management surveillance of union meetings or openly photographing those engaged in picketing have been held to violate section 8(a)(1).[358] Similarly, asking job applicants if they are union members is an unfair labor practice under this section.

On the other hand, burdening the other side with a lawsuit in retaliation for the exercise of rights protected by NLRA section 7 is not an unfair labor practice unless no reasonable litigant would expect to win the suit.[359]

Because supervisors are not 'employees', under the NLRA, the Act does not provide them with any direct protections. Nevertheless, the Act is violated if the action against a supervisor affects section 7 rights of employees.[360] Thus, it has been held that the Act is violated if a supervisor is disciplined for providing testimony that is favorable to a union. Such action against the supervisor is deemed to have a coercive impact upon employees who witness what can happen to even a supervisor who acts contrary to management's wishes.[361]

378. Union coercion to gain employee support or to deter them from supporting a rival labor organization is an unfair labor practice. Thus, a union cannot threaten to seek a worker's dismissal because the worker is engaged in anti-union activity or supports a rival union. If that worker is a union member, however, the union can

358. *See*, for example, *Local Joint Executive Board* v. *NLRB*, 515 F.3d 942 (9th Cir. 2008)(however, brief, casual, unintrusive observations are not an unfair labor practice).
359. *BE&K Construction Co.*, 351 NLRB 451 (2007).
360. *NLRB* v. *Better Monkey Grip Co.*, 243 F.2d 836 (5th Cir. 1959) (*per curiam*), *cert.* denied 355 US 864. *See also*, *Delling* v. *NLRB*, 869 F.2d 1397 (10th Cir. 1989) (supervisor must be reinstated if dismissed for refusing to falsify reasons for discharging workers who in fact were terminated for engaging in union activity) and *Kenrich Petrochemicals, Inc.* v. *NLRB*, 907 F.2d 400 (3d Cir.), *cert.* denied 498 US 981 (1990) (supervisor reinstated by NLRB where dismissed because family members supported unionization).
361. *Parker-Robb Chevrolet*, 262 NLRB 402 (1982), appeal denied 711 F.2d 383 (DC Cir. 1983) (supervisors not protected if simply acting in concert by themselves or together with protected employees).

use its internal disciplinary machinery, including fines and suspensions from membership, to deter conduct that undermines the union's status.[362]

379. There is some uncertainty respecting the need to prove wrongful intent with regard to an employer's interference with protected employee rights. The Supreme Court has held that a violation is established if the employer's conduct probably has the effect of restraint or coercion.[363] On the other hand, the Court has also held that, absent proof of intent to interfere with employee rights, conduct that tends to deter concerted activity does not constitute an unfair labor practice if it is justified by 'legitimate and substantial' business considerations and is not so inherently destructive of the right to engage in concerted activities that the employer must have known that it would have such a deterrent impact.[364]

Much of the Supreme Court's discussion of whether wrongful motive must be proven to establish an unfair labor practice has arisen in the context of cases involving alleged employer discrimination based on union activity. Such discrimination is a violation of section 8(a)(3) of the NLRA and is a derivative violation of 8(a)(1). Thus, it has been argued that while proof of intent is relative to establishing the unfair labor practice of interfering with employee rights by discriminating against union activity, proof of wrongful motive is not relevant to cases involving independent 8(a)(1) violations.[365] Moreover, whether the degree of inherent destructiveness to protected rights caused by the challenged conduct is so great as to justify treating it as irrebutable evidence of the employer's discriminatory motive is a matter of judgment based on the decision maker's perceptions of worker vulnerability to coercion and of employer propensities to undermine union activities. Thus, the outcome in many cases turns on the seeming worker-friendly or management-friendly propensities of the Board and the reviewing judges, and on the latters' willingness or unwillingness to defer to the NLRB's supposed expertise regarding such matters.[366]

380. An employer's liability for unlawful coercion under the NLRA extends to the conduct of any person acting directly for the employer and to any person whose conduct would be reasonably construed by workers to have the employer's blessings. For example, in one case, the mayor of a town helped persuade an employer to open a plant there and was a friend of the company president. When a union began organizing the company's workers, the mayor paid for newspaper advertisements that posed threats of dire consequences if the workers voted in favor of the union. These ads were also distributed by the mayor to workers whose names and

362. Compare. *Tri-Rivers Marine Engineers Union*, 189 NLRB 838 (1971) with *NLRB* v. *Teamsters Local 745*, 462 F.2d 201 (5th Cir. 1972).

363. *NLRB* v. *Burnup and Sims, Inc.*, 379 US 21 (1964).

364. *NLRB* v. *Great Dane Trailers, Inc.*, 388 US 26, 34 (1967).

365. *See* for example, W. Oberer. 'The Scienter Factor in sections 8(a)(1) and (3) of the Labor Act', 52 *Cornell L.Q.*, 491 (1967). In *Meijer, Inc.* v. *NLRB*, 463 F.3d 534 (6th Cir. 2006), the court held that proof of an 8(a)(1) violation includes showing that the employer knew that protected conduct was affected by its challenged action. On the other hand, the court agreed that the NLRB can establish general rules barring employer conduct that experience shows generally tends to interfere with section 7 rights. In such situations it is not necessary to prove that the employer knew that its action would interfere with protected employee rights.

366. *Metropolitan Edison Co.* v. *NLRB*, 460 US 693, 701–704 (1983).

addresses the mayor obtained from the company. A federal court of appeals upheld the NLRB's finding that the mayor's conduct was to be imputed to the employer.[367]

B. Distinguishing between Coercive Expression and Protected Expression

381. Threats designed to deter workers from supporting a labor organization are common in the United States even though they are violations of NLRA section 8(a)(1). A difficulty faced by the NLRB is distinguishing between a threat and a mere statement of information or opinion designed to help the worker reach a non coerced conclusion that unionization would not be beneficial. Because freedom of expression is constitutionally protected in the US, it is assumed that employers and their agents cannot be prohibited from expressing merely their opinions about labor organizations or offering accurate information respecting the effects of unionization. This principle is reflected in section 8(c) of the NLRA which limits the extent to which expression can be used as a basis for finding an unfair labor practice.

382. The NLRB, with the approval of the courts, takes the position that whether an employer's statement constitutes a threat must be determined by examining the context in which the statement is made and not just the content of what is said or written. Thus, if the company president makes a speech to all employees at an assembly and states he thinks that unions are rotten, that they do not serve the workers' best interests and that they are bad for business, in the absence of other words or conduct indicating intolerance for those who disagree with that expressed opinion, the NLRB will not treat the speech as an unfair labor practice. An unfair labor practice will be found only when the workers are likely to understand the employer's statements as a threat or when the circumstances create a coercive environment that is likely to cause the workers to construe the words as coercive. Accordingly, the NLRB weighs the totality of circumstances in each individual case in order to discern the probable impact of the employer's statements on the workers.[368] For example, even when a company president called most of the workers into his office one at a time to ask if they had any questions about the company's prior statements opposing the union's organizing efforts, and specifically urged some of them to vote against the union, the Board found no violation because, citing such facts as that employees often met the president in his office and addressed him by his given name, it concluded that the evidence did not demonstrate that it was a coercive atmosphere.[369]

383. It has been argued that systematic visits by supervisors to the employees' homes in order to urge a 'no union' vote should be treated as *per se* coercive, but the Board has avoided reaching the issue. Rather, in such situations it usually finds

367. *Henry I. Siegel Co., Inc.* v. *NLRB*, 417 F.2d 1206 (6th Cir. 1969), *cert.* denied 398 US 959 (1970).
368. *NLRB* v. *Virginia Electric Power Co.*, 314 US 469, 477 (1941).
369. *Flex Products, Inc.*, 280 NLRB 1117 (1986).

additional facts present, such as interrogation or threats of adverse consequences, that corroborate the assertion of coercive behavior.[370]

384. Once workers are organized, an employer is allowed to inform them of their right to resign or to revoke a dues checkoff agreement and for the employer to explain how such actions can be taken. But the NLRB has held that it is unlawful coercion for the employer additionally to urge each employee to take such steps.[371] There is division of opinion, moreover, respecting how far an employer may go in encouraging and assisting workers to withdraw union authorization cards.[372] In some cases such employer encouragement has been treated as inherently coercive and, therefore, in violation of section 8(a)(1).[373]

385. The Supreme Court has provided some guidance respecting the distinction that must be made between lawful employer statements and those that constitute unprotected threats. It has held that an employer can express its opinion regarding the perceived evils of unionization and can even make predictions regarding the adverse impact of employee concerted activities. However, such predictions 'must be carefully phrased on the basis of objective fact' and not contain any implicit or explicit statement of dire consequences that will be brought about by the employer's exercise of its own discretion in responding to the workers' decision to organize.[374] On the other hand, in *dicta*, the Court has said that there is at least one situation in which it is permissible for an employer to inform workers of its commitment to impose dire consequences if they unionize. If the employer has in fact made a decision to close the entire operation should the workers select a collective bargaining representative, the Supreme Court has said the employer may threaten the workers by informing them of that decision during the organizing campaign.[375]

If the Court adheres to this position when directly faced with the issue, it will be approving what has become a significant means of deterring unionization. If an employer's announced decision to close the business is effective in deterring unionization, the employer will not need to close and, therefore, will be able to continue to operate with the benefits of its successful threat. But, if the workers select a bargaining representative despite the announcement of the decision to close, what is to keep the employer from 'reconsidering' that decision and remaining open? After all, what remedy will the NLRB impose on such an employer? Surely, the agency will not order the employer to keep its promise and terminate the business. Thus, the

370. For example, *Double J Services, Inc.*, 347 NLRB No. 58 (2006).
371. *Perkins Machine Co.*, 141 NLRB 697 (1963). *Space Needle, LLC,* 363 NLRB No. 11 (2015), held it was an unfair labor practice to urge employees to resign their union membership as a more expeditious way to terminate their dues checkoff consent.
372. Union authorization cards state that the employee designates the named union to act as collective bargaining representative and are a basis for initiating an NLRB representation election or establish the union's support from an employee majority if the employer's unfair labor practices have made it impossible to conduct a fair election.
373. *See*, for example, *Mohawk Industries, Inc.*, 334 NLRB 1170, 1171 (2001).
374. *NLRB* v. *Gissel Packing Co.*, 395 US 575, 618 (1969). For examples of lax appellate court application of these restrictions on employer predictions, *see NLRB* v. *Village IX Inc.*, 723 F.2d 1360 (7th Cir. 1983) and *Be-Lo Stores* v. *NLRB*, 126 F.3d 268 (4th Cir. 1997).
375. *Textile Workers Union* v. *Darlington Mfg. Co.*, 380 US 263 at footnote 20 (1965).

employer has no motivation to not make the threat. Therefore, it is possible that when faced with the question more directly, the Court might be persuaded to limit the availability of threats to close a business to those rare situations in which the employer's commitment to that course of action has in some way been made irrevocable.

Such an approach was adopted by an appellate court in *Wiljef Transportation, Inc.* v. *NLRB*, 946 F.2d 1308 (7th Cir. 1991). In that case the employer had announced to the workers, about two months prior to a scheduled NLRB representation election, that about eleven years earlier it had adopted a corporate by-law stating that it was the company's policy to dissolve the corporation in the event of unionization. The union lost the election but filed an unfair labor practice based on the announcement. The court, affirming the NLRB's finding that the announcement was an unfair labor practice, explained that by-laws are easy to ignore or rescind. Because the corporation had not shown what concrete steps it had taken in preparation for the prospective need to go out of business, the court concluded that the bylaw announcement was not a protected 'prediction grounded in reality' but rather was a threat that violated the NLRA.[376]

§2. Preserving Laboratory Conditions for Representation Elections

386. The NLRB imposes some restrictions on non-coercive expression when an NLRB election is pending and the parties are attempting to persuade employees to vote for or against union representation. However, rather than deal with a party's misconduct as an unfair labor practice, the Board sets aside the results of the representation election if it is won by the party that violated the NLRB's rules for fair discourse. The Board's underlying doctrine, in such cases, is that it will not certify the results of an election that was held in circumstances that might momentarily divert the workers from recording their best judgment respecting their desire to be collectively represented. In its well-worn, and often criticized phrase, the Board insists that its elections be held under 'laboratory conditions'. However, as explained below, its perception of what constitutes violation of such conditions has undergone several revisions.

One basic principle respecting the preservation of laboratory conditions is that the election result will be set aside if the prevailing party engaged in any unfair labor practices after the filing of the election petition. On the other hand, conduct falling short of an unfair labor practice can be grounds for finding an interference with laboratory conditions requiring that the election result be set aside. For example, the NLRB has held that, absent mitigating circumstances, an election won by a union will be set aside if during the campaign period a supervisor actively solicited union support and that support tended to influence the election result.[377]

376. 946 F.2d at 1312. Accord, *Farris Fashions, Inc.* v. *NLRB*, 32 F.3d 373 (8th Cir. 1994).

377. *Harborside Health Care, Inc.*, 343 NLRB 906 (2004); *NLRB* v. *Family Fare, Inc.*, 205 Fed. Appx 403 (6th Cir. 2006).

Another illustration of the 'laboratory conditions' concept is the NLRB prohibition against an election campaign speech to an assembly of workers whose attendance is compelled if made within 24 hours of the commencement of a representation election. According to the Board, such speeches disrupt the workers' need for a reasonable period of undisturbed deliberation. Thus, if the party that violated the 24 hour rule wins the election, the losing party can have the results set aside by timely filing an objection to the conduct of the election based upon that violation. As a result, a new election will be conducted.[378]

The Board also sets aside election results if it finds that the election campaign atmosphere was poisoned by emotionally inflammatory, though non-threatening, communications. Accordingly, on a number of occasions NLRB election results have been set aside because either those favoring or those opposing a union made blatant appeals to the racial, religious or ethnic prejudices of a group of employees.[379]

387. The Board for many years followed the rule that it will set aside an election on the grounds that the winning party engaged in substantial and material misrepresentation of facts at a time when the opposing side or sides did not have an adequate opportunity to respond prior to the election.[380] It deviated from that approach for a short period in the late 1970s, reinstated it and then, in 1982 announced, by a 3–2 vote, that it was again abandoning the rule.[381] Thus, the NLRB's present position is that campaign rhetoric is almost as boundless as that used in American political elections. Lies, distortions and misrepresentations are permissible so long as they are not coercive or emotionally inflammatory. The majority justified this approach as a more efficient rule that acknowledges the voter's maturity and intelligence, and resolves the representational issue without procedural delay.

One segment of the rule against material misrepresentation survives. The NLRB will set aside an election if the successful side represented the NLRB as supporting that party. In order to reduce the prospect of this occurring, the NLRB's election ballot now states: 'The National Labor Relations Board does not endorse any choice in this election. Any markings that you may see on any sample ballot have not been put there by the National Labor Relations Board.' Additionally, the Board's election rules require that statement to appear on any reproduction of its ballot that parties

---

378. *Peerless Plywood Co.*, 107 NLRB 427 (1953); *Falmouth Co.*, 115 NLRB 1533 (1956). This rule was extended to treating as an election interference the practice of giving employees two paychecks, one the amount of their pay less union dues, the other the amount of the union dues, within 24 hours of the election. *Kalin Construction Co.*, 321 NLRB 649 (1996). In *Bro-Tech Corp.*, 330 NLRB 37 (1999) it was held that broadcasting union songs from a truck parked outside a plant on election day is a 24-hour rule violation if the music can be heard in the plant.

379. *KI(USA) Corp.* v. *NLRB*, 35 F.3d 256 (6th Cir. 1994); *NLRB* v. *Katz*, 701 F.2d 703 (7th Cir. 1983); *NLRB* v. *Schapiro & Whitehouse*, 356 F.2d 675 (4th Cir. 1966). *See also*, *NLRB* v. *Flambeau Airmold Corp.*, 178 F.3d 705 (4th Cir. 1999) (holding that the inflammatory statement must be attributable to the party that won the election).

380. *General Knit of California, Inc.*, 239 NLRB 619 (1978); *Hollywood Ceramics Co.*, 140 NLRB 221 (1962); *The Gummed Shoe Products Co.*, 112 NLRB 1092 (1955).

381. *Midland National Life Insurance Co.*, 263 NLRB 127 (1982); *Riveredge Hosp.*, 264 NLRB 1094 (1982).

use in their election campaign literature. Failure to include the statement is grounds to set aside an election won by the wrong-doer.[382]

388. The NLRB does not attempt to curb defamatory statements, other than those defamatory remarks that inflame racial, religious or ethnic hatred. Despite this policy of allowing free expression in carrying out the various facets of labor–management relations, the Supreme Court has held that state courts are not preempted by that federal labor policy from imposing liability for defamation arising in a labor–management relations context. Nevertheless, such suits are not totally free from federal standards. Because federal statutory policy favors free and open exchange of ideas in the labor relations context, and because there is a need to protect the free exercise of the right to organize and the right to act in concert, the Supreme Court has held that in a defamation suit arising in such a context, the plaintiff must prove that the defamer knew that the statement in question was false or that the defamer published the statement with reckless disregard for the truth or falsity of the statement. The Court has also required that actual damage be proven in order for there to be a recovery and that damages must not be excessive.[383]

§3. Prohibition Against Inducements to Refrain from Exercising Section 7 Rights

389. A worker's freedom of choice respecting concerted activities may not be interfered with by purchasing his vote. Thus, neither side may make gifts of substantial value to workers shortly before an NLRB election even if the gift is not expressly conditioned upon the worker agreeing to support the position espoused by the gift giver.[384] Promises of benefits are similarly treated. However, minor amenities are permitted if provided in circumstances in which the gift does not carry an implication of an expected reciprocation by the worker. Accordingly, providing low cost refreshments to those who attend a pre-election campaign rally is not treated as interfering either with employee rights or with the election process.

In contrast, it has been held to be an unfair labor practice for an employer to tell workers he would 'look after' those who oppose a union.[385] Similarly, a company president committed an unfair labor practice when, after reminding an assembly of his workers that he would be breaking the law if he made any special promises respecting their decision at the next day's election, went on to say: 'But, thank heavens, after tomorrow we'll have the right to talk to you freely. It's only natural for

382. *Ryder Memorial Hospital*, 351 NLRB 214 (2007).
383. *Linn* v. *United Plant Guard Workers*, 383 US 53 (1966).
384. *Mailing Services, Inc.*, 293 NLRB 565 (1989) (set aside union election victory because two days prior to the election it provided free medical examinations to workers 'as a first union service'); *B & D Plastics*, 302 NLRB 245 (1991) (election rejecting a union set aside where two days before the election workers received an unscheduled paid holiday on which day they were invited to attend a company picnic where anti-union propaganda was presented).
385. *NLRB* v. *Scoler's Inc.*, 466 F.2d 1289 (2d Cir. 1972).

management to want to clean up all gripes as quickly as possible if not hampered by the union.'[386]

390. A difficult problem arises if, when a union starts to organize the workers, the employer was in the process of seriously weighing whether to improve worker benefits. The Supreme Court has ruled that giving an unexpected benefit during an organizational drive carries the implication that the employer can also withhold benefits if it is dissatisfied with the workers' choice. 'The danger inherent in well-timed increases in benefits is the suggestion of a fist inside the velvet glove' (*NLRB* v. *Exchange Parts*, 375 US 405, 409 (1964)). As a result, the employer must maintain the *status quo* during the course of an election campaign. However, this duty includes the responsibility of putting into effect any improvements that would have been implemented in the normal course of events. Thus, the union organizational effort should neither prompt a sudden improvement in benefits nor provoke a withholding of planned improvements. In the words of the NLRB: '[A]n employer is obliged to carry out his wage-setting practices during a union campaign in the same manner as it would have done in the absence of the campaign.'[387]

Similarly, it is an unfair labor practice for an employer, in response to a union organizing campaign, to solicit employee grievances inasmuch as the activity carries the implication that the employer will now resolve those grievances on its own initiative.[388]

391. Normally, remedies under the NLRA are designed to restore the status quo existing prior to the unfair labor practice and give employees the benefits they would have received but for the violation. This approach is self-defeating, however, if the employer's violation was to promise or give new benefits. It does not promote the union's right to a fair opportunity to organize the workers if, based on the union's unfair labor practice charge, the NLRB orders the employer to take away such benefits even though giving them was an unfair labor practice. Thus, in the previously discussed *Exchange Parts* case, the Board simply ordered the employer not to repeat its violation and to post a notice acknowledging that its conduct had been held to be an unfair labor practice. Once an employer has committed an unfair labor practice and has been ordered not to repeat the violation, if the NLRB obtains a court order enforcing its unfair labor practice finding, any repetition of the unfair labor practice is a contempt of court which can be punished by criminal or civil penalties. Nevertheless, it is questionable whether the availability of such an order is an adequate deterrent to prevent a first-time offense.

392. The Supreme Court has ruled that if a union waives initiation fees for those who become members before the election, this waiver induces or coerces them into joining at that time and thereby creates an inflated impression of the extent of fellow employee support. In addition, the Court said workers who joined the union to

386. *NLRB* v. *Spotlight Company, Inc.*, 462 F.2d 18, 20 (8th Cir. 1972).
387. *Comcast Cablevision*, 313 NLRB 220, 248 (1993); *McCormick Longmeadow Stone Co.*, 158 NLRB 1237 (1966).
388. *Leland Stanford Jr. University*, 240 NLRB 1138 n. 1 (1979).

avoid having to later pay an initiation fee might feel obligated to vote for the union in the NLRB representation election. The net result, held the Court, is to sufficiently interfere with the free choice at the NLRB polls so as to require setting aside the results if the union is victorious.[389] A later appellate decision held, however, that a union can waive initiation fees if the waiver applies to all who join either before or within a stated time after the NLRB election.[390]

§4. Unlawful Discrimination Based on Union Membership

I. Generally

393. Section 8(a)(3) of the NLRA prohibits employers from encouraging or discouraging union membership by discriminating with respect to hiring, job tenure or conditions of employment. Section 8(b)(2) places a similar prohibition on labor organizations. The Supreme Court has broadly construed this language to prohibit any discrimination based on an employee's activities in support of or in opposition to a labor organization.[391]

An explicit statutory exception to this general prohibition permits employers and unions to enter into and enforce agreements requiring workers to pay the financial obligations of union membership unless state law prohibits such agreements or the employee's religious convictions conflict with that obligation. These so-called union security provisions can take several lawful forms and are discussed in greater detail in paragraphs 403-406 and 645-649, below.

Section 2 Fourth and Fifth of the Railway Labor Act, as amended in 1934, prohibited railroads from imposing union security arrangements on workers. However, that authority was reinstated in 1951 (by which time the RLA also covered airlines) with the addition of section 2 Eleventh to that statute.

A related NLRA provision, section 8(b)(5), makes it an unfair labor practice for a union to impose excessive or discriminatory fees as a condition of becoming a member. As discussed in greater detail below at paragraph 405, the NLRB has held that whether an initiation fee is excessive must be determined in light of the wage levels paid in the industry serviced by the union and in light of the traditional norms of the trade.

394. Until the early 1980s, about two thirds of all unfair labor practice cases initiated against employers contained at least one charge of an 8(a)(3) violation. By the 2010 fiscal year the portion of cases that included an 8(a)(3) charge had declined substantially and the most common charge against an employer was for refusal to bargain. Starting with fiscal year 2011, the NLRB ceased publishing detailed data respecting the various categories of filed charges or issued complaints.

Often 8(a)(3) charges often involve close factual questions. Typically, the employer claims that its treatment of an employee or a job applicant was justified

389. *NLRB* v. *Savair Mfg. Co.*, 414 US 270 (1973).
390. *NLRB* v. *VSA, Inc.*, 24 F.3d 588 (4th Cir.), *cert.* denied 513 US 1041 (1994).
391. *Radio Officers' Union* v. *NLRB*, 347 US 17, 39–40 (1954).

by legitimate business concerns but the hearing reveals evidence suggesting that the employer's conduct was motivated, at least to some degree, by antagonism toward the worker's union activities or affiliations. For many years the NLRB and several appellate courts disagreed about the proper test to be applied to resolve mixed motive cases. The NLRB attempted to remove this conflict by adopting in *Wright Line*, 251 NLRB 1083 (1980), enforced 662 F.2d 899 (1st Cir. 1981), *cert.* denied 455 US 989 (1982), a modified statement of its analytic approach. It explained that the General Counsel has the burden of proving by the greater weight of the evidence that the worker's exercise of protected rights was a motivating factor in the employer's adverse conduct toward the employee. Thereafter, the charge will be dismissed only if the employer shows, by a preponderance of the evidence, that its conduct would have been the same even in the absence of the protected activity. The Supreme Court approved the Board's approach in *NLRB* v. *Transportation Management Corp.*, 462 US 393 (1983).

395. The basic elements of an 8(a)(3) or 8(b)(2) violation are:

(a) there was discrimination that classified an employee because of union activity or affiliation,
(b) there was either adverse or favored treatment of a person so classified, and
(c) that treatment tended to encourage or discourage union membership or activity.

The classification based on union activity or membership need not be explicit. If the employer or union adopts a policy that has the impact of treating union members one way and non members another way, it is a classification encompassed by sections 8(a)(3) and 8(b)(2). Similarly, the purpose of encouraging or discouraging union activity or affiliation need not be proven by direct evidence. Illegal intent is presumed if the circumstances reveal that such encouragement or discouragement was the natural consequence of the conduct in question.[392]

396. In some situations, an unfair labor practice is found where a person who is discriminated against is not himself affiliated with a union or engaged in union activities. For example, in one case it was found that the employer discharged some non union workers together with union supporters in order to disguise the discriminatory purpose of its action. The NLRB concluded that 8(a)(3) protected the non-union workers as well as the union adherents and ordered both groups reinstated with backpay.[393]

In another case, the Board held that a worker's rights under section 8(a)(3) are violated if an employer discriminates not because of the worker's union activities but because of the union activities of the worker's relative.[394] In still another situation, the Board held that the Act had been violated when an employer fired a

392. *Metropolitan Edison Co.* v. *NLRB*, 460 US 693 (1983).
393. *Howard Johnson Co.*, 209 NLRB 1122 (1974).
394. *Amerace Corp.*, 217 NLRB 942 (1975).

worker in the mistaken belief that the worker had been engaged in union activities.[395] In effect, the remedy was not designed to protect the individual worker's rights, which in essence were non existent under the circumstances, but rather to enforce the Act's prohibitions inasmuch as the primary function of the NLRA is to serve the public interest by establishing a code of fair conduct for labor management relations.

397. Union organizers sometimes seek employment with a targeted enterprise so that they will have an opportunity to organize from within the workforce (sometimes called 'salting'). The Supreme Court has upheld the NLRB's ruling that even though an organizer remains on the union's payroll during an organizing effort, an employer cannot refuse to hire such an otherwise qualified worker, and cannot dismiss such a worker simply because his only interest in the job is the opportunity to more effectively organize employees.[396] The Court explained that at common law it is recognized that an employee can have two masters. Therefore, since the term 'employee' is broadly defined by the NLRA, a paid union organizer can also be an 'employee' of the targeted enterprise and, hence, is within the Act's protection.[397]

On the other hand, when an employer is charged with refusing to hire a job applicant because of the applicant's pro union sympathies, in a 3–2 decision the NLRB has held that the General Counsel must show that the alleged discriminatee was genuinely interested in seeking to establish an employment relationship with the employer and did not apply merely to demonstrate that the employer discriminates against union supporters.[398]

II. Runaway Shops

A. Generally

398. The introduction of a labor organization into an employer's relationship with its workers undoubtedly produces great anxiety for many American employers. The history of some industries has been characterized by the sequence of organizational success followed by the termination of operations at the scene of that success and a transfer of operations to a different locale. One recent change in the pattern is that whereas in prior decades the flight frequently meant a move from the industrialized north or far west to the more rural southern or central states, starting in the 1980s the flight now often involves moving operations out of the US to a low wage country or contracting the work to a company whose workers are unorganized.[399]

395. *Henning and Cheadle*, 212 NLRB 776 (1974), rev'd on other grounds 522 F.2d 1050 (7th Cir. 1975); *Cedar Falls Health Care Center*, 276 NLRB 1300, 1302 n. 14 (1985).
396. *Sunland Construction Co.*, 309 NLRB 1224 (1992).
397. *NLRB* v. *Town & Country Electric, Inc.*, 516 US 85 (1995).
398. *Toering Elec. Co.*, 351 NLRB No. 18 (2007); *Massey Energy Co.*, 358 NLRB No. 159 (2012).
399. *See*, for example, *Vico Prods. Co.* v. *NLRB*, 333 F.3d 198 (DC Cir. 2003).

399. An employer's flight from union representation is referred to as the 'runaway shop' syndrome. Such flight from unions, the NLRB has reasoned, is a form of discrimination against those who seek to join or remain members of unions and, therefore, violates section 8(a)(3) of the NLRA.[400] The Board's remedies in such cases have included ordering the employer to make jobs available at the new site for its prior workforce and finance the cost of any change in residence necessitated by the move to the new location.[401] Alternatively, on occasion the board has ordered the employer to reopen and resume closed operations.[402]

400. Normally an employer charged with a runaway shop violation asserts that its move was motivated by business considerations. This has been held to be a good defense even when those business considerations include the employer's concern that the costs of employing workers under union standards will make the business operation unprofitable.[403] A related issue, discussed in paragraph 707, below, is the extent to which the employer has a duty to bargain with the union concerning the decision to make such a move and to bargain concerning the impact the move will have upon bargaining unit employees.

B. Termination of Business and Partial Closings

401. The prohibition against employers discriminating based on an employee's union membership or activity does not prevent an employer from totally terminating a business to avoid having to deal with a union. The Supreme Court has held that the choice to terminate a business is a property right that is preserved absent an explicit legislative encroachment upon it. The Court's discussion suggests that, in any event, the constitutional protections of an owner's right to control its property might prohibit Congress from interfering with an employer's decision to terminate its business in order to avoid dealing with a union.

Partial business closings, on the other hand, are not sacrosanct. Accordingly, it is an unfair labor practice for an employer to close one part of a business operation for the purpose, or with the apparent likelihood, of dissuading workers employed in another part of the owner's enterprise from engaging in union activities.[404]

---

400. *ILGWU* v. *NLRB*, 374 F.2d 295 (DC Cir.), *cert.* denied 387 US 942 (1967), held, however, that the employer cannot be ordered to bargain with the union as representative of the employees at the new site unless there is evidence that a majority of the new workforce supports the labor organization.
401. *Philadelphia Dress Joint Board* v. *NLRB*, 305 F.2d 825 (3d Cir. 1962) affirming 133 NLRB 547 (1961).
402. *Mid-South Bottling Co.* v. *NLRB*, 876 F.2d 458 (5th Cir. 1989).
403. For example, *NLRB* v. *Rapid Bindery, Inc.*, 293 F.2d 170 (2d Cir. 1961). But *see*, *Statler Industries, Inc.* v. *NLRB*, 644 F.2d 902, 909 (1st Cir. 1981) (suggesting that the employer's defense is limited to situations involving economic necessity accelerated by the prospect of increased costs due to unionization).
404. *Textile Workers Union* v. *Darlington Mfg. Co.*, 380 US 263 (1965). In some licensed industries, such as railroads and public utilities, a condition of licensing is agreement to not close without obtaining the regulatory agency's permission so that the public convenience will not be unduly injured.

III. Union Hiring Halls

402. The prohibition against discrimination based on union membership requires that labor organizations treat all workers equally with respect to their job interests. Thus, a union cannot seek favored treatment for its members as opposed to non-members in the same bargaining unit. Similarly, to the extent that the union itself controls work opportunities, it is prohibited from giving favored treatment to its own members. Thus, in operating a hiring hall that is the sole source through which an employer recruits new workers, a union may not discriminate in favor of union members or against dissident members.[405] Unions can, however, give hiring hall preference on the basis of prior work experience in the industry – a characteristic that normally gives some priority to union members. Unions can also give preference to local residents in referring job applicants to employers pursuant to a hiring hall agreement.[406] And, unions can charge non members a fee for the hiring hall service, but that fee must be less than the amount of the union's dues.[407] On the other hand, if a union has an agreement making its facility the exclusive hiring hall for an employer, it can insist that an employee be discharged if hired without being referred by the union.[408]

IV. Union Security and Preferred Status

403. Union violations of the prohibition against causing an employer to discriminate based on union activity often involve a union's efforts to enforce a union security agreement. Although section 8(a)(3) and 8(b)(2) appear to allow unions and employers to enter into and enforce agreements compelling union membership, a union may not request or require an employer to use job actions or contractual arrangements as a means of enforcing the union's rules or policies with respect to membership. Thus, a union violates section 8(b)(2) if it invokes a union shop clause in order to have an employee discharged for non-membership when the employee was denied or lost union membership for some reason other than a failure to pay dues. For example, it has been held that if union membership is denied to a worker because he refused to participate in a strike or because he assisted a rival union, it is an unfair labor practice for the union to attempt to enforce the union shop provision by demanding that the worker be discharged.[409] Furthermore, in *NLRB* v. *General Motors Corp.*, 373 US 734, 743 (1963), the Supreme Court stated: 'If an

---

405. *Carpenters Local 537 (E.I. Dupont)*, 303 NLRB 419 (1991); *Dist. Council 91 Int'l Union of Painters*, 2013 NLRB LEXIS 170 (2013).

406. *Metro. Dist. Council, Carpenters (Jamestown Metal Prods. Co.)*, 194 NLRB 159 (1971); *Local Union 8, I.B.E.W. (Romanoff Elec.)*, 221 NLRB 1131 (1975).

407. *NLRB* v. *Local 138, Operating Engineers*, 385 F.2d 874 (2d Cir. 1967), *cert.* denied 391 US 909 (1968) (The union was required to rebate $3.50 per month from $10 monthly 'permit fee' paid by non-members to use union hiring hall. Monthly dues were $10.) *Simms* v. *Local 1752*, 838 F.3d 613 (5th Cir. 2016)(state law cannot prohibit exclusive hiring halls or requiring the payment of fees to use such facilities).

408. *Construction and General Laborers Local 596*, 216 NLRB 778 (1975).

409. *Local 1104 Communications Workers* v. *NLRB*, 520 F.2d 411 (2d Cir. 1975), *cert.* denied 423 US 1051 (1976).

employee in a union shop unit refuses to respect any union-imposed obligations other than the duty to pay dues and fees … the employee may not be discharged for non membership even though [as a result] he is [no longer] a formal member.' Therefore, if a worker tenders the payment of union dues, the worker cannot be refused a job or be discharged even though he quit the union rather than participate in a strike or simply refused to join the union.[410]

Moreover, in *Communication Workers* v. *Beck*, 487 US 735 (1988), the Supreme Court ruled that if an employee fulfills the union security clause's financial obligation but refuses to become a union member, the worker can only be assessed for the portion of union dues that represents the cost of the union's activities 'germane to collective bargaining, contract administration, or grievance adjustment'. In an earlier decision, *Ellis* v. *Brotherhood of Railway, Airline and S.S. Clerks*, 466 US 435 (1984), arising under the Railway Labor Act, the Court had found that an unwilling employee cannot be compelled to contribute to a labor organization's expenses for activities such as lobbying Congress to increase the minimum wage or organizing workers in other enterprises or litigating cases that involve principles that generally protect worker interests but do not directly involve the employee's own bargaining unit.

In reaching decisions such as *General Motors, Beck* and *Ellis*, the Supreme Court has observed that because the parties are compelled by law to engage in collective bargaining when a labor organization has the support of a majority of employees, the system of collective bargaining in the US carries the government's stamp of approval and, as such, may be subject to the same constitutional restrictions that would limit actions of a government agency. Because the Constitution implicitly protects freedom of association and freedom of expression, the Court has suggested that it might be impermissible for government to compel union membership or compel financial support for expressions of opinion with which the payer disagrees. Thus, the Court has expressed unwillingness to assume that Congress intended to authorize the parties to engage in actions that might be constitutionally forbidden to a government agency. Hence, although the union security proviso of NLRA section 8(a)(3) on its face says that it is permissible for a union and employer to agree to require employees to become and remain union members (after a minimum 30-day waiting period), the Supreme Court decisions limit the extent to which such provisions can be enforced.[411]

A collective bargaining provision that on its face requires a worker to become and remain a union member is known in the US as a 'union shop' provision. The type of provision that the Supreme Court has held to be functionally permitted by the union security proviso in section 8(a)(3) is known in the US as an 'agency shop' provision. The latter requires employees to do no more than pay their *pro rata* share of the costs of the union's services in directly serving as the collective bargaining agent of the bargaining unit. In *Marquez* v. *Screen Actors Guild, Inc.*, 525 US 33

---

410. *Booster Lodge 405, IAM* v. *NLRB*, 412 US 84 (1973); *NLRB* v. *Hershey Foods Corp.*, 513 F.2d 1083 (9th Cir. 1975). *See also*, *Pattern Makers' League* v. *NLRB*, 473 US 95, 106 n. 16 (1985).
411. *See*, A. Goldman, 'Industrial Democracy – Slogan or Metaphor?' in *Liber Amicorum Roger Blanpain* (M. Weiss & C. Engels, eds. 1998) for a discussion of a doctrinal approach under which union shop provisions constitutionally could be enforced in the manner specified on the face of §8(a)(3).

(1998), the Supreme Court ruled that it is not an unfair labor practice for a union and employer to adopt a union shop provision in their collective agreement without explaining in the agreement that employees need do anything beyond paying an agency shop fee. The Court expressly did not reach the question of whether the union has a separate duty to inform the workers that they satisfy the requirement by paying their *pro rata* share of the costs of the union's representational activities and do not actually have to become a member of the labor organization. However, after *Beck*, the NLRB ruled that a union violates its duty of fair representation by failing to notify bargaining unit employees that they cannot be required to join the union and have a right to limit payment of their union-security dues and initiation fees to moneys spent on activities germane to their union's role as the bargaining representative.[412] It thereafter held that once employees elect to exercise their right to not be members and pay only an agency shop fee, it is a violation of the duty to bargain in good faith for the union to require employees to annually notify it that they continue to elect to pay only that part of membership dues that is used for the union's bargaining unit representation activities.[413]

404. In 1980, section 19 of the NLRA was amended in an effort to accommodate persons with religious objections to union membership. It says that an adherent of a religious group that conscientiously objects to joining or supporting labor organizations is entitled, as an alternative to paying union dues, to make a charitable contribution to a tax exempt non religious organization. Section 19 also provides that the labor organization is permitted to charge a reasonable service fee for processing a grievance on that worker's behalf. One appellate court, however, has held that this provision violates the First Amendment's constitutional separation of church and state because it gives a special privilege to members of only certain religious groups.[414]

405. Closely related to the section 8(b)(2) prohibition against a labor organization causing an employer to discriminate based on union activity is section 8(b)(5) which prohibits unions from charging excessive initiation fees as a condition of employment under a union security agreement with an employer. Section 8(b)(5) states that in determining whether an initiation fee is excessive, the Board must consider the customs of labor organizations in the industry and the wage level paid to the affected worker. To illustrate, in one case, a local union representing graphic artists employed in the television broadcast industry was faced with a need to increase its per capita dues payment to its parent organization. In order to find the finances to do this, the union doubled the initiation fee charged new members. That fee previously had been two weeks' salary. In amount, the new initiation fee ranged from about $900 to $1,000 depending on the wage rate for the particular job. This increase discouraged some non-union member job applicants from accepting work

---

412. *California Saw & Knife Works*, 320 NLRB 224 (1995).

413. *Communication Workers of America (AT&T Teleholding),* 359 NLRB No. 131 (2013); *L-C Communications*, 355 NLRB 1062 (2010).

414. *Wilson* v. *NLRB*, 920 F.2d 1282 (6th Cir. 1990), cert. denied 505 US 1218 (1992); S. Irion, 'The UnConstitutionality of the NLRA's Religious Accommodation Provision', 44 *Gonz. L. Rev.* 325 (2009) (examining both sides of this issue).

with a broadcaster who had a collective agreement containing a union shop clause. The employer filed charges with the NLRB asserting that the real motive for the increase in the initiation fee was to obtain more job opportunities for the local union's unemployed members – which, at the time, constituted close to half of the membership. The employer testified that the union had previously requested favored treatment for job applicants who were union members. Since the union's unemployed members would not have to pay an initiation fee to the union, the increased fee demanded by the union made the job opportunities with the employer more attractive to them than to non-members since the latter would have to join the union and pay the fee pursuant to the union security clause of the collective agreement. The NLRB agreed that the initiation fee was both discriminatory and excessive. It ordered the fee reduced back to the original level and required the union to pay back any excess that had been collected from new members. In reaching its decision, the Board reviewed the initiation fees and wage rates for this type of work at bargaining units in various locations throughout the country and found that the highest initiation fees were no more than about two weeks' salary and that the wage rates at these other locales generally were higher than in the bargaining unit at issue.[415]

406. Offering or giving special benefits for union membership or activity violates the section 8(a)(3) prohibition against discriminatory treatment relating to union activities. (Such special treatment may also violate section 8(a)(2).) This prohibition is not applied, however, to those privileges given to employees who have union representation responsibilities in administering the collective agreement. Thus, it is not a violation of the Act if shop stewards (workers appointed by the union or elected by the membership to investigate grievances, counsel grievants and present grievances to management) are permitted to perform their representational responsibilities on company time while receiving company pay. Similarly, it is not an unfair labor practice if the employer provides such workers with office space and equipment to carry out those responsibilities.[416]

Collective agreements often give special seniority to the workplace representatives of the union so as to protect them from layoff and grant them early recall, in preference to workers with greater job longevity. Such 'super-seniority' provisions are not an unfair labor practice so long as the benefited workers in fact need to be available in the workplace to perform their responsibilities administering the collective agreement. The rationale for permitting this form of favored treatment is that the employer benefits from the ready availability of the union's representative to resolve problems concerning the application of the agreement. Thus, the employer is serving its own needs and not merely granting a special favor to union activists.[417]

415. *IATSE, Local 841 (National Broadcasting Co.)*, 225 NLRB 994 (1976).
416. *Baker Mine Services, Inc.*, 279 NLRB 609 (1986). Section 8(a)(2) of the Act, which prohibits most forms of employer assistance to unions, recognizes the right of an employer to 'confer' with employees during paid work hours and, thereby, implicitly acknowledges the legitimacy of allowing shop stewards to conduct the business of representing bargaining unit interests while on paid work time.
417. *Local 1384, UAW* v. *NLRB*, 756 F.2d 482 (7th Cir. 1985).

On the other hand, it is a violation of section 8(a)(3) for an employer to give shop stewards or officers job benefits that are unrelated to facilitating the union representative's ability to counsel and speak for the workers. For example, it has been held to be an unfair labor practice to give a shop steward special consideration in making delivery route assignments.[418] Regardless of whether the steward has a more or less lucrative route assignment, he is working and available to help administer the collective agreement.

V. Remedying Unlawful Discrimination under the NLRA

407. The basic remedy in an NLRA discrimination case is for the NLRB to attempt to place the discriminatee in the position he would be in but for the unfair labor practice. This involves awarding the worker backpay, with interest, plus reinstatement with all of the rights and privileges to which the employee would be entitled had the employee not been discharged or in some other way disciplined or disadvantaged. If the job is not available at the time reinstatement is ordered, the worker is entitled to the next available opening. Backpay is owed for those hours for which work would have been available and for which the worker would have been able to work during the period of the discriminatory separation. Earnings from other employment during that period are a set-off deducted from what is owed. In addition, if the worker did not make good faith efforts to mitigate damages by trying to find other employment, a deduction is made for the estimated amount that would have been earned from other employment. On the other hand, the employee is entitled to be reimbursed for reasonable expenses incurred in searching for other work and that reimbursement, with daily compounded interest, is not subject to an offset based on interim earnings.

Backpay and any set-offs to backpay are calculated on a quarterly basis so as to reduce an employer's motive to delay the offer of reinstatement in the hopes that the discriminatee's higher earnings in a different job will, as a result of the set-off rule, eventually reduce the employer's liability. Interest on any amounts owed is compounded daily.

For many years, interest on backpay had been calculated at the rate of 6 percent. In 1977, the NLRB ruled that interest will be at the same rate as is awarded in federal income tax cases – a rate that is tied to the prime interest rate charged by commercial banks. In 1987, the Board abandoned that method for calculating interest and adopted the approach of the newly adopted federal Tax Reform Act which sets the rate to be charged based on the interest rate paid by the federal government for its own short term borrowing. These varying rates are considerably lower than the rates wage earners typically pay for consumer borrowing. Because the collection of backpay in a single year may cover several years, it could put the employee in an income tax bracket that is higher than it would have been had there been no suspension of earnings. Therefore, the Board will also award an added amount to offset any resulting higher tax liability imposed on the employee.

418. *NLRB* v. *Teamsters Local 338*, 531 F.2d 1162 (2d Cir. 1976); *Local 1384, United Auto.* v. *NLRB*, 756 F.2d 482 (7th. Cir. 1985). *See also*, *Frankline, Inc.*, 287 NLRB 263 (1987).

The make-whole remedy also extends to all benefits such as accrual of paid vacation, paid holidays, pension benefit contributions or credit, Social Security contributions, disability and medical insurance protection, and the like.[419]

408. If both a union and employer are found guilty of discrimination, backpay liability is joint and severable. That is, the entire amount can be collected from either respondent and that respondent, in turn, can seek a recovery of half from the other. Backpay liability is measured as of the employer's offer of reinstatement, and in the case of joint liability, it is measured as of the employer's reinstatement offer plus the union's notification to the employer that it does not object to reinstatement. In the fiscal year that ended in October 2016, the NLRB recovered $52.3 million in backpay for workers whose NLRA rights had been violated and over $0.4 million for employees who were reimbursed for improperly levied union fees, dues or fines.

In many cases a worker receives backpay but agrees not to seek his job back. This is done to hasten the receipt of backpay as a result of the employer's agreement to forgo appeals. Such a settlement requires the consent of the NLRB's General Counsel. Settlements based on backpay without reinstatement have been criticized on the ground that the remaining workers are likely to be left with the impression that the employer can successfully discharge workers because of their union activities. In fiscal year 2016, 1,648 employees were offered reinstatement of which only 595 accepted the offer.

409. In addition to the foregoing, the employer is also required to post in a prominent place at the work premises a notice to employees acknowledging the finding of a violation and the issuance of the cease and desist order. In cases involving egregious or frequently repeated employer unfair labor practices, management has been ordered to assemble the employees at the premises so that the notice could be read to them or to allow union access to plant bulletin boards or even access to meet with employees on the employer's premises to provide an opportunity for the union to offset the chilling effects of the employer's unfair labor practices.[420]

Unions found guilty of unfair labor practices often are required to mail notices to bargaining unit members. (See also, discussion at paragraphs 803–804, below.)

§5. Unlawful Interference with Labor Organizations

I. Employer Domination or Interference

410. NLRA section 8(a)(2) prohibits employers from dominating unions, interfering with their formation or organization, or from giving them financial or other support. These prohibitions are largely the product of widespread pre-Wagner Act

419. NLRB General Counsel Memos 11-07, 08 (2011).

420. *See generally, United Steel Workers of America (Florida Steel Corp.)* v. *NLRB*, 646 F.2d 616 (DC Cir. 1981); *Beverly Health & Rehabilitation Services, Inc.* v. *NLRB*, 317 F.3d 316 (DC Cir. 2003) (where appropriate, required posting can be enterprise-wide even though the violation involved a more confined bargaining unit).

efforts by employers to promote employer-dependent labor organizations by coercing workers into joining company designed 'employee associations' that were dominated by workers whose loyalty management regarded as assured. In a few cases, these organizations, generally referred to as 'company unions', eventually were captured by more independent workers who were prepared to engage in arm's length collective bargaining. And, in some situations, workers at an enterprise established their own independent union without employer interference or domination. But, most commonly, the company union was a propaganda medium for persuading workers that the employer's treatment of them was fair and generous.[421] Although the company-dominated union has become a rarity in American labor–management relations, the statutory principles designed to combat this phenomena continue to regulate important aspects of the employer-union relationship.

411. Of critical importance in applying section 8(a)(2) is the definition of 'labor organization'. This is found at section 2(5) of the NLRA which states that a labor organization is a group in which employees participate and which exists, at least in part, for the purpose 'of dealing with employers concerning grievances, labor disputes, wages, rates of pay, hours of employment, or conditions of work'. As a result of this very broad language, groups such as works councils or shop committees, that are treated as distinct from labor organizations in the labor law systems of most other industrial nations, are by definition 'labor organizations' under American law.[422]

412. Because American labor law is structured on the principle that the representative designated by a majority of workers is the exclusive bargaining agent of bargaining unit employees, it is an unfair labor practice for an employer to bargain with any group of workers other than the collective bargaining agent unless that agent gives its consent. Even in the absence of a majority representative, section 8(a)(2) makes it an unfair labor practice to assist or dominate a labor organization. Thus, at least to the extent that a works council or similar group is established at an employer's urging, or with the employer's aid, the employer is guilty of an unfair labor practice unless the workers are represented by a majority designated bargaining agent and that bargaining agent agrees to the establishment of the council or group.[423]

The foregoing is illustrated by the situation that came before the United States Supreme Court in *NLRB* v. *Cabot Carbon Co.*, 360 US 203 (1959). At the urging of the War Labor Board, the employer established a series of employee committees, elected by the workers, that met periodically with employer representatives. Its

421. D. Brody, *Labor Embattled*, 49–57 (2005).

422. *Electromation, Inc.*, 309 NLRB 990 (1992), affirmed 35 F.3d 1148 (7th Cir. 1994); *NLRB* v. *American Medical Response, Inc.*, 438 F.3d 188 (2d Cir. 2006).

423. Federal Credit Unions, which are savings and loan institutions controlled by the employee depositors, are found in many places of employment. Section 158(a) of US Code Title 29 states that employer assistance to a Federal Credit Union shall not constitute the sort of aid or interference with a labor organization that is prohibited or regulated by the NLRA.

discussions with the committees covered plant and personnel problems ranging from safety, improvement of efficiency, conservation of materials, the installation of roof vents, individual employee grievances, and establishing a system for the assignment of overtime work. The employer provided clerical assistance to the committees and conducted the elections at which the committee members were chosen. The Supreme Court upheld the NLRB's finding that even though the committees never attempted to engage in bargaining with the employer, and submitted their proposals solely in the form of requests, not demands, the committees were labor organizations as that term is defined by the NLRA because they were 'dealing with' the employer concerning those issues. Accordingly, the assistance given by the employer to the committees was an unfair labor practice. The Court observed that when Congress reexamined the NLRA for the purpose of amending it in 1947, the legislature rejected a proposal that would have authorized employers to establish and aid worker committees designed to facilitate the discussion of matters of mutual interest. It should be noted that the Court did not state that such committees cannot exist. Its holding dealt only with the situation in which a committee receiving employer assistance engages in the sort of activities that constitutes it to be a labor organization.

413. More recently the NLRB has held that employee committees that, within defined spheres of discretion, perform managerial functions such as making job assignments, assigning job rotations, scheduling overtime, interviewing job, making safety inspections, and modifying starting and stopping times, are not *dealing with* management but rather *are* management and, therefore, 8(a)(2) is inapplicable to them.[424] Similarly, the NLRB has held that a joint employer-employee committee formed by an employer and charged solely with the responsibility of hearing and ruling on employee grievances is not a labor organization. Therefore, the employer's conduct in establishing such a committee does not constitute a violation of section 8(a)(2). The Board reasoned that to fit within the definition of a labor organization, a group must in some way act as an advocate of worker interests and not serve a wholly impartial function.[425] The Board also has held that section 8(a)(2) does not prohibit an employer from convening an employee meeting to request employee ideas for improving the operation or management of the facility. Nor does the Board consider it unlawful for an employer to establish a committee to provide information to the employer so long as 'the employer simply gathers the information and does what it wishes' with it.[426] Rather, it has been held that to be a 'labor organization' the group must have a bilateral relationship with the employer and a

424. *Crown Cork & Seal*, 334 NLRB 699 (2001).

425. *Sparks Nugget, Inc.*, 230 NLRB 275 (1977). The Board held, however, that the employer's failure to negotiate with the Union concerning this change was a breach of the duty to bargain. The Board's decision was enforced as modified on other grounds in *NLRB* v. *Silver Spur Casino*, 623 F.2d 571 (9th Cir. 1980). Compare *Magan Medical Clinic, Inc.*, 314 NLRB 1083 (1994) finding an 8(a)(2) violation where the employer formed a grievance committee to provide an alternative to union organizing and the committee dealt with the employer about grievances rather than resolving them on its own authority.

426. *E.I. duPont de Nemours & Co.*, 311 NLRB 893, 894 (1993).

pattern or practice of submitting proposals for changes in wage, hours or other terms or conditions of employment.[427]

A different aspect of this issue arises when a social action organization that assists low-income workers calls upon employers to improve benefits or working conditions for a group of its workers. It has been suggested that because the social action organization is not the representative selected by a majority of workers in an appropriate bargaining unit, it is a violation of the NLRA to exert social or economic pressure in support of getting the employer to change its policies. To answer this question it is necessary to decide whether such organizations are labor organizations under the Act and whether calling for greater fairness or decency in the treatment of workers constitutes 'dealing with' employers within the context of the NLRA. Such questions have been discussed but not resolved.[428]

414. The issue of whether an employer–employee consultation arrangement constitutes a labor organization becomes more complicated in the setting of bargaining units containing professional employees. Professional employees frequently look upon such consultation as a professional prerogative through which they provide their expertise and ensure that the entity's procedures and policies conform to the profession's standards of care, performance, quality and ethics. On the other hand, professional employees often regard such joint consultation as the mechanism through which they participate in and are part of management.

In one case, an appellate court held that it was lawful for a university to financially support the activities of a group elected by about one-third of the non faculty employees even though this group proposed benefits changes and served as a conduit for presenting employee problems to the institution's management. The court did not discuss the previously cited Supreme Court's decision in *Cabot Carbon*. Instead it praised the system as a cooperative alternative to the traditional adversary model and said that it had special appropriateness in a university setting.[429]

In *NLRB* v. *Yeshiva University*, 444 US 672 (1980), the Supreme Court ruled that extensive teacher consultation respecting promotions to a higher academic rank, the grant of tenure, curriculum design, and standards for being awarded a degree constitute managerial activities and remove the teachers from the status of 'employee'. Accordingly, the university teachers were not entitled to file a petition with the NLRB to obtain an election in which they could establish that a majority of them wanted to be represented by a bargaining agent. The *Yeshiva* decision, therefore, suggests that taken far enough, employee participation in management can be a means by which employers can avoid having to bargain collectively with a labor

---

427. *Electromation, Inc.*, 309 NLRB 990 (1992), affirmed 35 F.3d 1148 (7th Cir. 1994); *Waugh Chapel South, LLC* v. *United Food & Comm. Workers Union Local 27*, 728 F.3d 354, 361 (4th. Cir. 2013)(the parties 'must reciprocally interact'). *Also, see NLRB* v. *Peninsula General Hosp. Med. Center*, 36 F.3d 1262 (4th Cir. 1994).

428. E. Naduris-Weissman, 'The Worker Center Movement and Traditional Labor Law: A Contextual Analysis', 30 *Berkeley J. Emp. & Lab. L.* 232 (2009). Unions, too, have sponsored similar non bargaining efforts. M. Oswalt, 'Improvisational Unionism', *104 Calif. L. Rev. 597* (2016).

429. *NLRB* v. *Northeastern University*, 601 F.2d 1208 (1st Cir. 1979).

organization. It should be noted, though, that in *Yeshiva* it was found that the teachers additionally played a significant role in setting tuition rates, appointing administrators, and shaping the institution's programs.

II. Employer Assistance

415. A few appellate courts have allowed some employer assistance to employee groups without classifying that aid as a violation of section 8(a)(2). In one case an employer convened a meeting after a union lost a close NLRB election and acknowledged to the workers that it was evident there was some employee dissatisfaction. In response to the employer's inquiry as to whether there might be a way to resolve these problems, employees proposed a system of joint management–employee committees to discuss the problem areas and make recommendations to management. The proposal was accepted and became the subject of an unfair labor practice charge. Emphasizing that the proposal originated with the workers and was enthusiastically endorsed by them, a Court of Appeals held that the establishment of the joint committees, the participation of management in their operation, and the conduct of committee business at the employer's premises on paid work time, did not constitute unlawful assistance to a labor organization.[430]

In another case, a federal appellate court held it was not an unfair labor practice for an employer to permit a union to operate and receive the profits from food and beverage sales in the plant where the annual profits were less than $1,000 and the funds were used to provide social amenities beneficial to employees. The court characterized the employer's action as 'a permissible form of friendly cooperation designed to foster … harmonious labor–management relations' and not a 'form of 'support' designed to interfere with' the employees' free exercise of protected organizational rights.[431] (In both of the foregoing cases the court was setting aside an NLRB determination that the employer's conduct constituted an unfair labor practice.) See, also, paragraphs 422–431, below.)

III. Remedial Distinction between Domination and Interference

416. The NLRB and the courts distinguish between employer domination of a labor organization and less intrusive forms of interference or support. The purpose of this distinction is to determine the extensiveness of the remedy needed in the event of a violation. If the employer dominated a labor organization, the remedy is to disestablish that organization. The underlying assumption is that this is the only way to ensure the independence of labor organizations. If it is found that the employer interference does not prevent the organization from regaining the

430. *Hertzka & Knowles* v. *NLRB*, 503 F.2d 625 (9th Cir. 1974) *cert.* denied 423 US 875 (1975). *Compare, NLRB* v. *Fremont Mfg. Co.*, 558 F.2d 889 (8th Cir. 1977) (*per curiam*) (violation found where committee brings worker complaints to the employer).

431. *NLRB* v. *Post Pub. Co.*, 311 F.2d 565, 569–570 (7th Cir. 1962). But *see* the same court's affirmance of the NLRB's decision in *Electromation Inc.*, 309 NLRB 990 (1992), enforced 35 F.3d 1148 (7th Cir. 1994).

capacity for independent action, the remedy is to prohibit continuation of employer activity that interferes with or tends to interfere with the union's independence.[432]

IV. Limits on Supervisory Participation in a Labor Organization

417. Because supervisors are not 'employees', as that term is defined by the NLRA, they do not have a protected right to engage in concerted activities. Nevertheless, supervisors sometimes become or remain union members because they were members before becoming supervisors and do not wish to lose benefits financed by union dues. These may include life insurance, cooperative consumer purchasing programs, low cost housing, recreational facilities, and the like. Supervisors employed in industries, such as building construction, in which many workers frequently switch back and forth between supervisory and non supervisory jobs (often based on their being the most senior person on the job), may find continued payment of dues less confusing and less expensive than resigning and rejoining when they take and later lose a supervisory position. Still other supervisors are employed in an enterprise in which management voluntarily bargains collectively with the representatives of its lower level supervisors.[433] In still other situations, such as nursing, a supervisor may be a member of a profession in which the professional association also engages in collective bargaining representation. Thus, the supervisor maintains membership in the labor organization in order to maintain professional affiliations.

418. Section 8(a)(2)'s prohibition against employer interference with labor organizations could be construed to prohibit supervisory membership in a union on the ground that, as an agent of the employer, the supervisor's presence in a labor organization might constitute prohibited employer interference with or support of the union. However, section 14(a) of the NLRA accommodates the desires of some supervisors to retain their union membership. It states that nothing in the NLRA prohibits a supervisor from becoming or remaining a union member.

419. Despite the language of section 14(a), there are NLRB and judicial decisions holding that a supervisor's presence violates section 8(a)(2) if the supervisor has an active role in the labor organization and, thereby, could influence union policies in accordance with the employer's desires. Additionally, in one case a federal appellate court noted that because a supervisor can influence a worker's job status and benefits, non supervisory union members might be reluctant to express views within the union if those views are contrary to the position of the supervisor-member. Accordingly, it was held that an employer must prohibit its supervisors from actively participating in a labor organization if that active participation might interfere with the rights of non supervisory employees to freely conduct union

432. *NLRB* v. *District 50, United Mine Workers of America*, 355 US 453, 458 (1958).
433. *See*, for example, *Florida Power & Light Co.* v. *International Brotherhood of Electrical Workers, Local 641*, 417 US 790, 792 (1974).

affairs.[434] Proof of such interference is satisfied by showing a potential conflict of interest; it is not necessary to prove actual sacrifice of representational integrity.[435] On the other hand, a supervisor's participation as an active union member does not violate the NLRA if no conflict of interest is created. Hence the NLRB has indicated that it is not an unfair labor practice for a supervisor-member to serve on the union's finance committee or on a committee that reviews grievances involving bargaining units whose workers are employed by other employers.[436]

420. The position taken by the Board and the courts leaves considerable uncertainty as to whether a particular supervisor's union activities will cause problems for his employer. One solution, adopted by many employers, is to forbid supervisors from being union members since they are not employees as defined by the NLRA and, therefore, do not have a protected right to organize. In industries such as printing and construction, in which there is a long and strong tradition of union membership irrespective of supervisory status, an employer prohibition against such membership might prove counterproductive for the employer. Moreover, in those sectors in which the same organizations serve both as bargaining agent and professional association, considerable tension and dislocation would result from an employer ban on supervisory membership in the labor organization.

Although one appellate court has suggested that a labor organization should not be permitted to obtain NLRB certification as bargaining agent if that organization permits supervisors to be members,[437] section 14(a) of the NLRB appears to reject that suggestion. More persuasive is the position of the NLRB that a union loses its right to be a bargaining agent if the presence of supervisors prevents the organization from approaching the bargaining table with the single purpose of protecting and advancing the interests of its members.[438]

421. Some of the more frequently cited decisions in which an unfair labor practice has been found based on the active role a supervisor played in union affairs predate the adoption of the LMRDA. That Act established a series of protections for union members including the right 'to express any views, arguments, or opinions' respecting the business of the labor organization or candidates for union office. It also protects the right of members to vote in elections, to nominate candidates for union office, and to be a candidate for office. These rights are subject to 'reasonable rules and regulations' and to 'reasonable qualifications' uniformly imposed. Inasmuch as these rights are extended to all members in good standing, and the term 'member' is defined in the Act as including all persons (not just 'employees'), there is a question as to the extent to which it is appropriate, in carrying out the section 8(a)(2) prohibitions against employer interference in union affairs, to place

434. *Local 636, United Ass'n of Journeymen and Apprentices of the Plumbing and Pipe Fitting Indus.* v. *NLRB*, 287 F.2d 354 (DC Cir. 1961).
435. *NLRB* v. *General Steel Erectors, Inc.*, 933 F.2d 568 (7th Cir. 1991).
436. *Hoyt, Brumm & Link, Inc.*, 292 NLRB 1060 (1989).
437. *NLRB* v. *Annapolis Emergency Hosp. Ass'n*, 561 F.2d 524 (4th Cir. 1977).
438. *Desert Hospital* v. *NLRB*, 91 F.3d 187 (DC Cir. 1996); *NLRB* v. *North Shore University Hospital*, 724 F.2d 269 (2d Cir. 1983); *Sierra Vista Hospital*, 241 NLRB 631 (1979).

restraints upon the rights of supervisor-union members to participate in the governance of their unions. A union prohibition against a supervisor holding union office, for example, is not a uniformly imposed qualification; thus, arguably it would violate the LMRDA. However, this argument has been rejected by one appellate court based on section 603(b) of the LMRDA (229 US Code §523(b)) which provides that nothing in the LMRDA shall impair any rights nor confer any defenses on employers under the NLRA. Therefore, the appellate court reasoned that in the event of a conflict, the NLRA policy is controlling.[439]

V. Recognition of a Minority Union

422. An employer is prohibited from recognizing a labor organization as the exclusive bargaining representative of its employees unless that organization in fact has been designated by a majority of employees. Thus, in what is known as the *Bernhard-Altmann* case,[440] an employer was held guilty of violating section 8(a)(2), and a union was held guilty of violating section 8(b)(1)(A), where the employer had voluntarily recognized a union in the good faith, but mistaken, belief that the union had received cards from a majority of the bargaining unit employees authorizing the union to represent them in collective bargaining. The Court ruled that this violation was not cured by the union's subsequent receipt of enough additional authorization cards to constitute a majority inasmuch as the solicitation of those cards was tainted by the fact that the union had by then received the unlawful assistance of premature employer recognition. As a remedy, the employer and union were ordered to discontinue the bargaining relationship, including the enforcement of a collective agreement that had been negotiated as a result of the voluntary recognition. At such time as the union received NLRB certification as majority representative, the union and employer could commence a collective bargaining relationship.

A premature recognition of a union, however, is not treated as a continuing unfair labor practice. Thus, the NLRA's six month time limitation on the filing of unfair labor practice charges will bar such a challenge to the recognition of a minority union if the charge is not timely filed after the unlawful recognition.[441] (At an appropriate time, the union's status could, nevertheless, be challenged through a representation proceeding.)

423. A statutory exception to the rule that makes it unlawful for an employer to recognize a union as exclusive bargaining representative prior to that union obtaining the support of a majority of workers is found in section 8(f) of the NLRA which permits employers 'engaged primarily in the building and construction industry' to enter into collective agreements with minority unions in that industry. Such agreements are referred to as 'pre-hire' agreements because often they are negotiated before the first worker has been hired.

---

439. *NLRB* v. *General Steel Erectors, Inc.*, 933 F.2d 568, 572 (7th Cir. 1991).
440. *International Ladies' Garment Workers' Union* v. *NLRB*, 366 US 731 (1961).
441. *Local Lodge No. 1424* v. *NLRB*, 362 US 411 (1960).

The building construction industry in the United States is largely composed of small employers that specialize in performing the work of a single trade craft – e.g. carpentry, plumbing, painting, iron work, and the like. Rather than maintain a permanent crew of workers, many hire employees as needed to work on particular jobs – commonly lasting no more than a few weeks at a time. Therefore, the justification for the exception found in section 8(f) is that employment for a particular employer in that industry usually is for so brief a time that the employment normally would be terminated before a union could negotiate a collective agreement. Pre-hire agreements additionally serve construction industry employer interests because they enable the contractor to know in advance what it will be paying for labor and, therefore, more accurately calculate costs before bidding on the project.

Pre-hire agreements between an employer and a construction industry union are enforceable. The NLRB has held that a union may engage in recognitional picketing for a reasonable period of time in support of its demand for a pre-hire agreement but cannot coerce an employer into accepting a pre-hire agreement by, for example, engaging in recognitional picketing under circumstances that violate the restrictions of section 8(b)(7).[442] In addition, the Board has held that a pre-hire agreement does not bar an election petition, later filed with the NLRB, that challenges the union's representational status.[443]

424. The contention that the NLRA requires members-only collective bargaining in the absence of a majority representative is made by Prof. Charles Morris in *The Blue Eagle at Work* (2005) and has dicta support in the NLRB's decision in *Dana Corp.*, 356 NLRB 256 (2010). That dicta asserts that in *Consolidated Edison Co.* v. *NLRB*[444] the Supreme Court upheld the legitimacy of minority bargaining. Although the Court in *Consolidated Edison* said that the NLRA does not prohibit an employer and minority union from entering into a members-only contract, the question of whether bargaining with a minority union is required or is permitted to establish terms and conditions of employment for the minority union's members was not before the Court and was not decided by it. The unfair labor practice charges in *Consolidated Edison* asserted that rival union members were victims of coercion, discriminatory restrictions, and discriminatory discipline. The Board, without any discussion, dismissed the 8(2) charge in which the complaint had also asserted employer domination or assistance to the labor organization. However, the dismissal of that charge was not appealed to the Supreme Court and, most significantly, the Court explicitly stated: 'the validity of the contracts had not been, and was not, in issue'.[445]

---

442. *Laborers' Local Union No. 1184 (NVE Constructors, Inc.)*, 296 NLRB 1325 (1989), enforced 934 F.2d 1084 (9th Cir. 1991); *Ryan Heating Co., Inc.* v. *NLRB*, 942 F.2d 1287 (8th Cir. 1991). Section 8(b)(7), among other things, places time limits on such picketing. *See* paragraphs 444-450, below.
443. *Deklewa & Sons*, 282 NLRB 1375 (1987), enforced 843 F.2d 770 (3d Cir.), *cert.* denied 488 US 889 (1988). Other courts have noted that an employer can repudiate the pre-hire agreement based on the union's failure to obtain support from a majority of those hired. *Mesa Verde Constr. Co.* v. *No. Calif. Dist. Council of Laborers*, 820 F.2d 1006 (9th Cir. 1987).
444. 305 US 197, 237 (1938).
445. 305 US at 235.

Although the Supreme Court has held that a federal court can enforce an agreement between an employer and a minority representative concerning the reinstatement of union members who had been on strike, representation in that situation involved advocacy respecting enforcement of employee rights; it was not an interests dispute in which a minority union was engaging in collective bargaining respecting future terms and conditions of its members' employment.[446]

The generally accepted proposition that members-only bargaining is not an alternative available under the NLRA is supported by statements made by Senator Robert F. Wagner during the hearings that preceded adoption of the National Labor Relations Act and in the House and Senate reports leading to the Act's adoption.[447] The rejection of members-only collective bargaining is based on the proposition that such bargaining constitutes the bestowal of unlawful employer assistance to the minority union as well as unlawful favored (discriminatory) treatment of its members.[448] Should the employer, alternatively, extend to all workers any benefits obtained by the minority union, the employer would be treating the minority representative as representative of all the employees. This, too, would be contrary to the policies of the NLRA because only a majority representative is entitled to speak for the entire bargaining unit.[449] On the other hand, if a minority union separately bargains with an employer on behalf of each individual member, this might be permissible under the Act. The employer in that situation would not be dealing with the union as a collective representative; rather, the union would be acting as an individual agent of the several employees who are members.[450]

VI. The Employer's Duty of Neutrality between Competing Unions

425. As a general rule, an employer must remain neutral in its conduct with respect to the employee's protected choice as to whether to engage in concerted activities. It must also remain neutral in its conduct as between competing labor organizations. There are four basic exceptions to these principles. First, the employer's neutrality does not require the employer to cease making decisions designed to maintain a prospering business so long as the means chosen for accomplishing that end are not calculated to interfere with the employees' freedom to choose or reject union activity. Secondly, the employer remains free to express its opinion and offer accurate information respecting the merits or lack of merits of labor organizations, or of particular labor organizations, and of concerted employee activities. Third, an employer can cooperate with a recognized labor organization so as to facilitate the

---

446. *Retail Clerks Int'l Ass'n* v. *Lion Dry Goods, Inc.*, 369 US 17 (1962). Such a settlement involves a rights grievance, not collective bargaining over terms and conditions of employment. Therefore, the decision reflects the intent of a proviso to section 9(a) respecting an employer's right to deal with individual employee representatives in resolving grievances.

447. NLRB, *Legislative History of the National Labor Relations Act 1935*, 1419, 1422, 2312-13, 3069, 3073 (1959). *See also*, S. Fine, *The Automobile Under the Blue Eagle*, 191-92 (1963).

448. Sections 8(a)(2) and (3) prohibit such conduct.

449. *International Ladies' Garment Workers Union* v. *NLRB*, 366 US 731 (1961).

450. M. Finkin, 'The Road Not Taken: Some Thoughts on Nonmajority Employee Representation', 65 *Chi.-Kent L. Rev.* 195 (1993).

collective bargaining process. Fourth, even if more than one union seeks recognition, an employer that has not previously recognized a labor organization is free to recognize a union as its employees' bargaining representative if the recognized union has authorization cards from a majority of the workers and if an election petition has not been filed with the NLRB.

426. Just as an employer is free to express its anti-union opinion in a non coercive manner, the NLRB has ruled that 'an employer does not improperly interfere with an election by expressing a preference for one of the two competing unions'.[451]

Nor is it an unfair labor practice for an employer to cooperate in a union's efforts to communicate with employees. Thus, it is not a violation of the NLRA for an employer to introduce a union representative to the employees or to allow the representative to make an organizational speech to workers on company time and property unless another union is engaged in organizational activity and is not given equal opportunities.[452] The latter situation is an unfair labor practice because it gives special assistance to a particular union.

Further, the NLRB has held that it is permissible for a union and employer to enter into an agreement laying the framework for a collective bargaining relationship should the union attain support from the majority of bargaining unit employees.[453]

For many years the NLRB treated as a breach of neutrality an unorganized employer's recognition of a labor organization at a time when another union was also seeking recognition. In 1982 the Board modified its position and ruled that so long as an election petition has not been filed, the employer can recognize a union that has authorization cards signed by a majority of workers.[454] If an election petition has been filed, then the NLRB representation proceeding provides the sole method for determining which union, if any, is entitled to recognition.[455]

427. An employer crosses the line of permitted expression of support for a particular union if it creates an impression that it has already recognized that union even though the latter has not yet achieved evidence of majority support. Similarly,

---

451. *Stewart-Warner Corp.*, 102 NLRB 1153, 1157 (1953).
452. *Coamo Knitting Mills, Inc.*, 150 NLRB 579 (1964); *Local 1325, Retail Clerks Int'l Ass'n* v. *NLRB*, 325 F.2d 293 (1st Cir. 1963). *Compare*, *Farmers Energy Corp.*, 266 NLRB 722, enforced 730 F.2d 1098 (7th Cir. 1984), finding that an employer gave unlawful support to a union, in violation of §8(a)(2), when it required employees to attend on paid time a union organizing meeting.
453. *Dana Corp.*, 356 NLRB No. 49 (2010), rev. denied *sub nom Montague* v. *NLRB*, 698 F.3d 307 (6th Cir. 2012). Laying the framework for bargaining is not, of course, the same as establishing the terms and conditions of employment.
454. However, authorization cards signed by employees who also signed such cards for a rival union cannot be counted toward that majority. *Human Development Association* v. *NLRB*, 937 F.2d 657 (DC Cir. 1991).
455. *Bruckner Nursing Home*, 262 NLRB 955 (1982). In *American Nat'l Can Inc.*, 321 NLRB 1164 (1996), the Board confirmed its later modification of the *Buckner* rule and stated that voluntary and good-faith recognition of a union by an employer based on an unassisted and uncoerced showing of interest from a majority of employees bars a representation petition by a competing union (*see* paragraphs 430 and 795, below) unless that union demonstrates that prior to the recognition at least 30 percent of the employees showed interest in being represented by the rival union.

it is an employer unfair labor practice if supervisors solicit union authorization cards or are present while union organizers solicit and indicate the employer's approval of that union.[456]

428. It is an unfair labor practice, as well, for an employer to assist a union by checking off union dues from an employee who has not voluntarily executed a dues check off authorization that satisfies the requirements set out in LMRA section 302(c)(4).[457]

If dues have been unlawfully checked off, the employer and union are jointly and severally liable to reimburse employees for any amounts that were not owing to the union. Amounts owed as a result of a lawful union security provision or voluntary union membership, however, are not reimbursable. In recovering reimbursable dues, the NLRB's policy is to first attempt recovery from the union as the party that ultimately received the funds.[458]

Early in its history, section 2 Fourth of the Railway Labor Act made it unlawful for an employer to enforce a dues check-off arrangement but a later amendment included section 2 Eleventh which removed that prohibition.

429. Once a labor organization has been recognized as the bargaining agent selected by a majority of employees, mere expansion of the number of workers in the bargaining unit is referred to as an 'accretion' and the collective agreement for the existing unit, including any union security provisions, must be applied to the added employees. But if the expansion is more than a mere growth of the exiting bargaining unit, the employer is guilty of unlawfully assisting the union if the employer applies the agreement to the added workers unless the majority of workers express a desire to be represented by the union by, for example, signing cards designating the labor organization as their bargaining representative.

The NLRB has expressed reluctance to find that a new group of workers constitute an accretion to an existing bargaining unit. This reluctance is an acknowledgment that such a finding deprives the new employee group of an opportunity to separately determine whether they want a bargaining representative, and if they do, whether they want the incumbent representative.[459]

430. Probably the most difficult issue respecting the rules for maintaining employer neutrality concerning the employees' choice of a union representative involves what is known as the *Midwest Piping* doctrine,[460] a principle established

456. *Tuschak/Jacobson, Inc.*, 223 NLRB 1298, 1307–1309 (1976); *Northern States Beef, Inc.*, 226 NLRB 365 (1976).

457. *Jo-Jo Management Corp.*, 225 NLRB 1133 (1976). Section 302(c)(4) prohibits an employer from deducting union dues unless the worker signed a written assignment of the dues and the assignment can be revoked either after the termination of the collective agreement or after one year.

458. *Hermet Inc.*, 222 NLRB 29 n. 1 (1976).

459. *Meijer's Thrifty Acres*, 222 NLRB 18 (1976), enforced 564 F.2d 737 (6th Cir. 1977); *Sheraton-Kauai Corp.* v. *NLRB*, 429 F.2d 1352 (9th Cir. 1970); *Sunset House*, 167 NLRB 870 (1967), enforced 415 F.2d 545 (9th Cir. 1969). Also, *KR Contracting, Inc.*, 2017 Reg. Dir. Dec. LEXIS 111.

460. The doctrine was announced in *Midwest Piping & Supply Co.*, 63 NLRB 1060 (1945).

in 1945, but significantly modified in 1982, that regulates the relationship between an employer and an incumbent union when a rival labor organization is engaged in organizational activities.

To fully understand the NLRB's approach to bargaining with an incumbent whose majority status has been challenged by another union, it is necessary to be familiar with the NLRB's contract bar rule. This rule, which has received judicial approval and indirect statutory recognition,[461] provides that the NLRB will not entertain a representation petition during certain time periods if the affected employees are covered by a bona fide, executed collective agreement. The contract bar rule is intended to carry out the statutory goal of establishing stable industrial relations by encouraging the parties to enter into collective agreements and is premised on the proposition that having entered into a collective agreement, the parties should be able to live under that agreement without the disruptiveness of a challenge to the authority of the collective bargaining agent. Since section 8(d) of the NLRA allows a new bargaining agent to renegotiate the terms and conditions of employment irrespective of the existence of a current collective agreement with a prior bargaining agent, the stability achieved by such an agreement is disrupted if the incumbent representative's authority can be challenged during the life of the agreement. However, balanced against the statutory goal of establishing stable bargaining relations is the equally important legislative policy of assuring that employees are free to select their bargaining agent by majority vote. Thus, allowing the collective agreement to bar an NLRB representation proceeding has the impact of reducing the employees' opportunity to rid themselves of a bargaining representative who is no longer desired by a majority of the workers. The contract bar rule accommodates these competing concerns by permitting a current collective agreement to bar a representation proceeding only if:

(a) it is for a specific duration but has not been in existence for more than three years,
(b) it is a written, signed contract that to a substantial extent regulates the terms and conditions of employment and has been ratified by constituents when required by the parties' internal governing rules,
(c) the labor organization continues to be a functioning entity and has not gone through the sort of internal schism that would destroy the identity of the original bargaining agency,
(d) there has not been such a substantial change in the size and nature of the bargaining unit so as to destroy its original identity, and
(e) the agreement contains neither racially discriminatory provisions nor a union security or dues checkoff provision that is illegal on its face.

In addition to these rules regulating the circumstances under which an existing collective agreement will bar the NLRB from entertaining a petition for a representation proceeding, under the contract bar rule an existing collective agreement does not bar a representation proceeding if the petition is filed during the 30-day period

461. *See*, for example, NLRA §8(b)(7)(A). The rule is described in detail at chapter 9 of NLRB General Counsel, *An Outline of Law and Procedure in Representation Cases* (2017).

falling between the 90th and 60th day prior to the termination date of the agreement. (In the health care industry it is the 30-day period falling between 120 days and 90 days prior to the agreement's expiration date.) This qualification creates what is called the 'open season' and is designed to ensure an opportunity to challenge an incumbent's representational status even if it has the capacity to execute a new collective agreement with the employer. The open season qualification prevents a union and employer from entering into successive collective agreements in whole or in part so as to prevent the employees from ousting the incumbent union through an NLRB representation election.

The *Midwest Piping* doctrine operated on the assumption that if more than one union seeks to be bargaining representative, the very process of an employer negotiating for a new collective agreement with one of those unions gives unfair assistance to that union. Accordingly, in its original form the *Midwest Piping* doctrine made it an unfair labor practice for an employer to bargain with a union if, at a time when a representation petition could be entertained by the NLRB, another union claimed to be majority representative and that claim had some apparent support.[462] Thus, an employer violated section 8(a)(2) if it negotiated with a challenged incumbent union even though the incumbent demonstrated its continued majority support (through authorization cards, voluntary dues checkoffs, or union membership not compelled by a union security provision). However, the NLRB did not treat as an unfair labor practice the employer's continued dealing with the incumbent union in administering the terms of the unexpired current agreement.[463]

431. Appellate courts were not receptive to the *Midwest Piping* doctrine. The bench expressed fear that the instability generated by the hiatus in bargaining relations created by the doctrine exceeded the unfair advantage possibly gained by mistakenly recognizing a non majority union during a period of open rivalry. Therefore, most appellate courts took the position that the employer's duty of neutrality is satisfied in a rival union situation if the employer recognizes and negotiates with that labor organization which, based on reliable indicators of voluntary employee support, in fact appears to represent the bargaining unit's majority.[464]

In 1982, in *R.C.A. del Caribe, Inc.*, the NLRB, by a 3–2 vote, modified the *Midwest Piping* doctrine.[465] Under this modified approach the Board requires an employer to continue to recognize and negotiate with the incumbent union even though a rival has shown sufficient support to file an election petition (support from at least 30 percent of the bargaining unit employees) and the NLRB has issued a direction for an election to be conducted. Of course, if an election is conducted, the rival's subsequent victory in that election will oust the previously recognized union from its status as collective bargaining agent, the collective agreement negotiated with it is unenforceable, and a new agreement can be negotiated. However, the

---

462. *Buck Knives, Inc.*, 223 NLRB 983 (1976), enforcement denied 549 F.2d 1319 (9th Cir. 1977).
463. *Seaboard Terminal and Refrigeration Co.*, 114 NLRB 754 (1955).
464. 63 NLRB 1060 (1945). For appellate court review, *see*, for example, *Buck Knives, Inc.* v. *NLRB*, 549 F.2d 1319 (9th Cir. 1977).
465. 262 NLRB 963 (1982).

previously negotiated agreement will have established the status quo from which bargaining must begin. That is, the terms and conditions of employment established by the predecessor union's collective agreement cannot be changed unilaterally until there has been bargaining to impasse respecting the proposed changes.[466]

Under the revised doctrine, the employer must also continue to bargain with the incumbent union even if a decertification petition has been filed unless the employer has a good faith doubt respecting that continued majority status based on the fact that the decertification petition was signed by a majority of the employees.[467] Similarly, if a rival union's petition is supported by objective evidence that the incumbent labor organization has lost its majority status, such as when a majority of employees signed cards authorizing the rival to be their bargaining agent, then the employer commits an unfair labor practice if it executes a new collective agreement prior to the NLRB's resolution of the representation issue.[468]

§6. Balancing the Employer's Property Interests against the Workers' Statutory Rights

I. Generally

432. The most effective location for communicating with workers in an effort to organize them, or to urge their support for concerted worker activity, often is at the place of work due to the relative ease of identifying the workers and the absence of distractions from demands or activities of family or other non work related concerns or pressures. Of course, there is a disadvantage to this site if the workers fear employer surveillance and retribution.

One opportunity to discuss union affairs with workers at the work site is when they are arriving for work or leaving at the end of their shift. This poses some difficulties inasmuch as often they are pressed for time. In addition, many work sites are in locations in which it is difficult to identify those who work at the targeted enterprise (e.g. office buildings, construction sites or retail malls housing employees of many different companies). Therefore, often the best opportunity for a union to communicate with workers is on the employer's premises during the work day.

433. Most American employers object to unions using their premises for organizing or other union activities and assert that as a matter of constitutional protection of property rights they ought to be able to exclude those they do not want on their property or restrict the purposes for which strangers can enter the property.

Labor organizations generally insist that union access to employees while on the employer's premises is a necessary opportunity in order to have a meaningful right to organize and engage in concerted activity.

---

466. *More Truck Lines, Inc.*, 336 NLRB 772 (2001), enforced 324 F.3d 735, 355 US App. DC 355 (DC Cir. 2003).
467. *Dresser Indus. Inc.*, 264 NLRB 1088 (1982).
468. *Point Blank Body Armor, Inc.*, 312 NLRB 1097 (1993). For further discussion of the conditions under which recognition can be withdrawn *see* paragraph 797, below.

434. The NLRB and the courts, balancing the competing contentions respecting use of employer property for concerted activities, have reached results that vary according to whether:

(a) the persons seeking to engage in the concerted activities are themselves employees,
(b) business activities might be disrupted by the proposed mode of communication, and
(c) alternative channels are available for communicating with the employees.

II. Employees' Limited Right to Organize Fellow Workers on the Employer's Premises

435. In establishing rules governing the extent to which employees can engage in organizational activities on their employer's premises, the NLRB makes a distinction between:

(a) oral solicitation of support and
(b) the distribution of organizational leaflets or pamphlets.

One principle underlying the Board's rules is that an employer is entitled to direct the conduct of its workers during that time when they are paid to be engaged in work duties. Another principle is that the mere fact that a worker is on the employer's property during non-work time does not entitle the employer to direct that person's conduct so long as that conduct does not interfere with work activities. Thus, an employer is permitted to prohibit the distribution of literature in areas where work is performed. In other areas, such as locker rooms, lounges, lunch rooms, and parking lots, the employer can only restrict distribution of union or antiunion literature to the extent of prohibiting persons from handing out or receiving such material when they are scheduled to be performing work. The employer's protest against resulting litter is not accepted as an excuse for prohibiting distribution of union literature. Instead, the employer is confined to punishing those who in fact spread the litter by failing to dispose of it in appropriate receptacles.[469] The right to distribute union literature, moreover, applies to materials that address labor related political issues as well as materials urging unionization.[470]

436. Workers can be prohibited from orally soliciting another worker's support of a labor organization, or from soliciting other concerted activity, if the solicitation involves one or more persons who are supposed to be performing work. An employer is also permitted to ban all solicitation in those places to which the general public has access if such solicitation is likely to disrupt the employer's primary

469. *Stoddard-Quirk Mfg. Co.*, 138 NLRB 615 (1962); *Litton Indus., Inc.*, 192 NLRB 793 (1971), enforced 465 F.2d 104 (3d Cir., 1972); *Essex Int'l, Inc.*, 211 NLRB 749 (1974).
470. *Eastex, Inc.* v. *NLRB*, 437 US 556 (1978).

business activities.[471] However, an employer's reason for its no solicitation rule must be based on business necessity. Therefore, if it allows solicitation for some causes (for example, charitable or political), it cannot justify prohibiting union solicitation. Accordingly, it is an unfair labor practice for the employer to adopt an otherwise valid no solicitation rule that is directed only at union activity.[472]

The wording of the rule banning solicitation can also make a difference. If the rule prohibits solicitation during 'working time', it is presumptively valid; if it states that solicitation is prohibited during 'working hours' or 'business hours' it is presumptively invalid because the wording is likely to be understood by workers as prohibiting solicitation at all times while on the employer's premises.[473] The presumption of invalidity can be overcome, however, if the employer's rules make it clear that employees are free from the restriction when not performing work duties or can demonstrate an objectively observable decline in worker output coincident with the onset of the solicitation activity.[474]

The NLRB has held that even if an employer uses its email system to express anti-union views, it can bar employees from using the system to communicate respecting organizing or other union activities so long as the restriction on employee use does not favor one union over another or anti-union views over pro-union views and extends to other types of non charitable use of the system by outside organizations. In the same decision the Board also stated that this principle is to be applied to the use of other employer property such as bulletin boards.[475] Restrictions on use of an employer's email system during nonwork time must be justified by productivity or disciplinary necessities.[476] The NLRB's decisions have involved employees who had frequent opportunities for face-to-face interactions with each other. The decisions do not reach situations in which employees are telecommuters a large part of the time and, therefore, have few, if any, opportunities for interacting with other employees other than through the employer's email system.

437. Wearing union buttons or insignia while at work generally is treated as privileged from employer interference. However, if workers have contact with the general public, their employer is entitled to insist that such insignia be unobtrusive and not mar the appearance of a required uniform. In addition, if the buttons or

---

471. *May Department Stores, Co.*, 59 NLRB 976 (1944) (solicitation may be prohibited on the selling floor of a retail store); *Beth Israel Hospital* v. *NLRB*, 437 US 483 (1978) (hospital cannot prohibit union solicitation in cafeteria used by patients and visitors as well as staff); *NLRB* v. *Baptist Hospital,* 442 US 773 (1979) (hospital can prohibit solicitation in public corridors and waiting rooms on patient care floors where evidence indicates that such activity disrupts tranquil atmosphere beneficial to patients and visitors); *Montgomery Ward & Co.*, 256 NLRB 800 (1981), affirmed 692 F.2d 1115 (7th Cir. 1982) (store cannot prohibit union solicitation in store's public restaurant).

472. *Premier Maintenance, Inc.*, 282 NLRB 10 (1986); *Brigadier Indus. Corp.*, 271 NLRB 656 (1984). The Board's position was rejected in *Salmon Run Shopping Ctr. LLC* v. *NLRB,* 534 F.3d 108 (2d Cir. 2008) on the ground that charitable and public service activities bring more people into the shopping mall whereas union solicitation and distribution of union literature does not have that benefit for the mall.

473. *Our Way*, 268 NLRB 394 (1983).

474. *Bankers Club Inc.*, 218 NLRB 22 (1975).

475. *The Guard Publ. Co.*, 351 NLRB 1110, n.17, 18 and accompanying text (2007).

476. *Purple Communic., Inc.,* 361 NLRB 126 (2014).

insignia are provocative (for example, use strong language directed at other workers) and have in fact provoked altercations or present safety hazards, employers are entitled to prohibit their use.[477] Finally, it is not an unfair labor practice for an employer to prohibit all additions to uniforms, such as union buttons or other insignias, if worn in patient care areas of health care facilities or if the uniform is supplied by the employer and there is no showing that the rule was adopted to thwart the right to organize union support.[478] Some appellate courts broadly apply the presumptive rule to all employees who wear an employer provided uniform and deal directly with customers, others follow the Board's approach of requiring a showing of special circumstances justifying the restriction.[479]

438. American labor law is less welcoming to allowing a non-employee to use company property for organizing activities than it is to giving access to the premises for that purpose by the company's own employees. In part this is a reflection of the greater risk to the employer of allowing someone on the property over whom it has no control and little, if any, background knowledge. However, the business justifications are less compelling for excluding its own workers from the premises, even when they are not working, since the employer knows who they are, has found their presence acceptable for other purposes, and has control over them if they abuse the privilege of accessing the property.

439. For the reasons discussed in the above paragraph, the NLRB protects the right of workers to use the employer's premises for union solicitation or distribution during the time the workers are leaving from or arriving for their work shift. It also treats as presumptively invalid an employer rule that tries to totally exclude workers from the premises during hours when they are not scheduled to work. However, an employer is permitted to have a rule that excludes from interior areas and other work areas all persons other than those who are present for work or business. But, unless it can show special business justification, such as substantial malicious damage to property or government security requirements, it is an unfair labor practice for an employer to exclude from exterior non work areas, such as parking lots and entrance areas, its own employees who seek to engage in union organizing activities.[480]

---

477. Compare *Caterpillar Tractor Co.* v. *NLRB*, 230 F.2d 357 (7th Cir. 1956) with *NLRB* v. *Mead Corp.*, 73 F.3d 74 (6th Cir. 1996).

478. *St. John's Health Center*, 357 NLRB 2078 (2012), explaining that a prohibition on wearing union insignia in patient care areas is presumptively permitted but the same prohibition applied to other areas of the facility is presumptively invalid. However, because the hospital selectively banned a specific union ribbon but not others, and also allowed political buttons to be worn in patient care areas, the hospital had the burden of proving the necessity for the particular restriction.

479. *See*, *Meijer, Inc.* v. *NLRB*, 130 F.3d 1209, 1214–1216 (6th Cir. 1997); *Titus Elec. Contr., Inc.*, 355 NLRB 1357 (2010).

480. *Meijer, Inc.* v. *NLRB*, 463 F.3d 534 (6th Cir. 2006); *NLRB* v. *Southern Maryland Hospital Center*, 916 F.2d 932 (4th Cir. 1990).

III. Non-employee Organizing on Employer's Premises

440. In *Babcock & Wilcox*, the Supreme Court upheld the authority of the NLRB to treat as an unfair labor practice an employer's refusal to allow nonemployees to enter the company's premises for union organizing purposes where alternative opportunities to communicate with the workers are not available.[481] This rule has been applied to grant non employee union organizers access to workers in remote work sites such as logging camps, docked ocean-going vessels, and vacation resort hotels.[482] However, the Court has rejected the NLRB's effort to give non employee union organizers access to exterior non work areas, such as employee parking lots, even when the organizers encounter great difficulty contacting employees away from the job because their residences are widely dispersed in a large metropolitan area. The Court stated that an employer's property right should not be balanced against the union organizing activities of non employees unless off premises access to the employees is nearly impossible.[483]

The NLRB distinguishes the situation in which a property owner allows non-union solicitors to use its premises for activities unrelated to work. Based on the proposition that the employer is clearly discriminating on the basis of union affiliation, the NLRB has found an unfair labor practice when union sponsored solicitation is banned by the property owner even though other outsiders are permitted to engage in such activities.[484] However, more recent decisions limit the finding of disparate treatment to situations in which the allowed outside activity is of a similar nature to union organizing as contrasted with activities such as charitable solicitation or other beneficent acts.[485] Appellate courts have split over the question of whether in such cases the Supreme Court's decisions allow property interests to prevail over the statutory right of workers to act in concert in support of worker interests.[486]

Even in some remote work area situations, union organizers can be denied access to the employer's premises. For example, it has been held that safety considerations justify excluding non-employee union organizers from offshore petroleum extraction platforms even though workers remain on the platforms for several weeks at a time. However, the NLRB has required employers of offshore platforms to provide an onshore opportunity for the organizers to meet with employees.[487]

481. *NLRB* v. *Babcock & Wilcox Co.*, 351 US 105 (1956).
482. *NLRB* v. *Lake Superior Lumber Corp.*, 167 F.2d 147 (6th Cir. 1948).
483. *Lechmere, Inc.* v. *NLRB*, 502 US 527 (1992). The employer must have a property right to exclude others from the property in order to invoke the right to expel non employee organizers. *Roundy's Inc.* v. *NLRB*, 674 F.3d 638 (7th. Cir. 2012) (tenant in shopping mall guilty of unfair labor practice if it does not have a property right to control the common areas of a shopping mall and calls police to eject union organizers from the area outside its store).
484. *Be-Lo Stores* v. *NLRB*, 126 F. 3d 268, 284-86 (4th Cir. 1997).
485. *The Guard Publ. Co.*, 351 NLRB 1110 (2007); *Salmon Run Shopping Ctr. LLC* v. *NLRB*, 534 F.3d 108 (2d Cir. 2008).
486. Compare *Cleveland Real Estate Partners* v. *NLRB*, 95 F.3d 457 (6th Cir. 1996) with *Four B Corp.* v. *NLRB*, 163 F.3d 177 (10th Cir. 1998).
487. *McDermott Marine Construction*, 305 NLRB 617 (1991).

441. For a brief time a separate line of Supreme Court decisions provided that non employee union organizers had a right to access workers on the employer's premises whenever the employer generally provided the public with uncontrolled access to those premises. This most typically occurs in the case of a large shopping center or shopping mall. The Court's rationale was that such large, comprehensive shopping areas are functionally equivalent to downtown business areas and that, by dedicating the private property to such public use, the owner must abide by the constitutional protections available to those who use publicly owned property. Since the constitutional protections of freedom of assembly and freedom of expression protect the right to use public sidewalks of a downtown shopping area for public discourse, so long as it does not obstruct their general use, so, too, the constitutional protections were held to prohibit the shopping center or mall owner from restricting such activities. However, when a change in membership on the Supreme Court shifted the majority from those with propensities to give priority to the protection of civil liberties to those with propensities to preserve the prerogatives of the owners of private property, the Court overruled this line of decisions.[488]

442. The California Agricultural Labor Relations Board, which regulates farm labor relations in that state, has adopted regulations allowing union organizers to have a limited degree of access to farm workers while on the employer's property during their meal and other break periods. The constitutionality of these regulations has withstood challenge.[489]

Agriculture is a major industry in California. Union organizing, which generally has been unsuccessful in that industry, gained considerable headway in California in the 1970s and its farm labor laws are the most extensive of any state. Because this industry is excluded from the NLRA,[490] the policies adopted in California farm labor relations initially were expected to have considerable influence on legal developments in this industry. However, no such trend developed. By the 1990s the farm labor movement in California was itself struggling for survival.[491]

IV. Union Access to Worker Names and Addresses

443. Another form of employer property to which those seeking to organize workers are given limited access is the employer's knowledge of the workers'

488. *Hudgens* v. *NLRB*, 424 US 507 (1976).

489. *Agricultural Labor Relations Board* v. *Superior Court,* 16 Cal. 3d 392, appeal dismissed for want of a substantial federal question 429 US 802 (1976).

490. J. Perea, 'The Echoes of Slavery: Recognizing the Racist Origins of the Agricultural and Domestic Worker Exclusion from the National Labor Relations Act', 72 *Ohio St. L.J.* 95 (2011).

491. J. Gordon, Law, Lawyers, and Labor: 'The United Farm Workers' Legal Strategy in the 1960s and 1970s and the Role of Law in Union Organizing Today', 8 *U. Pa. J. Lab. & Emp. L.* 1 (2005); M. Ontiveros, 'New Perspectives on Labor and Gender: Lessons from the Fields – Female Farmworkers and the Law', 55 *Me. L. Rev.* 157, 174–175 (2003). Use of foreign guest workers has been one tool for frustrating organizing farm workers. H. Bernton, 'Foreign Farm Workers' Unusual Strike in Central Washinton', *The Seattle Times*, 1 October 2017.

names and addresses. Under a doctrine known as the Excelsior Rule, the NLRB routinely orders employers to submit, within 10 days after the NLRB orders that a representation election be conducted, the names and addresses of all employees eligible to vote in the election. The submitted data is now required to include known email addresses and known home and personal cell phone numbers. The NLRB then makes a copy of this list available to any petitioning or intervening unions so as to facilitate their communicating with workers regarding the impending NLRB election. Failure to provide the list, and omissions of names from the list, are grounds for setting aside the election if the majority vote in a way that is contrary to the interests of any group prejudiced by the failure to supply the list.[492] If the election is set aside, a new election is directed and the Board, this time, will apply to a US District Court for a subpoena requiring the employer to provide the list of employee names and addresses. The Supreme Court has upheld the NLRB's authority to require the employer to submit this information.[493]

In contrast with the rule under the NLRA, the federal Privacy Act has been held to bar providing similar information to unions seeking to represent or already representing federal employees unless the employees consent to having that information released to the union.[494]

§7. Legal Restrictions on Obtaining Support from Others

I. Organizational and Recognitional Picketing

444. During the mid-1950s, a committee of the United States Senate conducted a highly publicized series of hearings and investigations into the internal operations of labor organizations. These explored the variety of ways in which some unions engaged in coercive practices to increase membership or to extract bribes from the business community. Among the abuses of power brought to light was the practice of some unions to engage in extensive organizational picketing against an employer with the implicit or explicit assurance that any resulting economic pressure on the employer would be removed if it would require the workers to join the union or pay bribes to the union leadership. In the former situation, the union's majority status was gained not because of the free choice of the workers but because the employer, motivated by a desire to remove any economic pressures that accompanied the picketing, coerced its workers to join. This technique was particularly successful against retail establishments in communities in which unions enjoyed wide public support. It was also successful in situations in which workers making deliveries of needed supplies or pickups of goods, or who provided important services to the employer, would as a matter of conscience, or because of their own union's policies, refuse to

492. NLRB, *Rules and Regulations* §§ 102.62(d), 102.67(l). *Thrifty Auto Parts*, 295 NLRB 1118 (1989); *Excelsior Underwear Inc.*, 156 NLRB 1236 (1966). In deciding whether to set aside the election result, the Board weighs the number of excluded names in comparison with the margin of the election result, whether the percentage of those excluded was high or marginal, and the justification, if any, for the error. *Automatic Fire Systems*, 357 NLRB No. 190 (2012).

493. *NLRB* v. *Wyman-Gordon Co.*, 394 US 759 (1969). Disobedience of the subpoena is a crime.

494. *Department of Defense* v. *FLRA*, 510 US 487 (1994); 5 US Code §552a.

cross such picket lines. Even without the employer being coerced, if the picketing reduced business and work opportunities, the employees themselves might 'choose' to join the union rather than continue to see their jobs threatened.

A related use of organizational picketing that became a subject of congressional scrutiny was the practice of subjecting an enterprise to pickets posted by a union that was a rival of a union that represented the employees of that enterprise. Such inter-union rivalry was not uncommon prior to the merger of the AFL and CIO.

Public and congressional sentiment sought to eliminate the coercive use of picket lines. On the other hand, it was recognized that organizational picketing can be, and generally was, for the legitimate purpose of communicating with workers and consumers respecting the desirability of concerted activity and the merits of labor organizations. Such uses of picketing are consistent with the purposes of the NLRA and are constitutionally protected by the guaranties that government will not interfere with the freedoms of expression, association and peaceful assembly. In an effort to accommodate these competing concerns, in 1959 Congress adopted, as part of the Landrum–Griffin Act amendments, section 8(b)(7) of the National Labor Relations Act which is a compromise provision that has been condemned for its lack of clarity as well as for its failure to reflect concrete policy choices.

445. Section 8(b)(7) of the NLRA restricts the right to engage in or threaten to engage in picketing when the communicated objective of that picketing is to organize workers or obtain their employer's recognition as the workers' bargaining agent. If picketing does not have an overt organizational or recognitional objective it cannot constitute an unfair labor practice under section 8(b)(7). If it does have such an objective, except as further explained in the next numbered paragraph, the picketing is an unfair labor practice if the picketing union is not the workers' certified bargaining agent and:

(a) the workers in question are presently represented by an exclusive bargaining agent and, under the NLRB's rules, a representation petition could not be entertained at this time, or
(b) a valid NLRB representation election was conducted for the bargaining unit within the past 12 months, or
(c) the picketing has been conducted without a representation petition being filed with the NLRB within a reasonable period of time after the commencement of picketing which, in any event, cannot exceed 30 days.

The situation described by subsection (a) refers to instances in which the contract bar rule, which is described above at paragraph 430, would prevent the successful filing of a representation petition.

In the situation described in subsection (c) of 8(b)(7), the NLRB can determine that, under the circumstances of the particular case, a petition reasonably should have been filed earlier than thirty days after the commencement of picketing. Thus, in some cases organizational picketing that continues for one or two weeks without the filing of a representation petition will be found excessive and, therefore, an unfair labor practice under section 8(b)(7)(c). On the other hand, if a timely election petition has been filed by the picketing union, it can continue the picketing until the election results have been certified.

446. If there is not already a recognized bargaining agent, or there has not been a valid NLRB election in the past year, picketing that does nothing more than inform the public about the unorganized status of the picketed establishment is permitted, no matter how protracted, so long as its impact is not to cause workers employed by other employers to refuse to pick up or deliver goods at the picketed establishment or to refuse to perform services for that establishment. Picketing that satisfies these conditions is referred to as 'informational' picketing or 'proviso' picketing. Moreover, it is not an unfair labor practice even if the picketing persuades those employed by the picketed establishment to strike in support of the organizational effort.[495] Thus, picketing to solicit sympathetic consumer pressure designed to reinforce the union's organizational or recognitional demand is not an unfair labor practice unless either:

(a) it results in workers from other establishments refusing to cross the picket line, or
(b) it is aimed at an establishment that already has a recognized bargaining agent or has had a valid NLRB election within the past year or continues for an unreasonable duration.

447. The word picketing originally was used to describe patrolling by soldiers who walked within a confined area when posted on guard duty. In labor relations practice, the term generally has been understood in the United States to describe the activity of someone walking back and forth carrying a placard in the vicinity of the entrance to a business establishment. In applying section 8(b)(7), it has been held that the term 'picketing' does not require the presence of all of the characteristics of the normal form of that activity. Thus, physical presence near the entrance of an establishment accompanied by some effort to convey the labor organization's or strikers' message regarding the existence of a labor dispute and the desire that people stop dealing with the business is adequate to bring the conduct within the scope of section 8(b)(7).[496] However, where union supporters did nothing more than distribute handbills in a parking area adjacent to a place of employment, the NLRB held that this was not a signal to others to stop dealing with the employer and, therefore, was not picketing.[497]

448. To violate section 8(b)(7) there must be more than just picketing during a proscribed period of time. As previously noted, the picketing must convey an

495. *Hotel and Restaurant Employees (Crown Cafeteria)*, 135 NLRB 1183 (1962), enforced 327 F.2d 351 (9th Cir. 1964); *Electrical Workers Local 3*, 144 NLRB 5 (1963); *Smitty's Supermarkets, Inc.*, 310 NLRB 1377 (1993).

496. *Lawrence Typographical Union No. 570*, 169 NLRB 279, 283 (1968), enforced 402 F.2d 452 (10th Cir.) (*per curiam*).

497. *Teamsters, Local 688 (Levitz Furniture)*, 205 NLRB 1131 (1973). See discussion of characteristics of picketing in *Sheet Metal Workers (Galencare, Inc.)*, 356 NLRB 1290, 1291-92 (2010).

organizational or recognitional intent. Occasionally, union supporters make it easy to prove this element of the unfair labor practice by carrying a placard that calls upon the workers to join the union or that demands that the employer recognize and bargain with the union. Often, however, proof of the organizational or recognitional goal must come from collateral sources. This is the case, for example, if the picketing is preceded by a demand for recognition and a warning by the union representative that the premises will be picketed if the union is not recognized. Similarly, although the placards being carried say nothing more than that the employer is unfair to its workers, the picketing is treated as coming within the scope of 8(b)(7) if it is accompanied by handbills, or statements made by the pickets that the nature of the employer's unfairness is that it does not have a collective agreement with the picketing union.

In contrast, picketing to protest an employer's unfair labor practice is not treated as organizational or recognitional picketing and, therefore, cannot be a violation of section 8(b)(7).

Nor is it a violation of section 8(b)(7) for a union to picket solely for the purpose of informing the public that the employer does not provide workers with the level of benefits that is provided by most local employers for similar work. This type of picketing is known as 'area standards' picketing. However, if the labor organization is not able to objectively support its contention that the picketed employer does not provide the level of benefits generally given by employers in that area, the picketing is treated as recognitional or organizational and, thus, comes within the scope of the section 8(b)(7) prohibitions. Furthermore, the mere fact that the benefits provided by the picketed employer are below those given by employers with collective bargaining agreements does not justify area standards picketing unless such collective agreements in fact represent the general standard of employee benefits paid in the locale. Finally, if picketing qualifies as area standards picketing, it does not lose its protected status even if it results in interruptions in services provided by others or in disrupted delivery or pick-up of goods at the picketed premises.[498]

449. In addition to the cease and desist order that, under section 10(c) of the NLRA, is available as a remedy for all unfair labor practices, section 10(l) of the Act requires the NLRB Regional Attorney to seek a temporary federal district court injunction against unlawful organizational or recognitional picketing if, after a preliminary investigation of the unfair labor practice charge, the Regional Attorney concludes that there is reasonable cause to believe that the charge is true and that, therefore, a complaint probably will be issued. This is done prior to issuing the complaint.

However, section 10(l) injunction proceedings have become rare in part because there has been a decline in the use of organizational picketing. (*See* discussion at paragraph 817, below.) In addition, practical considerations induce unions to terminate such picketing prior to the filing of an unfair labor practice charge and to quickly settle such cases when charges are filed. One reason a union charged with

498. *Houston Building & Construction Trades Council*, 136 NLRB 321 (1962).

an 8(b)(7) violation often agrees to discontinue its picketing is that the employer has agreed to a prompt election and once the picketing has been discontinued the NLRB will not seek an injunction unless it has cause to suspect that the picketing will be resumed. In addition, under certain situations, an expedited election is held where there has been organizational or recognitional picketing and, frequently, the prospect of the expedited election is enough to cause the union to discontinue its picketing. Also, an expedited election might be held prior to the NLRB being able to have its injunction petition heard by the federal court, thus eliminating the need for an injunction.

Finally, with some frequency an 8(b)(7) charge is combined with charges of unlawful secondary activity under section 8(b)(4) of the NLRA. (*See* paragraphs 451–490, below.) Because section 303 of the LMRA provides a private damages cause of action for victims of 8(b)(4) violations, a union charged with such violations has a strong incentive to enter into a settlement agreement requiring it to withdraw from all objectionable activity in exchange for the employer's agreement not to sue. The NLRB cooperates in such settlements by not seeking an injunction, especially since the objectionable picketing will have been discontinued as part of that settlement. Thus, labor organizations generally avoid violating 8(b)(7) and when there is a violation, enforcement of the policy against organizational and recognitional picketing is almost always achieved through the informal processes for litigation settlement rather than through any formal judicial or administrative procedures. For example, in the Fiscal Year that ended in September 2010, only 34 cases against labor organizations included a charge of an 8(b)(7) violation. This was barely one half of one percent of all unfair labor practice charges brought against unions that year and all were resolved without a court order.

450. In 1974 the NLRB's jurisdiction was expanded to cover the health care industry. Prior to that time nonprofit hospitals had been excluded from coverage. In the exercise of its discretion, the Board for some years had also declined to handle disputes involving proprietary hospitals. In expanding the NLRB's jurisdiction to cover the entire health care industry, Congress adopted several special provisions aimed at meeting what it understood to be problems particular to health care institutions. One change was the addition of paragraph (g) to section 8.

Among other things, section 8(g) requires unions to give 10 days' written notice to the employer and to the Federal Mediation and Conciliation Service, prior to picketing a health care institution. The NLRB takes the position that this notice requirement applies only to picketing directed at the health care institution. Picketing on behalf of persons who are not employees of that institution – such as construction workers engaged in erecting an addition to a hospital – are not required to comply with 8(g) so long as their dispute is directed at their own employer and not at the health care facility.[499] In addition, the NLRB has held that the 8(g) notice is not applicable to a stoppage whose purpose is to protest a serious unfair labor practice.[500]

499. *Laborers' Int'l Union (St. Mary's Hospital)*, 248 NLRB 244 (1980).
500. *Park Inn Home for Adults*, 293 NLRB 1082, 1087 (1989).

II. Prohibited Secondary and Sympathetic Activities

A. Constitutional Protection of Appeals for Support from the Public or from Sympathetic Employers

451. The US Constitution prohibits government interference with the freedoms of expression, peaceful assembly, and association. But the freedoms of expression, peaceful assembly, and association do not encompass all expression, all peaceful assembly, or all association. For example, the US Supreme Court has held that freedom of expression does not protect expression that appeals to prurient interest in sex in a manner that, judged by contemporary standards of the community where the alleged offense occurred, is patently offensive. As a result, such expression is not constitutionally protected and hence can be restrained or punished.[501] Similarly, the Supreme Court has held that expression that is used in conspiring to commit a crime, or that creates an imminent danger of violence or a similar serious evil, is not constitutionally protected.[502] The Court has, in like regard, held that peaceful assembly on private property, or on public property that is dedicated to a limited use, can be regulated or prohibited despite the constitutional protection of the freedom of assembly.[503] In all of these decisions, the Court has been divided. In each, some members dissented either on the ground that the majority was adopting a doctrinal approach that gives too narrow a reading to the scope of constitutionally protected liberty, or because the majority was responding to the facts out of authoritarian fear of freedom rather than with libertarian faith in the strength of an open society.

452. The American legal system accepts numerous restrictions on expression and association in the conduct of commercial activities. Thus, antitrust laws prohibit businesses from combining together in restraint of trade or to monopolize an industry. Laws regulating the sale and transfer of corporate securities prohibit transactions and communications that are not accompanied by approved statements covering prescribed areas of information. Such laws also restrict various financial transactions by or among certain classes of people. The merchandising of goods in the United States is also subject to many restrictions and requirements regarding what information can, or must, or may not, be conveyed on labels and in advertisements. And, the foregoing is but a partial survey of the sorts of regulations or restraints that the Supreme Court has permitted despite the broadly phrased constitutional protections of the freedom to engage in expression, peaceful assembly, and association. Nevertheless, in the area of labor relations activities, these constitutional freedoms have on occasion been held to provide important limitations upon government regulation or restraint of the parties.

---

501. *Miller* v. *California*, 413 US 15 (1973).
502. *See*, for example, *Scales* v. *United States*, 367 US 203 (1961); *Feiner* v. *New York*, 340 US 315 (1951).
503. *See*, for example, *Hudgens* v. *NLRB*, 424 US 507 (1976); *Adderley* v. *Florida*, 385 US 39 (1966).

453. At various times in American history, union organizers or striking workers have been confronted with laws challenging their right to picket, to distribute leaflets, to withhold work, and even to make speeches. In some of these situations the courts eventually struck down such restrictions on the grounds that the conduct in question was constitutionally protected or the law in question was constitutionally defective. In other situations, however, the restrained party was financially unable to judicially test the validity of the restraint or was too fearful to do so. In still other situations, such challenges undoubtedly have been foregone or abandoned because the eventual legal victory would not materialize for months or years, by which time the underlying cause for the conduct would long since have disappeared.

Most Americans believe that in the US those realities approach the ideals of an open society to a greater degree than in any other nation. Moreover, it is clear that the growth of the political influence of organized labor since the mid-1930s was accompanied by substantial improvements in the willingness of law enforcement officials to respect the constitutional rights of union organizers and strikers. Thus, at the grass roots level, the constitutional rights of labor organizations today are most often a reality.

454. Two constitutional doctrines that lend assistance to the protection of the freedoms of peaceful assembly, expression, and association are:

(a) excessively vague laws violate the constitutional guaranty of due process of law, and
(b) due process is violated by laws that reach so broadly that they regulate not only conduct that constitutionally is subject to regulation but also appear to limit constitutionally protected rights.

The rule against excessive vagueness ensures that a person will not be punished for conduct he could not have reasonably determined was illegal at the time he engaged in it. It also ensures that there is adequate ability to understand what the law prohibits so as to make it possible to prepare a defense against a charge of violation. Finally, it eliminates the prospect that those who enforce the law will have such an unbridled scope of interpretive discretion that the law will in fact be not what was prohibited by the legislature but rather what the enforcement authorities choose to enforce as law.

The rule against overly broad laws has often been referred to as a dimension of the due process doctrine. Alternatively, it can be viewed as a necessary correlative of the specific guaranties of constitutional liberty. The overbreadth doctrine is designed to avoid the situation in which people are deterred from engaging in constitutionally protected conduct out of fear of breaching a law that seems to prohibit such conduct as well as forbid similar conduct that constitutionally can be regulated.

455. In the labor relations field, constitutional protection of the freedoms of expression, peaceful assembly, and association often have been achieved through the invocation of either the vagueness or overbreadth rule, or both, rather than through the direct application of the substantive constitutional freedom at issue. For example, in the 1930s, Jersey City, New Jersey, a medium sized city with a large concentration of manufacturing and commercial activities, was under the tight political control of Mayor Frank Hague. Hague was pledged to 'protect' Jersey City businesses from the industrial union organizing of the CIO. Ordinances had been adopted giving the police commissioner total discretion in deciding when public parks could be used for delivering speeches. The distribution of handbills on city streets and sidewalks was totally banned and these ordinances were vigorously and summarily enforced by police officers against union organizers. Eventually, however, a federal district court enjoined these restraints on union organizing activities and the injunction was upheld by the Supreme Court of the United States. The majority of the Supreme Court divided over the reasons for reaching its result. Much of what had been done by the city officials was attacked as being in direct conflict with constitutionally protected rights. But in discussing the ordinance respecting the use of the park by public speakers, the plurality opinion particularly called attention to the evil of giving a public officer 'uncontrolled' discretion in licensing who can and who cannot make a speech.[504]

456. In another case, *Thornhill* v. *Alabama*, 310 US 88 (1940), the Supreme Court struck down, as an excessively 'sweeping proscription of freedom of discussion', a state law prohibiting picketing by strikers near a place of business. Although there was evidence that the defendant in the case may have been trespassing on the employer's property, the Court refused to confine itself to determining the constitutionality of the statute as applied in that instance. The perniciousness of an overly broad regulation of expression that encroaches upon constitutionally protected liberty, explained the Court, is not only in the application of that law but in what it threatens to punish as well. 'The existence of such a statute, which readily lends itself to harsh and discriminatory enforcement by local prosecuting officials, against particular groups deemed to merit their displeasure, results in a continuous and pervasive restraint on all freedom of discussion that might reasonably be regarded as within its purview'. The Court went on to hold that the dissemination of facts concerning a labor dispute is 'within that area of free discussion that is guaranteed by the Constitution'. Therefore, by restraining all communication by means of picketing at the place of business, this law was unconstitutional because the dangers of permitting such dissemination of information by means of peaceful picketing are neither so serious nor imminent as 'to justify the sweeping proscription of freedom of discussion'.[505]

In *AFL* v. *Swing*, 312 US 321 (1941), the Court extended its reasoning by protecting unions from sweeping injunctions that would bar picketing of establishments by non-employees who seek to communicate with the public respecting a dispute they have with the target employer. In both the *Thornhill* and *Swing* cases, however, the Court noted that labor dispute picketing is not constitutionally protected under all circumstances. Violent picketing and mass picketing that intimidates or interferes with entering or leaving private property are frequently cited in the opinions as the sort of conduct that is not constitutionally protected.

504. *Hague* v. *CIO*, 307 US 496, 516 (1939).
505. 310 US at 97–98, 102, 105.

457. The Supreme Court illustrated the limits on expression that it is prepared to accept when it decided *Giboney* v. *Empire Storage Co.*, 336 US 490 (1949). In that case truck drivers who had been hired by customers to pick up goods were deterred from doing so by picketing at the location at which the pick-ups were to be made. (The drivers would have been fined by their union had they crossed the picket line.) The goal of the picketing was to get the target employer to refuse to sell its product to non-union self-employed retailers. The Court concluded that the picketing was designed to further an unlawful restraint of trade by coercing the seller to cease doing business with non-union customers. Therefore, the Court held, the picketing was not merely lawful assembly or expression. Rather, it was illegal conduct and, therefore, could properly be enjoined. The distinction between pure expression and picketing was, perhaps, best explained by a statement Justice Douglas made in a concurring opinion in another case:

> No one may be required to obtain a license in order to speak. But once he uses the economic power which he has over other men and their jobs to influence their action, he is doing more than exercising the freedom of speech protected by the First Amendment. That is true whether he be an employer or an employee. But as long as he does no more than speak, he has the same unfettered right, no matter what side of an issue he espouses.[506]

An interesting variation of the *Giboney* principle is found in *Hughes* v. *Superior Court*, 339 US 460 (1950). In that case civil rights demonstrators asked the public to cease patronizing a store because its management refused to hire only black employees until it reached a quota of half of the workers being members of that race. The Supreme Court upheld a state court injunction against the picketing on the ground that the quota hiring it was aimed at imposing on the employer would have violated a state policy of assuring job applicants equal employment opportunity regardless of race, religion, or national origin.

458. As discussed in paragraphs 449–454, above, the 1959 amendments to the NLRA placed restrictions on organizational and recognitional picketing. The foundation for explaining the constitutionality of these restrictions on expression was supplied by the Supreme Court a couple of years earlier in its decision in *Teamsters Union* v. *Vogt, Inc.*, 354 US 284 (1957), a case that involved a state court injunction against picketing with placards that declared that the workers at a job site were not union members. Some union truck drivers who worked for other employers refused to cross this picket line to pick-up and deliver goods and materials. The state court concluded that the picketing, with the anticipated sympathetic conduct by union truck drivers, was designed to coerce the employer into forcing its workers to join the union. Emphasizing that the state court had drawn a reasonable inference respecting the unlawful coercive goal of this picketing, the majority of the Supreme Court concluded that the picketing was not constitutionally protected. In section 8(b)(7) of the NLRA, a similar inference was adopted by Congress in limiting the organizational picketing privilege to those situations in which there has not in fact

506. *Thomas* v. *Collins*, 323 US 516, 543–544 (1945).

been an accompanying refusal by the workers of other employers to pickup, deliver, or provide services at the establishment of the employer that is the target of the picketing.

B. Limitations on Appeals for Support or Sympathy

459. When it adopted section 8(b)(4) of the NLRA in 1947, and when it amended that section in 1959, Congress sought to protect at least some opportunities for labor organizations to appeal to public sympathy as a source of pressure available for organizing and adjusting economic disputes. On the other hand, Congress also was determined to insulate employers who do not have a stake in a particular labor–management conflict from becoming embroiled involuntarily in the conflict and suffering economic consequences for doing nothing more than conducting their normal business activities.

Concerted appeals by labor for public sympathy puts pressure on management if there is a prospect either that: (a) the public will directly reduce the level of business with the employer, or b) other enterprises that are intermediaries between the public and the employer involved in the labor conflict will discontinue doing business with that embroiled employer in order to avoid loss of business to themselves. When it enacted section 8(b)(4) and its amendments, therefore, Congress tried to balance (a) the competing consideration of preserving the workers' right to inform their friends of their plight and win sympathetic responses, against (b) the desire to protect enterprises that are not direct participants in the labor–management conflict from suffering economic consequences particularly when such enterprises likely are unable to alter the conditions that gave rise to the conflict. The available points at which to draw this balance are many and the legislative history of the provision does little to provide definitive guidance respecting the precise points of balance intended by Congress.

In contrast to the NLRA, the RLA does not restrict union activity based on the identity of the target of the exerted pressure.[507]

460. Some parts of section 8(b)(4) of the NLRA are difficult to follow. Generally, this provision allows a union to put direct economic pressure on the employer with whom the union has a dispute and does not allow a union to put economic pressure on other enterprises. What often is unclear, though, is how to determine when an enterprise should be treated as the employer, or one of the employers, directly involved in a particular labor–management conflict and when it should be treated as a victimized neutral.

There are several focal problems in applying the broad, somewhat jumbled language of section 8(b)(4). First, in determining whether particular concerted activity is prohibited by that provision, a decision must be made as to whether the activity is directed at the employer that has a dispute with the union (the 'primary'

507. *Burlington Northern Railroad* v. *Brotherhood of Maintenance of Way Employees*, 481 US 429 (1987).

employer) or at some other employer (a 'secondary' employer). For example, appellate court decisions hold that section 8(b)(4) is not violated when strikers physically prevent deliveries or pick-ups from being made at their employer's business site even though that conduct may be criminally punished, is ground for civil suits by any victims of the assault, and is an unfair labor practice under section 8(b)(1). Even though unlawful, the conduct is at the primary site and is directed at the primary employer and, therefore, is beyond the scope of section 8(b)(4).[508] As a consequence, neither the NLRB nor the affected employers can resort to the special remedies that are available when there is a section 8(b)(4) violation.[509]

Secondly, in some situations, conduct overtly aimed solely at one employer may be understood by union supporters to signal a desire that pressure be directly brought to bear upon an enterprise that deals with the primary employer. Thus, a picket line at the site of the primary employer normally signals a request that those employed by other enterprises not perform any work that requires crossing the picket line. It might also signal to those employed by others that they should refuse to work with, or on, the goods produced by that primary employer irrespective of the place where that work is to be performed.

Third, even though pressure is directed solely at the primary employer, as for example in a request for a consumer boycott of that employer's products, that pressure may have a significant impact upon those who do business with that employer. Thus, the NLRB and the courts have had to answer the question: To what extent did Congress intend to shelter employers from pressures that, though incidental to pressures directed at a primary employer, are substantial in their impact upon the secondary employer?

461. Two principal cases in this area are *NLRB* v. *Servette, Inc.*, 377 US 46, and *NLRB* v. *Fruit and Vegetable Packers*, 377 US 58, both decided in 1964. The latter case is more popularly known among labor relations specialists as the *Tree Fruits* case. (*Tree Fruits* was the name of the employer with which the union had its primary dispute.) In these cases the Supreme Court decided that Congress intended to allow workers who have a dispute with an employer to lawfully ask the public to stop doing business with that employer and to communicate their request through any peaceful technique, including picketing, at a place not owned by the employer but at which its goods are being sold or its services are being performed. Thus, it was lawful for the union, in the *Tree Fruits* case, to picket outside the entrance of a supermarket with which it had no dispute, and to ask customers not to purchase products sold there that were packed and distributed by the employer with whom the union did have a dispute. The Court made it clear, however, that it would have been unlawful for the union to request the public to stop doing business with the supermarket just because the supermarket was handling the goods of the struck employer.

---

508. *Landgrebe Motor Transport, Inc.* v. *District 72, IAMAW*, 763 F.2d 241 (7th Cir. 1985).

509. When there is good cause to believe that 8(b)(4) is being violated, the NLRB can seek, and usually must seek, a temporary injunction under section 10(l). If an 8(b)(4) violation is proved, aggrieved parties can sue for damages under LMRA section 303.

The Supreme Court also held in these decisions that it is lawful for a union to ask enterprises that do business with a struck employer to cease doing such business for the duration of the labor–management dispute. This is similar to a non coercive appeal for sympathetic support from the public.

However, it is unlawful to threaten or otherwise coerce an employer to cease doing business with a struck employer. Similarly, in an effort to get an enterprise to cease doing business with the employer with which the union has a dispute, it is unlawful to request a person employed by that enterprise to refuse to work until its employer ceases doing business with the targeted employer. Thus, it was lawful, in *Servette*, for the union to inform supermarket managers that handbills would be distributed outside the store requesting customers not to buy the struck employer's goods which were being sold at the store. It also was lawful for the union to request the managers to have the store discontinue handling these products for the duration of the union's dispute with the struck employer. The Court construed the latter request as being directed at the managers in their managerial capacity – requests, therefore, for them to exercise their managerial discretion in a particular manner. The Court noted that had the union instead asked the managers to stop working with the struck goods, this would have been an unfair labor practice because the union would have been guilty of asking persons employed by someone with whom the union does not have a dispute to cease working until their employer stops doing business with the target of the union's dispute. The Court emphasized that in the *Servette* situation, the union was asking, not coercing, the managers to make a business decision to stop dealing with the struck employer. Moreover, because the handbilling seeking consumer support for the union's cause was itself lawful activity, the Supreme Court refused to treat as a threat the fact that the union informed the managers that such handbilling would be conducted if the supermarkets continued to handle the struck goods. Had the Court decided that conditioning the handbilling on the supermarkets' continued sale of the struck goods constituted a threat or coercion, the union would have been found guilty of the unfair labor practice of not merely requesting sympathetic conduct by another employer but rather of unlawfully trying to impose such sympathetic conduct through threats or coercion. A dissenting opinion questioned the court's assumption that it is not coercive to threaten to engage in conduct that is itself lawful. In analogous contexts, similar conduct constitutes unlawful coercion. For example, if business A tells business B that unless B loans A money, A will advertise the fact that B's product is unhealthy, the threat is an unlawful extortion even if B's product is unhealthy and even though the advertising of that fact is lawful.

In deciding *Servette*, the Court did not determine whether section 8(e) would have been violated had the employer agreed that it would not handle the struck products. (See paragraph 473, below.)

462. A provision in section 8(b)(4), known as the 'publicity proviso', permits workers to appeal to the public to stop doing business with even a 'neutral' employer in order to get that neutral employer to cease dealing with an employer with whom there is a labor dispute so long as:

(a) the appeal is publicized through means other than picketing, and
(b) the appeal does not result in refusals by the neutral employer's workers to perform services or refusals by the workers of other enterprises to pick up or deliver goods at the neutral site or to refuse to service that neutral employer.

Thus, in *International Union of Operating Engineers, Local No. 139 (Oak Construction)*, 226 NLRB 759 (1976), a union was attempting to gain recognition from a company that constructed underground conduits for the telephone company. The union, among other things, distributed handbills at the telephone company's business offices requesting customers to withhold 20 percent of their telephone bill payments until the company ceased using a non union contractor to construct underground conduits. The NLRB held that this appeal was protected by the publicity proviso of section 8(b)(4). Had the same appeal been made by means of picketing, however, it would not have been protected by the publicity proviso nor by the *Tree Fruits* decision inasmuch as the economic pressure would have been directed not at a struck product but at an employer other than the one with which the union was directly engaged in a dispute.

Although the publicity proviso itself was not applicable, the Supreme Court emphasized this statutory distinction between picketing and other forms of communication when, in *Edward J. DeBartolo Corp.* v. *Florida Gulf Coast Building & Construction Trades Council*, 485 US 568 (1988), it held that a union could lawfully distribute handbills urging people to not patronize a shopping mall because the union had a dispute with a construction contractor building a store for one of the mall's tenants.

463. The *Operating Engineers* case, discussed in the preceding paragraph, dealt as well with another problem encountered in drawing a line between permissible pressure placed directly on the 'primary' employer with which the union has a dispute, and unlawful, indirect pressure that asks people not to do business with a 'secondary' employer because that employer deals with the enterprise that is the target of the union's dispute. In the *Operating Engineers* case the work being done by the primary employer, the target of the union's dispute, was an integral part of the telephone company's operations. Moreover, at the time in question, over 99 percent of the primary employer's business income was derived from the work performed for the telephone company. Can it be said, therefore, that the two businesses were so interrelated as to obliterate the distinction between primary and secondary employer? At times the NLRB has resorted to such a functional analysis of business relationships in determining whether an enterprise is a primary party to a labor dispute. However, in the *Operating Engineers* case the Board rejected such a functional analysis. Unlike the handbilling, that was held protected under the publicity proviso of 8(b)(4), the picketing at the telephone company was held to violate 8(b)(4) because it was aimed at a reduction of payments to the telephone company which, according to the NLRB's analysis, was a neutral party to this dispute.

464. Even though a union does not have a direct dispute with Enterprise X, the NLRB has held, under a concept known as the 'ally doctrine', that if Enterprise X is performing the work of the employer that is the primary target of the union's dispute, the union can treat Enterprise X as though it is the employer with which the union has its direct dispute. Thus, an 'ally' is equal to a primary party. For example, if the employees of an employer that manufactures bed sheets for a department store engage in a work stoppage, and their employer contracts with another bed sheet manufacturer to produce enough sheets so that it can continue to supply the demands of the department store, the union striking the first manufacturer can direct its strike at the second manufacturer including engaging in picketing that asks people not to do the work of producing the struck goods nor deal with that employer until it ceases to do the struck work.[510] On the other hand, if the department store on its own initiative shifts orders to a different manufacturer, that second manufacturer is a 'neutral' employer. Therefore, any picketing or other activity seeking to get that neutral employer's workers to refuse to produce the goods for the striking employer's customers would constitute unlawful secondary pressure.[511]

465. Under limited circumstances the ally doctrine has been applied to those situations in which the struck operation is functionally integrated with an enterprise that, though legally separate from the struck enterprise, is under common ownership and control with the second organization. However, the Board insists that all three conditions – integration of the operation, common ownership and substantial common control – must be wholly satisfied. Indeed, the NLRB treats divisions of the same company as separate employers if all three conditions are not met. This approach is known as the 'reverse ally doctrine'. For example, in *International Brotherhood of Teamsters Local Union No. 391* v. *NLRB*, 543 F.2d 1373 (DC Cir. 1976) (*per curiam*), *cert.* denied 430 US 967 (1977), a labor organization was engaged in bargaining with a multi-division company at a facility producing crushed stone. When negotiations reached an impasse, the union called a work stoppage at the facility. Several weeks later it set up a picket line at a division of the same company located several hundred miles away. This other division produced crushed stone but did not serve the same marketing area. Moreover, there was no interchange of workers between the two divisions and, although managerial personnel from the corporation's headquarters consulted with each division's manager, the division heads had substantial autonomy and operated through separate channels of communications directly with the top executives of the corporation. In addition, workers at the picketed plant were represented by a different union from the one that struck. Nevertheless, the workers at the picketed plant respected the picket line and refused to cross it. The Court of Appeals affirmed the NLRB's conclusion that the union had violated the secondary boycott prohibitions of section 8(b)(4) of the NLRA. The court reasoned that because the divisions operated independently, they were entitled to be treated as separate employing entities for purposes of section 8(b)(4). Although the corporate headquarters had potential controlling power over the business and personnel decisions of both divisions, this did not destroy the separateness of the two divisions for purposes of section 8(b)(4). Thus, the appellate

510. *See*, for example, *Blackhawk Engraving Co.* v. *NLRB*, 540 F.2d 1296 (7th Cir. 1976).
511. *Maritime Union Local 333 (Dixie Carriers)*, 131 NLRB 693 (1961).

court concluded that the union had unlawfully caused a work stoppage at an employer other than the one with which it had its dispute.

466. Just as it is lawful to call for a work stoppage at, or a boycott of, an employer that is allied with the primary employer, it is lawful as well for a union that is engaged in a dispute to follow the work of the target employer to inform all persons that this product or work is produced or performed by an employer with which it has such a dispute. It was this permissible form of ambulatory picketing or handbilling that was involved in the *Servette* and *Tree Fruits* cases described, above, in paragraph 461. The ambulatory nature of some work also leads to another important and controversial line of decisions respecting section 8(b)(4) of the NLRA. These decisions involve what is known as the common site picketing problem.

467. In order to properly examine the common site picketing issue, it is necessary to be familiar with one other principle regulating picketing and strike activity. A proviso in section 8(b)(4) specifically states that it is lawful for workers to refuse to cross, and for a union to order its members to not cross, a picket line that is established by a recognized union at the site of an employer that is directly engaged in a labor dispute. This is true even though such a refusal to cross a picket line at the primary employer's work site is, in effect, a partial refusal by the workers of other employers (secondary or neutral employers) to do their own work – a refusal that, if sponsored by a union, would otherwise fall within the prohibitions of section 8(b)(4).

What rule controls, then, when the labor dispute concerns work performed at a site at which workers employed by several different enterprises are present? If the striking workers establish a picket line, can all persons employed at the site lawfully refuse to cross the picket line and can the union request all workers to respect their picket line even though this results in direct economic pressure on enterprises that are not directly involved in the labor dispute?

468. The common site picketing issue can arise in two contexts. One is where persons working for employers other than the one with whom a union has a dispute, are performing their work at the premises of the employer whose employees are engaged in a dispute. Although it is lawful for the picketing union to appeal to those other workers to respect their picket line, and although it is lawful for unions representing those other workers to require their members to respect that picket line, under a principle known as the 'reserved gate doctrine', it has been held that it is unlawful to picket at a separate entrance whose use is reserved for those employed by the enterprises that are not engaged in the labor dispute so long as the work performed by these other workers is not part of the normal operations of the facility.[512] That is, the picketing must be confined to entrances that are assigned for the use of those doing the normal work of the employer with whom the union has its dispute. If, however, the workers assigned to use the separate gate are engaged in work that is integrated into the normal operations at the premises, their entrance is treated the same way as entrances for all other workers. In such situations, therefore, picketing

512. *Local 761, IUE* v. *NLRB*, 366 US 667 (1961).

can be conducted at all entrances – including the gate reserved for workers of employers that are not directly in dispute with the union.

469. The other context in which the common site picketing issue can arise is where the workers who have a dispute with an employer perform their work at a site owned by someone other than their employer and persons who work for other employers are also employed there. Picketing is permitted at a common site owned by a neutral employer if it is conducted only at times when:

(a) those employed by the employer with whom the union has a dispute are actually engaged at the site in their normal work activities,
(b) the picketing is located reasonably close to the place where that employer is operating, and
(c) the picket signs clearly designate that the dispute is solely with the specified target employer.[513]

By establishing an entrance reserved for the workers of the employer with which the union has its dispute, however, the owner of the premises can isolate lawful picketing activity so that it affects only the workers of the primary employer.

470. One form of common site picketing occurs at building construction sites. Typically, the owner contracts with a general contractor for the construction of the planned building and that general contractor subcontracts with enterprises that specialize in performing the work of the various construction trades such as carpentry, plumbing, heating and air conditioning installation, elevator installation, plastering, structural steelwork, and the like. If, for example, the plumbers' union has a dispute with the plumbing contractor (normally referred to in the industry as the plumbing 'subcontractor'), to what extent can they picket the construction site and seek support from the other building trades workers? A simple solution would be to treat all of the workers as jointly employed by the general contractor or by the owner of the building site. That would result in permitting picketing directed at all persons working at the job site. That simple solution, however, was rejected by the Supreme Court in *NLRB* v. *Denver Building & Construction Trades Council*, 341 US 675 (1951), on the ground that in the construction industry the law long has recognized the business relationship between general contractor and sub contractors as being separate and independent.

Underlying the application in the construction industry of the reserve gate doctrine, discussed in paragraph 469, above, is the concept that different building trades contractors operate in a separate and unrelated manner – a legal fiction that has no

513. *Sailors' Union of the Pacific (Moore Dry Dock Co.)*, 92 NLRB 547 (1950); *Electric Workers Local 861 (Plauche Elec.)*, 135 NLRB 250 (1962). *See also Sheet Metal Workers' Local 15* v. *NLRB*, 491 F.3d 429 (DC Cir. 2007) (ruling that an orderly mock funeral about 100 feet from a hospital, by a union whose members were doing construction work at the hospital, did not carry the coercive impact of picketing and, therefore, was a protected means of seeking a sympathetic customer boycott of the hospital).

relationship to the actual integration of building construction work. This legal fiction, moreover, ignores the fact that in section 8(e) of the NLRA, Congress expressly permitted unions and employers in the construction industry to enter into agreements requiring contractors to not engage union workers on the same job sites with non-union workers. Thus, the proviso recognized the extent to which the integrated nature of construction industry work can lead to serious personal conflicts between union and non union employees who perform their work at the same job site. The reserved gate doctrine as applied to construction sites also ignores the Board's own experience with the frequency with which the different construction industry trades engage in work assignment disputes due to the overlapping nature of much of their work.

A vigorous effort to legislatively reverse the *Denver Building Trades* decision was successful in both houses of Congress in 1975 but was defeated by a presidential veto that Congress failed to override.

471. Another example of the difficulty encountered in trying to distinguish what is primary activity, and therefore lawful under section 8(b)(4) of the NLRA, and what is secondary activity, and therefore unlawful under section 8(b)(4) of the NLRA, is found in the attempt to apply the rule of the *Tree Fruits* case, discussed above in paragraphs 461 and 466, to the situation in which the struck work product is the sole focus of another employer's business. This situation often is referred to as the 'merged product' problem. To illustrate, in one case, striking bakery workers picketed at the premises of a restaurant that sold mostly sandwich items. The picket signs asked customers to not buy the bread produced by the struck bakery. In another case, a union having a labor dispute with a gasoline refinery picketed auto service stations that, though independently owned, sold little else besides gasoline produced by the struck refinery. The pickets requested customers to not purchase the gasoline. In both cases the NLRB ruled that the picketed product was so entwined with the business of the 'neutral' employer that picketing against the product was equal to asking customers to cease doing business with that neutral employer and, therefore, was unlawful secondary picketing.[514]

472. In a 6–3 decision, known as the *Safeco* case, the Supreme Court upheld the NLRB's approach to the merged product situation. It stated that 'product picketing that reasonably can be expected to threaten neutral parties with ruin or substantial loss' violates section 8(b)(4)(ii)(B) of the NLRA.[515] Two concurring justices complained that the Court's decision gave inadequate consideration to the serious constitutional problem of making the legality of picketing turn upon the content of the picketer's message. Justice Stevens, one of the concurring justices, explained that since picketing 'calls for an automatic response to a signal, rather than a reasoned response to an idea', the statutory restraint is regulating conduct, not expression, and

514. *American Bread Co.*, 170 NLRB 91 (1968), enforced 411 F.2d 147 (6th Cir. 1969); *Dow Chem. Co.*, 211 NLRB 649 (1974), rev'd 524 F.2d 853 (DC Cir. 1975), vacated for remand to NLRB for reconsideration 429 US 807 (1976), dismissed for mootness due to dissolution of the respondent local union, 229 NLRB 302 (1977).

515. *NLRB* v. *Retail Store Employees*, 447 US 607, 614 (1980).

therefore does not violate the Constitution.[516] The dissenters argued that the Court's approach is an 'unsteady standard' because it turns upon the extent to which the secondary firm will suffer from the picketing. They also noted the irony of giving to the business that has entwined its fate with that of the primary employer, greater protection from economic pressure than is given to the business having only an incidental contact with the party to the labor dispute.

473. Another form of secondary boycott designed to reach the employer with which a union has a dispute is a refusal by workers to handle goods produced by the primary employer. Such a refusal is known as 'hot cargo action' – goods produced by the target employer constitute cargo that is too 'hot' for union sympathizers to handle. Prior to the adoption of the 1959 amendments to the NLRA, it was permissible for unions to enter into agreements with employers obligating the employer to not handle goods produced by employers that were engaged in a dispute with a union. This type of undertaking, characterized as 'secondary boycotts by advance commitment',[517] was made an unfair labor practice when the Landrum–Griffin Act amendments altered section 8(b)(4) to address this type of activity. The Landrum–Griffin Act also added to the NLRA section 8(e) which declares hot cargo agreements void and unenforceable and makes it an unfair labor practice to enter into such agreements.

474. Section 8(e) of the NLRA excludes the clothing manufacturing industry from the hot cargo prohibition and the construction industry is excluded to the extent of permitting employers and unions to execute hot cargo agreements with respect to work performed at a construction site. The exclusion for the clothing manufacturing industry is broad enough to make lawful not only the execution of a hot cargo agreement but also the use of concerted activities designed to obtain or actions to enforce such agreements. The exclusion respecting on-site construction work, however, is more narrowly worded with the result that although it is lawful to use concerted activities to get a hot cargo provision, and it is lawful to execute a hot cargo provision and enforce it through a judicial or arbitration proceeding, it is not lawful to enforce it through picketing or coercive activity such as a work stoppage or threat of a stoppage.[518]

475. The prohibition against hot cargo agreements has been broadly interpreted to ban contract provisions that exempt workers from disciplinary action if they refuse to handle goods produced by a non-union company or a company with which there is a union dispute. The prohibition also has been held to invalidate contractual

516. 447 US at 619.

517. R. Goetz. 'Secondary Boycotts and the LMRA: A Path Through the Swamp', 19 *Kan. L. Rev.* 651, 683 (1971).

518. *Woelke & Romero Framing, Inc.* v. *NLRB*, 456 US 645 (1982) (holding that such provisions are lawful even when not confined to a specific job site); *Ryan Heating Co.* v. *NLRB*, 942 F.2d 1287 (8th Cir. 1991); *United Brotherhood of Carpenters and Joiners* v. *NLRB*, 533 F.2d 1136 (DC Cir. 1975).

provisions that make the collective agreement terminable or renegotiable upon the employer doing business with an enterprise that is engaged in a labor dispute.[519]

476. In some situations it has been held that the hot cargo agreement prohibition was violated by a provision in a collective agreement that prohibited the employer from selling assets to purchasers who were not signers of a collective agreement. The cases reaching this result involve the maritime industry where the Board has found that the sale of vessels is part of the ongoing process of engaging in that business. The NLRB decisions emphasize that although it is lawful for a collective agreement to contain a provision seeking to ensure the perpetuation of the bargaining unit despite a sale of the business, it is unlawful to seek to ensure the perpetuation of the union's bargaining status irrespective of what happens to the employee unit. The disputed provisions in the maritime cases did not ensure the perpetuation of the jobs of the bargaining unit employees but, instead, unlawfully ensured that whoever was employed by the new employer would be represented by the union.[520]

In contrast to the above described maritime cases, the NLRB has upheld the validity of a collective agreement provision prohibiting the sale of the business except to a buyer that undertakes to continue the operations subject to the collective agreement. In reaching this conclusion the NLRB noted that because the collective agreement limited the causes for discharge, the bargaining unit workers were directly protected by the provision at issue.[521] It has been explained that a provision requiring that the present work force will be maintained by a new employer under the existing terms and conditions of employment reflects a primary objective of protecting the interests of the current bargaining unit workers. Because the objective directly affects the bargaining unit members, the hot cargo clause prohibition of the NLRA does not apply. However, if the clause does nothing more than protect the union's interest in perpetuating itself as bargaining representative, regardless of who is in that unit, the provision's impact potentially is upon workers other than the ones in the negotiating unit and, therefore, is secondary and unlawful. An alternative rationale for the result in these cases is that section 8(e) restricts only those agreements affecting ongoing employment activities and not what happens after the business has terminated.[522]

477. In *Dowd* v. *International Longshoremen's Association*, 975 F.2d 779 (11th Cir. 1992), the NLRB sought a court injunction against alleged pressure a union representing Florida longshore workers was placing on secondary employers, in violation of NLRA section 8(b)(4)(ii)(B), who were engaged in a dispute with US stevedoring companies that employed non union dock workers. The alleged unlawful pressure was through gaining the cooperation of unions representing Japanese dock workers who warned Japanese importers that they would not unload citrus fruit if it was loaded by non-union American workers for shipment from the US to

519. *Truck Drivers Local 413* v. *NLRB*, 334 F.2d 539 (DC Cir.), *cert.* denied 379 US 916 (1964); *Employing Lithographers* v. *NLRB*, 301 F.2d 20 (5th Cir. 1962).

520. For example, *National Maritime Union (Commerce Tankers Corp.)*, 196 NLRB 1100 (1972), enf'd 486 F.2d 907 (2d Cir. 1973), *cert.* denied 416 US 970 (1974).

521. *District 71, IAM (Harris Truck & Trailer Sales)*, 224 NLRB 100 (1976).

522. *Lone Star Steel Co.* v. *NLRB*, 639 F.2d 545 (10th Cir. 1980), *cert.* denied 450 US 911 (1981).

Japan. The Court of Appeals for the 11th Circuit, in upholding the injunction, emphasized that the impact of the threat not only fell on Japanese citrus importers but also upon US citrus exporters. However, the US Court of Appeals for the District of Columbia rejected this analysis when it reviewed the NLRB's subsequent unfair labor practice finding against the American longshore workers' union. In denying enforcement of the NLRB decision, the latter appellate court explained that a union cannot be held responsible for the conduct of another unless that other party acts as the union's agent. It concluded that because the essence of an agency relationship is the principal's right to control the agent's actions and because the Japanese unions are independent and have no legal obligation to the American union, their conduct could not be charged to the respondent American longshore workers' union. Hence, it held, the US union was not guilty of coercing the secondary parties, an element necessary to sustaining the illegal secondary boycott charge.[523]

478. The NLRB and courts recognize other limits on the restraints imposed by the hot cargo clause prohibition. For example, a provision in a collective agreement protecting the worker's rights to refrain from crossing a primary picket line (that is, one located at the site of the work where the union and employer are in dispute) arguably is a refusal to handle the products of another employer and, therefore, a violation of section 8(e). Nevertheless, the law is well settled that the prohibition against hot cargo clauses was not intended to interfere with the lawfulness of respecting primary picket lines. Accordingly, it is lawful for a collective agreement to protect workers from being disciplined for having refused to cross a primary picket line.[524]

479. It is also lawful for a union and employer to enter into an agreement prohibiting the employer from assigning workers to perform struck work – that is, the work normally performed by workers who have a dispute with a labor organization. The rationale for this position is based on the ally doctrine, discussed above starting at paragraph 464. When workers are asked to do work that is normally performed by those employed at an establishment at which there is a labor dispute, their employer has become an ally of the primary employer to that dispute and, therefore, is to be treated as a primary employer. Thus, the refusal to do the work of those who are engaged in a labor dispute is a primary, not a secondary, concerted refusal.[525]

480. As seen above, section 8(e) is not violated by agreements that allow workers to refuse to cross primary picket lines, or that allow workers to refuse to do work normally performed by those employed by an employer engaged in a labor dispute. However, the NLRB has held that section 8(e) is violated when a clause in a collective agreement that protects the workers' right to refuse to cross a picket line is

523. *International Longshoremen's Association* v. *NLRB*, 56 F.3d 205 (DC Cir. 1995).

524. *Truck Drivers Union Local No. 413* v. *NLRB*, 334 F.2d 539, 543 (DC Cir.) *cert.* denied 379 US 916 (1964).

525. *Blackhawk Engraving Co.* v. *NLRB*, 540 F.2d 1296 (7th Cir. 1976); *NLRB* v. *Amalgamated Lithographers of America*, 309 F.2d 31, 38 (9th Cir. 1962), *cert.* denied 372 US 943 (1963).

written in language that is broad enough to cover secondary as well as primary picket lines. Rather than uphold such provisions to the extent of their legality, the NLRB's policy is to strike them in their entirety.[526]

481. Because section 8(e) is not intended to limit concerted activities that are directed at protecting the interests of the workers engaged in conduct in relation to their own employer, it is lawful for a labor organization to demand agreement by the employer to preserve the bargaining unit work for the bargaining unit members. Thus, a decision of the Supreme Court ruled that it was not an unfair labor practice for a union to negotiate a provision requiring an employer to assign to construction site carpenters all of the work of cutting and fitting doors rather than use doors that had been pre-cut and fitted at a factory – work traditionally performed by the on site carpenters.[527]

482. The principle of allowing workers to contractually preserve their work opportunities has led to the rule that it is not a violation of the hot cargo clause prohibition for an employer and a labor organization to agree that any contracting out of bargaining unit work will be restricted to enterprises that provide at least the same level of wages as is provided under the bargaining unit's collective agreement. A provision limiting such contracting out of work to unionized enterprises, on the other hand, is an unlawful hot cargo violation - except in the clothing manufacturing industry where such agreements are specifically allowed under section 8(e). Limiting the contracting out of work to unionized enterprises shifts the focus of the agreement from preserving work for the bargaining unit, which is a lawful primary objective, to preserving work for union members no matter where employed.[528]

483. In recent years many unionized construction industry employers have engaged in the practice known as 'double-breasting'. Such employers operate two separate businesses performing the same type of work. One business, however, solicits only those jobs in which the general contractor or owner has agreed to use only contractors that provide their employees with union wages and benefits; the other business solicits only those jobs that do not have those restrictions. Construction industry unions object to double-breasting because the profits made on union jobs help finance the survival of the commonly owned business that promotes non union work, a problem for them because the increased number of nonunion employers undermines the union's strength in the industry. Unions also object because some workers employed by nonunion employers gained their trade skills in union sponsored apprenticeship programs. Therefore, in an effort to combat double-breasting, some unions have negotiated provisions in their collective agreements stating that the agreement terminates upon the employer affiliating with a non union shop. Others have negotiated provisions that prohibit the unionized employer from

526. *Bricklayers, Local 2 (Associated General Contractors)*, 224 NLRB 1021 (1976), enforced 562 F.2d 775 (DC Cir. 1977).
527. *National Woodwork Manufacturers Association* v. *NLRB*, 386 US 612 (1967).
528. *Retail Clerks, Local 770 (Hughes Markets, Inc.)*, 218 NLRB 680 (1975).

operating a non-union entity and still others have sought provisions making the collective agreement applicable to all work done by any entity controlled by the owners or managers of the employer that is the party to the collective agreement.

The NLRB treats such provisions as a violation of section 8(e) if the employer runs the non-union entity as a wholly separate operation. If it is not a separate operation, the Board treats the non-union entity as an alter ego of the unionized employer and allows restrictions in collective agreements that prevent the employer from engaging in double-breasting. In deciding if commonly owned entities are separate, the NLRB weighs such facts as whether the non-union entity serves different customer markets and has separate labor relations policies, employees, supervisors, office locations, bank accounts, insurance policies, and business licenses.[529]

In one case[530] an appellate court rejected an employer's argument that section 8(e) is violated where the union seeks to extend the collective agreement to any entity controlled by the owners or managers of the unionized employer. The court noted that because the employer had previously engaged in double-breasting practices, the provision's primary objective was work preservation. Therefore, it concluded that the proposed provision did not violate section 8(e) even though the non-union shop could operate with a separate employment policy and with different customers, supervisors, facilities and workers. The court reasoned that because the union-represented employees had been losing work to construction jobs that operated using non-union workers, when the employer's non-union operation obtained jobs this was part of the process of taking from the union-represented employees work they traditionally performed. Hence, it found the situation analogous to the type of work preservation declared lawful by the Supreme Court in *National Woodwork Manufacturers Association* v. *NLRB*.[531] (See paragraph 481, above.)

484. Unless tasks have in fact traditionally been the work of the bargaining unit employees, it is unlawful for a labor organization and an employer to agree to restrict work assignments in such a way as to allow bargaining unit members to refuse to handle work on the ground that preparatory tasks were performed outside the bargaining unit. In a closely divided decision, the Supreme Court ruled that so long as the union seeks to preserve the employees' traditional work patterns, work preservation provisions are valid even if, in response to technological modifications, the nature of the protected work changes. The Court explained that in analyzing such situations, the fact finder must first determine what work the provision allegedly seeks to preserve and then examine how the parties have attempted to do that in the face of technological change. If the provision reflects an objective of preserving the traditional work pattern, even though the work itself is changed, the provision does not violate the prohibition against hot cargo agreements.[532]

529. *United Brotherhood of Carpenters and Joiners of America, Local No. 745 (SC Pacific Corp.)*, 312 NLRB 903 (1993).
530. *Becker Elec. Co.* v. *IBEW Local Union No. 212*, 927 F.2d 895 (6th Cir. 1991) (*per curiam*). For similar analysis by the NLRB, *see Int'l Ass'n of Bridge, Structural and Ornamental Iron Workers (Southwestern Materials & Supply, Inc.)*, 328 NLRB 934 (1999).
531. 386 US 612 (1967).
532. *NLRB* v. *International Longshoremen's Ass'n*, 447 US 490 (1980).

485. Another restriction on the ability of labor organizations to contractually preserve work opportunities for bargaining unit members is the 'right of control' test used by the NLRB and approved by the Supreme Court. The right of control test is a limitation not on the work preservation agreement but on its enforcement. This test narrows the type of situation in which enforcement of a work preservation provision can survive a challenge under the section 8(b)(4) restrictions upon hot cargo activity. The test states that a labor organization may not attempt to enforce a valid work preservation agreement against an employer if the employer lacks the authority to make the disputed work assignment to bargaining unit workers.

In the leading decision, the Supreme Court held that even though a plumbing contractor agreed not to use pre-cut or pre-threaded pipe, the union engaged in unlawful secondary activity when it sought to enforce that agreement where the plumbing contractor, in bidding on a job, had obligated itself to adhere to work specifications requiring the use of pre-cut or pre-threaded pipe. The Supreme Court reasoned that since a party other than the bargaining unit employer had the sole right to control the decision to use non pre-cut or non pre-threaded pipe, the enforcement of the work preservation clause was directed at altering the conduct of a secondary employer (the general contractor), an employer with whom the union did not have a direct dispute.[533]

Ultimately, of course, by trying to remove the market for the product, the union's efforts in enforcing the work preservation clause was directed at influencing the producers of pre-cut and pre-threaded pipe to cease engaging in that type of work. But this was the aim of enforcing the work preservation clause whether or not the plumbing contractor had authority to use non pre-cut and non pre-threaded pipe. Thus, it can be argued that the Court's right of control test draws a distinction that is more responsive to a widespread antagonism toward agreements that restrict technological advancement than it is to any functional differences in the objectives or impact of the union's work preservation effort.

486. Section 8(b)(4) also protects an employer from concerted activity in which it is squeezed between the economic pressures exerted by competing labor organizations. This situation is generally referred to as a jurisdictional dispute and has two variations, one of which can best be described as a work assignment dispute and the other as a representation dispute.

The representation type of jurisdictional dispute is a proper subject for a unit clarification procedure under the NLRB's section 9(b) authority to determine the appropriate bargaining unit in which a union can establish its status as bargaining representative. This type of dispute involves a situation in which two or more unions represent workers in the same enterprise and both unions claim the right to represent the interests of particular employees.

The other type of jurisdictional dispute situation is regulated under the NLRB's unfair labor practice machinery. It arises when two or more labor organizations each claim that particular work tasks should be performed by the workers that union represents. That is, the conflict concerns which bargaining unit's workers are entitled to be assigned particular tasks.

---

533. *NLRB* v. *Enterprise Ass'n*, 429 US 507 (1977).

In both situations, two or more labor organizations or groups of employees are demanding recognition from the employer for the same status. Satisfying the demand of one group or organization means rejecting the claim of another union or the employees it represents. The employer often has a preference between the competitors based on its perception of the more efficient work process, but other times is indifferent as to who wins the jurisdictional claim. Either way, though, the employer has no desire to be caught in the pull of this conflict.

487. The work assignment variety of jurisdictional dispute often arises when the employer, as a result of business expansion, modification, or technological change, must assign a new work task. Two or more groups of workers may seek to have the work assigned to them either to increase their potential earnings, provide greater job security, or to replace other work that is no longer available to them. To obtain that work assignment, one or more of the groups may decide to resort to, or may threaten to resort to, concerted activity. Often, all of the worker groups that claim the right to perform the new task assert a contractual right to do so. Whatever decision the employer reaches may result in the disfavored group or groups trying to alter that decision through the coercion of contractual enforcement or by resorting to concerted activities.

488. Labor organizations are prohibited by section 8(b)(4)(D) of the NLRA from engaging in or threatening to engage in a work stoppage or otherwise threatening or coercing persons for the purpose of forcing them to assign particular work to members of a particular union, or to those in a particular work classification, unless such work assignment has been approved by a Board order or by a bargaining unit certification. If this provision is violated, however, the Act does not call for the usual remedies to be invoked – at least not in the first instance. Instead, through a special procedure established by NLRA section 10(k), described in paragraphs 819–823, below, the Act encourages the interested parties to privately resolve their differences through settlement or through submission to arbitration. If this is unsuccessful, the NLRB must then determine what the work assignment should be. Only if the parties fail to abide by that determination is the situation subject to the usual cease and desist remedies. In addition, in such disputes the normal unfair labor practice remedies are supplemented both by NLRA section 10(l)'s provision for the NLRB to obtain temporary injunctive relief, and by the injured parties' ability to bring a damages cause of action under LMRA section 303.

489. Often a jurisdictional dispute combines both a conflict over representation and a conflict over work assignments. This happens, for example, if two different departments of an enterprise are separately represented by different bargaining agents and, due to technological changes, work previously performed in the different bargaining units is combined and assigned to a new job classification. Each of the two groups likely will claim for themselves both the job assignments and the representational responsibilities. Technically, the job assignment aspect of this conflict should be resolved under the section 8(b)(4) and 10(k) procedures of the

NLRA, and the representational aspect should be resolved in a unit clarification proceeding under section 9 of the Act. In fact, the NLRB often deals with both aspects in a section 8(b)(4)/10(k) proceeding.[534]

490. When the NLRB first received its authority to resolve work assignment disputes, it refrained from using it. Among other things, it disclaimed having the necessary expertise to deal with such matters. The Supreme Court, however, decided that in the absence of the parties' ability to resolve such disputes for themselves, the Act gave the Board the responsibility to decide these matters and it ordered the NLRB to do so.[535] The Board has since done this whenever necessary, but has continued to reflect its own discomfort with making work assignment determinations by following a pattern of decisions which gives a great deal of weight – almost always determinative weight – to the employer's judgment regarding to whom work should be assigned.[536] Moreover, the parties generally choose to resolve the case without an NLRB determination. For example, in the Fiscal Year that ended in 2009, the dispute was settled or decided without an NLRB 10(k) hearing in three-fourths of the cases and a formal decision was issued in less than 10 percent of the cases.

There is no comparable statutory machinery for resolving such disputes in the rail and air transportation industries. Instead, under the Railway Labor Act the parties must resolve such disputes through negotiation or arbitration.

§8. Access to the NLRB and Other Tribunals

491. The NLRA prohibits an employer from imposing any sanctions on an employee because that individual has filed charges with the NLRB or testified at a hearing under the Act. An equivalent prohibition has been held to implicitly apply to a labor organization's interference with a worker's access to the processes of the NLRB.[537]

492. The prohibition against interference with concerted worker activities also protects employee access to tribunals other than the NLRB where that access is sought in furtherance of collective interests. The protected right to press concerted interests also includes the right to file a claim for individual benefits with the employer where those rights arise under a collectively bargained agreement.[538]

534. *See*, *Carey* v. *Westinghouse Electric Corp.*, 375 US 261 (1964).
535. *NLRB* v. *Radio and Television Broadcast Engineers Union*, 364 US 573 (1961).
536. *Laborers' International Union of North America (Anthony Allega Cement)*, 336 NLRB 358 (2001); *Machinists Local 724 (Holt Cargo Services)*, 309 NLRB 377 (1992), enforced 30 F.3d 1487 (3d Cir. 1994).
537. *NLRB* v. *Industrial Union of Marine & Shipbuilding Workers*, 391 US 418 (1968).
538. *NLRB* v. *City Disposal Systems, Inc.*, 465 US 822 (1984).

Chapter 3. Labor Unions, Employee Associations and Employer Organizations

§1. Worker Organizations

I. Unions

493. Collective bargaining is the focal point for modern American labor organizations. Although American law permits an individual to serve as a collective bargaining agent, the collective representative in the US almost always is a labor organization established in the form of a private membership association.

In addition to being organized to act as a collective bargaining representative, labor organizations often perform other functions ranging from operating trade skills training programs, conducting recreational activities, and sponsoring retirement homes, to raising money for charities, engaging in political lobbying, and supporting political campaigns. In large measure, such collateral functions are intended to improve group solidarity, organizational loyalty, and enhance the memberships' financial security, income, and welfare.

494. As observed in paragraph 42, above, union membership has declined significantly in recent decades. Explanations for the decline are varied. Some attribute it to the labor movement's lack of sufficient investment in education and training and to its failure to adapt its organizing activities to new worker life styles and values. In addition, many employees have been deterred from supporting labor organizations due to highly publicized situations of corrupt, undemocratic union leadership, sometimes tied-in with organized criminal syndicates.[539] A related explanation for the decline in union membership may be the influence of cultural norms generated by national political leadership and mass media that question the beneficial role of labor organizations. A manifestation of this characteristic is the frequency with which relatively conservative political candidates publicly condemn their opponents as 'dominated by union bosses' and the frequency with which relatively liberal candidates try to understate the importance of support received from labor organizations. Furthermore, some employees no doubt have been discouraged from supporting some unions due to rigid adherence to outmoded work rules that hamper industry viability and due to unrealistic bargaining demands that sometimes cause prolonged work stoppages. Many commentators also point to increased intensity of employer resistance to unions, the lack of adequate legal remedies to respond to violations of the right of workers to select union representation, the fear of unionized jobs being eliminated or out-sourced to non-union facilities in other parts of the country or abroad, the tactic of shifting large portions of enterprise work to the purportedly self-employed (the gig economy), and an imbalance in the tools of economic warfare available to management as contrasted with those allowed for

539. J. Jacobs, *Mobsters, Unions and Feds* (2006).

labor.[540] Finally corporate takeovers and accompanying reorganizations sometimes appear to target unionized firms with the strategy of ousting union influence and transforming past union gains for workers into a financial bonus for the controlling corporate managers and controlling shareholders.[541]

495. As detailed in paragraph 42, above, union membership is unevenly distributed among different industries and types of work. It is also very unevenly distributed geographically.

496. The only significant union growth since the 1960s has been among government employees. Most categories of workers employed by the federal government and by state and local governments had been largely unorganized until the 1960s. In addition to the dramatic increase in unionization of government workers, the 1970s saw statistically less spectacular, but nevertheless very visible, unionization of professional athletes in the sports of baseball, football (American style), and hockey. (Soccer was unionized in the 1990s.) Other important areas of union growth in the 1970s were the organization of hospital and other health care workers, some farm workers in California, small pockets of such workers in Texas and Florida, and some organizing of university and college teachers. The momentum of these organizing efforts disappeared in the 1980s and in non government employment the portion of unionized workers had declined so substantially by the mid-1990s that the survival of organized labor had become a topic of serious discussion. In the late 1990s, new national labor leadership dedicated substantial financial resources to reverse the membership decline of the previous two decades. However, the reversal has yet to become evident.

497. With a few exceptions, such as the short lived Knights of Labor, most early American unions were organized along job skills (trade or craft) lines. Although industrial unions had thrived for some time in the coal and textile industries, the momentum toward organizing along industrial lines did not increase dramatically until the late 1930s with organizational successes in the automotive and steel industries. Many unions continue to organize and bargain along trade lines and others along industrial lines. A few labor organizations, such as the Teamsters, are eclectic. One might say that their motto is: If they draw pay, sign them up.

For several decades the International Brotherhood of Teamsters held the distinction of being the nation's largest labor union. In 1980 its membership was about 1.8 million; in 2017 it reported its membership at about 1.4 million and had been surpassed by the American Federation of State, County and Municipal Employees (1.6 million) and the Service Employees International Union (1.9 million). The United

540. *See*, R. Adams, *Industrial Relations Under Liberal Democracy*, Columbia, SC, 1995; V. Dubal, 'Wage Slave or Entrepreneur'", 105 *Calif. L. Rev.* 65 (2017); K. Andrias, 'The New Labor Law', 126 *Yale L.J.* 2 (2016). A political event often cited as encouraging management resistance to unions was President Ronald Reagan's wholesale dismissal of federal air traffic controllers when they engaged in an illegal work stoppage in 1981.

541. For a study observing this trend, *see* B. Becker, 'Union Rents as a Source of Takeover Gains Among Target Shareholders', 49 *Indus. & Lab. Rel. Rev.* 3 (1995).

Auto Workers, which was the nation's second largest union in 1980, with 1.35 million, had declined to a membership in 2017 of 415,963. The United Steelworkers had 1.2 million in 1980 and claimed the same membership size in 2017 by including retirees and members in Canada and the Caribbean as well as active US members. The differences are more dramatic than the figures indicate because during this time many small unions were merged into the larger ones thereby increasing the size of the surviving unions.

II. Employee Associations

498. Several million workers are members of various types of employee associations that bring together workers who have a common occupation or profession or who work in the same industry. The distinction between a union and an employee association is difficult to define. Essentially, a union is organized for the purpose of collective bargaining representation but also engages in collateral activities that benefit members in their capacity as workers. An employee association is organized for several principal purposes, one of which may be to engage in collective bargaining representation. Many professional associations are learned societies that bring together people who share similar intellectual interests and institutional concerns regardless of whether they are employees, managers or owners. Often collective representation plays a small role to the other activities of such associations. On the other hand, collective bargaining has come to play a central role in the organizational life of many associations that until the 1970s or 1980s were models for distinguishing employee associations from unions. For example, the National Education Association (NEA) had for decades been a professional association of teachers and school administrators whose activities focused on the improvement of educational institutions. Among the more important policies adopted and promoted by the NEA was its condemnation of collective bargaining in education. With the growth, in the early 1960s, of the American Federation of Teachers (a union claiming 1.5 million members in 2016), the National Education Association reconsidered its policy toward collective bargaining and eventually altered its position. As a result, by the mid-1970s, organizing for collective bargaining and representation had become one of its principal activities. By 2017, claiming about 3 million members, it was the nation's largest organization serving as a collective bargaining agent, though for much of its membership its efforts to improve their terms and conditions of work focus on legislation rather than collective bargaining.

Some professional associations have an affiliated organization to engage in collective organizing and representation in order to separate the focus on professional standards as contrasted with efforts to improve employment conditions and remuneration. This division is also necessitated by the fact that many members of the professional association work in unorganized establishments or are self-employed or have managerial positions that exclude them from bargaining units. In addition to possible conflicts of interests, such members do not wish to pay dues that finance activities from which they do not derive any direct benefits. An example of the division of responsibilities that emerged is the establishment of the National Federation of Nurses which is affiliated with the American Nurses Association, a professional organization of registered nurses. In 2013 the National Federation became an affiliate of the American Federation of Teachers. Another, and larger, AFL-CIO union representing nurses is National Nurses United.

499. In gathering labor relations statistics, the Department of Labor counts employee associations as labor organizations if they engage in collective bargaining representation. Government employees constitute the bulk of the membership of employee associations that are so counted. Excluded from this category are professional organizations that tend to represent the proprietary interests of professional workers, rather than the employee interests of the members of the profession. Two groups that best illustrate the excluded type of association are the American Medical Association and the American Bar Association. The Union of American Physicians and Dentists, an AFL–CIO affiliate, has entered into memoranda of understanding and collectively bargained agreements covering a variety of health care professionals primarily employed by local governments in the state of California. It has been expanding its representational activities to other locales as well as begun to represent health care professionals as a collective bargaining agent in the private sector.

III. AFL–CIO

500. Early in the history of American labor unions there were a few short-lived national or regional union federations. The American labor movement did not become a truly coordinated national force, though, until the foundation of the American Federation of Labor in 1886. Several unions split off from the AFL in the late 1930s to protest the lack of industrial organizing effort by the trade union dominated federation. These unions eventually formed the Congress of Industrial Organizations (CIO) whose constituent member organizations were responsible for a substantial portion of the growth in union membership that took place during the 1940s and early 1950s. The two federations merged to become the AFL–CIO in 1955. Since then the number of affiliated unions has declined from 135 to 56 in 2017 due largely to mergers necessitated by the excessive administrative expenses to service small memberships. In 2017 the AFL–CIO claimed to represent 12.5 million workers.

501. Structurally, the AFL–CIO primarily is an organization composed of other organizations and is financed by per capita dues paid by the member organizations. The federation's affiliate member organizations are national unions. (Some are international unions to the extent that they have membership both in the United States and Canada.) In addition to its affiliate national unions, the AFL–CIO has had several independent local unions attached to it.

502. The AFL–CIO does not enter into collectively bargained agreements. This is the responsibility of its member organizations. Rather, the federation serves as the political lobbying arm for organized labor and as a source for improved public relations and general education. In addition, it provides financial and staff assistance in targeted organizing efforts, US union representation for international agencies such as the ILO, research activities, training programs, information exchange, and liaison with unions in other countries. It also mediates inter-union disputes, polices the ethical conduct of unions and union officials, and provides arbitration machinery for resolving certain types of inter-union conflicts. Through its regional, state and local federations or councils, the AFL–CIO coordinates union organizing activities at state and municipal levels and engages in more localized forms of political lobbying. (*See also*, paragraph 66, above.)

503. To a large degree, the AFL–CIO has cast its lot with the Democratic Party. With the exception of the 1972 Presidential election between Richard Nixon and George McGovern, the AFL–CIO has consistently supported Democratic presidential candidates. In the 1972 election, the AFL–CIO adopted an embargo on union political support for either candidate. A few AFL–CIO unions, nevertheless, gave their endorsement to McGovern, the Democratic candidate, but that endorsement was not adequate to get him elected and some analysts concluded that the withholding of AFL–CIO endorsement from the Democratic candidate insured Nixon's election. Interestingly, the next year the AFL–CIO, together with other organizations, pressed for Nixon's impeachment due to his participation in trying to hide his and his associates' participation in efforts to steal strategic planning information from the Democratic Party headquarters during the presidential election campaign. A year later, largely as result of the pressures that had developed from impeachment directed investigations, Nixon became the only President in American history to resign from office.

§2. Regulation of Internal Union Affairs

I. Basic Union Structure

A. The Local Union

504. The term 'local union' is most commonly used to refer to the basic subdivision of national unions. Some unions traditionally refer to their locals as 'chapters' or 'lodges'. It was estimated by one source that in 1978, there were approximately 75,000 local unions in the United States. In the early 1990s approximately 41,000 union locals were filing annual financial reports with the Department of Labor as required by the LMRDA.[542] Although some locals are independent of any other labor organization and a few are affiliated on a separate, individual basis with the AFL–CIO, most local unions are subdivisions of a national labor organization.

On occasion a local union changes its national affiliation or an unaffiliated local becomes affiliated with a larger organization. The US Supreme Court has held that a union need not allow bargaining unit members who are not members of the union vote on the question of whether to change the union's affiliation and that the

542. The Department of Labor no longer publishes such data.

employer must continue to bargain with the union after a change of affiliation. However, the Court left open the possibility that the NLRB could find that a change of affiliation is a sufficient disruption of the labor organization's representational continuity so as to permit it to entertain a petition for a representation election that otherwise would be barred by the existence of a current collective agreement.[543]

505. Local unions (frequently referred to as 'locals') vary greatly in membership size. Most have from a few hundred to several thousand members. A few have had tens of thousands of members and are large scale operations. For example, Local 721 of the Service Employees International Union, which represents local government workers in Southern California, claimed over 95,000 public sector members in 2017. Local 1, of the same international union, headquartered in Chicago has members in 11 cities in 5 states performing such diverse jobs as commercial office and residential janitors and maintenance workers, residential doormen, security officers, window cleaners, light manufacturing workers, school bus drivers, retail workers, cemetery workers, nurses, laboratory technicians, ushers in sports and theater complexes, and security scanners at the airports.

Local unions sometimes are established for the purpose of representing workers in a single bargaining unit. More often, the local represents workers in several different bargaining units located within close geographic proximity.

506. Under the LMRDA (29 US Code §401 *et seq.*), the ultimate policy making authority of American unions must reside with the membership or with officials who are elected by the membership. The daily administrative responsibility of the local often is assigned to an individual who is employed full time by the union to serve one or several locals. Frequently, that person is an elected local officer or an elected local administrator. Often, however, the person in charge of the daily administrative responsibilities of the local is appointed either by the local's officers or by the national union's national or regional officers or administrators. In contrast, it is common for the local union's presiding officers to be full-time workers employed in one of the bargaining units for which the local is the recognized collective representative. Although that elected officer may preside over meetings, often the presiding officer's influence is limited. In contrast, the person who administers the local's affairs frequently is a full-time official given the title 'business agent' or 'business representative' or 'secretary-treasurer'. When there is a full-time paid administrator of the local's affairs, that person generally has determinative influence over what is decided in the local union's name because this person is the one individual in the local union who regularly has an opportunity to meet all of the members and give assistance to them in dealing with their personal problems as workers and as union members. Thus, he or she is the most visible person within the local union. In addition, this individual likely has the most thorough familiarity with the union's constitution, by-laws, customs, national officers and national policies, and the most available local experience in organizing non union workers, in seeking assistance or protection from government agencies, in negotiating a collective agreement, and in

543. *NLRB* v. *Financial Institution Employees*, 475 US 192 (1986); *Minn Dak Farmers Cooperative*, 311 NLRB 942 (1993), enforced 32 F.3d 390 (8th Cir. 1994).

enforcing the collective agreement. Hence, the business agent, or other full-time paid administrator of the union, is the local's expert; the person the members most often turn to for aid and advice, the person who has most often assisted in resolving a member's personal problems. Accordingly, the full-time paid administrator is in a position to adversely affect the affairs of disfavored members by influencing the union's response to that member's grievance under a collective agreement, or that member's requests for negotiating priorities, or that member's claim filed against a union administered or influenced health care or retirement fund, or that member's use of the union's job referral machinery. Therefore, the extent to which the full-time paid local administrator is inclined to operate in a democratic or a dictatorial manner often determines the extent to which the members in fact enjoy self-determination within the union.

A study of local union officers who, in the mid-1990s, characterized themselves as the 'top' official found that about three-fourths were full-time employees and only part-time union officers. The most common title was President. The typical top official was a 46 year old male with a high school diploma (12 years of education). Close to 10 percent were women and close to 8 percent were non white. (Both figures are substantially lower than the general membership having these characteristics.) Full-time local officers are even more likely to be white males and generally are older and better educated than the part-time officers. In addition, while the average length of time in office for a part-time top local union officer was 6.9 years, it was 8.7 years for full-time officers. Finally, only about a third of those studied had first attained that position as a result of a contested election. The remainder were elected without an opposing candidate. Since the study dealt only with local unions representing non government workers, the patterns may not represent the entire labor movement.[544]

507. Prior to World War II, most union members were active in their union's affairs. The union frequently served as a social club and adult education center. A high percentage of members regularly attended union meetings which generally were followed by a social hour or professional entertainment. A decade after World War II, union members were drifting away from attending union meetings. The distractions of television, increased living standards and the accompanying obsession with consumerism, the growth of suburban living and the accompanying dispersion of membership residences far from the site of the union meeting hall, perhaps coupled with the transformation from ideological identification with a common cause to cynical acceptance of the union as a profiteering amalgam of power brokers, all contributed to the decline of active membership participation in the routine affairs of American labor unions.

508. Despite the decline in union activism, members have not totally surrender their prerogatives of self-governance. Rebellion against the local leadership breaks out frequently enough in most unions to make the elected and appointed officials aware of their vulnerability to an aroused and disgruntled membership. In the 1980s

544. M. Goldberg, 'Top Officers of Local Union', 19 *Lab. Studies J.* 3 (1995).

dissident movements resulted in changes in the top leadership of several major unions, including the United Mine Workers of America and the International Brotherhood of Teamsters, but in large measure were precipitated by government investigations and prosecutions of union leaders accused of corrupt practices.

In addition, committees of worker-members often participate in collectively bargaining new contracts and in determining which grievances to process through the full series of grievance-arbitration dispute settlement stages. The authority to call a strike normally requires a favorable membership vote and the constitutions or by-laws of most unions condition acceptance of a collective agreement upon membership ratification (usually by majority vote).

B. Regional Divisions

509. Many national unions have intermediate administrative and even executive structures separating the local from the national organization. These bodies typically are regionally based and are presided over by elected vice-presidents of the national union. In addition to exercising delegated authority from the national union to act in its behalf with respect to the locals and members, the regional divisions generally provide staff assistance and guidance to the locals and coordinate activities, such as organizing efforts and political lobbying, that often involve the interests of many or all of the locals within the region. The regional structure for coordinating the activities of locals of the same national union sometimes is called a joint board or joint council to which each local in the region has a voting representative. On occasion, the joint board or joint council is recognized or certified as bargaining representative or is recognized or certified as bargaining agent jointly with one or more local unions. This occurs, for example, where the bargaining unit is geographically dispersed and cuts across the jurisdictional boundaries of several locals.

C. National Organizations

510. National unions are autonomous entities whose structures and methods of governance vary in accordance with the provisions of their constitutions or charters. Among other things, the national union's charter describes the types of workers eligible for membership. Often these definitions are narrow, particularly for trade unions. Industrial unions generally define their scope of activity more broadly. National unions that have, or at one time had, locals in Canada often use the title 'International' in their organizational name.

Many American labor unions at one time had formal or informal restrictions on membership based on race, sex, religion, nationality or ethnic background. By the 1940s the labor movement was trying to eliminate such restrictions and NLRB decisions and the Civil Rights Act of 1964 now prohibit most forms of discrimination. Although there continues to be some covert racial and other discrimination by a few unions, this vestige of the past has largely faded under the pressure of court suits,

NLRB proceedings, the so-called federal affirmative action programs, changing cultural attitudes, AFL–CIO policy, and the pressures of financial survival.

511. National unions sometimes act directly as a bargaining representative. More often this is the responsibility of a local union chartered by the national. On occasion, the local and national jointly represent the bargaining unit. However, even if the local is the sole bargaining representative, the national union often has considerable influence over the local's conduct as a result of the national's charter or by-law requirement of consultation and as a result of the degree to which the local relies on the national for staff assistance and expertise. Perhaps of greatest importance, many national unions control the right of the local to engage in a work stoppage or to draw upon union funds established to financially assist strikers.

512. The LMRDA requires that national union officials be elected by the union membership. This election can either be direct or can be through the indirect method of the members electing representatives to a national union convention that in turn elects the national officers. On a few occasions, pursuant to the LMRDA and federal anti-racketeering laws, federal courts or the Department of Labor have supervised such elections to ensure their integrity.

Most presidents of national unions are older men who have held office for many years. Progression up the hierarchy of union leadership is not too different from progression up the corporate hierarchy with the exceptions that union leaders tend to remain in office longer once they reach the top rank and it is rare for them to move from one organization to another.

The annual salaries of national union presidents are substantial when compared to average worker earnings but most pale in comparison with the salaries of the top executives of major and not so major US corporations. As with corporative executive salaries in the United States, there appears to be little or no correlation between compensation and the size or success of the enterprise. For example, in 2004, the highest paid union official was the president of the Laborers' International Union (reported to have a bit over 363,500 members at that time) who received a reported $405,620, while the president of the Service Employees International Union (reported at that time to have over 1,400,000 members) was paid an annual salary of $222,792.

513. National union charters and by-laws structure the manner in which the national union is governed and shape the relationships between the national and local organizations including the procedures and grounds for intervention by the national organization into the affairs of a local union. Lawful intervention by the national entity can include such matters as conducting or coordinating collective negotiations involving more than a single local; overruling a local's decision adversely affecting the interests of individual members; requiring locals to merge or dissolve in order to promote organizational efficiency or get rid of corrupt local leadership; or in response to corruption or disarray, appointing a trustee to preside over the local's affairs for a period of time.

The national union's charter or by-laws often also regulates the amount of dues to be collected by locals and the amount to be allocated to the national office and to strike or other welfare reserve funds. (See paragraphs 528–533, below, for federal legal restraints on the relationship between national and local unions.)

514. A substantial number of national unions have their headquarters in Washington, DC. Some are headquartered in population centers such as New York City, or in industrial centers or former industrial centers such as Detroit and Pittsburgh.

II. The Law of Private Associations

515. In addition to being controlled by their charters and by-laws, labor unions are regulated in accordance with the common law of private associations. For many years some jurisdictions rejected the standing of private associations to sue or be sued as separate entities. This rule has largely been altered by statute or case law and even when still recognized generally can be avoided by using the procedural device of a class action.[545] Furthermore, the LMRA and the LMRDA permit unions to sue and be sued for most purposes in the federal courts.[546]

516. The preemptive impact of federal labor law has substantially limited the extent to which labor organizations are subject to the body of state law that regulates the internal affairs of private associations. A narrow exception is recognized to allow states to prohibit union officers or other agents from receiving dues or administering pension and welfare funds if they have been convicted of a felony or are close associates of persons engaged in racketeering.[547] State private association law also is recognized to the extent of imposing general standards of fiduciary responsibility upon union officers and grants members a right to fair treatment. For example, under the law of private associations a union cannot expel a member because he refused to disobey a court order or because he testified against the union's interest in a public hearing.[548] In addition, the common law of private associations generally has required groups such as labor organizations to follow at least

545. Note, 'Private Associations,' 76 *Harv. L. Rev*. 983, 1081 (1963); *United States* v. *White*, 322 US 694 (1944); *United Mine Workers* v. *Colorado Coal Co*., 259 US 344 (1922).

546. *Plumbers & Pipefitters* v. *Local 334*, 452 US 615 (1981) (suit by local respecting rights under the union's constitution can be brought in federal court and is governed by federal substantive law); *Wooddell* v. *IBEW*, 502 US 93 (1991) (individual member can bring LMRA section 301 suit against local union to enforce protections under national union's constitution); *Freight Drivers* v. *Gordon*, 576 F.2d 1285 (8th Cir. 1978) (local union has standing to file a voluntary bankruptcy petition).

547. *Brown* v. *Hotel and Restaurant Employees Union*, 468 US 491 (1984).

548. Note, 'Private Associations,' 76 *Harv. L. Rev*. 983, 1006–1007 (1963); J. Baird and M. Player, 'Free Speech and the Landrum-Griffin Act', 25 *Ala. L. Rev*. 577, 582–583 (1973). The LMRDA imposes a statutory duty of fiduciary responsibility upon union officials but some courts have held that this provision relates only to custody and use of the organization's finances. (*See* paragraphs 534–539, below.) Other courts have held that the duty extends to all aspects of conduct involving the interests of members. Compare *Lodge 1380* v. *Dennis*, 625 F.2d 819, 828 (9th Cir. 1980) with *Hoffman* v. *Kramer*, 362 F.3d 308, 316 n. 4 (5th Cir. 2004).

minimal standards of procedural fairness in dealing with their members and to adhere to their own internal procedures before taking adverse action against members.[549] In addition, challenges by members based on the local union's by-laws or other contractual undertakings with members are resolved under local, not federal, law.[550] Nevertheless, most internal disputes involving labor organizations are resolved by courts either pursuant to statutory standards established under the LMRDA or pursuant to the duty of fair representation that the courts have ruled is implicit in the NLRA.

III. Regulation of Internal Union Affairs under the LMRDA

517. The LMRDA (29 US Code §401 *et seq.*) regulates certain aspects of the internal affairs of those organizations that themselves or through their subsidiary or affiliate bodies either represent or seek to collectively represent workers in employment units that are covered by the NLRA or the RLA. Thus, the only unions not covered are those that solely represent workers who are excluded from the two basic labor relations statutes such as farm workers and government workers.

The LMRDA was adopted after a long series of highly publicized Senate hearings which revealed that: a number of unions were governed by dictatorial power brokers, on occasion national union leaders perpetuated themselves in office through the support of representatives from fictitious locals, some national unions exploited locals by imposing trusteeship control over locals whose leadership was independent or whose treasuries were fat, union members often were fearful of violent retribution or job loss if they voiced objections to union leadership, union finances often were poorly managed and susceptible to embezzlement, and management sometimes received favorable treatment by bribing union officials. To combat these evils, Congress adopted a variety of remedial devices in the LMRDA.

A. *The Right to Vote*

518. The LMRDA guarantees to all members of covered labor organizations equal rights to participate in the election of officers (29 US Code §411). This includes the right to nominate the candidates and to vote. The Act also requires that officers of national unions be elected at least once every five years by a secret ballot of the membership or by a convention of delegates chosen by secret ballot of the membership. A similar requirement is imposed for the election at least every four years of officers of any intermediate bodies, such as regional boards. Local union officers must be elected at least every three years by a secret ballot of the membership.

549. Note, above at 76 *Harv. L. Rev.* 1027, 1033.
550. *See*, for example, *Casumpang* v. *ILWU Local 142*, 121 P.3d 391 (Hawaii 2005).

In each of the above elections all members in good standing have a right to run for office subject to reasonable standards of qualification. Such qualifications must permit a substantial portion of the membership to qualify as candidates for office.[551]

Access to lists of eligible voters is guaranteed to the candidates and discrimination among candidates is prohibited.[552] When the membership elects officers, each eligible voter must be sent an election notice to his home at least 15 days prior to the date of balloting, the voting procedures must be fair, and the ballots must be retained for at least one year.

The Secretary of Labor investigates violations of LMRDA election requirements. If the Secretary finds probable cause to believe a violation has occurred, he or she can sue to set aside election results and order a new election to be conducted under the Department of Labor's supervision. To prevail, the Secretary must prove that an interference with a reasonable opportunity to be a candidate or nominate a candidate may have affected the election outcome.[553] In addition, a private cause of action is available to any individual member who was deprived of the right to vote or to nominate a candidate.

519. The right to vote also includes the right to equally participate in any membership vote concerning union business.[554] Moreover, a membership vote must precede an increase in local dues or a special financial assessment by the local. Dues increases or special assessments by the national union must also be approved by a vote either of the members or by officers expressly authorized by the union's constitution to impose such obligations.

In addition, if the Secretary of Labor finds, after a hearing, that a union's constitution or by-laws do not provide adequate procedures for the removal of an elected officer who is guilty of serious misconduct, the Secretary can supervise a secret ballot election enabling the membership to remove such an officer.

However, a membership vote need not precede the elimination of an established union program such as one to organize new workers.[555]

An appellate court has rejected the argument that a union has a duty under the LMRDA to fully disclose all material information to the members before submitting a new collective agreement for a membership ratification vote. The court reasoned that since the LMRDA does not require that collective agreements be submitted for membership ratification, the broad duties of democratic procedure provided by the Act do not impose a duty of fair disclosure respecting balloting that is available only because union by-laws provided for such a vote.[556]

551. *Local 3489, United Steelworkers of America* v. *Usery*, 429 US 305 (1977).

552. *Int'l Org. of Masters* v. *Brown*, 498 US 466 (1991).

553. *Reich* v. *Local 89, Laborers*, 36 F.3d 1470 (9th Cir. 1994).

554. *Alvey* v. *General Electric Co.*, 622 F.2d 1279 (7th Cir. 1980) (the Act was violated where laid off members were denied the right to participate in a referendum to ratify a contract that affected their interests); *Sergeant* v. *Inlandboatmen's Union of the Pacific*, 346 F.3d 1196 (9th Cir. 2003) (the Act was not violated where members who were only casual employees at the bargaining unit were excluded from participating in a ratification vote).

555. *Corea* v. *Welo*, 937 F.2d 1132 (6th Cir. 1991).

556. *Ackley* v. *Western Conference of Teamsters*, 958 F.2d 1463 (9th Cir. 1992). The court acknowledged that the duty of fair representation may be applicable in such cases but stated that relief under

520. Americans are shockingly apathetic about voting for their leaders. For example, in the typical Presidential election in recent decades only a little over half of the voting age population cast ballots and since the early part of the 20th century seldom has participation exceeded 60 percent. Similarly, union members often do not bother to vote. Thus, in the highly publicized 1972 re-run election for the presidency of the United Mine Workers, about one third of the members did not cast ballots.

B. Freedom of Expression

521. Section 101(a)(2) (29 US Code §411(a)(2)) of the LMRDA explicitly protects the right of union members to 'express any views, opinions or arguments'. The Act limits this right, however, to the extent of permitting a union to enforce reasonable rules as to the member's responsibility toward the union as an institution. The Act also allows a union to require that members refrain from interference with the union's performance of its legal or contractual obligations. Under these limitations, a union can discipline members for violating reasonable rules of decorum in the conduct of meetings but cannot silence a member's criticism of its conduct or its officers – even when that criticism is defamatory.[557] Nor can a union impose rules of conduct that reflect personal values as contrasted with rules necessitated by the need to operate in an orderly and efficient way. Thus, in one case it was held that the LMRDA prohibited a union from barring certain members from the opening ceremonies of the union where those members refused to participate in the salute and pledge of allegiance to the American flag.[558]

522. The job security of union officers or staff, however, is not protected by the LMRDA's free speech provision. The Act protects the freedom of expression of such persons only in their capacity as union members. Accordingly, the Supreme Court has indicated that the Act is violated only if the union's challenged conduct altered the official's or staff member's membership status in some way. Removal from office or from a staff job is not itself a violation of the LMRDA because it involves the official or employment status of the affected individual instead of that person's membership status. In reaching this determination the Court expressly avoided dealing with the question of whether disciplining a union official would be actionable if it was part of a purposeful attempt to suppress membership dissent. In

---

that theory would require proof both that the undisclosed information would have altered the outcome of the vote and that it would have resulted in a more favorable collective agreement for the employees - matters that are not likely susceptible of proof since they would appear to be wholly speculative.

557. *Salzhandler* v. *Caputo*, 316 F.2d 445 (2d Cir.) *cert.* denied 375 US 946 (1963); *Pearl* v. *Tarantola*, 361 F. Supp. 288 (SDNY 1973). *See also*, *Helton* v. *NLRB*, 656 F.2d 883 (DC Cir. 1981) taking guidance from §101(a)(2) in holding that a union violated §8(b)(1)(a) of the NLRA when it refused to allow a member to post a statement criticizing the union leadership on a union bulletin board located in the employee rest area at the employer's terminal. In contrast, threatening language or aggressive use of discourteous language has been held unprotected. *Hylla* v. *Transp. Communs. Int'l Union,* 536 F.3d 911 (8th. Cir. 2008).

558. *Stachan* v. *Weber*, 535 F.2d 1202 (9th Cir. 1976) (*per curiam*).

applying these principles, the Court has found that the dismissal of members from their positions as appointed business agents is merely the exercise of traditional patronage by a newly elected officer and is justified by the need to assure that the policies of newly elected officials are diligently carried out. However, it expressly left open the question of whether the result should be different if the union members work for the labor organization in non confidential, non policymaking positions or hold elected office.[559]

Several years later, the Supreme Court dealt with the latter issue when it held that an elected local union officer cannot be removed from office in retaliation for statements made at a union meeting in opposition to the actions of an official appointed by the national union. The Court distinguished this situation on the ground that the members' freedom to vigorously debate and criticize union policy within the organization would be unduly chilled if an elected officer was removed for engaging in such discourse. In addition, it observed that the removal of an elected official because of a policy disagreement had the impact of depriving the membership of an effective ballot.[560] Similarly, a lower court has held that in contrast with the leadership's right to demand loyalty from its appointed staff, elected union officials cannot be removed or otherwise disciplined for expressing opposition to the hierarchy's policies.[561]

Lower federal courts have applied the LMRDA to other aspects of freedom of expression claims. Several appellate courts have ruled that although a union member does not lose LMRDA freedom of expression by becoming a union official, it is reasonable to prohibit appointed officials or staff from expressing opposition to the leadership's announced policies. However, some courts have indicated that such removal is not permitted if it is part of a scheme to repress the membership's free speech.[562] Regardless of whether removal from an appointed position is allowed, removal from union membership is not an available sanction against a member who expresses opposition to union policies.[563] A distinction is made, however, between expressed opposition to union policies as contrasted with statements that support a rival union's organizing efforts or an effort to defeat the representational status of the member's labor organization. In the latter situations, courts permit ouster from union membership on the ground that the express limitation to the LMRDA's free speech provision allows a union to remove members who are undermining the union's status and effectiveness as a collective representative.[564]

559. *Finnegan* v. *Leu*, 456 US 431 (1982).
560. *Sheet Metal Workers* v. *Lynn*, 488 US 347 (1989).
561. *Schermerhorn* v. *Local 100, Transport Workers Union of America*, 91 F.3d 316, 324 (2d Cir. 1996).
562. Compare, *Cotter* v. *Owens*, 753 F.2d 223 (2d Cir. 1985) and *Grand Lodge, IAM* v. *King*, 335 F.2d 340 (9th Cir. 1964), *cert.* denied, 379 US 920 with *Witmeyer* v. *BRAC*, 779 F.2d 206 (4th Cir. 1985); *Miller* v. *Holden*, 535 F.2d 912 (5th Cir. 1976); *Newman* v. *Communication Workers*, 570 F.2d 439 (2d Cir. 1978), review on remand 597 F.2d 833 (1979).
563. *Thompson* v. *Office and Professional Employees Int'l Union*, 74 F.3d 1492 (6th Cir. 1996), *cert.* denied 519 US 993.
564. *Aircraft Mechanics Fraternal Association* v. *Transport Workers Union, Local 514*, 98 F.3d 597 (10th Cir. 1996).

C. Freedom of Assembly and Other Limitations on Internal Union Actions

523. Section 101(a) (2) of the LMRDA (29 US Code §411(a)(2)) protects the right of union members to meet and assemble freely with other members. This provision prohibits a union from disciplining dissident members who caucus or convene meetings to organize a challenge to the union leadership. The Courts of Appeals have divided over the question of whether and when this provision requires the convening of a membership meeting or referendum if one is demanded by the requisite number of members in accordance with the union's constitution or by-laws.[565] Even if the LMRDA does not provide a means for enforcing the union's regulations for the convening of a special meeting, a remedy might be available through a suit brought under the law of private associations on the theory that federal law does not attempt to control the particular question or a contractual action might be available under the LMRA to enforce the membership contract.[566]

By a 5–4 vote, the Supreme Court has held that a union member's freedom of association, implicitly protected by the LMRDA, is not violated by a union rule prohibiting members from accepting contributions from non-members to support a campaign for election to union office. The Court stated that reasonable restraints upon campaign activities are permissible under the Act and that the disputed rule was a reasonable effort to protect the organization from undue outside interference with its internal affairs. The dissenters argued that less restrictive rules (e.g. required disclosure of contributors and a ceiling on the amount of contributions) were adequate to meet the union's legitimate concern and, therefore, the total bar to such contributions was an unreasonable restraint upon the protected right of association.[567]

D. Right to Sue the Union

524. The strength of labor organizations depends in large part upon membership solidarity – that is, the members' mutual loyalty. It is not surprising, therefore, that unions frequently display intolerance toward conduct that suggests lack of solidarity. If a member has a grievance regarding the conduct of the union or a union official, the member is expected to resolve that dispute within the union family. Often, internal procedures are available for airing such grievances and for appealing from the adverse decisions of lower ranking officials. Nevertheless, a member may not trust the justice of such internal dispute resolution mechanisms, especially since the decision makers often have close working relationships with those involved in the disagreement. Accordingly, union members sometimes seek redress from outside the organization by filing a charge with the NLRB or by suing in state or federal

565. *Compare Yanity* v. *Benware*, 376 F.2d 197 (2d Cir.), *cert.* denied 389 US 874 (1967) and *Grant* v. *Chicago Truck Drivers*, 806 F.2d 114 (7th Cir. 1986) with *Lodge 1380* v. *Dennis*, 625 F.2d 819 (9th Cir. 1980).

566. Such a suit may be available only in state court. *See* the discussion in the next numbered paragraph respecting unavailability of federal court suits to enforce local by-laws as contrasted with enforcement of the national unit's constitution or by-laws.

567. *United Steel Workers of America* v. *Sadlowski*, 457 US 102 (1982).

court. The NLRB has held that it is an unfair labor practice for a union to fine or expel a member for having filed an unfair labor practice charge against the union.[568]

Moreover, the LMRDA, at section 101(a)(4) (29 US Code §411(a)(4)), provides broad protection of such efforts to seek redress by expressly prohibiting labor organizations from limiting the right of members to sue or to appear as a witness before any court, administrative or legislative body. A statutory limitation on this prohibition, however, is that a union can require members to first exhaust the organization's own hearing procedures before bringing suit or seeking help from an administrative agency so long as that internal remedy does not take more than four months. The Supreme Court has construed this latter provision as permitting a court or agency to stay its proceedings for up to four months while requiring the grievant to first seek relief through the labor organization's own internal processes. On the other hand, the failure to exhaust the union's internal remedies for even a four month internal appeal effort cannot be used as a basis for imposing disciplinary sanctions against the member.[569] Moreover, lower federal courts have held that there is no need to exhaust internal procedures of the union if to do so would frustrate the opportunity to exercise statutory rights or if the procedures are inadequate to remedy the wrong.[570] (*See, also*, paragraph 855, below.)

A somewhat different approach was taken in *Breininger* v. *Sheet Metal Workers*, 493 US 67 (1989), where a member brought suit asserting that because of his opposition to the union's leadership, local officials who operated the union hiring hall were not referring him to available jobs. The Court held that the worker had stated a valid claim of breach of the duty of fair representation, and therefore allowed his suit to go forward on that claim. (Section 301 suits for breach of the duty of fair representation are described in section V, below.) However, the Court rejected that part of the suit that was based on the LMRDA on the ground that the alleged wrong was the act of individual officers, and not of the union as an entity, and that only discrimination by the labor organization gives rise to an individual suit under the LMRDA.

The Supreme Court has also ruled that a union member can bring a suit in federal court under section 301 of the LMRA where the member asserts that the national union breached its responsibility toward a local union under the national organization's constitution. The Court explained that federal courts have authority to hear such suits because the national union's constitution is a contract between it and the local unions and section 301 expressly includes jurisdiction over contract suits

568. *NLRB* v. *Industrial Union of Marine & Shipbuilding Workers of America*, 391 US 418 (1968); *Roberts* v. *NLRB*, 350 F.2d 427 (DC Cir. 1965). *NLRB* v. *UAW*, 690 F.2d 82 (6th Cir. 1982) (unfair labor practice to remove an appointed union officer for filing an unfair labor practice charge).

569. *NLRB* v. *Industrial Union of Marine & Shipbuilding Workers of America*, 391 US 418 (1968). In *United Steelworkers of America* v. *Sadlowski*, 457 US 102, 119–120 (1982), the Court indicated that the right of members to sue may include the right to receive financial assistance from nonmembers in bringing the suit.

570. *Mallick* v. *IBEW*, 644 F.2d 228 (3d Cir. 1981); *Bise* v. *IBEW*, 618 F.2d 1299 (9th Cir. 1979), *cert.* denied 449 US 904 (1980).

between different labor organizations.[571] Relying on that decision, a federal appellate court has held that the same statute makes the federal courts available for a union member's damages suit against a union official if it is based on the official's alleged breach of the union constitution.[572] In contrast, it has been held that a section 301 suit is not available where a member claims that a local union has breached its local constitution or by-laws. The court explained that while a national union's constitution or by-laws is a contract with its constituent local unions, a local union's constitution or by-laws is a contract between the union and its members. Section 301 suits are available to enforce contracts between unions, not those between unions and their members.[573]

Based on the protection of an employee's right to sue the union, a court has rejected a collective bargaining provision that attempted to impose on an employee the union's costs of defending an arbitration decision whose validity is challenged in court by the employee.[574]

E. Right to Full and Fair Hearing

525. Section 101(a)(5) of the LMRDA (29 US Code §411(a)(5)) requires adherence to basic rules of fairness when a labor organization disciplines a member. Accordingly, the member must receive a written statement of the specific charges, have a reasonable opportunity to prepare a defense, and be afforded a full and fair hearing before an impartial decision maker. The statutory right to a full and fair hearing also includes the right to present one's defense and to confront the adverse evidence. It additionally includes the requirement that there be some evidence to support the tribunal's finding.[575]

The impartial tribunal requirement can be particularly troublesome inasmuch as most unions turn to their officers to preside over such hearings and review hearing findings. Since these same officers often are the source of authority for initiating disciplinary actions, the disciplinary tribunal may have difficulty qualifying as impartial. One approach to dealing with this problem is the Public Review Board (PRB) system used by the United Automobile Workers. The PRB is composed of outstanding members of the general community who are experts in the field of labor law and ethics–all are non members, non employees, and non officers of the union. The Review Board has authority to make final decisions that bind the union in situations in which constituent locals have a dispute with the parent organization or in which a union member is dissatisfied with local disciplinary action that has been upheld by the parent union's executive board. The Public Review Board's authority

---

571. *Wooddell* v. *IBEW*, 502 US 93 (1991).
572. *Shea* v. *McCarthy*, 953 F.2d 29 (2d Cir. 1992).
573. *Korzen* v. *Local Union 705, Int'l Bro. of Teamsters*, 75 F.3d 285 (7th Cir. 1996).
574. *Moore* v. *Local 569 of Intern. Broth. of Elec. Workers*, 53 F.3d 1054 (9th Cir. 1995), *cert.* denied 516 US 1111 (1996).
575. *English* v. *Cowell*, 10 F.3d 434 (7th Cir. 1993). The court indicated that a summary procedure is allowed if no facts are in dispute but held that in the case before it the expelled member was entitled to show that prior practice in applying the union's by-laws was inconsistent with the action taken against him.

does not extend to grievances respecting the union's administration of collective agreements.

Although the right to a fair hearing includes the right to be represented, some courts hold that the union can limit representation to lay counsel and bar lawyers from these hearings.[576]

F. Union's Duty to Inform Members

526. Section 105 of the LMRDA (29 US Code §415) requires labor organizations to inform members respecting their rights under that law. Accordingly, courts have ordered unions to inform new members about all rights protected by the Act.[577]

The LMRDA, at section 104 (29 US Code §414) further requires a local labor organization to give a requesting worker a copy of each collective bargaining agreement affecting that worker. Unlike other provisions of the LMRDA, such as section 105, this right extends to all affected employees regardless of whether the worker is a union member. Collective agreements negotiated by union organizations other than local unions must be provided to each local affected by the agreement and affected workers have a right to inspect such agreements.[578]

A lower court has ruled that a union has a statutory duty to make available to members copies of its constitution and by-laws and that right can be enforced by the member.[579] In addition, most material provisions must be reported to the Department of Labor and unions have a duty to make available to members the information contained in such reports. Also, the LMRDA requires every labor organization to adopt a constitution and bylaws and file copies with the Secretary of Labor. Such filed documents become public records that can be inspected at the Department of Labor or on-line, and anyone is entitled to obtain a copy from the Department for the cost of copying.

Since members of an association, such as a union, are in a contractual relation to the organization and its members and since contractual obligations are based on voluntary, knowing consent, it stands to reason that under the general law of associations a union also has a duty to make a copy of its charter and by-laws available for membership inspection.

527. Unions are required by the LMRDA to file annual financial reports with the Secretary of Labor. Because these reports become public documents, copies can be inspected at the Department of Labor and anyone can view on-line the individual

576. *Curtis* v. *Int'l Alliance of Theatrical Stage Employees*, 687 F.2d 1024 (7th. Cir. 1982).

577. *Knight* v. *International Longshoremen's Association*, 457 F.3d 331 (3d Cir. 2006); *Callihan* v. *United Association of Journeymen and Apprentices of the Plumbing and Pipefitting*, 349 F.3d 704 (DC Cir. 2003).

578. *Gardner* v. *Int'l Tel. Employees Local No. 9*, 850 F.2d 518, 521 (9th. Cir. 1988) (refusal to provide such documents also breaches the duty of fair representation and, therefore, is an unfair labor practice).

579. *Forline* v. *Helpers Local No. 42*, 211 F. Supp. 315, 319 (ED Pa. 1962).

reports for recent years or obtain a copy from the Department for the reproduction cost. The reporting forms require greater detail if the labor organization has annual receipts of $250,000 or more. Included in these reports is a statement of opening and closing assets for the year, receipts of any kind, salaries and other disbursements to each officer and employee who received more than $10,000 during the Fiscal Year, loans to officers or employees in excess of $250 for the year, loans to any businesses, and all disbursements required by the Secretary of Labor to be detailed in the report. In addition, the LMRDA entitles union members to inspect the union's books, accounts and records which provide the information used in preparing these annual reports if the members have 'just cause' to inspect such documents. The courts have held that the just cause requirement is satisfied if a member has a reasonable basis for suspecting falsities, errors or wrong-doing as indicated by the reported information, such as substantial changes in reported amounts, or by other information reaching the member.[580]

The right of members to inspect a union's books and records extends as well to the books and records of any affiliated entity whose activities affect the organization's finances. In one case, for example, the members were entitled to inspect the books, records and accounts of a funeral home, a pharmacy and a recreational organization, all of which were owned by the union. That right of inspection, moreover, includes the right to have the inspection performed by professional auditors rather than by the union members themselves.[581]

G. Right to Local Self-determination

528. Parent labor organizations may seize control of the operations of subordinate units only under limited circumstances specified by LMRDA section 302 (29 US Code §462). Commonly, the parent requires the local to adhere to national bargaining policies and make proportionate contributions to the costs of national activities. Similarly, the parent organization may be entrusted with custodianship over the union's strike fund and control the conditions under which moneys may be drawn from that fund. On occasion, the parent may find that a local union is corruptly or ineptly managed and intervene on behalf of the local membership or to preserve the integrity of the overall labor organization. However, national unions have occasionally wielded control over subordinate units for inappropriate or illegal reasons.

529. The device by which national unions typically impose control over local units in the United States is the trusteeship or receivership. Under this practice, the national union's leadership declares that the local unit is unable to attend to its own affairs properly and appoints a trustee or receiver to administer the local's affairs until it once again is able to look after its own needs.

The LMRDA places both substantive and procedural restraints upon the imposition of trusteeships or receiverships.

---

580. *Mallick* v. *IBEW*, 814 F.2d 674 (DC Cir. 1987); *Fruit & Vegetable Packers* v. *Morley*, 378 F.2d 738 (9th Cir. 1967).

581. *Mallick* v. *IBEW*, above; *Local No. 1419, ILA* v. *Smith*, 301 F.2d 791 (5th Cir. 1962).

530. The LMRDA provisions speak specifically of trusteeships as the restricted form of control over a subordinate unit's affairs. Trusteeships are defined by the LMRDA as a method of supervision or control whereby a subordinate's otherwise available autonomy has been suspended. Consistent with the broad statutory definition, courts have applied the statutory label 'trusteeship' independent of the union's own classification of its action. Thus, where the union placed a local under 'supervision', the court held the action to be the imposition of a 'trusteeship' inasmuch as the local organization had been deprived of the autonomy it normally enjoyed and the members had been disenfranchised with regard to determining the local's policies.[582] On the other hand, some courts have not applied the trusteeship rules to situations in which the national union has merged different locals because in such situations the membership continues to exercise its franchise by electing those charged with the management of the surviving local. Other courts have held that a merger imposed for the purpose of ousting dissidents from control is a constructive trusteeship and can be challenged if the procedure or justification is not permitted under the LMRDA's standards.[583]

Federal appellate courts have allowed local unions to evade a trusteeship by disaffiliating themselves from the national organization before the completion of the imposition of the trusteeship.[584]

531. Trusteeships may be imposed only in accordance with the parent union's constitution and by-laws and only for the purpose of correcting corruption or financial malpractice, restoring democratic procedures, assuring the performance of the local unit's representative responsibilities, 'or otherwise carrying out the legitimate objectives' of the labor organization. This last provision has been cited to justify a trusteeship imposed because a local union repudiated a no-strike provision in a current collective agreement.[585] Also based on the last provision, a divided Court of Appeals upheld the legitimacy of imposing a trusteeship over a local that sought to withdraw from a multi-union bargaining unit which the parent union judged was the preferred arrangement.[586] A different court, however, rejected the use of a trusteeship to force a local union to join in a district council with other locals of the parent organization in order to facilitate making union job referrals over a wider geographical district.[587]

---

582. *Sawyers* v. *Grand Lodge, International Association of Machinists*, 279 F. Supp. 747 (E.D. MO, 1967).
583. *San Filippo* v. *United Brotherhood of Carpenters*, 525 F.2d 508 (2d Cir. 1975); *Local No. 48, United Brotherhood of Carpenters* v. *United Brotherhood of Carpenters*, 920 F.2d 1047 (1st Cir. 1990).
584. *Int'l Brotherhood of Boilermakers* v. *Lodge D129*, 910 F.2d 1056 (2d Cir. 1990). Contra, *International Brotherhood of Boilermakers* v. *Olympic Plating Industries, Inc.*, 870 F.2d 1085, 1088 (6th Cir. 1989) (under its constitution the parent organization had a continuing claim on the local's assets).
585. *Benda* v. *Grand Lodge of International Ass'n of Machinists & Aerospace Workers*, 584 F.2d 308, 317 (9th Cir. 1978).
586. *Executive Board Local 1302* v. *United Bro. of Carpenters*, 477 F.2d 612 (2d Cir. 1973).
587. *United Bro. of Carpenters* v. *Brown*, 343 F.2d 872 (10th Cir. 1965).

532. The LMRDA, at section 304 (29 US Code §464), makes a trusteeship presumptively valid for 18 months if it is imposed in accordance with the union's constitution and by-laws after a fair hearing before a union tribunal. The presumption is overcome only by clear and convincing proof that the national organization acted without good faith, failed to follow the union's constitutional procedures, or acted for reasons not authorized by the LMRDA.[588] After 18 months, the continuation of the trusteeship is declared presumptively invalid. The courts are divided over the significance of the hearing requirement. Some take the view that a fair hearing is necessary in order for the trusteeship to ever be valid. Others reason that the absence of a fair hearing raises a refutable presumption of invalidity and that a trusteeship can be proved valid if the parent organization overcomes that presumption of invalidity.[589]

533. In addition to giving local units a statutory right to sue for relief if a trusteeship is imposed in an improper manner or for illegitimate purposes, the Secretary of Labor has the power to intervene and challenge the legality of a trusteeship or its continuance. To facilitate the Secretary's policing of trusteeships, the Act requires the parent organization to file an information report with the Secretary within 30 days after imposing a trusteeship and to up-date that report every six months. The report must contain specified financial and organizational information. Willful failure to file these reports is a crime.

In a further effort to discourage the use of the trusteeship in inappropriate situations, the LMRDA removes the voting power of the delegates from a supervised local unit except where they have been elected by the membership in secret ballot elections. In addition, the Act limits the types of fund transfers that may be made between the supervised local unit and the supervising organization during the life of a trusteeship.

IV. Restraints upon the Use of Union Funds

A. Union Funds Used for Union Elections

534. Under section 501 of the LMRDA (29 US Code §501), union officials are expressly held to fiduciary responsibilities toward the union and its finances. Consistent with that status, the Act also expressly prohibits the expenditure of union funds or the use of union facilities in support of any candidate for union office. Union facilities and funds, on the other hand, must be used to notify members about an impending election of union officers and may be used for the distribution of campaign literature so long as all candidates are treated equally. It has been held that

588. *IBT* v. *Local Union Number 810*, 19 F.3d 786 (2d Cir. 1994).

589. *National Ass'n of Letter Carriers* v. *Sombrotto*, 449 F.2d 915, 920 (2d Cir. 1971). In the *Local Union Number 810* case, cited in the previous footnote, the union constitution allowed the parent organization to impose a temporary trusteeship in emergency circumstances and the court permitted that action without a prior union hearing establishing that there was an emergency.

distributing to the membership a union financed newsletter shortly before a contested election violated these restrictions where the newsletter had quoted remarks from the national president praising a candidate for local office.[590] Similarly, it has been ruled that the Act is violated even if the value of the union facilities used by a candidate is minimal and there is no proof that this misuse of union facilities affected the election results.[591]

B. Union Funds Used for Political Activities

535. American labor unions have long been prohibited from giving direct financial support to candidates for elected public office in the federal government. (*See* 2 US Code §441b.) However, as individuals, union leaders and members could endorse particular candidates and communicate that fact directly to the membership. Also, general funds of a union may be used for programs designed to persuade union members and sympathizers to vote in a particular election–even though a heavy turnout of such voters is expected to favor particular candidates. In addition, a union may use its general funds to engage in lobbying activities and public education designed to promote the bargaining interests of the membership or gain passage of legislation that union leaders believe will promote the workers' interests. Union leaders and members may also join together in organizations separate from their unions to give direct financial and other support to the election activities of particular candidates for public office so long as participation is voluntary.[592] Such efforts are generally known as PACs, an abbreviation of the term Political Action Committees. In fiscal years 2015 and 2016 (the latter a Presidential Election year), PACs identified as corporate or trade expended $533.9 million while those identified as labor expended $331.5 million. A PAC can expend money in support of a political party or particular candidate. However, there are limits on the amount of money a PAC can contribute to a particular candidate or party ($15,000 and $5,000 respectively). A Super PAC is a committee that can spend an unlimited amount of money solely to advocate for or against a particular political idea or program—an expenditure that often indirectly supports a candidate or party that favors that idea or program. In fiscal years 2015 and 2016 Super PACs spent over $1.8 million promoting their causes.

The Federal Election Campaign Act imposes on PACs and individual political contributors, political parties, and campaign committees a variety of financial record keeping and reporting requirements as well as limits on the amount of money an individual can contribute to a particular PAC. The Federal Election Commission (FEC) administers these regulations. Even under the lavish standards by which American political campaigns have come to be financed (largely due to the cost of

590. *Usery* v. *Int'l Organization of Masters*, 538 F.2d 946 (2d Cir. 1976); *Donovan* v. *Metropolitan District Council of Carpenters*, 797 F.2d 140 (3d Cir. 1986) (union newsletter reports of the remarks incumbent officers make during a union election campaign do not require equal coverage for opposing candidates if the remarks are pertinent to the normal course of conducting the union's affairs).

591. *Shultz* v. *Local Union 6799, United Steelworkers*, 426 F.2d 969 (9th Cir. 1970), affirmed 403 US 333 (1971).

592. *Pipefitters Local Union No. 562* v. *US*, 407 US 385 (1972).

television advertising), union related campaign contributions remain a significant but minor source for campaign funding. The two principal national political parties, the Republican Party and the Democratic Party, are well financed from individual and group contributions. Another potential source of campaign finance in a Presidential election is from the federal government. However, receipt of that money imposes spending limits on the campaign. In recent years, candidates have elected to forego the federal contribution in favor of their own fund raising and the ability to spend well in excess of the federal limits. State law governs the extent to which labor organizations and corporations are prohibited from giving financial assistance to candidates for state or local government office.[593]

In *Citizens United v. Federal Election Commission*, 558 U.S. 310 (2010), the US Supreme Court held, 5–4, that the Constitution does not permit the government to prevent corporations from directly supporting political parties or the election of particular political candidates. This decision is generally understood to invalidate laws prohibiting direct union financial support of candidates and political parties as well. (*See* paragraph 558, below, for additional discussion of this decision.)

536. The political activities of federal government employees, and of those state and local government employees whose work is financed by federal funds, are subject to extensive regulations under the Hatch Act (5 US Code §§1501–1503) and the federal criminal code (18 US Code §§600–603, 610). These laws permit such government workers to make individual financial contributions to political campaigns and be members of political parties but at the same time protect such workers from job related threats or promises aimed at coercing or enticing them into engaging in political activities. In addition, these statutes bar the covered workers from performing campaigning tasks and from being candidates for elected political office or office in political parties.[594] Finally, federal law prohibits use of government work time and property for political fund-raising activity.

State laws often impose similar restrictions on state and local workers not covered by the Hatch Act.[595]

537. Many contend that the barriers to labor organization participation in the political process should be more complete; that a union's only legitimate role is to act as a bargaining agent. A justification offered for greater restrictions on union political activity is that the authority which government gives to a labor organization to serve as the exclusive bargaining agent of a group of workers bestows quasi-governmental power. That government bestowed power, it is argued, must not be wielded in a manner that would be constitutionally forbidden to the government itself and should not be used in a way that infringes on such basic liberties as freedom of expression and association. Accordingly, it is contended, unions must

593. The Campaign Finance Institute's web site (http://www.cfinst.org/law/states.aspx) provides links to detailed information about state laws restricting union, corporate and government employee political campaign activity and contributions and imposing financial reporting requirements for such contributions.

594. *US Civil Service Comm'n* v. *Nat'l Ass'n of Letter Carriers*, 413 US 548 (1973).

595. *Broadrick* v. *Oklahoma*, 413 US 601 (1973). *Also, see* The Campaign Finance Institute's web site (http://www.cfinst.org/law/states.aspx).

respect the constitutional freedoms of all bargaining unit employees to speak and act for themselves in all matters not directly involved in carrying out the process of negotiating and administering collective agreements. Based on these premises, it is asserted, unions should not be permitted to use funds or paid staff time financed by the dues of dissenters for purposes unrelated to their narrow, institutional mission of negotiating and enforcing collective agreements.

A competing thesis is that as the elected representatives of a community of workers, labor organizations are the elected officials of that special type of domain and have the authority and responsibility to take all measures the elected leadership deems appropriate to improve the economic and social welfare of that employee community. Therefore, it is argued, labor organizations should have the same freedom as other elected political entities, such as municipalities, to expend their resources on all avenues they judge may achieve those improvements, including influencing legislative and administrative policies, reshaping public opinion, electing more sympathetic political leaders, and encouraging the appointment of more sympathetic judicial, executive and administrative decision makers. Under this thesis, it is asserted that those community members who disagree are free to try to persuade a majority of the bargaining unit either to dissolve the communal system of representation or to elect wiser leaders. However, until dissenters succeed in persuading the majority to take another course of action, their share of the dues, the functional equivalent of tax revenues, can be expended for whatever legal purposes the elected officials deem appropriate.

In *Citizens United* v. *Federal Election Commission*, 558 US 310 (2009), the US Supreme Court held, 5–4, that the Constitution does not permit the government to prevent corporations from directly supporting political parties or the election of particular political candidates. Just as the Court in that case held that 'corporate democracy' adequately protects the interests of shareholders of a business corporation with respect to the expenditure of their funds for political purposes by those who control the corporation's treasury without receiving individual or group shareholder consent, the same rationale could be applied to justify such use of the union's general treasury for direct support of political candidates and activities without membership consent. (*See* paragraph 554, below, for a more complete discussion of this decision.)

On their face, the NLRA and RLA allow unions and employers to agree that, after a statutory grace period, employees shall be required to join the union that is the duly selected bargaining representative and pay dues or a service fee to the collective bargaining representative (these are negotiated union security provisions).[596] However, the Supreme Court has held that although the collective agreement can state that employees are required to become and remain union members, at most the union security provision can be enforced to require all employees who are not union

596. NLRA §8(a)(3); RLA §2 (Eleventh). RLA §2 (Eleventh) superseded RLA §2 (Fourth and Fifth) which originally prohibited such arrangements. The Acts impose a minimum grace period of 30 days under the NLRA and 60 days under the RLA before the union security agreement can be enforced.

members to pay a service fee for the union's representational services.[597] Moreover employees who pay such fees can insist that their service fees not be used to finance activities or programs not directly related to negotiating or administering a collective agreement covering the worker's employment or the costs of the union's institutional existence.[598] The Court has reached this conclusion as a constitutionally required rule when government employees are involved, explaining that to decide otherwise would constitute prohibited government participation (the government employer's agreement to impose the union security requirement) in a scheme that interferes with the government employees' liberties of expression and association. In cases involving non government employees, the Court has reached the same conclusion as a matter of interpreting the legislative intention behind the NLRA and RLA and, thereby, has avoided reaching the question of whether Congress has the constitutional authority to allow unions and employers to compel workers to contribute dues that can be used for activities, such as support of a political candidate, not directly involved in negotiating and enforcing collective agreements.

538. The Supreme Court's decisions that entitle those paying service fees to refrain from giving financial support to a union's non-representational activities require unions to reduce the service fees paid by objecting employees in the proportion that expenditures for political and other ideological activities have to the union's overall expenditures. Unions must adopt procedures for excluding from an objecting employee's service fees the pro rata share of financing activities not directly involved in negotiating and enforcing the collective agreement, provide sufficient annual financial information so that objecting employees can determine whether their contributions are being misapplied, and provide a reasonably prompt procedure for objecting employees to receive an impartial resolution of any challenges to being charged for particular expenditures and receive a rebate for their share of expenditures not involving the union's bargaining agent activities.[599] Once a union provides the required information, the burden is on the objecting employee to prove that the expenditure could not be properly charged to a non member. Disputes as to which expenditures are attributable to such activities can be submitted to

---

597. *Marquez* v. *Screen Actors Guild, Inc.*, 525 US 33 (1998). *See*, however, the discussion of the duty of fair representation beginning at paragraph 540, below. That duty requires the union to inform employees concerning their option to pay a service fee in lieu of becoming union members.

598. *Abood* v. *Detroit Board of Educ.*, 431 US 209 (1977); *Ellis* v. *Bro. of Ry. Clerks*, 466 US 435 (1984); *Communication Workers of America* v. *Beck*, 487 US 735 (1988); *Lehnert* v. *Ferris Faculty Ass'n*, 500 US 507 (1991). In *Davenport* v. *Wash. Educ. Ass'n*, 551 US 177 (2007), the Court ruled that a state can require a union to annually obtain from government employees who are not union members an authorization for any expenditures from their agency fee for purposes related to political elections.

599. *See*, for example, *Chicago Teachers Union Local No. 1* v. *Hudson*, 475 US 292 (1986); *Price* v. *UAW*, 927 F.2d 88 (2d Cir.), *cert.* denied 502 US 905 (1991); *Grunwald* v. *San Bernardino*, 994 F.2d 1370 (9th Cir.), *cert.* denied 510 US 964 (1993); *Knight* v. *Kenai Peninsula Borough School Dist.*, 131 F.3d 807 (9th Cir. 1997), *cert.* denied 524 US 904 (1998); *Int'l Ass'n of Heat and Frost Insulators*, 311 NLRB 969 (1993), enforced *NLRB* v. *Int'l Ass'n of Heat and Frost Insulators*, 35 F.3d 554 (2d Cir. 1994); *Office & Professional Employees International Union, Local 29*, 331 NLRB 48 (2000).

an outside arbitrator or arbitration board for resolution, but such decisions are binding on objecting employees only if they have consented to arbitral resolution.[600]

The NLRB and courts have established some guidance respecting the type of information that must be provided to bargaining unit employees so that they can be assured that they are receiving the full rebate to which they are entitled. However, there remain many unanswered questions respecting which expenditures can be assessed to all employees, including those who involuntarily pay a service fee to the labor organization, and which expenditures can be allocated only to the finances supported by union members.

For example, the Supreme Court has ruled that non member railroad workers could not be required to contribute to the costs of organizing other workers in the industry.[601] Nevertheless, the NLRB has held that it was not bound by that railroad industry decision when confronted with the same issue respecting union expenditures to organize workers in the retail food industry. The NLRB distinguished the Supreme Court's railroad decision on the ground that the Court there cited legislative history under the RLA showing that the industry was already largely organized and that added union representation would not increase bargaining strength. In contrast, the Board noted that the stated purposes of the NLRA reflects Congressional awareness that lack of widespread union representation generally weakens bargaining strength and expert testimony in the specific case showed that in fact unions gain at least some bargaining strength in the retail food industry when a greater portion of the employers must engage in collective bargaining.[602]

In still another case, this one arising under the RLA, an appellate court held that the evidence supported the pilots' union's contention that mandatory contributions to a strike fund that aided pilots of another airline, who were in a separate bargaining unit, were justified because negotiations in the contributing employees' own bargaining unit were significantly influenced by collective agreements reached with other airlines.[603]

The impact the decision in *Citizens United* v. *Federal Election Commission*, 558 U.S. 310 (2009), discussed in the previous paragraph, upon the above rules regarding use of membership dues will have to be resolved by the courts. If corporate officials can expend general treasury funds for political purposes without the individual or group consent of shareholders, arguably the same rule should apply to union officers. (*See* paragraph 554, below, for a more complete discussion of this decision.)

600. *Air Line Pilots Association* v. *Miller*, 523 US 866 (1998).
601. *Ellis* v. *Bro. of Ry. Clerks*, 466 US 435 (1984).
602. *UFCW, Local 1036* v. *NLRB*, 307 F.3d 760 (9th Cir.), *cert.* denied *sub nom Mulder* v. *NLRB*, 537 US 1024 (2002).
603. *Crawford* v. *ALPA*, 992 F.2d 1295 (4th Cir.), *cert.* denied 510 US 869 (1993). However, also see *Beckett* v. *ALPA*, 59 F.3d 1276 (DC Cir. 1995) questioning whether the same reasoning applies in the event of a union's special dues assessment to provide benefits for pilots at another airline who struck in sympathy for machinists at that same airline.

C. Other Expenditures of Union Funds

539. Labor unions often participate in socially beneficial programs either in the direct interest of their membership or in the more general community interest. So long as such expenditures are permitted under the union's charter and by-laws, they are permissible. Thus, the statutory fiduciary responsibility of union officials is not violated when union funds are expended for the purpose of improving community and social conditions even though union members are not directly benefited and even though some union members may be opposed to the particular programs receiving the union's help.[604]

V. The Union's Duty of Fair Representation

540. The National Labor Relations Act has been held to impose on collective bargaining agents the duty to give fair representation to all workers represented by the union. The union's responsibility as exclusive bargaining agent is to fairly represent all bargaining unit workers, regardless of their membership or non membership in the union. This duty was first established in a series of Supreme Court cases decided in 1944.[605] There the Court explained that in giving the majority union the status of exclusive bargaining agent, it was Congress' implicit intent that the union would represent all bargaining unit workers fairly, impartially and in good faith. This is the standard of fiduciary responsibility normally expected of persons entrusted by law to represent the interests of others. Therefore, it was reasonable to assume that in placing the union in a statutorily sanctioned representative role, Congress expected the union to live by the standards applicable to other types of legally imposed representatives.

Had the Court not implied a duty of good faith representation, it would have had to face the difficult question of whether it is a violation of the constitutional prohibition against taking property without due process of law for Congress to give a union the authority to fix the terms of employment for a worker unless that representative, in its quasi-governmental role, is required to adhere to strict standards of good faith and fairness–standards comparable to those imposed on government itself by the due process and equal protection provisions of the US Constitution. The Court acknowledged its desire to avoid such questions by finding that Congress had in fact intended to impose the standard of fair representation upon the exclusive bargaining agent.

541. The union's duty of fair representation is a responsibility of fairness to individuals it represents. Counterbalancing it is its responsibility to the collective. Therefore, the Court has further explained that the latter responsibility can prevail

604. *McNamara* v. *Johnston*, 522 F.2d 1157 (7th Cir. 1975), *cert.* denied 425 US 911 (1976).
605. *Steele* v. *Louisville & Nashville RR*, 323 US 192 (1944); *The Wallace Corp.* v. *NLRB*, 323 US 248 (1944). *See generally*, J. McKelvey, ed., *The Duty of Fair Representation*, Ithaca, NY (1977).

over the interests of individual workers in the bargaining unit so long as the union makes its choices in good faith and without discriminatory or invidious intent.[606]

Violation of the duty of fair representation can be the basis for remedies provided by the courts and for remedies provided by the NLRB.

A. NLRB Enforcement of the Duty of Fair Representation

542. The NLRB's requirement that labor organizations give fair representation to all bargaining unit employees was adopted as early as 1938 when it refused to treat race as an appropriate criterion in defining the workers to be included in a bargaining unit. This decision thwarted the widespread practice of totally excluding non whites from union membership or maintaining racially separate locals. Nevertheless, the Board presented its decision not as a legal standard but as a reflection of the mainstream principles of the American labor movement by citing to the fact that at its 58th annual convention, on 7 October 1938, the American Federation of Labor unanimously adopted a resolution calling upon all unions 'to eliminate the color bar and all forms of discrimination which serve to exclude workers from membership on account of race or color'.[607] A few years later, the Board announced that it was its duty 'to see to it that any organization certified under section 9(c) as the bargaining representative act … as a genuine representative of all the employees in a bargaining unit'[608] and it warned that it would revoke the certification of a bargaining representative that failed to live up to the duty to represent all bargaining unit employees.

543. The threat of certification removal did not significantly affect a union whose organizational strength was sufficient to compel employers to bargain. The more effective NLRB remedy for improper conduct is an unfair labor practice proceeding which results in a remedial order that ultimately is backed by the contempt power of the federal courts. However, under the original Wagner Act it was not possible to apply the unfair labor practice remedies to situations in which a union breached the duty of fair representation–even after the Supreme Court had endorsed the concept in 1944 because until the adoption of the Taft-Hartley Act amendments in 1947, unfair labor practice charges were available only against employers. With the passage of Taft-Hartley, though, unions too became subject to NLRB remedies for various forms of misconduct. However, none of the enumerated union unfair labor practices specifically condemn the misdeed of failing to provide fair representation to bargaining unit workers.

544. Hughes Tool Company, 104 NLRB 318 (1953), involved a bargaining unit located in a state in which it was unlawful for the collective agreement to require

606. *Ford Motor Co.* v. *Huffman*, 345 US 330 (1953); *Humphrey* v. *Moore*, 375 US 335 (1964); *ALPA* v. *O'Neill*, 499 US 65 (1991).

607. *American Tobacco Co.*, 9 NLRB 579 (1938); *Union Envelope Company*, 10 NLRB 1147 (1939); *Interstate Granite Corp.*, 11 NLRB 1046 (1939).

608. *Larus & Bros. Co.*, 62 NLRB 1075, 1082 (1945).

employees to contribute to the costs of financing union representation. (This was a so-called 'right to work' law authorized by NLRA §14(b). *See* paragraph 649, below.) Despite the Board's previous decisions condemning racial discrimination by unions, a local that accepted only white workers and a local that accepted nonwhite workers were jointly certified as bargaining representative. The white local adopted a schedule of payments to the union that non members would have to make if they wished the union to process a grievance to arbitration. The non white local did not adopt such a payment schedule. In protest against the action by the white local, a petition was filed with the NLRB asking it to remove its certification on the ground that the white local's fee schedule discriminated against non union members. A majority of the NLRB ruled in favor of the petition in an opinion that stated that as exclusive bargaining representative a union must provide impartial representation for all bargaining unit employees. The Board majority concluded that charging non-members the fees as a condition of processing their grievances violated the requirement of impartiality. The Board did not base its decision on the unreasonableness of the amount the union wanted to charge nor did it discuss the legality of segregating the locals' membership by race. The Board's decision stated: 'Discrimination in the performance of the duties of the representative designed to deny equal treatment to those of the minority is to subvert the privilege and rights granted by the statute. Whether such discrimination is based on union membership or the lack thereof, rather than on considerations of race, creed, or color is, in our opinion, irrelevant.'[609] The Board ordered the joint certification of both locals revoked unless the white local rescinded its special fee charges within 10 days. Two Board members dissented on the ground that the case should be resolved through processing a pending unfair labor practice charge brought against the white local rather than by using the proceeding that sought to have the certification withdrawn.

545. Some twenty years after *Hughes Tool*, and a decade after Congress adopted the Civil Rights Act of 1964 barring unions from engaging in any racial discrimination, the NLRB adopted the rule that an employer can challenge a union's qualification for certification, after winning an NLRB election, on the ground that the union has a policy of discrimination against members or applicants on the basis of race, sex or ethnic origin or that the union has a 'a propensity to fail fairly to represent employees'. However, this policy, adopted by a 3–2 vote in June of 1974,[610] was abandoned with only one dissenting vote in early 1977.[611] In the initial decision the Board majority reasoned that as a government agency it could not lend its name to a proceeding that recognizes a labor organization that engages in discrimination. Upon reconsideration, the NLRB majority explained that its certification of election results: 'does not place its imprimatur on all the organization's activity, lawful or otherwise ... A certification is neither more nor less than an acknowledgment that a majority of the employees in an appropriate bargaining unit have

609. *Hughes Tool Company*, 104 NLRB at 326.
610. *Bekins Moving & Storage Co.*, 211 NLRB 138 (1974).
611. *Handy Andy, Inc.*, 228 NLRB 447 (1977).

selected the union as their exclusive representative.'[612] The Board also noted that before condemning a union for discriminatory conduct, the labor organization should have a chance to defend itself through the adversarial proceedings of an unfair labor practice case. (A representation proceeding is administrative, not adversarial.) It noted, however, that it was not rejecting its prior practice of revoking the certification of a labor organization that has been guilty of a pattern of discrimination against a class of employees. In addition, the NLRB reaffirmed its policy of not recognizing collectively bargained agreements that contain provisions calling for invidious discrimination.

546. Normally, under a doctrine known as the 'contract bar rule', for up to the first three years of a collective agreement the NLRB will not entertain an election petition challenging the representative status of the bargaining agent that signed the agreement. However, the Board does not recognize for this purpose a collective bargaining agreement that treats employees differently on the basis of race.[613]

547. In 1962, by a 3–2 vote, the NLRB decided that sections 7 and 8 of the NLRA impose on labor organizations the duty of fair representation and that breach of that duty constitutes an unfair labor practice. The majority reasoned that the section 7 right of workers 'to bargain collectively through representatives of their own choosing', gives the bargaining unit workers 'the right to be free from unfair or irrelevant or invidious treatment by their exclusive bargaining agent in matters affecting their employment'.[614] The union's breach of that right, through unfair or invidious discrimination, is an interference with section 7 rights and, thus, a violation of section 8(b)(1)(A) of the NLRA. Moreover, the Board ruled that to the extent that an employer participates in the union's unlawful conduct, the employer, too, interferes with protected section 7 rights and, therefore, violates section 8(a)(1) of the NLRA. In addition, the NLRB majority held that to the extent that the unfair treatment or invidious discrimination is designed to encourage union membership, the union's action violates section 8(b)(2) and the employer's participation is an 8(a)(3) violation (discrimination because of union activities). In later cases, the NLRB expanded the statutory basis for remedying a breach of what is now generally referred to as the 'duty of fair representation'. The Board added to the above rationale the argument that implicit in the duty to bargain in good faith is the duty to give fair representation to its constituents. Accordingly, breach of the duty of fair representation also violates section 8(b)(3) of the NLRA which requires unions to bargain in good faith.[615]

548. The doctrine is now well settled that if the NLRB finds that union conduct toward bargaining unit members has been invidious or arbitrary it will provide a

612. 228 NLRB at 450.
613. *Pioneer Bus Company*, 140 NLRB 54 (1962).
614. *Miranda Fuel*, 140 NLRB 181 (1962), rev'd 326 F.2d 172 (2d Cir. 1963).
615. *Independent Metal Workers Union*, 147 NLRB 1573 (1964); affirmed by implication in *Breininger v. Sheet Metal Workers Int'l Ass'n Local Union No. 6*, 493 U.S. 67, 77 (1989).

remedy through an unfair labor practice proceeding.[616] And, the greater weight of court decisions supports that approach.[617]

B. Private Suit for Enforcement of the Duty of Fair Representation

549. In *Vaca* v. *Sipes*, 386 US 171 (1967), the Supreme Court recognized a cause of action by an employee against his exclusive bargaining agent based on the latter's alleged breach of its duty of fair representation.[618] That duty, the Court held, is implicit in the exclusive bargaining status Congress bestows under NLRA section 9(a). Moreover, the Court ruled that the duty of fair representation is enforceable in a state or federal court suit despite the possible availability of a remedy under the NLRA. The Court declined to impose what is known as the 'primacy doctrine' (giving an administrative agency, here the NLRB, exclusive jurisdiction over conduct that is either protected or made unlawful by the statute enforced by that agency) on the grounds that Congress probably did not intend to remove the jurisdiction of the trial courts in these matters and that often the courts can provide a more complete remedy in this type of case. In a later decision the Court explained that the statutory basis for federal court jurisdiction to hear such suits against the bargaining representative is found in 28 US Code §1337(a).[619]

550. Whether brought in state or federal court, a suit against a union for breach of the duty of fair representation is governed by federal law.

The typical case arises when an employee's grievance under a collectively bargained agreement has been rejected by the employer and the bargaining representative has refused to process the grievance to arbitration. The employee then sues on the theory that the union's refusal to process the grievance was not based on the merits but rather was based upon some invidious consideration or sheer neglect. Normally, only the union, as a party to the collective agreement, has the authority to enforce it. Hence, the employee's claim against the labor organization is that but for the breach of the duty of fair representation, the employee's rights under the collective agreement would have been vindicated through the contractual grievance and arbitration processes. The Supreme Court's decision in the *Vaca* case, referenced in paragraph 549, above, recognized the employee's right to sue the union to recover losses incurred by the union's breach of the duty of fair representation. But the *Vaca* decision went a step further by holding that, based on the employee's rights under the collective agreement, the employee can also sue the employer for what the employee would have recovered had the union not breached its duty of fair representation. Professor Clyde Summers argued that the proper understanding of this latter aspect of the Court's decision is that the collective agreement bestows rights

616. *See*, e.g. *International Brotherhood of Painters Local 1066*, 205 NLRB 651 (1973).
617. *See* cases compiled in *Breininger* v. *Sheet Metal Workers*, 493 US 67, 76 –77 (1989).
618. The underlying rationale of *Vaca* had long been recognized. *Steele* v. *Louisville & Nashville RR*, 323 US 192 (1944) and *The Wallace Corp.* v. *NLRB, 325 US 335 (1944)*. It was applied in support of a suit to remedy a breach of the duty of fair representation at least as early as *Syres* v. *Oil Workers Int'l Union*, 350 US 892 (1955) (*per curium*).
619. *Breininger* v. *Sheet Metal Workers*, 493 US 67, 76–77 (1989).

that become part of the employee's individual contract of employment. Thus, the employee can sue to enforce those contractual rights unless barred from doing so because the union has provided fair representation in pursuing them through the procedure established under the collective agreement.[620] The problem with that approach is that the authority of federal courts to hear such cases is based on section 301 of the LMRA. That provision allows for suits 'for violation of contracts between an employer and a labor organization'; it does not allow for suits based on contracts between employers and employees. An alternative understanding of the employee's suit against the employer is that, if the bargaining representative has unlawfully failed to enforce the collective agreement, the *Vaca* decision construes section 301 as allowing the affected employee, in the capacity of a third party beneficiary of the collective agreement, to enforce substantive rights granted employees by the agreement. Still another reading of the Supreme Court's decisions is that implicit in section 301 is the right of an injured employee to enforce the collective agreement on behalf of the labor organization if the latter's misconduct has caused it to refrain from doing so.[621]

The employee may sue the employer, the union, or both. In the suit against the union the employee must show both that the union breached the duty of fair representation and that, had it not done so, the employee's claim against the employer would have prevailed. Similarly, in the suit against the employer, the employee must prove that the union breached its duty of fair representation, thereby allowing the employee to bring suit to enforce rights under the collective agreement, and that the employer's conduct respecting the aggrieved employee was a breach of that collective agreement.

The Supreme Court has further explained that the employer's liability encompasses that part of the damages that would have been suffered because of the breach of the collective agreement even if the union had properly represented the employee's interests. In contrast, the union's liability encompasses any additional injury suffered as a result of its failure to provide fair representation. (This includes backpay and benefits for the period of delay in obtaining a remedy as well as the litigation costs in vindicating rights under the collective agreement.) The Court has not, however, fixed the appropriate form of remedy for these cases. Instead, it has left to the lower courts the responsibility for shaping a remedy to meet the special circumstances of each case. In some cases, the Court suggested, the most appropriate remedy is to compel the parties to reinstate the grievance and arbitration procedures in the collective agreement. In other cases equitable relief for the employee (presumably in the form of reinstatement) and money damages against both the union and the employer may be the most appropriate remedy. However, the Supreme Court has ruled that one form of remedy not available in such suits is an award of punitive damages.[622]

Finally, the Supreme Court has held that before bringing a suit based on a breach of the duty of fair representation and a breach of the collective agreement, the

620. C. Summers, 'The Rights of Individual Workers', 52 *Ford. L. Rev.* 1082, 1093 (1984).
621. The lack of clear doctrinal explanation by the Court is well illustrated by its opinion in *Hines* v. *Anchor Motor Freight, Inc.*, 424 US 554 (1976).
622. *IBEW* v. *Foust*, 442 US 42 (1979).

employee must attempt to exhaust any exclusive grievance and arbitration procedures that are available. The employee need not exhaust internal union procedures, however, unless they are capable of restoring the contractual dispute resolution process or of providing the worker with the complete remedy sought.[623] The latter exception is especially important since such suits must be filed within 6 months of the contractual breach.[624]

C. Standard of Conduct under the Duty of Fair Representation

551. The nature of the duty of fair representation has been defined as the 'statutory obligation to serve the interests of all members without hostility or discrimination toward any, to exercise its discretion with complete good faith and honesty, and to avoid arbitrary conduct'.[625] The Court, on one occasion, indicated that proof of a breach of the duty of fair representation requires a substantial showing of deliberate and severely hostile and irrational treatment. Similarly, it has spoken of the need to prove fraud, deceit or dishonesty.[626] On the other hand, it has ruled that the duty also prohibits a union from processing an employee's grievance in a perfunctory fashion, a standard that would not appear to require a showing of hostility.[627]

Additionally, the Supreme Court has held that the duty of fair representation standards are the same regardless of whether the labor organization is dealing with a rights dispute, an interests dispute, or an administrative task.[628]

552. The decisions concerning the duty of fair representation are difficult to reconcile with respect to the degree of negligence that is tolerable without violating the duty. While in one case the Supreme Court held that the duty of fair representation is breached if the union's preparation of a case for arbitration is so perfunctory that it fails to discover material evidence that would raise serious doubt respecting the credibility of the key evidence relied on to discharge the grieving employee,[629] it also has held that mere negligence and judgmental errors that are not wholly irrational do not constitute a breach of the duty.[630] Appellate courts draw a line between mere negligence, which does not violate the duty, and gross negligence. Thus, where the evidence shows that union lacked 'concern or solicitude' for an employee's contractual claim, such as being months overdue in filing a demand for arbitration, a

623. *Clayton* v. *UAW*, 451 US 679 (1981).
624. *DelCostello* v. *Teamsters Union*, 462 US 151 (1983).
625. *Vaca* v. *Sipes*, 386 US 171, 177 (1967).
626. *Amalgamated Motor Coach Employees* v. *Lockridge*, 403 US 274 (1971).
627. *Hines* v. *Anchor Motor Freight, Inc.*, 424 US 554 (1976).
628. *ALPA* v. *O'Neill*, 499 US 65 (1991).
629. *Hines* v. *Anchor Motor Freight, Inc.*, 424 US 554 (1976).
630. *United Steelworkers of America* v. *Rawson*, 495 US 362, 376 (1990) (union's negligence in carrying out its authority under the collective agreement to prevent unsafe conditions not a violation of the duty of fair representation). *See also*, *Steamfitters Local Union No. 342*, 336 NLRB 549 (2001) (mere negligence in the operation of an exclusive hiring hall does not violate the union's duty of fair representation), review denied *Jacoby* v. *NLRB*, 325 F.3d 301 (DC Cir. 2003).

court has held that there was a breach of the duty of fair representation because such behavior constitutes arbitrary, not merely negligent, conduct.[631]

Moreover the duty of fair representation does not mean that the union may never act adversely to the interests of a particular worker or group of employees. The Court has noted that in representing the collective interests of all bargaining unit members often it is necessary for the labor organization to make choices from among competing interests and that the practicalities of representation often make it necessary to do so in situations in which reliable information is incomplete or inaccessible, goals are unclear, and wisdom is elusive. Accordingly, the Court has held that the duty of fair representation is not breached by favoring one group over another so long as a union's judgments are made in good faith and honesty and are not wholly irrational or arbitrary.[632]

553. The duty of fair representation has been characterized by the Supreme Court as 'akin' to the duty fiduciaries owe their beneficiaries.[633] Consistent with that characterization the NLRB has held that once a union undertakes to represent a grievant, it must do so as an advocate. Thus, it was a breach of the duty of fair representation for a union representative to state to a joint grievance board that he did not think the grievant's claim was valid.[634] Similarly, the Board has held that once a union initiates a grievance it cannot drop that grievance on the basis of the employer's response without investigating the grievant's plausible rebuttal to the response.[635] On the other hand, in one arbitration case where grievants were allowed to introduce witnesses who testified to the union business agent's alleged bias against them, the union's attorney cross-examined those witnesses and challenged this aspect of their defense in his own closing argument to the arbitration tribunal. Nevertheless, in a split decision the NLRB held that the duty of fair representation was not breached by the refusal of the union's attorney, in the arbitration hearing, to attack the credibility of the union business agent's testimony which was adverse to the grievants.[636]

In other cases the NLRB has held that a labor organization that refuses to pursue the collective bargaining agreement rights of an employee without giving a legitimate explanation for that refusal breaches the duty of fair representation. Moreover, the NLRB has ruled that the mere opposition of a majority of union members who have an interest that conflicts with the contractual right asserted by the grievant is

---

631. *Beavers* v. *United Paperworkers Int'l Union, Local 1741*, 72 F.3d 97 (8th Cir. 1995). Accord, *Hinkley* v. *Roadway Express, Inc.*, 249 Fed. Appx. 13 (10th Cir. 2007).
632. *ALPA* v. *O'Neill*, 499 US 65 (1991) (strike settlement agreement that presumptively gave employees less than they would have achieved by unilaterally abandoning the strike not a violation of the duty of fair representation).
633. *ALPA* v. *O'Neill*, 499 US 65, 74–75 (1991).
634. *Truck Drivers, Local* 705, 209 NLRB 292 (1974), aff'd 532 F.2d 1169 (7th Cir. 1976).
635. *United Steelworkers of America*, 223 NLRB 1184 (1976).
636. *Teamsters Local Union No. 542*, 223 NLRB 533 (1976).

not of itself an adequate explanation for refusing to represent the grieving employee's claim to the contractual right.[637]

A few cases have explored the impact of the duty of fair representation upon contract negotiations. In *Teamsters Local 860* v. *NLRB*, 652 F.2d 1022 (DC Cir. 1981), the court affirmed the NLRB's decision that the duty placed an affirmative responsibility upon the union to inform a group of clerical workers of the employer's repeated threat to discontinue their jobs if they insisted upon the same wage increase as other workers in the bargaining unit. In contrast, in *Ackley* v. *Western Conference of Teamsters*, 958 F.2d 1463 (9th Cir. 1992), members asserted that the duty of fair representation had been breached by the union leadership's failure to disclose material changes in non-compensation provisions of a collective agreement being submitted for the membership's ratification vote. The court observed that a number of cases have held that misrepresentation of a collective agreement can constitute a breach of the duty of fair representation but that, even assuming that the union's failure to disclose material facts similarly breached the duty, the members' suit could not succeed because they had not established that the result of the ratification vote would have been different had there been full disclosure by the union.

In still another decision, *Letter Carriers Branch 6000* v. *NLRB*, 595 F.2d 808 (DC Cir. 1979), the court upheld the NLRB's finding that the duty of fair representation requires a union to allow all bargaining unit employees, not just union members, to vote in a referendum to choose which of the alternative leave provisions established by the collective agreement would be selected for the local operations. The Board and the court emphasized that this situation is distinguishable from a ratification vote for a new contract – a situation in which normally only union members have a vote.[638] Case decisions have held that confining contract ratification votes to union members does not breach the duty of fair representation.[639]

§3. Employer Associations

I. National Organizations

A. *Generally*

554. Most industries in the United States have a national association. Subgroups within an industry often are represented by their own organizations as well. A

637. *General Truck Drivers, Local 315*, 217 NLRB 616 (1975), aff'd 545 F.2d 1173 (9th Cir. 1976). Also, *Smith* v. *Hussman Refrigeration*, 619 F.2d 1229 (8th Cir. 1980) (*en banc*) (duty of fair representation required union to give junior employees an opportunity to assert their position before compromising their seniority rights in an arbitration proceeding).

638. *See also*, *United Auto Workers* v. *NLRB*, 168 F.3d 509 (DC Cir. 1999) (all employees, not just union members, must have access to a union's internal procedures for appealing from a grievance committee's decision to not take a grievance to arbitration).

639. *International Longshoreman's Association, Local 1575 (Navieras, NPR, Inc.)*, 332 NLRB 1336 (2000); *Standard Fittings Company* v. *NLRB*, 845 F.2d 1311, 1318 (5th Cir. 1988). In *IBT* v. *NLRB*, 587 F.2d 1176 (DC Cir. 1978) the court found a breach of the duty of fair representation where the members of one union in a multi-union bargaining unit were, contrary to past practices, excluded from the opportunity to engage in a ratification vote.

principal function of these industry organizations is to audit legislative and administrative agency activities at the state and federal government levels and advocate on behalf of the industry's perceived self-interests respecting local and national economic and social policies that are translated into statutes, administrative regulations, or judicial doctrine.

Federal law long prohibited corporations, government contractors, and banks from using funds in the organization's treasury for contributions affecting federal election campaigns and most states have laws imposing similar prohibitions concerning financing state and local level elections.[640] Nevertheless, political campaign contributions commonly have been solicited by the leaders of these organizations from among the members' higher paid staff and officers. The funds are then donated to certain political candidates as a symbol of the industry's support for those who have been, or promise to be, sympathetic to the industry's self-proclaimed needs. With the high cost of political campaigning in the United States, such contributions do not go unnoticed or unappreciated. It is generally recognized that the representatives of some industries, such as the tobacco, petroleum, airline, aerospace manufacturing, pharmaceuticals, insurance, banking and even milk and gun manufacturing, have a very powerful influence on key Congressional leaders and even on Presidents. These influences shape important policies relating to taxation, foreign relations, employment, business regulation, and government investment as well as the appointment of federal judges and administrative officials. Most often such influence is brought to bear through confidential communications.

Congress attempted to reduce such financial influences by providing government financing for federal election campaigns and limiting other sources of contributions to those campaigns. (*See* paragraph 535, above.)

In addition to contributions to a candidate's or political party's election campaign, individuals or interests groups, including unions and business entities, can finance without limit their own literature and mass media advertising expressing a point of view respecting the merits of particular political policies and proposals or criticizing past political actions.[641]

The Supreme Court, in *Citizens United* v. *Federal Election Commission*, 558 US 310 (2009), held, 5–4, that the Constitution does not permit the government to prevent corporations from directly supporting political parties or the election of particular political candidates. Thus, corporate officers can support candidates and political parties not only with their own funds but with the shareholders' funds as well. This decision overruled over a hundred years of federal statutes restraining corporate contributions to political election campaigns and over six decades of legislative prohibitions of direct corporate and union advertisements supporting or opposing political parties or candidates. The Court's decision preserved the authority of the legislature to require corporations to reveal that they are the source of any specific political election advertising. The Court added that because the statute

640. *See* 2 US Code §441b. See paragraph 535, above, for a description of the impact on political elections of campaign contributions from businesses and business groups. The Court held in *First Nat'l Bank of Boston* v. *Bellotti*, 435 US 765 (1978), that restrictions on political contributions cannot prevent a corporation from spending funds to urge voters to vote in a particular manner in a public referendum affecting the enterprise's interests.

641. *Federal Election Comm'n* v. *Wisconsin Right to Life, Inc.*, 551 US 449 (2007).

being challenged did not treat foreign sources of contributions separately, it was not reaching the question of whether the government can prevent foreign individuals or associations from influencing the nation's political process.

The *Citizens Union* decision is based on the proposition that constitutionally protected freedom of expression extends to corporations (citing numerous decisions allowing incorporated newspapers, magazines, book publishers, film makers and other media to defend against censorship) and reasons that the challenged statutory ban on corporate political activity violates free expression because it broadly applies to opinion media corporations and to corporations with single shareholders. (The dissenters observed that freedom of the press is separately guaranteed by the Constitution and, therefore, the protected free expression of opinion media should be distinguished from that of other enterprises.) Additionally, the Court rejected the proposition that the challenged restrictions of corporate political activity protect the right of shareholders who invest in business entities for the purpose of engaging in commercial activity and not to have their investments used for political expression with which they disagree. The Court contended: 'There is ... little evidence of abuse that cannot be corrected by shareholders "through the procedures of corporate democracy"', 558 US at 361–62, a proposition the dissenters characterized as unrealistic, adding:

> [C]orporations have no consciences, no beliefs, no feelings, no thoughts, no desires. Corporations help structure and facilitate the activities of human beings, to be sure, and their 'personhood' often serves as a useful legal fiction. But they are not themselves members of 'We the People' by whom and for whom our Constitution was established. (558 US at 466)

Moreover, much of the ownership of larger corporations is indirect with the shares held by mutual investment companies and similar entities that invest money on behalf of individuals but control how the shares in those investments are voted when the corporate directors are elected. In addition, normally a few directors act as a committee to nominate persons to hold vacant director seats on the corporate board and those nominees are unopposed. Furthermore, in widely held companies, typically a few large shareholders can control the election results because of a range of reasons for most shareholders not participating in board elections. Additionally, the performance of those in control of a commercial enterprise normally focuses on short term financial success; the directors' utilization of a small portion of shareholder assets to further the directors' political preferences is likely to be lost in the investors' investment decisions.

The Court's decision in *Citizens United* indicates that all political expression by unions, similarly, is constitutionally protected from government constraints. That result, of course, is more readily defensible inasmuch as union members, unlike shareholders, have an equal say in electing union officials and can opt out of participating in the financial support of the organization's political activities. (See paragraphs 537–38, above.)

555. On occasion, political influence is wielded through subtle and not so subtle forms of bribery. Generous personal gifts to government officials of money, travel, free use of vacation villas, entertainment, access to special investment opportunities, contributions to a favorite charity or favors to the official's relatives and friends, and the like, too frequently are provided to those in power whose favor is sought. Conflict of interest laws prohibit most but not all such intrusions on independent political, administrative and judicial judgment.

A common means of evading restrictions on improper financial influence is to invite the official to deliver a supposedly informative speech at an organization meeting and then to show appreciation by bestowing warm hospitality and a very generous honorarium. In recent years, restrictions have been adopted that limit the amount of such income federal officials can receive. Some states have adopted similar limits respecting outside income for state officials.

Although the salaries of elected and appointed officials in the United States often are generous, they are far from sufficient to enable a person of modest means to gain any considerable wealth. Yet, with some frequency, high officials have entered government service with far less wealth than they have had upon leaving it. The explanation has not always been left to speculation. From time to time bribery has been revealed – often as a result of the official's failure to report these gifts as income for income tax purposes. Such failure is a crime punishable by fines and even jail terms. The administrative agency that collects federal income taxes, though itself occasionally the subject of revealed corruption, has been a moderately effective investigator and prosecutor of bribe takers who do not pay income taxes on such earnings. In perhaps the most notorious case of this sort, Spiro Agnew resigned from the office of Vice President of the United States and pleaded no contest to criminal charges that he had failed to declare as income certain money received from business interests while he served as a state governor.

556. Some corrupt forms of influence probably have shaped labor and employment law and policies. It should be noted, however, that the NLRB is among the few federal government agencies that has never been the focus of a major scandal respecting corrupt forms of misconduct. There was a minor scandal in 2012, however, when Board Member Terence F. Flynn resigned after the NLRB Inspector General released reports concluding that while serving as chief counsel to a Board member, Flynn had violated ethics rules by disclosing confidential information about Board cases and activities to former Board members, one of whom was then serving as outside counsel for the National Association of Manufacturers and the other as a labor advisor to the presidential campaign of former Massachusetts Governor Mitt Romney. To protect against such abuse of power, the NLRB's internal regulations are designed to eliminate ex-parte communications concerning the merits of matters in issue and reduce the prospects for any conflict of interest influencing the investigatory, prosecutorial or decisional activities of the agency. Many of these regulations are also more generally imposed by federal statutes adopted for the purpose of reducing the ability of special interest groups to influence government by appealing to the personal interests of public officials.

B. Chamber of Commerce

557. The Chamber of Commerce of the United States, whose headquarters is in Washington, DC (1615 H St., NW, Washington, DC 20062; telephone 202 659-6000; www.uschamber.com), was founded in 1912. It is a national federation of state and local chambers of commerce and is recognized as one of the two principal voices of the American business community. It claims to represent more than 3 million businesses of all sizes and about 200 state and local chambers are accredited members.

A primary function of the Chamber of Commerce of the United States is to communicate its recommendations to government officials concerning national issues. It frequently conducts special studies and issues reports on important economic issues and its representatives often testify at legislative hearings. The federation maintains a digital blog site and issues a weekly e-mail that includes coverage of labor relations issues. In addition, the Chamber often appears *amicus curiae* to advocate its version of the business community's position in important cases heard by federal and state administrative agencies and courts. Similarly, these advocates generally submit the Chamber's views to administrative agencies engaged in making rules including those that regulate various aspects of labor management relations and labor standards.

C. National Association of Manufacturers

558. The National Association of Manufacturers is the other principal recognized representative of the American business community. Like the Chamber of Commerce of the United States, the National Association of Manufacturers has its headquarters in the nation's capitol (733 10th Street NW, Suite 700, Washington, DC 20001; telephone 202 637-3000; www.nam.org). The Association represents manufacturing industry views on national and international problems through a public information program and by testifying at legislative and administrative hearings and by submitting *amicus curiae* briefs in important judicial and administrative litigation. It maintains a digital magazine, weekly e-mail newsletters on economic and legislative news and activities, and monthly e-mail updates on litigation and global economic policy trends. It also compiles reports on issues and manufacturing, financial, and trade data.

559. Neither the Chamber of Commerce of the United States nor the National Association of Manufacturers acts as a collective bargaining representative. In important national negotiations, however, these organizations occasionally make public statements regarding the reasonableness or unreasonableness of certain bargaining positions. (Typically these support management's bargaining position.)

II. Multi-employer Bargaining

A. The Process

560. Collective bargaining between a union and a group of employers (multi-employer bargaining) was an established practice in American labor relations when the NLRA was adopted in 1935. It continues to be an important mode of bargaining in a few industries but its role has declined since the 1970s. The largest bargaining unit described by the NLRA's language respecting the procedure for NLRB bargaining unit certification is the employer-wide unit. Nevertheless, in the interest of stable labor–management relations, the NLRB and the courts treat bargaining on a multi-employer basis as a legitimate approach to the bargaining process and the Board sometimes conducts elections in a multi-employer unit to ascertain whether the majority of all workers in the unit wish to be represented by a particular labor organization.[642]

Most often, multi-employer bargaining involves a local group of businesses in the same industry competing for the same work force. Occasionally it involves all, or a substantial majority of all, employers in an industry on a regional or national level.

561. Multi-employer bargaining is lawful only to the extent that all of the negotiating parties consent to engage in that bargaining format. Consent need not be formal and is operative so long as the employers have indicated an intention to be bound by group rather than individual action in collective bargaining and the union has indicated a willingness to negotiate with the employer representatives on a group basis. That willingness can be indicated by a history of group bargaining. Moreover, the multi-employer structure is not defeated by the fact that the parties negotiate some contract issues using a format other than bargaining for the entire group as a unit.[643] Indeed, a commonly used technique is for the multi-employer group to negotiate a master agreement covering all enterprises but leave certain terms open for variation or special provisions through supplemental agreements separately negotiated with the individual employers.

562. Multi-employer collective bargaining sometimes is conducted by an informally affiliated group of employing enterprises. Alternatively the multi-employer group forms or utilizes a formal employers' association as the structure for representing management in negotiating with the union. That association sometimes also serves other purposes such as establishing uniform standards or terminology for identifying product variations in the industry, generating greater consumer interest in the industry's products, scrutinizing industry related legislative or administrative activities, lobbying, and the like. The Board has not attempted to regulate the internal governance methods of an association that represents multi-employer bargaining interests. For example, in one case the Board held a group of employers bound

642. *Charles D. Bonanno Linen Service. Inc.* v. *NLRB*, 454 US 404 (1982); *Rock Springs Retail Merchants Ass'n*, 188 NLRB 261 (1971); *Dover Tavern Owners' Ass'n*, 164 NLRB 933 (1967).
643. *Charles D. Bonanno Linen Service. Inc.* v. *NLRB*, 454 US 404 (1982); *H.S. CARE, L.L.C.*, 343 NLRB 659 (2004). *See also*, *Brown* v. *Pro Football*, 518 U.S. 231, 240 (1996).

to their multi-employer bargaining relationship even though two of the six employers had the right to veto any proposal on behalf of all of the employers.[644]

Mere membership in the representing association, however, does not place an employer within the multi-employer bargaining unit. The association member must affirmatively manifest an intention to be represented by the association for collective bargaining in order to be bound by its collective agreements.[645]

563. Because multi-employer bargaining is a consensual format in which all participants must agree to participate, prior to the scheduled commencement of negotiations either the union or any employer may unilaterally withdraw from the multi-employer bargaining structure by giving adequate notice to the other participants. This includes the right of the union to withdraw from dealing on a multi-employer basis with respect to some of the employers but not as to the rest.[646] Once bargaining begins, however, it must continue on a multi-employer basis unless there is mutual consent to abandon that format or extraordinary circumstances, such as an employer's insolvency, intervene to a sufficient degree to justify unilateral withdrawal from the multi-employer bargaining. If an impasse is reached in negotiations, the union is permitted to separately settle with individual members of the multi-employer bargaining group on an interim, temporary basis pending a unit-wide settlement. However, even after a bargaining impasse, individual parties are not permitted to abandon the multiemployer bargaining format over the objection of any other participants because an impasse is not considered an extraordinary event in the collective bargaining process.[647] The restrictions on withdrawing from multi-employer bargaining have been justified as necessary to promote stable collective bargaining relationships.

B. Antitrust Limitations

564. Multi-employer collective bargaining poses questions related to national legislative policies designed to promote competition among business enterprises. These policies, generally referred to as antitrust laws, prohibit excessive concentration of the number of enterprises in any particular product or service market and outlaw concerted actions among enterprises that reduce their level of design, market, price or services competition. However, section 6 of the Clayton Act, adopted in 1914, declared that human labor is not a commodity or article of commerce (15 US Code §17). Accordingly, the antitrust laws do not encompass restrictions on competition respecting labor standards. Thus, American antitrust policy has long treated collectively bargained efforts to stabilize and fix wages and other terms and conditions of employment as lawful restraints on competition.[648] In contrast, the

644. *Weyerhaeuser Co.*, 166 NLRB 299 (1967), enforced 398 F.2d 770 (DC Cir. 1968).
645. *Charles D. Bonanno Linen Service. Inc.* v. *NLRB*, 454 US 404 (1982); *Rock Springs Retail Merchants Ass'n*, 188 NLRB 261 (1971).
646. *Pacific Coast Ass'n of Pulp and Paper Mfgs*, 163 NLRB 892 (1967).
647. *Charles D. Bonanno Linen Service. Inc.* v. *NLRB*, 454 US 404 (1982).
648. *Apex Hosiery* v. *Leader*, 310 US 469 (1940).

antitrust exemption is not available to employers that adopt uniform employment standards as a means of thwarting labor organizing.[649] Moreover, as discussed in paragraph 594, below, antitrust law restricts the extent to which employers engaged in multi-employer bargaining can enhance their bargaining power by acting as a single economic unit.

565. The immunity of labor–management relations from the antitrust laws presumes that concerted action to stabilize employment standards is designed to serve the goals and interests of workers. However, when the setting of labor standards is used in part or in whole to restrain the terms of business competition, that immunity is lost. Thus, the Supreme Court has explained:

> [A] union forfeits its exemption from the antitrust laws when it is clearly shown that it has agreed with one set of employers to impose a certain wage scale on other bargaining units. One group of employers may not conspire to eliminate competitors from the industry and the union is liable with the employers if it becomes a party to the conspiracy. This is true even though the union's part in the scheme is an undertaking to secure the same wages, hours and other conditions of employment from the remaining employers in the industry.[650]

Accordingly, although competing employers that are engaged in the multi-employer bargaining can adopt uniform employment standards, even if they are unable to reach a collective agreement with the union,[651] they cannot try to impose those standards upon competitors who do not choose to join in this bargaining approach. Nor can they accomplish that goal by obligating the union to try to impose the standards of the multi-employer collective bargaining agreement upon competitors who are not part of the negotiating group.[652] In contrast, on its own initiative and in its own interests, a union is permitted to attempt to attain uniform standards of employment in reaching agreement with all employers in an industry.[653] Clearly, a union's opportunities for doing so are greatly enhanced to the extent that the multi-employer bargaining format is used. Moreover, setting uniform employment standards may at times directly dictate the terms of competition. For example, if a collective agreement restricts the hours during which retail employees may be required to work, that labor contract term generally will dictate the hours during which stores are open for business. A business that wants to capture the late night trade is, therefore, prevented from doing so if it is a party to a collective agreement that permits work only between sunrise and sunset.

The effort to impose work standards beyond the bargaining units for which it is the bargaining agent violates the prohibitions against secondary pressures designed to force union recognition by employers whose employees are not represented by

649. *Detroit Auto Dealers Ass'n* v. *FTC*, 955 F.2d 457 (6th Cir.), *cert.* denied 506 US 973 (1992).
650. *United Mine Workers* v. *Pennington*, 381 US 657, 665–666 (1965).
651. *Brown* v. *Pro Football, Inc.*, 518 US 231 (1996).
652. *United Mine Workers* v. *Pennington*, above at 665–666 (1965).
653. *Local Union No. 189, Amalgamated Meat Cutters* v. *Jewel Tea Co., Inc.*, 381 US 676 (1965).

the union. Accordingly, in one case an appellate court ruled that antitrust law is violated if a union persuades a multi-employer group to not contract the work of hauling construction site waste to companies that pay less than the truck driver rates in the collective agreement unless such haulage was work traditionally done by members of the union's own bargaining unit. In the latter situation, the union is trying to protect the jobs of its members–a permitted activity; in the former situation, the union is merely trying to exclude non-union trucking companies from a segment of the waste hauling market.[654] In contrast, the same court has ruled that a union can try to preserve work opportunities for its members by agreeing to permit unionized employers to pay a lower hourly rate than that normally required under the collective agreement when workers are employed on construction sites where the employer had to bid against non union companies in order to get the contract.[655]

566. Obviously, in a multi-employer bargaining setting the temptation is great and the means are readily available for employers to establish uniform non-competitive terms for at least some aspects of marketing their products and services. The antitrust law exemption for labor–management negotiations does not apply if the employers' intent is to restrain competition and if the union consciously cooperates. In contrast, if the uniform terms are the result of the union's arm's length bargaining to establish what it considers to be in the workers' best interests, the antitrust exemption applies. It ordinarily would not be too difficult to elicit proposals from the union for employment standards that facilitate the elimination of areas of competition under the guise of adhering to the terms of the collectively bargained agreement. Normally, of course, it is difficult to prove the essential elements for establishing a violation of the antitrust laws. Thus, while the goals of labor relations policy and antitrust policy are in competition in permitting the multi-employer bargaining format, in balancing those competing concerns, Congress has permitted labor relations stability to prevail.

---

654. *Maui Trucking, Inc.* v. *Operating Engineers Local Union No. 3*, 37 F.3d 436 (9th Cir. 1994).

655. *Phoenix Elec. Co.* v. *National Elec. Contractors* Ass'*n*, 81 F.3d 858 (9th Cir. 1996). In the particular situation at issue, the union established a fund financed by a tax union workers paid from the wages earned on jobs covered by its collective agreements. Contractors that were parties to the collective agreement could get authorization to bid on jobs in competition with non-union contractors by pricing their bids on the assumption they would pay a lower wage similar to that paid by non-union contractors. If a union contractor won the job bid, the union contractor would then receive a subsidy from the fund to make up the difference between the union wage it paid its workers and the non-union wage it assumed in pricing its bid.

Chapter 4. Worker Participation in Management through Collective Bargaining

§1. Written, Comprehensive Agreements of Specific Duration

567. Collective bargaining is a method for establishing rules regulating work relationships, the work environment, and work benefits. In the United States the results of collective bargaining are committed to a written, signed document that normally is of considerable length. Most collective agreements continue for a specified number of years. Collective agreements in the railroad and airline industries traditionally were for indefinite periods of time and continued in effect until changed or modified by following the RLA's prescribed procedure for making such changes. Although agreements for set periods have become the norm in these two industries, the RLA's mandatory procedures governing collective bargaining have the effect of continuing the established employment terms and conditions for an indefinite period even after the date of termination set forth in the agreement.

568. The NLRA expressly requires the parties to commit a collective agreement to writing upon the demand of either side. Although the Act does not expressly require that collective agreements be negotiated for a fixed period of time, the NLRB has recognized that agreements for a fixed duration are the norm in American labor–management relations and has stated that a fixed period of agreement promotes the underlying NLRA policy of facilitating stability in labor–management relations. Accordingly, under what is called the 'contract bar rule', the NLRB recognizes a collective agreement that has been in effect for less than three years as barring the processing of a petition for a representation election only if that agreement is for a fixed duration and only if it contains provisions substantially regulating the labor–management relationship (*see* paragraph 430, above).

§2. The Duty to Bargain Collectively

569. The RLA and the NLRA impose upon the employer a duty to bargain collectively with the representative duly recognized by the employer or certified by the appropriate government agency as the agent chosen by a majority of employees as their collective bargaining representative. The collective bargaining agent has the same duty to bargain with the employer. Section 8(d) of the NLRA defines the duty of bargaining collectively. Among other things, it is a responsibility 'to meet at reasonable times, and confer in good faith with respect to wages, hours, and other terms and conditions of employment'. The duty to bargain collectively also obligates both sides to meet and confer in good faith regarding questions arising under a collective agreement between them. Thus, even without a contractual grievance procedure, the parties have an obligation to discuss in good faith any grievances or other disputes concerning the meaning or requirements of their agreement.

Importantly, section 8(d) expressly states that the duty to bargain collectively 'does not compel either party to agree to a proposal or require the making of a concession'. For this reason, it can be argued that in essence the duty to bargain is no more than a duty to meet and confer.

Another section 8(d) requirement of bargaining collectively is to satisfy statutory procedures for notifying the other side and various government agencies of bargaining conflicts before making unilateral changes or resorting to economic pressure.

I. Mandatory and Non-mandatory Topics for Collective Bargaining

570. Because the statutory description of the duty to bargain under the NLRA refers to 'wages, hours, and other terms and conditions of employment', the Supreme Court has held that there is no duty to bargain with regard to subjects that do not fall within one of those specified categories.[656] Accordingly, one question to be resolved is whether particular bargaining demands fall within the scope of these so-called 'mandatory' bargaining topics. Wage rates, work schedules, vacation benefits, and the like, are obvious topics with respect to which bargaining is mandatory. Other topics have raised closer questions. For example, it took a decision of the Supreme Court to resolve a debate over whether a change in prices employees pay in a company cafeteria is a mandatory topic of bargaining. (The Court decided that it is a mandatory topic.)[657] Similarly, although the NLRB decided that an employer's offer to retirees, giving them an option to elect certain benefits in lieu of participating in an employee health insurance program, was a mandatory bargaining topic, the United States Supreme Court disagreed on the ground that the duty to bargain concerns the benefits of current employees, including their retirement benefits, but does not include proposed new benefits for those who are retired.[658]

Mandatory bargaining topics have been held to include such things as use of plant bulletin boards, performance of non-supervisory work by supervisors, required physical examinations, and testing for drug abuse.[659] In contrast, a demand that employees be allowed to vote on whether to accept a contract offered by the employer has been held not to be a mandatory bargaining topic.[660] The NLRB has also ruled that because employers have a right to hire striker replacements, it will not complicate that process by compelling the employer to bargain concerning the terms and conditions of the replacements' employment during a strike.[661] On the other hand, an employer was held guilty of an unfair labor practice when it advertised for striker replacements and offered them higher wages than it was

656. *Allied Chem. and Alkali Workers* v. *Pittsburgh Plate Glass Co.*, 404 US 157 (1971).
657. *Ford Motor Co.* v. *NLRB*, 441 US 488 (1979).
658. *Allied Chem. and Alkali Workers* v. *Pittsburgh Plate Glass Co.*, 404 US 157 (1971).
659. *See* for example, *Johnson-Bateman Co.*, 295 NLRB 180 (1989).
660. *NLRB* v. *Wooster Div. of Borg-Warner Corp.*, 356 US 342 (1958).
661. *Detroit Newspaper Agency*, 327 NLRB 871 (1999).

paying current union represented workers. The Board explained that such action unlawfully disparages and discriminates against union representation.[662]

571. Those subjects that are not mandatory topics of bargaining fall into two categories: permissive and illegal. Permissive bargaining topics are those with respect to which the parties may bargain if both sides are willing to negotiate regarding them. Examples of permissive bargaining include demands concerning the terms and conditions of supervisory employment, arrangements permitting or requiring the employer to place a label on its product showing that it is made by union labor, employer and union contributions to a fund used to promote the industry, changes in benefits given to persons who are already retired, and changes in an employer's product line or other alterations of the manner in which an employer conducts its business.[663]

Bargaining demands that elicit unlawful conduct are illegal demands. For example, a closed shop provision–one that prohibits the employer from employing nonunion members–is an unfair labor practice and, therefore, seeking such a provision is an illegal bargaining topic. Making an illegal proposal is evidence of the unfair labor practice of failing to bargain in good faith; insisting upon such a demand to the point of a bargaining impasse is itself an unfair labor practice.[664]

572. If the bargaining topic for which a change is sought is one that is covered by an existing collective agreement, the NLRA does not require further bargaining about the issue or the duration of the collective agreement unless there is a provision in the agreement specifying that the issue can be reopened after a designated time.[665] Thus, such a proposal is a permissive but not mandatory topic of bargaining.

II. Maintaining the Status Quo until there is a Bargaining Impasse

573. If a term or condition of employment constitutes a mandatory bargaining topic, section 8(d) of the NLRA prohibits changes in that term or condition until:

(a) both sides mutually agree to the change or
(b) the parties have reached a bargaining impasse.

The unilateral alteration of a term or condition of employment prior to a bargaining impasse is an unfair labor practice.[666]

662. *Beverly Health & Rehab. Serv., Inc.* v. *NLRB*, 317 F.3d 316 (DC Cir. 2003) (enforcing NLRB decision).
663. *See* generally, *First National Maintenance Corp.* v. *NLRB*, 452 US 666 (1981).
664. *See*, for example, *Local 1367, International Longshoremen's Association*, 148 NLRB 897, 899–900 (1964), enforced 368 F.2d 1010 (9th Cir. 1966) (*per curiam*), *cert.* denied 389 US 837 (1967).
665. *NLRB* v. *United States Postal Service*, 8 F.3d 832 (DC Cir. 1993).
666. *NLRB* v. *Katz*, 369 US 736 (1962); *Bryant & Stratton Business Inst., Inc.* v. *NLRB*, 140 F.3d 169 (2d Cir. 1998).

Whether there has been a bargaining impasse is determined based on all of the issues affecting the agreement– there cannot be an issue by issue impasse since accommodation respecting one item may affect willingness to modify bargaining positions regarding other items. Assessment of whether there is a bargaining impasse weighs such factors as the duration of bargaining activities, the number of bargaining sessions, previous concessions made, prior bargaining history, the presence or absence of bad faith bargaining tactics, a mediator's continuation or abandonment of efforts, and the complexity of the unresolved issues. There is, however, no single test of whether bargaining has reached an impasse. Rather, the NLRB weighs the totality of the negotiating conduct in order to assess whether there is a realistic possibility that continued discussions will lead to additional accommodations.[667]

Generally, once there is a bargaining impasse, a party can unilaterally implement its most recent bargaining proposal (but not make changes that it did not offer at the bargaining table). However, some terms and conditions of employment, such as a dues check-off provision, a union security provision, an arbitration provision, and a no work stoppage provision, require mutual consent[668] and, therefore, it is not an unfair labor practice to unilaterally abandon such a condition of employment if the parties are no longer bound by a prior agreement respecting the subject nor is it an unfair labor practice to unilaterally resume protected conduct (such as picketing) unless contractually waived.[669]

Even though a bargaining impasse has been reached, that does not permanently relieve the parties of the duty to bargain. Negotiations must be resumed if changed circumstances or new proposals indicate agreement may be possible.[670]

Moreover, impasse does not insulate all previously proposed changes from challenge as unfair labor practices. For example, an appellate court upheld the Board when it treated as an unfair labor practice an employer's unilateral implementation, at impasse, of a bargaining proposal that would have allowed the employer to grant individual wage increases without being confined by specific criteria and without conditioning such an increase on union representation and bargaining concerning the individual change. The court noted that such changes would inherently undermine the union's status as bargaining agent and that the Board could reasonably find that bilateral determination of wage changes or the criteria for such changes is at the core of the duty to bargain collectively. Therefore, unilateral implementation of proposed unfettered management authority to increase wages without first meeting and conferring with the union made the union's bargaining status meaningless and hence violated the duty to bargain in good faith.[671]

---

667. *Truserv Corp.* v. *NLRB*, 254 F.3d 1105, 1114 (DC Cir. 2001), *cert.* denied 534 US 1130 (2002).

668. *Litton Financial Printing Division* v. *NLRB*, 501 US 190 (1991).

669. *McClatchy Newspapers, Inc.* v. *NLRB*, 131 F.3d 1026, 1030-1031 (DC Cir. 1997) *cert.* denied 524 US 937 (1998). In *Lincoln Lutheran of Racine*, 362 NLRB No. 188 (2015), the Board held that a dues check-off agreement cannot be unilaterally discarded by an employer upon the expiration of the collective agreement.

670. *McClatchy Newspapers, Inc.* v. *NLRB*, 964 F.2d 1153, 1164–1165 (DC Cir. 1992).

671. *McClatchy Newspapers, Inc.* v. *NLRB*, 131 F.3d 1026 (DC Cir. 1997) *cert.* denied 524 US 937 (1998). Contrast *Mail Contractors. of Amer.* v. *NLRB*, 514 F.3d 27 (DC Cir. 2009) (after impasse

III. Notice of Intent to Modify the Collective Agreement

574. Section 8(d) of the NLRA provides that if there is an existing collective agreement, before either side may initiate a change in a term or condition of employment, at least 60 days' prior written notice of the intended modification must be given to the other side and at least 30 days' prior written notice must be given to the Federal Mediation and Conciliation Service and to any state mediation agency having jurisdiction over the work site. Longer notice requirements are imposed for the health care industry (90 days to the other side and 60 days to the federal and state mediation agencies). Violation of the notice provisions is a failure to bargain collectively and, therefore, an unfair labor practice under NLRA sections 8(a)(5) and 8(b)(3).

IV. Resort to Pressure Tactics as Part of the Bargaining Process

575. Either side may use lawful economic pressure (such as work stoppages, primary boycotts, picketing, contracting out work, work performance by supervisors, etc.) in support of a demand regarding a mandatory bargaining topic so long as:

(a) the statutory notice requirements have been satisfied (*see* paragraph 574, above),
(b) the issue is not already settled by an existing collective agreement, and
(c) the parties have not entered into a no-work stoppage or similar peace agreement waiving their right to resort to such pressures.[672]

576. If a topic is a permissive subject of bargaining, a unilateral change can be made with regard to that subject without committing an unfair labor practice. Similarly, the statutory notice requirements do not apply to making changes regarding permissive subjects of bargaining. On the other hand, resort to economic sanctions in support of a demand regarding a non-mandatory bargaining topic is an unfair labor practice. Also, it is an unfair labor practice to insist, to the point of reaching a bargaining impasse, upon a proposed change involving a permissive subject of bargaining.[673]

§3. Regulation of Bargaining Table Conduct

577. A basic principle of the duty to bargain is that the employer and the recognized bargaining agent are the parties to collective negotiations. Therefore, an

---

a unilateral change that shifted work from one worker group to another was an operational decision that did not undermine or render meaningless the union's bargaining status even though it had an impact on employee earnings).

672. *Allied Chemical and Alkali Workers* v. *Pittsburgh Plate Glass Co.*, 404 US 157 (1971); *NLRB* v. *Insurance Agents' Int'l Union*, 361 US 477 (1960); *NLRB* v. *Wooster Div. of Borg-Warner Corp.*, 356 US 342 (1958).

673. *Allied Chemical and Alkali Workers* v. *Pittsburgh Plate Glass Co.*, 404 US 157 (1971).

employer must negotiate with the labor organization and not with individual employees respecting terms and conditions of employment unless the union consents to individual bargaining. Moreover, an employer may not insist to the point of a bargaining impasse that the union give such consent.[674]

The duty to bargain in good faith also involves the duty, on request, to provide the other side with information that is directly related to the controversy. Thus, the Supreme Court has held that if an employer asserts inability to pay more, the union is entitled to reasonable access to information respecting the employer's financial position.[675] On the other hand, the appellate courts have read this information access requirement narrowly and have held that if the employer's rejection of a union demand is based on unwillingness to pay or an assertion that accepting the union's demand would place it at a competitive disadvantage, the employer has not claimed it is unable to pay and the union is not thereby entitled to examine the employer's financial records.[676]

Other requested information that is essential to formulating demands must be provided by the other side. Thus, it is an unfair labor practice for an employer to refuse to provide a certified or recognized labor organization with information regarding the wages received by bargaining unit employees.[677] However, in determining whether particular information sought by a labor organization must be provided by the employer, the NLRB balances the union's need for the information against any legitimate employer or individual worker interests in maintaining secrecy or confidentiality.[678]

578. Ascertaining when a party has failed to bargain 'in good faith' can be an extremely difficult fact finding task. Occasionally, an angered spokesperson openly declares a lack of intention to find a common ground for agreement. More often, evidence of a lack of good faith must be discovered in a party's overall conduct that is found to be inconsistent with good faith bargaining behavior. Thus, dilatory bargaining tactics, failure to give a negotiating representative responsible authority, broken promises to respond to an offer, false statements, unexplained withdrawal

---

674. *Toledo Typographical Union* v. *NLRB*, 907 F.2d 1220 (DC Cir. 1990), *cert.* denied 498 US 1053 (1991).

675. *NLRB* v. *Truitt Mfg. Co.*, 351 US 149 (1955).

676. *See*, e.g. *CONAGRA, Inc.* v. *NLRB*, 117 F.3d 1435 (DC Cir. 1997). However, it has been held that a union is entitled to demand data specific to verifying the accuracy or inaccuracy of an employer's claim that acceding to demanded concessions will put it at a competitive disadvantage. *KLB Indus., Inc.* v. *NLRB,* 700 F.3d 551 (DC Cir. 2012). Commentators have long urged an expansion of the duty to disclose such information. *See*, for example, C. Estlund, 'Economic Rationality and Union Avoidance', 71 *Tex. L. Rev*. 921, 985 (1993); K. Dau-Schmidt, 'A Bargaining Analysis of American Labor Law and the Search for Bargaining Equity and Industrial Peace', 91 *Mich. L. Rev*. 419 (1992); B. Lawniczak, 'Substantiating 'Competitive Disadvantage' Claims', 87 *Mich. L. Rev*. 2026 (1989).

677. *Int'l Woodworkers of America* v. *NLRB*, 263 F.2d 483 (DC Cir. 1959).

678. *Detroit Edison Co.* v. *NLRB*, 440 US 320 (1979) (four dissenting Justices would have required the employer to give the union the demanded aptitude test scores of named individual test takers where the scores affected promotion decisions).

from a less extreme position that had been taken earlier, by-passing the bargaining representative, and the like, have been treated as evidence of bad faith bargaining.[679]

579. Although section 8(d) of the NLRA expressly states that the parties have a duty to bargain in 'good faith', it also says that the duty to bargain collectively does not necessitate making a concession. Therefore, a difficult distinction must be made between bad faith bargaining and tough bargaining. In some cases in which a party has been found guilty of failure to bargain in good faith, the NLRB and the courts have cited to the party's rigidity in adhering to a bargaining position. Some court and NLRB decisions suggest that a party must be prepared to make at least some concessions if that party is to be found to be bargaining in good faith. Other decisions emphasize that willingness to make concessions is not required for good faith bargaining. And, there has been much debate concerning whether a 'take-it-or-leave-it' bargaining position is a lawful strategy or a failure to bargain in good faith. The prevailing view is that good faith bargaining must be assessed by looking at the totality of the parties' conduct and that while rigidity is not itself a violation of the duty to bargain in good faith, it is evidence that the party has not come to the bargaining table with the requisite willingness to try to reach an agreement.[680]

580. For many years it was unclear whether an employer can resort to self-help tactics during the course of negotiations without violating the NLRA duty to bargain in good faith. It had long been settled that workers can strike and picket during negotiations without breaching the bargaining duty, but it was less clear as to whether an employer can lock-out workers in support of its bargaining position.

In American industrial relations law a lockout is distinguished from a dismissal and a layoff. Dismissal is the total severance of the employment relationship at the employer's initiative. Layoff is the suspension of the relationship due to lack of work but the employee on layoff has a contractual right to resume full employment status when work becomes available. (In non-collective bargaining relationships employers often use the term layoff to denote a reduction in force in which the employment relationship of those affected is permanently severed. Many human resource managers apparently regard the term layoff as having a less harsh connotation than the terms termination, dismissal or discharge although, as the term layoff is used in such situations, they all mean the same thing.) In contrast, in a lockout the work opportunities that otherwise would be available to the employees are withheld by the employer in an effort to coerce their union to accept the employer's bargaining proposals.

The Supreme Court has ruled that it is not an unfair labor practice for an employer to lockout employees as a means of putting economic pressure on them in

679. For example, *Carey Salt Co.* v. *NLRB*, 736 F.3d 405 (5th Cir. 2015). *See* R. Gorman and M. Finkin, *Labor Law*, 2d ed., 2004, at §§20.17–20.19.

680. E.g. *NLRB* v. *General Electric Co.*, 418 F.2d 736 (2d Cir. 1969), *cert.* denied, 397 US 965 (1970), enforcing 150 NLRB 192 (1964), *Golden State Bottling Company* v. *City of Los Angeles*, 475 US 608 (1986); *Frankl ex rel. NLRB* v. *HTH Corp.*, 650 F.3d 1334 (9th. Cir. 2011); NLRB v. Hardesty Co., 308 F.3d 859, 865–867 (8th Cir. 2002); *Borden, Inc.* v. *NLRB*, 19 F.3d 502, 512 (10th Cir.), *cert.* denied 513 US 927 (1994); *Teamsters Local No. 515* v. *NLRB*, 906 F.2d 719, 726 (D.C. Cir. 1990), *cert.* denied 498 US 1053 (1991).

support of the employer's bargaining demands. The NLRB and courts hold that an employer can use this tactic prior to as well as after the parties reach a bargaining impasse so long as the use of the tactic has a business or bargaining justification and is not designed to destroy the union.[681]

A few decisions allow an employer to hire temporary replacements for locked out employees or temporarily contract-out their work in order to keep its business going even when the lockout is initiated by the employer solely as an offensive measure to put economic pressure on the union. It has been held, however, that at the end of the lockout the locked out employees are entitled to return to their jobs to the extent the jobs remain available.[682]

On the other hand, overruling a divided decision by the NLRB, an appellate court held that it was an unfair labor practice for an employer to lockout employees who had ended their strike where it did not lock out workers it had temporarily hired during the strike nor lock out those who previously had abandoned the strike. The court explained that such discrimination against those who had exercised their right to strike, without regard to seniority or any other criteria relevant to maintaining business efficiency, constituted unlawful punishment of those who stood with their union and gave unlawful benefits to those who crossed lawful picket lines.[683] Similarly, overruling a divided NLRB decision, an appellate court held that it was unlawful discrimination for an employer to lock out the regular workforce, all of whom were union members, but not lock out probationary employees who were not members of the union.[684] (*See* additional discussion in paragraphs 768–772, below.)

581. The National Labor Relations Act protects workers when they resort to strikes, picketing and primary boycott action to pressure an employer into making concessions. Thus, an employer cannot discharge an employee for engaging in such activity. Any disabilities imposed upon a worker as a result of such concerted activity constitute an unfair labor practice.[685] However, the courts and NLRB distinguish between dismissing a striker or picketer and permanently replacing that worker. As discussed in paragraphs 739–742, below, replacement, as contrasted with dismissal, is permitted unless it is shown that the employer's action was motivated by a desire to destroy the system of collective representation.

---

681. *American Ship Building Co.* v. *NLRB*, 380 US 300 (1965); *Lane* v. *NLRB*, 418 F.2d 1208 (DC Cir. 1969); *Ottawa Silica Co.*, 197 NLRB 449 (1972), enforced 482 F.2d 945 (6th Cir. 1973), *cert.* denied 415 US 916 (1974); *Central Illinois Public Service Co.*, 326 NLRB 928 (1998), rev. denied *sub nom Local 702 IBEW* v. *NLRB*, 215 F.3d 11 (DC Cir.), *cert.* denied 531 US 1051 (2000).

682. *Int'l Brotherhood of Boilermakers* v. *NLRB*, 858 F.2d 756 (DC Cir. 1988); *Pankratz Forest Indus.*, 269 NLRB 33 (1984). However, *see also*, *Int'l Paper Co.* v. *NLRB*, 115 F.3d 1045, 1051 (DC Cir. 1997), where the court held that if the employer showed it was much less expensive to contract out certain work than continue to have it done by its own employees, it was not an unfair labor practice for it to institute a lockout and then permanently contract that work while the lockout was in effect and while bargaining continued. The court noted, however, that the result might not be the same if the employer hired permanent replacements during a lock-out instituted to put bargaining pressure on the union.

683. *Local 15 IBEW (Midwest Generation, EME, LLC)* v. *NLRB*, 429 F.3d 651 (7th Cir. 2005), *cert.* denied 127 S. Ct. 42 (2006).

684. The NLRB's decision, on remand, applying the DC Circuit's decision is reported at *Bunting Bearings Corp.*, 349 NLRB 1070 (2007).

685. *NLRB* v. *Fleetwood Trailer Co.*, 389 US 375 (1967).

Moreover, if employees engage in strikes, slowdowns or picketing during a time when the bargaining unit is covered by a collective agreement that contains a 'peace' or 'no work stoppage' provision prohibiting such conduct, the economic activity is unprotected. This means that the employer is free to discipline, including discharge, employees who resort to such economic pressure. In theory, the employer is not punishing them for exercising the protected right to engage in concerted activities; rather, the employer is punishing them for violating a duty established by the collective agreement. If the underlying dispute is also covered by an arbitration provision, then, under what is known as the 'Boys Markets doctrine', the employer may be able to obtain a court order enjoining the pressure tactic.[686]

582. Section 8(d) of the NLRA also removes statutory protection from employees who engage in work stoppages prior to the expiration of the 60-day or 90-day notice required by the statute before a collective agreement can be modified or terminated. (*See* paragraph 574, above.) Those who engage in a stoppage in violation of the notice requirement are treated as unprotected and, therefore, can lawfully be dismissed.

Employees are also unprotected, and, therefore, are subject to employer punishments, including dismissal from work, if they engage in forms of concerted activity that violate the employer's right to control its property and direct its operations. Thus, employees who engage in a sit-in strike can be discharged and those who engage in partial disruptions of work activity may be dismissed, disciplined in other ways or locked out, depending on the nature of the disruption. For example, refusals to leave the employer's premises are unprotected; peaceful refusals to go back to work are protected.[687] (See further discussion in paragraphs 743–750, below.)

§4. Bargaining Practices

I. Reliance on Work Stoppages

583. The work stoppage lies at the heart of the collective bargaining process in the private sector of American labor–management relations. Resort to economic weapons is expected whenever the power of persuasion, including the threatened consequences of resort to economic warfare, fails to adjust the parties' differences. In the words of the Supreme Court of the United States: 'The presence of economic weapons in reserve and their actual exercise on occasion … is part and parcel of the system that the Wagner and Taft-Hartley Acts have recognized'.[688]

686. *Boys Markets, Inc.* v. *Retail Clerks Union, Local 770*, 398 US 235 (1970). *See* additional discussion at paragraphs 715–716 and 830, below.

687. *NLRB* v. *Insurance Agents Int'l Union*, 361 US 477 (1960) (*dicta*); *NLRB* v. *Fansteel Metallurgical Corp.*, 306 US 240 (1939); *Lodge 76, IAM* v. *Wisconsin Employment Relations Comm'r.*, 427 US 132 n. 14 (1976); *Molon Motor and Coil Corp.* v. *NLRB*, 965 F.2d 523 (7th Cir. 1992); *Fortuna Enters., LP* v. *NLRB*, 665 F.3d 1295, 1300 n. 3 (D.C. Cir. 2011) (list of criteria for determining whether an at-work stoppage is protected).

688. *NLRB* v. *Insurance Agents Int'l Union*, 361 US 477, 489 (1960).

584. In the public sector of American labor–management relations, work stoppages generally are expressly prohibited by statute[689] or by judicial determination. Even in the 12 states[690] that permit at least some public employees to strike, restrictions are imposed on the procedure leading to stoppages and the right to engage in a work stoppage is not available to all public employees. Justification for prohibiting stoppages by public employees is based on the delegated authority of elected public officials to determine management policy and carry on governmental functions free from interference.[691]

Under 5 US Code §7311(3), federal employees who violate the work stoppage prohibition lose their eligibility to hold federal government jobs and, under 18 US Code §1918, are subject to imprisonment for up to one year and a day plus a fine. In addition, a labor organization supporting such a strike can lose its representational status.[692]

Penalties often are not imposed on government workers who remain out during a prohibited strike. In the case of state workers, officers charged with enforcing such laws often are elected officials who are reluctant to antagonize the workers and their families and friends–all of whom may be voters. In addition, some who do not work during such stoppages later claim that their absence was not in support of the strike but resulted from fear of reprisals from fellow workers. In federal government employment, the absent employee is excused if he or she meets the burden of proving that the fear was sufficiently great so as to go beyond what a person of ordinary firmness would be expected to resist.[693]

585. A variety of alternative methods for exerting pressure are used by employees where strikes are prohibited. One method is for the government employees to 'work to rule'. This results in the workers performing their duties without exercising any discretion. Instead, they perform exactly what is required by official work rules and, thereby, often create chaos and inefficiency.

Another method is the sick-in (workers claim to be too ill to work). This is sometimes referred to as the 'blue flu' due to the color of the uniforms often worn by police officers. In addition to requiring workers to provide medical verification of the claim, at least one court has permitted the government to use an anticipatory lockout in the face of a pattern of such conduct.[694]

Political action (voting for more sympathetic elected officials) and picketing at the homes and social clubs of elected officials are among the other methods sometimes used.

---

689. For example, Florida, Ohio, New York.
690. Alaska, California, Colorado, Hawaii, Illinois, Louisiana, Minnesota, Montana, Ohio, Oregon, Pennsylvania, and Vermont.
691. *United Federation of Postal Clerks* v. *Blount*, 325 F. Supp. 879 (DDC) affirmed without opinion, 404 US 802 (1971); *City of New York* v. *De Lury*, 23 N.Y.2d 175 (1968), appeal dismissed 394 US 455 (1969). See generally, R. Perry, 'Strike-Out', 66 *Ala. L. Rev.* 445, 479-81 (2017).
692. *PATCO* v. *FLRA*, 685 F.2d 547 (DC Cir. 1982); *Dehainaut* v. *Peña,* 32 F.3d 1066 (7th Cir. 1994), *cert.* denied 514 US 105 (1995).
693. *Schultz* v. *Department of Transportation*, 773 F.2d 296 (Fed. Cir. 1985).
694. *Utility Workers of America* v. *Labor Relations Comm'n*, 451 N.E.2d 124 (Mass. 1983). *See also*, text at note 5 in paragraph 584, above.

Strike substitute techniques, including various approaches to compulsory interests arbitration, have been statutorily adopted in an estimated thirty states or localities within those states. Although the courts have upheld most of these laws, a few state courts have invalidated such statutes as an unconstitutional encroachment on legislative or executive authority.[695]

II. Sequence of Events in Collective Bargaining

586. Traditionally, in bargaining units covered by the Railway Labor Act collective agreements did not have a fixed termination date and bargaining began whenever a party gave the required notice for initiating what is called the major dispute procedure. (A major dispute is one involving a proposed change in a term or condition of employment; that is, it is an interests dispute.) Contracts of fixed duration are now the norm in the US, including the rail and airline industries.

In most collective bargaining relationships in the United States, bargaining begins a few months prior to the termination of an expiring collective agreement. The initiating event is to give written notification to the other side, a requirement of section 8(d) of the NLRA (*see* paragraphs 574, above, and 745, below). Shortly thereafter the parties meet and typically the union submits a list of demanded improvements. Since the late 1980s, as a result of increased employer outsourcing of the production of products and components, outsourcing service activities, and downsizing of larger operations, management now often also has its list of demands for reductions in the benefits levels or expansion of the work force's flexibility.

Initial demands, and the responses to them, typically are exaggerated to leave room for 'compromise' and to take into account the imperfections of available information, uncertainties of predicting future business and labor market developments, and possible miscalculations regarding the other side's willingness or ability to meet particular demands. The demands list also often contains some 'throw away' items which the union or employer does not realistically expect to achieve. Occasionally, 'throw away' items are presented to induce the other side to begin thinking about particular changes that the may be proposed in earnest at some future contract negotiation.

Generally, bargaining focuses upon each item in the proposed contract with the understanding that any concessions can be conditioned upon counter concessions regarding some other item. That is, negotiations ultimately look to the final package

695. *See*, for example, *County of Riverside* v. *Riverside Sheriff's Ass'n*, 66 P. 3d 718 (Calif. 2003) (state constitution's delegation of authority to county government to conduct local affairs was violated by state legislation requiring impasse arbitration of disputes with county employees). M. Malin, 'Does Public Employee Collective Bargaining Distort Democracy? A Perspectivefrom the United States', 34 *Comp. Lab. L. & Pol'y J.* 277 (2013); B. Malloy, 'Binding Interest Arbitration in the Public Sector', 55 *Hastings L.J.* 245 (2003). From 2010-2012 several states adopted legislation severely curbing public employee collective bargaining. See, M. Malin, 'Sifting Through the Wreckage of the Tsunami that Hit Public Sector Collective Bargaining' 16 *Empl. Rts. & Employ. Pol'y J.* 533 (2012).

of modifications in the terms and conditions of employment so that an improvement in the direction of meeting one demand might be offset by an improvement, no change, or a concession with regard to some other item or group of items.

587. The technique of 'continuous' bargaining involves exploring possible solutions to problems as they arise, or as they are anticipated, regardless of how much time must pass before the existing collective agreement expires. This approach has enabled some parties to successfully accommodate their mutual and competing interests concerning complex problems. For example, continuous bargaining has proven useful in dealing with the impact of technological and regulatory changes. Even when solutions are not reached by the joint effort, often it encourages the parties to investigate the issue with enough thoroughness so that when they later approach the bargaining table, there is agreement on the facts underlying their differences and the unresolved issues are more clearly and narrowly defined.

588. Normally, mediators are invited into collective bargaining under the LMRA when a deadlock appears imminent or when the parties' communications have broken down. Mediation is voluntary under the LMRA except in the health care industry and in the occasional situation in which national emergency dispute machinery is invoked. The Federal Mediation and Conciliation Service (FMCS) provides staff specialists to mediate disputes in industries covered by the LMRA. Upon request, the FMCS also aids dispute settlement in state and local government collective bargaining. In the private sector, the parties sometimes retain the services of their own mediator in lieu of, or in addition to, the services of the government mediator.

In the case of the airline and railway industries, mediation of bargaining issues is mandatory and is conducted by full time officials or staff of the National Mediation Board. However, in these two industries, as in other industries, parties sometimes seek the services of their own mediator in addition to those of the government mediator.

589. In some industries, unions have a tradition of striking during any period in which a collective agreement is not in force. An alternative, in order to avoid a strike, is for the parties to agree in advance that the new contract will be retroactive to the termination date of the expired collective agreement. Bargaining can, must, and normally does continue during the course of a work stoppage[696]– though the emotions generated by the stoppage may require a temporary suspension of bargaining table efforts.

590. At the bargaining table it is common for the employer to be represented by a lawyer or have lawyers actively participating on its negotiating team. Also, it is not uncommon for management representatives, other than legal counsel, to have legal training. Sometimes they are top management officials who were previously employed as corporate counsel or labor counsel. Although unions, too, use lawyers as negotiators, they do so less often than does management.

---

696. *Poultrymen's Service Corp.*, 41 NLRB 444, 461 (1942).

The union officials at the bargaining table often are accompanied by, or are required to report regularly to, an elected committee of bargaining unit workers. Moreover, both sides normally bargain with the understanding that any agreed new contract is subject to submission to the bargaining unit for ratification by majority vote of the union members. Some employers similarly condition agreement upon ratification by the corporate directors.

In some situations, particular segments of the bargaining unit are given the power to veto the agreement if their special bargaining interests are not satisfied. This arrangement has been used, for example, by the United Auto Workers union to assure the skilled trades employees, who are a small minority of the total employee complement, that their interests have not been neglected.

591. Contract rejection by the union membership is the exception. In the mid-1960s, some American labor relations commentators expressed alarm at what they characterized as a dramatic increase in such rejections. However, studies showed that the rejection rate peaked at less than 15 percent in 1967 and continued at less than 12 percent for the following decade. The issue faded away in the 1980s in part because the risks to workers of rejecting proposed contracts increased as a result of the decline in union membership, the increased frequency with which employers permanently replaced strikers, and the growing trend to outsource bargaining unit work. In addition, union leaders and employers discovered that there is greater assurance of ratification when the collective agreement includes a lump sum payment to the workers in the form of a 'ratification bonus'.

III. Strike Insurance and Other Mutual Aid

592. Part of the economic muscle parties bring to the bargaining table is their respective abilities to withstand a work stoppage. In some industries one side is greatly aided by the technological characteristics of the industry or the structure of the market. Thus, a highly automated industry, such as telecommunications, can withstand a long strike with little loss in income and little increase (and possibly even decrease) in operating expenses; whereas, in an industry such as building construction, often all work must cease if a particular segment of the workers (for example, crane operators) engage in a stoppage. In addition to such built-in strategic characteristics, American labor unions generally attempt to supplement their strength by improving their ability to prolong a work stoppage. This is accomplished by establishing a fund to financially assist striking workers (strike fund).

593. A strike fund is usually controlled by the union's national or international headquarters. Some unions rely on the ability of their general fund to finance strikes, but most large American unions maintain a reserve fund for this purpose and regularly allocate to it a set portion of dues income. Strike benefits are usually available only if the national or international headquarters of the union authorizes or approves the strike. Generally, there is a one or two week waiting period before the strikers are entitled to draw upon the fund and they must be available to perform strike tasks, such as picketing, if they are to receive the benefits.[697] A study conducted in the early 1970s revealed that close to one-third of the larger unions in the United States further conditioned the receipt of funds upon some showing of need. The rest paid the funds to all strikers as a matter of right; in some unions the amount of benefits differed based upon the number of dependents in the striker's family.[698] Whatever the amount, strike benefits are not generous.

The strike funds of national unions may at first impression sound imposing. For example, in 2000 it was reported that the Communication Workers of America had 630,000 members and a $210 million strike fund. However, that averaged less than one week's wages per member. Although only a small portion of the members are likely to go on strike in any year, in light of the fact that strikes in the US can last for several weeks, and sometimes for months, the fund can quickly be depleted resulting in benefits being small.[699] For example, starting in 2002, the United Auto Workers union increased its weekly strike benefit to $200 plus the payment of health and life insurance premiums. That level of cash benefit was less than the minimum wage for a full-time worker.

594. American employers, too, have attempted to improve their ability to withstand the pressures of economic warfare in labor–management relations. One approach is to establish a strike insurance fund or commitment. For example, for many years the American Newspaper Publishers Association sponsored a program under which individual participating newspaper publishers paid an annual premium and in return received insurance payments in the event of a strike lasting for more than a week. A condition for receiving strike benefits was the struck publisher's willingness to submit deadlocked issues to arbitration.

Another early development of employer strike insurance was a program adopted by railroads in the late 1950s that the insurance industry administered but whose premiums were based on an assessment system rather than on an actuarial formula. The benefits of this plan covered the struck railroad's fixed costs and assessments were apportioned based on each carrier's fixed costs relative to the other participating railroads. However, the plan covered only limited categories of strikes.

From 1958 to 1975, several major airlines had a Mutual Aid Pact that paid the struck carrier a percentage of its normal operating expenses. Funds primarily came from any excess above normal operating revenues received by the non struck participants during the strike. To the extent such windfall revenues did not cover the insured percentages of operating expenses owed to the struck airline, the other airlines contributed on an assessment basis out of their general revenues. The Mutual

---

697. In *Kolinske* v. *UAW*, 712 F.2d 471 (DC Cir. 1983), 30 percent of the agency shop fee paid by nonmembers was deposited into the union's strike fund from which payments were made only to those who performed strike duties. The court rejected the assertion that constitutional and statutory protections of free expression were violated when the union refused to give this benefit to a non member who would not perform picket line or similar tasks. The court ruled that there was no violation since the union administered the strike funds in the manner it reasonably thought would maximize the effectiveness of a work stoppage.

698. S. Kline, 'Strike Benefits of National Unions', 98 *Monthly Lab. Rev.* 17 March 1975.

699. FMCS data shows that 44 percent of strikes that ended in 2016 were of more than ten calendar days' duration. Most did not endure for more than a month.

Aid Pact was blamed by some for prolonging strikes and was abolished by the Airline Deregulation Act which restricts airline industry strike insurance plans by prohibiting payments for the first 30 days of a work stoppage, requires recipients to agree to submit disputes to interests arbitration, bars payments in excess of eight weeks, and limits them to 60 percent of the airline's operating expenses.[700]

Doubt as to the lawfulness of such arrangements was created by *California ex rel. Harris*, 651 F.3d 1118, 1120 (9th Cir. 2011), a case in which the appellate court ruled that when a group of grocers which was engaged in multi-employer collective bargaining adopted a revenue sharing arrangement to combat strikes, they were pursuing an anti-competitive practice in violation of federal anti-trust law. The court distinguished the revenue sharing scheme from the lockout tactic described in paragraph 595, below.

595. Similar to the mutual aid provided through a strike insurance fund is a special type of mutual assistance pledge sometimes given by employers who bargain on a multi-employer basis. Unions bargaining with a multi-employer group sometimes use the so-called 'whipsaw' bargaining technique, whereby the union separately strikes one employer at a time, often financing the strike in part by special assessments imposed on those employed in the non striking bargaining units. This technique is intended to gain interim individual concessions from the struck employer that might not be achieved from a united employer group. The strategy assumes that such concessions will become a benchmark for the ultimate group settlement. As a counter tactic, the multi-employer group may pledge that if any member is struck, the remaining employers will in turn lock out their employees. For a number of years it was uncertain as to whether such lockouts are legal, but in *NLRB* v. *Truck Drivers Local 449*, 353 US 87 (1957) (known as the *Buffalo Linen* case) and *NLRB* v. *Brown*, 380 US 278 (1965), the Supreme Court of the United States held them to be lawful.

§5. Bargaining in the Public Sector

I. State and Local Employment

596. Until the late 1960s, most government employees were not permitted to have collective representation. In the 1960s and 1970s, numerous states adopted statutes allowing at least some categories of government employees to have such bargaining representation. As a result, 47 states, Puerto Rico, and the District of Columbia, now permit at least some categories of government workers to engage in collective bargaining. A few other states implicitly acknowledge some role for union representation by allowing government employees to direct that their union dues be deducted from their pay. In states that have laws providing for the recognition of government employee unions, collective representation generally follows

700. S. Unterberger and E. Koziara, 'The Demise of Airline Strike Insurance', 34 *Indus. & Lab. Rel. Rev*. 82 (1980).

the NLRA principle that the representative selected by a majority of bargaining unit employees is the exclusive representative of the entire bargaining unit.

Bargaining unit composition varies greatly from state to state. Some favor bargaining based on administrative and budgetary units, others focus greater attention on common work skills and responsibilities.

Those who manage government workers generally do not engage in active campaigns to persuade their employees to reject the collective bargaining approach when it is available. As a result, well over a third of state and local government employees are now covered by collective agreements; over three times the portion covered in the private sector. The portion is much higher if one counts only those state and local government employees who are legally permitted to have collective representation. Some scholars as well as most labor leaders argue that this demonstrates that the decline in private sector union representation is primarily the product of fear of employer retribution for union activity, not lack of employee interest in having such representation.

Because most government employees in the US are prohibited from engaging in work stoppages, collective bargaining procedures in public employment differ from those encountered in the private sector of the American economy. In most states, either side can call for the intervention of state mediation officials and in at least two states, Kansas and New York, the state mediation agency can intervene on its own initiative. Although most states use a single mediator, some use a panel on which each side selects an even number of mediators and then those mediators select an additional one.

597. A substantial number of states also provide for either side to be able to initiate a fact-finding procedure if bargaining approaches or reaches an impasse. Under some statutes the fact finder's report is kept confidential pending further negotiations; under other statutes it is automatically made public. Although a few states permit the same person to combine the fact-finding and mediation roles, in most jurisdictions they are separate.

598. Most states with public employee collective bargaining statutes encourage the parties to submit bargaining impasses to arbitration; some make such submission mandatory and binding. However, the courts of a few states have held such legislation to be in violation of the constitutional responsibility of state legislative bodies to establish the terms of government employment.[701] In a number of states, interests arbitration is compulsory for some, but not for all types of public employee bargaining disputes. In addition, some local governments, especially larger cities, have established their own impasse resolution machinery.

Impasse arbitration in public employment often utilizes the final-offer format. That is, the arbitrator must choose one or the other side's final bargaining offer and cannot make an award that constitutes a compromise between bargaining positions. There are two forms of final-offer arbitration. One requires the arbitrator to select

701. *County of Riverside* v. *Riverside Sheriff's Association*, 66 P.3d 718, 730 (Calif. 2003). *See* J. Grodin, 'Judicial Response to Arbitration' in *Public Sector Bargaining*, 2d ed. (B. Aaron, J. Najita and J. Stern, eds., 1988), at p. 253.

the entire contract proposed by one side or the other; the other format allows the arbitrator to select provisions, issue-by-issue, from among the two final offers.

In a few jurisdictions the legislature has authority to reject an interests arbitration award affecting government employees.[702]

599. A specific time-table often is established for third party intervention in those states that impose mediation, fact finding or arbitration in the event of negotiation impasses in government employee collective bargaining. In Oregon for example, either party may notify the Employment Relations Board (ERB) if an agreement is not reached after 150 days of good faith bargaining. The ERB then assigns a state mediator to assist the parties. If a settlement is not reached after 15 days of mediating, either party may declare an impasse. Alternatively, the mediator may declare one at any time. Upon an impasse being declared, each side has seven days to submit a final offer which is made public by the mediator. The parties may then jointly request appointment of a fact finder. Thirty days after the fact finding report (which is preceded by a hearing), the government employer may implement its final offer and the employees may engage in a work stoppage unless employed in a category prohibited from striking. (Police, firefighting, prison and mental health facility guards, deputy district attorneys, emergency call telephone operators, and parole and probation officers, and those who have custody or supervision of youthful offenders, are prohibited from striking.) In the absence of a joint fact finding request, the public employer may implement its final offer and the employees may engage in a work stoppage unless employed in a category barred from striking. For those Oregon employees who are barred from initiating work stoppages, binding arbitration is mandatory if mediated bargaining becomes deadlocked. Factors to be weighed by the arbitrator are specified by statute.[703]

Other states have procedures that vary considerably from the above Oregon example. In Ohio, for example, the fact finding report is submitted for a vote by the union membership and the heads of the government entity, and becomes binding on the parties unless rejected by at least 60 percent of those voting on one side or the other. If the recommendation is rejected, the unresolved bargaining impasse eventually is submitted for resolution by arbitration.[704]

II. Federal Employment

A. *Postal Employees*

600. The Postal Reorganization Act of 1970, as amended (39 US Code §§1004, 1201–1209) established a separate system of regulations for the United States Postal Services' labor–management relations. Under that Act, federal postal employees

702. *See*, for example, *Minnesota Education Association* v. *Minnesota,* 282 N.W.2d 915 (Minn. 1979), appeal dismissed 444 US 1062 (1980); *Alaska Public Employees Association* v. *City of Fairbanks*, 920 P. 273 (Alsk. 1996).

703. Ore. Rev. Stat. §§243.712, 742, 746.

704. Oh. Rev. Code §4117.14. The statute mislabels the arbitral decider a 'conciliator'.

who have neither management nor supervisory functions have the same rights to organize and be collectively represented as do workers in the private sector. For this purpose, the Postal Reorganization Act makes the NLRA largely applicable to postal workers. The labor–management provisions in the Postal Reorganization Act, however, require that collective agreements be for a minimum of two years and establish special bargaining impasse resolution machinery. Because Postal Service employees are prohibited from engaging in strikes, the Act gives the parties a specified period for bargaining without intervention. If during that time an agreement is not reached between the Postal Service and the employees' exclusive bargaining agent, or if the parties have not, alternatively, mutually selected a method for resolving a bargaining impasse, a procedure is imposed by law for a panel to investigate the facts of the dispute and report to the parties, with or without recommendations, within a specified time. However, if the parties do not thereafter reach agreement within a specified time, a tripartite arbitration panel is selected with each side naming an arbitrator. Those two arbitrators, if able, select the third arbitrator by mutual agreement. If unable to do so they then receive from the Director of the FMCS a list of nine persons who are members of the National Academy of Arbitrators and select from that list the third arbitrator. Within 45 days after its appointment, the arbitration panel must make its award resolving any issues submitted by the parties. The arbitration award is final and binding and is part of the parties' collective agreement.

Three national postal workers' organizations represent postal employees. While the threat of work stoppages has occasionally been heard in Postal Service collective bargaining, it has not been a major factor in the parties' relations under the Act. On several occasions, however, the parties have resorted to interests arbitration to resolve bargaining impasses.

601. The Postal Reorganization Act also states that if a supervisors' organization represents a majority of supervisors, that organization has a right to 'participate directly' in planning pay policies and schedules, fringe benefits and other programs relating to supervisors. The Act similarly gives the same 'direct participation' rights to an organization representing other managerial personnel if it has the support of 'a substantial percentage' of such employees. The Act provides for a system of monthly meetings through which direct participation is conducted and impasse resolution procedures similar to those established for collective bargaining with non-managerial Postal Service employees with the exception that there is no provision for ultimate resolution of impasses by binding interests arbitration. Instead, the Postal Service is directed to give 'full and fair consideration' to recommendations of a fact-finding panel and provide a written explanation for its rejection of any such recommendation.

Several organizations, including one representing Postmasters, the executive in charge of each postal facility, participate in the determination of supervisory and management employment conditions under this system. Generally, though, issues raised in such consultations have been resolved without resorting to fact-finding.

B. Federal Workers Other than Postal Employees

602. The federal government did not have a formal system of collective bargaining relations with its employees until 1962 when a Presidential decree, in the form of an Executive Order, was adopted. Executive Order 11491 was the last of a series of amended Orders regulating federal employment labor–management relations. It was superseded by the Civil Service Reform Act of 1978, also known as the Federal Services Labor–Management Statute (5 US Code §§7101–7106, 7111–7123, 7131–7135).

The Reform Act protects the right of federal government workers to join unions and regulates both the process for selecting labor organization representatives and the bargaining and contract administration processes for executive branch federal employees. The Act created the Federal Labor Relations Authority (FLRA) to administer the rights and responsibilities created under the Act, and the Federal Services Impasses Panel, an agency responsible for assisting in the resolution of deadlocked disputes between federal government departments and agencies and their employees' collective bargaining representatives. Excluded from the Act's coverage are those employed by the Postal Service. In addition, excluded from the right to union representation are aliens employed by the US government outside the United States, members of the military forces, supervisors and managerial officials, employees of the Department of State and of other agencies dealing with foreign affairs, employees of security agencies such as the FBI and CIA, those employed by the General Accounting Office, the FLRA, the Federal Service Impasses Panel, and the Tennessee Valley Authority. The President of the United States can exclude additional agencies when deemed necessary for reasons of national security. In addition, when it consolidated 22 existing agencies into the Department of Homeland Security, Congress authorized that department to develop its own system of human resource administration subject to several conditions, including a requirement that 'employees may organize, bargain collectively, and participate through labor organizations of their own choosing in decisions which affect them, subject to any exclusion from coverage or limitation on negotiability established by law'.[705] It has been held that definitions contained in the Civil Service Reform Act of 1978 govern the meaning of the right to engage in collective bargaining and participate in labor organizations when construing employee rights and agency responsibilities preserved by the statute which created the Department of Homeland Security and that the Civil Service Reform Act similarly controls the permissible role that can be assigned to the FLRA in administering the labor– management relations system established by the Department of Homeland Security.[706]

The Civil Service Reform Act adopts the principle of exclusive collective bargaining representation by a labor organization selected by a majority of employees in a bargaining unit. In addition to the majority union's right to negotiate collective agreements, the Reform Act protects the right of federal government workers to be

705. 5 US Code §9701(b)(4).

706. *National Treasury Employees Union* v. *Chertoff*, 452 F.3d 839 (DC Cir. 2006).

represented by their union in grievances, disciplinary proceedings, and discussions of personnel policy and employment conditions.[707]

Civilian employees of the Department of Defense have collective bargaining rights under the Civil Service Reform Act. Pursuant to temporary Iraq War legislation, collective bargaining rights of the Department's civilian employees were restricted by the Secretary of Defense. Later changes restored their bargaining rights subject to the Secretary's authority to conduct bargaining on the national level regardless of the level at which a bargaining unit is established.[708]

603. The Civil Service Reform Act of 1978 expressly reserves to management the authority to select, direct and discipline the work force. However, it requires management to negotiate with the workers' exclusive representative, determined by a majority of the employees, concerning the structure of the work force, the methods of performing work, and procedures to be followed by management in exercising its authority.[709] The Act additionally requires collective agreements to provide for grievance resolution procedures and for binding arbitration of unresolved grievances. The parties cannot negotiate for an arrangement that is inconsistent with a statute or a government-wide regulation if that regulation serves a compelling need that is essential to: (a) accomplishing the agency's functions, (b) maintaining the basic merit principles for appointment, assignment, and promotion, or (c) achieving a specified legal mandate given to the agency.

The FLRA has oversight authority for determining whether a particular issue is subject to negotiations.[710] It can also find that the Act has been violated where a department or agency refuses to sign a lawful agreement reached by a subordinate unit.[711] Although the Reform Act requires an agency to give a bargaining representative information needed to carry out its responsibilities, the Supreme Court has held that the Privacy Act exceptions to the Freedom of Information Act prevent a federal agency from providing the majority representative with the home addresses of the employees in the bargaining unit represented by a union.[712]

Because wage rates for most federal employees are established by statutory schedules, bargaining cannot affect wages. An exception to the latter principle has been created for federal government employees in skilled trades who are employed at jobs that in 1972 were subject to negotiated adjustment of wages and other terms

707. *See*, for example, *Department of Veterans Affairs* v. *FLRA*, 16 F.3d 1526 (9th Cir. 1994).

708. *American Federation of Government Employees* v. *Gates*, 486 F.3d 1316 (DC Cir. 2007). 5 US Code § 9902(e).

709. For example, in *Department of Veterans Affairs* v. *FLRA*, 33 F.3d 1391 (DC Cir. 1994), the court upheld the FLRA's decision that although the content of a standard established for evaluating employee performance is not a negotiable subject, an agency is required to negotiate with a labor organization respecting the statistical method used for measuring an employee's rate of errors in applying the performance standard. In *INS* v. *FLRA*, 12 F.3d 882 (9th Cir. 1993), it was held that although the decision to require law enforcement employees to wear uniforms and to make the wearing of bullet proof vests optional are non-negotiable, management was required to negotiate with the union respecting proposals to reduce the discomfort of complying with regulations that required that such vests be worn inside the uniform even in very hot working conditions.

710. *National Fed. of Federal Employees* v. *US Dep't of the Interior*, 526 US 86 (1999).

711. *Montana Air Chapter No. 29* v. *FLRA*, 898 F.2d 753 (9th Cir. 1990).

712. *Department of Defense* v. *FLRA*, 510 US 487 (1994).

of employment (this group is known as 'prevailing rate employees').[713] Congress has excluded wage rates of some other federal employees from those established by the Civil Service laws and thereby subjected such wages to collective negotiations.[714] (*See*, *also*, paragraphs 903-905, below.)

604. In those situations in which a majority of workers have not selected an exclusive bargaining representative, the Civil Service Reform Act of 1978 permits a labor organization that represents a 'substantial number' of an agency's employees, as determined by the FLRA, to have national consultation rights. National consultation rights consist of the right to be informed of proposed substantive changes in conditions of employment, an opportunity to present views respecting the proposed changes, and the right to have those views considered by the agency and receive a written statement of the agency's reasons for its final action respecting the proposals.

605. The Federal Mediation and Conciliation Service provides assistance to management and labor organizations that reach negotiations impasses under the Civil Service Reform Act of 1978. In addition, the Federal Service Impasses Panel, which consists of at least seven members who are appointed by the President and serve at the President's pleasure, may assist the parties in finding a resolution or a method for reaching a resolution. At the parties' initiative and with the approval of the Federal Service Impasses Panel, impasses may be submitted to final resolution by arbitration. The Panel also has the authority to conduct hearings and impose upon the parties either a resolution or a procedure for achieving a resolution of their impasse if voluntary efforts are unsuccessful. However, a federal court has held that when an agency is required by the Impasses Panel to arbitrate an issue that has reached impasse, the arbitral decision is only advisory to the agency and cannot bind it.[715]

§6. The Impact of the NLRB upon Bargaining Structure

I. Generally

606. Bargaining structure in the United States is regulated to some extent both by explicit provisions of the National Labor Relations Act and by the Act's delegation to the NLRB of authority to determine the composition of bargaining units (*see*

713. *See*, for example, *US Information Agency* v. *FLRA*, 960 F.2d 165 (DC Cir. 1992). *See also*, *Bureau of Reclamation* v. *FLRA*, 23 F.3d 518 (1994) (agency did not have to bargain for supervisor wage rates even though supervisors previously had been included in the prevailing rate employees' bargaining unit).
714. In *Fort Stewart Schools* v. *FLRA*, 495 US 641 (1990), the Court upheld the FLRA's decision that the federal agency had a duty to bargain respecting the union's request for reimbursement of teacher travel expenses, a salary increase, and other benefits, where the salaries and benefits of the represented teachers are statutorily excluded from the Civil Service salary schedules.
715. *Dep't of Agriculture* v. *FLRA*, 895 F.2d 1239 (9th Cir. 1990).

NLRA §9). For example, the NLRA states that workers who are members of a profession cannot be placed in the same bargaining unit as non professionals unless a majority of the professionals choose to be in such a unit. Also, those employees assigned to perform plant security work are banned by section 9 from being in the same certified bargaining unit as other employees and cannot elect as their bargaining agent a union other than one that represents only those employed in security work.[716]

On the other hand, section 9 of the NLRA gives discretion to the Board to determine whether the unit for which a labor organization seeks certification is 'an appropriate unit' for bargaining. Section 9 also states that the bargaining unit can be an employer unit, a craft unit, a plant unit, or a subdivision of these. Acting under this authority, the NLRB has held that, in deciding if a unit is appropriate, it will weigh whether the included employees have the necessary 'community of interests' and constitute a sufficiently cohesive and non fragmented group so as to ensure their ability to viably engage in collective bargaining.

Factors the NLRB considers relevant to deciding whether the workers have a community of interests include similarity of work environment; benefits; methods of computing compensation; work hours; background training, experience and skills; functional integration of work activity; physical proximity of their respective work activities; frequency of transfers; and common lines of promotion and labor relations oversight. None of these factors is individually controlling. However, considerable weight in persuading the NLRB that the unit is appropriate is given to evidence that there is an established pattern of bargaining between the parties or in the industry.[717]

The NLRB also approves multi-employer and multi-union units where the parties agree to such groupings. Additionally, it approves units consisting of employees in particular geographic or operational divisions of an enterprise. And, when competing unions seek to represent employees in overlapping groups, if the Board finds that each alternative would be appropriate, it structures the election in such a way as to give the voting workers a voice in determining which grouping they want for representational purposes.[718]

607. Even though the NLRB has certified a particular bargaining unit, this does not prevent the parties from conducting their actual bargaining on some other structural basis that they mutually find to be more satisfactory. For example, if a union separately organized the employees at two plants owned by the same employer, the

716. *Henry Ford Health System* v. *NLRB*, 105 F.3d 1139 (6th Cir. 1997). *Also, see Velez* v. *Puerto Rico Marine Mgmt.*, 957 F.2d 933 (1st Cir. 1992), where the court, in agreement with NLRB case decisions, held that section 9 does not prohibit guards from joining a labor organization that includes non security workers and that it does not prohibit an employer from voluntarily recognizing a union as bargaining representative for such a unit. Therefore, if an employer voluntarily enters into a collective agreement covering a bargaining unit combining guards with other employees, the agreement is enforceable for its full duration and cannot be rescinded unilaterally. Accordingly, a union that is a party to such an agreement has a duty of fair representation to enforce employee rights established by the agreement.

717. NLRB, *An Outline of Law and Procedure in Representation Cases*, pp. 146–58 (2017).

718. *See*, for example, *New York University*, 205 NLRB 4 (1973).

union and employer can negotiate a single collective agreement for both bargaining units. Absent such mutual agreements to deviate from the certified or recognized bargaining unit, however, any insistence upon bargaining on some other basis constitutes the unfair labor practice of refusing to bargain.

608. Because supervisory personnel are excluded from the Act's definition of 'employee', they do not have protected rights to engage in concerted activity under the NLRA. (See paragraph 609, below.) Therefore, the Board always excludes supervisory personnel from its description of the certified bargaining unit. Nevertheless, just as the parties may mutually agree to bargain on a unit basis other than that certified, so, too, they may mutually agree to include supervisory personnel within all or some of the terms of agreement. Total exclusion of supervisors, however, is the normal pattern.

609. The NLRA protects the right of 'employees' to organize and bargain through representatives selected by the majority of employees in an appropriate bargaining unit. The Act's definition of 'employees' is sufficiently broad so that on its face it would appear to include the chief executive officer and other policy-making managers of a large enterprise. However, the Act expressly excludes 'supervisors' and 'independent contractor' from the definition of 'employees' and defines who is within those two categories.

The definition of 'supervisors' requires the person in that status to have authority in the interest of the employer to hire, discipline, resolve grievances or direct work or effectively recommend such action in a manner that requires independent judgment. The Supreme Court has upheld the NLRB's ruling that the party asserting that someone is a supervisor has the burden of proving the truth of that assertion.[719]

The assumption behind the exclusion of supervisors from the Act's protection is that an employer is entitled to rely on the undivided loyalty of those who manage the enterprise and that supervisors are among those who manage. For this reason, as well as to protect the independence of labor organizations, those who formulate and administer personnel policy long have been treated as excluded from collective bargaining units. Although excluded from the right to participate in a bargaining unit, however, confidential employees continue to be protected from unfair labor practices.[720]

Under the Act's literal meaning, a high level staff assistant who plays a key advisory or even a controlling role in shaping investment, merchandising, human resource, or other policies, would be a protected 'employee' unless that person exercises supervisory authority over others. Nevertheless, those employed to exercise managerial discretion over investment, personnel, production, development, and

---

719. *NLRB* v. *Kentucky River Community Care, Inc.*, 532 US 706 (2001).
720. *NLRB* v. *Hendricks County Rural Elec. Membership Corp.*, 454 US 170 (1981). *Peavey Co.*, 249 NLRB 853 (1980), enforced in relevant part 648 F.2d 460 (7th Cir. 1981). For an assessment of the merits of the *Peavey* doctrine, *see* R. Fischl, 'Self, Others and Section 7', 89 *Colum.L. Rev.* 789, 823–825 (1989).

similar decisions, are excluded from NLRB certified bargaining units regardless of whether their responsibilities satisfy the definition of 'supervisor'.[721]

The fact that the Act provides specific criteria for determining who is a professional employee, and contains special provisions for establishing bargaining units for professional employees, arguably supports interpreting narrowly the provisions regarding who is excluded from the Act's protections even though the professionals exercise policy making influence, have considerable discretion in carrying out their responsibilities and give some direction to the work of others. Nevertheless, a majority of the Supreme Court has excluded from the Act's protections both those who direct others to help them carry out their professional discretion and those whose professional decisions give significant direction to the enterprise. For example, in *NLRB* v. *Yeshiva University*, 444 US 672 (1980), the majority of the Supreme Court held that full-time university professors who effectively determine academic policy, programming, matriculation standards; hiring and promotion policies and selections; and who have an effective voice in setting tuition rates, student body size and school location; are managerial personnel and, therefore, are not entitled to petition for an NLRB election to certify the bargaining agent selected by a majority of the professors.

Additionally, in cases involving nurses, a closely divided Supreme Court has held that directing the patient care activities of less professionally trained or untrained health care workers is sufficient to constitute supervisory activity that removes the Act's protection from the person who guides the performance of health care work even though such oversight involves exercising professional judgment primarily to serve the interests of the patients as contrasted with exercising judgment in the interest of the employer.[722]

Commentators have observed that the Court's failure to distinguish the exercise of professional judgment and prerogatives from the entrepreneurial decision-making of managerial executives, indicates, somewhat bizarrely, that the greater the degree of worker participation in shaping work policy, the greater the likelihood that the workers will be found to have lost their protected status as 'employees' under the NLRA.[723]

610. Generally, the NLRB places part-time employees and seasonal employees in the same bargaining unit as regular full-time workers. It excludes casual workers from bargaining units but includes temporary workers. For a brief time, under what was referred to as the *Sturgis* rule, the NLRB held that if workers are provided by an employee leasing agency but have a clear community of interest with the rest of

---

721. *NLRB* v. *Textron, Inc.*, 416 US 267 (1975); *NLRB* v. *Health Care & Retirement Corp. of America*, 511 US 571 (1994).

722. *NLRB* v. *Kentucky River Community Care, Inc.*, 532 US 706 (2001) and *NLRB* v. *Health Care & Retirement Corp. of America*, 511 US 571 (1994). *See also*, *Oakwood Health Care*, 348 NLRB 686 (2006).

723. *See*, for example, J. Getman and R. Marshall, 'Industrial Relations in Transition' 102 *Yale L.J.* 1803, 1894 (1993); M. Crain, 'Building Solidarity Through Expansion of NLRA Coverage', 74 *Minn., L. Rev.* 953, 979 (1990); D. Rabban, 'Can American Labor Law Accommodate Collective Bargaining by Professional Employees?', 99 *Yale L.J.* 689 (1990); K. Stone, 'Labor and the Corporate Structure', 55 *U. Chi. L. Rev.* 73, 137 (1985).

the bargaining unit and the employer of the rest of the bargaining unit workers possesses or shares authority to determine essential employment terms and conditions of the leased employees, the latter could be placed in the larger bargaining unit regardless of the consent of the respective employers.[724] However, the Board reconsidered that decision a few years later and concluded that, under the wording of NLRA §9(b), absent consent of both employers and the union, it cannot impose a bargaining unit larger than that of a single employer. Therefore, the jointly employed leased workers could not be placed in the larger bargaining unit over the objections of any of the parties. In reaching this decision, the NLRB distinguished the situation of a joint enterprise in which the employers are unable to independently enter into an agreement establishing employment terms and conditions.[725]

However, a dozen years later, the Board returned to the *Sturgis* rule stating: 'Employer consent is not necessary for units that combine jointly employed and solely employed employees of a single user employer.' Additionally, 'there is no statutory impediment to processing petitions that seek units composed only of the employees supplied to a single user, or that seek units of all the employees of a supplier employer and name only the supplier employer.'[726]

II. Examples of Bargaining Structures

611. The construction industry in the United States, except for very specialized types of projects such as highways, skyscrapers, dams and bridges, largely is locally owned and operated. In addition, employment generally is confined to workers in a single craft and the industry is composed of tens of thousands of enterprises, many of which dissolve or become insolvent within a few months to a few years. There is also great fluidity in the industry's work force. Thus, because of turnover, although about five to six million jobs are provided by employers, they employ about twice that number of different persons each year.

Generally, in the unionized segment of the construction industry local unions bargain on a craft basis with an association representing most of the local employers that enter into contracts to perform work involving that craft skill. There are many variations within this pattern as well as variations from this pattern. In the western part of the United States, for example, regional or metropolitan area bargaining is prevalent. Additionally, throughout the industry the major employers that install elevators, fluid and gas transmission pipelines, and sprinkler systems, negotiate industry-wide agreements. Regional agreements are encountered for boilermakers, those engaged in dredging work, and ironworkers (though many work under local collective agreements).

Even when bargaining is local, the local union's bargaining autonomy often is subject to significant restraints. For example, 14 international unions represent

724. *M.B. Sturgis*, 331 NLRB 1298 (2000).

725. *H.S. Care Center, LLC*, 343 NLRB 659 (2004).

726. 184. *Miller & Anderson, Inc.*, 364 NLRB No. 39 (2016). The split in these cases has reflected the political affiliations of the Board members. In 2017 the Board majority shifted back to the Republican members. Accordingly, there is some question as to whether the NLRB will soon abandon the *Sturgis* rule once more.

workers in the construction industry and most of the internationals have authority to veto local strike demands – at least when the payment of strike benefits is sought. This authority is used largely for the purpose of cajoling the locals into keeping within the international union's guidelines and policies. (It is rare, however, for the international to withhold strike approval from a construction industry local that militantly insists on pressing its bargaining position to the point of a work stoppage.)

612. Superimposed on the bargaining structure in the construction industry is the use of national agreements between groups such as the Associated General Contractors and various national unions. These contracts deal with only a small portion of the range of negotiated terms and conditions of employment and anticipate local bargaining as the basis for providing the details establishing those terms and conditions of work.

613. Contract termination dates usually differ from craft to craft in the construction industry and bargaining demands tend to leapfrog successively as each craft in turn tries to improve upon the gains of the group that most recently completed negotiations. Moreover, bargaining gains in one sector of the industry, such as commercial construction, often set the pattern for other sectors, such as residential construction.

614. A different type of bargaining structure is encountered in the automotive industry where a single union, the United Auto Workers, represents most of the industry's workers in bargaining with the small number of giant enterprises on an employer-by-employer basis. Although the main focus of bargaining in the industry is at the enterprise level, the resulting contracts are supplemented by localized plant-wide agreements. In addition to the giant companies that assemble automobiles and trucks, a substantial portion of manufacturing in the industry is performed by smaller companies that make parts for new vehicles and replacement parts for used vehicles. Bargaining more typically is conducted on a plant-wide basis for these suppliers.

Those automotive plants in the US that manufacture vehicles for companies that traditionally were headquartered in other countries[727] largely are unorganized. Unionization of such plants has been deterred by the fact that when they have been built, the wages and benefits have been provided and maintained at a level comparable to that established by collective bargaining in American headquartered companies. In addition, foreign headquartered companies venturing into the automotive industry in the US largely have selected plant locations where the bulk of the work force has not had prior experience as union members and, therefore, are more difficult to organize.

727. International mergers in the industry in the last part of the 20th century, as well as joint manufacturing ventures, have complicated the description of some auto manufacturers.

615. In the steel industry, for decades industry-wide bargaining between an employers' association and a single union was the basic pattern. That system dissolved in the 1980s and thereafter enterprise bargaining became the normal pattern. The enterprise agreements typically are supplemented by additional contracts at the mill or plant level.

In the 1970s, when bargaining in the steel industry was still predominantly multi-employer and the union strike threat still carried considerable power, the parties adopted a no work stoppage pact under which bargaining impasses had to be submitted to arbitration. That approach disappeared in the 1980s.

616. In the appliance manufacturing industry, bargaining often is on a plant-wide basis with separate representation and bargaining for particular skilled workers or classes of technical workers. Thus, production workers and unskilled maintenance workers often are represented separately from skilled maintenance workers. In addition, power plant employees, drivers, and office clerical workers often are each separately represented or have no union representation. Since the late 1960s, coordinated or multi-union bargaining by labor organizations has been adopted for some enterprises, and plant bargaining is the pattern for the industry's larger bargaining units.

III. NLRB's Power to Stabilize Bargaining Unit Structure

617. Through its control over bargaining unit elections, the NLRB has considerable authority to standardize the structure for collective bargaining in the United States. However, the agency has done little in this direction. Instead, it gives great weight to the historical patterns established for bargaining in various industries and, thereby, accepts much of the haphazard approach that existed when it was established in the mid-1930s. Because the NLRA speaks in terms of 'a unit appropriate for bargaining', not 'the most appropriate bargaining unit', the NLRB has construed its function as limited to determining whether a representational unit sought in an election, or challenged after voluntary recognition, is an appropriate unit. It does not reject a unit merely because some other unit might be a 'more appropriate' or 'the most appropriate' bargaining structure.

In determining appropriateness, traditionally the Board has explained that it must balance the Act's protection of the right to self-determination against the need for bargaining units that have sufficient coherence and potential effectiveness to provide through their bargaining efforts the stabilization of industrial relations that the Act is designed to achieve. When weighing the impact of the Act's preservation of collective worker self-determination, the Board tries to avoid the danger that the interests of individuals who have little in common with the interests of the mass of bargaining unit employees will be ignored in the representative's exercise of bargaining discretion. When weighing the Act's goal of ensuring effective representation, the Board tries to avoid the danger that overly fragmented groupings of employees will lack the concerted power needed to achieve change through collective bargaining agreements.

618. Even when it treads on relatively virgin soil, the NLRB has avoided providing clear guidance in structuring the bargaining relationship. For example, it was in the late 1960s that collective bargaining began to be an active force in university faculty employment (in the US, 'faculty' refers to the instructional staff–professors, instructors, and lecturers). Thus, there was no industry bargaining history to inhibit the Board's choices. Nevertheless, rather than establish its own notions of what should be the bargaining structure, the Board's bargaining unit decisions largely responded to the particular characteristics of each individual case. To illustrate, it established multi-campus units in some situations but in others opted for separate units for each individual campus of the same university. Although it generally places all full-time faculty in the same bargaining unit, the NLRB has allowed professional school faculties, such as those in law and medicine, to have separate bargaining units when that school has demonstrated relative autonomy and uniqueness on the campus.[728] Similarly, depending upon the specific nature of their individual assigned responsibilities, sometimes the NLRB includes and other times excludes associate and assistant deans and department chairpersons from faculty bargaining units.

In more recent years, on several occasions the NLRB has found that a particular faculty had effective authority to determine or responsibly recommend changes in the school's policies concerning curriculum, grading, academic calendar, hiring, tenure, promotion and similar matters, and, therefore, were managers and not employees. Accordingly, under the Supreme Court's rulings respecting the distinction between managerial and professional responsibilities, the faculty was not entitled to elect a certified representative under the NLRA.[729]

619. Even if it sought to actively shape the structure of collective bargaining in higher education, the NLRB's lack of authority over public employees, coupled with the large numbers of public institutions of higher education in the US, would prevent it from ever fully establishing a standard bargaining structure for that field of employment. In addition, because the structure of collective bargaining can influence the availability and viability of operational choices, it can be argued that a flexible administrative approach to the structure of collective bargaining might be a better policy for higher education and other fields in which there is no accepted preferred operational or job structure.

620. On the other hand, the NLRB's approach to bargaining unit selection sometimes appears to lack unifying principles. For example, even though in other industries the NLRB normally includes part-time workers in units with full-time workers,[730] in the area of higher education the Board at times has excluded from all bargaining units those part-time campus workers who are students employed as

728. Salary levels in the US generally vary considerably based on the professors' field of specialty. Medical, law, and business teachers typically are the highest paid. Therefore, teachers in these fields often are reluctant to be in the same bargaining unit as faculty in lower paid specialties.

729. *NLRB* v. *Yeshiva University*, 444 US 672 (1980); *College of Osteopathic Medicine and Surgery*, 265 NLRB 295 (1982).

730. *Bachman Uxbridge Worsted Corp.*, 109 NLRB 868 (1954).

teaching assistants, examination proctors or research assistants.[731] Accordingly, while students employed part-time by a college were excluded from a bargaining unit of the college staff, fellow students with identical part-time jobs off campus (e.g. at a private bookstore, a private language school, or an independent laboratory) could be included in a bargaining unit with their full-time fellow workers. After about a dozen years, the NLRB reversed its position regarding students employed by their school.[732]

For many years the NLRB excluded medical interns and residents, who are licensed physicians completing their apprenticeship requirement, from all NLRA protections and rejected their recognition petitions on the premise that they are students, not employees, and, therefore, have no rights under the Act. However, eventually it overruled those decisions.[733]

IV. Bargaining Unit Size

621. An examination of the available data respecting bargaining units sheds some light and much fog upon the structure of collective bargaining in the United States. A few collective agreements cover very large bargaining units. For example, the United Auto Workers contract with General Motors covers over 50,000 workers and the Teamsters Union claims that its contract with United Parcel Service covers over 250,000 employees. In the first nine months of 2017, the Federal Mediation and Conciliation Service received notification of an intention to negotiate or renegotiate over 13,790 public and private sector collective agreements. Because the duration of the average collective agreement probably exceeded three years, and because the notification requirement does not apply to the initial collective agreement, a conservative estimate is that there are over 50,000 such agreements in effect of which probably over 90 percent are private sector collective agreements.[734]

622. In many situations, such as in construction craft units and newspaper craft units, a collective agreement covers less than a dozen employees. Nevertheless, it probably is accurate to say that the pattern of collective bargaining is set in large part by the dozen or so agreements negotiated each year that involve highly visible, widely publicized labor–management relations concerning very large numbers of workers. Thus, the benchmarks for private sector collective bargaining throughout

731. *Brown University*, 342 NLRB 483 (2004). For a brief period, the Board allowed students to be represented in a separate bargaining unit. *New York University*, 332 NLRB 1205 (2000).

732. *The Trustees of Columbia Univ.*, 364 NLRB No. 90 (2016). The overruled *Brown* decision was made by a Republican majority on the Board. The *Columbia University* decision was by a Democratic majority of the Board. In 2017 the majority shifted back to the Republican members. Accordingly, there is some question as to whether the NLRB will soon revert to the position it took in *Brown*.

733. *Cedars-Sinai Med. Ctr.*, 223 NLRB 251 (1976) overruled in *Boston Medical Ctr. Corp.*, 330 NLRB 152 (1999).

734. Since the early part of the 21st century, efforts to reduce federal government spending have eliminated many government financed information-gathering programs. This has greatly reduced the amount of reliable data available for accurately portraying labor-management relations activities.

the nation are set by the settlements reached in the automotive, over-the-road transportation, communications, and airplane manufacturing industries, and a few other industries in which bargaining is either conducted on a national or regional multi-employer basis, or in which the organized segment of the industry consists of no more than a handful of very large enterprises.

§7. Bargaining Structure in Public Employment

I. State and Local Employment

623. Bargaining structure for government employees follows a variety of patterns in the United States. The approaches of the various states and localities that have adopted public employee bargaining laws are diverse.

However, one common characteristic for laws that authorize collective bargaining is the adoption of the so called 'exclusivity doctrine' which recognizes the labor organization selected by a majority of employees in a bargaining unit as the sole collective representative of all employees in that unit regardless of their union membership or non-membership. Most states do not give any representational rights to organizations that have the support of only a minority of employees. However, some jurisdictions give 'consultation' status, as contrasted with 'bargaining' status, to such organizations in the absence of a representative selected by an employee majority.

624. Some bargaining unit boundaries are imposed by the government's structural design and distribution of responsibilities. Thus, if public education and police and fire protection are the responsibilities of country or municipal level governmental bodies, bargaining units of such employees can be expected to be confined to, and likely include, all of those employed by the individual local governmental units. Accordingly, in one jurisdiction firefighters may negotiate with the county government but in a neighboring local jurisdiction within the same state firefighters may negotiate with the municipal government.

Complicating matters is the fact that governmental responsibility for certain services often is divided among several entities. In many states, for example, public education is partially financed with general state-wide revenue resources (obtained, for example, by a sales tax), and partly with specific local revenue resources (obtained, for example, by a property tax). Similarly, a state level entity may be responsible for setting various minimum standards of operation for the public schools and regulate certain aspects of their operations, while a local level entity may have separate and independent authority to make policy choices that do not conflict with the state minimum standards and full discretion with respect to those matters not covered by the state level entity's responsibilities. Nevertheless, choices made by both the state and local officials often significantly affect the terms and conditions of teacher employment, thereby posing problems in creating a rational bargaining structure.

625. Another bargaining unit problem in government employment, as in private sector labor relations, is deciding which groupings of workers are appropriate for bargaining. For example, should teachers and firefighters be in the same unit? Should supervisors have collective bargaining rights? Should they bargain separately from, or jointly with, non supervisors? Should maintenance personnel working for recreational facilities be in the same bargaining unit as those working for transportation facilities?

At the state level, due to the large size of some states, there also is the question as to the appropriateness of including in the same bargaining unit those employees whose jobs, though identical, might be located hundreds of miles apart. Some states, such as Hawaii, which is composed of a series of islands (some of which are hundreds of miles apart), require state employees to be in statewide bargaining units.[735] Although there are exceptions, generally government management representatives favor broadly defined bargaining units. At the same time, public employee labor organizations, in part concerned with the problems of organizing and representing widely dispersed workers with divergent job responsibilities and differing work problems, often prefer more narrowly structured bargaining units.

626. The states have followed a variety of paths in dealing with unit determination problems. For example, Ohio permits professional and non professional employees to decide whether they wish to be together in a bargaining unit but prohibits including fire fighters or police officers in bargaining units with other classes of employees and further prohibits including higher ranking police officers in the same unit as lower ranking ones.

Hawaii has established 14 state-wide bargaining units based upon the broad job classifications of the employees. Students, confidential and top-level managerial employees, and short-term temporary employees, among others, are excluded from the right to bargain, but lower level supervisory personnel may bargain, although they are in separate bargaining units under the Hawaiian statutes.

Wisconsin was a leader in accepting public employee collective bargaining. However, in 2011 it substantially curbed the scope of that right and eliminated union security protections. The state law continues to provide for statewide bargaining units for various categories of classified employees. At the same time, the statute cautions against excessive fragmentation of bargaining units. . Although the Illinois law gives attention to the same concern, it provides a different emphasis by stating 'fragmentation shall not be the sole or predominant factor used by the Board in determining an appropriate bargaining unit'.[736] In Michigan, state employee bargaining units are required to be 'the unit appropriate' for bargaining as determined by the state Employment Relations Commission.[737]

---

735. Employer authority to enter into a collective agreement is divided based on the category of employees involved. For example, for primary and secondary school teachers, the Governor has three votes, the Board of Education has two votes and the Superintendent of Education has one vote. For firefighters and police officers, the Governor has four votes and the mayors each have one vote. Hawaii Rev. Stat. §89-6.
736. 5 IL Comb. Stat. § 315/9(b).
737. Mich. Comp. L. § 423.213.

At the local government level, bargaining unit determination often is resolved by a state agency on a case-by-case basis. Many states give considerable discretion to a public regulatory agency to determine whether a local government public employee bargaining unit is appropriate or, in some cases, whether a unit is 'the most appropriate' one available for the employees in question. Finally, teachers, firefighters and police often are covered by separate labor relations laws.

II. Federal Employment

627. The Civil Service Reform Act of 1978, at 5 US Code §7112, gives the Federal Labor Relations Authority responsibility for determining whether 'the appropriate' bargaining unit of federal employees should be established on an 'agency, plant, installation, functional or other basis'. The Act states that the Authority shall consider whether the unit ensures employees the fullest freedom in exercising their rights to collective representation as well as whether the unit will 'ensure a clear and identifiable community of interest among the employees in the unit and will promote effective dealings with, and efficiency of, the operations of the agency'.

The Act prohibits employee bargaining units from containing any management officials, supervisors, confidential employees, employees engaged in national security intelligence and counterintelligence responsibilities, employees who audit the honesty and integrity of agency performance, employees engaged in personnel work other than in a purely clerical capacity, and those excluded from the coverage of the Act. Professional employees must be in a separate unit unless a majority agree to be included with non professionals. Those engaged in administering labor– management relations laws may be represented only by wholly separate and independent organizations.

Section 7114 of Title 5 US Code adopts the 'exclusivity doctrine' which recognizes the labor organization selected by a majority of employees in a federal employee bargaining unit as the sole collective representative of all employees in that unit regardless of their union membership or non membership.

628. Bargaining unit determinations concerning postal service employees are excluded from the Civil Service Reform Act because the Postal Reorganization Act assigns these questions to the NLRB.

§8. Scope and Coverage of Collective Agreements

629. A distinguishing characteristic of American labor–management relations is the degree to which the parties use collective bargaining to resolve the details of employment terms and conditions. As a consequence, in the United States collective agreements are lengthy documents that include many details respecting working conditions, assignments and benefits which would be determined by other methods in most other labor relations systems. Often lawyers participate in the negotiation of such agreements and normally the agreement has been prepared and reviewed by lawyers regardless of whether the lawyers actively participated in the negotiations.

Until recent years, considerable information about collective bargaining practices was available from federal government agencies. However, political pressures to reduce the size of the federal government have resulted in curtailment of many governmental data collection efforts such as those previously conducted by the US Department of Labor's Bureau of Labor Statistics. Similarly, there has been a marked reduction in privately sponsored studies of such activities. Therefore, the descriptions that follow are based on older data supplemented by sporadic news reports and the authors' experiences and informal sources.

I. Duration

A. Length

630. In NLRA's early years, most collective agreements were for a year. The historic trend has been toward longer contracts, though volatile economic conditions have resulted in occasional, temporary reversals of that trend. Information compiled by an annual survey conducted in 1993 by the publishing company Bureau of National Affairs, Inc., found that 64 percent of the collective agreements were for three years. This was a decline from 80 percent in 1989. The change largely came from an increase in the percentage of contracts for four or more years. It was 9 percent in 1989 but had grown to 30 percent in 1993. Of the major industrial groupings, the construction industry long had a tendency to prefer shorter contracts, but even in that industry by 1993 most contracts were for three or more years. Although data respecting agreement duration no longer is compiled on a regular basis, news reports and other sources have made it evident that since the last decade of the 20th century, parties often enter into five-year collective agreements.

Until the 1960s, the tradition in the railroad and airline industries had been for collective agreements to be for an indefinite duration. However, since that time these industries have shifted to agreements with specific termination dates.

631. The duration of collective agreements in government sector labor management relations, a newer area of collective bargaining experience in the United States, initially leaned toward one- and two-year agreements. However, by the 1990s, their typical duration had lengthened and in 1994 it was reported that collective agreements covering 1,000 or more state or local government employees had an average duration of 22.4 months. Although about half were for less than two years, about 30 percent were for three or more years.

Two year collective agreements are the most common in federal government employment and statutory minimum and maximum terms for collective agreements are often found in collective bargaining laws regulating state and local government employment.

B. Automatic Renewal and Intervals between Contracts

632. Collective agreements in the United States normally contain an automatic renewal provision that typically states that unless 60 days prior to the termination date one of the parties gives a written notice of an intent to modify or terminate the agreement, the contract will be extended for an additional year beyond the original termination date. The 60-day notice provision in an automatic renewal clause coincides with the 60-day notice that section 8(d) of the NLRA requires as a condition to making unilateral changes in employment terms and conditions and as a condition of resorting to strikes or lockouts at the termination of a collective agreement. The NLRA requires that a 90-day notice be given before changes can be made or economic warfare can be resorted to in relation to collective agreements in the health care industry. Accordingly, automatic renewal clauses in that industry generally contain a 90-day pre-termination notice requirement to prevent the automatic renewal clause from being operative.

If notice of intent to modify or terminate is given within the contractual time limit, the contract, of course, terminates at the end of its designated duration. Resolution of disputes arising during the life of the contract continues to be controlled by its terms.[738]

633. The NLRA prohibits either side from altering employment terms and conditions, even after contract expiration, until the parties have negotiated to impasse respecting the proposed changes.[739] Thus, as a matter of law, not contract, the terms and conditions of employment established by the expired collective agreement remain binding on the parties until changed by agreement or the parties have bargained to impasse. However, in *Litton Financial Printing Division* v. *NLRB*, 501 US 190 (1991), the Supreme Court held that the grievance-arbitration process established by an expired collective agreement does not necessarily remain enforceable. The Court explained that the arbitration provision in a collective agreement presumptively is intended by the parties to provide the mechanism for resolving disputes concerning rights that accrued or vested prior to the termination of the agreement and any rights that the agreement expressly requires to continue after the contract's expiration. But, the Court ruled, the collective agreement's grievance-arbitration machinery presumptively is not intended to govern the resolution of those claims arising after the termination of the collective agreement unless the claim accrued prior to the agreement's expiration. In the *Litton* case the claimant asserted a right to be recalled from layoff based on seniority. The expired collective agreement recognized that right but the employer successfully argued to the Court that since the layoff and recall occurred after the agreement had expired, the seniority claim had not accrued or vested during the agreement and, therefore, the

738. *Nolde Bros.* v. *Bakery & Confectionery Workers*, 430 US 243 (1977).

739. *NLRB* v. *Katz*, 369 US 736 (1962); *New York Dist. Council No. 9, Painters* v. *NLRB*, 453 F.2d 783 (2d Cir. 1971), *cert.* denied 408 US 930 (1972); *Carey Salt Co.* v. *NLRB*, 736 F.3d 405, 430 (5th. Cir. 2013) (expired collective agreement's provision for seniority-based recall from layoff applies to those who return at the end of a work stoppage where there had not been bargaining to impasse respecting merit based recall to work).

employer was not required to resolve the dispute under the arbitration provision of the parties' expired collective agreement. The Court did not address the question of whether the refusal to recognize seniority after the contract had expired was itself an unfair labor practice. That contention could be made since the refusal to continue to recognize employee seniority in effect was a change in that term of employment and, as observed above, the duty to bargain in good has been held to require parties to maintain the *status quo* respecting terms and conditions of employment until they have bargained to impasse.[740] Nor did the Court discuss the right of the seniority claimant to sue in federal or state court to enforce the layoff recall claim.

The Court did note in *Litton* that the parties can by explicit provision in the collective agreement extend the grievance-arbitration dispute resolution mechanism to any grievance respecting rights of workers during the period between contracts.

C. *Reopener Clauses*

634. Even though a collective agreement is for a fixed duration, it is not unusual for the parties to include a 'reopener' provision that allows specified terms or conditions established by the agreement to be renegotiated during the life of the agreement. Such reopener provisions most often deal with the contractual wage rates, especially in agreements that are for a longer duration. The vast majority of such clauses designate a specific date or time period when the option to reopen the contract may be exercised.

II. Parties to the Collective Agreement

A. *Generally*

635. Section 8(d)'s definition of the duty to bargain includes the duty to execute written agreements when reached. Those charged with that responsibility are: (a) the certified representative, if a certification has been issued by the NLRB; (b) those specified in any recognition agreement entered into by management and a labor organization; or (c) those who have customarily represented the parties if there is no NLRB certification or a formal recognition agreement. The certification may include one or more employers and one or more unions. Often it includes the national labor organization and the local division that has responsibility for representing the union in day-to-day activities.

636. In most situations, a responsible corporate official signs on behalf of the employer[741] and one or more responsible local union officials sign on behalf of the

740. *See Carey Salt Co.* v. *NLRB*, in the previous footnote.

741. A non-government employer can be owned and operated as a proprietorship, a partnership, business trust, limited liability company, or a corporation. Most employers in the US are owned and operated as a corporation or limited liability company. The formation of ownership associations is regulated by state law. In all American jurisdictions a corporation is a legal entity whose equitable

labor organization. But complications can arise. When the employing enterprise is a subsidiary of a larger company, the union may want an officer of the parent organization to execute the agreement. Similarly, management may see some advantage in having an agreement executed by a representative of the national or international union as well as by a local union official. In some situations, such approval by the national or international officers may be required under the union's own constitution or bylaws. If the parties mutually agree, or if such additional parties are named in the certification or the recognition agreement, it is proper for representatives of parent or subsidiary groups to join in executing the agreement. But absent such recognition or certification, neither side can lawfully insist on execution by those who are not certified or recognized parties to the collective bargaining relationship.[742]

B. Change of Union

637. If a labor organization ceases to be the representative of a bargaining unit, under section 8(d) of the NLRA, the collective agreement no longer contractually controls the terms and conditions of employment whether or not the employees are represented by a new bargaining agent. However, if a successor labor organization has been elected or selected by a majority of bargaining unit employees as the new exclusive bargaining agent for the employees, the employer must bargain in good faith with that successor organization before making any changes in the terms and conditions of employment including those established by the defunct collective agreement.[743]

It is unclear whether a decertified union, a successor labor organization, or individual employees, can enforce rights that vested before the union lost its representational status. In theory, such enforcement should be permitted by a successor union selected by the employees inasmuch as the agreement ultimately represents the employees' collective undertaking with the employer and the new labor organization is the agent of that collective even if it was not the party that signed the contract.[744] Similarly, if there is no successor union, there is a clear basis for contending that the beneficiary of the vested contract rights should be entitled to

---

ownership resides in the shareholders. Civil liability for the corporation's conduct normally is limited to the entity's assets. There is only one form of corporate entity in American law, although for some regulatory and tax purposes distinctions are made between corporations whose shares are held by a relatively small number of persons and those whose equitable ownership is widely dispersed. A limited liability company is an amalgamation of a partnership and corporate entity in which liability generally is limited to its assets but the owners (which in some jurisdictions can be or include partnerships and corporations) have equal voting authority regardless of the amount invested. In some jurisdictions voting in limited liability companies can be based on the amount invested, and for some regulatory and tax purposes limited liability companies are treated in the same manner as corporations.

742. *NLRB* v. *Wooster Div. of Borg-Warner Corp.*, 356 US 342 (1958).

743. *American Seating*, 106 NLRB 250 (1953), cited with approval *NLRB* v. *Burns Int'l Security Services, Inc.*, 406 US 272 at n. 8 (1972).

744. *United States Gypsum Company* v. *United Steelworkers of America*, 384 F.2d 38 (5th Cir. 1967), *cert.* denied 389 US 1042 (1968). Accord, *UAW* v. *Telex Computer Prods., Inc.*, 389 F.2d 1042 (10th Cir. 1987).

enforce them just as an employee can directly enforce a collective agreement when the union breaches its duty of fair representation.[745]

638. Under the Railway Labor Act, a duly negotiated collective agreement continues in full force until modified pursuant to the major dispute negotiating procedures. This rule holds true even if there is a change in the employees' bargaining agent.[746] However, the Surface Transportation Board has authority to override obligations arising under collectively bargained agreements if it deems it necessary in approving a consolidation of railroads.[747]

C. Change in Enterprise Ownership

639. In the railway industry, change of ownership normally takes the form of a corporate merger or consolidation. Starting in 1940, a federal agency (now the Surface Transportation Board) has been required to ensure that employee job security, remuneration and other interests are protected before approving a railroad merger or consolidation. (49 US Code §11326) Until the early 1980s, based on its authority under this provision, affected rail carriers had to negotiate an agreement with the affected railroad unions respecting the impact of a merger or consolidation submitted for its approval.

From 1982 to 1994 the Interstate Commerce Commission (the agency then responsible for enforcement) adopted a policy of requiring such labor protective provisions only in extraordinary circumstances.[748] This policy of administrative neglect of the statutory directive conformed with the Reagan–Bush administrations' goal of reducing regulatory restraints on business. While that enforcement policy was in effect, there was not a single instance, out of the many hundreds of approved rail line ownership changes, in which the ICC found that there was an extraordinary circumstance requiring labor protective provisions.[749] ICC commissioners appointed by the Clinton administration announced that the determination of whether labor protective provisions were required would be done on a case by case basis.[750]

In 1995, Congress amended the law to explicitly require that 'the employees of the affected rail carrier will not be in a worse position related to their employment

745. *See Vaca* v. *Sipes*, 386 US 171 (1967).
746. Nat'l Med. Bd., *39th Ann. Report*, p. 30 (1973).
747. *Norfolk & Western Ry. Co.* v. *American Train Dispatchers' Ass'n*, 499 US 117 (1991). (The Board's functions at that time were performed by the Interstate Commerce Commission.)
748. W. Thoms and F. Dooley, 'Collective Bargaining Under the Railroad Labor Act', 20 *Transp.L.J.* 275 (1992); P. Dempsey and W. Mahoney, 'The US Short Line Railroad Phenomenon', 21 *Transp. L.J.* 383, 387–389 (1993).
749. In one case, court approval was given to a transfer arrangement that was structured as an abandonment of service followed by a sale of the line, without requiring the ICC to even go through the pretense of considering whether adequate provision was made for the interests of the workers who lost their jobs due to the transfer. *Simmons* v. *ICC*, 934 F.2d 363 (DC Cir. 1991).
750. 'Case-by-Case Approach to be Used in Future Section 10901 Applications', *Journal of Commerce*, 31 October 1994, p. 43; 'RailTex Job Plan Wins OK to Buy Central Vermont', *Journal of Commerce*, 19 December 1994, p. 34.

as a result of the transaction during the 4 years following the effective date of the final action of the [Surface Transportation Board]'.[751] However, an appellate court decision subsequently held that this protection is limited to 'incidents of employment, or fringe benefits … and does not include … seniority provisions' established by a collective agreement.[752] Moreover, as a result of earlier consolidation of the industry, there soon was little left to merge.[753]

Beginning in the early 1950s, the Civil Aeronautics Board imposed labor protective provisions (requirements that worker job security and benefits not be adversely affected) as a condition of approving airline mergers, consolidations and airline route transfers. This created pressure for collective bargaining concessions to resolve issues arising from the change. Moreover, if the transfer or sales agreement did not resolve these questions, the Board imposed labor protective terms.[754]

The Airline Reorganization Act of 1978 eliminated the Civil Aeronautics Board and transferred regulation of airline mergers, consolidations, and route transfers to the Department of Transportation. During the Reagan–Bush years, the Department followed the ICC policy of leaving the question of labor protective provisions in sales and transfer arrangements solely to the negotiating power of the employee representatives and opposed efforts to statutorily mandate the inclusion of labor protective provisions.[755]

In limited categories of business transfers federal law requires a successor to assume its predecessor's collective bargaining obligations and the obligations of the collective agreement, such as under the Urban Mass Transportation Act, where the work project receives federal financial assistance.[756] However, it has been held that that Act does not provide a private cause of action in support of such claims.[757] Thus, affected employees are dependent upon administrative discretion to enforce the requirement that successor owners assume existing collective agreements or the terms established thereunder.

A very different situation exists outside the transportation sector of the economy where regulatory agencies rarely exercise oversight respecting decisions to merge or consolidate enterprises. Even when such oversight exists, rarely is administrative consent conditioned on the existence of labor protective provisions in the merger or consolidation agreement.

The NLRA is silent respecting change of employer ownership. If the change takes the form of a change of ownership of the shares of a corporation's voting stock, the employing entity, the corporation, continues unaltered as a legal entity and, therefore, there is no impact on the employer's duty to recognize an incumbent union or abide by the previously negotiated collectively bargained agreement. However, if the change of stock ownership is accompanied by a merger or consolidation of the

751. *See generally*, *Norfolk & W. Ry.* v. *Brotherhood of R.R. Signalmen*, 164 F.3d 847 (4th Cir. 1998).
752. *United Transp. Union* v. *Surface Transp. Bd.*, 108 F.3d 1425 (DC Cir. 1997).
753. P. Dempsey, 'Transportation: A Legal History', 30 *Transp. L. J.* 235, 359–360 (2003).
754. *See*, S. Rosenfield, *Labor Protective Provisions in Airline Mergers* (1981).
755. 'Airlines, DOT Criticize Employee Protection Bill', *Aviation Daily*, 4 May 1992, p. 198; 'DOT Tentatively Gives PanAm Latin American Routes to United', *Aviation Daily*, 18 May 1992, p. 288.
756. See, for example, Urban Mass Transportation Act, 49 USC §5333(b) and Service Contract Act 41 USC §353(c).
757. *Jackson Transit Auth.* v. *Local Division 1285*, 457 US 15 (1982)

purchased corporation with one or more other corporations, the original legal entity does not survive and, as indicated in the paragraphs below, the effect is less certain and is partly dependent upon the rules of corporate securities law of the state which issued the corporate charters of the acquired and acquiring corporations.

If the change of ownership takes the form of a purchase of the selling enterprise's assets, separate rules established by the Supreme Court, as detailed below, govern: (1) whether the employer has a continuing duty to bargain with the labor organization that was recognized as the bargaining agent of the predecessor owner's work force, and (2) whether the collective agreement can be enforced against the new owner.

Both judicial rules and statutory legal principles in the US require the new owner of realty to accept the obligations and relationships established by leases, covenants, encumbrances (such as mortgages), and easements negotiated by predecessors. Similarly, judicial and statutory principles require purchasers of other forms of property to accept the obligations and relationships established by the predecessor's licenses and encumbrances (such as creditor security interests and conditional endorsements of negotiable paper), and sometimes obligations created by the predecessor's other contracts (*see*, for example, bulk sales laws). Nevertheless, the US Supreme Court has rejected that approach in dealing with changes of ownership as they affect the work force. The Court's principal explanation for its special approach to successorship obligations in the labor law area is that it is confident that in enacting federal labor legislation, Congress did not intend to unduly interfere with the flexibility of owners to alter where they invest their capital. (No legislative history is cited in support of that assumption.) The Court has reasoned that entrepreneurs might be deterred from making socially desirable investments if the purchases are by law accompanied by the prior owner's obligations to engage in collective bargaining or the terms and conditions of any unexpired collective agreements. The Court has not discussed the socially desirable investment the workers made in committing themselves to an enterprise in expectation of continued employment and contracted benefits.

640. Under the Supreme Court's interpretation of the rules imposed by the NLRA upon succession in ownership, the purchaser of enterprise assets has no obligation to retain the predecessor's workforce unless the buy-sell agreement expressly includes that obligation. If the successor employer fails to hire a significant portion of the work force, or if the successor employer makes substantial changes in the nature of the business operation, the Court has held that the representational status of the labor organization (and the employer's duty to bargain with it) terminates with the change of ownership and must be established anew with respect to the new owner unless the new owner agreed to recognize the union. This is true even if the collective agreement contains a provision asserting that it is binding upon successor owners. (In contrast, property law and the law of secured interests in the US generally requires the new owner to undertake such obligations unless it makes special arrangements with the beneficiaries of the obligations to be released from those encumbrances.) In the event of such a sale of the enterprise's assets, the union still has contractual remedies against the first owner including a right to damages for breach of the agreement to sell only to successor owners that continue the workforce and collective agreement.[758]

In contrast, if the ownership change is in the form of a purchase of corporate shares, the contracting entity has not changed. Therefore, the collective agreement remains enforceable against the enterprise even though it now has new owners.

If ownership change involves a corporate merger or consolidation with another company, not only has the enterprise structure been altered, often the equitable ownership has changed as well. (This is not true if the absorbed entity was already a wholly owned subsidiary or affiliate of the dominant entity.) Sometimes in such situations a collective agreement remains enforceable as a contractual obligation, even in the absence of a successor provision in the collective agreement against the surviving entity, if, as is generally true in the case of corporate mergers and consolidations, state law holds the surviving entity responsible for contractual obligations of its predecessor entities.[759]

Although the NLRA does not require the new owner to hire the previous owner's workforce, it is an unfair labor practice for an employer to refuse to hire members of the predecessor's work force if the new owner's motivation is to avoid having to recognize the union that represented the predecessor's employees. Thus, although the new owner can refuse to hire the former bargaining unit workers because it thinks that other job applicants are better qualified to do the work, it cannot reject the former employees because it expects them to support union representation. The NLRB remedies such discrimination by ordering the successor employer to hire those who otherwise would have been hired and pay them for lost wages based on the terms and conditions of their former employment.[760]

641. The NLRB's initial encounter with the problem of change of ownership arose in a case in which the assets of a business that had committed an unfair labor practice were sold before the unfair labor practice was remedied. At issue was whether the new owner could be required to remedy the unfair labor practice. The Board ruled that if the new owner was merely an alter ego of the old owner (that is, ownership had only nominally changed hands), the remedy could be enforced against the alter ego. In addition, the Board held that if at the time the enterprise assets were transferred the new owner had actual knowledge of the unfair labor practice, or if unfair labor practice charges had been filed with the NLRB against the prior owner, then the new owner is responsible for remedying the unfair labor practice so long as the new owner carries on the operation without substantial

758. *Howard Johnson Co., Inc.* v. *Detroit Local Joint Exec. Bd.*, 417 US 249 (1974). If it learns of the impending sale, the union also might have a right to enjoin the transfer. *Howard Johnson Co.* at 258 n. 3 (1974).

759. *John Wiley & Sons. Inc.* v. *Livingston*, 376 US 543 (1964).

760. *US Marine Corp.* v. *NLRB*, 944 F.2d 1305 (7th Cir. 1991), *cert.* denied 503 US 936 (1992). However, appellate courts are divided respecting whether the Board should impose the terms of the prior collective agreement only for a period allowing for a reasonable opportunity for collective bargaining. *Capital Cleaning Contractors, Inc.* v. *NLRB*, 147 F.3d 999, 1011 (DC Cir. 1998).

changes in the work force, supervisory personnel, or methods of operations. The Supreme Court affirmed the proposition that new owners of business assets have an obligation to remedy the unfair labor practices of the prior owner so long as there is substantial continuity in the way the business operates.[761]

When the question to be answered is whether the new owner of the enterprise's assets has an obligation to recognize and bargain with the union that represented the previous owner's workforce, the Board and the courts apply a more specific test of enterprise continuity. The basic rule regarding a new owner's duty is that the successor enterprise must bargain with the union that represented its predecessor's work force if at the point at which the labor organization demands recognition from the new owner: (a) the new owner has hired a 'substantial and representative complement' of its work force, (b) a majority of the successor's work force had been employed by the previous owner of the business assets, and (c) the business operations largely continue unchanged. The successor is deemed to have hired a substantial and representative complement of its work force when the job classifications for the operation have been substantially filled and normal operations have substantially begun. The fact that future expansion is planned does not defeat the finding that a substantial and representative complement of the work force has been hired. The business operations will be found to be continued largely unchanged if the enterprise is essentially performing the same type of production or service with a work force performing substantially the same jobs, under the same working conditions and supervisors, and for substantially the same customers. Minor changes in these aspects do not alter the result. Nor does the fact that the operation was closed for a number of months prior to the transition defeat the finding that the successor has a duty to bargain with the labor organization that represented the prior owner's work force.[762]

642. Once the successor has a duty to bargain with the labor organization that represented the prior owner's work force, it cannot make changes in the terms and conditions of employment without first bargaining to impasse with that union concerning such changes. The successor is not, however, bound by the collective agreement negotiated with the prior owner unless it chooses to be bound. Accordingly, the existing terms and conditions of employment, including those established by the collective agreement with the first employer, may continue in force under the new employer, but only until such time as the successor employer exhausts its duty to negotiate regarding any changes it wishes to make. When establishing the terms and conditions of work for its newly hired workers, the new owner may disregard the employment terms and conditions established by the collective agreement between

761. *Golden State Bottling Co.* v. *NLRB*, 414 US 168 (1973). This approach to successorship responsibilities for a predecessor's violations of federal law has been applied as well to the Fair Labor Standards Act, the Equal Employment Opportunity Act, the Mine Safety and Health Act, the Age Discrimination in Employment Act, and the Employee Retirement Income Security Act. *Steinbach* v. *Hubbard*, 51 F.3d 843 (9th Cir. 1995).

762. *Fall River Dyeing & Finishing Corp.* v. *NLRB*, 482 US 27 (1987).

the union and the prior owner until such time as it has hired or decided to hire a majority of its workers from its predecessor's work force.[763]

643. Unions, in anticipation of the problems posed by the sale of a business, sometimes obtain a provision making the collective agreement enforceable against successor owners or obtain one that requires the original employer to condition sale of the business upon the purchaser assuming the obligations of the collective agreement including its job security and union recognition provisions. Although there is some judicial precedent asserting that such successor provisions constitute an unlawful 'hot cargo' agreement,[764] the better reasoned view would appear to accept such provisions as enforceable.[765]

On occasion the contractual obligation to sell only to a buyer that will retain the work force and accept the collective agreement is enforced by means of an injunction issued to prevent the sale of business assets pending an arbitrator's determination of whether the sale would violate the successorship provision.[766] It has also taken the form of a damages award issued by an arbitrator charged with enforcing a collective agreement covering a bargaining unit that was sold to a buyer that did not, contrary to the agreement's successor provision, agree to accept the terms of that collective agreement.[767]

Local legislation requiring a successor employer to hire the prior owner's work force for at least a specified minimum period of time has been challenged as preempted by the NLRA. However, at least one federal appellate court has held that such legislation is lawful and not preempted by the Labor Act.[768]

644. Decisions respecting the impact of changes in business ownership upon collective agreements have generated considerable controversy.[769] One outgrowth is that legislative proposals have been offered to make collective agreements binding upon successor owners of businesses in all or in most situations. None has been adopted by Congress.

---

763. *NLRB* v. *Burns Int'l Security Services Inc.*, 406 US 272 (1972).

764. *NLRB* v. *Hotel & Restaurant Employees Local 531*, 623 F.2d 61 (9th Cir. 1980). *See generally*, G. Crandall, S. Starrett and D. Parker, 'Hiding Behind The Corporate Veil: Employer Abuse of The Corporate Form To Avoid Or Deny Workers' Collectively Bargained And Statutory Rights', 100 *W. Va. L. Rev.* 537 (1998).

765. *Lone Star Steel Co.* v. *NLRB*, 639 F.2d 545 (10th Cir. 1980), *cert.* denied 450 US 911 (1981). By 1995, the issue of the provision's legality was not even raised on appeal in *United Mine Workers of America* v. *Basin Cooperative Services*, 53 F.3d 222 (8th Cir. 1995), a case upholding damages award in a suit to enforce the restriction requiring a purchaser of the business assets to assume the collective agreement.

766. *Local Lodge No. 1266 IAMAW* v. *Panoramic Corp.*, 668 F.2d 276 (7th Cir. 1981).

767. *Zady Natey, Inc.* v. *United Food & Commercial Workers*, 995 F.2d 496 (4th Cir.), *cert.* denied 510 US 977 (1993).

768. *Washington Service Contractors Coalition* v. *District of Columbia*, 54 F.3d 811 (DC Cir. 1995), *cert.* denied 516 US 1145 (1996).

769. For example, *see*, H. Northrup and P. Misscimarra, *Government Protection of Employees Involved in Mergers and Acquisitions* (1989).

III. Union Security Agreements

A. Closed Shop, Union Shop, Agency Shop, Other Variations

645. The overwhelming majority of collective agreements contain a provision giving the union some degree of protection of its continued status as bargaining agent.

The strongest form of protection for a union's continued majority status is an agreement requiring persons to become union members prior to becoming employed. Such provisions, known as closed shop clauses, are illegal under sections 8(a)(3) and 8(f) of the NLRA. In the building and construction industry, NLRA §8(f) states that an employee must be given at least seven days on the job before his continuation in employment can be conditioned upon 'joining' the recognized employee bargaining representative. In all other industries covered by the NLRA, §8(a)(3) states that an employee cannot 'be required to join' the recognized employee bargaining representative until the expiration of 30 days on the job or 30 days after the execution of the current collective agreement, whichever is later. Such a requirement of post employment union membership is called a 'union shop'. A union shop provision in a collective agreement is legal under the National Labor Relations Act but as explained below, it cannot be enforced beyond the requirements of an agency shop provision.[770] Over two-thirds of collective agreements in the United States have been estimated to have a union shop clause.

646. An 'agency shop' provision is one that gives the worker the choice either of union membership or paying the union a fee equal to union dues in order to continue in employment after expiration of the statutory minimum waiting period described in the previous numbered paragraph. As a matter of law, although it is legal to have a union shop or agency shop provision in a collective agreement, they cannot be enforced beyond requiring the payment of a fee equal to that portion of union dues that is expended for collective representation as distinguished from expenditures for union organizing, political, charitable and social action activities. That is, a collective agreement can require a person to submit to the *pro-rata* financial obligations of union representation (the agency shop requirement) but cannot actually force the person to become or remain a union member or finance union activities that do not directly involve representing bargaining unit interests.[771]

If contracts with union shop or agency shop provisions are combined, the vast majority of collective agreements have such a provision.

647. A small percentage of collective agreements require current members to retain their union membership but do not require others to join. This is called a 'maintenance of membership' clause. Presumably such provisions cannot be

770. *Marquez* v. *Screen Actors Guild, Inc.*, 525 US 33 (1998).

771. *Marquez* v. *Screen Actors Guild, Inc.*, 525 US 33 (1998); *NLRB* v. *General Motors Corp.*, 373 US 734, 742 (1963). For more detailed discussion, *see* paragraphs 534–539, above. *Also*, K. Dau-Schmidt, 'Union Security Agreements Under the National Labor Relations Act', 27 *Harv. J. of Legis.* 51 (1990).

enforced beyond requiring current members to continue to pay agency fees subject to the limits described in the previous paragraph.

648. Section 19 of the NLRA, adopted in 1980, states that workers who belong to religious organizations that have conscientious objection to financially supporting a labor organization may elect to pay to a non religious tax exempt charity an amount equal to the agency fee required under a union security provision. One court has held that section 19 violates the constitutional principle of equal protection and unconstitutionally prefers some religious beliefs over others because it does not give this privilege to those having a religious objection to union support but who do not belong to a formal religious organization.[772] On the other hand, it has been held that the option of paying the union fee to a charity is a reasonable accommodation to employee religious practices required by the 1964 Civil Rights Act's protections against religious discrimination and that the Civil Rights Act's protections apply so long as the religious belief is bona fide regardless of whether the employee belongs to any formal religious organization.[773] Although it can be argued that section 19's constitutionality is saved by accommodating it to the Civil Rights Act, a companion federal statute, the soundness of that contention is questionable in light of the fact that the language of the NLRA provision is very precise as to who can exercise this privilege and it was added to the NLRA after the adoption of the 1964 Civil Rights Act. Hence, it would appear to modify the right created by the earlier Civil Rights Act.

649. In addition to the above discussed prohibition against closed shops and the statutory waiting periods before union and agency shop provisions can be enforced, three other restrictions reduce the ability of unions to extract from employers an arrangement to ensure that bargaining unit members will pay for the representation services.

First, under section 14(b) of the NLRA, all of the above discussed types of union membership or financial support provisions can be made unlawful by state law. Twenty-eight states have laws prohibiting, to a greater or lesser degree, union security provisions. In addition, two states allow union security provisions only if ratified by a favorable employee vote equal to three-fourths, in one state, and two thirds in the other. States laws adopted pursuant to 14(b) are popularly known as 'right-to-work' laws. Union leaders prefer to call them 'right-to-scab' laws[774] or 'right to work for less' laws. The labor movement continues to seek repeal of section 14(b) in order to make it possible to negotiate union security provisions anywhere in the United States.

---

772. *Wilson* v. *NLRB*, 920 F.2d 1282 (6th Cir. 1990), *cert.* denied 505 US 1218 (1992).
773. *Tooley* v. *Martin-Marietta Corp.*, 648 F.2d 1239 (9th Cir.), *cert.* denied 454 US 1098 (1981).
774. 'Scab' is a derogatory term for someone who replaces a worker who is on strike. According to a report prepared by AFL–CIO statisticians, employees in states without right-to-work laws in 1993 averaged 18 percent higher earnings than those in right-to-work states. In addition, workers in states without such laws had a 23 percent higher rate of health insurance coverage than those employed in right-to-work states and workers' compensation benefits generally were lower and injury rates higher in right-to-work states.

The second problem unions face respecting the adoption of collective agreement provisions requiring employees to financially support their bargaining representative is that NLRA section 9(e) states that the NLRB must hold an election to determine the will of the bargaining unit members if 30 percent of the employees file a petition seeking deauthorization of the parties' right to include union security provisions in the collective agreement. If a majority vote for deauthorization, any existing union security provision is nullified. In the fiscal year that ended September 30, 2017, the NLRB conducted 20 deauthorization polls in which a majority of workers favored deauthorization in 12 of the pollings.

The third restriction on union security provisions is that although the language of section 8(a)(3) of the NLRA literally permits union shop provisions, as is explained in paragraphs 534–539 and 624, above, the Supreme Court has held that in fact employees cannot be required to become union members but can only be required to share in paying for representational activities. This presents the question of whether a union breaches its duty of fair representation if it negotiates a collective agreement that contains a provision stating that, after the statutory waiting period, employees must become and remain union members – the type of language that section 8(a)(3) of the NLRA on its face appears to allow – even though judicial decisions do not permit union shop provisions to be enforced in that manner.

The Supreme Court addressed that issue in *Marquez* v. *Scen Actors Guild, Inc.*, 525 US 33 (1998), where it held that it is not an unfair labor practice for a union to negotiate a union security provision that tracks the statutory language and does not reveal that case decisions hold that employees need not become actual union members in order to retain their jobs. However, the Court also observed: 'If a union negotiates a union security clause, it must notify workers that they may satisfy the membership requirement by paying fees to support the union's representational activities, and it must enforce the clause in conformity with this notification': 525 US at 43.

When a collective agreement contains a union shop provision, the NLRB holds that the union's duty of fair representation requires that, prior to demanding dues payments, the labor organization notify employees that they have the right to be non members and that non members have the right to object to paying for union activities that are not germane to the union's duties as bargaining agent and to obtain a reduction in fees to the extent that they are used for such activities. The Board also requires the labor organization, as part of its duty of fair representation, to provide bargaining unit employees with a description of the procedure for registering their objection to participating in supporting particular expenditures being charged to non members and sufficient information about expenditures to enable them to decide intelligently whether to make such an objection.[775]

775. *Prod. Workers Union, Local 707* v. *NLRB*, 161 F.3d 1047 (7th Cir. 1998); *California Saw & Knife Works*, 320 NLRB 224 (1995), enforced *sub nom Machinists* v. *NLRB*, 133 F.3d 1012 (7th Cir. 1998), *cert.* denied *sub nom Strang* v. *NLRB*, 525 US 813 (1998).

B. Hiring Halls

650. Unions sometimes serve as employment agencies or 'hiring halls' that receive requests from employers to refer qualified workers to fill job vacancies. The NLRA has been interpreted as requiring that if an employer agrees to use the union hiring hall as a first source for filling vacancies, the hiring hall must be equally available to union and non-union members and job referrals must not be made based on whether the job seeker is a union member.[776] Nevertheless, as a practical matter, union members are more likely to be familiar with the location and mode of operation of a union hiring hall. Thus, the use of hiring halls tends to promote greater employment of union members. Most often this arrangement is found in the performing arts and related trades, printing, construction, and maritime industries.

C. Dues Check-off

651. Of additional aid to a union in maintaining its status as majority representative is a provision commonly found in collective agreements requiring the employer to deduct union dues periodically from the workers' pay and remit that money to the union. Section 302 of the LMRA requires that dues check-offs be confined to those employees who have, in a signed, written agreement, individually authorized the payroll deduction. Further, it requires that the employee have the right to rescind that authorization at least once every year and upon the termination of the collective agreement.

Dues check-off provisions are lawful even in right-to-work states. (*See* paragraph 649, above.)

Section 2 Fourth of the Railway Labor Act (45 US Code §152 Fourth) outlawed dues check-offs in the rail and air transportation industries. However, in 1951 Congress added paragraph Eleventh of the same section where it restored the authority of labor organizations and employers covered by that Act to adopt check-off arrangements (although the prohibition was not deleted from section 152 Fourth).

D. Public Sector Union Security Provisions

652. In public sector employment there has been some resistance to union security provisions based on the argument that the constitutional guaranty of freedom of association does not permit forcing someone to give financial support to a particular organization as a condition of government employment. At least in so far as the federal constitution is concerned, this objection was rejected by the Supreme Court in *Abood* v. *Detroit Board of Education*, 431 US 209 (1977). In that decision the Court

776. *Teamsters Local 357* v. *NLRB*, 365 US 667 (1961). If the employer is not contractually compelled to use the union hiring hall, the union can lawfully favor its members or be available only to them. *United Bro. of Carpenters and Joiners, Local 537*, 303 NLRB 419 (1991). The 1964 Civil Rights Act prohibits unions from discriminating based on race, religion, gender or national origin in making hiring hall referrals.

held that the encroachment upon associational freedom imposed by compelling a public employee either to join a union or pay a service fee not in excess of dues is justified by the state's interest in minimizing employee conflicts and gaining the stability of being able to negotiate a single contract with a common bargaining representative. However, the Court also held that an employee cannot be compelled to pay as a service fee any monies that will be used by the union for political activities or for ideological activities that are not germane to its role as collective bargaining representative. (For further discussion concerning restrictions on the portion of union dues that can be charged to non-members as a service fee, *see* paragraphs 534–539, above.)

653. Dues check-off by the US Postal Service on behalf of a certified exclusive bargaining agent (one that has demonstrated majority support) is mandatory under 39 US Code §1205; it is similarly mandatory under 5 US Code §7115 with respect to other federal employees. Under both provisions the check-off is permitted only if the employee has voluntarily authorized the deduction. Such dues deduction agreements once made cannot be revoked for a year so long as the employee has not been expelled from the union and continues to be covered by a collective agreement between the union and the employing agency. In the absence of an exclusive bargaining representative, 5 US Code §7115 entitles a union to negotiate a dues check-off provision (but no other provision) if it has the support of at least 10 percent of the federal agency's bargaining unit employees.

Although dues check-off provisions are common in state and local government employment, the Wisconsin Supreme Court ruled that a check-off provision cannot be limited to the majority representative but must be available, as well, to rival organizations.[777]

IV. Contractual Status of Probationary Workers

654. Collective agreements generally provide for some special treatment of newly hired workers in recognition of the need to train them for their jobs and give management a reasonable opportunity to evaluate their suitability for the work. A majority of collective agreements give management unbridled discretion to discharge probationary employees, except where dismissal is for union activity, and most contracts do not extend seniority privileges to these workers. Frequently, the probationary worker receives a separate, lower pay rate than regular employees. The probationary period is normally calculated in calendar days starting from the date of hire. Sometimes it is based upon a given number of days or hours worked. The most common probationary periods are 30, 60, and 90 days. However, the probationary period for teaching positions normally is for a number of years, most commonly up to seven years.

777. *Board of School Directors* v. *WERC*, 168 N.W.2d 92, 97–98 (1969). *See also*, *National Education Association* v. *Unified School District 259, Wichita*, 608 P.2d 1367 (KS 1980) (not violation of law or collective agreement for school district to voluntarily provide such deductions for members of rival organization).

V. Wages

A. Generally

655. Wages paid under collective agreements most often are negotiated and paid on an hourly basis. This system is in part encouraged by the overtime pay requirements of the Federal Fair Labor Standards Act (FLSA), 29 US Code §201 *et seq.*, which for most workers provides that a minimum 50 percent premium above the hourly wage rate be paid for hours worked in excess of a given number per week (40 hours in most situations).

Alternatively, productivity based wages in the form of piece work can be paid under the FLSA so long as workers earn at least the statutory minimum hourly rate and the statutory premium is paid for hours worked in excess of 40 hours a week. Accordingly, some collective agreements specify a schedule of piece work pay.

656. Negotiated wage schedules can fix a minimum rate, a uniform rate, or a rate range. Whether the wage schedule is stated as a minimum or as a uniform rate, the wage rates set forth in the collective agreement are most often the rates actually paid to the workers.

The rate which the individual worker is entitled to be paid normally varies depending on the job classification that is worked. Often, too, rates are greater for those who have longer periods of service at that job or with the employer (longevity increases).

B. Scheduled Wage Increases

657. Because most collective agreements are in effect for several years, the negotiated wage schedule typically provides for a series of periodic wage increases that become effective during the life of the contract. Most often, these specified increases are at yearly intervals.

C. Cost-of-living Increases

658. On a monthly basis, the Bureau of Labor Statistics calculates and publishes a series of consumer price indices (CPI) designed to reflect changes in the cost-of-living. Some collective agreements provide for periodic cost-of-living wage rate adjustments using an agreed formula based on changes in a CPI. Most of these agreements use as the determining index the Consumer Price Index for Urban Wage Earners and Clerical Workers (CPI-W).

In the early 1990s, government studies indicated that in about one out of four private sector collective agreements covering 1,000 or more employees, the contractual wage rate schedule was periodically adjusted during the life of the contract to reflect significant increases in the cost-of-living. This was down from about 40 percent having cost-of-living provisions in the late 1980s. Since that time the federal government no longer conducts periodic studies of such data but estimates that the wages of about 2 million workers covered by collective agreements are periodically adjusted based on CPI changes. (The CPI has a wider impact upon retirement benefits including those provided through Social Security and recipients of various welfare benefits for the impoverished.) Wages of local and state government workers often are regularly adjusted to reflect CPI increases.

Where they are used, cost-of-living adjustment provisions often provide for quarterly adjustments in manufacturing industries and for annual adjustments in other industries. A significant minority of such provisions impose a maximum increase measured in specific amounts or percentages and many make the adjustment only after there has been a minimum specified increase in the cost-of-living. Some provisions distribute increases in the form of increased financing of particular social benefits programs as well as wage increases. Others exclude cost-of-living increases from the base used to measure other benefits. Very few collective agreements for government workers have cost-of-living adjustment provisions.

D. Merit Increases

659. Some collective agreements permit management to give wage increases based upon performance. Union participation in such merit evaluation varies. Often the collective agreement specifies a review procedure and criteria to be weighed and allows the union an opportunity to protest the denial of such an increase.

E. Pay Differences Based on Working Conditions

660. Most collective agreements provide for a shift differential – a small hourly premium paid to those scheduled to work during less desirable hours. Differentials also are frequently paid for performing especially dirty or hazardous work.

F. Work Incentive Systems

661. American employers use a variety of production incentive programs that are tied-in with pay schedules. One approach is the piecework system under which the worker receives an hourly rate plus payment based upon the amount of work produced or the amount produced beyond a standard level of production. Incentive systems sometimes focus upon the productivity of a work group rather than on the individual worker. Some American employers use a company-wide profit sharing plan as a work incentive system.

Piece work standards normally are subject to modification when there are changes in product designs, work methods or the introduction of new equipment and tools. Contract provisions regarding work incentive programs usually describe the procedures for setting and modifying the standards for measuring entitlement to such incentives, and procedures for challenging such changes.

VI. Work Schedules and Premium Pay

A. *Work Hours and Schedules*

662. Collective agreements in the United States almost always define the normal daily and weekly hours of work. An important function of these definitions is to provide an indisputable method for determining whether an employee is entitled to contractual or legally required premium pay for overtime. A Bureau of National Affairs, Inc. survey of collective agreements found in the mid-1990s that almost all specified eight hours as the standard work day and 40 hours as the standard work week. Most often, provisions defining the work day and work week are accompanied by a disclaimer asserting that they do not constitute a guaranty of this much work per week.

663. The distinction between a part-time and full-time employee is sometimes contractually defined in terms of a maximum number of hours after which an employee is treated as full-time. The Bureau of Labor Statistics defines a part-time work week as fewer than 35 hours. Specific statutes sometimes have their own definition. For example the Plant Closing Act (WARN) defines part-time employee as someone working fewer than 20 hours a week (29 US Code §2101(a)(8)) while the Affordable Care Act defines part-time as someone working fewer than 30 hours a week (26 US Code §4980H(c)(4)).

664. Most collective agreements place some restraint upon management's ability to reschedule the work week. The most common restraint is that there be a specified minimum advance notice of the work schedule change. Some collective agreements specify the work schedules.

Constraints are often placed on management's right to require overtime work and contractual provisions frequently prescribe the method for distributing such work. A significant minority of collective agreements specify a minimum amount of advance notice in order to compel the employee to do overtime work and many agreements limit the amount of overtime work that can be required. Agreements frequently impose a system that attempts to ensure equal distribution of overtime opportunities and burdens. Such equalization normally is confined to the particular job classification. A substantial portion of collective agreements make overtime voluntary or make it voluntary except in emergencies.

Although the flexible work schedule is becoming less of a novelty in the United States, its use is largely confined to white collar workers. Collective agreements seldom reflect the use of flexible work schedules.

Some occupations are subject to statutory restrictions on the number of consecutive hours worked. Such restrictions prevail over any conflicting contractual provisions. Department of Transportation regulations (49 Code Fed. Reg. §395.3), for example, prohibit drivers of vehicles engaged in interstate transportation from driving without having had a 10 consecutive hour rest. Thereafter a driver may not drive for a 14-hour period. However, a driver may not drive more than a total of 11 hours during the 14-hour period. In addition, they are prohibited from being on duty more than 60 hours within a seven-day period nor more than 70 hours within an eight-day period. Similarly, by law, railroad workers involved in train operations must have at least 10 consecutive hours off duty during the prior 24 hours and not work more than 12 consecutive hours (49 US Code §21103). This law allows, in emergency situations, railroads to require employees to be on duty for up to 16 hours in a 24-hour period (49 US Code §21102). Railroad unions often complain that the long work hours in the industry are detrimental to safety.

B. *Work Shifts*

665. A 2004 Bureau of Labor Statistics study found that about two-thirds of all full-time wage and salary workers usually began work between 6:30 and 9:29 in the morning with the greatest number beginning work between 7:30 and 8:29 am. Over half usually left work between 3:30 and 6:29 pm with the greatest number leaving work between 4:30 and 5:29 pm. However, almost 15 percent of full-time wage and salary workers normally worked an alternative shift. Of all workers studied, 4.7 percent of the total normally worked an evening shift, 3.2 percent worked a night shift, 3.1 percent worked employer dictated irregular schedules, and 2.5 percent worked rotating shifts.

C. *Meal Periods*

666. State law often requires that an extended meal break from work of at least 30 minutes be provided during the course of a full work shift. Collective agreements, too, often specify that a meal period be scheduled. A 30-minute meal period is most common but some require as much as an hour. Only a minority of collective agreements provide for employees to be paid for a meal period occurring during normally scheduled work time. However, collective agreements often give the worker an allowance for a meal if the employee works a substantial period of daily overtime and often require the employer to pay overtime wages for the employee's time during that meal period.

Some collective agreements allow the employer to require that work continue through the meal period but normally such work must be compensated with premium pay.

D. *Rest Periods*

667. State law often provides for a minimal amount of rest time during the course of a work day. Collective agreements often contain specifications respecting the frequency, timing and duration of such 'breaks'. The duration normally is either 10 or 15 minutes. Some collective agreements also provide for paid personal wash-up or clothes changing times for employees. Normally it is a 5- or a 10-minute allowance.

E. Holidays and Other Leaves of Absence

668. In the US the term 'holiday' refers to time off from the regular work schedule due to a particular widely celebrated event as contrasted with 'vacation' which refers to time off from the regular work schedule that is unconnected with a widely celebrated event but is for the purpose of allowing the worker an additional personal respite. Some industries are closed by federal or state law on certain legal holidays. Normally these laws do not require employers to pay employees for the work missed due to the holiday. Almost all collective agreements and a high percentage of non union represented work places provide for paid holidays in addition to paid vacations.

A 2017 survey by the Bureau of Labor Statistics found that in the private sector 77 percent of all workers and 89 percent of union represented workers receive some paid holidays. Of these, employees without union representation on average received 9 paid annual holidays while those with union representation received an average of 8 such days. Only 4 percent of collective agreements provided for 14 or more paid annual holidays. According to the BLS, the average number of paid holidays for all private sector workers declined from 10 in 1993 to 8 in 2017.

A high percentage of government entities give employees 10 or 11 days of annual paid holidays.

669. Most collectively negotiated holidays correspond to legally recognized holidays such as Labor Day (the first Monday in September), Thanksgiving (the third Thursday in November), New Year's Day (1 January), Independence Day (4 July), Christmas Day (25 December) and Memorial Day (last Monday in May). The day after Thanksgiving is also commonly granted as a paid holiday in order to provide four consecutive days off. The day before New Year's Day and the day before Christmas are also frequently included to provide extended holidays. In addition, there is a trend both in the scheduling of national holidays, and in the shaping of holiday provisions in collective agreements, to tack paid holidays onto weekends (even though that practice adds to the motor vehicle mortality rates and to crowded transportation and resort conditions).

A 2012 survey by the Bureau of Labor Statistics found that in the private sector 37 percent of all workers and 57 percent of union represented workers were given a paid 'personal day'. A personal day gives an employee the right to take one or more paid days off from work on a day of special personal significance such as a wedding anniversary, the opening day of the hunting or fishing season, the day of a special baseball game, and the like. Some employers specify the extra day as being available only for the employee's birthday or a child's or spouse's birthday, or the employee's wedding anniversary.

670. The 2012 survey by the Bureau of Labor Statistics found that in the private sector 88 percent of union represented workers and 60 percent of non-union workers are entitled to take a specified amount of paid funeral leave or bereavement time off in situations in which a close relative has died.

By statute, employers in most states are required to give a few hours off from work on Election Day to permit the employee to vote. Some state laws require the employer to pay for that time. Collective agreements frequently require paid time off on Election Day even when such pay is not required by law.

State and federal laws require employers to give employees time off to serve on a jury or as a subpoenaed witness and normally the government provides a small amount of pay for that service. For example, federal jurors are paid $40 a day; $50 a day after serving 10 days on a trial. They also are reimbursed for reasonable transportation expenses and parking fees and receive a subsistence allowance covering their meals and lodging if they are required to stay overnight. According to the 2012 survey by the Bureau of Labor Statistics, in the private sector 67 percent of all workers and 90 percent of union represented workers receive paid time off from their employer for performing jury duty; often that pay is the difference between the worker's normal pay and what is received from the government for jury duty.

Federal law requires employers to release employees from work to perform military reserve service. The 2012 Bureau of Labor Statistics survey reported that 40 percent of all employees and 62 percent of union represented employees are paid by their employer for such leave. Typically, that pay is the difference between the pay received from the military and the employee's normal earnings for up to a specified number of days per year.

Employees disabled by extended illness or injury often are granted an unpaid leave of absence. However, employees receive workers' compensation insurance benefits during extended leaves resulting from work related injury or illness. Moreover, BLS data for a 2013 study found that 43 percent of full-time workers are covered by short-term disability compensation benefits (typically defined as up to one year) and about 41 percent are covered by long-term disability benefits under employer provided insurance. (Also see paragraphs 260, 262–264, above, for statutory requirements respecting leaves of absence.)

671. A substantial majority of collective agreements state that employees are entitled to an extended leave of absence to serve as a union official or attend union conventions. A majority of agreements covering larger bargaining units allow some paid time to be spent on work related union business such as safety inspections. Almost as prevalent are provisions allowing employees who are union officials to spend paid time investigating or processing grievances, including discussions with management seeking adjustment of a grievance. Section 8(a)(2) of the NLRA has been construed to exclude such provisions from the prohibition against employer assistance to labor organizations.

F. Vacations

672. In the US employers are not required by law to provide paid annual leave. Some enterprises shut down for a set vacation period once or twice a year during which time all workers receive the same amount of paid vacation. Most collective agreements, both in the private and in the public sectors, contain a graduated vacation benefit under which the employee is entitled to longer paid vacations as the employee increases his longevity with the employer. Seniority preference often is given in scheduling individual vacation days.

During 2017, 76 percent of all workers in the US received a paid vacation benefit. If only full-time workers are included, the percentage was 87 percent. A studying 2012 showed that of those private sector workers with 1 year of service who received paid vacation, 38 percent received between 5 and 9 paid vacation days per year and 35 percent received between 10 and 14 paid vacation days. On average, workers with 1 year of service received 10 days of paid vacation in 2012. In most establishments the amount of vacation increases with longevity. Thus, the mean number of paid vacation days was 14 days after 5 years of service, 17 days after 10 years of service, and 19 days after 20 years. Although the latest data does not separately show the duration of paid vacation benefits for union represented workers, earlier data showed that on average paid vacation for union workers was comparable to that non union workers for those with up to 5 years' longevity but after that was of greater duration. Union represented workers with 20 or more years of service averaged 22.2 paid vacation days a year.

673. Paid vacation for public employees outside of the education field most often reaches a maximum of less than 5 weeks, but some are given 6 weeks or even more. Teachers traditionally receive 8–12 weeks of summer vacation plus a winter and spring holiday of a week or longer. However, at the level of higher education, teachers often are expected to engage in scholarly activities during much of that time and those teaching in lower level schools often are expected or required to take courses or participate in teaching work shops during part of the vacation period.

674. In the 1980s, when unions still had considerable bargaining strength, a few major collective agreements, most notably in the primary metals production and fabrication industries, provided for extended paid vacation benefits every fourth or fifth year. Depending on the contract, the extension consisted of 2 to 13 weeks added to the regular paid vacation.

675. Because of the high mobility of the American work force, a large portion of workers retire without ever accumulating 20 years' service with any one employer and, therefore, never enjoy the longer paid vacation periods often granted to employees who have substantial longevity with the same employer. In addition, a shrinking portion of the work force is employed in heavy industries where collective agreements most often provide more generous paid vacation benefits.

676. A significant minority of the collective agreements prohibit the accumulation of vacation benefits from year to year. Many collective agreements that permit accumulation of vacation limit the total amount that may be accumulated.

677. Some collective agreements expressly permit vacations to be split over different times of the year; very few expressly prohibit it.

678. Some collective agreements prohibit employees from working during vacation. Others allow work during vacation shutdowns (a time when major equipment repairs, modifications or replacements often are scheduled) but many of those agreements specify that vacations will be rescheduled for those who do shutdown work.

Earlier surveys showed that a substantial majority of collective agreements expressly provide that those who work during vacation shutdowns are paid the vacation pay as well as be paid for the hours worked.

679. Collective agreements often require an employee to have worked a minimum amount of time during the previous year to qualify for full vacation benefits and adopt a variety of techniques for determining the amount of vacation pay. Although most calculate vacation pay based on straight time pay for the standard work week, a substantial minority calculate vacation pay based on the worker's average earnings for a defined 12-month period. The latter approach provides higher pay if substantial overtime was worked but lower vacation pay if there were layoffs, reduced hours, or frequent absences. Only a small minority of agreements grant extra pay for the vacation leave.

680. Collective agreements also vary respecting whether a vested right to vacation pay is granted an employee who quits, is terminated, or is laid off. Most agreements provide for a *pro rata* vesting based on the amount of time worked since the most recent vacation or since the beginning of the most recent defined vacation year. Many collective agreements provide that vacation pay, or a portion thereof, will be given if separation was due to the employee's death, retirement, or discharge for other than disciplinary cause, but will not be paid to those who leave of their own choice or who are discharged for just cause.[778]

G. Premium Pay

681. The Fair Labor Standards Act requires that a 50 percent premium be paid above the regular wage rate for work performed in excess of 40 hours per week. (There are a number of statutory exemptions from this requirement.) The 40 hour week is used as the standard for overtime pay in most collective agreements but some begin paying an overtime premium after 37 or 37½ hours. In a few industries that are not covered by the FLSA overtime law, collective agreements permit a slightly longer workweek before the hourly overtime premium must be paid. The FLSA itself permits flexibility from the weekly overtime pay requirement in some situations if that flexibility has been negotiated into an individual or collective agreement and there is a weekly pay guaranty that includes a specified number of hours at the overtime rate and the number of hours worked do not exceed specified statutory parameters (29 US Code §207(f)).

682. Almost all collective agreements require that a 50 percent hourly premium be paid for any work in excess of 8 hours a day and a few agreements call for such premium pay after 7 or 7.5 hours in a workday.

---

778. Unless a collective agreement provides otherwise, California law requires an employer to pay a terminated worker the *pro rata* share of any unused paid vacation. Cal. Lab. Code §227.3. *Boothby* v. *Atlas Mech., Inc.*, 6 Cal. App. 4th 1595 (1992).

683. Premium pay is required by most collective agreements for work performed on the weekend or outside of the employee's normally scheduled workweek. If employees are normally scheduled to work on the weekend, the premium pay entitlement typically is based upon working on the sixth or seventh day of the workweek. The premium rate for Saturday, or the sixth day, generally is fixed at a 50 percent addition to the regular pay rate, whereas the pay rate for Sunday, or for a seventh day of work, is generally set at double the normal rate of pay.

684. Many agreements also try to deal with the conflicts surrounding the distribution of work paid at premium rates. Longevity with the employer, in the department or in the job classification, is often given some weight in resolving such matters. Most often contracts provide for equal distribution of such work on a rotating basis, sometimes with a limited right of refusal. Frequently, the most senior employees have the first option to volunteer for such work and the most junior have the burden of being drafted for such work if volunteers are not forthcoming or equalization of the burden is not mandated.

685. A substantial majority of collective agreements prohibit what is called pyramiding of premium pay. Pyramiding is the payment of all premiums that are literally applicable to the work. Under such a prohibition, a worker who works 10 hours on a seventh day would receive pay at double his normal rate (the rate normally paid for seventh day work) but would not receive an added 50 percent for the two hours beyond the first eight hours worked on that day even though the agreement specifies a 50 percent premium for hours worked in excess of eight per day.

VII. Insurance and Pension Benefits

A. Life, Accident and Health Insurance

686. Government mandated unemployment compensation, statutory disability protection programs, and old age benefits programs generally provide but a bare survival level of benefits or only a little better than that. The individual is expected to use his own financial resources to supplement these protections through savings, private insurance schemes or supplementary benefits from his employer. Collective bargaining agreements generally have been responsive to the need for supplemental protection. The 2010 Affordable Care Act, imposed a high tax on so-called Cadillac insurance plans – plans with monthly premiums in excess of $10,800 for individuals and $29,500 for families. (The threshold premium amount is to be adjusted based on changes in the Consumer Price Index.) Such plans typically are found in executive compensation packages and in some collective agreements for higher wage employees and provide not only comprehensive full coverage but also for luxuries such as private hospital rooms. It is contended that such very generous benefits have contributed to the extreme high cost of health care in the US by encouraging expensive practices that do not achieve better medical results. Political pressure from labor organizations and employers have resulted in special legislation that has delayed imposing the tax prior to 2020.

687. Eighty-three percent of union represented employees in the private sector and 53 percent of non-represented employees had employer sponsored life insurance according to a Bureau of Labor Statistics 2017 survey. The survey showed that only a very small percentage of plans require an employee premium contribution. A 2012 study showed that the available life insurance benefit was a fixed multiple of earnings for 38 percent of union represented workers and for 54 percent of non-represented workers and a flat dollar benefit amount was payable for 53 percent of the plans for union represented workers and 33 percent of those for non union represented workers. In 2012 flat dollar benefit plans for union and non-union represented workers most often had a maximum benefit of $50,000.

Short-term disability insurance is provided for 47 percent of employees covered by collective agreements and 37 percent of such workers receive long-term disability insurance. (*See also*, paragraph 670, above, respecting disability insurance.)

688. Most American workers depend on private health insurance to pay the major costs for medical care and prescription drugs. Typically, to discourage unnecessary use, beneficiaries must co-pay a small amount of each fee and the benefit does not begin until a modest threshold amount has been paid by the beneficiary to service providers during an annual benefit period. Additionally, workers often are required to pay part of the insurance premium. A Bureau of Labor Statistics survey for March 2017 found that 85 percent of the union represented civilian workers and 53 percent of the non-represented civilian workforce had some form of employer sponsored group medical insurance. These figures can be misleading inasmuch as some workers decline to participate in their employer's healthcare plan because they are covered by a spouse's less expensive or more comprehensive family plan.

The Affordable Care Act (42 US Code §18001 *et seq.*) requires most legal residents in the US to have some form of health care insurance. Older persons have part of their coverage through a the national Medicare insurance system, impoverished persons have health insurance coverage through the national and state operated Medicaid insurance system, some persons have coverage through the national health care insurance system for military veterans, and the rest must obtain insurance through private insurers. The federal law sets minimum standards for the types of care that must be provided by insurance, provides substantial premium subsidies for low income persons, entitles parents to continue to include their children under a family insurance plan until they reach age 25, and makes unlawful any limits on the maximum amount an insurer will pay for an illness or over the course of an insured's lifetime.

B. Negotiated Retirement Benefits

689. Most collective agreements contain a program of employer contributions to a funded retirement benefit. There are two types of plans, those with a defined benefit and those with a defined contribution. (See paragraph 269, above.)

The LMRDA section 302 (c)(5) (29 US Code §186(c)(5)) requires retirement and similar funds established pursuant to a collectively bargained agreement to be controlled by trustees appointed in equal numbers by the management and union representatives. Decisional deadlocks are resolved by an impartial third party jointly selected by those trustees or, if they cannot agree on a third party, one is appointed by a federal district court.

In 1981 the AFL–CIO initiated a special program to press efforts to increase union participation in retirement fund management including shaping the investment policies of those controlling the vast sums held by such retirement trusts. (For further discussion, see paragraph 273, above.)

According to the Bureau of Labor Statistics' 2017 survey, 72 percent of union represented employees in the civilian work force participated in an employer sponsored defined benefit retirement plan as compared with 15 percent of unrepresented civilian workers. About 30 percent of represented workers and 42 percent of unrepresented workers participated in a defined contribution plan. (Some collective agreements provide a defined benefit plan and an optional defined contribution plan.) Defined benefit plans were the norm until the last decade of the 20th Century. Overall, however, defined contribution plans are now more common with about 40 percent of all workers participating in a defined contribution plan and 23 percent participating in a defined benefit plan. In 2017 over two-thirds of all defined contribution plans required at least some employee contribution and over 80 percent allowed the employee to also make an optional contribution to the plan.

690. Age 65 is the most common retirement age used in pension plans provided by collective agreements. However, the Age Discrimination in Employment Act of 1978, as amended, prohibits most workers from being compelled to retire based on their age. (See paragraphs 346–351, above.)

Negotiated pension plans often permit early retirement at a reduced benefit level. Sometimes such early retirement rights are conditioned upon a showing of disability or unemployment.

691. A significant minority of collectively bargained retirement benefits plans for non government employees are multi-employer programs. That is, the employees of two or more enterprises are covered by a single plan. This approach is prevalent, for example, in the construction and trucking industries where an advantage for employees who are covered by multi-employer plans is that if workers change jobs and the new employer is covered by the plan, they can continue all of their pension benefits intact, a feature referred to as pension portability.

692. Collective agreements give employees a vested interest in defined benefit pensions after a period of time. (See paragraph 270, above.) When the benefit becomes vested, the employee's right to draw the pension is not affected by termination of employment prior to retirement. The employee can either withdraw the value of his vested interest from the fund, or can draw benefits from the former employer's fund upon retirement.

693. The absence of a negotiated retirement program in a collective agreement does not necessarily mean that the employees are without such a benefit. Railroad workers have a statutorily mandated retirement program (see 45 US Code starting at §231a) and the Social Security Act provides a safety net retirement insurance system for most other workers and their spouses. In addition, government employees normally have supplemental retirement insurance benefits based on a special state or federal statutory scheme and non government workers sometimes are covered by retirement benefits programs adopted by their employer outside the scope of their collective agreement.

The Employee Retirement Income Security Act of 1974 (ERISA) regulates non-government retirement plans that are employer financed in whole or part and which are not established under a collective agreement. This Act introduced a minimum statutory requirement of vesting pension benefits on a graduated basis as the worker accumulates longevity with the employer. Prior to the adoption of the Act, the vesting of worker benefits in pension plans often was deferred for such a long period that, due to the high degree of worker mobility in the US, for many workers the benefits were illusory. That is, a high percentage of workers never remained with an employer long enough to qualify for plan benefits. (See paragraphs 269–270, above, for a description of ERISA's minimum vesting requirements.)

Under certain circumstances, as an incentive to save money for retirement, federal income tax laws shelter from income taxes the investment income earned on funds held in an individually established retirement plan. In addition, depending on the type of plan, income taxes either are not assessed on the earned income originally deposited in the retirement account or are not assessed on the benefits paid out upon retirement. (See, for example, 26 US Code §§401, 408, 501.)

VIII. Job Security

A. Restraints upon Disciplinary Action

694. An almost universal provision in American collective agreements is the assurance that, after completion of the probationary period, disciplinary action will not be unfairly imposed. The most common way of expressing this is to include in the collective agreement a provision that prohibits discharge or other disciplinary action except when there is 'good cause', 'proper cause', 'sufficient cause' or 'just cause'. (The terms are used interchangeably.) Most collective agreements rely on the expression of this general standard but many add specific illustrations or enumerations of various forms of conduct that constitute 'just cause' for disciplinary action. Typically, such enumerations include: violation of the collective agreement's prohibition against work stoppages or picketing; failure to return to work after a leave of absence; excessive absenteeism or tardiness; and violation of reasonable company rules against violence, theft, dishonesty, insubordination, possession of illegal substances at work, or working under the influence of a regulated substance.

695. Disciplinary procedures vary. Some agreements require prior oral or written warnings against the misconduct, or both. Usually, various types of blatantly improper actions are excluded from the warning requirement. Many contracts require the employer to discuss the intended disciplinary matter with the employee and a union representative prior to making a final disciplinary decision.

An appeal from the disciplinary action normally is processed as a grievance that is reviewed through several steps involving discussion and settlement attempts by increasingly higher levels of management and union representatives. (*See* paragraphs 718-722, below.)

696. Some collective agreements establish a system of progressive or graduated disciplinary action. Under this system, except for the most serious types of worker misconduct, less severe disciplinary sanctions (such as oral or written warnings or reprimands) are imposed for the worker's initial infractions. However, the severity of the penalty, including short periods of suspension from work without pay, increases with each additional infraction. Generally, if the employee makes it through a specified prolonged period without any additional infractions (usually one or two years), the record of those infractions is removed and any later infraction will again be punished by the least severe penalty in the disciplinary schedule. For example, the first infraction may result in an oral reprimand plus a notation of that reprimand in the employee's work record (usually with notification being given to the union as well). The next infraction might be punished by a written warning plus a copy of that warning being placed in the employee's work record. After that an infraction might be punished by a two-day suspension without pay; the next, by a one-week suspension without pay; and the next, by termination of employment.

B. Seniority

697. In American labor relations, a person's longevity in a job (generally referred to as 'seniority') often brings specified benefits and privileges. For example, wage rates frequently are graduated based upon longevity in that wage classification. In part, this may be justified as a reflection of the efficiency gains from increased skill or knowledge that comes with experience in performing a task. But the degree of increase and the period over which these increases are spread often bear no concrete relationship to productivity improvements that come with experience. Longevity benefits can also be justified as an acknowledgment of the employee's 'investment' in the employing enterprise – an inducement to not seek employment elsewhere.

698. Collective agreements measure longevity in a variety of ways. In some industries where employees are highly mobile and collective agreements tend to involve a number of different employers, longevity or seniority is measured by the amount of time the worker has been employed in that industry, or more commonly, by the time employed at that job skill in the industry. In such situations, the parties tend to rely on the union to maintain records verifying claims to seniority status. More often, longevity is measured by the amount of time the employee has been continuously employed by the enterprise, or in the particular division, plant, office, or store, or in the particular department, or in the particular job classification. Seniority distinctions can also be based upon the employee's assigned work shift.

By law, within statutorily specified parameters, breaks in continuity of work due to military service or a family or medical leave of absence, cannot be counted against the employee, and collective agreements normally allow seniority to be counted for up to specified periods during leaves of absence for maternity leave, sick leave, military leave, and leaves to perform union related responsibilities.

699. Many collective agreements measure seniority by longevity in one status for one purpose, and by longevity in another status for other purposes. For example, a worker's wage rate within a pay scale that is graduated to reflect seniority may look to the amount of time the worker has been employed in the particular job classification. On the other hand, under the same collective agreement the duration of a worker's vacation benefit may be based upon longevity with the enterprise regardless of the fact that the worker accrued some of that longevity while employed in some other job classification.

700. Most collective agreements provide some special benefits or protections, such as promotion opportunities based on an employee's seniority; that is, the worker's continuous service in the enterprise, plant, department, job classification, or other work status.

Short term temporary and probationary employees usually do not have recognized seniority status. The probationary period prior to which an employee can assert seniority rights most often is 60 or 90 days. Collective agreements covering professional or highly skilled workers (for example, teachers) often establish a much longer period of probation.

701. Special seniority, generally called 'superseniority', is often given to union officials, including shop stewards. Those with superseniority are placed at the top of the seniority list regardless of their actual employment longevity. Because such superseniority rewards union activity it is unlawful discrimination under the NLRA unless it is justified by the union and employer's mutual administrative needs. Thus, such special seniority provisions are presumptively valid only with respect to layoffs from and recalls to work and only to the extent that the union official has regular responsibility for handling grievance resolution so that his or her continued presence in the work place materially facilitates enforcing the collective agreement. Superseniority can lawfully extend to such decisions as job or shift transfers to the extent that giving the union official that preference is the only way to preserve the official's ability to provide continuity of representation respecting day-to-day contract administration.

Superseniority, however, cannot be used merely to enable the union's shop floor representative to retain his or her most favorable job position. Thus, in one case, because he could have remained on the shift by taking a lower paid position in the work group to which he currently was assigned, a shop steward was denied the right to use his superseniority to transfer to another work group in order to maintain his pay level as well as remain on the shift he represented.[779]

---

779. *NLRB* v. *Joy Technologies, Inc.*, 990 F.2d 104 (3d Cir. 1993).

702. Seniority rights most often include the privilege of 'bumping' a less senior person from another job in the event of layoff. Bumping rights are based on a broader measure of seniority, such as the department or plant, and are conditioned upon the more senior person being qualified to perform the job of the person being bumped. For example, due to a reduction in operations, a plant may eliminate the use of one of several cranes. Typically, the least senior crane operator will be laid off. When notified of this layoff, if that person has bumping rights based, for example, on departmental seniority, that junior crane operator will look to the next highest paying job in the department that he can perform at which someone with less departmental seniority is employed. That job might, for example, be as a crane operator's helper. The bumped crane operator's helper is then notified of his layoff and will, in turn, look for someone with less departmental seniority in a position that he is qualified to fill. As can be seen, if a collective agreement recognizes seniority and bumping rights, a layoff can start a chain reaction resulting in considerable shifting of job assignments before it is determined which employee is actually left without work.

703. Some collective agreements provide for work-sharing in order to reduce the frequency of resort to layoffs in the event of a reduction of available work. Work-sharing requires a reduction of weekly work hours for designated groups of employees prior to resorting to layoff. In many agreements, certain categories of workers are not protected by these requirements and often the union must be consulted before work-sharing is implemented.

One limit upon the practical effect of work-sharing is the level of insurance benefits provided for those who are unemployed. If the state's unemployment insurance law does not permit benefits to be drawn by employees working a reduced schedule (something that varies from state to state), at a particular level of work reduction due to work sharing the individual worker may be better off financially if laid off and then collect unemployment insurance benefits rather than remain employed at a reduced work schedule. This is less likely to be true for higher paid workers since unemployment benefits typically are one half of normal wages up to a maximum based on the average wage level in the state. Thus, the income from even one or two days of work for a higher paid worker may exceed the maximum that can be collected from unemployment insurance.

704. A high percentage of collective agreements make some provision respecting the standards and procedure for employee promotions to higher classifications and for transfers to more desirable work situations. A common employee benefit is the requirement that job vacancies be filled from applicants who are already part of the enterprise work force before giving consideration to applicants from outside that work force. Another common protection mandates that notice of promotion or transfer opportunities be prominently posted to allow potentially interested employees to learn about and apply for the position before decisions are made regarding those opportunities.

705. Some collective agreements specify seniority as the controlling or primary factor to consider in making promotions and transfers, and in most other agreements it is a factor that management must take into account in making such decisions. A significant portion of collective agreements make seniority the controlling factor in promotion so long as the employee meets minimum standards of qualification, or minimum standards of performance on the new job during a trial period. In still other agreements, seniority is made the controlling factor if all other criteria are satisfied to an equal degree. Among the competing factors often stated by the collective agreement as properly guiding promotion and transfer decisions are: skill and ability, physical fitness, education, training, and test or examination scores.

Many collective agreements also require management to consider seniority in making promotions to supervisory positions.

A substantial portion of collective agreements state that seniority is the sole or primary factor in deciding who to retain in case of layoff and in deciding who should be recalled from layoff. However, a minority of agreements specify that longevity is to control only if ability and fitness are equal.

Shift transfers based solely on seniority also are common.

706. As a practical matter, seniority probably plays a more important role in promotion and transfer decisions than is indicated by the percentage of collective agreements requiring that it be given substantial weight. So long as seniority is designated as a factor to be considered in any degree, it is likely that a promotion or transfer awarded to a less senior employee will be challenged through the grievance process. Administrative convenience, therefore, weighs heavily toward making the decision in favor of the most senior worker unless that person's competence for the new position is in serious doubt and unless a clear case can be presented in favor of the less senior applicant.

C. Transfer of Operations, Training and Retraining

707. Annually, thousands of US enterprises are discontinued either due to financial failure or a transfer of ownership and thousands of other new enterprises are started. The location of on-going enterprises that are good targets for partial or total acquisition or merger has become an important business activity in the US. Such changes can disrupt the workforce and its collective bargaining relationship. Technological dislocation also poses serious problems for the local work force as can the impact of cyclical fluctuations in economic activity. Nevertheless, the Supreme Court has rejected the right of labor organizations to participate in making many such decisions. The Court's position is based upon its proclamation that in adopting the NLRA and its amendments, Congress did not intend to force employers to share purely entrepreneurial decisions with collective bargaining representatives.[780]

However, when an employer desired to terminate an operation by substituting contracted workers employed by another entity to do the same work that had been performed by bargaining unit workers and under the same conditions, the Supreme

780. *Textile Workers Union* v. *Darlington Mfg. Co.*, 380 US 263 (1965).

Court ruled that the employer had to bargain to impasse with its workforce's collective bargaining agent before reaching a final decision to make that change.[781] Nevertheless, in *First National Maintenance Corp.* v. *NLRB*, 452 US 666 (1981), the Supreme Court ruled that an employer has no duty to bargain concerning a decision to terminate all or part of an operation, so long as the decision is motivated purely for economic reasons. However, it held that the employer does have a duty to bargain regarding the impact of the decision upon the work force. In reaching this result the Court stated that the employer need not notify the labor organization of its decision to terminate the operation until after the decision has been made. On the other hand, the Court also stated that bargaining over the effects of the decision must be conducted at a meaningful time and in a meaningful manner. This latter observation may in many situations require that the union in fact be notified about the intended termination decision before it has become final. The Court expressly did not reach the question of whether the same rule applies to decisions to transfer the employer's operations from one location to another.

The NLRB addressed the issue respecting the employer's duty to bargain concerning transfers of operations from one location to another in the *Dubuque Packing* case.[782] There, the Board, with the approval of an appellate court, held that if the relocation of work is not accompanied by a basic change in the enterprise's operations, the employer must offer to bargain with the union about the change before the work transfer decision is made unless: (a) the transferred work will be performed in a substantially different manner at the new location; (b) the transferred work is part of a substantial change in the scope and direction of the enterprise; (c) labor costs were not a factor in making the decision to transfer the work; or (d) although labor costs were a factor in the decision, the union could not have offered cost concessions that would have been adequate to alter the decision.

Underlying the Board's *Dubuque Packing* criteria is the assumption that decisions to alter the nature of enterprise operations are outside a union's right to participate in decision making through collective bargaining. The Board's criteria regarding when the labor organization has a right to prior consultation also assumes that the right to participate in decision making through collective bargaining is limited to matters involving labor costs that can be adequately altered through amending the collective agreement. The fact that such decisions often affect whether the employee will have continued employment is not sufficient for the Board to include a transfer determination within the scope of mandatory collective bargaining. At

---

781. *Fibreboard Paper Products Corp.* v. *NLRB*, 379 US 203 (1964). An appellate court has ruled that the duty to bargain concerning decisions to contract out bargaining unit work applies only if the employer's contracting-out motivation involves factors that could be altered through collective bargaining. *Furniture Renters of America* v. *NLRB*, 36 F.3d 1240 (3d Cir. 1994). *See also*, *Regal Cinemas, Inc.* v. *NLRB*, 317 F.3d 300 (D.C. Cir. 2001)(management must bargain with the union before transferring bargaining unit work to non-members of the bargaining unit such as managers).

782. *United Food & Commercial Workers, Local 150-A* v. *NLRB*, 1 F.3d 24 (DC Cir. 1993), *cert.* dismissed 511 US 1138 (1994), affirming *Dubuque Packing Co.*, 303 NLRB 386 (1991); accord, *NLRB* v. *Solutia, Inc.*, 699 F.3d 50 (1st. Cir. 2012)(employer must bargain before consolidating the work of two separately represented laboratories at different nearby locations and transferring the work of one group to other's site); contra, *Dorsey Trailers, Inc.* v. *NLRB*, 233 F.3d 831 (4th Cir. 2000) (holding that decisions concerning where to locate business operations are not subject to the duty to bargain).

least partially ameliorating the impact of these limitations upon the union's right to bargain concerning decisions to transfer operations is the presumed duty of the employer, under the *First National Maintenance Corp.* decision, to negotiate at a meaningful time concerning the impact the decision will have on bargaining unit employees.

708. Under the federal WARN Act, or plant closing act (29 US Code §§2101–2109), adopted in 1988, an employer, prior to termination or long term lay-off of a significant number of employees, must give 60 days' notice or a form of severance pay if notice is not given. The Act expressly states that its remedies are in addition to, and not in lieu or alteration of, contractual or statutory remedies, except that the 60 day notice period runs concurrently with any notification period required by statute or contract. (The Act is discussed more detail at paragraph 155, above.) In many situations, an employer's efforts to comply with the WARN Act, plus its NLRA duty to bargain with respect to the impact a change will have on bargaining unit employees, as a practical matter provides the labor organization with an opportunity to participate in shaping the underlying decision regardless of whether it falls within the scope of the Board and Court's standards concerning when the employer must bargain about a proposed operational change. In the course of such bargaining, the parties may agree that the employer can go forward with its plans conditioned upon severance pay arrangements, job placement assistance, job transfer opportunities, and other special benefits for the displaced employees even though those benefits were not provided in the original collective agreement. As a practical matter, once the workers learn of the impending change, such benefits may be necessary to induce them to remain and cooperate with the work activities involved in the transition with its ultimate loss of their jobs.

709. Apprenticeship programs are often encountered in the skilled trades and may be regulated by collective agreements. Enrollment in, or completion of, such a program is frequently made a condition of employment for particular job categories. Normally, a specified limited number of apprentices can be employed in the establishment or the number is limited based on a ratio to those workers who are graduates of such a program (journeymen or masters). Generally, the administration of an apprenticeship program is entrusted to a joint union-management committee. (Deadlocks among the trustees are resolved in accordance with the dispute resolution mechanism established by section 302(c) of the LMRA.) The apprentice is required to spend a certain amount of time in on-the-job training and to take a specified amount of classroom instruction. Many collective agreements require the employer to pay apprentices for time spent in classroom instruction whether or not that part of the program is administered during regular work hours.

The Department of Labor establishes standards for certifying apprenticeship programs. Certification is important to the employer in order to exempt certain training time from minimum wage and overtime pay requirements.

A significant number of collective agreements make provision for non-apprenticeship employee training. These programs fall into two categories: (a) those designed to upgrade or maintain current employee skills, and (b) those designed to replace obsolete employee skills or develop new skills. Three international unions, the Steelworkers, the Auto Workers, and the International Brotherhood of Electrical Workers, have been especially active in negotiating provisions for employee training and retraining programs. Such provisions are more likely to be found in agreements with large employers. Most of these programs involve on-the-job training, either by itself or in conjunction with other training and retraining techniques. Some involve employer conducted classroom instruction, others provide for the employer to pay all or part of the tuition for job-related classroom instruction offered by an outside institution.

IX. Paid Sick Leave

710. The Bureau of Labor Statistics estimates that in 2016 paid sick leave was available to 86 percent of union represented and 65 of unrepresented civilian workers. Normally, a specified number of days is allocated per year and up to a certain number can be accumulated from year to year. A BLS survey in 2009 found that private sector workers who had a paid sick leave benefit were allowed on average 8 annual paid sick leave days after their first year of service. The annual average allowed for government workers was 11 days.

711. In the private sector, some collective agreements provide employees with some form of sickness and accident insurance benefit in lieu of paid sick leave earnings. Such benefits generally pay less than the full amount of lost earnings and normally are not paid until and unless the employee is out of work for at least a minimum number of days.

Private sector collective agreements often determine the number of available sick leave days whether paid or unpaid based on the number of weeks or months or years worked. Generally, absences in excess of the allowed number of sick leave days are treated as an attendance infraction and can become the basis for disciplinary action.

Some agreements provide for employees to receive an annual bonus for unused sick leave. Often, unused sick leave is paid upon separation from employment for other than disciplinary reasons.

X. Working Conditions and Safety

712. Surveys indicate that most collective agreements contain language relating to the safety and health conditions of the work environment, but most often these are general statements of employer responsibility. Nevertheless, some agreements specify various types of safety measures or equipment to be used and the majority require the employer to provide or pay for all personal safety equipment such as eye shields and safety boots. Only a small percentage specify that a medical professional be present at the facility.

Physical examinations of workers are mandated by some collective agreements but most do not specify anything other than a periodic checkup. Many also require a medical check-up of employees at the time of hire or recall from layoff.

Some agreements give the union a specific role in investigating accidents or employee complaints regarding unsafe working conditions including establishing joint union-management safety and health committees. A small portion of agreements give employees a right to refuse to perform work they believe unsafe. A significant minority require the employer to identify harmful substances to which workers are exposed.

713. Some collective agreements deal with those aspects of working conditions that might be described as the amenities of the work environment. Included are such items as provision for clean and adequate toilet and cleanup facilities, the right of each employee to a clean and secure locker, adequate drinking fountains, the availability of soft drink vending machines, and comfortable facilities for taking meals and rest breaks. Some collective agreements give employees a right to purchase a limited quantity of the employer's product or merchandise at a discount. And, a few collective agreements still require the employer to provide a pint of beer for each employee at break time – a long standing but disappearing tradition in a few construction industry trades in some parts of the country and in the brewing industry.

XI. Strikes and Lock-outs – Peace Clauses

714. Most collective agreements in the United States contain a provision renouncing work stoppages and related economic pressure activities during the life of the agreement. The overwhelming majority of these no stoppage provisions include unconditional no-strike agreements. Most of the remaining contracts permit strikes only under limited conditions such as a party's refusal to take an issue to arbitration, a refusal to abide by an arbitration award, an impasse arising under a wage reopener procedure, or employee confrontation with primary picket lines.

Prohibitions against employer lockouts are almost as common. A small minority (about one out of five collective agreements when such data was still collected by the BLS) permit lockouts under circumstances such as the union's refusal to arbitrate a dispute or abide by an arbitration award or in the event of a deadlock when negotiating pursuant to a provision for reopening the terms of a portion of the collective agreement.

715. Because the right to strike is treated as a collective right in American labor law, the Supreme Court has held that it can be waived by the bargaining unit's collective bargaining agent.[783] Thus, although the protected right to engage in concerted activity prohibits an employer from disciplining an employee who engages in a lawful sympathy work stoppage, such as refusing to cross a picket line established by employees who are striking for higher benefits, that employee protection may be waived by a no stoppage agreement that covers such work refusals.[784] The

783. *Emporium Capwell Co.* v. *Western Addition Community Organization*, 420 US 50 (1975); *NLRB* v. *Sands Mfg. Co.*, 306 US 332 (1939).

784. *NLRB* v. *Rockaway News Supply Co.*, 345 US 71 (1953); *R.L. Coolsaet Construction Co.* v. *Local 150, International Union of Operating Engineers*, 177 F.3d 648 (7th Cir.) *cert.* denied 528 US 1004

legally recognized justification for dismissal in such a case is that the worker was terminated not because of refusing to engage in a work stoppage; rather it was because the employee violated the no stoppage provision of the collective agreement. Another way to characterize the employer's action in such a situation is that the employee's breach of his obligation to work without stoppage, as established by the collective agreement, was a material failure of performance allowing the employer to exercise a right to rescind the individual employment contract.

A no stoppage provision in a collective agreement will not be construed to prohibit a stoppage whose purpose is to protest a significant unfair labor practice unless it explicitly applies to such protests.[785] Nor may a no stoppage provision be enforced to prevent workers from refusing to do work that they honestly believe, based on objective evidence, poses an abnormally dangerous working condition.[786]

Even though a collective agreement does not contain an explicit no stoppage provision, one will be implied by the NLRB and the courts for the duration of any dispute resolution procedures that the agreement requires the parties to follow. In addition, if the dispute resolution procedure covers the underlying dispute being protested by the work stoppage, the stoppage can be enjoined by a federal court pending exhaustion of the contractual procedure, and the federal as well as state courts can provide injunctive relief to enforce an arbitrator's order ending the stoppage if such an order is issued under the contractual dispute resolution procedure.[787]

Unless a particular procedure is contractually designated as final, or the collective agreement limits resort to alternative procedures, upon exhaustion of any contractual dispute resolution procedures the parties are free to resort to judicial enforcement of the alleged contractual claim or to economic pressure tactics including a work stoppage.[788]

If a union authorizes a work stoppage in violation of a no stoppage provision in the collective agreement, the employer may bring a damages action in court or in an arbitration proceeding (depending upon whether the arbitration provision of the collective agreement covers the employer's grievance respecting the contract violation).[789]

(1999) (holding that a broad no stoppage provision waives the right to engage in sympathy action if there is extrinsic evidence showing that the parties intended that result).

785. *Mastro Plastic Corp.* v. *NLRB*, 350 US 270 (1956); *Servair, Inc.* v. *NLRB*, 726 F.2d 1435 (1984).

786. *Gateway Coal Co.* v. *United Mine Workers*, 414 US 368 (1974). For more detailed discussion *see* paragraphs 754–755, below.

787. *Local 174, Teamsters* v. *Lucas Flour Co.*, 369 US 95 (1962); *Boys Markets, Inc.* v. *Retail Clerks Union*, 398 US 235 (1970); *Jacksonville Bulk Terminals* v. *Longshoremen*, 457 US 702 (1982). State courts often have broader authority to enjoin violations of no stoppage provisions, *William E. Arnold Co.* v. *Carpenters*, 417 US 12 (1974), but that authority can be avoided through the procedural device of removing such cases to federal court. *Avco Corp.* v. *Aero Lodge No. 735*, 390 US 557 (1968).

788. *Groves* v. *Ring Screw Works*, 498 US 168 (1990).

789. *Drake Bakeries* v. *Local 50*, 370 US 254 (1962). For rules insulating the individual employees and parent union from liability, *see Carbon Fuel Co.* v. *United Mine Workers of America*, 444 US 212 (1979) and *Complete Auto Transit, Inc.* v. *Reis*, 451 US 401 (1981).

716. Many no-strike provisions place an affirmative duty upon the union to make every effort to get employees who are engaged in an unauthorized strike (a 'wildcat strike') to return to work. An employer cannot punish union officials, such as shop stewards, more severely than it punishes other employees for engaging in the same conduct unless the collective agreement required the officials to perform duties to end the stoppage and they failed to do so.[790] Some agreements specify that the union's liability for such strikes is limited to making good faith efforts to return the strikers to work. Collective agreements often spell out the disciplinary sanctions that can be imposed upon workers who strike in violation of the no-stoppage pledge. Typically, dismissal is the specified penalty.

717. In those industries in which the production machinery, such as a high temperature furnace, is subject to damage if suddenly shut down, the collective agreement often imposes a duty on the union and the employees to provide a skeletal work force during the first stage of any stoppage to enable management to discontinue production gradually and protect the production equipment from damage. Even when not specified, typically self-interest has made such procedures customary.

XII. Conflict Resolution Machinery

A. Grievance Procedure

718. Almost every collective agreement establishes a procedure for joint discussion of grievances arising under the contract. Even if the collective agreement does not contain such a provision, section 8(d) of the National Labor Relations Act entitles either side to require the other to discuss a grievance.

Grievance provisions in collective agreements describe a particular procedure for discussing disputes arising during the life of a collective agreement. Sometimes they additionally impose limitations respecting appropriate subjects for grievance discussion and normally include time limits for initiating or resolving them. Most often, the collective agreement states that a grievance covered by the procedure can concern any matter regarding the agreement's interpretation or application.

719. Subjects contractually excluded from grievance procedures primarily are topics that are not mandatory subjects of bargaining. These include such issues as the selection and assignment of supervisors, the enterprise's investment decisions, and the like. In addition, however, decisions concerning particular issues affecting terms or conditions of employment often are expressly left to management's sole discretion. Such matters typically include promotions, contracting out work or certain types of work (for example, maintenance work), work and vacation schedules, and testing and training requirements. See also, paragraph 725, below.

---

790. *Metropolitan Edison Co.* v. *NLRB*, 460 US 693 (1983).

720. Grievance procedures usually state the maximum period for initiating a grievance after the event in question has occurred. Sometimes the limit is as short as one day, more often it is a stated number of days or weeks and, generally, is not more than a month.

721. Grievance procedures normally are designed to resolve issues raised either by individual workers or groups of workers. A minority of these provisions, however, spell out separate procedures for union initiated complaints based on questions of collective interests. Additionally, some agreements spell out a procedure for management initiated grievances.

722. Although grievance procedures vary considerably, the basic pattern is for the manner of presentation to become more formal with each step and for persons in higher positions of authority to become involved with each step. Often, the first step may be initiated by the employee alone, but further processing requires union participation. However, many agreements require union participation at every step of the procedure. Based on data compiled in the early 1990s, it can be said that three and four step grievance procedures are most common. Frequently, the first step is an oral presentation by the grievant and his shop steward to the grievant's immediate supervisor or that supervisor's superior. A majority of those agreements that specify the manner for taking the first step state that it must be submitted in writing. Time limits are generally established for management's response. Some agreements treat management's failure to respond within the time limit as an acceptance of the merit of the grievance; other contracts treat it as an automatic rejection of the grievance. Time limits also are generally imposed on the union's right to move the grievance to the next step in the process. Failure to so move within the time limit is usually treated as union acquiescence in management's resolution at the prior step. Time limits upon management's response, and on the union's appeal to the next step of the grievance process, most often allow two to five days. In actual practice, often extensions of time limits are routinely granted by the other side.

723. The Civil Service Reform Act of 1978 (5 US Code §7121) requires federal employees to elect between pursuing a grievance under the appeals procedures presided over by the Merit Systems Protection Board, which is a governmental agency, and the grievance-arbitration machinery established by collective agreement where the latter is available. However, claims based on alleged race, sex, age or nationality discrimination may be pursued through both avenues for relief. (See 29 Code Fed. Reg. §1614.401.)

B. Arbitration

724. Collective agreements in the US almost always specify a procedure for submitting unsettled grievances to arbitration. Although some disputes reach arbitration without going through a grievance process, most often the exhaustion of the grievance machinery has preceded submission of the dispute to arbitration. The vast majority of disputes are resolved through the grievance process. For example, a study of grievances filed by General Motors workers during one period showed that all but 0.05 percent were resolved without going to arbitration.[791] Although this settlement rate is exceptionally high, it is indicative of the important role played by grievance procedures.

There is no systematic annual collection of data respecting the number of labor arbitration cases decided and while the public and private agencies that provide parties with lists of qualified labor arbitrators publish annual data reporting the volume of appointments and reported decisions, a significant portion of arbitrator selections are made by the parties without using the services of those agencies. Accordingly, only a rough estimate can be made of the number of labor arbitration cases decided annually. Extrapolating from the available data, it is reasonable to estimate that between 15,000 and 25,000 labor arbitration cases are submitted for arbitration annually. The vast majority of these cases are settled without a hearing or decision. Nevertheless, a reasonable estimate is that over 10,000 labor arbitration cases are decided each year.

Initiation of arbitration normally can come from either side but most often it is the union that seeks such relief. Some collective agreements require the parties to attempt mediation after exhausting the grievance procedure and before submitting the dispute for arbitration. Most contracts require that some step be taken toward initiation, such as a request to the FMCS or the American Arbitration Association for a panel of arbitrators, within a specified time limit. Ten days and 30 days are the most common time limits for this purpose. The arbitration process is described in greater detail in paragraphs 881–900, below.

XIII. Management and Union Rights and Zipper Provisions

A. Management Rights

725. A management's rights or management's prerogatives provision in a collective agreement expressly preserves for management's sole discretion certain broad areas of policy formation and decision making. Almost every collective agreement contains such a provision. Most often these provisions explicitly give management the sole right to direct the work force, schedule and assign work, conduct the business, and control production, except as otherwise specifically limited in the collective agreement.

Unions frequently try to limit certain aspects of managerial authority to make core business decisions such as the right to contract out to other enterprises work that can be performed by the bargaining unit. Similarly, collective agreements sometimes prohibit supervisors from performing bargaining unit work. Such restrictions usually make exception for supervisory work that is necessitated by emergency conditions or by instructional activities.

Collective agreements occasionally impose a procedure for introducing technological changes. The restriction might require prior consultation with the union or impose obligations to retrain current employees.

---

791. *Vaca* v. *Sipes*, 386 US 171, 192 n. 15 (1967).

Some collective agreements also impose restrictions on the procedure for plant shutdowns or relocations including giving the current work force express transfer rights to the site of relocated work and may include a requirement for employer payment of at least part of the worker's cost of moving to the new location.

B. Union Rights

726. Many collective agreements expressly protect the right of employees to engage in collective activities free from employer discrimination. While the law itself protects this right, if such a provision is included in the collective agreement, contractual remedies become available in addition to statutory remedies. A principal advantage of the contractual remedy is that generally it can be processed more expeditiously than the statutory remedy.

Another type of provision that significantly strengthens the union's representational role is a contractual right granted non-employee union representatives to enter the employer's premises to discuss union matters with management, with the union's shop representatives, or with individual employees. Such provisions are common, as are those giving the union the right to post notices on company bulletin boards. Some contracts expressly give the union a right to various types of information including the names and addresses of new employees, the seniority list, work assignment and work schedule information, individual wage data, data used for establishing production standards, and the like. Collective agreements also often specify the degree to which union shop representatives can, during paid work time, engage in union business such as handling grievances. Often, however, arrangements such as permitting shop stewards to handle grievances during paid work time are accomplished informally and are not mentioned in the collective agreement.

727. Related to both management and union rights provisions are mutual cooperation clauses. Most often these are stated in broad hortatory language in which each side pledges to cooperate in solving problems peacefully so as to avoid unnecessary conflict. Sometimes they are accompanied by more concrete commitments to contribute funds and other aid to joint industry-union programs to promote employee training, or improve the status, technology, standards, and prosperity of the industry and of those employed in the industry.

C. Zipper Provisions

728. The duty to bargain does not end with the execution of a collective agreement. If a mandatory subject of bargaining is not resolved by the agreement, either side may demand changes concerning that subject during the life of the agreement and may bargain about that subject to impasse and invoke economic pressure in support of those demands unless barred by a no work stoppage provision in the agreement. Similarly, because established practices constitute part of the existing terms and conditions of employment, they cannot be changed unilaterally during the life of the collective agreement even though it is silent respecting the subject of the past practice such as, for example, coffee being provided free of charge during rest periods. On the other hand, the parties can waive the right to negotiate respecting a mandatory subject of bargaining. However, such a waiver is recognized only if it is explicitly stated or if the parties' conduct shows clearly and unmistakably that the matter was fully discussed and one side consciously yielded to its not being subject to control by the collective bargaining contract or procedure.[792]

Some collective agreements contain a provision, commonly called a 'zipper' provision, broadly waiving any further bargaining during the life of the agreement and limiting claims to those supported by the explicit language of the agreement. The purposes of a 'zipper' provision are to prevent a party from insisting on bargaining during the life of a collective agreement respecting matters not covered by the agreement and, equally, to eliminate either side's right to rely on established prior practices as constituting enforceable terms or conditions of employment beyond those specified in the collective agreement. A typical zipper provision might state, for example, that the collective agreement constitutes the sole and entire agreement of the parties, superseding all prior agreements and practices, and that neither side shall have an obligation to bargain respecting any subject during the duration of the agreement even though that matter may not have been a topic of negotiations or may not have been within the knowledge or contemplation of either or both parties at the time of negotiations.

Because it is usually management that is in a position to make unilateral changes respecting the terms and conditions of employment, a zipper provision generally works to the employer's advantage. However, a zipper provision can be worded in such a way as to preclude changes respecting matters not covered by the collective agreement.[793]

The NLRB and the courts do not give a zipper provision controlling effect unless broad enough in the scope of its express language, or as evidenced by the bargaining history, so that it is clear and unmistakable that there was an intentional and express waiver of the right to bargain respecting the specific proposal or change at issue.[794]

The General Counsel of the Board has observed that the NLRB more readily gives effect to a zipper provision when it is used as a defense to an effort to institute bargaining over new subjects during the life of the collective agreement than when used as a means of asserting that established practices provide terms and conditions beyond those stated in the collective agreement.[795]

---

792. *NLRB* v. *C & C Plywood Corp.*, 385 US 421 (1967); *Metropolitan Edison Co.* v. *NLRB*, 460 US 693 (1983); *Provena Hospitals*, 350 NLRB 808 (2007). But *see NLRB* v. *US Postal Serv.*, 8 F.3d 832, 836 (DC Cir. 1993) and *Bath Marine Draftsmen's Ass'n* v. *NLRB*, 475 F.3d 14, 22 (1st Cir. 2007) (holding that if the subject is 'covered' in the collective agreement, that coverage satisfies the requirement of reaching agreement even if the specific proposed changes at issue are not addressed by the contract's language). However, in *Local Union 36 IBEW* v. *NLRB,* 706 F.3d 73 (2d Cir. 2013) the court cautioned that waiving the right to bargain over making a change does not unmistakably waive the right to bargain respecting the effects of the change.

793. *The Mead Corp.*, 318 NLRB 201, 202 (1995).

794. *Gannett Rochester Newspapers* v. *NLRB*, 988 F.2d 198 (DC Cir. 1993).

795. NLRB General Counsel, *Quarterly Report*, June 1979 at 101 LRR 173.

XIV. Pay Without Work – Featherbedding

729. An assertion made by some antagonists of union representation is that labor organizations seek to extract pay for not working. Attempts to preserve work opportunities have at times generated union demands that provide evidence in support of this criticism. Additionally, corrupt practices sometimes produce situations in which employers pay fictitious workers or non-workers as a way to bribe union officials. In an early case, for example, a former employee charged that he was dismissed because he shifted his loyalties from a company dominated union to an independent CIO union. In defense of its action, the employer asserted that this employee had not been doing any work, did not even know what his assigned job was, often reported to work late, often went home early, and had on occasion reported to work while intoxicated. Even though the NLRB found in favor of the employer's factual assertions, it held the employer guilty of unlawful discrimination because of union activity. It was noted that the worker's non performance was the same for several years and had been tolerated by the employer because he was instrumental in maintaining worker support for the company dominated union. Only when he shifted his support to the independent union did the employer decide that the worker's lack of performance required that he be discharged. Thus, although the worker was not entitled to hold a job without working, the real reason for dismissal was unlawful because it was based on his union activity.[796]

730. In American labor relations jargon, drawing pay without producing any work is known as 'featherbedding' (sleeping on a feather bed and being paid for work). The first federal law prohibiting featherbedding was aimed at the musicians' union. Because of improvements in sound reproduction and recordings, in the mid-1940s many American musicians were unemployed since live music no longer was needed in many settings. In an attempt to preserve work opportunities, their union established minimum standards specifying the number of musicians who would have to be engaged for various types of musical performances. The minimum number of musicians generally increased with the probable increase in the size of the listening audience. Radio broadcasting stations, which for almost two decades had employed large orchestras to provide background music for dramatic programs and musical entertainment, were among the first to replace live musical performances with recorded reproductions. This resulted in considerable potential savings for the broadcasters by enabling them to reduce the number of musicians in their workforce. Faced with union demands for minimum numbers of broadcasting studio jobs for musicians, the broadcasters succeeded in getting Congress to adopt the Lea Act, in 1946, which made it a crime to coerce a broadcasting station into employing more musicians than it needed.

James C. Petrillo, President of the American Federation of Musicians, challenged the validity of this law by personally demanding that a studio comply with the union's minimum staffing requirement. When Petrillo was charged with criminal violation of the Lea Act, his lawyer argued that the law was unconstitutionally vague and moved to have the case dismissed. The case made its way to the US

---

796. *Edward G. Budd Mfg. Co.* v. *NLRB*, 138 F.2d 86 (3d Cir. 1943).

Supreme Court which upheld the Act's constitutionality.[797] At about the same time, Congress adopted the Taft–Hartley Act which added section 8(b)(6) to the NLRA making it an unfair labor practice for a labor organization to cause an employer to pay anything of value for services which are not performed or are not to be performed. Thus, featherbedding could no longer legally be required by a collectively bargained agreement.

731. The Supreme Court, in construing NLRA §8(b)(6), has drawn a distinction between work preservation or make-work provisions and a provision designed to extract compensation without any services being given. The Court decided that only the latter is an unfair labor practice under the NLRA because the legislative history of the Taft–Hartley provision indicates that Congress did not wish to restrain the sort of demands made by the musicians' union in the *Petrillo* case. Thus, it is not featherbedding under the NLRA for a union to insist upon the employment of a minimum number of musicians for the band in a musical play, nor is it a violation of 8(b)(6) for a union to insist that workers be paid to do work that is unnecessary because it merely duplicates work performed by machines or by contractors.[798] So long as the employees are working, the Act does not treat the inefficiency or unnecessary nature of their work as featherbedding.

§9. Effect of Bankruptcy on the Collective Agreement

732. American bankruptcy law is national (federal) in scope and is administered by special bankruptcy judges whose decisions are reviewed, in the first instance, by the federal district courts which are the federal courts of general trial jurisdiction.[799]

Bankruptcy procedures can be initiated either to liquidate and distribute the debtor's assets or to reorganize the debtor's financial affairs. When reorganization is undertaken as a result of a petition filed with a bankruptcy court, the normal procedure in the US is to permit the debtor to retain custody of its assets rather than place them in the custody of an independent trustee. The owner's status is referred to as the 'debtor-in-possession'. The bankruptcy court, with the advice of a creditors' committee, must approve various legal alterations of the debtor's affairs. Because payroll debts often are a major liability of an enterprise that has filed for, or been forced into, bankruptcy reorganization, employee representatives sometimes are included on the creditor's committee.

One privilege of an enterprise undergoing bankruptcy reorganization is to cancel (reject) its contracts. The obligee then becomes a creditor to the extent of any damages caused by the early termination of the contract and can collect those damages to the extent that assets were secured for performance of the contract (a secured creditor). To the extent the debt was not secured by specific assets, the claim is a

797. *United States* v. *Petrillo*, 332 US 1 (1947). (The charges against Petrillo eventually were withdrawn and the Lea Act was repealed in 1980.)

798. *American Newspaper Publ. Ass'n* v. *NLRB*, 345 US 100 (1953); *NLRB* v. *Gamble Enterprises*, 345 US 117 (1953).

799. An alternative procedure is available in many districts that allows a party to present the first appeal, instead, to a panel of bankruptcy court judges.

general claim and, on a *pro-rata* basis subject to some limitations based on the nature of the contract, is satisfied from any remaining assets to the extent that the creditors and court have approved a plan for the payment of such debts.

In the mid-1980s Congress amended the Bankruptcy Code to impose special regulations on the procedure for rejecting a current collectively bargained agreement. Section 1113 of the Bankruptcy Code (11 US Code §1113) establishes the procedures and standards that limit the authority of a bankruptcy trustee or debtor-in-possession to reject a current collectively bargained agreement.[800] Under the Code provision, prior to rejection the debtor-in-possession must propose to the collective bargaining representative such modifications of the agreement that it considers 'necessary to permit the reorganization of the debtor'. The modifications are to assure 'fair and equitable treatment' of all affected parties. The debtor-in-possession also must provide the labor organization with information that is relevant and necessary to evaluate the proposal and must negotiate in an attempt to reach a mutually satisfactory modification of the agreement. The collective agreement cannot be rejected without bankruptcy court approval and the court's approval can be granted only if the statutory procedure for proposing modifications was followed, the labor organization refused the proposed changes 'without good cause', and 'the balance of the equities clearly favors rejection'. Expedited procedures are provided for completing the rejection process and interim changes may be approved by the court pending completion of those procedures.

Although obligees of other types of rejected executory contracts are entitled to submit claims for their contractual losses as general claims against the person or entity undergoing liquidation or reorganization, an appellate court has held that such claims are not available to the union or employees when their collective agreement has been modified in a reorganization procedure.[801]

The appellate courts have divided over whether the test of what is 'necessary to permit reorganization' should look only to those changes required to maintain the enterprise's ability to pay its current debts or whether it can include changes required over the longer term for the enterprise's successful reorganization.[802]

The rejection of a collective agreement does not alter the labor organization's status as collective bargaining representative and once the collective agreement is rejected, under the NLRA the bargaining unit employees are free to resort to economic pressure in support of demands for restored or improved terms and conditions of employment. Accordingly, an appellate court has held that in balancing the equities respecting whether a collective agreement should be rejected, the bankruptcy court must include consideration of the likelihood that rejection will result in

800. Excluded from these procedures are railroad industry collective agreements governed by the Railway Labor Act (11 US Code §1113(a)). Air carrier collective agreements, which are also regulated by the RLA, are not within the §1113(a) exclusion.

801. *United Food & Commercial Workers, Local 328* v. *Almac's Inc.*, 90 F.3d 1 (1st Cir. 1996). But *see*, M. Baxter, 'Is There a Claim for Damages from the Rejection of a Collective Bargaining Agreement under section 1113 of the Bankruptcy Code?', 12 *Bank. Dev. J.* 703 (1996).

802. *Compare In Re Mile Hi Metal Systems, Inc.*, 899 F.2d 887 (10th Cir. 1990) and *Truck Drivers Local 807* v. *Carey Transportation*, 816 F.2d 82 (2d Cir. 1987); with *Wheeling-Pittsburgh Steel* v. *United Steelworkers of America*, 791 F.2d 1074 (3d Cir. 1986).

a sustained work stoppage.[803] On the other hand, an appellate court has ruled that if a collective agreement regulated by the Railway Labor Act is rejected, the modifications accepted by the Bankruptcy Court become the new status quo and the union must go through the normal RLA procedures, including the prohibition against work stoppages until an impasse has been declared by the NMB.[804]

§10. Alternative Methods of Worker Participation

733. In addition to collective bargaining, four alternative avenues enable American workers to participate in some forms of managerial decision-making. Three are based on exercising share-holder influence, the other on direct participation through employee committees or joint worker-management committees authorized to make policy or shop decisions or policy recommendations.

Employee ownership of the voting shares of common stock in the corporations for which they work is widespread. For example, in 2011 the Department of Labor's Employee Benefits Security Administration reported that, based on filings with it, over 13 million employees owned at least some of their employer's stock shares through an employer sponsored stock ownership plan. A study conducted that year found that employees owned more than half the shares of well over 800 corporations.[805]

Majority ownership of shares is not essential for employee owners to have significant influence in a widely held corporation. As a rule of thumb, if the shares of a corporation are held by a widely diverse group of shareholders, because most shareholders do not exercise their voting rights, control of 5 percent or more of the voting shares generally is sufficient to constitute a controlling interest over the enterprise. This suggests considerable potential for employees to exercise shareholder power in order to influence management decision-making. However, some of the shares cited in the above statistics were owned by managers and a significant portion were owned by employees who, though protected by the NLRA in their right to organize a union, nevertheless do not have a collective bargaining representative to assist in coordinating efforts to vote shares in a way that supports particular employee goals. In addition, not all shares owned by employees have voting rights and a substantial portion of employee ownership is controlled by retirement funds that do not provide employees with the right to vote shares held for their benefit.[806] That is, the shares are voted by the trustees or administrators who themselves may be officers of the corporation or are dependent on the corporation for their continued service in that capacity.

803. *Truck Drivers Local 807* v. *Carey Transportation*, 816 F.2d 82, 93 (2d Cir. 1987).

804. *Northwest Airlines*v. *Ass'n of Flight Attendants*, 483 F.3d 160 (2d Cir. 2007). *See* note 769 above regarding the railroad industry's exclusion from the rejection procedure.

805. E. Olsen, *Majority Employee Owned Enterprises in the U.S.: A Profile* (2011).

806. The ERISA prohibits an employer operated retirement fund from investing more than 10 percent of its assets in its own shares. For some funds, however, a 10 percent investment in the employer's shares represents a controlling block of corporate stock. *See*, for example, *Donovan* v. *Bierwirth*, 680 F.2d 263 (2d Cir.), *cert.* denied 459 US 1069 (1982).

Federal income tax law encourages one form of employee ownership of the shares of the employing enterprise by giving favorable tax treatment to programs for investment or for profit sharing bonuses in the form of stock shares. These generally are known as employee stock ownership plans, or ESOPs, and stock bonus plans.[807] Such plans represent a form of deferred compensation–the employer gives employees corporate shares in lieu of higher wages or retirement benefits. Often, the plans governing such distribution of corporate shares, much like employer sponsored retirement plans, place assets in a trust governed by company appointed trustees–most often officers of the employing corporation. In the case of ESOPs involving corporations whose shares are owned by large numbers of shareholders, the beneficiary employees are legally entitled to vote those shares in which they have a vested interest. However, ESOPs of closely held corporations need not 'pass through' voting rights except for decisions involving fundamental changes in the corporation's structure. A majority of ESOPs with significant blocks of the employing company's shares are those formed by such closely held corporations.[808]

In addition to the direct employee ownership of shares of their employing company, employee benefit programs in the form of ESOPs, stock bonus plans, and retirement plans, own a substantial portion of all securities of publicly owned companies in the US. Thus, some argue that organized labor could greatly increase its influence over general corporate employment policies by providing leadership to coordinate the shareholder power of employees and of fiduciaries who hold shares for their benefit. However, there may be legal limits to the availability of this strategy. Although an employer would not have a means of punishing a union for engaging in such efforts, the NLRB has held that the NLRA does not protect employees from being dismissed for efforts to coordinate employee shareholder efforts to gain managerial control of the employing entity.[809] In addition, the Board has ruled that employees or a group of employees lose the right to participate in collective bargaining under the protections of the NLRA if their corporate share ownership gives them actual control over management affairs.[810]

The other potential alternative to collective bargaining as a method of employee participation in management decision-making is through employee committees or joint worker-management committees. Such committees that help make management policy or shop decisions or recommendations have been established by some enterprises in the US. As is discussed above at paragraphs 410–414, with very limited exceptions, employers are not required to establish such committees in the US

807. *See* 26 US Code §§401(a) & 409. ESOPs and stock bonus investment plans are not subject to ERISA's prohibition against more than 10 percent of fund assets being invested in the employing institution. This poses a danger of undermining the security of employee interests. *See* M. Hylton, 'The Changing World of Employee Benefits', 79 *Chi.-Kent. L. Rev*. 625 (2004); R. Hockett, 'What Kinds of Stock Ownership Plans Should There Be? Of ESOPS, Other SOPS, and "Ownership Societies"', 92 *Cornell L. Rev*. 865 (2007).

808. *See*, B. McDonnell, 'ESOPs' Failures: Fiduciary Duties When Managers of Employee-Owned Companies Vote to Entrench Themselves', 2000 *Colum. Bus. L. Rev*. 199 (2000).

809. *Harrah's Lake Tahoe*, 307 NLRB 182 (1992). For a discussion questioning the wisdom and correctness of this decision, *see* J. Hirsch, 'Labor Law Obstacles to the Collective Negotiation and Implementation of Employee Stock Ownership Plans', 67 *Ford. L. Rev*. 957 (1998).

810. *Science Applications International Corp*., 309 NLRB 373 (1992).

and, unless established by a collective agreement, the scope of their lawful activities is very limited. Moreover, labor organizations often are not receptive to establishing such committees through collective bargaining because they fear that such participation may become a means of by-passing or co-opting union organized collective action.

Chapter 5. Industrial Action

§1. Right to Strike

I. Generally

734. Section 501(2) of the LMRA defines the term 'strike' as any concerted stoppage of work, concerted slowdown or 'other concerted interruption of operations by employees'. Since the definition is not confined to concerted actions by an employer's own workers, it includes situations such as a refusal to deliver goods to, or service the operations of, an unorganized establishment or an enterprise whose workers are on strike. It also includes concerted action by two or more workers whether or not they have a bargaining representative. This definition applies to all provisions within the LMRA, including its first title, the NLRA.

Section 7 of the NLRA declares that employees have a right to engage in concerted activity for collective bargaining and other mutual aid and protection and §8(a)(1) of the NLRA makes it an unfair labor practice for an employer to interfere with an employee's exercise of a right protected under §7. These provisions establish the principle that employees have a right to withhold their labor, that is to strike, for their mutual aid and protection.[811] Hence, as a general rule, employers cannot penalize employees or discriminate against them because they have exercised the right to strike.[812] However, court decisions hold that an employer is permitted to permanently replace strikers. See paragraphs 739–742, below.

Although the RLA is silent respecting the right to strike, case decisions hold that the Act's mandatory arbitration procedure for resolving rights disputes arising under collective agreements implicitly prohibits the resort to work stoppages involving claims of contract violation. (Rights disputes in the context of the RLA are referred to as 'minor disputes'.) On the other hand, the courts have interpreted the RLA's mandatory mediation procedure as permitting strikes over interests disputes (that is, disputes seeking a modification of existing contractual terms and conditions of employment – or 'major disputes' as they are referred to under the RLA) so long as there has been compliance with and exhaustion of the RLA's mandatory mediation procedures.[813]

---

811. *Santa Cruz Fruit Packing Co.* v. *NLRB*, 303 US 453 (1938).

812. *NLRB* v. *Mackay Radio & Telegraph Co.*, 304 US 333 (1938). Challenging a striker's unemployment compensation claim, however, is not considered a penalty. *Baker* v. *General Motors*, 478 US 621 (1986). Nor did one appellate court think it was a penalty when an employer, whose workers were on strike, refused to comply with its normal practice of matching employee contributions to a Christmas savings account. The court noted that the employer had a history of not matching such savings for employees who were on a layoff or leave of absence and reasoned that the employer was simply treating the striking workers as being in a comparable status. *Forest Products Company, Inc.* v. *NLRB*, 888 F.2d 72 (10th Cir. 1989).

813. *Brotherhood of Locomotive Engineers* v. *Louisville & Nashville R.R.*, 373 US 33 (1963); *Chicago & North Western Ry.* v. *United Transportation Union*, 402 US 570 (1971).

735. Unlike many other legal systems, American law does not constitutionally protect the right to engage in a work stoppage. Rather, that right is established by statute and is less than complete.

The policy underlying the National Labor Relations Act reflects an understanding that the right to withhold work is an integral part of American labor relations law. However, the NLRA places specific limitations on that right. The Act's express limitations include notice requirements that must be satisfied under certain situations as a prelude to a strike, prohibitions against the use of strikes to put pressure on employers who do not have a direct dispute with their workers, limitations on the use of strikes for organizing and gaining union recognition, and time periods during which strikes are forbidden. Other limitations have been imposed by administrative and judicial interpretation. Despite these limitations, however, work stoppage activity historically was relatively high in the United States as compared with other industrial nations, although strike activity has declined significantly since the early 1980s.

The tables contained in paragraph 736, below, indicate the level of work stoppage activity in the United States. Although this data combines union initiated work stoppages (strikes) and employer initiated work stoppages (lock-outs), the former is by far the predominant cause of stoppages in the United States. One characteristic of American work stoppages has been that their average duration generally has exceeded that encountered in most other industrial nations.

736. Work stoppage data in the United States has always been incomplete. For decades the Bureau of Labor Statistics (BLS) has gathered work stoppage data, combining strikes and lockouts, principally based on newspaper accounts and follow-up inquiries by the BLS staff. Until December 1981, the Bureau's data included work stoppage information involving six or more workers. However, significant reductions in its staff during the early 1980s caused the BLS to confine the scope of its inquiries to those stoppages involving 1,000 or more employees.

An alternative source of work stoppage information is provided in the reports of Federal Mediation and Conciliation Service mediators. Its data is only partial because FMCS mediators often have no awareness of stoppages involving efforts to organize a bargaining unit or to negotiate a first contract. Also, its data on work stoppage frequency is incomplete because, although the agency is notified that the parties are initiating contract renewal negotiations, it is not necessarily notified that there has been a work stoppage. Furthermore, there is no procedure ensuring that the federal mediators are informed of stoppages concerning government employees. In addition to the incompleteness of the work stoppage data routinely submitted to the FMCS, until the late 1980s the agency did not regularly report the work stoppage information to be found by culling its records. Finally, inconsistent information is sometimes found in the FMCS's annual reports when listing data for prior years and the data does not include the number of employees involved in the stoppages, although the reports sometimes attempt to estimate the number of work hours lost from stoppages. Nevertheless, though recognizing the short comings in these sources, the tables below offer data from the BLS and FMCS in an effort to provide at least a fragmented picture of work stoppage experience in the US.

Table 4 Work stoppages – BLS data for selected years (1,000 or more employees)

Year	*Number of stoppages that began in the period*	*Number of workers (thousands)*	*Days idle working time (thousands)*	*Percent of estimated working time*
2016	15	99	1,540	less than 0.005
2000	39	394	20,419	0.06
1995	31	192	5,771	0.02
1990	44	185	5,926	0.02
1980	187	795	20,844	0.09
1970	381	2,468	52,761	0.29
1960	222	896	13,260	0.09
1950	424	1,698	30,390	0.26

* With the small numbers of strikes in recent years, a single prolonged strike can significantly alter the data.

Table 5 Work stoppages – BLS data for selected years (six or more employees – private non-farm)

Year	*Number of stoppages*	*Average duration (calendar days)*	*Number of workers involved*	*Percent of total employed*	*Percent of estimated total working time*
1930	637	22.3	183,000	0.8	0.05
1935	2,014	23.8	1,120,000	5.2	0.29
1940	2,508	20.9	577,000	1.7	0.10
1947	3,693	25.6	2,170,000	4.7	0.41
1955	4,320	18.5	2,650,000	5.2	0.26
1965	3,963	25.0	1,550,000	2.5	0.18
1970	5,716	25.0	3,350,000	4.7	0.44
1975	5,031	26.8	1,746,000	2.2	0.16
1980	3,855	35.4	1,366,000	1.5	0.14

Table 6 Work stoppages – FMCS data

Year	*Number of stoppages beginning in year*	*Average duration (calendar days)*
1985	801	40.3
1990	733	43.9
1995	409	55.9
2000	400	40.7
2016	108	not calculated

The level of work stoppage activity has varied among different industries. For example, the Bureau of Labor Statistics reported that the average frequency of worker idleness in the clothing industry due to strikes and lockouts as a percent of total days worked in 1967–1969 was 0.06 and for 1973–1975 it was 0.20. The same data for the rubber industry was 1.12 percent for 1967–1969 and for 1973–1975 it was 0.58 percent. In the mining industry the figure for 1967–1969 was 1.42 percent and it was 1.27 percent for 1973–1975. Among the causes for these variations is the extent to which workers are unionized in the particular industry, the competitive structure of the industry, the labor–management bargaining structure in the industry, its level of prosperity, and the characteristics of both union and management leadership.

Although a small percentage of strikes (perhaps about 5 percent per year) involve workers' efforts to gain union recognition, the overwhelming majority result from unsatisfied demands for increased wages or other forms of financially related benefits. Studies show that job security issues and disputes regarding plant conditions and supervisory policy also account for a small but significant portion of all work stoppages. As indicated above, it has become apparent that work stoppages have declined significantly in the past couple of decades.

II. Public Employees

737. Until well into the 1960s, it was extraordinary for public employees to engage in a work stoppage. By the late 1960s, however, such strikes were no longer a rarity. There were 300–400 public employee strikes each year starting in 1969 and into the mid-1970s. By the late 1970s the annual number of strikes involving government workers had increased. For example, in 1979 there were 593 strikes involving 254,100 government workers that resulted in a total of 2,982,500 lost work days. Of all those strikes, only a little over a dozen involved federal government workers. Most were strikes of municipal or school district employees.

Systematic data reporting government employee strike activity was discontinued in the 1980s but general impressions are that it declined although perhaps not to the same degree as the decline in private sector work stoppage activity.

738. The vast majority of public employee strikes in the United States have been unlawful inasmuch as most jurisdictions by statute or judicial decree prohibit public employees from resorting to work stoppage activities.[814] In the minority of states that permit public employee strikes, the right to strike is not extended to all government workers.[815]

Legal restraints on public employee work stoppages often are ignored or evaded due to reluctance of publicly elected officials to enforce such laws. This has caused many state legislatures to seek new techniques for enforcing the no-strike prohibition. Injunctions and criminal contempt proceedings have had some success in deterring or terminating such strikes but often the vast numbers of workers involved, and political pressures, promote prosecutorial and judicial leniency. Reluctance of elected prosecutors to seek injunctions against large numbers of strikers has been combated in some jurisdictions by giving any local citizen or taxpayer the right to sue to enforce the anti-strike legislation. Automatic dismissal or suspension imposed by statute has also been resorted to as a means of discouraging public employee strike activity. Similarly, some public employee laws disqualify strikers from receiving pay increases for a specified period.

Another problem in enforcing legal standards prohibiting government employee strikes is defining when an absence from work is an illegal stoppage. Often government workers involved in a labor dispute notify their employing agency that they are too ill to work, a tactic known as the 'blue flu'. A common response is to impose on the workers the burden of producing clear and convincing evidence to prove their actual illness. Courts have also had to deal with claims by absent employees that their failure to report for work was not strike participation but rather was a response to fear of reprisals from militant union supporters if they went to work.[816] The most highly publicized effort to enforce prohibitions against public employee work stoppages was President Reagan's 1981 dismissal of some 11,000 federal air traffic controllers.

In addition to disqualifying a federal employee who engages in a work stoppage from further federal government employment for an indefinite period, federal employees can be enjoined from striking and imprisoned for contempt of court if they disobey the injunction. They can also be prosecuted and punished by up to a

814. B. Aaron, 'Unfair Labor practices and the Right to Strike in the Public Sector', 38 *Stan. L. Rev.* 1097, 1109 (1986). At 5 US Code §7311 the federal statute disqualifies a person from holding a government job for merely asserting the right to strike against the government or belong to an organization that asserts that right. The constitutional protection of expression bars enforcing this provision where the accused merely has stated an opinion but not engaged in a work stoppage. *US* v. *Taylor*, 693 F.2d 919 (9th Cir. 1982) (*dicta*).

815. B. Aaron, above, at 1111–1112. For an examination of the history of public employee bargaining and recent political threats to the collective rights of government workers see J. Slater, 'The Strangely Unsettled State of Public-Sector Labor in the Past Thirty Years', 30 *Hofstra Lab. & Emp. L.J.* 511 (2013).

816. Federal and state courts reject such excuses unless the employee proves a specific basis for the fear, such as actual threats, and that the resulting fear goes beyond what a person 'of ordinary firmness' would be expected to resist. *Schultz* v. *Department of Transportation*, 773 F.2d 296 (Fed. Cir. 1985); *Zaner* v. *Board of Education of Farmingdale*, 429 N.Y.S.2d 725 (App. Div., 2d Dep't 1980).

year and a day of imprisonment and up to a $250,000 fine.[817] A union that tells federal workers to engage in a work stoppage may lose its certification as their bargaining representative.[818]

III. Rights and Risks of Private Sector Strikers

A. *Right to Replace Strikers*

739. In an early case, the Supreme Court discussed the question of whether an employer can discharge a striker and hire a replacement in order to keep the business operating. Because an employer who does not reinstate a returning striker penalizes the worker for exercising the protected right to act in concert for mutual aid, a literal application of NLRA section 7's broad protection of concerted employee activities would appear to prohibit an employer from imposing any disadvantage on someone who resorts to the concerted activity of striking. The Supreme Court, however, assumed that an employer faced with a strike is implicitly entitled to try to keep its business operating. To do so, it explained, an employer is permitted to hire workers on a temporary or permanent basis to replace the strikers. Although the Court actually decided the case at issue on other grounds, its observations respecting the employer's right to keep its business operating by using striker replacements was thereafter treated by the NLRB and the courts as though it was the ruling in the case. Thus, American labor law allows an employer to refuse to reinstate a worker while that worker's job is occupied by a replacement hired when the worker was on strike. However, if less than all of the workers are replaced, the employer's decision respecting which strikers shall be permitted to return to the available jobs cannot be based upon the extent of their participation in, or leadership of, the strike. A distinction based on such union activity is anti-union discrimination and, therefore, an unfair labor practice.[819]

The rule is different if workers engage in a stoppage to protest against a substantial employer unfair labor practice. If the employer in fact was guilty of that unfair labor practice, the employee is entitled to his job back even if replaced by another worker during the strike.[820] This type of stoppage is called an unfair labor practice strike as distinguished from organizational or economic strikes.

---

817. 5 US Code §7311(3); 18 US Code §§1918(3), 3559(a)(5), 3571(b). By regulation, a federal employee who has been dismissed for at least 3 years, as a result of engaging in a work stoppage, can be rehired if the Office of Personnel Management finds that the applicant is 'fit for appointment'. *Korte* v. *Office of Personnel Management*, 797 F.2d 967 (Fed. Cir. 1986). However, with respect to air traffic controllers, the President's dismissal and disbarment of them was held to have superseded the administrative regulation. *Clarry* v. *US*, 85 F.3d 1041 (2d Cir. 1996).

818. *PATCO* v. *FLRA*, 685 F.2d 547 (DC Cir. 1982).

819. *NLRB* v. *Mackay Radio & Telegraph Co.*, 304 US 333 (1938). A striker or strike leader, however, can be dismissed for violating the collective agreement if it contained a peace clause. *See* paragraph 715, above.

820. See, for example, *Teamsters Local Union No. 515* v. *NLRB*, 906 F.2d 719 (DC Cir. 1990). Employees who strike in protest against a substantial unfair labor practice are not entitled to be paid while engaged in the work stoppage. However, once they offer to return to work, if the employer refuses to take them back they are entitled to pay from that point forward.

In summary, therefore, generally the NLRA places upon workers a threefold economic risk when they engage in a stoppage to place pressure on their employer. First, they risk whether their ability to go without the financial returns of their jobs will be greater than the employer's ability to get along without their work. Secondly, they risk that the economic harm the strike inflicts on the employer will permanently damage the employer's prospects of operating at an improved level of worker benefits. Third, they risk that their jobs will be occupied by others when the conflict ends.

Often, when an employer attempts to keep operating by hiring replacements for striking workers, the union extracts an agreement that all strikers will be permitted to return to work as one of the terms for settling the strike.[821]

The NLRB has held that an employer has no duty to bargain with the incumbent union respecting the terms under which striker replacements are hired.[822] In contrast, it has been held that an employer cannot 'permanently' contract out bargaining unit work that will displace strikers unless the employer has bargained to impasse with the labor organization respecting that proposed change but can enter into such an agreement if there has been such bargaining and the impact is not inherently destructive of the bargaining unit.[823]

740. In 1995, President Clinton issued Executive Order 12954 authorizing the Secretary of Labor to 'debar' from contracting with the federal government the units of businesses that have permanently replaced lawfully striking employees. The order made such businesses ineligible from receiving federal government contracts until the Secretary determined that the labor dispute that precipitated the permanent replacement of strikers was resolved or the head of the contracting agency determined that a compelling reason existed to lift the debarment. Because the federal government is the nation's single largest purchaser of goods and services, the Executive Order had significant potential leverage in discouraging employers from permanently replacing strikers. A legal challenge to the President's constitutional and statutory authority to issue such an order was promptly initiated and the federal courts eventually ruled that the Executive Order conflicted with the policies of the NLRA and, therefore, was void. The Clinton administration did not try to appeal that decision to the US Supreme Court.[824]

741. The NLRA's definition of 'employee' includes a worker who is on strike until that worker obtains other and substantially equivalent employment. Upon

---

821. See, for example, *Belknap, Inc.* v. *Hale*, 463 US 491 (1983) where the 'permanent' replacements were held to have a possible action against the employer for misrepresentation or breach of contract because the employer dismissed them as part of a settlement in which strikers were reinstated. For a more detailed examination of work stoppages under US law, *see* A. Goldman. 'The USA'. in 'Strikes and Lock-outs in Industrialized Market Economies', 29 *Bull of Comp. Lab. Rel.* at 199–230 (R. Blanpain, ed.; R. Ben-Israel, Guest ed., 1994).

822. *Leveld Wholesale, Inc.*, 218 NLRB 1344 (1975); *Capitol-Husting Company, Inc.* v. *NLRB*, 671 F.2d 237, 246-48 (7th Cir. 1982).

823. *International Paper Co.* v. *NLRB*, 115 F.3d 1045 (DC Cir. 1997).

824. *Chamber of Commerce* v. *Reich*, 74 F.3d 1322 (DC Cir.), rehearing *en banc* denied 83 F.3d 442 (DC Cir. 1996).

obtaining and accepting such employment, the striker loses his right to reinstatement in his old job. If a worker is not replaced in his job while he is on strike, the NLRA's recognition of the right to engage in concerted activity gives the worker a right to be reinstated to his job upon abandonment of the strike. Moreover, even if the job is occupied by a replacement when the strike is abandoned, or is unavailable because the workforce has been reduced in size, the former striker is entitled to reinstatement in that job, or a substantially equivalent job, when it next becomes available. This rule results from the NLRA language specifying that the striking worker remains in the status of an employee.[825] The unavailability of a job when the striker offers to return to work in effect transforms the returning striker to the status of a laid off employee.[826]

Not all strikers retain their status as employees. As is discussed below, a striker ceases to have statutory protection as an employee if the strike itself is an unfair labor practice, or is in violation of a no-strike provision in a collective agreement, or is in support of a demand that has already been resolved in a current collective agreement, or the striker has engaged in the sort of misconduct that the courts have held removes the worker from the protection of the NLRA. In the latter situation the worker's misconduct gives the employer a right to rescind the individual employment contract and terminate the employment status.

If an employer fails or refuses to reinstate a worker who is entitled to reinstatement, that worker is entitled to recover the wages and other financial benefits he would have received had he been reinstated. The backpay award is enforced by the NLRB as an unfair labor practice remedy.

On the other hand, American labor law does not give an employee a claim to pay while engaged in a strike, even if the strike is to protest the employer's unlawful conduct. One way to understand the doctrinal structure of the American approach is to distinguish between the employee's contractual and equitable job interests. A work stoppage relieves the employer of contractual obligations to remunerate the striking employees but the NLRA preserves their equitable status as employees. When the strike ends, the employees' equitable status entitles them to resume their contractual relationship with the employer upon a job opening being available if that job is substantially equivalent to their prior work position. If the employer unlawfully withholds that right to reinstatement, backpay benefits must be paid to remedy the lost opportunity to work.

742. The Strikebreaker Transportation Act (18 US Code §1231) makes it a federal crime to transport people across state boundaries for the purpose of using threats or violence to interfere with those engaged in a peaceful labor dispute. When applicable, the Wagner–Peyser Act (29 US Code §49j) requires the US Employment Service to notify applicants who it refers to available jobs that there is a strike or lockout at the premises. The latter provision has little significance because

825. But the employer does not have to offer an entry level job to the displaced experienced striker when such jobs become available. Rather, the right to reinstatement is to a substantially equivalent job. *Rose Printing Co.*, 304 NLRB 1076 (1991); *Medite of N.M., Inc.* v. *NLRB*, 72 F.3d 780 (10th Cir. 1995).

826. *Laidlaw Corp.*, 171 NLRB 1366 (1968), enforced 414 F.2d 99 (7th Cir. 1969); *Brooks Research and Mfg., Inc.*, 202 NLRB 634 (1973).

federal job placement services are not extensive. However, state employment agencies, operating in conjunction with the administration of state unemployment compensation insurance, do a considerable amount of job placement and receive part of their financial support from the federal government. Therefore, of greater significance is a long-standing regulation of the US Department of Labor prohibiting state employment agencies receiving federal financial assistance from making job referrals that would fill a vacancy that resulted from a strike or lockout and requiring them to notify the referred applicant if there is a labor dispute involving other jobs at the establishment.[827]

Many states require private employment agencies and temporary help companies to inform clients or employees of the presence of a labor dispute before referring them to a job vacancy. Some states go further and prohibit temporary employment companies and employment agencies from supplying workers as striker replacements. However, there is some question as to whether the National Labor Relations Act preempts states from placing the latter type restrictions on the recruitment of lawful striker replacements.[828]

B. Rights of Strikers and Returning Strikers

743. Because strikers remain employees even while on strike, they have a claim to participate in any NLRB elections during the strike. However, the NLRA expressly imposes a one year limit on the right of strikers to vote in NLRB elections. On the other hand, court decisions hold that the one year limit does not apply to those who strike in protest against an unfair labor practice so long as it is determined that, in fact, there had been such a violation.[829]

Consistent with the concept that strikers continue to be employees, a striker who returns to work must be treated as a returning worker – much as one who had been on a layoff or leave of absence – and not as a new employee. Adverse changes in the striker's tenure or seniority status, for example, are treated as an unfair labor practice on the theory that the employer is thereby discriminating against those who engaged in concerted activities. To illustrate, it has been held that an employer violated §8(a)(3) when it gave to all workers who did not participate in a strike, and to all who abandoned the strike early, seniority privileges greater than those enjoyed by the workers who participated in the strike for its entire duration.[830]

Employees returning to work after a strike do not have a statutory right to displace employees who remained on the job during a strike or who returned to their jobs before the strike ended or who were hired as 'permanent' replacements during a strike. There is, however, a presumption that replacements are temporary and the employer has the burden of proving that the replacements were hired with a mutual

827. 20 Code of Federal Regulations §652.9. It is anticipated that the Trump administration will rescind this regulation.

828. *Compare*, *Chamber of Commerce* v. *State*, 445 A.2d 353 (NJ 1982); *International Union, UAW* v. *C. M. Smillie Co.*, 362 N.W.2d 780 (Mich. App. 1984) (*per curiam*); and *Kapiolani Medical Center for Women and Children* v. *Hawaii*, 82 F. Supp. 2d 1151 (D. Hawaii 2000).

829. *Larand Leisurelies, Inc.*, 222 NLRB 838 (1976).

830. *NLRB* v. *Erie Resistor Corp.*, 373 US 221 (1963).

understanding between the employer and worker that they would continue to hold the jobs after the strike ended.[831] Moreover, the employer cannot give job or shift preferences to those who worked during the strike except with respect to the jobs and shifts they worked during the strike.[832]

A further rule is that if the striker replacements are later laid off due to a reduction of operations but with an expectation of returning to the jobs when operations expand and workers are recalled, the employer is allowed to recall the striker replacements to their jobs in preference to more senior employees who had stayed out for the full duration of the work stoppage and were never returned to their jobs after the strike.[833] (Arguably, in order to uphold the statutory prohibition against discrimination based on union activity, competition for jobs between employees who are returning strikers and those who were their replacements should be based on factors unrelated to exercising or refraining from exercising the right to engage in concerted activity – such as seniority, job experience, or job performance.)

744. In the early 1990s unions mounted an unsuccessful political effort to amend the NLRA in order to reduce the circumstances under which employers can lawfully replace striking employees. Some proposals would have banned all replacement for a minimum period such as the first sixty days of a work stoppage. Another proposal would have entitled replaced workers to displace their replacements at the end of the stoppage.[834] Part of the debate concerned the extent to which employees have been losing their jobs as a result of employers using the technique of hiring striker replacements. One government study showed that in 1985 and 1989 at least some strikers were unable to return to work in about 17 percent of all strikes because their jobs were occupied by a permanently hired striker replacement. The study also found that 4 percent of all strikers in 1985 and 3 percent of all strikers in 1989 were unable to return to work at the end of the stoppage because their job was occupied by a permanently hired striker replacement.[835] Perhaps even more significant, the study found that employers threatened to hire permanent replacements for strikers in about 23 percent of the 1985 strikes and in about 30 percent of the 1989 strikes.[836] As a result of its perception that employers increasingly resorted to the striker replacement weapon, in 1990 the AFL–CIO filed a complaint with the ILO asserting that the lack of statutory protection from striker replacement places the US in violation of ILO Convention 87 on the freedom of association. A few years later,

831. *Jones Plastic & Eng. Co.*, 351 NLRB 61 (2007) (the fact that the replacements are employed 'at will' does not detract from their being 'permanent' replacements); *O.E. Butterfield, Inc.*, 319 NLRB 1004 (1995).
832. *Waterbury Hosp.* v. *NLRB*, 950 F.2d 849 (2d Cir. 1991).
833. *Aqua-Chem, Inc.* v. *NLRB*, 910 F.2d 1487 (7th Cir. 1990), *cert.* denied 501 US 1238; *Medite of New Mexico, Inc.* v. *NLRB*, 72 F.3d 780 (10th Cir. 1995).
834. For examples of such proposals *see* Senate Bill 55 and House Bill 5 of the 1st Session, 102nd Congress.
835. Study conducted by the General Accounting Office and reported in *BNA Daily Labor Reports* on 13 Mar. and 1 Apr. 1991.
836. M. Finkin, 'Labor Policy and the Enervation of the Economic Strike', 1990 *U. Ill. L. Rev.* 547, 548–549 n. 12.

when the business community gained greater legislative influence through the election of a Republican Party majority in both houses of Congress, statutory proposals were offered by conservative legislators to require US withdrawal from the ILO.

The US continues to be an ILO member but no change has been made in US law respecting the availability of striker replacements to counteract employee work stoppages.

C. Strikes in Violation of Statutory Notice Requirements

745. Section 8(d) of the NLRA imposes certain procedural requirements before a work stoppage can lawfully be initiated if the stoppage seeks a change in terms or conditions of work (as contrasted with a stoppage protesting an alleged violation of the current agreement, a stoppage in support of union organizing efforts, or a stoppage in support of demands for an initial collective agreement). Under §8(d), a stoppage in support of bargaining demands is an unfair labor practice unless: (a) one of the parties has been given a 60 day prior written notice of the intention to terminate or modify the existing collectively bargained agreement, and (b) at least 30 days' prior written notice of the labor dispute has been sent to the Federal Mediation and Conciliation Service and to any pertinent state mediation agency. The NLRB has held that it is an unfair labor practice for a union to strike prior to the expiration of both notice periods. As a result, if a union gives notice to the employer at least 60 days prior to the date of the expiration of the collective agreement, but does not give notice to the FMCS until the date of the contract expiration, it cannot resort to a strike until at least thirty days have expired since the notice was given to that federal agency.[837] In addition, the expiration of the notice period does not by itself release the parties to resort to a work stoppage unless either the most recent collective agreement has expired by the end of the notice period or the agreement provides for pre-expiration renegotiation of the subject at issue.

Under the explicit language of NLRA §8(d), the Act gives no job protection to a worker who, before the notice requirements have been satisfied, participates in a strike seeking a change in terms or conditions of work. Accordingly, such a striker does not have the normal statutory right to reinstatement upon termination of the strike.

The notice requirements of the NLRA do not apply to employees who do not have a collective bargaining agent. Therefore, such employees can engage in work stoppages without giving the statutory notices.[838] In addition, a spontaneous walkout by workers who did not consult the union is not in violation of the notice provisions because the duty to give notice is imposed on the parties to the collective agreement – the employer and the union; it is not imposed on the employees.[839] Whether the employer can discipline such workers is examined in paragraphs 747–55, below.

837. *See*, for example, *Nabors Trailers, Inc.* v. *NLRB*, 910 F.2d 268 (5th Cir. 1990).
838. *NLRB* v. *Washington Aluminum*, 370 US 9 (1962).
839. *East Chicago Rehabilitation Center, Inc.* v. *NLRB*, 710 F.2d 397 (7th Cir. 1983), *cert.* denied 465 US 1065 (1984).

746. In the health care industry, written notice must be given 90 days, instead of 60 days, prior to the collective agreement's expiration and the notice to the FMCS and any pertinent state mediating agencies must be 60 days, instead of 30 days in advance. Moreover, §8(g) of the NLRA makes it an unfair labor practice to resort to a strike, picketing or other action in a dispute with an employer in the health care industry unless at least 10 days' prior notice has been given by the labor organization respecting that intended industrial action.

D. Strikes without Union Approval

747. A strike can occur without union approval in three different situations. The first is when workers do not have a bargaining representative, the second is when they have a bargaining representative but it has not taken a position regarding the workers' decision to strike, and the third situation is when workers strike despite the union's announced decision that they should not engage in a work stoppage.

748. Because the statutory right to engage in concerted activity is not dependent upon the workers having a recognized collective bargaining representative, a group of unrepresented workers have a protected right to act in concert to protest against an employment or work policy. For example, in a leading case a group of unrepresented workers walked off the job in protest against the unusually cold condition of the work area. The Supreme Court held that this was a protected work stoppage even though the workers did not articulate to management a specific demand for improvement. Several workers had, prior to the walkout, complained of the cold. 'Having no bargaining representative and no established procedure by which they could take full advantage of their unanimity of opinion in negotiations with the company, the men took the most direct course to let the company know that they wanted a warmer place in which to work'. This, the Court concluded, was enough to bring the conduct within the protection of the National Labor Relations Act.[840]

749. Insubordination, which an employer can punish, is distinguishable from a concerted work stoppage, which is activity protected by the NLRA. If the workers are union represented, the concerted nature of the conduct is more likely to be in the form of a challenge using contractual procedures such as the grievance and arbitration mechanisms. But when such procedures have not been established, what the workers consider to be a labor dispute protest, the employer might characterize as a refusal to follow management's direction of work. There are case decisions holding that workers cannot remain in work status while engaging in a protected concerted work stoppage. That is, to engage in protected concerted activity the workers must stop work completely and not merely disregard the work rule that is the focus of their protest. If they only partially cease working, the employer can treat the conduct as insubordination and impose disciplinary penalties, including dismissal from

840. *NLRB* v. *Washington Aluminum Co.*, 370 US 9, 15 (1962).

employment.[841] However, these case decisions fail to discuss the impact of §501(2) of the LMRA which includes concerted 'slowdowns' in the definition of 'strike' as used in that Act. Since the NLRA is a 'title' or portion of the LMRA, and §13 of the NLRA states that the right to strike shall not be diminished except as specifically provided for in the NLRA, it would seem that a concerted refusal to perform some aspect of work is a protected slowdown. Thus, although in order to maintain its operations an employer can place such workers on suspension until they are ready to perform all of their duties, dismissing them would appear to be an unfair labor practice since such action is unnecessary in order to maintain business operations. That is, the necessities of maintaining business operations are met by using supervisors, contractors or hiring others to perform their work during the time when they are unwilling to do so. However, once there is a vacancy and they are ready and willing to end their slowdown and perform all of their job functions, allowing the employer to treat them as dismissed would appear to unlawfully penalize them for having exercised their right to engage in a concerted slowdown.[842]

750. If workers are represented by a collective bargaining agent, that agent has the statutory status as exclusive representative of their collective interests. Under American law, a corollary of this principle is that all concerted activity must be channeled through that bargaining representative and is protected only if approved by the representative. Concerted activity that is disapproved by the bargaining agent is unprotected activity. The participants in such disapproved concerted conduct, therefore, can be disciplined by the employer without violating the NLRA.[843] (If they are union members, they also may be disciplined by the union through its own internal procedures.) Such disapproved concerted activity by a group of workers is known as 'wildcat' activity.

Less certain, however, is the status of concerted activity that is in furtherance of the collective's objectives but neither has been expressly authorized nor disapproved by the bargaining representative. The NLRB takes the position that unless disapproved, the concerted activity is protected so long as it is in furtherance of union authorized goals. Although the law in this area is not settled, the prevailing approach is that collective action taken without the union's approval does not lose its status as protected activity so long as it does not constitute an effort by a minority of workers to impose their will on the majority and is not designed to denigrate or interfere with the union's ability to carry out its responsibility as bargaining representative. For example, it has been held that when employees, without first consulting the union, refuse to work in order to demonstrate the intensity of their support for particular demanded changes in the collective agreement, it is an unfair labor practice for the employer to terminate their employment.[844]

---

841. *Excavation-Construction, Inc.* v. *NLRB*, 660 F.2d 1015 (4th Cir. 1981); *Elk Lumber Co.*, 91 NLRB 333 (1950).
842. *Laidlaw Corp.*, 171 NLRB 1366, enforced 414 F.2d 99 (7th Cir. 1969) (once a strike is abandoned, the employees have a right to reinstatement when their former job is available).
843. *Emporium Capwell Co.* v. *Western Addition Community Organization*, 420 US 50 (1975); *NLRB* v. *Draper Corp.*, 145 F.2d 199 (4th Cir. 1944).
844. *NLRB* v. *Bridgeport Ambulance Service*, 966 F.2d 725 (2d Cir. 1992).

E. Peace Clauses – Waiver of the Right to Strike

751. Because the recognized or certified bargaining agent has exclusive authority to represent the workers' collective interests, that bargaining agent has the power to contractually waive the right to strike.[845] Thus, regardless of whether a striker acts with union approval, acts without union consent, or is involved in wildcat activity, the employer lawfully may terminate the worker's employment for breaching the peace provision of the collective agreement. Such peace provisions, most often referred to as 'no-strike clauses', must be expressly made part of the collective agreement. However, a peace provision will also be found by implication to the extent that there is an express undertaking to resort to arbitration or to resolution through a specific grievance procedure as the exclusive means for resolving disputes.[846]

752. An employer can sue for breach of contract or initiate an arbitration proceeding (if such a breach is covered by an arbitration provision in the collective agreement) to recover damages from the labor organization if the union authorized a work stoppage in violation of an express or implied peace agreement.[847] To recover such damages from the union, however, it must be shown that the union made itself a party to that stoppage. The union is not liable for damages arising out of a stoppage it neither authorized nor ratified. Therefore, a parent organization, such as a national union, cannot be held liable for damages resulting from an affiliate or subordinate organization's strike, such as a strike by a local union, unless the parent organization encouraged or adopted the action. Nor is a union liable for damages for failing to take affirmative steps to end a wildcat strike unless it has contractually undertaken that responsibility.[848]

Although an employer may dismiss workers who violate a no stoppage provision of a collective agreement, it is not permitted to sue those employees for damages.[849]

753. The NLRB generally holds that a broad no stoppage provision in a collective agreement does not waive the right to act in concert with the employees of other employers by refusing to cross a lawful primary picket line. (A primary picket line is one located at the work site of the employer with whom the picketing labor organization has its dispute.) To be effective as a waiver of the qualified right to respect picket lines the no stoppage provision must make that waiver in clear and

845. *NLRB* v. *Sands Mfg. Co.*, 306 US 332 (1939). On the other hand, a labor organization cannot waive the individual's right to refrain from participating in concerted activity. *NLRB* v. *Magnavox Co.*, 415 US 322 (1974).
846. *Local 174, Teamsters* v. *Lucas Flour Co.*, 369 US 95 (1962); *Groves* v. *Ring Screw Works*, 498 US 168 (1990).
847. *Drake Bakeries* v. *Local 50, American Bakery Workers*, 370 US 254 (1962).
848. *Carbon Fuel Co.* v. *United Mine Workers*, 444 US 212 (1979).
849. *Complete Auto Transit, Inc.* v. *Reis*, 451 US 401 (1981).

unmistakable language. Alternatively, that intention may be established by comparable collateral evidence respecting the parties' mutual understanding.[850]

Although, if not waived, the NLRA protects the right to cross a primary picket line, the employer can treat the worker who refuses to cross a picket line as himself a striker and replace him if it can show that the refusal to cross the picket line resulted in a material interference with the employer's operations and that the employer had no reasonable alternative means for getting that work done (such as by sending another worker to do the work or having it done by a supervisor or directing the employee in question to use an alternative entrance not covered by a picket line).[851] Such replacement is not the same as a dismissal from employment. The employee must be allowed to do other available work assignments and if none are available, the replaced worker can be sent home and need not be recalled until his job is available to be performed without his causing the material interference resulting from his refusal to cross primary picket lines. Under this line of reasoning, drawing the analogy to replacement of strikers, if the worker has been replaced by someone hired on a permanent basis he need not be recalled until the position becomes vacant because the replacement has left or until more positions of the same type have been created.[852]

At least one federal appellate court, however, has refused to treat a refusal to cross a picket as analogous to a strike. It decided that if the employer has compelling business reasons to hire a replacement who will cross the picket line, and is not acting with an intent to harm the employees' organizational rights, the employer may discharge a worker who refuses to cross the picket line even without a collective agreement waiver of the right to engage in such activity.[853]

Since the worker who refuses to cross a primary picket line is not seeking changes in his own collective agreement, and since the conduct is that of an individual and not the labor organization, the notice requirements of §8(d) of the NLRA are inapplicable.

By adopting a provision in the collective agreement that in clear and unmistakable language waives the employee's qualified right to respect primary picket lines, the employer obtains the authority to discharge or in some other manner discipline a worker who refuses to cross a picket line, regardless of whether the employer can maintain its operations without that work being performed by the worker who insists on respecting picket lines.[854]

Collective agreements sometimes contain the opposite type of provision; one that recognizes a worker's right to respect any picket line, or any picket line recognized

---

850. *Keller-Crescent Co.*, 217 NLRB 685 (1975), enforcement denied on other grounds 538 F.2d 1291 (7th Cir. 1976).

851. *Torrington Construction Company*, 235 NLRB 1540 (1978); *Newberry Energy Corp.*, 227 NLRB 436 (1976); *Butterworth-Manning-Ashmore Mortuary*, 270 NLRB 1014, 1015 n. 7 (1984).

852. *NLRB* v. *Fluor Daniel, Inc.*, 161 F.3d 953 (6th Cir. 1998).

853. *Business Service by Manpower, Inc.* v. *NLRB*, 784 F.2d 442 (2d Cir. 1984). The NLRB has not accepted this approach and continues to limit the employer's remedy to replacement if business necessity requires hiring a new person to do work involving crossing a picket line. *Whayne Supply Co.*, 314 NLRB 393 (1994).

854. *NLRB* v. *Rockaway News Supply Co.*, 345 US 71 (1953).

by his union, regardless of the impact upon the employing enterprise. In such situations, the worker is contractually protected against disciplinary action or job loss resulting from refusing to cross a picket line. However, the NLRB has held that a provision in a collective agreement that prohibits the employer from disciplining workers who refuse to cross picket lines is insufficient to waive the employer's right to hire a replacement.[855]

F. Work Stoppages Due to Unsafe or Unhealthy Conditions

754. Section 502 of the LMRA states:

> Nothing in this Act shall be construed to require an individual employee to render labor or service without his consent, nor shall the quitting of labor by an employee or employees in good faith because of abnormally dangerous conditions of work at the place of employment be deemed a strike under this Act.

This has been held to prohibit treating as an unfair labor practice a work stoppage whose sole purpose is to avoid abnormally dangerous conditions.[856] Moreover, an employer who disciplines a worker for engaging in such a walkout has been held to be guilty of the unfair labor practice of interfering with the protected right to engage in mutual aid and protection.[857] In addition, the Supreme Court has stated that the courts should neither grant a damage award nor an injunction in a suit brought as a result of a work stoppage that satisfies the conditions of §502.[858] This means that such a walkout is permissible even if the collective agreement contains a no-strike undertaking. Such a work stoppage, however, must be based on more than an honest belief that abnormally dangerous conditions are present. To gain the immunity granted by §502, the employees must show that their fear of abnormal danger was based on objective evidence of such danger and not merely upon the speculation of those who are fearful.[859]

755. In some circumstances the OSHA additionally protects workers from employer sanctions if they walk off the job due to hazardous conditions. Under the Department of Labor's interpretation, this work stoppage immunity from employer sanctions is available 'if the employee, with no reasonable alternative, refuses in good faith to expose himself' to a condition that threatens imminent risk of serious

855. *Butterworth-Manning-Ashmore Mortuary*, 270 NLRB 1014 (1984), rev. denied 767 F.2d 933 (9th Cir. 1985).
856. *Clark Engineering & Construction Co.* v. *United Brotherhood of Carpenters*, 510 F.2d 1075, 1079 (6th Cir. 1975) (*dicta*).
857. *NLRB* v. *Knight Morley Corp.*, 251 F.2d 753 (6th Cir. 1957), *cert.* denied 357 US 927 (1958); *TNS, Inc.* v. *NLRB*, 296 F.3d 384 (6th Cir. 2002), *cert.* denied 537 US 1106 (2003) (rejecting the contention of other courts that §502 applies only when there is a collective agreement).
858. *Gateway Coal Co.* v. *United Mine Workers*, 414 US 368, 385 (1974) (*dicta*).
859. *Gateway Coal Co.* v. *United Mine Workers*, 414 US 368 (1974). *See also, Plain Dealer Publ. Co.* v. *Cleveland Typographical Union*, 520 F.2d 1220, 1228 (6th Cir. 1975) (it cannot be treated as a violation of a collective agreement's requirement that workers cross picket lines if there is honest fear, supported by objective evidence, that crossing the line would result in violent injury).

injury or death. The Department of Labor regulation additionally limits the worker's right to situations where a reasonable person would have such apprehensions.[860] This protection is available even if a worker acts individually and not in concert with others. In addition, it is available to employees, such as supervisors, who are not protected by the NLRA.

Because §§7 and 8(a)(1) of the NLRA together with §502 of the LMRA entitles workers to collectively walk off the job if there is objective evidence of abnormal danger even though that danger does not threaten imminent harm, in the mid-1970s an NLRB General Counsel announced a policy of deferring to OSHA proceedings where a walkout occurs under conditions that are covered by the Safety and Health statute. But, if the conditions prompting the work stoppage do not satisfy the imminent danger standard used by the Department of Labor, the NLRB's General Counsel will issue an unfair labor practice complaint if the employer disciplines workers who, supported by objective evidence, walk out in protest against abnormally dangerous working conditions.[861]

G. Striker Misconduct

756. Strikers who engage in certain types of conduct lose their statutory right to reinstatement at the end of the strike. The NLRB and the courts often characterize such conduct as 'unprotected' activity. Yet, the NLRA is silent regarding the loss of statutory protection except in the limited situation in which workers strike over a demand for a new collective agreement prior to the expiration of the statutory notice periods for renegotiating such agreements.

A better explanation of the result in cases involving striker misconduct is that even though an employer is prohibited from disciplining a worker for engaging in concerted activity, the employer may discipline a worker for misconduct that occurs during a strike if that misconduct seriously impairs the future employer–worker relationship. In such situations, it is not the concerted nature of the activity that gives rise to the employer's right to sever the relationship; rather it is the individual misconduct that gave rise to the employer's response.

Section10(c) of the NLRA describes the NLRB's remedial power as being subject to the limitation that the backpay and reinstatement remedy shall not be available if an employee was discharged or suspended 'for cause'. Strikers, under the NLRA, remain employees. Therefore, the employer can discipline (including dismiss) 'for cause' the employee, who, as a striker, engaged in misconduct.

757. Striker violence is the most obvious form of misconduct that is outside of the statutory protection of concerted activity. Thus, the Board and the courts have held that an employer does not commit an unfair labor practice if it discharges a striker who resorts to violence regardless of whether that violence is directed at

---

860. The regulation was upheld in *Whirlpool Corp.* v. *Marshall*, 445 US 1 (1980).

861. J. Irving, 'Effect of OSHA on Industrial Relations and Collective Bargaining', in ABA, *Nat'l Institute on Occupational Safety and Health Law* at 123, 128–129 (1976).

other workers, law enforcement officers, customers, managerial personnel or property belonging to the company or others. The threat of violence similarly gives the employer legally recognized 'cause' to discharge a striker. In applying this principle, however, the NLRB and the courts acknowledge that, in the context of a strike, the language and manners of participants must not be judged by the standards of conduct normally encountered in polite and restrained settings. In the context of a labor dispute, mere use of crude or offensive language or of obscene gestures is not enough to justify disciplinary action. Similarly, physical offenses of a minor or incidental nature, such as mutual shoving, waiving of picket signs in front of people's faces, and the like, do not rise to the level of seriousness required to remove the striker's protection from disciplinary sanctions. Rather, an employer can impose disciplinary sanctions based on a striker's hostile acts only when the conduct involves use of significant force or is destructive or may reasonably tend to coerce or intimidate others.[862] In assessing whether a striker's hostile words or conduct were truly threatening, the Board considers the extent to which it was a reaction to provocation or was a momentary impulsive response without long term significance.[863]

758. Ever since the decision in *NLRB* v. *Fansteel Metallurgical Corp.*, 306 US 240 (1939), the NLRB and the courts have held that an employer may discharge workers who engage in sit-in or sit-down strikes. In the *Fansteel* case some of the workers resorted to considerable violence in resisting their ejection from the plant. The Court's opinion treated the sit-in strikers' conduct as rendering them outlaws who forfeited their claim to legal protection. The Court did not explore the question of whether those sit-in strikers who had not engaged in violence were capable of returning to the mill and resuming a constructive working relationship with management.

More recent cases have applied the *Fansteel* principle even when violence has been absent. Without specifically finding that the workers' conduct damaged the employer in some manner other than through the withholding of expected work, some courts, and to a lesser extent the NLRB, have concluded that mere participation in a refusal to leave the premises, after being told to do so, constitutes conduct that justifies disciplinary action including dismissal from employment. In contrast, other courts have held that the threat to an employer's right to control its property must be balanced against the workers' collective right to show chagrin at the employer's actions and demonstrate their solidarity. On occasion, the NLRB has attempted to avoid the *Fansteel* doctrine by finding that the employees did not

862. *Associated Grocers of New England* v. *NLRB*, 562 F.2d 1333 (1st Cir. 1977); *NLRB* v. *McQuaide*, 552 F.2d 519 (3d Cir. 1977). In *Universal Truss, Inc.*, 348 N.L.R.B. 733 (2006) the Board held that the employer's honest belief that a striker was guilty of serious misconduct is enough to justify dismissal unless it is proven that the returning striker did not in fact engage in the misconduct or that the conduct was not serious enough to forfeit the protection of the Act.

863. *Precision Window Mfg., Inc.* v. *NLRB*, 963 F.2d 1105 (8th Cir. 1992). In *ABF Freight System, Inc.* v. *NLRB*, 510 US 317 (1994), the Court upheld the Board's reinstatement award even though the employee had been guilty of giving false testimony in the NLRB proceeding.

intend to engage in a sit-down but merely were insisting on remaining in a supervisor's office, or similar location, until a grievance had been fully discussed.[864]

759. When workers strike, management likely regards that conduct as a manifestation of disloyalty. Although the law of individual employment agreements includes a duty of loyalty to the employer, disloyalty in the form of a concerted work stoppage is statutorily protected under the National Labor Relations Act. Some concerted activities, however, do give the employer a right to impose disciplinary sanctions based upon the manifest disloyalty involved in those activities. For example, the Supreme Court upheld the right of a broadcasting company to discharge workers who, during non-duty hours, distributed handbills that criticized the quality of their employer's programming.[865] In another case, strikers carried placards warning customers against the alleged inferior quality of paint produced by their temporary replacements. The NLRB held that this disparagement of the employer's product was a sufficiently serious offense to justify the employer's resort to disciplinary sanctions.[866] Insofar as the employer's public image is concerned, it is questionable whether the above unprotected concerted activities harmed the employer to any greater extent than the long recognized and protected activities of carrying placards condemning the employer as 'unfair' and urging customers not to do business with the struck employer. Thus, commentators have questioned the continued viability of these earlier 'disloyalty' decisions. More recent decisions have been responsive to such criticism. Thus, in *MasTec Advanced Technologies*, 357 NLRB 103 (2011), the NLRB ruled that the employees were protected from dismissal where the employees' public statements were related to their labor dispute with the employer and, to the extent that they were inaccurate, were merely mistaken and not malicious falsehoods calculated to harm the company's reputation.[867]

In a different type of 'disloyalty' case, a divided NLRB held that it was not an unfair labor practice for an employer to dismiss an employee for having attempted to persuade the employee stock ownership plan trustees to buy a controlling interest in the employer corporation. The Board based its decision on the proposition that the Act only protects concerted employee conduct when directed at the workers'

864. *See*, for example, the discussion in *Molon Motor and Coil Corp.* v. *NLRB*, 965 F.2d 523 (7th Cir. 1992); *Advance Indus. Div.* v. *NLRB*, 540 F.2d 878 (7th Cir. 1976); *Quietflex Mfg. Co.*, 344 NLRB 1055 (2005); *Fortuna Enterprises, LP* v. *NLRB*, 665 F.3d 1295 (DC Cir. 2011).
865. *NLRB* v. *Local Union No. 1229, IBEW*, 346 US 464 (1953). The Court particularly emphasized that: (1) the employees did this while still on the employer's payroll; and (2) the handbills did not reveal that the employees were involved in a labor dispute. This suggests that the outcome may have been different if the employees were engaged in a work stoppage, and therefore were not being paid, or if the employees made it clear to the public that the criticism was coming from participants in a labor dispute. However, in the case cited in the next endnote, the NLRB allowed an employer to discipline for 'disloyalty' even where there was a strike and the public was alerted to the existence of the labor dispute.
866. *Patterson-Sargent Co.*, 115 NLRB 1627 (1956).
867. Accord, *DirecTV, Inc.* v. *NLRB*, 837 F.3d 25 (DC Cir. 2016) (disparaging statements are protected if related to the underlying dispute, not maliciously untrue or aimed at doing gratuitous harm, and are primarily aimed gratuitously aimed at drawing a third party into the dispute).

interests as employees and that the concerted activity involved in this case was directed at the employees' interests as owners.[868]

760. If a striker's misconduct constitutes a crime, the normal criminal laws can be enforced against the striker without regard to the employer's disciplinary action. Similarly, the striker can be held liable under the law of tort for any damages to property or persons so long as the theory of the action is one that is generally available, is not specific to labor disputes, does not conflict with rights protected by the NLRA, is not rooted in the collectively bargained agreement, and does not turn on the merits of an underlying labor dispute. For example, because the NLRA protects the right of workers to engage in concerted activity for mutual aid, an employer cannot recover for business losses due to a work stoppage based on a theory of action that the stoppage was a tortious interference with the employer's beneficial contractual relations. In contrast, a tort action will be allowed against a striker or manager who punched someone during an argument at a picket line.

Tort actions brought to recover for damages caused by striker misconduct generally are governed by state law. However, some federal law doctrine is superimposed when tort law is applied to disputes arising out of labor–management conflicts. For example, in an action for emotional distress arising out of statements made in the course of a labor dispute, the Supreme Court has held that, at the minimum, the state must condition recovery upon a showing that the tortious conduct was 'outrageous' and further must assure that awarded damages are not excessive.[869] Similarly, the Supreme Court has held that a recovery for defamation arising in the context of a labor dispute can be available only upon proof that the tortious statement was made with actual knowledge of its falsity or with reckless disregard for the truth and, additionally, courts must assure that awarded damages are not excessive.[870] The Supreme Court also has indicated that in a state court action the union cannot be held liable for its members' misdeeds unless there is clear and convincing evidence that union officials actually authorized, ratified or participated in the wrong doing; nor can members be held liable for the union's misdeeds in which they did not personally participate.[871]

H. Partial Strikes and Specially Timed Strikes

761. There are several limitations on a union's timing of a strike. For example, it has been held that an employer can discharge workers who walk out without prior warning if that sudden walkout poses a serious threat of damage to the employer's equipment.[872] In addition, in an early decision the technique of a series of short, or 'quickie', strikes was held by the Supreme Court to be unprotected. In reaching that

---

868. *Harrah's Lake Tahoe*, 307 NLRB 182 (1992).

869. *Farmer* v. *United Brotherhood of Carpenters*, 430 US 290, 304-306 (1977).

870. *Linn* v. *Plant Guard Workers*, 383 US 53 (1966).

871. *Atkinson* v. *Sinclair Refining Co., 370 US 238 (1962). See also*, Norris–LaGuardia Act §6 and *United Mine Workers of America* v. *Gibbs*, 383 US 715 (1966).

872. *NLRB* v. *Marshall Car Wheel and Foundry Co.*, 218 F.2d 409 (5th Cir. 1955). The *Marshall* case involved walking out while molten metal was in a cupola. Thus, the threatened damage involved

conclusion the Court also decided that such conduct was subject to state regulation.[873] However, a later decision overruled that part of the holding that permitted state regulation of such activity and cast some doubt upon the unprotected status of the 'quickie' strike.[874]

Inasmuch as the statutory definition of strike, at LMRA §501(2), includes slowdowns and 'other concerted interruptions of operations', there is reason to anticipate that reconsideration of the issue may lead the Court to treat such actions as 'protected'. In any event, although the NLRB has held that a series of short strikes is unprotected activity, it also has ruled that such stoppages are protected if the evidence does not demonstrate an intentional strategy of harassing the employer. Similarly, it has determined that if there is separate provocation for strikes of brief duration or intermittent strikes, they are protected forms of concerted activities.[875] Although the employer cannot discipline such strikers, under more general principles adopted by the Supreme Court (*see* paragraph 739, above) it should be entitled to hire replacements during the stoppage and refuse to reinstate any replaced strikers so long as the conduct that provoked the stoppage was not a significant unfair labor practice.

762. The most common form of partial strike is a slowdown–the refusal to work at a normal work pace. An employer is entitled to insist that workers perform at a reasonable level of effort and perform all tasks. Therefore, it can be argued that an employer has good cause to discharge workers who fail to work at a normal pace or who refuse to perform certain tasks or who refuse to work overtime even if that failure is pursuant to a concerted effort to put negotiating pressure on the employer to make some change in the terms or conditions of work. Moreover, some NLRB and court decisions support that position.[876]

On the other hand, as noted in paragraph 761, above, the statutory definition of 'strike' expressly includes slowdowns or other concerted interruptions of operations. Accordingly, while an employer can lay off and replace workers who are not willing to work at the standard work pace, the statute would appear to prohibit dismissal of such workers if engaged in a concerted slowdown, overtime refusal, or refusal to perform certain tasks. Interestingly, the cases allowing employers to dismiss workers engaged in such partial strikes do not discuss the impact of LMRA §501(2) or the related provision at NLRA §13 which states that nothing in the Act, except as specifically provided, shall be construed to 'diminish in any way the right to strike, or to affect the limitations or qualifications on that right'. Therefore,

---

more than the lost production, it posed a real and imminent prospect of causing considerable physical damage to the mill's equipment. *Columbia Portland Cement Co.* v. *NLRB*, 915 F.2d 253 (6th Cir. 1990).

873. *United Automobile Workers* v. *Wisconsin Employment Relations Board*, 336 US 245 (1949).

874. *Lodge 76, IAM* v. *Wisconsin Employment Relations Comm'n*, 427 US 132 (1976).

875. *Roseville Dodge, Inc.* v. *NLRB*, 882 F.2d 1355 (8th. Cir. 1989); *NLRB* v. *Empire Gas Inc.*, 566 F.2d 681 (10th Cir. 1977); *NLRB* v. *Robertson Indus.*, 560 F.2d 396 (9th Cir. 1976). Typically, in analyzing these cases, neither the NLRB nor the courts discuss the impact of LMRA §501(2)'s definition of 'strike'. *See*, too, the next paragraph.

876. *Elk Lumber Co.*, 91 NLRB 333 (1950); *Yale University*, 330 NLRB 246 (1999); *Vencare Ancillary Services, Inc.* v. *NLRB*, 352 F.3d 318 (6th Cir. 2003).

although there is some case law supporting the proposition that a concerted refusal to work overtime or perform certain tasks is an unprotected partial strike, the Supreme Court has indicated that it is prepared to apply the usual work stoppage protections to such refusals.[877]

In any event, if the employees have a recognized or certified bargaining representative, and if the dispute involves a demand for changes in the terms or conditions of work, the notice requirements of §§8(d) and (g) (*see* paragraphs 745–746, above) must be satisfied regardless of whether a work stoppage is total or partial.[878]

I. Unlawful Strikes

763. There is support for the proposition that strikers have no protection if their work stoppage is unlawful under the National Labor Relations Act or, perhaps, under other federal legislation. Thus, in one case an appellate court indicated that an employer could have lawfully discharged unrepresented employees who struck for the purpose of demanding that foreign workers be dismissed.[879] There also is case law supporting the proposition that those who engage in secondary boycotts that are unfair labor practices are unprotected by the NLRA and, therefore, can be dismissed or otherwise disciplined because the employer acted with good cause within the meaning of NLRA §10(c).[880] Such unlawful secondary boycott activity inevitably involves employee refusals to do a particular work task or work in a particular manner or with particular people. Because the conduct is itself an unfair labor practice, §7 of the NLRA does not protect it and, therefore, the employee's failure to follow management's directions constitutes good cause for imposing a disciplinary penalty that, under NLRA §10(c), cannot be set aside by the NLRB.

---

877. *Lodge 76, IAM* v. *Wisconsin Employment Relations Comm'n*, 427 US 132 (1976); *Local 1229, IBEW* v. *NLRB*, 202 F.2d 186 (DC Cir. 1952). Also, *C.G. Conn. Ltd.* V. *NLRB*, 108 F.2d 390 (7th Cir. 1939). In *NLRB* v. *GAIU Local 13-B*, 682 F.2d 304 (2d Cir. 1982), *cert.* denied 459 US 1200 (1983) the court upheld an NLRB finding that it was an unfair labor practice for a union to fine members who refused to abide by the union's ban on overtime work imposed during contract negotiations. Of course, the right to engage in such concerted activity can be waived through a non stoppage provision in a collective agreement. In that event, employees engaged in a partial strike can be disciplined by the employer for violating their obligations under the collective agreement.

878. *SEIU, United Healthcare Workers-West* v. *NLRB*, 574 F.3d 1213 (9th. Cir. 2009); *New York State Nurses Ass'n*, 334 NLRB 798 (2001).

879. *Zartic, Inc.* v. *NLRB*, 810 F.2d 1080 (11th Cir. 1987). Had there been a recognized bargaining agent in the particular case, the demand would have violated its duty of fair representation since the union has a duty to represent all bargaining unit workers. However, the workers were unrepresented. Their work stoppage included a demand for union recognition and certain other changes, as well as the demand that foreign workers be dismissed. It is the labor organization, not the employees, who have a duty of fair representation. Therefore, because a recognized union was not making the demand, it is unclear how the workers' collective action constituted an unfair labor practice under the NLRA. On the other hand, it is clear that the employer would have committed a civil rights violation if it acceded to such a demand. Without discussing these complications, the court stated that the stoppage in support of the demand for dismissal of foreign workers had an illegal purpose and, therefore, the dismissal of the strikers would have been permitted had the employer taken such action.

880. *See*, for example, *NLRB* v. *International Union of Elevator Constructors*, 902 F.2d 1297 (8th Cir. 1990).

In an interesting special situation, the Supreme Court has held that seafarers may not engage in a work stoppage under any circumstances in which they are aboard ship – even if the ship is in port. The majority of the Court reasoned that under American law it is mutiny for a sailor to refuse to follow the orders of a ship's officer at any time that the sailor is aboard ship. Because a strike at any time while on board is mutiny, the Court majority concluded that Congress could not have intended to protect such 'mutineers' from disciplinary sanctions.[881]

J. Injunction against Stoppages in Emergency Circumstances

764. Both the Railway Labor Act, at §10, and the LMRA, at §§206–210, provide special machinery for delaying or enjoining a work stoppage under certain 'emergency' circumstances in order to encourage resolution of the labor dispute without a stoppage. Those who strike in violation of such prohibitions are unprotected from employer disciplinary sanctions, including discharge, and may be subject, as well, to judicially imposed penalties for violating a court order. Section 213 of the LMRA provides for a more limited work stoppage delay in disputes affecting health care institutions that threaten a substantial interruption of care in the community concerned. These provisions are discussed further in paragraphs 833–834 and 873.

§2. Right to Refrain from Striking

765. Section 7 of the NLRA protects the right to refrain from concerted activities as well as the right to engage in them. Thus, it is an unfair labor practice for a union to coerce or attempt to coerce a worker into joining a strike. However, if the worker is a union member, the labor organization is entitled to use its internal organizational sanctions to coerce compliance with organizational policy including a work stoppage decision. Such internal sanctions might involve suspension or expulsion from membership, loss of certain membership privileges, or the imposition of a fine. The Supreme Court has held that the enforcement of such sanctions against a union member who violated union policy by refraining from participating in a strike is not an unfair labor practice. However, the Court has drawn a distinction between a union's attempt to enforce its policies by altering a member's employment status and a union's reliance solely upon its internal regulations to shape that member's conduct. Resort to employment sanctions, such as demanding that an employer dismiss a worker who did not join a walkout, is an unfair labor practice, but reliance upon internal union remedies is not.[882] As a result, in *NLRB* v. *Allis-Chalmers Mfg. Co.*, 388 US 175 (1967), the Court held that a union may expel or fine a member who crosses a picket line in violation of union rules. Moreover, such fines can be collected in a court suit. Underlying the Court's decision are the assumptions that:

---

881. *Southern Steamship Co.* v. *NLRB*, 316 US 31 (1942).
882. *Teamsters Local 1040*, 174 NLRB 1153 (1969).

(a) the union rule was properly adopted,
(b) the union rule reflects a legitimate union interest,
(c) the union rule is not itself in violation of federal labor laws, and
(d) the members can escape the rule by resigning from the union.[883]

An exception from the rule allowing a union to use internal disciplinary measures against members who work during a strike is imposed when the member is employed in a position that has supervisory responsibilities or other responsibilities respecting the development or implementation of labor–management policy. Based on the premise that NLRA §8(b)(1)(B) prohibits a union from interfering with an employer's choice of bargaining agent, in a closely divided decision the Supreme Court held that a union cannot discipline or threaten to discipline a member who works during a strike if that member is employed as a supervisor in a position that includes responsibilities for adjusting employee grievances and if that member-supervisor is required to work during the strike performing supervisory duties only.[884] The NLRB, with approval of appellate courts, has extended that reasoning to include prohibiting union discipline of a member who refused to assist the union in obtaining information to help organize an unorganized employer while that member was employed in a position having supervisory responsibilities including dealing with employee grievances of the unorganized employer.[885]

766. It has been argued that even though a union can use its internal disciplinary authority to coerce membership compliance with its decisions, unreasonably severe sanctions violate the workers' §7 right to refrain from concerted activities. This view found encouragement in earlier Supreme Court decisions. However, over the dissent of three justices, the Supreme Court eventually held that even an unreasonably severe fine does not constitute an unfair labor practice so long as the criteria for imposing such internal sanctions have been met. The Court observed that the severity of the fine or other sanction might make it unenforceable under the state law of voluntary associations or related legal principles that would be applicable in any suit brought by the union to collect its fine or otherwise enforce its disciplinary action.[886]

In addition, the NLRB has held that an employee who resigns during a work stoppage and then returns to work while the stoppage is in progress cannot be required by the union to reimburse it for strike benefits the employee received while he participated in the stoppage.[887]

767. The Supreme Court has upheld NLRB rulings that it is an unfair labor practice for a union to prevent a member from resigning during a strike or penalize a member for resigning during a strike. Accordingly, a union member who does not

883. *Scofield* v. *NLRB*, 394 US 423, 430 (1969).
884. *American Broadcasting Co.* v. *Writers Guild*, 437 US 411 (1978).
885. *NLRB* v. *IBEW, Local 1547*, 971 F.2d 1435 (9th Cir. 1992) (*per curiam*).
886. *NLRB* v. *Boeing Co.*, 412 US 67, 74 (1973).
887. *United Mine Workers of America (Canterbury Coal Co.)*, 305 NLRB 516 (1991).

want to join a strike, or who wishes to abandon a strike (referred to as a 'crossover'), can resign from the union and then return to work without facing any penalties from the union. The Court's explanation for this ruling is that it is a necessary result of NLRA §7's explicit protection of the right to refrain from concerted activities.[888]

The Supreme Court has also held that an employer can induce employees to not join or to abandon a work stoppage by ensuring them that when the stoppage ends they will not be displaced from the jobs they hold at the end of the stoppage.[889] The Court reached this conclusion despite the fact that the assurance that non strikers will remain in the job positions they hold at the end of the strike is, in effect, a unilaterally imposed new term or condition of employment that it adopted without first bargaining to impasse with the union respecting that change.[890]

In holding that at the end of a strike an employer can keep non strikers in job positions previously held by returning strikers, the Court approved employer conduct that discriminates against those who exercise their statutory right to strike. Such discrimination would appear to be evident where the striker seeking to return to work has longer experience on the job or demonstrably better job skills or knowledge. In such a case, as between the competing claims to the job, the employer gives favored treatment to the non-striker with the result that the striker who wishes to return does not get the job because he or she exercised the statutory right to strike. The Court's justification for this result was that it could 'see no reason why those employees who chose not to gamble on the success of the strike should suffer the consequences when the gamble proves unsuccessful'.[891] Thus, the Supreme Court ignored those competing job claims that normally determine who prevails and, instead, gave controlling weight to an employee's willingness to 'gamble' on the success or lack of success of the union effort in deciding between the statutory option of whether or not to participate in a work stoppage.[892]

In reaching its decisions allowing employers to favor striker replacements and crossovers, the Supreme Court has relied on its contention that the NLRA does not deprive an employer of the right to try to keep its business operating despite a work stoppage. However, although that consideration explains why an employer can hire replacements during a strike, it does not compel the preference given to non strikers when the stoppage ends. In addition, unlike its approach to some other forms of employer economic pressure, the Court does not limit the employer's right to favor striker replacements and crossovers to those situations in which there is a showing that the employer could not keep its business operating without hiring striker

888. *Pattern Makers' League of North America* v. *NLRB*, 473 US 95 (1985); *NLRB* v. *Granite State Joint Board*, 409 US 213 (1972); *NLRB* v. *Local 73, Sheet Metal Workers*, 840 F.2d 501 (7th Cir. 1988). For a critique of the Court's decision, *see* D. Abraham, 'Individual Autonomy and Collective Empowerment in Labor Law', 63 *N.Y.U.L. Rev*. 1268 (1988).

889. *Trans World Airlines* v. *Independent Federation of Flight Attendants*, 489 US 426 (1989).

890. The general principle is that changes in terms and conditions of employment may not be made unilaterally unless there has been an opportunity to bargain to impasse respecting the proposed change. *NLRB* v. *Katz*, 369 US 736 (1962).

891. *Trans World Airlines* v. *Independent Federation of Flight Attendants*, 489 US 426, 438 (1989).

892. For further examination, *see* A. Goldman, 'The USA' in 'Strikes and Lock-outs in Industrialized Market Economies', *Bull. of Comp. Lab. Rel.*, No. 29 (R. Blanpain and R. Ben-Israel, eds. 1994).

replacements on a 'permanent basis' or inducing employees to abandon their stoppage by assuring them that they will not be displaced by returning strikers.[893] Moreover, it has been argued that the Court's decision gives inadequate weight to the stated purposes of the NLRA that includes 'restoring the equality of bargaining power between employers and employees' and 'encouraging the practice and procedure of collective bargaining'.[894]

§3. Employer's Right to Lock out Workers

768. Most terms and conditions of employment are within the control of management. Hence, management's ability to maintain the status quo or to unilaterally change terms and conditions of employment constitute basic forms of economic leverage available for resolving labor disputes in a manner favored by management. Management has additional economic power in its ability to hire other workers if its present work force engages in a stoppage or, alternatively, it can displace workers with machines or contract its work to other employers. Each of these techniques represents a form of withholding work from employees who are unwilling to work based on the terms and conditions offered by management. A lockout – that is, a management imposed work stoppage–is a more direct method of financially pressuring employees in an effort to coerce them into acceding to the employer's proposals respecting the terms and conditions of employment. In American law a lockout is distinguished from dismissals because an employer that imposes a lockout is not asserting that the employment relationship is ended; it is just suspending the contract until the workers are willing to accept the terms and conditions of employment offered by the employer.

To the extent that it is a response to labor's collective demands, a lockout constitutes adverse treatment of workers because of their union activity. For this reason, labor organizations long argued that lockouts were an unfair labor practice. The administrative and judicial decisions have only agreed in part. A lockout is an unfair labor practice if it is used as a response to a labor organization's demand for recognition or as a means of purging union supporters from the payroll.[895] But, under the doctrine of the *American Ship Building* case, it is now settled that lockouts generally are lawful when used as a response to collective bargaining demands.[896] And, just as a strike can be called prior to a bargaining impasse, so, too, can management lock-out employees to put pressure on the union even though progress is being made

893. *See*, for example, *NLRB* v. *Fleetwood Trailer Co.*, 389 US 375 (1967).

894. The quoted language is found in the third and fifth paragraphs of NLRA §1. For critiques of the Supreme Court's striker replacement decisions *see*, for example, J. Getman and R. Marshall, 'Industrial Relations in Transition', 102 *Yale L.J.* 1803 (1993); P. Weiler and G. Mundlak, 'New Directions for the Law of the Workplace', 102 *Yale L.J.* 1907 (1993); M. Finkin, 'Back to the Future of Labor Law', 32 *William and Mary L. Rev.* 1005, 1019–1020 (1991); D. Pollitt, 'Mackay Radio: Turn it Off, Tune it Out', 25 *U. San Francisco L. Rev.* 295 (1991); P. Weiler, *Governing the Workplace: The Future of Labor and Employment Law* at 267–268 (1990); M. Finkin, 'Labor Policy and the Enervation of the Economic Strike', 1990 *U. Ill. L. Rev.* 547.

895. *NLRB* v. *Schmutz Foundry and Machine Co.*, 678 F.2d 657 (6th Cir. 1982); *DRC, Inc.*, 233 NLRB 1409 (1977).

896. *American Ship Building Co.* v. *NLRB*, 380 US 300 (1965).

toward a negotiated settlement. However, there is some judicial authority indicating that a lockout imposed prior to a bargaining impasse is an unfair labor practice unless there is a business justification for such early resort to this form of economic leverage.[897]

Although the NLRA does not specifically address the question of the legal status of a lockout, in support of its position that lockouts are a lawful method of asserting economic pressure in the course of collective bargaining, the Supreme Court has been able to cite language in the federal labor laws that imply that the lockout is the legitimate counterpart of the strike.[898] In *American Ship Building* the Court also found in one part of the legislative history of the NLRA support for its conclusion that Congress intended to permit employers to lock-out workers as a bargaining pressure technique. The original proposal for the Labor Act included an express prohibition against lockouts but that language was deleted in response to criticism that since the Act protected the right to strike, it would not be even-handed to prohibit the lockout. (For further discussion *see* paragraph 580, above.)

769. There are a number of restrictions upon the use of a lockout. First, it is an unfair labor practice for an employer to lock out employees in support of demands to change terms and conditions of employment established by an existing collective agreement without first satisfying the notice requirements of NLRA §8(d). In addition, a lockout is an unfair labor practice if it is in support of an unlawful demand or a demand that does not concern a mandatory subject of bargaining. If a lockout is initiated for such a purpose, the locked out workers are entitled to backpay for the entire period of the illegal lockout.[899] It also has been held that an employer commits an unfair labor practice when it locks out union represented employees to coerce their acceptance of a change in employment conditions made unilaterally by the employer prior to a bargaining impasse.[900] Additionally, an appellate court has held that it is unlawful discrimination for an employer to lock-out those who offer to return from a strike but not those who previously abandoned the strike because the employer offered no legitimate and substantial business justification for making the distinction. Hence, the employer's conduct merely punished those who stood with the union and awarded those who crossed the strikers' picket lines.[901]

770. The bargaining power gained by an employer that engages in a legitimate lockout is offset by the impact of the stoppage in restricting the employer's own economic activity. That impact can be minimized to the extent that the employer can stockpile the work in advance of a lockout or engage people to perform the work of

---

897. Business justification would include, for example, preventing the union from waiting to launch a strike at a time when replacement workers would no longer be available. *Blue Grass Precision Co., Inc.* v. *NLRB*, 636 F.2d 1127 (6th Cir. 1980), *cert.* denied 452 US 915 (1981); *Lane* v. *NLRB*, 418 F.2d 1208 (DC Cir. 1969).

898. *See* NLRA §8(d)(4) and LMRA §§203(c), 206, 208, and 213(a).

899. *Movers and Warehousmen's Ass'n*, 224 NLRB 356 (1976), affirmed 550 F.2d 962 (4th Cir. 1977).

900. *Teamsters Local 639* v. *NLRB*, 924 F.2d 1078 (DC Cir. 1991).

901. *Local 15, IBEW* v. *NLRB (Midwest Generation)*, 429 F.3d 651 (7th Cir. 2005), *cert.* denied 127 S. Ct. 42 (2006).

the locked out employees. There are several potential ways this can be accomplished. One is for non-bargaining unit employees, such as managers, to perform bargaining unit work during the lockout. Another is to contract the locked out work to another enterprise. And still another approach is to hire new employees to perform that work.

The Supreme Court has approved the hiring of temporary replacements for locked out workers in at least one situation. That is where the lockout was instituted to protect the employer from suffering exceptionally severe affects from the union timing a stoppage so as to impose it when the employer is most vulnerable. Such a lockout is often characterized as 'defensive'. Where, for example, a business is seasonal, a lockout well in advance of the busy season is defensive in that it is designed to bring about a settlement prior to the busy season, thereby reducing the level of business lost from the work stoppage. (Unions, of course, prefer to strike immediately prior to the busy season so as to maximize the impending business loss and, thereby, maximize the economic pressure the stoppage imposes on the employer.) Similarly, a lockout is defensive if it is designed to gradually shut down an operation in which a sudden shutdown is likely to seriously damage equipment (for example, a steel furnace). In the specific case in which the Supreme Court allowed a lockout to be accompanied by the hiring of temporary replacements, collective bargaining was being conducted in a multiemployer bargaining unit and the union had already struck one of the employers. To protect against this divide and conquer technique being used by the union, the other employers locked out their workers. All of the employers then continued their operations through the work efforts of supervisory personnel and people hired as temporary replacements for the strikers. Rejecting the assertion that this lockout penalized workers because of their collective activities, the Court held that it was a legitimate economic countermeasure. The Court reasoned that since the struck member of the multi-employer bargaining unit could hire temporary, or even permanent, replacements for the strikers, it was permissible for the cooperating employers engaged in the lockout countermeasure to be able to continue their operations on a parity with their struck colleague.[902]

771. Some appellate courts and the NLRB have ruled that so long as there is no proof that the employer's real aim is to rid itself of the union, an employer is permitted to hire temporary replacements for locked out workers even though the employer is not responding defensively but rather seeks to maximize its bargaining leverage.[903] However, it can be argued that, in violation of NLRA §8(a)(3), such conduct inherently discriminates against the locked out employees because of their union activity. That is, the employees who were locked out would have been working had they not made bargaining demands. Thus, the employer gave outsiders the jobs of bargaining unit members who were ready, willing and able to work and did this for no reason other than the fact that the employees through their representative made demands for changes in the terms and conditions of employment. Moreover, unlike the situation in which an employer hires striker replacements, when an

902. *NLRB* v. *Brown*, 380 US 278 (1965).

903. *International Brotherhood of Boilermakers* v. *NLRB*, 858 F.2d 756 (DC Cir. 1988); *Local 825, Int'l Union of Operating Engineers* v. *NLRB*, 829 F.2d 458 (3d Cir. 1987).

employer locks out bargaining unit employees, it cannot justify its conduct, as the courts have done in the case of striker replacements, on the ground that the employer has a right to keep its business operating. But for the lock-out, the business would have continued to operate with its regular workforce.[904]

772. There are no clear holdings respecting whether an employer can lock out and then hire permanent replacements. Although case decisions hold that an employer is entitled to hire replacements to keep its business going during a strike, it is difficult to see how hiring permanent replacements after locking out the organized work force can be viewed as anything other than an effort to be rid of the organized workers.[905] From that perspective it would appear to be an unfair labor practice whether hiring permanent replacements accompanies an offensive or a defensive lockout. To look at it another way, hiring permanent replacements after locking out the workers arguably converts even a defensive lockout into an offensive one that does not merely generate pressure to get the union to accede to a more favorable agreement; rather, the lockout inherently serves to rid the employer of workers who make concerted demands.

Nevertheless, the influential Court of Appeals for the District of Columbia rejected an unfair labor practice finding by the NLRB where an employer locked out workers during negotiations and then entered into a 'permanent' contract for another company to do part of the bargaining unit work. The court noted that during negotiations the employer had notified the union that it was considering permanently contracting out the work in question and the union had an opportunity to negotiate changes that would have made such an option less attractive to the employer. Under the circumstances, the court ruled that the contracting out was not inherently destructive of the employees' rights to engage in concerted activity. In addition, it reasoned that since the employer's proven motivation was cost savings, it had not engaged in unlawful discrimination or a refusal to bargain in good faith. Although the contracted work did not cover the entire bargaining unit and did not involve hiring replacement employees, this decision suggests that it is permissible for an employer to combat bargaining demands by replacing its entire workforce with those willing to work for less than what is demanded by the current employees so long as it first warns the union at the bargaining table that it will take such action.[906]

§4. Appeals for Sympathetic Support

773. American workers commonly use a variety of techniques to enlist the support of fellow workers, consumers and even other employers in order to generate

904. *Inland Trucking Co.* v. *NLRB*, 440 F.2d 562 (7th Cir.), *cert.* denied 404 US 858 (1971) (it is an unfair labor practice for an employer to hire temporary replacements after initiating an offensive, as contrasted with a defensive, lockout).

905. *See*, for example, *Kelley-Goodwin Hardwood Co.*, 269 NLRB 33 (1984) (hiring a series of 'temporary' replacements for locked out employees was found to be permanent replacement which demonstrated the employer's union destroying purpose).

906. *International Paper Co.* v. *NLRB*, 115 F.3d 1045 (DC Cir. 1997).

boycotts of work or products. Such techniques are used to raise awareness of the value of solidarity in organizing workers into labor organizations, to persuade employers not to resist recognizing the employees' bargaining agent, and to pressure employers to resolve conflicts over the terms and conditions of employment. Picketing, handbilling, news media advertising, and other means of communication are utilized for these purposes.

There are two categories of restrictions imposed upon these techniques. One is the concept of illegal secondary activities; a concept based on the proposition that economic pressures in a labor dispute should be exerted directly against the parties to the dispute and should not directly burden others since only the parties to the dispute are capable of resolving it. The resulting limitations to appeals to sympathetic parties are discussed above at paragraphs 444–480 and 486.

The other restriction on obtaining the support of others in a labor dispute is that economic and other pressure must not violate the right of property owners to control the use of their premises or jeopardize any person's safety or health. For example, picketing is unprotected if it creates a physical barrier to entering, leaving or using property or causes potential users to become fearful of entering or using the property. Such conduct, to the extent that it deters workers from performing their work, is an unfair labor practice because it interferes with their right under §7 of the NLRA to refrain from concerted activity. In addition, it is prohibited by state civil and criminal law doctrines such as trespass, assault and intimidation.[907] However, the Supreme Court has held that state law remedies must be restricted to regulating only the use of physical force or obstruction, intimidation, or incitement to violence and state remedies cannot address such issues differently in a labor dispute context than they are addressed in other contexts.[908]

907. For early examples of the prohibition against, and lack of protection of, coercive or destructive activity, *see Milk Wagon Drivers Union* v. *Meadowmoor Dairies, Inc.*, 312 US 287 (1941); *Electrical Workers (Cory Corp.)*, 84 NLRB 972 (1949).

908. *Youngdahl* v. *Rainfair*, 355 US 131 (1957).

Part III. Machinery for Enforcing Labor Laws

Chapter 1. The National Labor Relations Act

§1. Structure

774. The NLRB is a federal administrative agency created by the NLRA. Its five Board Members are nominated for staggered five-year terms by the President and are appointed upon the consent of the Senate. The President designates one of the members as Chairman. The General Counsel of the NLRB is nominated by the President for a four-year term and is appointed with the consent of the Senate. (Prior to the Taft–Hartley Act amendments of the NLRA, the General Counsel was appointed by the Board Members and the Board consisted of three rather than five members.)

By tradition, no more than three of the five Board Members belong to the same political party. Although most Board Members have been lawyers, this is not required by statute and a number of members, prior to their appointment, have been either non lawyer NLRB career employees, or non lawyers with some other exposure to the labor–management relations field. Most Board Members have served less than two full terms. However, John Fanning served for 25 years, including four as Chairman, and Howard Jenkins served for twenty years.

The title 'National Labor Relations Board' is both used to refer to the five Board Members who are the agency's final adjudicative officers, and to refer to the entire agency including its General Counsel, who is the agency's head prosecutorial officer, together with the various staff personnel that performs most of the agency's functions.

775. The NLRB's principal office is in Washington, DC (1015 Half St., SE, Washington, DC 20570-0001; telephone (202) 273-1000) but it has 26 regional offices plus a few sub-regional and resident offices located in major cities throughout the country. The Board Members, General Counsel and their immediate staff personnel work in the Washington, DC, headquarters. All NLRB proceedings are initiated either by petitions or by charges filed in writing with a regional office. These offices are staffed by lawyers, designated as field attorneys, and non-lawyer labor specialists, designated as field investigators, as well as by support staffs.

In charge of each regional office is a Regional Director who has considerable administrative and prosecutorial discretion delegated by the Board and by the General Counsel. Directly under the Regional Director is a Regional Attorney who supervises all litigation activities in the region. An agreement between the Board and the General Counsel gives the General Counsel administrative authority over the regional staff.

776. In the fiscal year completed at the end of 2017, written unfair labor practice charges were received by the NLRB in 19,280 cases in which it was asserted that a union or employer or both committed unfair labor practices in violation of the NLRA. (Unlike earlier years, the NLRB's published data no longer shows the portion of charges against unions separate from the portion filed against employers.) In the same period it received petitions in 2,236 situations raising questions concerning the representational status of a group of employees.

777. In addition to the regional offices, the General Counsel has a staff located in the agency's Washington, DC headquarters. This staff assists in administering the regional offices and includes lawyers who assist and advise the General Counsel in carrying out his or her responsibility for deciding whether there is probable cause for believing that charged violations of the NLRA in fact have occurred and that, as a result, a complaint should be issued in the name of the NLRB against the charged party. Washington based staff personnel also assist the General Counsel in carrying out the related responsibility of representing the NLRB in cases involving requests for injunctive relief from the federal district courts and in those cases in which the federal appellate courts review the decisions of the Board.

In addition to the staff supervised by the General Counsel, each Board Member has a personal staff of lawyers, plus supportive personnel, to assist in carrying out decisional responsibilities under the NLRA. The Board's case deliberations are open to the public except when public interest requires otherwise. Closed deliberations are transcribed and the public can access the transcripts except when secrecy is required to safeguard identities and other information in on-going criminal investigations or involves security classified foreign intelligence, counter-intelligence or international terrorism.[909] In the fiscal year that ended on 30 September 2017, the Board issued 158 decisions in unfair labor practice cases and 108 in representation cases.

Finally, there is an independent staff of law trained officials employed in the capacity of Administrative Law Judges (often referred to by the initials ALJ) assigned to the NLRB and organized as the NLRB's Division of Judges. Nineteen have their offices in Washington, DC. Nine are located in San Francisco, California, and five in New York City.

An Administrative Law Judge conducts the trial of an unfair labor practice case. This includes presiding over the hearing, ruling on evidentiary challenges, and issuing a written decision that includes findings of fact, conclusions of law, and an order either dismissing the complaint or providing a remedy for any unfair labor practices for which the charged party has been found guilty. If a timely appeal from the

909. 5 US Code §552(c).

Administrative Law Judge's decision is not taken to the five-member Board, the ALJ's order becomes the order of the Board. In earlier years, ALJs carried the title 'Trial Examiner'. Their decisions initially were known as 'Intermediate Reports' and later as 'Trial Examiner's Decisions'. They now are called 'Administrative Law Judge Decisions'.

The independence of an Administrative Law Judge is based on the fact that pursuant to the federal Administrative Procedure Act, decisions concerning the standards for promotion and salary increases of an ALJ are separately established by the Office of Personnel Management, an independent administrative agency, and, once appointed, an ALJ can be demoted in grade or pay, suspended or dismissed only upon a decision by the Merit Systems Protection Board, another independent administrative agency, based upon a hearing at which good cause is shown. (*See* 5 US Code §§3105, 5372, 7521 and 7532.) However, their offices are housed in the same buildings as the General Counsel's prosecuting staff.

778. The NLRB's decisions are publicly reported when issued. They are identified by the name of the respondent party (the party charged with an unfair labor practice) in unfair labor practice cases or the name of the employer in representation proceedings. In addition, the case is identified by a numerical designation of the case report. When a union is the respondent party in an unfair labor practice case, in order to help identify the particular decision, often the name of the employer is also parenthetically designated.

Each NLRB decision (the term used for unfair labor practice cases) or determination (the term used for representation cases) is initially available in stapled advance sheet form and identified by the number of the report volume in which it eventually will be reprinted plus an assigned advance sheet number. Thus, a case bearing the designation 208 NLRB No. 24 means that the decision eventually will be published in report volume 208 and that it has been issued as advance sheet 24. When volume 208 is printed, the case is thereafter officially identified by the volume number, followed by the designation 'NLRB', followed by the number of the page at which the case report begins.

779. By statute, the NLRB has the authority to issue regulations that interpret the NLRA as well as regulations that refine the details of what conduct is or is not required to comply with the statute. Unlike most other federal administrative agencies, the NLRB does not issue substantive regulations. Instead, it relies upon a case-by-case development for pronouncing its interpretation of the law and for exercising its discretion to shape the detailed rules for carrying out the broad policies of the NLRA. The NLRB has adopted regulations establishing procedural rules for conducting the agency's business including conducting investigations, elections, hearings, and appeals, and, on a few occasions, has used the power to issue regulations as a method for defining its standard for exercising jurisdiction over particular types of employment enterprises. In addition, occasionally it has issued regulations defining acceptable bargaining unit structures for particular industries. The official title of the regulations which have been issued by the Board is: 'National Labor Relations Board, Rules and Regulations'. Some commentators fault the Board for its failure to issue substantive regulations.

§2. The NLRB's Jurisdiction

780. The NLRB has jurisdiction[910] over labor disputes that by themselves or together with others in the same industry directly or indirectly burden or tend to burden interstate commerce. Expressly excluded from the Board's jurisdiction are persons subject to the Railway Labor Act, household servants, agricultural laborers, persons employed by their parent or spouse, independent contractors, and persons employed in a supervisory capacity. In addition, with one exception, excluded from the Act are all federal, state and local employees. However, under the Postal Reorganization Act of 1970, NLRB election procedures and most unfair labor practice provisions are applicable to federal postal workers.

781. In order to determine whether particular employment burdens or tends to burden interstate commerce, the Board uses guideline criteria based on the type of industry and the level of business activity. For example, employment of orchestra musicians is treated as within the Board's exercise of its jurisdictional power only if the gross annual receipts of the orchestra exceed $1 million. Similarly, persons employed by a newspaper are treated as covered if the paper has gross annual receipts of at least $200,000, but law firms must have gross annual revenues of at least $250,000 and hotels and motels must have gross annual business of $500,000 before the NLRB will exercise jurisdiction over them. Most jurisdictional standards have been announced by case decisions many of which were established decades ago. Therefore, inflation continually expands the agency's operational authority. The standards are summarized in *NLRB, Case Handling Manual, Part Two, Representation Proceedings,* which is available on-line.

§3. Determining Whether a Union is the Exclusive Bargaining Agent

I. NLRB Representation Proceedings

782. There are five basic categories of proceedings handled by the NLRB: (a) unfair labor practice charges, (b) representational certifications, (c) unit clarifications, (d) deauthorization certifications, and (e) work assignment determinations.

Representational proceedings determine whether a particular group of employees is an appropriate unit for the conduct of collective bargaining and, if so, whether a majority of that unit wants to be represented, or wants to continue to be represented, by a particular labor organization.[911]

910. American jurists and lawyers give the term 'jurisdiction' a broader meaning than it has in some other legal systems. It is the authority to rule on disputes involving particular persons or entities as well as the authority to regulate and resolve particular categories of conduct, rights, obligations, and disputes both generally and with respect to particular situations. Thus, as used in American jurisprudence, the term includes what other systems refer to as 'competence'. *See also*, paragraphs 49–50, above.

911. Although an individual can be certified as bargaining representative, this rarely happens. Therefore, the discussion is presented in terms of a labor organization being designated as bargaining representative.

783. Representation proceedings are governed by §9 of the NLRA and are initiated by the filing of a written petition with a regional office of the Board or a subdivision thereof. Filing need not be in person and the petition can be filed by a labor organization, a group of employees, or an employer. In the case of a petition filed by a union or a group of employees, it must assert that a substantial number of employees wish to be represented in collective bargaining by a named labor organization (or that they no longer wish to be represented), and that the employer has refused to recognize the union (or that the union continues to represent the employees). The petition does not explicitly request an election. The NLRB will dismiss a petition filed by a union or group of employees seeking representational status if it is not accompanied by evidence, such as union authorization cards signed by employees in the described bargaining unit, that at least 30 percent of the employees in the described bargaining unit want to be represented by the named union. This is referred to as the 'showing of interest' requirement. Once a valid petition has been filed, any other union interested in representing the employees can intervene if it shows that at least one bargaining unit employee favors it.

Alternatively, an employer can file a petition. If the petition is submitted by an employer, it need only assert that a particular labor organization demands recognition as the bargaining agent of the employees.

784. Often when a representation petition is filed, the parties agree that a question concerning the appropriate representational status of the bargaining unit has been properly raised and consent to the NLRB conducting a secret ballot election to determine the wishes of the majority of bargaining unit employees. Other times, objections are raised concerning the appropriateness of conducting such an election. These questions must be resolved, in the first instance, by the Regional Director (RD). The RD's determination is based upon either the findings of an investigation conducted by the regional staff or the record of a hearing conducted by a member of that staff. (Such 'hearing officers' are not Administrative Law Judges. *See* paragraph 777, above.)

Among the questions resolved in determining whether to proceed to an election are whether the NLRB will or can exercise its jurisdiction; the category of employer and employees in question; whether the bargaining unit is an appropriate one; whether an election cannot be conducted at this time because, under any one of several NLRB doctrines, conducting an election at this time is deemed inappropriate; whether particular employees do or do not belong in the bargaining unit; and the like. If the decision is in favor of an election, the balloting is conducted by Board personnel, usually at the employer's premises. If the workers are located in very widely dispersed areas, the Board may use the postal system for distributing and collecting ballots.

785. NLRB elections are conducted by secret ballot. A union must receive a majority of the votes validly cast (50 percent plus 1) in order to receive NLRB certification as the exclusive bargaining agent of the employees in the bargaining unit.

When it schedules an election the NLRB orders the employer to provide it with a list of the names and physical and email addresses of employees in the bargaining unit in which the election will be conducted. Unions on the ballot are given a copy of the list to assist them in contacting employees in their effort to solicit votes. During the election, the list (known as an *Excelsior* list due to the name of the case in which the requirement was first adopted) is used by the NLRB election officer to determine whether to challenge the eligibility of a person who seeks to vote. With some exceptions, employees are eligible to vote if they are on the payroll at the time of the election. This includes those absent for illness or on temporary layoff with a reasonable expectation of recall and those who are on vacation. Temporary employees whose employment is for a fixed time are not eligible to vote.[912] In the construction industry, and occasionally in other settings in which employment is for short but repeated durations, recently employed workers are eligible to vote.[913]

In order to be entitled to vote, a worker must be an 'employee' as defined by the NLRA and by judicial interpretation of the Act. (*See* paragraph 609, above.) A person whose eligibility to vote is challenged is given a special ballot envelope. (A double envelope system is used for challenged ballots so that ballot secrecy is preserved so long as there are at least two challenged ballots.) Challenges are resolved and challenged ballot envelopes are opened only if, after counting the other ballots, it is found that the number of challenged ballots is sufficient to change the result.

Once a representation petition has been filed, additional unions can petition to add their names to the ballot. One choice that is always on the initial ballot is 'no union'. If no available choice (including 'no union') wins a majority, a runoff election is held in which the employees select between the two choices that received the highest number of votes in the first balloting.

If a significant number of employees are literate in a language other than English, the NLRB provides a ballot with English and any other relevant language.

Under the language of §9(c)(3) of the NLRA, an employee engaged in an economic strike is eligible to vote for the first twelve months of the stoppage even if that person is not entitled to reinstatement.[914] During the first year of a strike, voter eligibility is lost only if the worker has abandoned the job. Employees engaged in an economic strike remain eligible to vote until permanently replaced even if the strike has continued in excess of twelve months.[915] Permanent replacements for strikers are eligible to vote but temporary replacements are not. (The employer has the burden of proving that a striker replacement has been hired as a permanent, not a temporary employee.)[916] Employees on strike to protest a proven, substantial unfair labor practice are eligible to vote even if the strike has lasted more than twelve months and their replacements, even though 'permanent', are not eligible to vote.[917]

912. *Caribbean Communications Corp.*, 309 NLRB 712 (1992); *NLRB* v. *SRDC, Inc.*, 45 F.3d 328 (9th Cir. 1995).
913. *See*, for example *Steiny and Co., Inc.*, 308 NLRB 1323 (1991).
914. If the job is no longer available, an employee is not entitled to reinstatement. Case decisions hold that a permanently replaced striker is not entitled to reinstatement because the employer need not terminate the permanent replacement and, therefore, the striker's job no longer is available. *See* paragraph 739, above.
915. *Gulf States Paper Corp.*, 219 NLRB 806 (1975).
916. *O.E. Butterfield, Inc.*, 319 NLRB 1004 (1995).
917. *Larand Leisurelies, Inc.*, 222 NLRB 838 (1976).

For many years the NLRB set aside elections unless a significant portion of the work force cast ballots. In *Lemco Construction, Inc.*, 283 NLRB 459 (1987), it reversed that rule and held that, even with a small voter turnout, it will certify the election results of an otherwise proper election so long as the employees were afforded a reasonable opportunity to participate.

786. In the fiscal year ending in September 2017, the NLRB conducted 1,391 representation elections. In the early 1980s the NLRB conducted over three times that number of representation elections. Indeed, the number of elections in 2017 was over 1,000 fewer elections than in 2005.

Most NLRB representation elections involve small bargaining units. For example, 40.2 percent of all new bargaining unit election cases that were closed in the fiscal year that ended in 2010 involved 19 or fewer eligible employees while only 15.4 percent involved bargaining units with 100 or more employees and the median bargaining unit size was 27. In the 2017 fiscal year the median size of bargaining units in election cases was 24. These figures can be misleading, however, because some smaller employee units are divisions or separate facilities of enterprises employing far larger numbers of workers.

Employers filed 2 percent of the 2,236 representation petitions filed slightly more than in the 2017 fiscal year. The rest were filed by unions or employees.

Of the 1,560 representation cases closed in fiscal year 2017, 168 involved elections in which employees were seeking to terminate a union's representational status (a decertification election). Unions retained their representational status in 35 percent of those elections.

787. A party that is displeased with the Regional Director's determinations in ordering an election can request the NLRB to review the Regional Director's decision. Such review is discretionary and is granted in only a very small percentage of these proceedings. As is discussed below, normally the decision of the NLRB to hold or not to hold an election is not directly reviewable by the courts.

788. The Board also conducts elections in cases in which at least 30 percent of the bargaining unit employees petition the Board stating their desire to rescind the union's authority to enter into a union shop agreement (an agreement that requires all employees to join the union within a given amount of time in order to retain their jobs). Such proceedings are referred to by the Board as 'deauthorization polls'. The NLRB has held that prior to such polling a union may caution the employees that if they vote for deauthorization by a decisive margin it will consider disclaiming recognition.[918] There were 19 such elections cases completed in fiscal year 2017.

789. After an NLRB election has been held, the results are not certified until there has been an opportunity to file objections regarding the way in which the election was conducted and to resolve any challenges to a voter's eligibility – if such challenged ballots would be enough to change the election results. The Regional Director conducts an investigation regarding such objections or challenges, and if

918. *Production and Maintenance Union, Local 101 (Bake-Line Products, Inc.)*, 329 NLRB 247 (1999).

deemed necessary, has a staff member conduct a hearing into the disputed matters. Unless the parties have conducted the election pursuant to an agreement with the RD for all such objections to be transferred directly to the Board for decision, the RD decides the questions raised by any challenges and objections. If the issues raised are novel, the RD can transfer the matter to the Board instead of making his or her own determination.

If the election was conducted after a contested hearing regarding the propriety of conducting an election, the Regional Director's determination concerning any objections or concerning vote challenges is final unless the NLRB grants a request to review that decision–a grant that normally it does not make.

Determinations concerning objections raised about the way an election was conducted, or challenges to ballots which were cast, are not subject to direct judicial review. Instead, such determinations are reviewed as part of any unfair labor practice case resulting from the losing party's decision to ignore the result of the representation determination and the NLRB's subsequent finding of an unfair labor practice based on that refusal. By appealing the NLRB's resulting unfair labor practice decision, or defending against the Board's effort to obtain a judicial order enforcing that decision, the objecting party can challenge the unfair labor practice decision on the ground that it was based on an invalid election certification.[919]

790. If the NLRB or Regional Director, upon review of the election, concludes that there was an irregularity, the Board will not certify the election results. Upon such a refusal, one possibility is to order another election, or 'rerun' election. In election cases completed in the Fiscal Year ending in 2010 only 21 were rerun elections. Of these, the original outcome was reversed in 8 of the elections; the union won 12 of the rerun elections that year. The Board no longer publishes this data.

As discussed in paragraphs 795–796, below, an alternative to ordering a rerun election is to find, under the so-called *Gissel* doctrine, that it is unlikely that a rerun election can be conducted in an atmosphere that is not burdened by prior or current coercion. In such situations the NLRB can order the employer to bargain with the union based on other evidence that it had the support of a bargaining unit majority prior to the employer's misconduct.

791. The NLRB General Counsel has no decisional authority in representation procedures. Although the Board has the ultimate authority to shape policy and resolve individual cases in the representation area, it has delegated to the Regional Directors the responsibility for day-to-day implementation of its authority over this area. The practical effect is that in most representation proceedings the RD's determination is the final source of law at the agency level. Inasmuch as most NLRB decisions are not judicially reviewed, this means that in most representation proceedings the RD is the final decision maker.

919. *American Federation of Labor* v. *NLRB*, 308 US 401 (1940). This is explained in more detail in paragraph 794, below.

792. During the 2017 fiscal year initial elections in union representation cases were conducted in a median of 23 days from the filing of the petition, and 98.5 percent of all elections were conducted within 56 days of the filing of the petition. Elections are delayed if a hearing is needed to resolve objections concerning such questions as jurisdiction, the appropriate bargaining unit, and whether there is a contract bar. The completion of the representation process is further delayed in cases in which the Regional Director or Board is required to resolve challenges to ballots or objections to the manner in which, or circumstances under which, the election was conducted.

793. There are a few exceptions to the rule that decisions concerning representation proceedings are not directly reviewable by the courts.. One is that a direct appeal can be taken to a federal district court to stay the Board's proceedings if the election in question is challenged on a jurisdictional basis having an impact upon American foreign relations. In *McCulloch* v. *Sociedad Nacional De Marineros de Honduras*, 372 US 10 (1963), the Supreme Court of the United States held that the NLRB does not have jurisdiction over labor–management relations concerning personnel employed aboard foreign flag vessels. The Court went on to say that the Board's attempted exercise of such jurisdiction raised a question so highly charged with foreign affairs considerations that it was appropriate for a federal district court to intervene to terminate the Board's representation proceeding. (It is note worthy that the Court rejected the NLRB's jurisdiction even though the foreign shipping company was owned and operated by US citizens.)

794. Normally a party obtains judicial review of the NLRB's determination in a representational proceeding by conducting affairs as though that determination was void. For example, an NLRB certification of the majority status or nonmajority status of a labor organization is not valid for any of the following reasons: (a) the Board did not have jurisdictional authority to conduct the representation proceeding, (b) the NLRB election included employees who do not constitute an appropriate bargaining unit, (c) one of the parties committed unfair labor practices, (d) there was some other interference with the proper conduct of the election, or (e) the facts present other grounds for objecting to the Board's representation determination (such as a breach of the security of the ballot box).

If an employer is displeased with the result of the NLRB's representational proceeding it can simply refuse to bargain with the certified employee bargaining agent. That bargaining agent must then file an unfair labor practice charge accusing the employer of violating the NLRA by refusing to bargain with the certified majority representative. The employer can then defend itself against the practice charge by asserting that the Board's certification was contrary to law and, therefore, was void and unenforceable. The unfair labor practice charge is heard by the NLRB and, with rare exceptions, the Board reaffirms the correctness of its earlier representation determination, finds the employer guilty of refusing to bargain, and orders it to bargain with the certified labor organization. However, because the Board's order does not carry direct penalties or enforcement power, the NLRB must apply to a US Court of Appeals for a court order requiring compliance with the Board's order to bargain. Alternatively, the respondent (the party charged with the unfair labor practice) can itself appeal to a US Court of Appeals asking it to vacate the NLRB order. Regardless of who takes the initiative in bringing the case before the Court of Appeals, in the appeal or enforcement proceeding the employer can again challenge the validity of the Board's underlying representation determination. At that point the merits of the challenged NLRB representation determination are weighed by the court and, thereby, the employer receives judicial review of the Board's determination. Sometimes, rather than pursue this indirect route, an employer accepts the result of the NLRB's representation proceedings even though it thinks there in fact was a deficiency that constituted good cause for setting aside the election.

It is more difficult for a labor organization to obtain judicial review of what it considers to have been an incorrect representation determination since, unlike an employer that can force the union's hand by refusing to bargain, the union may find it more difficult to force the employer to file an unfair labor practice charge. If the union refuses to bargain, the employer can be expected to carry on its business as though the employees are unrepresented. Often, though, in such a situation the union can engage in picketing that would be unlawful if the NLRB's decision was correct and for the employer to file an unfair labor practice charge to obtain relief from that picketing. At that point, by resisting the NLRB's resulting unfair labor practice orders, in the subsequent enforcement proceedings the union can obtain judicial review of the Board's underlying representation determination.

II. Alternatives to NLRB Election Proceedings

795. The National Labor Relations Act does not require that the representative status of a union be established through an NLRB conducted election. As an alternative, an employer can voluntarily recognize a union as bargaining agent for an appropriate bargaining unit if it has a reliable basis for believing that the majority of bargaining unit employees support that union as their bargaining agent.[920] The most common means of providing that proof is in the form of cards signed by the employees authorizing the union to be their bargaining agent. To ensure the authenticity and reliability of the cards, employers and unions sometimes agree to submit them to an impartial party for verification. The past two decades have witnessed an upsurge in the number of unions seeking recognition through the use of authorization card recognition by employers.

Many unions are successful in negotiating agreements that provide for employers to remain neutral during an organizing campaign. These 'neutrality agreements' often include language providing that the employer will not exercise its right to a Board-supervised election, but will recognize a union as exclusive representative of its workers if a majority of them sign valid authorization cards.[921] This 'card check' recognition has proved controversial in the broader political context, and the more business oriented Bush Board moved to regulate its use in 2007 by providing that

920. *NLRB* v. *Gissel Packing Co.*, 395 US 575 (1969).

921. *See generally* James J. Brudney, 'Neutrality Agreements and Card Check Recognition: Prospects for Changing Paradigms', 90 *Iowa L. Rev.* 819 (2005).

any union recognized by 'card check' was required to file a notice of such recognition with the NLRB, which would require the employer to then post a notice informing the workers that they had a forty five day window period after recognition to file a decertification petition with the Board.[922] That decision was reversed by the Obama Board in 2011.[923] The Board also clarified that 'card check' recognition by an employer brings with it a reasonable period of time of no less than six months but no more than one year from the time the employer engages in good faith bargaining with the union during which the union's majority status cannot be questioned.

Another alternative is for the employer to ascertain the majority's wishes by polling the employees respecting their desire for union representation. Because of the potential for intimidation in conducting such a poll, the NLRB has established criteria that must be satisfied so that the results of the poll can be accepted and will not itself be treated as coercive and, therefore, an unfair labor practice. Known as the *Struksnes* guidelines, these criteria require that the poll be by secret ballot conducted in an atmosphere free of coercion and unfair labor practices, that the employees be informed of the poll's purpose, and that they be given assurances against reprisals resulting from the outcome.[924] If the poll is an effort to establish grounds for discontinuing recognition of an incumbent union, the employer must notify the union that it intends to conduct such a poll.[925]

796. The NLRB sometimes is faced with a situation in which a union's seemingly successful organizing efforts were thwarted by an employer's unfair labor practices. In such situations, one possibility is for the NLRB to remedy those unfair labor practices and thereafter conduct a representation election or a rerun election. In recognition of the fact that it is not always possible to effectively remedy unfair labor practices, the Supreme Court has held that if the NLRB finds that due to their seriousness or pervasiveness it cannot adequately remedy the effects of unfair labor practices, it may order the employer to recognize and bargain in good faith with the union based upon the union's demonstration that a majority of employees (at least 50 percent plus one) supported it prior to the commission of those unfair labor practices and that the union had demanded recognition. Evidence of majority employee support normally is in the form of signed 'authorization cards' that state that the signer authorizes the labor organization to be his or her collective bargaining representative with the employer. An employer can challenge reliance on such cards if they are forged or coerced or were obtained through misrepresentation respecting the purpose for requesting the employee's signature, or were signed long prior to the union's demand for recognition. It can also challenge such a bargaining order request on the ground that the bargaining unit in question is not an appropriate unit under the Act.[926]

---

922. *Dana Corp.*, 351 NLRB 434 (2007).
923. *Lamons Gasket Co.*, 357 NLRB 739 (2011).
924. *Struksnes Construction Co.*, 165 NLRB 1062 (1967).
925. *Texas Petrochemicals Corp.*, 296 NLRB 1057 (1989), enforcement denied on other grounds 923 F.2d 398 (5th Cir. 1991).
926. *NLRB* v. *Gissel Packing Co.*, 395 US 575 (1969). On rare occasion the NLRB has ordered an employer to bargain to cure 'pervasive and outrageous' unfair labor practices even in the absence

Appellate courts often reject the NLRB's finding that it cannot effectively remedy unfair labor practices that interfered with holding a fair election. In such cases, despite the availability of authorization cards from a majority of bargaining unit employees, the appellate courts refuse to enforce the agency's bargaining order.[927] Eventually, in an effort to reduce the frequency with which bargaining orders are rejected by the courts, the NLRB General Counsel issued guidelines respecting when *Gissel* bargaining orders will be sought.[928]

III. Removal of Union's Representational Status

797. The opposite of voluntary employer recognition of a labor organization is an employer's withdrawal of recognition of an established employee bargaining agent. A basic principle affecting the rules concerning withdrawal of recognition is the doctrine is that once recognized as bargaining agent, a labor organization is presumed to have continued support from the majority of bargaining unit employees regardless of whether there has been a change in the bargaining unit personnel. If majority status was attained through winning an NLRB representation election, pursuant to §9(c)(3) of the NLRA, the presumption of continued majority support cannot be rebutted for the first 12 months after the NLRB certifies the election results. A slightly different rule applies if majority status was attained through voluntary recognition. In that instance, the NLRB also presumes continued majority status for up to the first year after recognition subject to the exception that the presumption is overcome if there are extraordinary circumstances justifying a conclusion that the union lacks majority support (for example, discovering that the cards on which recognition was based had been fraudulently obtained by the union organizers).[929] (*See also*, paragraph 795, above.) Moreover, under the doctrine of the 'contract bar rule', the presumption of a union's continued majority status cannot be challenged so long as the union continues to be available to function as the employees' representative, there has not been such a substantial alteration of the size and work tasks of the bargaining unit so as to constitute it as an essentially new and different workforce, and a current collective agreement has been in force for less than three years.[930]

However, once the first year of recognition or certification has expired, the presumption of continued majority support can be challenged and rejected if, under the mechanics of the contract bar rule, a party is able to file an NLRB representation

---

of a showing that the labor organization was ever supported by a majority of bargaining unit workers. However, in *Gourmet Foods*, 270 NLRB 578 (1985), it announced that it had abandoned that approach.

927. *See*, for example, *Kinney Drugs* v. *NLRB*, 74 F.3d 1419 (2d Cir. 1996).

928. Memorandum GC 99-8.

929. *NLRB* v. *Tahoe Nugget, Inc.*, 584 F.2d 293 (9th Cir. 1978), *cert.* denied 442 US 921 (1979). The rule respecting certification elections was upheld in *Brooks* v. *NLRB*, 348 US 96 (1954).

930. *Auciello Iron Works* v. *NLRB*, 517 US 781, 787 (1996); *NLRB* v. *Curtin Matheson Scientific, Inc.*, 494 US 775, 778, (1990). For more details, *see* paragraph 430, above.

petition.[931] Such a challenge either can be made: (1) through the NLRB election process, (2) by the employer's administration of a poll of employee sentiment (so long as the poll meets the *Strucksnes* guidelines discussed, above, in paragraph 799),[932] or (3) by the employer refusing to continue its recognition of the union under circumstances in which the employer has reliable proof that the union no longer enjoys majority status.

If a representation or decertification petition is filed by employees or a labor organization, it must assert that the incumbent union no longer has the support of a majority of employees. In addition, the petition must be supported by evidence, such as a signed petition or signed deauthorization cards, showing that at least 30 percent of the bargaining unit have expressly stated that they no longer wish to be represented by that labor organization. Alternatively, an employer can initiate the NLRB representation process by filing a petition making the same assertion. However, the employer's petition must be supported by some objective evidence that the employees' designated representative no longer enjoys majority support and, therefore, the employer has a good-faith basis for entertaining reasonable uncertainty respecting the desire of a majority of bargaining unit employees to continue to be represented by the incumbent representative.[933] As with a successful employee or union representation petition, if the above criteria are satisfied, the NLRB conducts a secret ballot election to determine whether a majority of employees continue to support the incumbent union.

In contrast, if an employer simply ceases to recognize the incumbent union in order to challenge its continued representative status, the employer's conduct is treated by the NLRB as an unfair labor practice unless the employer proves that the incumbent union in fact lost majority support.[934] What constitutes such evidence is less clear. For example, courts have noted that the fact that employees have not joined a strike, have abandoned a strike, or are replacements for strikers, does not permit the employer to assume that they do not support the union. Employees can desire continued union representation even though they do not have the fortitude to participate in or continue to participate in a work stoppage or disagree with the wisdom of the current stoppage.[935] Similarly, it has been held that the requirement of clear and convincing evidence of a reasonable, good faith doubt of continued majority status is not supported by the fact that some employees have complained to the employer that the union is not doing a good job of representing them or has not been in recent contact with them or that they are dissatisfied with the union.[936]

---

931. The NLRB processes a representation petition or decertification petition if it is filed after the earlier of: (a) the expiration of the collective agreement or (b) the agreement's first three years, or (c) during the contract bar rule's 30 day or 60 day 'open season' (*see* paragraph 430, above).

932. *Texas Petrochemicals Corp.*, 296 NLRB 1057, 1059 (1989), enforced as modified 923 F.2d 398 (5th Cir. 1991).

933. *Allentown Mack Sales and Service, Inc.* v. *National Labor Relations Board*, 522 US 359 (1998); *Levitz Furniture Company of the Pacific, Inc.*, 333 NLRB 717 (2001).

934. *Levitz Furniture Company of the Pacific, Inc.*, 333 NLRB 717 (2001).

935. *NLRB* v. *Curtin Matheson Scientific, Inc.*, 494 US 775 (1990); *Vanguard Fire and Supply Co., Inc.* v. *NLRB*, 468 F.3d 952 (6th Cir. 2006).

936. *NLRB* v. *Buckley Broadcasting Corp.*, 891 F.2d 230 (9th Cir. 1989), *cert.* denied 496 US 925 (1990); *Wagon Wheel Bowl, Inc.*, 310 NLRB 915 (1993).

The NLRB's most recent decision addressing the criteria for procedures by which a labor organization can lose its representative status leaves open the question of whether an employer implemented *Strucksnes* poll of employees is justifiable in the same circumstances that justify an employer petition for an NLRB representation proceeding or whether a more stringent standard will be applied.[937]

In any event, an employer cannot withdraw recognition, and an NLRB decertification petition will not be entertained, if loss of majority support for an incumbent labor organization was caused by unfair labor practices.[938]

§4. UNFAIR LABOR PRACTICE PROCEDURES

798. Section 7 of the National Labor Relations Act broadly declares that employees have a right to engage in or refrain from engaging in concerted activity for mutual support and protection and to organize for collective representation and engage in collective bargaining. Section 8 of the Act contains a variety of prohibitions against those forms of employer and labor organization conduct that Congress has deemed to violate the rights declared in §7 of the Act. Violation of a rule specified in §8 is designated an 'unfair labor practice' and §10 of the NLRA describes the procedures and standards to be followed in hearing and deciding unfair labor practice cases. The latter section includes authorizing the NLRB to order a party to cease and desist from unfair labor practices and to take 'such affirmative action including reinstatement of employees with or without back pay, as will effectuate the policies of the Act'.

I. Unfair Labor Practice Charge and Complaint

799. The Board cannot itself initiate an unfair labor practice case. Such a proceeding requires that someone file an unfair labor practice charge. That someone, however, need not be a party having a direct interest in the dispute. Accordingly, anyone who is upset by conduct that is believed to be in violation of the NLRA can file an unfair labor practice charge. The charge must be signed and filed in writing with an NLRB regional office or using the agency's electronic filing site. Upon receipt, the office notifies the party charged with wrongdoing. The party so charged is called the 'respondent'. The charge must be dismissed if it has been more than six months since the alleged unlawful conduct occurred. In applying this six month period of limitations, however, the NLRB treats some forms of misconduct as continuing in nature.

If the charge is filed in a timely manner and has merit on its face, that is, if the alleged facts constitute an unfair labor practice, the regional office conducts an investigation of the relevant facts. If the investigation shows good cause to believe that one or more unfair labor practices in fact were committed, the Regional Director issues a complaint, in the name of the NLRB, against the respondent setting forth

937. *Levitz Furniture Company of the Pacific, Inc.*, 333 NLRB 717 (2001).
938. *NLRB* v. *Gissel Packing Co.*, 395 US 575 (1969).

the nature of the alleged unfair labor practices. In the Fiscal Year that ended in 2017, regional directors issued 1,263 unfair labor practice complaints.

800. Although an unfair labor practice complaint is issued in the name of the NLRB, the Regional Director in issuing a complaint exercises power delegated by the General Counsel, not by the Board. The General Counsel's decision not to issue a complaint is final and is not subject to any form of review. This is referred to as absolute prosecutorial discretion.[939] If the RD decides it is inappropriate to issue a complaint, either because of a lack of adequate evidence of an unfair labor practice or because that the RD does not think the alleged misconduct constitutes an unfair labor practice, the charge is dismissed. The charging party may, however, within a designated amount of time, appeal that dismissal to the General Counsel who either affirms the RD's decision or orders that a complaint be issued.

If the RD issues a complaint, there is no appeal from that determination. Rather, its appropriateness is challenged in the ensuing unfair labor practice proceeding.

A very high percentage of unfair labor practice charge cases are resolved before a complaint is issued. In the fiscal year that ended in 2017, 24 percent were dismissed after investigation, 39 percent were settled, 35 percent were withdrawn before a complaint was issued and only 2 percent resulted in an adjudicated determination.

II. Hearing

801. Once a complaint has been issued, a hearing date is set and an ALJ is assigned to preside over that hearing. Unfair labor practice hearings normally are conducted at a place conveniently close to the location where the unfair labor practice allegedly occurred. Government hearing rooms or courtrooms are used if available; if not available, the hearing might be conducted in a motel conference room, a law school practice courtroom, or any similar compatible facility.

802. Prior to the start of the hearing, an ALJ explores the possibility of settlement. This task is assigned to specially trained ALJs, known as 'settlement judges', who attempt to mediate a case settlement. If this does not succeed, the unfair labor practice case is heard by a different ALJ. However, settlement can be reached during any stage of the proceeding. In the 2017 fiscal year ALJs decided 184 cases and 453 cases were settled while pending on the ALJ docket. An NLRB regional field attorney, who acts on behalf of the General Counsel, presents evidence and arguments at an unfair labor practice hearing to establish that the respondent committed an unfair labor practice. The charging party is entitled to be present, to be represented by counsel, and to participate in presenting the case against the respondent

939. The Supreme Court has not ruled directly on the question of whether, under compelling circumstances, the judiciary can order the General Counsel to issue a complaint. However, in *dicta*, the High Court has characterized the General Counsel's discretion in this regard as 'unreviewable'. *Vaca* v. *Sipes*, 386 US 171, 182 (1967). Some have urged that judicial intervention is appropriate under some circumstances. *See*, for example, J. Rosenblum, 'A New Look at the General Counsel's Unreviewable Discretion Not to Issue a Complaint Under the NLRA', 86 *Yale L.J.* 1349 (1977).

but only to the extent of supplementing the case put on by the regional field attorney. The respondent is entitled to be represented by counsel and cross-examine witnesses presented by the NLRB and the charging party, and to present rebuttal evidence and arguments. The ALJ makes any required evidentiary rulings. Subpoenas are available to both sides to facilitate the production of witnesses and documentary evidence. The NLRA provides that 'so far as practicable' the rules of evidence used in civil cases tried in federal courts govern NLRB hearings. A transcript is made of the hearing and a copy is available to the respondent at a reasonable cost.

Most unfair labor practice hearings are completed in one or two days. At the end of the hearing, the Administrative Law Judge returns to his or her home office to await the hearing transcript and receive any post-hearing briefs presenting the parties' arguments. Thereafter, the ALJ issues a decision presenting findings of fact and conclusions of law. If the ALJ concludes that an unfair labor practice has been committed, the Judge also prepares a remedial order. An unfair labor practice can be found only if proven by 'a preponderance of the evidence'.

III. Unfair Labor Practice Remedies

803. The typical remedy in an unfair labor practice case includes an order requiring the respondent to cease and desist from committing the unfair labor practice and to undo any damage resulting from the violation. The latter requirement includes reinstatement of any employee discharged, demoted or otherwise adversely affected due to violation of the employee's statutorily protected labor activities, plus payment, with interest,[940] and any pay or other benefits that the employee would have received but for the unfair labor practice.[941] Earnings from other employment that the worker had or could have obtained with reasonable efforts are set off against the back pay as calculated for each three month period since the unfair labor practice violation.[942] Unfair labor practices committed by unions sometimes are remedied by requiring the labor organization to reinstate workers to a hiring hall list or reimburse employees for lost earnings or for improperly collected dues, fines or assessments, together with interest on the amounts owed. In the 2017 fiscal year $73.6

940. Interest is accrued on a daily basis and the amount of backpay subject to interest is calculated quarterly based on the Department of the Treasury's quarterly determination of the rate it charges for unpaid taxes. *Kentucky River Medical Center*, 356 NLRB 6 (2010); *New Horizons for the Retarded, Inc.*, 283 NLRB 1173 (1987).

941. In *NLRB* v. *Ford Motor Co.*, 683 F.2d 156 (6th Cir. 1982), the court refused to enforce that part of the Board's order that would have required the employer to promote the discriminatee to a supervisory position. The court concluded that the legislative intent behind the NLRA does not permit it to require that a worker be promoted to a supervisory position even though the unfair labor practice consisted of bypassing workers for promotion in retaliation for their criticism of the company's promotion policies. The NLRB, however, has indicated that in an appropriate case it would have the power to order such a remedy. *Georgia Power Co.*, 341 NLRB 576, 577 (2004).

942. If the employer shows that other employment was available, to avoid the offset the General Counsel must show that the employee made reasonable but unsuccessful efforts to find such other employment. *St. George Warehouse*, 351 NLRB 961 (2007).

million was recovered on behalf of employees as backpay or reimbursement of fees, dues, and fines and 1,716 employees were offered reinstatement.

Reinstatement includes returning the employee to his job with all of the benefits of the work status that the employee would have received but for the unfair labor practice. It is a more complete remedy for the employee than is the rehire order encountered in some other labor law systems. The Supreme Court has held, however, that an employer can avoid being required to reinstate or give backpay to an employee if the employer establishes that the worker is not a lawful resident of the US.[943] The employer can also avoid reinstatement and backpay by showing that the worker was guilty of misconduct that would have been punished by termination of employment even if the employer had not interfered with the worker's exercise of rights protected by the NLRA.[944]

If the job from which an employee was unlawfully dismissed, or for which the worker was unlawfully denied employment, no longer is available due to business reductions, the employer must place the worker on a preferential hiring or recall list.

One adverse aspect of an unfair labor practice is to discourage statutorily protected activities even by those who were not directly affected by the unfair labor practice. In an attempt to combat that discouragement of protected activity, the NLRB's remedy normally includes the requirement that the respondent post, in prominent places, a notice to all employees acknowledging that the NLRB has found the respondent guilty of the particular unfair labor practices. This posted notice contains an assertion that the respondent acknowledges and will respect the statutory right of workers to engage in or refrain from engaging in concerted labor activities. In addition, the posted notice recites any other specific remedial action the respondent has been required to take, such as reinstating discharged employees with backpay. The Board tries to phrase these notices in non technical language so as to maximize the prospects that they will be read and understood by the average worker. If members of the workforce are known to be literate in a language other than English, a translated copy of the notice is also posted in that language or those languages.

If it finds that an unfair labor practice was committed in a manner that demonstrated flagrant defiance of the NLRA, the NLRB sometimes adds remedies such as requiring a representative of the respondent to read the NLRB remedial notice to the employees in addition to posting it. On occasion it also has ordered the guilty party to reimburse the NLRB and the charging party for all costs and expenses of investigating the unfair labor practice, and preparing and presenting the case against the respondent.[945]

Respondents with relatively small resources[946] that prevail in significant part in an unfair labor practice case can recover all or part of their litigation costs unless

---

943. *Hoffman Plastic Compounds, Inc.* v. *NLRB*, 535 US 137 (2002); *Sure-Tan, Inc.* v. *NLRB*, 467 US 883 (1984).

944. *NLRB* v. *Transportation Management Corp.*, 462 US 393 (1983).

945. *See*, for example, *Care Manor of Farmington*, 318 NLRB 330 (1995).

946. Individuals whose net worth do not exceed $2 million, proprietorships and corporations who employ up to 500 employees and whose net worth does not exceed $7 million, and non-profit organizations with not more than 500 employees. 29 Code Fed. Reg. §102.143.

the General Counsel shows that its litigation contentions were substantially justified.[947] The agency's report for the fiscal year that ended in 2017 provides no information respecting any applications for reimbursement being received or paid that fiscal year under the Equal Access to Justice Act.

804. Criminal penalties are not imposed on those who commit an unfair labor practice. Similarly, in an early case the Supreme Court ruled that the civil remedies provided by the NLRB are to be designed to 'make whole' the victims of an unfair labor practice but do not include the power to impose punitive damages against those who violate the NLRA.[948] However, it is a crime, punishable by a fine up to $5,000 and imprisonment for up to a year, for any person to interfere with the performance of duties of any member or agents of the Board.[949]

IV. NLRB Review of Hearing Decision

805. Either side, including the charging party, can appeal to the Board from the Administrative Law Judge's decision. If an appeal is not taken, the ALJ's decision becomes the decision of the NLRB. If an appeal is taken, the record of the hearing is transmitted to the Board Members and the parties can submit written briefs presenting their positions. In almost all cases the Board does not hear oral argument of an appeal but instead relies on any briefs filed by the parties plus the entire case record including the ALJ's opinion. All five Board Members can review the case or it can be decided by a panel of three members. Under the Board's rules, any one member can compel the entire Board to review a particular case. In any event, no decision is issued until every Board Member has had an opportunity to read it. Regardless of whether the case is reviewed by the entire Board or by a three-member panel, a majority vote controls and the decision is issued in the name of the entire Board. The Board can affirm, modify, reverse or remand the ALJ's decision.

In 2008 President Obama faced historically extraordinary resistance by the Republican minority in the Senate to giving consent to most of his judicial, cabinet and administrative agency nominations. Although the Constitution requires the consent of only a majority of Senators to approve such presidential nominations, a vote to consent to a nomination can be blocked by a filibuster – continuous argument by the opposition for an indefinite period. At the time, under Senate rules, a cloture vote to end debate on an issue required support by three-fifths of the Senators voting. As a result, the minority party in a closely divided Senate could block a vote on a nomination by mere threat of a filibuster since the majority did not have the votes to invoke cloture and a filibuster would bring all other Senate business to a halt. Because NLRB members serve for five years and their appointment requires Senate consent, by using the filibuster threat to block consent votes for NLRB member appointments or re-appointments, over a few years the minority party can reduce the number of NLRB members. The ability of the Republican Party to do this when

947. 5 US Code § 504, 28 US Code § 2412, 29 Code Fed. Reg. §102.144-46.
948. *Consolidated Edison Co.* v. *NLRB*, 305 US 197 (1938).
949. 29 US Code §162; *US* v. *Culy*, 790 F.2d 796 (9th Cir. 1986).

President Obama became President was accelerated by the fact that his Republican predecessor had not filled all of the Board member positions as they became vacant. Thus, by late 2007 the number of NLRB members had been reduced to two. Prior to this, however, anticipating the prospective problem, while there still were three Board members the Board voted to allow two members to issue NLRB case decisions. They reasoned that this is permitted under the NLRA since the vote of two members governs when a case is decided by a three-member panel. Accordingly, the NLRB issued unanimous decisions in the subsequent 27 months during which the minority party's blocking of new appointments left it with only two members. Some of the decisions it issued during this period were challenged as invalid because of the lack of an agency quorum and in *New Process Steel, L.P.* v. *NLRB*, 560 U.S. 674 (2010), the Supreme Court, examining the somewhat ambiguous language of the Act respecting the agency's quorum requirements, ruled, 5-4, that the NLRB must have a minimum of three members in order to issue a case decision.

The possible resumption of the strategy of a minority party in the Senate effectively eliminating the NLRB and other agencies by blocking the filling of vacancies was reduced in late 2013 when the Senate, ironically relying on a procedural ruling by a Republican Vice President in 2005, by majority vote modified its rules to establish the authority of the majority to impose closure on debate of executive branch and judicial nominees other than those for the US Supreme Court. (In 2017 it expanded the change to include the Supreme Court.)

It should be noted, however, that the Court's *New Process Steel* ruling leaves open the possibility that a President by not making nominations to fill agency vacancies, or a majority party in the Senate by not consenting to the appointment of any such nominees, can eliminate the authority of an agency such as the NLRB to carry out its responsibilities and, thereby, nullify an administrative statute without going through the normal requirement for passing a law repealing that statute. (*See* paragraphs 9 and 10, above.)

806. In reviewing an ALJ's decision, the NLRB must itself weigh the evidence in the entire record to determine whether an unfair labor practice has been proven by a preponderance of that evidence. In so doing, it must give some deference to the ALJ's findings with regard to the credibility of the witnesses. Such deference must be given because the ALJ heard the testimony and was able to assess veracity based upon nonverbal cues as well as by the content of what was said. Nevertheless, the Board can substitute its own judgment concerning the correct evaluation of the weight of testimony for that of the ALJ, including setting aside credibility findings, if the Board is persuaded that the ALJ was in error.[950]

807. The NLRB's decision affirming, modifying, reversing or remanding the decision of the Administrative Law Judge is accompanied by a written opinion. Often the Board's opinion is very brief and incorporates by reference, and adopts as its own, the ALJ's opinion. The practice of the Board is to issue opinions in the name of the Board together with a notation of which Board Members participated in the decision. The opinion, however, does not reveal which Board Member

950. *Universal Camera Corp.* v. *NLRB*, 340 US 474 (1951).

authored the majority opinion. (A major portion of the opinion writing is, in fact, done by the Board Member's staff – subject, of course, to the Board Member's final approval.) Occasionally, members file concurring or dissenting opinions and these are individually signed by the particular Board Member.

808. Commentators often characterize the decisional predilections of Board Members in relationship to the President who appointed the member. They, similarly, characterize the entire Board in terms of the President who appointed a majority of those members. Thus, many commentators have noted differences in the patterns of decision of the so-called Truman Board as compared with the Eisenhower Board or the Kennedy-Johnson Board or the Nixon-Ford Board, Reagan Board, etc. These discerned patterns generally focus on the agency's relative pro-union orientation versus pro-management orientation in deciding close factual and policy questions. Individual Board Members have made speeches and written articles denouncing such characterizations as inaccurate and unfair, and some observers have occasionally joined in rejecting this form of political analysis of the Board's shifts in decisional directions. However, there is empirical evidence that supports the charge that the agency's decisional propensities are related to the political source of appointment.[951]

V. Judicial Review in Unfair Labor Practice Cases

809. Decisions and orders of the NLRB are not self-enforcing; disobedience does not result in the imposition of any penalties. In order to put muscle behind the decisions of the NLRB, it is necessary to obtain a court order. If the court orders compliance with the Board order, any further disobedience is a contempt of court and is punishable by fine, imprisonment or both.

The Board can petition a federal Court of Appeals to enforce its decision. When the Board seeks an enforcement order, all parties to the Board proceedings are notified and have an opportunity to present to the court any arguments raised in the Board proceeding regarding the merits of finding an unfair labor practice or the appropriate nature of the remedy. Under NLRA §10(e), the reviewing court, or a district court, can in its discretion and upon the Board's application, grant temporary injunctive relief from an unfair labor practice pending a resolution of the appellate court's review of the NLRB decision. The Board rarely seeks this form of interim relief.

The reviewing court, if necessary, examines the entire record of the case. The court can issue a decree enforcing the Board decision in whole or as modified by the court, or can set the decision aside in whole or in part. The statutory standard is that fact findings of the Board are not to be set aside by the reviewing court if it concludes that the record, taken as a whole, contains substantial evidence to support those findings. This standard has been described as being satisfied if there is enough

951. *See* R. Turner, 'Ideological Voting on the National Labor Relations Board', 8 *U. Pa. J. Lab. & Emp. L.* 707 (2006); W. Cook and F. Gautschi, 'Political Bias in NLRB Unfair Labor Practice Decisions', 35 *Indus. and Lab. Rel. Rev.* 539 (1982).

relevant evidence in the record so that the court can understand how a reasonable mind might accept it as adequate to support the agency's conclusion.[952] (In practice, commentators find that the pro-business or pro-labor propensities of some judges and justices often appear to influence their perceptions of what is 'acceptable to a reasonable mind' based on the outcome of the case.)

The standard for reviewing the NLRB's interpretations of the law is sometimes stated as allowing the reviewing court to accept them only if the court decides that they are correct and consistent with the policies of the NLRA and the Constitution. However, the meaning of the often vague, broad language of the Labor Management Relations Act is not always self-evident. In addition, some legal conclusions made by the Board are of a rule-making rather than of an interpretive nature. That is, much of the language of the NLRA provides general policy guidance, but leaves to the NLRB the choice of the best means to apply the legislative policy. The stated legal standard for reviewing the Board's application of the Act both to situations in which the statutory language is vague and where the Act clearly anticipates that the agency will exercise enforcement discretion is that the courts should defer to the NLRB's reasonable exercise of discretion. For example, in sustaining the NLRB's restrictions on employer rules against in-plant union solicitation, the Supreme Court upheld the Board not because its approach was 'correct' under the NLRA, but rather because it was a reasonable exercise of the Board's delegated discretionary authority.[953] With some frequency, however, judges and justices differ respecting when such discretion is barred by the statute's 'self-evident' meaning.

810. An alternative route for obtaining judicial review of an NLRB decision is for a party aggrieved by the Board's decision to apply to a federal Court of Appeals, under §10(f) of the NLRA, for an order modifying or setting aside the Board's decision. The same standards for review apply as described in paragraph 809, above, respecting enforcement proceedings initiated upon the Board's petition to a Court of Appeals.

811. If the NLRB or some other party is displeased with the Court of Appeals disposition of a case, that party can petition the Supreme Court for a writ of *certiorari*. *Certiorari* is a discretionary writ. This means that the Supreme Court will review a decision if at least four Justices are persuaded that it warrants the high court's consideration. Denial of a petition for *certiorari* does not affirm the Court of Appeals decision. Rather, denial of *certiorari* simply means that whether right or wrong, the decision did not involve an issue meriting the attention of the Supreme Court at this particular time.

Sometimes the Supreme Court denies *certiorari* with regard to a particular issue because it wants several different Courts of Appeals to first have a chance to consider the problem so that it may have the benefit of their combined thinking respecting the best resolution. If the appellate courts all agree as to the correct rule of law, there is little prospect that the Supreme Court will review the issue. The Supreme

---

952. *Universal Camera Corp.* v. *NLRB*, 340 US 474 (1951).

953. *Republic Aviation Corp.* v. *NLRB*, 324 US 793 (1945). *See also*, *Chevron, USA. Inc.* v. *Natural Resources Defense Council, Inc.*, 467 US 837 (1984).

Court most often intervenes if the several Courts of Appeals have gone in different directions in resolving the same question.

VI. Measuring Case Handling Performance

812. The NLRB currently measures its case handling efficiency by looking at the percentage of unfair labor practice cases resolved within 120 days of the initial filing (68.9 percent in the fiscal year that ended in 2017) and within 365 days of the initial filing (82.4 percent in the fiscal year that ended in 2017). The quality of its performance is reflected in the frequency with which parties seek judicial review and with which appellate courts either affirm or reject the agency's decisions. In the 2017 fiscal year, in a little over half of the Board's decisions either the losing party sought judicial review or the NLRB applied for judicial enforcement. The Board's order was upheld in whole or in part in 69 percent of those cases.

From the above, it can be seen that the vast bulk of unfair labor practice cases are resolved through settlement and, therefore, with a minimum amount of agency or court litigation. It has often has observed that absent the frequency of voluntary settlement and adjustment of these disputes, the NLRB would be unable to handle its workload.

§5. Injunction Against Misconduct

I. Generally

813. Two provisions of the NLRA, §§10(j) and 10(l), both added by the Taft-Hartley Act, authorize the NLRB to apply to a federal district court for temporary injunctive relief to halt pressure tactics or preserve the *status quo* pending completion of the Board's unfair labor practice proceedings. Only the Board can apply for a temporary injunction under §10(j) and only the Regional Office of the NLRB can apply for a temporary injunction under §10(l). An individual party cannot initiate such proceedings. To the extent that these injunctions are available, they represent a modification of the Norris-LaGuardia Act's restrictions upon injunctions issued by the federal courts in situations involving labor disputes.

II. Section 10(j) Injunction

814. Section 10(j) gives the NLRB authority to petition a federal district court for temporary relief from an alleged unfair labor practice pending the completion of the Board's proceedings. The Board cannot seek such temporary relief until the General Counsel has issued a complaint. When it is issued, the Board decides whether temporary injunctive relief should be sought. In practice, the Board considers such matters upon the request of the General Counsel. The decision as to whether such relief is necessary and proper is a matter left to the court's discretion.

Issuance of an injunction does not resolve the underlying unfair labor practice complaint. However, once an injunction has been issued, it eliminates any benefits of procedural delay that might accrue to one of the parties. As a result, the parties' respective bargaining power positions are altered and often a settlement of the underlying issues is reached after the injunction has been issued. If the unfair labor practice is adjudicated and results in the complaint being dismissed, or if the case is settled, the injunction is dissolved.

815. For the first three decades after the Taft-Hartley Act was adopted, the Board showed great reluctance to seek relief under that provision and such petitions were rare. In the 1970s its policy gradually became a bit more aggressive so that by the 1980 fiscal year the NLRB filed injunction petitions under §10(j) in 50 cases. The Board partially retreated from its more aggressive approach to §10(j) during the Reagan and the first Bush administrations. For example, in the Fiscal Year that ended in 1992 the NLRB applied for §10(j) injunctions in 34 cases. During the Clinton administration the General Counsel and NLRB resumed a more aggressive policy of seeking §10(j) injunctions. For example, during the nearly three-year period from 3 March 1998, to 15 January 2001 the General Counsel requested authorization to seek such relief in 191 cases and the Board authorized a §10(j) suit in 164, or 86 percent, of the cases in which permission was sought. The agency settled 52 percent of the authorized cases before or after initiating a §10(j) suit and of the 64 cases resolved by the courts, injunctions were issued in whole or substantial part in 46, or 72 percent, of the cases. This success rate is comparable to that experienced during periods when the Board used this remedy less aggressively. Section 10(j) injunctions most often are sought against employers. A pattern has emerged in which 10(j) injunctions increase when a Democratic President has appointed the General Counsel and a Board majority, and decrease when they have been appointed by a Republican President. In the Fiscal Year 2017, the Board authorized 10(j) injunction requests in 37 cases. In seven of those cases the parties resolved the need for an injunction and went to court in the remaining 30 cases. In 75 percent of the 10(j) cases, the Board achieved its goal either by attaining a settlement or being granted the injunction.

III. Injunctions against Alleged Unlawful Union Pressure on Neutral Employers

816. Injunctive relief under §10(l) is available in response to a limited group of unfair labor practice charges respecting union conduct made unlawful by the unfair labor practice provisions added by the 1947 legislation. Unlike a §10(j) injunction, relief under §10(l) is initiated by the Regional Office, not by the Board, and the petition is filed with the court prior to the issuance of a complaint. However, the petition cannot be filed until an investigation reveals good cause to believe that the charged misconduct is true and that a complaint probably will be issued.

817. For several categories of cases qualifying for temporary relief under §10(l), it is mandatory that such injunctive relief be sought. These cases involve unlawful secondary boycotts, including 'hot cargo' activity, and violations of the NLRA restrictions upon organizational and recognitional picketing. The federal district court, nevertheless, has discretion to grant or deny such temporary relief based on whether it deems the relief to be just and proper under the circumstances. In addition, a temporary injunction may be sought by the NLRB's regional office in those cases involving so-called jurisdictional disputes if the regional office believes that such relief would be appropriate in the particular case. Section 10(l) injunctive relief is not available in any other categories of cases.

Although once common, in the past couple of decades, labor organizations have seldom resorted to the tactics that can lead to a 10(l) injunction. In part this is because the underlying unlawful secondary activity involved in such cases, if proven, can result in a damages suit under the LMRA §303. Over the years, a high percentage of these cases have been settled through an agreement to cease the disputed activity in exchange for a release from any damages claims, thus obviating the need for NLRB intervention.

818. An injunction issued by a court pursuant to §10(l) does not resolve the underlying unfair labor practice charge. Rather, the Regional Director must proceed to determine whether to issue a complaint and if issued, the Board must hold a hearing concerning that underlying complaint. If the underlying charge is dismissed (that is, a complaint is not issued) or if the adjudication of the complaint results in a decision that the respondent union was not guilty of the underlying unfair labor practice, the injunctive order is vacated.

§6. Determination of Disputes Concerning Group Work Assignments

819. Section 8(b)(4)(D) of the NLRA prohibits economic or other coercion designed to alter a group work assignment. This sort of conflict arises most often when different unions having status as certified or recognized bargaining agents claim the same work for their members. Because they assert that the work comes within their union's 'jurisdiction', these conflicts often are referred to as 'jurisdictional disputes'. The employer generally is caught in the middle of such a dispute. Whatever its preference may be, and sometimes it has none, the employer knows that whichever group is awarded the work, the other group, or groups, might resort to concerted action to alter that decision with the result that the employer will suffer.

820. Jurisdictional disputes interfere with the sort of inter-union solidarity that strengthens bargaining and organizing effectiveness. Accordingly, unions themselves have tried to eliminate such disputes and use their own means of resolving them when they arise. Pacts between unions have been negotiated from time-to-time that define their respective jurisdictions and provide a procedure for adjusting differences when disputes arise. Mergers among unions, reducing the number of competitors, have also contributed to the decrease in disputes of this nature.

The AFL–CIO Constitution prohibits affiliated unions from organizing or seeking work for members involving activities that are not within the scope of their traditional jurisdiction if such work is part of the traditional jurisdiction of other affiliated unions. In the case of jurisdictional disputes between affiliated unions, the AFL–CIO Constitution provides for their resolution under a system of arbitration. This system has reduced, but has not eliminated, the frequency with which unions charge each other with 'raiding' their territory. A factor contributing to this result is that not all unions are AFL–CIO members. In addition, AFL–CIO unions sometimes do not invoke the AFL–CIO machinery when they engage in such conflicts with each other, perhaps because both sides have more confidence in their ability to win the economic battle than to win the arbitration award. Finally, the AFL–CIO arbitration machinery relies on internal sanctions to enforce these awards and some affiliated unions are sufficiently powerful within the federation to have a sense of immunity from such sanctions.

821. Section 10(k) of the NLRA provides statutory machinery for resolving jurisdictional disputes if the parties are unable to peacefully reach their own agreement. The 10(k) process is initiated when a charge is filed under §8(b)(4)(D) asserting that a party has resorted to pressure tactics, or the threat thereof, in support of its work assignment demands. As a result of §10(k), an 8(b)(4)(D) charge is handled differently from the procedure followed for other unfair labor practice charges.

Under §10(k), when an 8(b)(4)(D) charge is filed, the affected labor organizations and the employer are given ten days to resolve their differences or enter into an agreement for a binding adjustment of their dispute. (Arbitration is the binding method of adjustment by which the parties can avoid the NLRB's authority to determine the issue.) If such an agreement or settlement is not reached during that period, the Board conducts a hearing regarding the dispute and, based upon its findings, decides the jurisdictional issue on the merits. Pending the final resolution of such disputes, the regional office in its discretion can seek temporary injunctive relief pursuant to NLRA §10(l).

822. A complaint is issued on a §8(b)(4)(D) charge only if the parties fail to find a mutually acceptable binding means for resolving their differences and fail to abide by the NLRB's determination regarding the jurisdictional dispute. Judicial review of the Board's resolution of the jurisdictional issue is obtained by continuing to place economic pressure on the other side or sides even though the NLRB has determined that it or they are entitled to the work. Such conduct triggers the issuance of an 8(b)(4)(D) complaint and an unfair labor practice decision against the party that refused to abide by the Board's determination. The merits of the Board's jurisdictional determination can then be challenged in the ensuing judicial proceeding to enforce or review the Board's unfair labor practice order.

823. In the fiscal year that ended in 2017, the NLRB did not separately report its case activity involving §10(k) or §8(b)(4)(D) – indicating it was not a significant part of its caseload. As with other cases involving charges under NLRA §8(b)(4), the parallel statutory money damages cause of action available under §303 of the LMRA no doubt influences the high rate of private adjustment in these cases.

§7. Money Damages for Unlawful Secondary Activity

824. As discussed in more detail in paragraphs 451–490, above, secondary activity involves imposing economic or other pressure on parties who are not themselves directly involved in the labor dispute and, therefore, are unable to resolve the underlying issue between the disputants. For example, if a union wants employer 'A' to reach an agreement with it, it would be a secondary activity to call the employees of employer 'B' out on strike so as to force employer 'B' to cease doing business with employer 'A' until 'A' reaches agreement with the union. Another example is where an employer is caught in the middle of a work assignment dispute in which two groups of employees go out on strike, each insisting that the employer assign certain work to their group.

If a union's conduct involves activity prohibited by §8(b)(4), §303(b) of the Labor Management Relations Act gives to 'whoever was injured' by that activity a right to sue the union in federal court for money damages. This right of action supplements the unfair labor practice remedies available under §8(b)(4) and the injunctive remedies available under §§10(l) and 10(j), discussed in paragraphs 813–21, above. The very threat of such a suit often induces unions to cease such activities and probably accounts for the very high rate of settlement of 8(b)(4) charges.

Because §303 provides a separate avenue for relief from unlawful secondary activity, a suit may be brought under §303 prior to the NLRB determining that the labor organization was guilty of an 8(b)(4) violation.[954] In addition, courts have entertained §303 suits even though there has been no charge or complaint under NLRA § 8(b)(4).[955] However, the findings in a final NLRB decision in an NLRB 8(b)(4) case controls when a later or pending suit is brought under §303.[956] On the other hand, fact findings in an NLRB proceeding need not be accepted as true in a §303 suit concerning the same events if newly discovered evidence, not discoverable in the NLRB proceeding, would make it unfair to hold a party bound by the fact findings of the administrative proceeding.[957]

Recovery in an LMRA §303 suit is limited to compensatory damages. Punitive damages and attorney's fees are not recoverable.[958] Although on its face the statute appears to provide such monetary relief to anyone who suffered as a result of the unlawful secondary activity, the courts, relying on legislative history respecting the purpose of this provision, have restricted recovery to those engaged in a closely integrated business relationship with the neutral or primary employer against whom

954. *International Longshoremen's Union* v. *Juneau Spruce Co.*, 342 US 237 (1952).

955. For example, *United Brick and Clay Workers* v. *Deena Artware*, 198 F.2d 637 (6th Cir.), *cert.* denied 344 US 897 (1952).

956. *Int'l Ass'n of Machinists and Aerospace Workers* v. *Stevens Pontiac-GMC-Honda, Inc.*, 1991 US App. LEXIS 23534 (9th Cir. 1991); *Consolidated Express, Inc.* v. *New York Shipping Association, Inc.*, 641 F.2d 90 (3d Cir. 1981); *Paramount Transportation System* v. *Teamsters Local 150*, 436 F.2d 1064 (9th Cir. 1971).

957. *Wickham Contracting Co., Inc.* v. *Board of Education*, 715 F.2d 21, 27 (2d Cir. 1983)(dicta).

958. *Summit Valley Industries* v. *Local 112, United Brotherhood of Carpenters*, 456 US 717 (1982); *United Mine Workers* v. *Gibbs*, 383 US 715 (1966).

the union took unlawful secondary action if that action caused reasonably foreseeable injury to the plaintiff and was a means by which the defendant sought to achieve its unlawful purpose. Thus, consumers or ordinary business affiliates who suffered as a result of the unlawful secondary activity cannot recover damages under LMRA §303(b).[959]

Section 303 precludes a claim for relief under state law for damages arising from peaceful, though unlawful, secondary pressure.[960]

959. *Charvet* v. *International Longshoremen's Ass'n.*, 736 F.2d 1572 (DC Cir. 1984).
960. *Teamsters Union* v. *Morton*, 377 US 252 (1964).

Chapter 2. Labor Management Relations Act's Preemption of Suits Affecting Collective Activities

§1. The Preemption Concept

825. A principle underlying the NLRA is that employee rights to engage in or refrain from collective action protects public as well as private, interests. Accordingly, although remedies for violations of the Act may make whole the individuals who have suffered losses from unfair labor practices, they also are a means of vindicating the public interests reflected in the standards of conduct imposed by the statute. Thus, the principal responsibility for prosecuting unfair labor practice cases is assigned to public officers and the enforcement machinery of the NLRA is assigned to public officials: the NLRB and its General Counsel or their subordinates.

Because it is a national administrative agency, the NLRB is able to apply the law of labor–management relations uniformly throughout the nation. In addition, the Board is presumed to administer the NLRA guided by its expertise formed from the learning, cumulative experience, and specialized knowledge of the Board Members and staff. Thus, the Supreme Court has adopted the doctrine that the procedures and jurisdiction of the NLRB presumptively preclude state and federal courts from entertaining suits involving questions concerning conduct that arguably is protected or prohibited by the NLRA - the preemption doctrine.[961] This doctrine is based on principles of constitutional law and interpretation of Congress's intent.

The Supremacy Clause of the US Constitution gives federal law priority over state law. Therefore, if the federal government has authority to act and exercises that authority, any conflicts between federal and state law must be resolved in favor of federal law. In addition, even if there is not a direct conflict with federal law, the Supreme Court has held that state law must give way to federal authority if federal law is designed to be the exclusive body of law governing an area of regulation that is within the federal government's constitutional competence. Hence, the question of whether federal law preempts (precludes) state law often depends upon whether Congress is found to have intended to exclude even those state regulations that are not in direct conflict with the federal regulations.[962]

826. In support of its preemptive authority, if necessary, the NLRB can obtain an order from a federal court staying any litigation that conflicts with the NLRB's exclusive jurisdiction over an issue.[963]

827. Not every question that is subject to the Board's jurisdiction is beyond the scope of private litigation. For example, section 303 of the LMRA expressly provides for a private party to sue for damages if injured by an unfair labor practice

961. *Motor Coach Employees* v. *Lockridge*, 403 US 274 (1971); *San Diego Building Trades Council* v. *Garmon*, 359 US 236 (1959).
962. *See*, for example, *Washington Service Contractors Coalition* v. *District of Columbia*, 54 F.3d 811 (DC Cir. 1995).
963. *NLRB* v. *Nash-Finch Company*, 404 US 138 (1971).

encompassed by NLRA §8(b)(4). In addition, a number of exceptions to the preemption rule permit state and federal courts and administrative agencies to provide remedies for various types of conduct that affect or are affected by labor–management relations even where federal legislation has not explicitly provided for such relief by processes beyond those contained in the LMRA. Moreover, those exceptions appear to be expanding.

§2. Suits to Enforce Collective Agreements

828. Unlike most other labor law systems, in the United States the personal job interests of an employee who is represented by a union normally are protected through the enforcement of the collective agreement rather than by enforcing the contract of employment. A suit to enforce a collective agreement can be brought in a state or federal court[964] and is not preempted by the NLRA even though in certain circumstances a refusal to adhere to a collective agreement constitutes an unfair labor practice.[965] Moreover, if the collective agreement involves a labor–management relations situation that affects interstate commerce to an adequate degree to bring it within the potential jurisdiction of the Labor Management Relations Act, state court litigation concerning the collective agreement is governed by federal substantive law, not by local law.[966]

Section 301 of the LMRA gives federal district courts authority to enforce collective agreements and union constitutions. This includes enforcement of collective agreement provisions for the arbitration of disputes between the parties. A suit brought to enforce an arbitration agreement or award under a collective agreement must be filed within 6 months after the contractual claim arises.[967] The same period of limitations likely applies to a comparable state court action.[968]

829. The vast majority of collective agreements in the United States require that some or all unresolved disputes concerning the interpretation or application of that agreement be resolved by final, binding arbitration. A party to a collective agreement can sue in federal or state court to require the other side to comply with the agreement's provision requiring arbitration of differences. Similarly, a suit can be

964. *Smith* v. *Evening News Ass'n*, 371 US 195 (1962); *Charles Dowd Box Co.* v. *Courtney*, 368 US 502 (1962).
965. *NLRB* v. *C & C Plywood Corp.*, 385 US 421 (1967).
966. *United Auto Workers* v. *Hoosier Cardinal Corp.*, 383 US 696 (1966); *Local 174, Teamsters* v. *Lucas Flour Co.*, 369 US 95 (1962). Nevertheless, local law is followed by the federal courts in applying procedural rules respecting the enforcement of such agreements unless the procedural rule has the effect of altering the parties' contractual rights. *United Parcel Service, Inc.* v. *Mitchell*, 451 US 56 (1981).
967. *Communications Workers of America* v. *AT&T*, 10 F.3d 887 (DC Cir. 1993) (the six-month period for filing an NLRA unfair labor practice charge is the appropriate period of limitations for filing an action to enforce the arbitration provision of a collective agreement).
968. *DelCostello* v. *Teamsters Union*, 462 US 151 (1983).

brought in state or federal court to compel a party to abide by an arbitrator's decision.[969]

Suits to enforce labor arbitration provisions are not preempted by the fact that the underlying claim might also raise issues under the National Labor Relations Act. Additionally, the NLRB abates processing some types of unfair labor practice cases pending the outcome of an active or impending resort to an arbitration tribunal. The scope of unfair labor practice charges for which the NLRB applies the abatement doctrine (actually the NLRB uses the term 'deferral', rather than abatement) has changed from time-to-time but currently requires that the charged unfair labor practice is cognizable under the collective agreement's dispute resolution procedure.[970] Under current doctrine, the NLRB holds the case in abatement unless the unfair labor practice charge indicates that the arbitration process cannot provide a prompt and fair hearing or that the Board's own processes have been compromised or it is alleged that a party is not providing information that must be exchanged as part of the duty of good faith bargaining.[971]

In addition, once a labor arbitrator decides the dispute the NLRB defers to the arbitration award if certain criteria are satisfied. The criteria for deferral to the award are: (1) The arbitration procedure was fair and regular; (2) the party seeking deferral shows that the arbitrator was explicitly authorized to decide the statutory issue; (3) the arbitrator was presented with and considered that issue, or was prevented from doing so by the party opposing deferral; and 4) the award was reasonably within the parameters of Board law.[972]

830. Under a principle known as the *Boys Markets* doctrine,[973] a federal court may enjoin a work stoppage if it is in violation of a collective agreement that contains a provision establishing a binding mechanism for the final resolution of disputes arising under the agreement. This encompasses both grievance and arbitration procedures established by the collective agreement. Such suits may be brought in federal court under §301 of the LMRA. If the action is brought in state court, it

969. *John Wiley & Sons, Inc.* v. *Livingston*, 376 US 543 (1964); *Textile Workers Union* v. *Lincoln Mills*, 353 US 448 (1957). Although courts are to resolve doubts in favor of arbitrability when enforcing arbitration provisions concerning disputes arising under a collective agreement, such provisions are presumed to not cover disputes involving statutory claims. *Wright* v. *Universal Maritime Serv. Corp.*, 525 US 70 (1998); *Manning* v. *Boston Med. Ctr. Corp.*, 725 F.3d 34 (1st. Cir. 2013). However, in *14 Penn Plaza* v. *Pyett,* 556 US 247 (2009) the Court held that a broad arbitration provision in a collective agreement precludes a claimant's suit to enforce a federal statutory right unless the statute explicitly excludes arbitration. The decision did not preclude enforcement of the statutory right by a federal agency charged with the duty of enforcing the statute and implied that judicial review of awards involving statutory claims may inquire into the correctness of the award's interpretation of the statutory right. 556 US at n. 10.

970. *Compare, General American Transp. Corp.*, 228 NLRB 808 (1977) overruled by *United Technologies Corp.*, 268 NLRB 557 (1984); *International Harvester Company*, 271 NLRB 647 (1984); *Superior Forwarding Company, Inc.*, 282 NLRB 806 (1987); and *Babcock & Wilcox Constr. Co.,* 361 NLRB No. 132 (2014).

971. See NLRB, *Casehandling Manual*, §10118.1.

972. *Babcock & Wilcox Constr. Co.,* 361 NLRB No. 132 (2014).

973. *Boys Markets, Inc.* v. *Retail Clerks Union*, 398 US 235 (1970). *See also*, *Buffalo Forge Co.* v. *Steelworkers*, 428 US 397 (1976) (an injunction is not available if the arbitrator does not have authority to decide the underlying dispute).

either can be decided there under state law or can be removed to federal court by the defending party. The *Boys Markets* doctrine has been held to permit a federal court to prohibit the alteration of the status quo pending arbitration of a dispute if a modification of the status quo would totally frustrate the arbiter's ability to remedy the alleged contractual violation.[974]

§3. Suits to Remedy a Breach of the Duty of Fair Representation

831. The union designated as the exclusive bargaining agent has a legal duty to provide fair and diligent representation for all employees in the bargaining unit regardless of their membership or non-membership in that union. Violation of the duty is an unfair labor practice.[975] Nevertheless, the Supreme Court has held that the possibility of NLRB jurisdiction over such cases does not preempt a right of action in state or federal court to recover from the union damages resulting from a breach of that duty of fair representation and, where applicable, against the employer for any contractual benefits that the employee would have enjoyed but for the union's breach of its duty.[976]

In federal court the suit against the union for breach of the duty of fair representation is based on 28 US Code §1337(a), a federal statute that broadly gives federal district courts authority to hear 'any civil action' arising under any Act of Congress regulating commerce. Since the duty of fair representation is derived from the NLRA, §1337(a) provides the federal trial court with authority to hear the suit. The suit against the employer in federal court is based on the federal courts' authority, under §301 of the LMRA, to hear suits to enforce collectively bargained agreements.

The parties have a right to a jury trial when a suit to recover damages is brought in federal court for breach of the duty of fair representation.[977] However, punitive damages cannot be recovered in such a suit.[978] Moreover, the Supreme Court has ruled that, inasmuch as the core of the claim in such suits is conduct that constitutes an unfair labor practice, it is appropriate to apply the same limitation period for bringing such actions as is applicable to filing unfair labor practice charges. Therefore, suits based on an alleged breach of the duty of fair representation must be filed within six months after the breach occurred.[979]

---

974. *Lever Bros. Co.* v. *Int'l Chem. Workers*, 554 F.2d 115 (4th Cir. 1976). Generally, courts limit such temporary relief to the most urgent situations where there are no possible alternative remedies if the status quo is altered. *See*, for example, *Indep. Oil and Chemical Workers* v. *P&G Mfg.*, 864 F.2d 927 (1st Cir. 1988).
975. *Local 12, United Rubber Workers* v. *NLRB*, 368 F.2d 12 (5th Cir. 1966), *cert.* denied, 389 US 837 (1967).
976. *Vaca* v. *Sipes*, 386 US 171 (1967).
977. *Teamsters Local No. 391* v. *Terry*, 494 US 558 (1990).
978. *IBEW* v. *Foust*, 442 US 42 (1979).
979. *DelCostello* v. *Teamsters Union*, 462 US 151 (1983).

§4. Other Court Actions

832. Actions in state court to remedy malicious libel and to enjoin and otherwise remedy physical violence to persons or property continue to be available even if the events occurred in the context of a labor dispute and an unfair labor practice was arguably involved in the conduct in question. Some torts against emotional well-being are also actionable in court even though an unfair labor practice is arguably involved. In all such suits, however, the claim for relief must be applicable for similar affronts to public policy that do not arise in a labor–management context. In addition, when the suits involve a labor relations context, they must be governed by standards of proof and pleadings that are designed to prevent the state remedy from coming into conflict with federal labor law. Those standards include assuring 'that the damages awarded are not excessive'.[980]

If the parties to a collectively bargained agreement have established a mechanism for interpreting the agreement, a suit under common law or state statute is preempted if its resolution requires that the collective agreement be interpreted by the court, agency or jury deciding that suit. However, a claimant can pursue state law claims for relief if the elements of proving the claim do not require an interpretation of the collective agreement. Thus, in one case the Supreme Court held that an employee working under a collective agreement permitting dismissal from work only for good cause could recover damages under a state law prohibiting retaliatory dismissal of workers who file workers' compensation claims. In reaching that conclusion, the Court noted that the issue of retaliatory dismissal could be resolved without addressing whether the contractual job security provision had been violated.[981] The Court has applied the same reasoning to limit the preemptive effect of the Railway Labor Act's mandatory arbitration procedure for resolving grievance ('minor') disputes.[982]

980. *Linn* v. *United Plant Guard Workers*, 383 US 53, 65–66 (1966); *Farmer* v. *United Brotherhood of Carpenters*, 430 US 290, 306 (1977).
981. *Lingle* v. *Norge Division of Magic Chef, Inc.*, 486 US 399 (1988); *Livadas* v. *Bradshaw*, 512 US 107 (1994).
982. *Hawaiian Airlines, Inc.* v. *Norris*, 512 US 246 (1994) (allowing a dismissed airline mechanic to bring a state wrongful discharge suit where he alleged that he was dismissed for refusing to certify that a repair conformed to federal safety regulations and for reporting his concerns regarding the repair).

Chapter 3. Resolution of Disputes that Threaten National or Local Welfare

833. Title II of the LMRA establishes a procedure to reduce the threat that certain work stoppages pose for national health or safety. It is initiated by the President who appoints a Board of Inquiry to investigate the issues involved in any work stoppage whose continuance might 'imperil' national health or safety. The Board of Inquiry is authorized to conduct a hearing and compel the presentation of evidence. Its report becomes a public record. On receipt of the report, the President may direct the Attorney General of the United States to petition a federal district court to enjoin the stoppage. The federal court is empowered to enjoin the stoppage and provide any other relief it deems proper if it finds that the stoppage affects at least a substantial part of an industry and that, if permitted to continue, the stoppage will imperil national health or safety. If the court issues the injunction, the parties have a statutory duty to cooperate with the mediatory efforts of the Federal Mediation and Conciliation Service and the Board of Inquiry is reconvened. The Board of Inquiry then audits the disputing parties' negotiations and, at the end of 60 days, reports on the status of their respective positions. Within 15 days after the receipt of that report, the NLRB conducts a secret ballot election of the employees to determine whether they are willing to accept the employer's most recent settlement offer. The results of that election must be certified to the Attorney General within five days. At that point, the injunction is dissolved and the President reports to Congress respecting the results of the inquiry and the election, and any recommendations thereon. Thus, under this procedure, the work stoppage can be enjoined for a maximum of 80 days, which is referred to as a 'cooling-off period' and is intended to encourage parties, with the help of federal mediation efforts, to find a peaceful, mutually satisfactory settlement by removing the distractions of the emotion-filled atmosphere that normally accompanies a work stoppage. If that does not succeed, the resulting information provides Congress with a basis for deciding whether to adopt special legislation to end the stoppage if it is resumed.

The success of the National Emergency Dispute procedure is far from clear. Between 1947 and 1977 it was used 35 times. In 31 of those situations, injunctions were requested and issued, and 13 of the issued injunctions ran for the full 80 days without a settlement being reached. In every case in which the last offer vote was conducted by the NLRB, the employees overwhelmingly rejected that offer. Criticism of the procedure includes the assertion that the greater weight of its burden falls upon the employees. Most often the back to work order interferes with the momentum of the strike – possibly at the very moment when the economic pressure on the employer is beginning to work its effects.

With the declining strength of unions, there have been few recent occasions to invoke the LMRA emergency procedures. The most recent event was in 2002 when, during negotiations for a new longshore workers' collective agreement for Pacific coast ports, employers locked out their employees with the explanation that the workers were engaged in a slowdown. A mediated settlement was reached within about three weeks prior to the expiration of the cooling-off period.

There are separate emergency dispute procedures for bargaining units covered by the Railway Labor Act (see paragraph 873, below).

834. A special mandatory mediation procedure is available under section 213 of the LMRA for work stoppages affecting health care institutions. These procedures are instituted if the Director of the Federal Mediation and Conciliation Service (FMCS) finds that a stoppage or threatened stoppage 'will, if permitted to occur or continue, substantially interrupt the delivery of health care in the locality concerned'. If §213 is invoked, the FMCS Director may appoint an impartial Board of Inquiry for the particular dispute. That Board can be comprised of one or more members, at the Director's discretion, and Board members may be, but need not be, government employees. The Board must, within 15 days of appointment, investigate the issues and prepare a written report setting forth its fact-findings and recommendations for settlement. Work stoppages and unilateral changes in terms or conditions of work are prohibited from the time the Board of Inquiry is appointed until 15 days have expired after the issuance of its report. In the 1980 Fiscal Year, 22 such boards were appointed. Since the early 1990s, use of such boards has diminished to the point that the Service no longer reports that activity.

Chapter 4. Federal Mediation and Conciliation Service

835. The origins of the FMCS can be traced to 1913 when, in establishing the US Department of Labor, Congress authorized the Secretary of Labor to act as a mediator and appoint commissioners of conciliation to promote industrial peace. Starting in 1918 and until the adoption of the Taft–Hartley Act in 1947, the United States Conciliation Service operated as a bureau within the Department of Labor. The Taft–Hartley Act substituted the present independent agency called the FMCS. The Service's headquarters is in Washington, DC (250 E Street, SW, Washington, DC; telephone: 202 606-8100; web site: fmcs.gov). It largely conducts its mediation activities through ten regional offices and 60 field offices located in major cities throughout the country. Fulltime mediators are assigned to the field offices. At the head of the agency is its Director who is nominated by the President and appointed with the consent of the Senate.

836. The FMCS has potential jurisdiction in all industrial disputes affecting commerce except those involving the rail and airline industries. Mediating services are provided for the latter industries by the National Mediation Board. The FMCS also provides labor-management mediation services for federal, state and local government agencies.

When parties seek to renew or renegotiate a collective agreement, the NLRA requires that prior notice of such intent be filed with the FMCS. Although such notices are not required respecting the negotiation of the first collective agreement between a union and employer, under an arrangement with the NLRB, the FMCS is notified whenever the Board certifies a union as a bargaining agent. The FMCS has a similar arrangement with the Federal Labor Relations Authority, the agency that supervises employee elections in federal government bargaining units.

837. American labor mediators generally view their role as facilitating communications between the disputing parties. At times mediators preside over the negotiating meetings and may separately consult with each side and act as a conduit for communications. If it appears to have promise of helping negotiations to progress, the mediator will 'pretest' new proposals for each side by suggesting to the other side that the proposer might be receptive to such a provision. Sometimes the mediator is able to encourage deadlocked parties to return to the bargaining table. The mediator might also attempt to resolve factual disputes by suggesting working assumptions that are acceptable to both sides. Federal mediators also occasionally suggest a possible new formula for settlement.

838. As a general policy, the FMCS recognizes that mediation is largely a matter of personal style and works best when the disputing parties accept the particular mediator and seek his or her assistance. Except for National Emergency Dispute situations and contract negotiations in the health care industry, the FMCS makes its personnel available to the parties but does not impose them on the parties. In the health care industry and in National Emergency Disputes, mediation is mandatory; that is, the parties have a legal duty to participate in the mediation efforts.

839. In the fiscal year that ended in 2016, the FMCS received over 11,734 notifications of contract expirations or renewals and its mediators were actively involved in 3,500 collective bargaining disputes, primarily in the private sector. It also mediated over 1,670 grievance disputes, primarily in the private sector.

840. Although the FMCS makes its services available in disputes involving government employees, the demands for its services in such disputes is offset by the fact that many states have their own mediation agencies to help parties negotiate collective agreements for state and local governments as well as private sector disputes and mandate participation with the state agency when a public sector dispute is at issue.

841. In addition to providing mediation services for parties engaged in collective bargaining, the FMCS offers educational and training services for management and union representatives to improve their understanding of methods for resolving labor–management problems with a minimum reliance upon confrontational techniques. This has included encouraging parties to develop shop floor committees and other worker consultation and relationship improvement programs. It also conducts negotiated rulemaking training programs to assist other US government agencies and has an international program that provides training in negotiating, mediating, problem solving, and dispute resolution and assists other countries in developing dispute resolution systems and organizations.

842. Another function of the FMCS is the maintenance of a national list of qualified impartial persons who are available to serve as labor arbitrators. The approximately 1,000 persons so listed are not government employees but instead are independent individuals who are privately retained by the disputing parties. Some are full-time labor arbitrators; many are academicians who specialize in labor law, labor economics, industrial engineering and related fields, or persons who are retired from such careers, and others are members of the clergy. The ranks of labor arbitrators also includes retired civil servants and persons who are retired after careers employed as representatives and officials either on the side of management or on the side of labor organizations.

On request and for payment of a small fee, the Service provides an odd numbered panel of names from this list to parties who are seeking an arbitrator. Occasionally, at the parties' joint request, the agency designates an arbitrator. There were over 12,250 arbitration panel requests submitted to the FMCS in the fiscal year that ended in 2016. In the same fiscal year arbitrators were selected from the requested panels in about 5,296 cases. Studies show that well over half of FMCS cases are settled between the time an arbitrator is appointed and the conclusion of the arbitration proceeding. Also, based on prior annual FMCS reports, it can be assumed that all but a couple dozen of these cases involved resolving grievances rather than collective bargaining deadlocks. The number of requests to the FMCS for arbitrators in 2016 was about a third less than the number 15 years earlier. In part this is attributable to the reduced level of union representation. Another possible cause may be that labor and management have become more effective at resolving their disputes without outside intervention. Still another possibility is that unions are financially weaker and less able to undertake the expenses of arbitration. Although difficult to document, it is also possible that the parties now use the FMCS less frequently for obtaining lists of potential arbitrators and, instead, establish the lists in their collective agreements or simply rely on their own familiarity with who is available and mutually select an arbitrator when disputes arise based on that knowledge.

In addition to maintaining its list of labor arbitrators, the FMCS engages in efforts to improve the quality and efficiency of labor arbitration by sponsoring training programs and conferences among arbitrators and the users of their services.

Chapter 5. Enforcement of Prohibitions against Certain Union–Management Transactions and Statutory Protections of Union Members

843. Section 302 of the LMRA, the LMRDA, and some provisions of the ERISA, protect workers from corrupt or inept management of employee benefit funds by prohibiting certain transactions between employers and unions and by requiring that specified financial information either be reported to affected fund beneficiaries or to public agencies. Similarly, certain conduct of unions in relationship to their members either is prohibited or subject to reporting requirements or regulations under the LMRDA. Several of these provisions are enforced through a private action brought in federal court by an aggrieved party. Other provisions are policed by investigative personnel of the US Department of Labor and enforced through civil damages suits or injunctive or criminal actions brought in federal district court either by lawyers on the staff of the Solicitor of the Department of Labor or by federal prosecutors (US District Attorneys).

§1. Office of Labor–Management Services

844. The initial investigative and enforcement responsibility concerning the regulation of financial transactions between unions and employers and the regulation of internal union affairs, is delegated by the Secretary of Labor to the Office of Labor–Management Standards which is located at 200 Constitution Avenue, NW, Washington, DC 20210. (Telephone (202) 693-0123; web site – www.dol.gov/dol/esa/olms_org.htm). Much of its compliance activity is accomplished by obtaining voluntary adherence to legal requirements.

I. Enforcement of Regulations Governing the Election of Union Officials

845. Union members can file a complaint with the Secretary of Labor within a month after exhausting internal union appeals procedures alleging violations of the various election requirements imposed by the LMRDA. The member's efforts to exhaust any internal union remedies need not exceed three months. When it receives such a complaint, Department of Labor personnel investigate and the Secretary of Labor has 60 days in which to determine whether the facts warrant filing a civil action for a remedy of the election violation. If the Secretary files suit and is successful, the district court directs a new election to be held under the supervision of the Secretary of Labor. Most often, new elections are conducted as a result of a voluntary settlement by the labor organization. For example, in the 2016 fiscal year unions entered into 17 settlements in election cases and the Department supervised 27 union elections.

II. Enforcement of Restrictions on Union Trusteeships

846. American labor unions normally are part of a national organization composed of local units called 'locals', 'lodges' or 'chapters'. The local units have varying degrees of autonomy. Generally, the national union retains authority to intervene local affairs in the event of irresponsible or dishonest handling of funds or representational responsibilities, or the proven inability of local officers to conduct the union's functions. Such intervention by the national often is in the form of appointing a 'trustee' to supervise the affairs of the local until its deficiencies are eliminated. (*See* paragraphs 529-533, above.)

847. The LMRDA places substantive and procedural restrictions upon the exercise of the power to impose a trusteeship over local units. Suits challenging a trusteeship can be filed in a federal district court by any union member or subordinate body of a union affected by the imposition of the trusteeship. Such a suit can also be brought by the Secretary of Labor if, after investigation of a complaint by a member or subordinate body of a union affected by a trusteeship, the Secretary finds probable cause to believe that a violation has occurred. The federal court can provide an appropriate remedy, including injunctive relief. Suits under this provision are uncommon but in the 2016 fiscal year the Office of Labor-Management Standards initiated nine trusteeship investigations to ascertain whether there were any legal violations.

III. Enforcement of Information Reporting Requirements

848. Unions, employers engaged in financial transactions with unions, persons who act as labor relations consultants for management, union officers and some union employees, must file annual financial reports with the Secretary of Labor. These statements contain information regarding certain types of financial transactions such as salaries and benefits paid or received for services, investment of union funds, a summary of operating expenditures, and the amount of money transferred between employers and unions. The financial reporting requirements can be enforced by the Secretary of Labor through an action brought in federal district court, but the Department resolves report delinquencies and deficiencies primarily through voluntary compliance. In the 2016 fiscal year the Office of Labor-Management Standards received 26,955 reports of all categories. These reports are public documents that are available on-line.

IV. Investigative Power of the Department of Labor

849. The Department of Labor has broad authority to subpoena witnesses and documents in the course of investigating whether the LMRDA has been violated. Because most compliance investigations are completed through informal techniques, the Department seldom issues subpoenas. Disobedience of the Department's subpoenas carries no sanctions. To enforce them, a civil suit must be brought by the Department in federal district court.

V. Enforcement of the Employee's Right to See the Collective Agreement

850. Employees covered by collective agreements are entitled, under the LMRDA, to receive from the union a copy of the agreement on request (29 US Code §104). An employee who is denied access to a copy may file a complaint with the Secretary of Labor and the Secretary or the employee may sue to enforce the employee's right. American unions normally give a copy of the agreement to all bargaining unit employees. Thus, it is rare for a suit to be filed in support of that right.

§2. Criminal Sanctions and Other Remedies

I. LMRDA Violations

851. A number of provisions of the LMRDA impose criminal penalties for willful violation. Such cases are prosecuted by the US District Attorney for the locale where the violation occurred. Criminal violations most often involve illegal political contributions, filing false reports, continuance in union office after being convicted of a felony (prohibited by the LMRDA), and misallocation or embezzlement of union funds. The latter is the most frequent violation. In the fiscal year that ended in 2015, 234 criminal cases were initiated, in the same fiscal year, 93 criminal indictments were issued in such cases and there were 87 convictions. The Department of Labor's Employee Benefit Security Administration (EBSA) exercises oversight for the financial integrity of those controlling and managing retirement and other welfare benefits plans, both those created by collective agreements and those unilaterally created by employers. (See paragraphs 264–267 and 269–273, above.) The EBSA estimates that in fiscal year 2016 the employer sponsored benefit plans that come under its scrutiny benefited about 149 million workers, retirees and their families and held $9.6 trillion in assets. In the fiscal year that ended in 2017, its enforcement actions recovered $355.6 million for the plans and $326.7 million directly for beneficiaries. It also assisted claimants in recovering $418.7 million through claims settlements.

II. LMRA Violations

852. The LMRA generally prohibits employers from paying, lending, or delivering anything of value to a union, union officer, or agent representing the employer's workers. The LMRA also prohibits union officers and agents from seeking or receiving such prohibited payments or gifts. Certain types of payments, however, are expressly permitted. These include such things as dues deducted from the employee's paycheck with the employee's permission, payment for union labels affixed to the employer's goods (showing that they were made by union workers), payments to jointly controlled trust funds that provide employee retirement or medical benefits, and the like. The Department of Labor investigates suspected violations of this law but violations are prosecuted by the Department of Justice's US District Attorneys. Often these prosecutions also involve LMRDA violations and violations of more general laws prohibiting corrupt practices.

III. Other Statutes

853. The Racketeer Influenced and Corrupt Organizations Act (RICO), 18 US Code §1964, was adopted in 1970 to provide federal law enforcement authorities with a means of combating syndicated criminal activity. It targets concerted actions that follow a pattern of using force or other illegal coercion to generate income. Violations of this anti-racketeering law are subject to substantial criminal penalties. In addition, the federal government or those injured by such violations can bring a civil suit against violators. In a successful civil action the court can require the defendant to surrender any illegal gains, enjoin the illegal activity, and order that wrongs resulting from the illegal action be rectified. In addition, an individual plaintiff in a civil RICO action can recover treble damages and reasonable attorneys fees. On occasion both the federal government and individuals have used this law to combat corrupt labor–management practices.

Of particular note was a civil RICO suit brought against the International Brotherhood of Teamsters in 1988, asserting that individual members of the international union's executive board and other officials of the union, and their associates, together with various reputed members of La Cosa Nostra, a criminal organization, had engaged in fraud, embezzlement, bribery and extortion to dominate the union for the benefit of themselves and their associates. Among other things, the suit asserted that these activities deprived union members of their right to free and fair elections. In 1989 the case was settled when the parties entered into a consent decree, approved by the trial court, that established a trusteeship consisting of three court appointed officers (Independent Review Board) who were given authority to: (a) investigate and initiate disciplinary charges against union officers, members and employees, and impose trusteeships over local unions and other affiliated entities; (b) conduct disciplinary hearings for those charged with wrongdoing; and (c) supervise elections for new union officers. The consent decree also made changes in the union's election and governance structure including providing for direct membership election of national officers.[983] Eventually, many officers were removed from the union through the disciplinary proceedings initiated under the consent decree, and new national union officers and many new local officers were elected in balloting supervised by the court appointed overseers. In 2016, the court agreed to allow the union to go through a five-year transition under which starting in 2021, the union will be granted the power to appoint the review board members.

---

983. *United States* v. *International Brotherhood of Teamsters*, 931 F.2d 177 (2d Cir. 1991).

§3. Public Information Regarding Union Activities

854. The LMRDA's required reports of financial and other information concerning union activities and union-management transactions are public documents that are available from the Department of Labor for a small copying fee. The reports provide union members (and most especially, dissident members), news reporters, and academic researchers with information concerning the activities of union leaders and probably deter some union leaders from actions they would expect to be unpopular with their members or the public. Management advocates sometimes use the reports to find damaging information for use in union representation election campaigns.

§4. Private Actions by Union Members

855. The LMRDA gives union members a right to sue to vindicate certain rights derived from their membership status. The first part of the LMRDA, entitled the 'Bill of Rights of Members of Labor Organizations', establishes substantive and procedural safeguards that promote democratic methods of internal union governance, ensure equal treatment for each member, and establish fair disciplinary procedures.[984] A member can enforce these rights by filing a suit in federal district court. (*See* paragraph 524, above.) No judicial deference is owed to the determination of an internal union tribunal with respect to the issue of whether the member's statutory rights were violated; that question is examined anew by the trial court. If malice is shown, punitive damages may be awarded in addition to compensatory relief.[985] Moreover, when such a claim is based on a union's alleged retaliation against a dissident member by failing to provide fair grievance representation in the member's dealings with an employer, that claim is separate from a claim for breach of the duty of fair representation.[986]

984. *Knight* v. *Longshoremen*, 457 F.3d 331 (3d Cir. 2006).
985. *Black* v. *Ryder/P.I.E. Nationwide, Inc.*, 970 F.2d 1461 (6th Cir. 1992).
986. *Black* v. *Ryder/P.I.E. Nationwide, Inc.*, 15 F.3d 573 (6th Cir. 1994); *Maddalone* v. *Local 17, United Brotherhood of Carpenters*, 152 F.3d 178 (2d Cir. 1998).

Chapter 6. Railway Labor Act Enforcement Machinery

§1. Generally

856. The RLA regulates labor–management relations in the airline and railroad industries. Excluded from coverage are local rail transportation systems serving urban and suburban areas and rail operations conducted as part of mining and transporting coal between the mine face and tipple.

857. The National Mediation Board administers those parts of the RLA that deal with establishing the representational status of a union and disputes arising out of bargaining for collective agreements. In the railway industry, the National Railroad Adjustment Board administers those provisions of the RLA designed to provide a method for resolving disputes arising out of the interpretation and application of collective agreements. The Surface Transportation Board has a small role to play in administering the RLA by resolving disputes concerning whether a particular employer does or does not engage in activities regulated by the Act.

§2. National Mediation Board

858. The National Mediation Board is an independent agency composed of three members who are nominated by the President and appointed with the advice and consent of the Senate for three-year terms. Its office is in Washington, DC (1301 K Street, NW, Suite 250 East, Washington, DC 20005-7011; telephone: 202 692-5000; web site: www.nmb.gov). The Board is assisted by a small staff of mediators (12 as of January 2017) selected through the civil service process.

I. Determining a Union's Representational Status

859. Under the RLA, bargaining units are based upon craft lines. That is, all employees performing a similar job function are in the same bargaining unit. Representation is system-wide rather than local. Therefore, all employees employed within a craft by a single air or railway system, no matter how geographically dispersed, are in the same bargaining unit.

860. The National Mediation Board (NMB) conducts a secret ballot election in a unit that does not have an existing representative if at least 50 percent of the employees in that unit signed cards within the past year requesting an election or authorizing a union to act as bargaining agent. To gain NMB certification as bargaining representative, the union must receive a majority of valid ballots cast by eligible voters. A second union that seeks to intervene in an election must present authorization cards from at least 50 percent of the employees who are eligible to vote.

861. The NMB does not conduct elections within two years of the last certified election in the bargaining unit. Even if the election results were not certified, under certain circumstances the NMB will not conduct an election for at least a year. If only one labor organization seeks certification, the NMB can certify it as bargaining agent if it finds that over 50 percent of the employees have executed valid cards authorizing the union to be their representative.[987]

862. Factual disputes respecting an application for a NMB election are investigated by staff mediators. At its discretion, the NMB may order a hearing concerning any issues raised regarding which employees are eligible to participate in the election.

863. To win an election conducted by the NMB, a union must receive votes from a majority of valid ballots cast. For many years the NMB did not list a 'no representation' option on the representation ballot. Submitting a blank ballot was the equivalent to voting against representation. That practice has been changed and a 'no representation' choice is part of the ballot.[988]

864. Because employees of a railway or airline often live in widely dispersed places, the NMB balloting is conducted by mail, telephone or internet using random separately assigned access identification codes provided to each voter.

If more than one labor organization is on a ballot and no one receives a majority of the votes cast, upon request the NMB conducts a runoff election between the two choices that received the highest number of votes. The NMB ballot also allows for 'write-in' votes–a vote for an organization that is not on the ballot. In at least one case the write-in candidate won the election.

The certification procedure of the NMB is treated as an administrative fact finding process, not an adjudicative process. Therefore, there is no direct review of the Board's determinations in these proceedings. Moreover, judicial review through ancillary actions, too, is very limited.[989]

865. The NMB conducts very few representation proceedings in comparison with the NLRB's comparable activity. For example, by the author's count, in the fiscal year that ended in 2017, the NMB concluded 27 representation elections of which 17 resulted in the certification of a bargaining representative.

II. Unfair Labor Practice Proceedings

866. The RLA imposes on both sides a number of duties designed to prevent interference with the right of self-organization and to protect the right to bargain

987. NMB, Rules and Regulations §§1206.2–1206.6.

988. *Brotherhood of Railway and Steamship Clerks* v. *Ass'n for Benefit of Non Contract Employees*, 380 US 650 (1965); NMB, *Representation Manual* §§13.203, 13,304-1.

989. *See* discussion in *United States* v. *Feaster*, 410 F.2d 1354, 1361–1364 (5th Cir.), *cert.* denied 396 US 962 (1969); *Am. Airlines, Inc.* v. *Nat'l Mediation Bd.*, 479 Fed. Appx. 657 (5th Cir. 2012).

collectively through an exclusive representative selected by an employee majority. However, unlike the NLRA, the RLA does not create special administrative machinery for the enforcement of these duties. Rather, they are enforced through private injunctive and declaratory judgment actions brought in the federal courts.[990] Alternatively, violation of the duties expressed in the Act is subject to criminal penalty. However criminal prosecution involving the Act is rare.[991]

III. 'Major Disputes' – NMB Role in Changing Terms and Conditions of Employment

867. The RLA divides conflicts between labor and management into two categories: 'major disputes' and 'minor disputes'. Depending upon the category into which a particular conflict falls, a specific procedure must be followed in seeking to adjust it. 'Major disputes' are interests disputes concerning modification of the terms and conditions of employment. Normally, such modifications involve proposed changes in the parties' collective agreement. 'Minor disputes', on the other hand, are those involving differences respecting the interpretation or application of the existing contractual terms and conditions of employment.

Occasionally close cases must be decided respecting whether a conflict is a major or a minor dispute. For example, when a railroad unilaterally added urine drug tests to its periodic physical examinations of employees, a divided Supreme Court decided that since the railroad was making a non-frivolous claim that the collective agreement entitled it to make the disputed change, the matter at issue constituted a minor dispute.[992]

868. The first required step in resolving major disputes is for the parties to try to reach a private settlement without government intervention. The RLA prohibits changes in the terms and conditions of employment until the party seeking the change gives the other side at least 30 days' written notice of the change it proposes. Within 10 days after the other side receives the notice, both sides have a duty of good faith bargaining and must agree upon a time and place to confer, beginning within 30 days of when the notice was given.[993] No change may be made in the terms and conditions of employment until a settlement has been reached or the parties become deadlocked. If there is a deadlock, no change may be made for another 10 days after bargaining has ceased. Furthermore, at the request of either side, or upon its own initiative, the NMB may intervene to assist the parties in their bargaining efforts and no change may be made in the terms and conditions of employment until the agency surrenders its jurisdiction by declaring that it finds that the parties have reached a deadlock.

990. *See* A. Harper II, 'Major Disputes Under the Railway Labor Act', 35 *J. of Air Law and Commerce*, 3, 5–6 (1969). *Virginian RR* v. *System Fed.*, 300 US 515 (1937).
991. *US* v. *Winston*, 558 F.2d 105 (2d Cir. 1977).
992. *Consol. Rail Corp.* v. *Ry. Labor Executives' Ass'n*, 491 US 299 (1989).
993. *See* RLA §6.

The requirement that no change be made during these bargaining and mediating periods has been held to also prohibit strikes or lockouts during this time. If either side makes a change or resorts to a work stoppage, the other side can obtain injunctive relief from a federal district court.[994]

Often the NMB retains jurisdiction and engages in mediatory efforts for many months. Even if there is an extended period without negotiations or the participation of the agency's mediators, the parties cannot treat their negotiations as deadlocked until the NMB declares that they are at impasse, a determination that the courts indicate is almost totally within the agency's discretion.[995]

869. At the point at which the NMB concludes that its mediatory efforts are fruitless, it urges the parties to submit the dispute to binding arbitration. The Act outlines the procedure to be followed if both sides choose to arbitrate, but the parties are free to reject the process.

870. If, as usually happens, one or both sides refuse to arbitrate, the NMB has two choices. One possibility is for it to withdraw from the conflict. If it does that, no change in the status quo may be made for another 30 days. After the 30 days, the parties are free to resort to unilateral action and engage in economic pressure tactics including work stoppages.

871. The other option for the NMB is to notify the President of the United States that in its opinion the conflict threatens to deprive a section of the nation of an essential transportation service or that it threatens to 'interrupt substantial' interstate commerce. If the NMB chooses the latter course, the President may create, but is not required to create, a Presidential Emergency Board which has 30 days to issue its report to the President, and no change in the status quo is permitted until 30 days after the Board's report is issued unless the parties reach a mutual agreement.[996] Since the beginning of the present century, Presidents have convened 15 Emergency Boards.

---

994. *Detroit & Toledo Shore Line RR* v. *United Trans. Union*, 396 US 151 (1969); *American Airlines, Inc.* v. *Air Line Pilots Ass'n*, 169 F. Supp. 777 (DCNY 1958).

995. *International Association of Machinists* v. *National Mediation Board*, 930 F.2d 45 (DC Cir.), *cert.* denied 502 US 858 (1991).

996. RLA §10 provides for the creation of a Presidential Emergency Board for privately owned rail and air carriers; section 9A separately provides for their creation for government owned carriers. In the latter case, a Presidential Emergency Board can be requested by a party or by a Governor and no change can be made for 120 days from the Board's creation. If a settlement does not result within the first 60 days of the Board's creation, the NMB conducts a hearing to ascertain why the parties have not accepted the board's recommendations. Thereafter, if not settled, the President may appoint a second Emergency Board to which the parties must submit final offers after which the Emergency Board reports its finding regarding which is the most reasonable offer. The freeze on changes remains for 60 days after that report. A carrier that does not accept the Board's recommendation is barred from taking work stoppage benefits under any agreement itr may have with other carriers; if a labor organization does not accept the recommendation, the employees may not draw work stoppage benefits under the Railroad Unemployment Insurance Act.

872. The NMB reports that since 1980, almost 99 percent of cases it has mediated have been resolved without public service interruptions. In addition to the mediated cases, each year the parties negotiate contract changes without reaching the point of having to notify the NMB.

IV. Emergency Dispute Procedure under the RLA

873. The size, compensation and budget of an Emergency Board are determined by the President. On occasion, if the parties at the end of the cooling off period have not resolved the dispute, based on the Emergency Board's recommendation or some other proposal, the President has requested Congressional intervention. For example, in 1992 Congress adopted Public Law 102-306 which prohibited the parties to several impasses in national railroad collective bargaining from resorting to work stoppages and required them to submit their differences to a Special Board appointed by the President. The Board was authorized, after conducting a hearing, to impose either side's last best offer as the final resolution of the dispute unless the parties mutually agreed to alter that arbitral process. In addition, upon appeal of a party, the President could, within three days after the award was issued, decide to set it aside. In the latter event, the parties would have been free to resort to work stoppage pressures.

V. 'Minor Disputes' – Resolving Grievances Respecting the Application of Terms and Conditions of Rail and Air Industry Employment

874. 'Minor disputes' are those involving day-to-day employee claims to rights and benefits including the application and interpretation of collective agreements. They are what in American labor relations law more commonly are referred to as grievances. The RLA imposes a form of mandatory grievance arbitration upon the railroad and airline industries. The mandatory minor disputes resolution procedures are the sole and exclusive remedy for resolving such conflicts.[997] The Act distinguishes, however, between the two industries with respect to procedures that must be followed.

Minor disputes arising in the railroad industry must be resolved under the National Railroad Adjustment Board procedures set forth in the RLA or through an authorized alternative procedure. An employee has a statutory right to select a representative of his own choice in the proceedings before the National Railroad Adjustment Board but the recognized bargaining unit agent can insist on acting as the grievance representative in seeking a settlement with the employer.[998]

The RLA allows the NMB to establish an industry-wide agency to provide dispute resolution services in determining the merits of minor disputes in the airline industry. However, this option has never been exercised by the NMB. Instead, in the airline industry the parties' collective agreements specify a required method for

997. *Andrews* v. *Louisville & Nashville RR.*, 406 US 320 (1972).
998. *Landers* v. *National RR Passengers Corp.*, 485 US 652 (1988).

selecting an impartial third party (usually called a 'referee' in the railroad and airline industries–an 'arbitrator' in most other American industries) who is authorized to make a binding decision concerning the controversy. Generally, the railroad industry's statutory procedures have influenced the airline industry's contractual arbitration procedures. Often, for example, the airline industry collective agreements call for the NMB to select a referee if the parties cannot themselves agree on the selection.

A. *National Railroad Adjustment Board (NRAB)*

875. Half of the NRAB members are chosen by, compensated by, and represent the railway unions; the other half are chosen by, compensated by, and represent the railroads.

The Board is divided into four divisions, each with equal numbers of employer and union members. Each division has jurisdiction over those disputes that involve employees in particular job classifications. For example, the First Division handles cases involving engineers, firemen, hostlers, outside hostler helpers, conductors, trainmen and yard service employees.

876. Minor disputes that cannot be adjusted by the parties must be submitted to the appropriate division of the NRAB. If the members of the division are unable to reach a decision by majority vote, they must attempt to agree upon a neutral to join them as an additional member and make an award. If, after ten days, the division cannot agree upon such a neutral, the NMB selects that neutral. The compensation and travel expenses of the neutral arbitrators selected for railway industry cases are paid for each case by the federal government.

In the fiscal year that ended in 2017, 344 new NRAB cases were filed, 311 were resolved during the year and 3,222, including those accumulated from prior years, were pending at the end of the year.

B. *Special Boards of Adjustment*

877. An alternative to using the NRAB is for the individual railroad and union, or for a group of railroads and a union, to agree to use a procedure known as a 'special board of adjustment'. Minor disputes covered by a special board of adjustment arrangement are not heard by the NRAB. The special boards retain their authority over disputes between parties to the arrangement until a party has given at least 90 days' notice of its desire to terminate its participation. Special boards consist of one representative of the railroad or railroads, and one of the union, plus an impartial chairperson selected by the two adversary board members. If they cannot agree upon that third person, the NMB designates one. Decisions are made by any two members of the board. At the end of the 2017 fiscal year, 49 special board cases were resolved and 306 cases, including those accumulated from prior years, were pending at the end of the year.

C. Public Law 89-456 Boards

878. A separate type of special board of adjustment is also available to the parties as a result of a law passed in 1966. That law, Public Law 89-456, was designed to ease some of the backlog of minor dispute cases. It provides that when a dispute has been pending before the NRAB for more than 12 months, either side may, upon written request, require that a special board of adjustment be established to resolve cases which are more than 12 months old. Thereafter, the procedures for setting up a Public Law Board are the same as those described in the preceding paragraph regarding special boards of adjustment. At the end of the 2017 fiscal year, 1,521 Public Law Board cases were resolved and 4,413 cases, including those accumulated from prior years, were pending at the end of the year.

D. Enforcement of Minor Dispute Awards

879. Federal court injunctive relief is available to prevent and terminate work stoppages concerning minor disputes or awards issued under the RLA for the resolution of such differences. The controlling principle is that the RLA has established the exclusive method for resolving such disputes and, therefore, parties cannot try to force a negotiated resolution by resorting to economic pressure. To gain enforcement of an award, the winning party must bring an action in federal district court for injunctive or similar relief ordering compliance.[999]

880. Until 1966, some types of awards in minor dispute cases were subject to judicial review by means of a trial *de novo* in federal district court. This meant that the trial court could displace all findings and conclusions based on its judgment without regard to the arbitral determination. Amendments to the RLA, adopted in 1966, essentially made all minor dispute awards final, binding and not subject to judicial review. The exceptions to this rule are that a federal court can set aside a minor dispute award if: (a) the proceedings violated the principles of fundamental procedural fairness, (b) the arbitration tribunal exceeded its jurisdiction, or (c) there was fraud or corruption.[1000]

The standard for judicial review of arbitration decisions in the airline industry is less clear.[1001]

---

999. *Locomotive Engineers* v. *Louisville & Nashville RR*, 373 US 33 (1963).

1000. *Shafii* v. *PLC British Airways*, 22 F.3d 59 (2d Cir. 1994). In *Shafii* the court examined the proposition that judicial review of RLA minor disputes awards includes the power to vacate decisions arising out of proceedings lacking fundamental fairness. Inasmuch as grievance arbitration is mandatory under the RLA, arguably constitutional standards of due process should be applicable because the dispute resolution procedure is required by statute and not contract. Hence, government conduct, which must adhere to due process, is involved in the RLA minor disputes resolution system. Contra, *Kinross* v. *Utah Ry.*, 362 F.3d 658 (10th Cir. 2004).

1001. A. Goldman, 'Selecting the Correct Standard for Judicial Review of Airline Grievance Arbitration Decisions', 9 *U. of Pa. J. Lab. & Emp. L.* 743 (2007).

Chapter 7. Arbitration of Disputes Arising under Collective Agreements

§1. Generally

881. In the private sector of labor–management relations in the United States, arbitration is the almost universal method for obtaining a final and binding resolution of at least some categories of disputes arising out of the interpretation or application of the collective agreement (grievances). By the early part of the 20th century, arbitration was already a familiar forum for resolving such differences. During the Second World War, the War Labor Board actively encouraged greater utilization of the technique and by the end of the war it had become the norm in collective agreements.

Although, as discussed below, the government encourages and assists in implementing labor arbitration arrangements, outside of the railroad industry and much of government employment, the process itself remains a voluntary, private arrangement controlled by the collective agreement.

Collective agreements in the government sector normally provide for grievance arbitration. In the federal portion of that sector, grievance arbitration awards are not final but rather are subject to review by the Federal Labor Relations Authority for the same grounds as are applicable to the private sector or to ensure that they are not contrary to any law, rule or regulation (5 US Code §7122).

Although grievance arbitration involving state and local government employees generally is final and binding, at least one state has rejected such provisions where the state constitution explicitly gives a government agency the authority to review issues concerning disciplining civil service employees.[1002]

§2. Tribunal Formats

882. Most collective agreements provide that a single arbitrator will decide the issues submitted to grievance arbitration. However, the most common alternative is a tripartite panel consisting of an arbitrator selected by management (and expected to represent management's interests), an arbitrator selected by the union (and expected to represent the union's and grievant's interests), and a third party selected jointly by the management and the union representatives and expected to function as a wholly impartial, independent decision maker. When collective agreement data was still being collected, around the 1980s, it was found that roughly 10 percent of collective agreements called for tripartite tribunals and less than 1 percent provided for a five-member arbitration board. However, even when a collective agreement provided for a multimember tribunal, the parties often waived that format and older studies indicate that in only a small portion of cases did the parties actually utilize their contractual arrangement for a multimember tribunal. Anecdotal evidence indicates that multimember tribunals have become rare.

1002. *State Personnel Board* v. *Department of Personnel Administration*, 123 P. 3d 169 (Calif. 2005).

883. Many collective agreements in the United States designate a permanent arbitrator, permanent arbitration board, or a permanent rotating panel of arbitrators. The permanent arbitrator is often called an 'umpire', 'referee', or 'impartial chairman'. Traditionally, the 'impartial chairman' served a broader role than the typical grievance arbitrator, whether permanent or temporary, because the traditional impartial chairman presided over the parties' collective bargaining sessions and acted as a private mediator as well as arbitrator.[1003] Such arrangements, however, have become rare. Far more common is the 'permanent' panel consisting of several arbitrators who, based on a fixed method of rotation, are appointed to hear cases as they arise. Regardless of the contractual designation of an arbitrator or panel of arbitrators as 'permanent', the parties can always mutually agree to replace such an arbitrator.

§3. Selecting an *Ad Hoc* Arbitrator

884. The majority of labor arbitration agreements provide that the parties will select an arbitrator each time a new grievance is submitted to arbitration. This approach is generally referred to as '*ad hoc* arbitration'. The collective agreement often specifies the FMCS or the American Arbitration Association (AAA) as the source from which the parties will receive a short, odd-numbered list ('panel') of names of available, qualified impartial, independent third persons. The most common practice is for the disputing parties then to alternately strike one name from that list. The person whose name remains after all but one have been stricken is designated as arbitrator for the case. Although the parties normally jointly appoint the arbitrator, because notification of that appointment typically is sent by the agency that provided the panel of names, the FMCS and AAA often are referred to as 'appointing' agencies. Occasionally parties request the 'appointing' agency to itself select the person to arbitrate their dispute.

885. Even when the collective agreement does not specifically designate any particular source for acquiring names of qualified arbitrators, the parties frequently seek this assistance from the FMCS or the American Arbitration Association (AAA). In practice, the AAA has become the primary agency used by parties in roughly the northeastern part of the nation; the FMCS is the primary agency used in the rest of the nation. About 20 states and a few municipalities have government agencies that maintain a list either of staff arbitrators or arbitrators who are not employed by the government, or both. Much like the FMCS, these government agencies variously prepare panels consisting of a short list of such names for requesting parties in disputes arising from collective agreements with government

1003. *See generally*, A. Zack, E. Goldstein and J. Sherman, 'Unique Problems and Opportunities of Permanent Umpireships – A Panel Discussion', *Proceedings of 42d Ann. Meeting of Nat'l Acad. of Arbitrators* (1989); C. Killingsworth and S. Wallen, 'Constraint and Variety in Arbitration Systems', *Proceedings of 17th Ann. Meeting of Nat'l Acad. of Arbitrators*, 56–72 (1964).

employees, with local non-government employees, or both.[1004] In other situations the parties rely upon their own knowledge of available, qualified impartial persons and agree upon a particular person for each case as it arises.

886. The FMCS's national list of arbitrators is compiled after it screens applicants in an effort to ensure impartiality, familiarity with labor–management relations, and the capacity to conduct a fair hearing. Arbitrators pay an annual listing fee. Normally, lists are sent to requesting parties, for a fee paid by them, based on the geographic region in which the hearing will be conducted. It assembles panel lists randomly based on the region and any special criteria requested by the parties. (Data and additional detailed description of arbitration activities assisted by the FMCS are at paragraph 842, above.)

887. The American Arbitration Association (AAA) (120 Broadway, 21st Floor, New York, NY 10271; telephone: 212-716-5800; web: www.adr.org) is a private, non-profit organization that promotes the use of arbitration, mediation and other conflict resolution mechanisms in all contexts including labor–management relations. It is financed by user service fees, membership dues and contributions, tuition for training programs, and book sales. It maintains a list of qualified labor arbitrators who either pay Association membership dues or pay an annual listing fee to the Association (that is considerably higher than that charged by the FMCS). If the parties have not agreed on the selection process, on request from the parties the AAA assembles a panel list from which they can select an arbitrator (or arbitrators in the rare case that the parties want more than one neutral). If they do not agree on one of the listed arbitrators, the parties each strike the names of those who are unacceptable to them and indicate their order of preference among the rest. Guided by that information, the AAA selects the arbitrator or arbitrators. The AAA has regional offices in several larger cities. In addition to providing lists of available arbitrators, the AAA assists the parties in making hearing arrangements.

888. The ultimate test for becoming a labor arbitrator is whether both sides find the individual acceptable. If they do not, the individual will not be chosen and eventually may be dropped from the lists for lack of use. Because listing involves an annual fee, eventually those who are not used can be expected to remove themselves from the lists.

Most of the more highly experienced labor arbitrators in the US and Canada are members of the National Academy of Arbitrators (1 North Main Street, Suite 412, Cortland, NY 13045; tel. (607) 756-8363, email: naa@naarb.org; web: www.naarb.org). The Academy has over 600 active members. To qualify for membership an applicant must show that he or she is of good moral character, adheres to the Code of Professional Responsibility for Arbitrators of Labor–Management Disputes, has established general acceptability as an impartial decision maker, and has current, substantial experience arbitrating labor–management disputes.

1004. *See* W. Gershenfeld and N. Nelson, 'The Appointment of Grievance Arbitrators by State and Local Agencies', *Survey Sponsored by the National Academy of Arbitrators* (2001).

Older studies of the labor arbitration profession, sponsored by the National Academy of Arbitrators (NAA)[1005] found that about 20 percent, including non Academy members, engaged in the profession as their primary source of earned income. That figure has probably become larger in recent years. The rest arbitrated on a part-time basis. Part-time arbitrators most often have full-time teaching positions, usually in a field related to labor relations, labor economics or labor law, or are retired from such positions or from government employment. The second most common primary occupation for part-time labor arbitrators is practicing law. A small number are in the clergy, serve as consultants, or are government administrators. Among members of the National Academy of Arbitrators, the majority are full-time arbitrators.

Almost all labor arbitrators have at least one university degree. Over half have law degrees and a majority of those who do not have a law degree hold a doctorate degree in some other field. A substantial portion of the remainder hold a master's degree. Most often the non-law degrees are in industrial relations, human resource management, or labor economics. (Law degrees are more common among Canadian labor arbitrators who are NAA members.)

American labor arbitrators normally have some prior or concurrent work background in labor–management relations, but the nature of those backgrounds is quite diverse. Some are former government officials such as former NLRB or FMCS staff. Others have held management or union positions of responsibility relating to personnel administration or labor–management relations or have practiced law representing parties in labor–management matters.

As of the early 1990s less than 2 percent of labor arbitrators were non white, only about 6 percent were women, and the average labor arbitrator was over 57 years of age. By the late 1990s the portion of female arbitrators in the NAA was about 12 percent and non-whites about 6 percent. The portion of both in the Academy appears to have continued to grow in the early 21st century and the average age probably has increased.

§4. Costs, Efficiency and Utilization

889. American labor arbitrators receive per diem fee compensation and their expenses are reimbursed by the parties. In over 90 percent of the cases, the collective agreement requires the parties to share equally the arbitrator's fee and expenses. About 5 percent of the agreements provide that the loser pays all fees and expenses. In about an equal portion of agreements, the division of fees and expenses is left to the arbitrator's discretion.

890. In the fiscal year that ended in 2015, the median per diem fee of arbitrators whose cases were obtained through the American Arbitration Association was $1,400. In the average case in which the parties secured their arbitrator through the

1005. *Labor Arbitration in America: The Profession and Practice*, NY, 1992 (M. Bognanno and C. Coleman, eds.); M. Picher, R, Seeber & D. Lipsky, *A Survey of the National Academy of Arbitrators* (2000).

FMCS's service in the fiscal year that ended in 2016, the arbitrator charged an average per diem fee of $1,314 and total fees of $7,490 representing 6.07 days' total billing time. Study and decision writing time averaged 3.42 days per case and hearing time 1.51 days. Travel time accounted for the remainder of the billed time. The average arbitrator's reimbursed expenses per case was $508. (Normally travel time and expenses are minimal if the hearing is held in a large metropolitan area but can be considerable if held in a small town that is distant from larger airports.) In 2017 both appointing agencies expressed concern that the 2016 arbitrator costs represented a five-year increase of over 80 percent. The per diem rate increased about 34 percent. Billed travel time was up more than two and a half times, for study days it was up over 44 percent, and for hearing days it had increased by over a third.

891. Although one advantage of arbitration as a means of dispute resolution is that it is supposed to be a quicker process than litigation, an FMCS study of the fiscal year that ended in 2013 showed that on the average 499 days elapsed between the filing of the grievance and the issuance of the award. Of that time 132 days represented the average time between the filing of the grievance and the request for a panel of arbitrators. It took about another three months, on average, for the parties to select an arbitrator from the list and almost six months after that before the hearing was conducted. The time between the hearing and the issuance of the award took an average of 95 days. A major portion of that time involves waiting for the parties' post-hearing briefs (almost two months) for those cases in which briefs are filed. Although the filing of post-hearing briefs was the exception until around the 1960s, by the 1990s the parties were filing briefs in the majority of cases and the use of transcripts and applications for subpoenas of witnesses has reportedly increased.

Arbitrators commonly report a high rate of settlements after they have been selected, a factor that may contribute to the delays in scheduling hearings.

892. In an effort to reduce delays, some collective agreements adopt an expedited process. Normally, expedited procedures are confined to more routine or less serious categories of cases. Typically, a rotating panel of permanent arbitrators is used and the parties must go to hearing within a specified short period after the last grievance step. Some expedited procedures limit the number of witnesses. In addition, hearing transcripts and post-hearing briefs are eliminated and the arbitrator is required to issue a decision within a specified amount of time (often 48 hours). Most expedited procedures specify that the arbitrator will issue the award without an explanatory opinion or with only a summary explanation and that the decision will not carry precedential weight in the parties' dealings.

893. In the fiscal year that ended in 2013, over 98 percent of the cases decided involved grievances arising under a contract as contrasted with resolving disputes resolving the terms of a new contract. Discharge and other disciplinary matters were involved, sometimes with other issues, in a little over half of the cases. Pay disputes and other benefits issues, management's scope of authority, and work hours and scheduling were among the other more commonly encountered issues. (More recent data have not been published.)

§5. THE ARBITRATION HEARING

894. American labor arbitration hearings are informal. Often they are conducted around a conference table in a lawyer's office, in a motel or hotel meeting room, or in a meeting room at the union's or employer's facility. As a theoretical matter, procedural details are largely governed by state law but not every state has fully defined these requirements.[1006] In most states the parties can obtain a subpoena requiring the attendance of witnesses or the production of evidence.[1007] Normally the subpoenas are issued by the arbitrator even though they are enforced by the courts. Preparation for the hearing is aided by the fact that the NLRB treats as an unfair practice a party's refusal to make information available to the other side if that information is relevant to evaluating and attempting to settle a grievance or preparing for arbitration.[1008] Generally, however, it is unnecessary to resort to formal methods to gain access to relevant evidence. The prospect of being in the opposite position in the next case encourages cooperation under the principle of reciprocity. In addition, in most cases unwillingness to antagonize the arbitrator, and fear that the arbitrator will make a negative assumption based on unwillingness to produce requested information, succeeds in bringing all relevant requested information into the hearing.

895. Although the parties at an arbitration hearing often are represented by an attorney, the representative need not be a lawyer. The actual presentation of evidence generally follows a trial format but trial court procedural rules and rules of evidence are used at most as a guideline, not as a governing standard. When all of the evidence has been presented and the witnesses have been subjected to cross-examination, each side may present a closing argument. If the parties choose to submit a written post-hearing brief, the closing argument usually is waived. If the parties choose, a court reporter may make a verbatim record of the hearing. This typically delays the preparation of post-hearing briefs for two to four weeks. In the absence of a transcript an arbitrator normally relies on exhibits plus the arbitrator's own notes in resolving any factual disputes.[1009] Some arbitrators supplement their note taking with an audio recording of the hearing.

896. Under the rules of the FMCS, the arbitrator has 60 days after the close of the hearing record to issue the opinion and award. Under the rules of the AAA that limit is 30 days. Alternatively, the parties specify that time limit in the collective

---

1006. *Auto Workers* v. *Hoosier Cardinal Corp.*, 383 US 696 (1966).

1007. *See*, for example, §7 of the Uniform Arbitration Act of 1956 and §17 of the Uniform Arbitration Act of 2000. According to the National Conference of Commissioners on Uniform State Laws, either the earlier or more recent version of the Uniform Act has been adopted by 35 states; 14 other states have adopted similar laws.

1008. *Detroit Edison Co.* v. *NLRB*, 440 US 301 (1979); *NLRB* v. *Acme Indus. Co.*, 385 US 432 (1967); *Fawcett Printing Corp.*, 201 NLRB 964 (1973).

1009. The level of formality and frequency of use of lawyers and transcripts varies regionally. Greater use of lawyers and increased hearing formality is encountered more often in major metropolitan areas. Many arbitrators take handwritten notes, but a growing number use laptop computers for note taking at the hearing or voice recording that is digitally transcribed. Most arbitrators look upon their notes as a personal work product and reject the notion that they can be treated as the hearing record and, thereby, subject to the parties' or a court's scrutiny.

agreement. The time limits can be extended by the parties but arbitrators who regularly delay issuing decisions are less likely to be selected by the parties and may be removed from the appointing agency lists. If briefs are submitted, the hearing record closes with their receipt by the arbitrator. Labor arbitration decisions are written and usually contain a moderately detailed discussion of the facts and the decision-maker's evaluation of the merits.

897. Those arbitration decisions that deal with more novel or more difficult questions often are, with the parties' consent, reported in publications of the Bureau of National Affairs, Inc., Commerce Clearing House, Inc., and the AAA. Also, some state agencies publish arbitration awards involving government units coming within their responsibilities.

Reported labor arbitration decisions are of persuasive value in presenting similar arbitration cases and provide guidance for grievance settlement by indicating how an arbitrator is likely to resolve a particular dispute. If the prior decision involved a dispute between the same parties, generally it is given considerably greater weight on the theory that arbitration decisions become an extension of the parties' collective agreement.

898. An arbitrator selected from a list of names submitted by the FMCS or the AAA, is required to abide by the procedural and ethical standards established by that agency. In 1951, the FMCS and the AAA adopted a Code of Professional Responsibility for Arbitrators of Labor–Management Disputes. This code was revised in 1974 by these two entities together with the National Academy of Arbitrators. It has been further amended in subsequent years. As described in paragraph 888, above, the Academy is a professional association whose members pledge to abide by the Code.

899. Under the authority of §301 of the LMRA, federal and state courts enforce arbitration agreements found in collective bargaining contracts by ordering parties to submit to arbitration and by issuing orders requiring parties to abide by the arbitrator's decision (generally referred to as the 'award').[1010] The scope of judicial review of an arbitrator's award is limited to assuring that it is within the boundaries of the contractually bestowed authority to determine the facts and interpret and apply the collective agreement, that it does not order anyone to do something illegal, and that the procedure was not marred by fraud, corruption or other basic procedural unfairness. However, the Supreme Court has not totally foreclosed the possibility of rejecting an award on 'public policy' grounds.[1011] Moreover, some federal appellate courts persist in trying to stretch the allowed scope of their reviewing authority.[1012]

1010. *John Wiley & Sons, Inc.* v. *Livingston*, 376 US 543 (1964).

1011. *Eastern Associated Coal Corp.* v. *UMW, Dist. 17*, 531 US 57 (2000); *United Paperworkers International Union* v. *Misco, Inc.*, 484 US 29 (1987).

1012. *See* S. Huber, 'The Arbitration Jurisprudence of the Fifth Circuit, Round II', 37 *Tex. Tech L. Rev.* 531 (2005).

900. In some cases, the NLRB abates dealing with an unfair labor practice charge until the arbitration process is completed if the issue to be arbitrated is the same as the issue involved in an unfair labor practice charge. In most situations, the NLRB accepts the arbitration award as controlling. The standards for such abatement and deferral are discussed above in paragraph 829.

Chapter 8. Regulation of Collective Representation of Federal Workers

§1. Postal Workers

901. The Postal Reorganization Act of 1970 established the Postal Service as an independent part of the federal government and largely subjects labor– management relations for postal employees, other than supervisors and management, to the regulations established by the NLRA. Postal employees are thereby granted NLRA rights to engage in or refrain from engaging in concerted activities. The NLRB enforces these rights and resolves representational questions including determining bargaining unit appropriateness. Where not inconsistent, federal civil service laws also apply to these workers. The latter afford some consultation rights to representatives of supervisory and managerial employees.

Because postal workers are prohibited from striking, the Postal Reorganization Act establishes special impasse resolution machinery for the parties. This special process uses the technique of fact finding and, absent its success, binding impasse arbitration.

§2. Other Federal Workers

902. The Constitution designates the President as Chief Executive officer of the federal government. Presidential Executive Orders have been issued from time to time establishing the rules for labor–management relations between the federal government and its employees. These orders were replaced by the adoption of the Civil Service Reform Act of 1978 which established the Federal Labor Relations Authority as the agency to regulate the relations of most segments of the federal government with labor organizations that represent the government employees.

See paragraph 602, above, for excluded federal employees.

I. Federal Labor Relations Authority (FLRA)

903. The Federal Labor Relations Authority (1400 K St., NW, Washington, DC 20424; telephone: 202-218-7770; web site: www.flra.gov) was established by the Civil Service Reform Act of 1978 as a three member body appointed by the President with the advice and consent of the Senate. Each member serves a five-year term and no more than two can be members of the same political party. The President also appoints the General Counsel of the Authority, with the advice and consent of the Senate, for a five-year term. However, while the three members of the Authority may be removed only upon notice and hearing and only for inefficiency, neglect of duty or malfeasance in office, the General Counsel may be removed at any time by the President. The Authority determines the appropriateness of bargaining units, supervises representation elections, adopts rules for carrying out the general policies of the Act, reviews arbitral awards, and adjudicates unfair labor practice complaints prosecuted under the Act. Its investigative activities, representation proceeding, and adjudicative duties may be delegated to regional directors or administrative law judges subject to a right to appeal to the Authority.

Although the FLRA can issue orders to other government departments requiring them to remedy unfair labor practices, the doctrine of sovereign immunity bars the Authority from providing a damages remedy in favor of persons injured by such misconduct.[1013]

The General Counsel of the Authority investigates unfair labor practice charges, issues complaints if in his judgment the investigation shows good cause for the charge, and prosecutes such complaints.

Arbitration decisions issued under collective agreements between federal agencies and labor organizations are subject to limited review by the FLRA. Appeals are not available in cases involving dismissal, suspensions or reduction in grade or pay. An appeal from an arbitration award must be filed with the Authority within 30 days and the award can be set aside only if contrary to a law, rule or regulation, or if the arbitrator exceeded his jurisdiction, or the hearing was fundamentally unfair or the proceeding was tainted by fraud or corruption.

II. Federal Service Impasses Panel

904. The FMCS mediates in the event there is a negotiation impasse between a federal agency and the exclusive bargaining representative of its employees. If mediation fails to resolve the impasse, the parties may jointly propose its resolution by arbitration or may submit the matter to the Federal Service Impasses Panel (1400 K Street, NW Washington, DC 20424, 202-218-7770, www.flra.gov/fsip/panel.html). The seven member Panel is attached to the FLRA but is separately appointed by the President. Each member has a six-year term but can be removed at the discretion of the President. Although Panel members do not serve full-time, it has a full-time staff. The Panel must approve any joint submission to arbitration of an unresolved interests dispute. In addition, it must investigate any other unresolved impasse submitted to it by either party and either recommend procedures for resolution or assist the parties in settling the impasse 'through whatever methods and procedures, including fact-finding and recommendations, it may consider appropriate'. On occasion, the Panel has imposed a solution on the parties. Work stoppages are prohibited by the Act.

III. Grievance-arbitration Process

905. The Civil Service Reform Act of 1978 requires covered collective agreements to include a grievance procedure with binding arbitration as a final step that can be invoked by either side. However, excluded from this process are certain categories of grievances such as claims relating to prohibited political conduct; retirement, life and health insurance; examination and appointment to positions; and

---

1013. *Department of the Army* v. *FLRA*, 56 F.3d 273 (DC Cir. 1995). Congress could expressly provide for damages relief.

classification changes that do not alter pay. Employees with complaints of discrimination based on race, religion, national origin, sex, age or physical handicap may elect to use: (a) the statutory appeal procedure administered by the Merit Systems Protection Board, or (b) arbitration. A similar election is available to employees grieving adverse actions respecting their employment, pay or classification status. In the latter situation, however, if the issue is arbitrated, the tribunal must abide by the standards of the Merit Systems Protection Board.

The Merit System Protection Board and the Equal Employment Opportunity Commission may review arbitral decisions involving assertions of racial, national origin, sexual, religious or handicap discrimination. In addition, as described in paragraph 903, above, there is a limited opportunity for review of other arbitration decisions covered by the Civil Service Reform Act.

Chapter 9. Enforcement of Federal Wage-Hour Laws

§1. GENERALLY

906. Enforcement of the various federal wage-hour and child labor laws is the joint responsibility of the Department of Labor and the individual worker. The government's enforcement responsibilities are assigned to the Secretary of Labor and to the Administrator of the Wage-Hour Division of the Department of Labor.

The Secretary's authority is to adopt rules refining the Act's definitions of various categories of employment that are fully or partially exempted from the minimum wage or overtime provisions and to impose rules concerning record keeping and public notices designed to facilitate enforcement of the minimum wage, overtime pay and child labor laws. The Secretary is appointed by the President with the advice and consent of the Senate but serves at the pleasure of the President. The Secretary's legal staff, presided over by the Solicitor of the Department of Labor, conducts federal court suits for enforcement of these laws.

The Administrator of the Wage and Hour Division is responsible for discovering, investigating and remedying violations of the minimum wage and overtime pay laws. The Administrator is subordinate to the Secretary of Labor but like the Secretary is appointed by the President with the advice and consent of the Senate and serves at the pleasure of the President. The Wage and Hour Division is headquartered in Washington (200 Constitution Ave., NW, Washington, DC 20210; telephone: 202 487-9243; web site: www.dol.gov/whd) but conducts its enforcement activities through regional, area and district offices. Staff from these offices visit places of employment to inspect wage records and interview employees concerning wage payments. They also investigate specific violation complaints received by their office. Additionally, special compliance investigations are directed at industries, enterprises and localities with a record of frequent violations. The Wage-Hour Administrator can subpoena records from uncooperative employers.

907. The Administrator of the Wage and Hour Division adopts regulations interpreting the federal wage, overtime pay, and child labor laws. These regulations are of particular importance because sections 9 and 10 of the Portal-to-Portal Act (29 US Code §§258, 259) state that good faith reliance on the Administrator's regulation or interpretation is a full defense to any liability under the Fair Labor Standards Act, the Walsh–Healey Act and the Davis–Bacon Act, even though the regulation or interpretation relied on is later held to be invalid. (Generally, in American law, good faith reliance upon an administrative regulation or interpretation is not a defense to an action if the regulation or interpretation is held to be invalid.)

908. The Department of Labor's Employment and Training Service sets minimum wage rates to be paid to alien agricultural workers. These rates normally exceed the minimum wage payable to farm workers and are designed to reduce the use of alien workers to displace American farm laborers.

909. To carry out its functions, the Wage and Hour Division distributes pamphlets informing workers of their rights and employers of their responsibilities under the federal wage, overtime pay, and child labor laws. Similarly, the Division has sponsored radio and television announcements reminding workers of those rights and informing them how to redress those rights if violated. In addition, employers must post notices on employee bulletin boards informing the workers of these same rights. Department of Labor rules also require employers to maintain ample records of hours worked and moneys paid and other information relevant to facilitating investigation of alleged violations.

§2. Setting Minimum Wages

910. The FLSA statutorily sets the minimum wage rates for most workers.

In addition to a general statutory minimum, the FLSA provides for administratively established special minimum rates for certain types of employment. For example, under FLSA §14(c) the Secretary of Labor can certify a lower minimum rate for disabled workers to reflect their reduced productivity in comparison with other workers performing the same tasks.

911. A different procedure is used for setting minimum wages for employees of federal government contractors. Under the Davis–Bacon Act, for example, the minimum wage rates vary both on the basis of the type of work involved and the location where the work is performed. The minimum wage is administratively established at the prevailing rate for that work in that locale. In setting these rates, interested parties are given an opportunity to submit evidence regarding the applicable prevailing wage rates for the type of work in question. This evidence can be in the form of executed collective agreements, certified wage schedules, and studies conducted by local officials. If there is a wage rate that is paid to a majority of persons performing the particular category of work in the locale where the work in question is to be done, it is deemed to be the prevailing wage rate. If a majority are not paid the same thing, the prevailing wage rate is that paid to the largest number of workers so long as that group constitutes at least 30 percent of those so employed. If neither test is met, then the prevailing wage is the average paid to such workers in that locale. As is apparent, the process for setting minimum wages under the Davis–Bacon Act is time consuming and costly and has been criticized for these and other reasons. Its justification is that since most contracts with the federal government are awarded on a low bid basis, without a prevailing wage standard government contracts would tend to drive down prevailing wages. Vigorous legislative efforts to amend or repeal the process have been attempted but to date have been unsuccessful.

§3. Backpay Settlements

912. When a Department of Labor inspection reveals payment or record keeping deficiencies, the investigator prepares a statement setting forth the finding and gives the employer an opportunity to clarify or correct the information and calculations. Because the facts are often in dispute, especially with respect to the number of overtime hours worked, a considerable amount of fact-finding compromise can take place in these discussions. If an agreement is reached respecting the needed corrections and the employer volunteers to pay any deficiencies, the employer pays the sum to the Wage–Hour Division and the inspector prepares a deficiency notice that is given to the affected workers. It states the amount the Division believes due, the employer's agreement to make payment, and the employee's option to accept that payment in full settlement of any claim or to reject settlement and bring his or her own suit in state or federal court. Most workers accept the settlement reached by the Wage–Hour Division. Acceptance of a backpay amount approved by the Division constitutes a statutory waiver of the employee's backpay claim.

If a settlement agreement is not reached with the employer, the Division can either request the Solicitor of Labor to bring an enforcement suit on behalf of the affected employees, or notify each employee of the amount the Division believes is owing and explain the alternative avenues for judicial enforcement that are available.

§4. FLSA Enforcement by the Worker

913. Employees need not wait for a Wage and Hour Division investigation or for the completion of such an investigation to bring their own private suit in federal or state court to recover back wages. However, if the Solicitor of Labor files suit, that action supersedes any pending or future private suits concerning the same events.

Suits for back wages for failure to pay the minimum wage or required overtime pay are limited to a period of two years dating back from the date the suit is filed (three years if the payment failure was 'willful').[1014] If the right to such back wages is proven in court, the employee additionally is entitled to receive an equal amount as liquidated damages (thus, the worker recovers double back wages) plus a reasonable attorney's fee and the costs of litigation. (In American jurisprudence, the unsuccessful defendant normally is not liable for the plaintiff's attorney's fee or for costs other than relatively nominal court filing costs.) However, section 11 of the Portal-to-Portal Act (29 US Code §260) gives the trial court discretion to reduce or eliminate the liquidated damages, but not the attorney's fee and costs, if it determines that the employer acted 'in good faith' and with a reasonable basis for believing that it was in compliance with the law.

A group of workers can join together in bringing a suit under the FLSA, but the Act expressly prohibits a union from bringing suit on their behalf even though it claims to be acting in its representative capacity. (See paragraph 970, below, respecting employer efforts to impose mandatory arbitration provisions that waive the right to jointly pursue statutory claims.)

1014. In *McLaughlin* v. *Richland Shoe*, 486 US 128 (1988), the Supreme Court defined the word 'willful' as knowledge or reckless disregard about whether its conduct was prohibited by the FLSA.

In addition to the liability of the employing enterprise for FLSA wage deficiencies, those managers and executives who have significant control over the employment relationship can also be held liable under the Act. This provision for personal liability of managers and executives takes on special significance if the enterprise is bankrupt.[1015]

914. Because of the costs of initiating suits to collect FLSA back wages, plus the bar's general lack of familiarity with these causes of action, employees have difficulty finding legal counsel to bring suit unless many workers are involved (which increases the potential recovery). Nevertheless, the number of wage and hour lawsuits tripled in number between 1997 and 2005. More recent statistics are not available in the annual reports of the Department of Labor or the Administrator of the US Courts. In the past it was observed that individuals often have access to state small claims courts, which follow very informal procedures. Nevertheless, only a very small portion of FLSA backpay recoveries are obtained through personal suit. Most are settled through the Department of Labor's enforcement efforts. By 2017 it could be added that because many state laws were providing higher minimum wage rates than the federal law, enforcement activity, both administrative and litigative, could be expected to shift in the direction of the state law systems.

§5. FLSA Enforcement by the Department of Labor

915. The Secretary of Labor has discretionary authority to sue in federal court to recover backpay owed under the FLSA. The recovery for the affected employees is the same as when the employee brings the suit. However, if an FLSA enforcement suit is brought by the Department of Labor, in addition to back wages it can obtain injunctive relief that prevents the employer from selling its goods in interstate commerce until it comes into compliance with the minimum wage or overtime payment laws.

In addition, an administrative proceeding can be initiated against an employer in which civil fines of up to $1,925[1016] per violation can be imposed against an employer for willful and repeated violations of the wage and hour laws. An employer subjected to such an administratively imposed fine can seek judicial review of the administrative determination.

One difference between a suit by the Secretary of Labor and an individual enforcement suit is that the latter can be a jury trial whereas the former is tried only by a judge.[1017]

916. If an employer violates the child labor restrictions, the Secretary of Labor can use an administrative process to impose a civil penalty in an amount up to

1015. For example, *see Reich* v. *Circle C Investments, Inc.*, 998 F.2d 324 (5th Cir. 1993); *Irizarry* v. *Catsimatidis*, 722 F.3d 99 (2d Cir. 2012).

1016. The amount was increased to this figure by 29 Code of Fed. Reg. §578.3 adopted pursuant to the Federal Civil Penalties Inflation Adjustment Act of 2015.

1017. *In re Hamilton Oil Co.*, 785 F2d. 151 (8th Cir. 1986).

$59,947 for each offense.[1018] Judicial review of a penalty is available in the federal courts. The Secretary can also bring a suit to bar such an employer from using interstate commerce to sell goods made in violation of the child labor laws and, in the case of repeat violators, can bring a criminal prosecution in federal court.

917. Violation of the FLSA is subject to criminal penalty if willful and the violator is a repeat offender. Prosecution is brought by the Department of Justice and each offense is punishable by a fine of up to $10,000. Violators with prior convictions are additionally subject to imprisonment of up to six months for each offense. Additionally, a civil penalty up to $1,954 may be imposed for each willful violation.[1019]

918. Discrimination against an employee for asserting rights under the Fair Labor Standards Act or for assisting someone in asserting such rights, can be remedied in the same manner as can violations of the Act's other provisions. In addition, the Secretary of Labor or the individual victim of such discrimination can also sue for injunctive relief to require reinstatement of the employee. At least one appellate court has held that civil damages in such actions can include relief for emotional distress as well as for lost earnings.[1020] Appellate courts have differed respecting the availability of punitive damages against an employer that dismisses an employee in retaliation for seeking or assisting in enforcement of the FLSA.[1021]

919. In the fiscal year that ended in 2016, the Wage and Hour Division reported it had recovered a record $77 million in back wages for more than 106,00 targeted low wage workers through its own investigations. In fiscal year 2017 it collected a total of over $270 million in back wages with the average recovery of over $1,120 per worker aided by it.

§6. ENFORCEMENT OF GOVERNMENT CONTRACTOR AND GRANTEE WAGE LAWS

920. The responsibilities of the Wage and Hour Division include enforcing the various minimum wage laws affecting those doing business with the federal government. One aspect of this responsibility is the issuance of prevailing wage and fringe benefits determinations which become the minimum standard for those contracting with the federal government or who work on projects financed by federal grants. Enforcement techniques include withholding from the contractor, on behalf

---

1018. The civil penalties stated in the FLSA were adjusted, pursuant to the 2015 Federal Civil Penalties Inflation Adjustment Act. The maximum is $12,529 if the violation does not result in death or serious injury to a child under 18 years of age. The maximum figure stated in the above text can be doubled if the violation is willful or repeated. 29 Code of Fed. Reg. §570.140.

1019. The maximum civil penalty was adjusted to this figure pursuant to the 2015 Federal Civil Penalties Inflation Adjustment Act. 29 Code Fed. Reg. § 579.1.

1020. *Avitia* v. *Metropolitan Club*, 49 F.3d 1219 (7th Cir. 1995).

1021. Compare *Shea* v. *Galaxie Lumber & Constr. Co.*, 152 F.3d 729 (7th Cir. 1998) with *Snapp* v. *Unlimited Concepts, Inc.*, 208 F.3d 928 (11th Cir. 2000), *cert.* denied 532 US 975 (2001).

of the underpaid workers, moneys equal to any underpayment of wages plus liquidated damages for such underpayments. Violators also can be suspended from doing business with the federal government for a period of up to three years.

In addition to the government's direct enforcement of the special standards for federal grantees and contractors, the Miller Act (40 US Code 3131–3133) requires contractors subject to the Davis–Bacon Act (contractors engaged in constructing, repairing or modifying buildings, highways, dams, and the like) to furnish a bond assuring payment of claims for labor and material expended on the project. An employee who has not been paid all wages and benefits due may sue the issuer of the bond. The suit, though brought by the individual worker, is filed in the US district court in the name of the United States.

Chapter 10. Enforcement of the Occupational Safety and Health Act (OSHA)

§1. Generally

921. The OSH Act, often abbreviated as OSHA, requires virtually all private employers to furnish employees with a work environment that is free from recognized hazards likely to cause death or serious physical harm. The employer is also required to satisfy the specific safety and health standards promulgated by the Secretary of Labor under the Act. To promote enforcement of the Act, employers must submit to government inspection of the work premises, maintain specified types of records regarding work safety and health experience, inform workers of their rights under the Act, and maintain a work environment and supervise employees in a way that avoids unnecessary and unlawful hazards. Although safety and health conditions in the mining industry are regulated by the Federal Mine Safety and Health Act (30 US Code §801 *et seq.*) and in some other industries are regulated in part by other statutes (for example, Railroad Safety Act, Atomic Energy Act, Pipeline Safety Act), OSHA provides the primary federal source of occupational safety and health protection for American workers in the private sector, including many excluded from the NLRA such as farm workers and supervisors. By Executive Order, OSH Act standards are also applied to the work environment of federal government employees. (In 2017 it was estimated that the OSH Act protected over 121 million workers in over 9 million establishments.) State and local government employees are not covered by OSHA unless the state has an OSHA program of its own that extends such coverage to its government workers.

922. The principal enforcement officer of the OSH Act is the Secretary of Labor who is responsible for issuing all safety and health standards adopted in accordance with the Act. The Secretary is also ultimately responsible for inspection, investigation and civil prosecution of violations.

923. The OSH Act also created the National Institute for Occupational Safety and Health (NIOSH) which serves as an advisory panel to develop a better understanding of the causes of, and cures for, occupational safety and health hazards. NIOSH is independent of the Secretary of Labor and is housed in the Center for Disease Control and Prevention (Centers for Disease Control and Prevention 1600 Clifton Rd. Atlanta, GA 30333; www.cdc.gov/niosh) which is part of the Department of Health and Human Services.

NIOSH is headed by a Director who is appointed by, and serves at the pleasure of, the Secretary of Health and Human Services. It sponsors its own studies respecting needed safety and health standards. In 2006, Congress amended the OSHA to permanently establish within the NIOSH an Office of Mine Safety and Health, which is administered by an Associate Director appointed by the NIOSH Director. The purpose of the Office is to enhance the development of new mine safety technology and technological applications and to expedite the commercial availability and implementation of such technology in mining environments.[1022]

924. Another agency created by the OSHA is the National Advisory Committee on Occupational Safety and Health (NACOSH). The 12-member NACOSH has two members representing management, two representing labor, two representing the occupational health professions, two representing the occupational safety professions, and four members representing the public. Two of the health representatives and two of the public members are designated by the Secretary of Health and Human Services, although actual appointment of these members, as well as all other members, is by the Secretary of Labor. The members serve two-year terms, and must have experience and competence in the field of occupational safety and health. Its responsibility is to advise the Secretary of Labor respecting the performance of his duties under OSHA.

925. The Occupational Safety and Health Administration (also abbreviated as OSHA) is the division of the Department of Labor established to enforce the Occupational Safety and Health Act. It is presided over by the Assistant Secretary of Labor for Occupational Safety and Health. The Assistant Secretary has a staff in Washington, DC (200 Constitution Ave., NW, Washington, DC 20210; tel: 202 693-1999, 1-800-321- 6742); www.osha.gov), plus additional staff in 10 regional offices and 85 state and local area offices.

Area offices are under the charge of Area Directors who oversee day-to-day enforcement activities. Compliance Officers, working out of the area offices, inspect work premises and investigate alleged violations of OSHA standards. OSHA has resources available for those who do not speak English. For example, the agency has a Spanish web page and Spanish speaking operators are available at the national call center. Many regional and area offices offer information in other languages such as Japanese, Korean, and Polish. The preliminary figures for Fiscal Year 2017 are that OSHA completed 26,510 safety inspections and 5,767 health inspections. (In addition, safety and health inspections were conducted by state agencies.)

926. Contested cases of alleged OSHA violations are presented to the Occupational Safety and Health Review Commission (OSHRC), a three-member body nominated by the President and appointed with the consent of the Senate. Each Commissioner serves for a six-year term. The Commission's office is in Washington, DC (1120 20th Street, NW, 9th Floor, Washington, DC, 20036; telephone: 202 606-5398; www.oshrc.gov). Its hearings are conducted by Administrative Law Judges in the locale where the alleged violations occurred.

§2. Establishment of Health and Safety Standards

927. The Secretary of Labor can adopt safety and health standards based upon standards that have previously been recommended to industry by national

1022. 29 US Code §671(h)(1)–(2) (2007).

organizations established to promote improved job safety and health. These are known as 'national consensus standards'. Within the first two years of the law's enactment, the Secretary of Labor was permitted to adopt such standards as OSHA standards without having to go through the normal rulemaking procedure.

Standards promulgated under the OSH Act may also be recommended to the Secretary of Labor by the National Institute for Occupational Safety and Health, by labor unions, trade organizations, advisory committees specially appointed by the Secretary to make such recommendations, or may be based on the Secretary's own initiative. Proposed new standards must be published in the Federal Register (a publication through which public notice is given of all official federal government actions). Within a specified period of time after initial publication in the Federal Register, any interested party may file objections to a proposed standard. Upon the filing of such objections, a formal hearing must be conducted respecting the proposal. If the Secretary thereafter decides to adopt the standard, it is published in the Federal Register, this time accompanied by an explanation of the reasons for adoption. Within 60 days thereafter, an adversely affected party can petition a federal Court of Appeals to vacate the standard. The Court of Appeals must uphold the standard unless it finds that it is not supported by substantial evidence upon the record taken as a whole. Some have asserted that the Courts of Appeals extend a greater degree of deference to the Secretary's standards than is strictly warranted under the substantial evidence standard for judicial review.[1023] On the other hand, some important standards have been rejected by the courts in decisions that arguably gave insufficient deference to the Secretary's judgment.[1024]

The normal procedure for establishing standards can be by-passed in emergency situations in order to protect workers from grave danger posed by toxic or physically harmful substances or from new hazards.

When adopting standards for protection against toxic substances, the Secretary is required to weigh whether the targeted level of risk-free environment is 'feasible' in terms of what the state of the art in technology is able to accomplish.[1025] The Supreme Court has held, however, that cost-benefit analysis is not an element to be considered in measuring feasibility.[1026]

928. The Secretary of Labor can grant a temporary variance from a safety or health standard if the employer is unable to comply immediately and if available

1023. B. Fellner and D. Savelson, 'Review by the Commission and the Courts', in American Bar Ass'n Nat'l Institute on Occupational Safety and Health Law, *Proceedings*, Chicago, 1976, pp. 101, 111–114.

1024. *See*, for example, *Usery* v. *Kennecott Copper Corp.*, 577 F.2d 1113 (10th Cir. 1977) (rejected the change of the word 'should' in a national consensus standard, to the word 'shall' when adopted under OSHA); *Asbestos Information Ass'n/North America* v. *OSHA*, 727 F.2d 415 (5th Cir. 1984) (rejecting a temporary emergency standard for asbestos exposure).

1025. In setting aside the Secretary's benzene exposure standard as lacking the proper evidence of sufficient risk, a closely divided Supreme Court in *Industrial Union Dep't* v. *American Petroleum Inst.*, 448 US 607 (1980), observed that the government's findings concerning such matters should be upheld 'so long as they are supported by a body of reputable scientific thought'.

1026. *American Textile Mfrs. Inst.* v. *Donovan*, 452 US 490 (1981).

safeguards are being used and compliance will follow as quickly as practicable. A variance is also available to permit participation in experiments or tests sponsored by the Department of Health and Human Resources for the purpose of advancing knowledge and technology in the occupational safety and health field.

929. A permanent variance from a safety or health standard is available from the Secretary of Labor upon a showing that the employer's operating conditions, practices or means are as safe as those achieved by the standards. A permanent variance is sometimes sought to enable an employer to achieve uniformity of operations where, due to an approved state program, the employer's operations are subject to different standards in different states. (State programs are described in paragraphs 945–950, below.)

§3. Federal Enforcement of Health and Safety Standards

I. Investigation

930. Enforcement begins with the inspection of the work premises by OSHA's field staff. This can be initiated by a private person's or labor union's complaint asserting the existence of specific unsafe or unhealthy working conditions, or can be generated by the agency's own program of workplace inspections, or by a workplace fatality or major accident reported to the Administration by the employer pursuant to reporting regulations adopted by the Secretary of Labor. Such reports must be submitted to OSHA within 48 hours of a fatality or an accident resulting in the hospitalization of five or more employees.

The Supreme Court has held that an employer has the right to refuse entrance to an OSHA inspector unless the inspector has obtained a court issued search warrant. However, the standards governing the issuance of such warrants make them readily obtainable.[1027] Although generally using the same enforcement mechanisms as OSHA, Mine Safety and Health Act inspectors have a right to inspect without obtaining a court order.[1028] The Supreme Court has set standards for warrantless searches of heavily regulated businesses. Those standards require that:

1. the business be subject to an extraordinary degree of regulation such as for businesses selling liquor, drugs, or firearms. OSHA regulation by itself is not sufficient;
2. the government has a substantial interest in regulating a particular aspect of the business or industry that has caused societal problems;
3. warrantless inspections are necessary to further the regulatory scheme and address the identified problem;
4. and the statute allowing warrantless searches provide a 'constitutionally adequate substitute for a warrant'. For example, the statute should give notice

1027. *Marshall* v. *Barlow's Inc.*, 436 US 307 (1978).
1028. *Donovan* v. *Dewey*, 452 US 594 (1981).

that warrantless searches are authorized and that the time, place, and scope of the search is limited.[1029]

The investigator, whose official title is Compliance Safety and Health Officer (often simply called a Compliance Officer) must give the employer and an authorized employee representative an opportunity to participate in the physical tour of the workplace (generally referred to as a 'walkaround'). The employee representative is selected by the recognized collective bargaining agent in unionized shops. Even if the employees are on strike, it has been held that the union is entitled to designate a striking employee as the walkaround representative.[1030] In unorganized establishments, the Act states that the investigator should consult with 'a reasonable number of employees' concerning the safety and health conditions. The right to accompany the inspector, however, is not absolute and must give way to the orderly conduct of the inspection. Thus, unless prejudice is shown, failure to ensure accompaniment on the walkaround is not grounds to set aside a citation.[1031] The courts have also held that the employer does not have to pay an employee for the time spent accompanying the inspector.[1032] Nevertheless, one survey indicated that 93 percent of the time, the employer pays the usual wage to such workers and that in about an additional 6 percent of the instances,[1033] the union makes up the lost wages. (For a brief period Department of Labor regulations treated an employer's failure to pay for walk-around time as unlawful discrimination against workers seeking enforcement of the Act. The regulation was repealed by the succeeding Administration before it was subjected to a court test.)

In the mining industry, under the federal Mine Safety and Health Act, an employee designated as a walkaround representative is entitled to regular pay during that activity. In that industry employees can designate a union organizer to be an employee walkaround representative even though the union has not established majority status and, therefore, is not the workers' bargaining representative.[1034] In addition, in the mining industry each work site must be inspected at least four times a year.

As a result of staffing shortages and employer complaints about the intrusiveness of walkarounds, Compliance Officers engaged in programmed inspections eliminate walkarounds if the employer's records show that its lost workday rate due to accidents is lower than the industry average.

In the Fiscal Year that ended in 2017, 1,410 employers had established a Voluntary Protection Program (VPP) with the federal OSHA, thereby exempting them from programmed inspections. A VPP must have workplace injury rates below the industry average for a three year period or a feasible plan to reduce rates to below

---

1029. *New York* v. *Burger*, 482 US 691 (1987). The standard for warrantless searches is, however, more rigorous in New York state under the state Constitution. *See People* v. *Scott*, 593 NE 2d 1328 (NY 1992).

1030. *In the Matter of Establishment Inspection of Caterpillar Inc.*, 55 F.3d 334 (7th Cir. 1995).

1031. *Chi. Bridge & Iron Co.* v. *OSHRC*, 535 F.2d 371 (7th Cir. 1971).

1032. *Leone* v. *Mobile Oil Corp.*, 523 F.2d 1153 (DC Cir. 1975).

1033. *Id.* at 1161.

1034. *Kerr-McGee Coal Corp.* v. *FMSHRC*, 40 F.3d 1257 (DC Cir. 1994), *cert.* denied 515 US 1159 (1995).

the industry average within two years; written safety and health rules and procedures; a cadre of employees trained in first aid procedures; a regular safety training program for employees; a procedure for surveying and evaluating existing hazards and the hazardous potential of new processes, materials and equipment. In addition, the employer must conduct monthly self-inspections and prepare an annual written safety and health performance evaluation, maintain a program through which employees may express their concerns and ideas respecting work health and safety, and a system for investigating and documenting accidents and utilize professional consultants in the field of work safety and hygiene.

931. At the end of the inspection tour, or within a few days thereafter, the Compliance Officer conducts a closing conference at which management and any worker representatives are told about the violations that have been found, the applicable safety and health standards, the opportunities for abatement that will be allowed, and the penalties for violations that will be proposed to the Area Director. OSHA's Field Inspection Reference Manual specifies that abatement shall be required within the shortest interval within which the employer can reasonably be expected to correct the violation. At this conference the interested parties can attempt to clarify any misunderstandings and offer explanations of mitigating circumstances.

932. When the OSHA was adopted in 1970, the annual rate of work related fatalities per 100,000 workers was about 18. In the fiscal year that ended in 2016, there were 3.6 work related deaths for every 100,000 full-time equivalent employees. Overall, road related fatalities constitute the largest category of work related deaths. The construction industry had the highest overall fatality rate with the leading causes being falls, followed by struck by object, electrocution, and caught in or between equipment or structural elements.

The rate of work related nonfatal injuries has also declined substantially since 1970. Safety data collected under state and federal OSHA programs indicate that many injuries result from muscle strains or sprains, being struck by objects, and falls on the same floor level. Such injuries occur most frequently in manufacturing, nursing home, and construction settings with the result that those industries are targeted for inspection more often than other places of employment. Work safety improvements no doubt are partly attributable to the shift from a predominantly manufacturing and extractive economy to an economy dominated by service industries.

II. Civil Fines and Abatement Orders

A. Citations and Notification of Proposed Penalties

933. Violations are divided into two classes – serious and non-serious. Serious violations are those conditions or practices the employer knew existed or with reasonable diligence would know to be present, and which pose a substantial probability that death or serious physical harm could result. Abatement is required both for serious and non-serious violations. Fines, however, are mandatory for serious violations but may be waived for non-serious violations. In the citation that is issued, the Compliance Officer specifies whether a violation is serious or non-serious and whether it is willful or repeated.

By regulation, a copy of the citation issued by the Compliance Officer must be posted near the site of the violation for a minimum three-day period. It is accompanied by a notice that states the precise penalty proposed for the violation, if any. Normally, the penalty is a civil fine that can be up to $12,934 for each violation and from $9,239 (minimum) up to $129,336 for each willful violation and up to $129,336 for each repeated violation.[1035] A willful violation of a standard resulting in the death of an employee is punishable by a court-imposed fine or by imprisonment for up to 6 months, or both (*see* paragraph 943 below). The OSHA Field Operations Manual provides guidance for determining the amount of the fine. The guidelines specify the amount of the fine based on the assessment of whether the gravity of the violation is high, medium or low, the size of the business, and the employer's good faith and history. The gravity assessment weighs the severity of the potential injury and the likelihood of an injury and specific benchmarks are specified by the guidelines for evaluating each of these factors.[1036] Although OSHA has discretion to prosecute less than all violations in cases of multiple offenses, it does not have discretion to consolidate violations and impose a single penalty.[1037]

934. An additional civil fine of up to $12,675 may be imposed for each violation of the posting requirement, and an added civil fine of up to the same amount per day may be imposed for each day's delay in removing a violation beyond the ordered abatement date.[1038]

935. OSHA protects employees from retaliation not only for reporting violations of the OSH Act but also for reporting violations of 21 other federal whistleblower protection laws. In Fiscal Year 2017 it completed 3,347 whistleblower investigations that resulted in $28 million recovered by victims and 81 employees reinstated.

B. Appeal to the Occupational Safety and Health Review Commission

936. An employer has 15 working days to file a notice of contest with the OSHA Area Director. Employees who are dissatisfied with the abatement period can also file a notice of contest. Failure to file a notice of contest results in the citation and proposed fine automatically becoming a final, enforceable order that is not subject

1035. The amounts stated in the OSH Act were adjusted pursuant to the Federal Civil Penalties Inflation Adjustment Act. 29 Code Fed. Reg. § 1903.15.
1036. OSHA, Field Operations Manual (2016) chap. 6.
1037. *Chao* v. *OSHRC*, 480 F.3d 320 (5th Cir. 2007).
1038. The amounts stated in the OSHA were adjusted pursuant to the Federal Civil Penalties Inflation Adjustment Act. 29 Code Fed. Reg. §1903.15.

to judicial review. Timely filing abates the employer's compliance duty until the OSHRC issues its own final order.

937. The notice of contest is forwarded to the Occupational Safety and Health Review Commission (OSHRC) which issues a complaint against the employer that it must answer. A hearing before an Administrative Law Judge (ALJ) is then scheduled near the place of employment. The Judge receives evidence, makes findings of fact, and reaches conclusions of law. It is an adversary hearing at which the staff of the Solicitor of the Department of Labor represents the prosecutorial interest and must prove the violation and justify the penalty and abatement order. Employees affected by a contested citation, or their labor union, may participate as a party whether or not they filed a notice of contest. Generally, the rules of evidence that apply in the federal district courts apply to these hearings. Limited pretrial discovery procedures are available to the parties. Interestingly, in a high percentage of appeals, the employer proceeds without the assistance of counsel. This probably reflects the relatively small amounts of the civil penalties at stake in most cases. OSHRC rules of procedure are designed to facilitate such *pro se* representation.

938. The ALJ can affirm, vacate, or modify in whole or in part the finding of violation and any remedies. The ALJ's decision becomes the decision of the Commission unless one of the three Commissioners grants review. Such grants are wholly discretionary. In its annual reports, the OSHRC asserts that there is an increase in the portion of appealed citations but does not offer supporting data. In fiscal year 2015, 2,165 new cases were filed with OSHRC and 888 cases were pending from previous years. Decisions were issued in 61 cases and 1,896 were settled.

C. Judicial Review of OSHRC Decisions

939. The Secretary of Labor, affected workers, and the employer all can appeal from an OSHRC decision to the appropriate US Court of Appeals or can seek the court's enforcement of the decision. The court can affirm, modify, or set aside the decision in whole or in part and can grant temporary relief pending its decision. Although the court owes no special deference to the Commission's determinations respecting questions of law, it is required to uphold the Commission's findings of fact if, on the record taken as a whole, they are supported by substantial evidence.

D. Constitutionality of Civil Penalty Procedure

940. The constitutionality of the procedure for levying civil fines under OSHA was unsuccessfully challenged on the ground that it violates the guaranty of jury trial found in the Seventh Amendment to the Constitution. The Supreme Court of the United States rejected the challenge in *Atlas Roofing Co., Inc.* v. *OSHRC*, 430 US 442 (1977) where it reasoned that actions by the government to enforce public rights are not common law type suits covered by the Seventh Amendment and, therefore, the fact finding responsibility in such cases can be assigned by Congress to an administrative tribunal.

III. Injunctive Relief

941. If an OSHA investigation reveals a hazard that is believed to pose a reasonable expectation of imminent death or serious injury, the inspector is required to immediately inform the employer and the endangered workers. In addition, the Secretary of Labor can petition a federal district court for injunctive relief to avoid, remove or correct the hazard. If the Secretary 'arbitrarily or capriciously' fails to seek such relief, an endangered worker or the worker's union can apply to a federal district court for a mandate requiring the Secretary to institute a suit for injunctive relief. The employer is not required to compensate employees whose work is unavailable because injunctive relief has been granted to protect them from the hazard.

In contrast, the federal Mine Safety and Health Act authorizes its inspectors to close a portion of a mining operation or the entire operation upon discovering imminent danger or repeated 'unwarrantable failure' to comply with safety or health standards. Mine employers must pay idled workers for up to the first week of such a closure.

942. The OSHA prohibits employers from discriminating against workers because they are whistleblowers (*see* paragraph 935 above) or participated in an investigation under the Act. If a violation is found, the Secretary of Labor sues in a federal district court asking that court for appropriate relief including backpay and worker reinstatement.

IV. Criminal Sanctions

943. A willful violation of OSHA that causes a worker's death may result in criminal prosecution. As a result of separate legislation dealing with the responsibility of corporate officials and corporations, and an increase in the level of fines for criminal violations (18 US Code §§ 2, 3571), the criminal sanction in the case of an individual owner includes a fine of up to $250,000 per violation or imprisonment for up to six months, or both. Persons with a record of prior convictions for such OSHA violations are subject to up to one year of imprisonment. Prison penalties can be imposed on responsible corporate officials and managers and the corporation can be fined for up to $500,000 for each such willful violation. Criminal cases are prosecuted by the Department of Justice in the federal district courts.

944. Criminal sanctions are also available against anyone who, without official authorization, gives advance notice of an impending OSHA inspection. The making of false statements or the supplying of false information to OSHA investigators also carry serious criminal penalties.

§4. State Regulations of Occupational Safety and Health

945. The federal OSHA permits a state to adopt its own program to regulate occupational safety and health if the state program is approved by the Secretary of Labor as being at least as effective as the federal program. An approved state program receives federal financial assistance for up to one half of the cost of operations. The US Department of Labor monitors state program performance to ensure quality. The provision for state programs was designed to combat criticism of ever-increasing centralization of government power and the asserted inability of Washington-based bureaucrats to regulate distant activities in a practical and efficient manner. A few states, such as California, have devoted significant resources for rigorous enforcement of their state OSHA programs. The rigor of enforcement in many other states is less apparent.

States that do not have a Department of Labor certified OSHA program cannot regulate occupational safety and health even if the regulations do not conflict with federal OSHA standards. Such states can, however, enforce general safety and health laws (such as motor vehicle traffic regulations and public sanitation laws) against employers, as well as against other persons and entities, so long as those laws do not conflict with OSHA regulations or standards.[1039]

946. As of 2017, 21 states and Puerto Rico operated approved OSHA programs covering at least private sector employees and five states and the Virgin Islands had OSHA approved programs covering public sector employees only. In several instances, approval has been revoked by the Secretary of Labor. In a few cases, states have discontinued their programs after several years of operation. The California legislature withdrew its plan in 1988 but later that year restored it as a result of a measure approved by a voter initiative.

947. A majority of the state plans fully incorporate the standards adopted by the Secretary of Labor as their own occupational safety and health standards. However, several major industrial states, such as California and Michigan, have adopted their own standards. This autonomy potentially can be used to deal with special local problems. California, for example, which experiences greater seismic instability than most other parts of the nation, can use its power to develop local standards in order to give special attention to making workplaces safe from the serious dangers of earthquakes. More rigorous procedural protections account for some state variations. For example, California has adopted procedures that give its agency broader power than is provided under the federal law to intervene directly in emergency situations.

948. Staffing of OSHA has been significantly reduced as a result of budget cuts with the result that it initiates fewer inspections. For some time, the AFL–CIO has been critical of state OSHA programs on the grounds that due either to corruption or ineptness, most state programs do not provide enforcement as rigorous as the federal government's. Employer representatives have been critical of the certified state

1039. *Gade* v. *National Solid Wastes Management Ass'n*, 505 US 88 (1992).

programs because the federal monitoring system sometimes results in duplicative plant inspections (first the state inspection, then a monitoring federal inspection) with the resulting extra burdens on operations and personnel. A criticism expressed by some larger employers is that the differences in standards and enforcement procedures from place to place reduce the employer's ability to maintain uniformity of operations among plants located in different states. Among other things, this may make it more difficult for the employer to compare efficiency of similar operations in different locales and to interchange administrative and supervisory personnel across state boundaries.

949. A broader criticism of OSHA is that the enforcement process does not give employers a sufficient financial incentive to make working conditions safer and healthier. Based on estimates for 2012, with over 8 million work sites being covered, an employer on average could assume it had less than a 2 percent chance of being inspected during the year. (For a few target, high-risk industries, the prospects for inspection were considerably greater.) The number of annual inspections in recent years had been roughly equal to the number of violations found by OSHA inspectors each year. Thus, even if an employer assumed a risk that 2 violations would be found and the penalty imposed would be the full $12,934 maximum per serious violation, a 2 percent risk of being fined $25,868 equals an annual risk of being fined $517.36 per violation. Thus, an employer that bases its business decisions on cost-benefit analysis is likely to conclude that it can well risk delaying removal of hazards not yet discovered by OSHA if the cost of correcting the situation is likely to be more than $517.36 a year.

950. Among amendments suggested from time to time to change the OSH Act is to permit employers to request OSHA inspectors to visit the workplace in a consulting capacity so as to facilitate compliance without fear of being penalized for less serious existing violations. Some state programs allow such advisory inspections. Another proposal is to impose penalties on workers who do not obey established safety and health standards or who disobey the employer's regulations designed to enforce those standards.

Many state workers' compensation programs indirectly penalize employees who violate safety standards by reducing disability recoveries for injuries resulting from such violations. These same laws often also increase the disability recovery, and thereby penalize the employer, if the injury was caused by the employer's violation of safety and health standards.

Still another recommendation for state programs is to combine OSHA administration with administration of the workers' compensation programs so as to provide more precise monitoring data respecting site safety and health as well as to facilitate educating employers respecting the long range savings from investing in safe and healthy work practices and surroundings.

Chapter 11. Enforcement of Equal Employment Opportunity

§1. Equal Employment Opportunity Commission

I. Commission

951. Title VII of the Civil Rights Act of 1964 created the Equal Employment Opportunity Commission (EEOC) as an independent administrative agency. As originally created, the EEOC lacked any real enforcement authority such as the cease and desist authority that had been conferred on the NLRB. Instead, the EEOC investigated charges of discrimination, determined whether there was probable cause to believe discrimination had occurred, and attempted to conciliate those claims. However, it did not have the power to bring suit to enforce Title VII or to order compliance with the law.

Although amendments to Title VII have expanded the EEOC's authority to enforce the Act. it still lacks the cease and desist authority possessed by the NLRB. However, it now has authority to initiate enforcement litigation against private employers. The responsibility for litigation against state and local governments resides with the Attorney General of the United States who also is in charge of EEOC litigation before the Supreme Court.

In 1978, the EEOC's responsibilities were expanded to include administration and enforcement of the Age Discrimination in Employment Act (ADEA) and the Equal Pay Act. This reorganization consolidated enforcement authority for job discrimination statutes in a single agency, rather than having such authority divided between the EEOC and the Department of Labor. In 1990, the EEOC's responsibilities were again expanded by passage of the Americans with Disabilities Act (ADA). Title I of the ADA incorporates the enforcement provisions of Title VII, making the EEOC responsible for administration and enforcement of the ADA's employment provisions. Finally, the EEOC has responsibilities for enforcing the Genetic Information Nondiscrimination Act. (*See* paragraph 359, above.)

Title VII, the ADEA and the ADA each requires an individual to file a charge with the EEOC prior to bringing suit. No such requirement exists for claims under the Equal Pay Act.

The EEOC has five commissioners, each of whom is appointed by the President, with the consent of the Senate, for staggered five-year terms. No more than three commissioners may be affiliated with the same political party. A quorum of the Commission is three members. The President designates one of the commissioners to serve as Chair and one to be Vice Chair.

The principal EEOC office is in Washington, DC (131 M Street, NE, Washington, DC 20507; eeoc.gov; telephone 202–663–4900). It has 53 offices around the country located in major and medium sized cities.

II. General Counsel of the EEOC

952. The President with the advice and consent of the Senate appoints the General Counsel of the EEOC to a four-year term of office. The General Counsel is responsible for the Commission's litigation against non-government respondents in all courts except the US Supreme Court.

III. EEOC Regulations and Guidelines

953. The EEOC has authority to promulgate procedural regulations under Title VII, and it has done so. The agency, however, lacks the authority to promulgate substantive regulations. Nonetheless, it has issued a number of Interpretive Guidelines that have been influential in the development of Title VII law. The EEOC also has a case-handling manual that provides useful information on how the agency processes charges of discrimination.

The EEOC has both procedural and substantive rulemaking authority under the ADEA and the ADA. It has been particularly aggressive in promulgating regulations under the ADA, perhaps because Congress expressly directed the agency to have such regulations in place one year before the ADA's effective date so that employers and employees would understand their responsibilities and rights under the statute. The EEOC also has adopted ADA Interpretive Guidances along with a Technical Assistance Manual.

IV. Processing a Charge of Discrimination under Title VII and the ADA

A. *Filing a Charge of Discrimination*

954. Because the ADA simply incorporates Title VII's enforcement provisions, the means of perfecting a charge under both of these statutes is the same. Violations of the laws administered by the EEOC are called 'unlawful employment practices'. An individual alleging that an unlawful employment practice has occurred must file a timely charge with the EEOC outlining the discrimination complained of. The time limits for filing such a charge varies, depending upon whether the practice occurred in a deferral or in a non-deferral jurisdiction. A deferral jurisdiction is one in which a state or local law prohibits the same unlawful discrimination and establishes a state or local agency to enforce that law. Such agencies are referred to as '706' agencies. In a non-deferral state, a charge of discrimination must be filed with the EEOC within 180 days of the occurrence of the allegedly unlawful employment practice. In a deferral state or locality[1040], the charge must be filed with the EEOC within 300 days of the act's occurrence, or within 30 days of the termination of state proceedings, whichever is earlier. However, no charge may validly be filed with the EEOC until 60 days after the charge has been presented to the 706 agency or the 706 agency has terminated its proceedings, whichever is earlier; the statute thus requires that charging parties in a deferral jurisdiction first seek relief from the state agency before turning to the EEOC.

1040. The ADA permits deferral to state agencies only; the deadline is not extended if only local law prohibits disability discrimination.

The EEOC has work-sharing agreements with many 706 agencies. These agreements generally treat charges filed by one agency as charges filed with the other and often waive the state's exclusive 60-day processing period. This reduces the difficulties of complying with the statutes' administrative procedures in deferral jurisdictions.

955. To be effective, a charge of discrimination must be in writing, sworn to, and signed. It can be filed by the aggrieved individual or by someone else on behalf of the aggrieved individual (this facilitates one person filing on behalf of an entire class of aggrieved persons), or by one of the EEOC's commissioners. Once a charge has been filed, the EEOC notifies the party charged with wrongdoing, the 'respondent', that a charge has been filed. The respondent has an opportunity to respond to the charge.

956. The EEOC investigates all charges of unlawful employment practices and determines whether there is probable cause to believe a violation occurred. If it finds probable cause, it attempts to conciliate the claim. If the claim is not settled, the EEOC issues a 'right to sue' letter, advising the charging party and respondent of the EEOC decision on probable cause and of the individual's right to bring suit if (s)he desires. Alternatively, the EEOC itself may decide to bring suit.

A charging party need not wait for the EEOC investigation to run its course. After a charge has been pending with the EEOC for 180 days, the charging party may request a right to sue notice and thereafter proceed to court. This allows an individual to circumvent the long delay that often accompanies exhaustion of the EEOC's investigation and conciliation process.

957. During Fiscal Year 2016, the EEOC received 91,503 charges. Many charging parties charge violations in more than one category. There were 35,411 charges of race or color discrimination; 26,934 charges of sex discrimination (including harassment and pregnancy discrimination); 9,840 charges of national origin discrimination; 3,825 charges of religious discrimination; 42,018 charges of retaliation; 20,857 charges of age discrimination; 28,073 charges of disability discrimination; 1,075 equal pay claims; and 238 charges of genetic information discrimination. Over the period from fiscal year 1997 through 2016, the most marked changes were in the increase in retaliation, and in disability and religion claims - all of which had significant percentage increases

The EEOC has a history of large backlogs of incompletely processed charges but that backlog has shrunk despite growth in the number of charges and considerable reduction in staff. In fiscal year 2016 it resolved 99,109 charges. The vast majority of charges result in a finding of no probable cause. Nevertheless, in fiscal year 2016 EEOC recovered for claimants through settlements or litigation about $484 million.

B. Suit by the EEOC

958. If the EEOC is unable to conciliate a charge that it has probable cause to believe to be true, and if the respondent is not a governmental entity, the EEOC may commence a civil suit seeking appropriate relief. If the charged party is a state or local government, a similar civil action may be initiated by the Attorney General of the United States. The person (or persons) aggrieved by the alleged unlawful employment practice have a right to intervene in the suit but may not bring their own suit if the EEOC or Attorney General already has filed suit.

959. The EEOC may bring suit in federal district court to enjoin a 'pattern or practice of resistance' to the rights secured by Title VII of the Civil Rights Act of 1964. This proceeding is designed to deal with systemic violations under either disparate treatment or disparate impact theories. Such proceedings are entitled to be placed at the head of the court's docket. The EEOC also faces fewer procedural requirements than private parties. In Fiscal Year 2016 it obtained favorable results in 90.8 percent of the 109 law suits concluded on behalf of 4,500 claimants.

C. Suit by an Individual

960. After receiving a 'right-to-sue' letter from the EEOC, a charging party may file suit in state or federal court under Title VII or the ADA. A right-to-sue letter is issued after the EEOC has made a determination of probable cause or no probable cause to believe discrimination has occurred. Whether or not probable cause has been found has no bearing on the individual's right to initiate suit. An individual need not wait for the EEOC's investigation to run its course but may instead request a right-to-sue letter after the charge has been pending with the EEOC for 180 days. Once the right-to-sue letter is received, the individual may proceed to court. A suit may be brought under the Equal Pay Act or the Age Discrimination in Employment Act without receiving a right-to-sue letter.

961. After receipt of the right-to-sue letter, the charging party in a Title VII action has 90 days to file his own private law suit in state or federal court. The plaintiff may apply to the court for appointment of counsel and waiver of fees, costs and security. Such appointments and waiver are at the court's discretion. A civil suit brought under Title VII results in a trial *de novo* of the issues raised in the EEOC charge. There is a right to a jury trial in claims alleging disparate treatment. No jury trial is available for disparate impact claims.

A charge may remain pending with the EEOC for several years and still result in a timely filed lawsuit, so long as the charge itself was timely filed and the lawsuit was brought within 90 days of the receipt of the right-to-sue letter.

962. Only issues presented or related to those filed with the EEOC or growing out of the EEOC's investigation may be the subject of the ensuing litigation.[1041] For example, a plaintiff may not file a charge with the EEOC alleging she was the victim of race discrimination and then sue alleging sex discrimination.

1041. *Sanchez* v. *Standard Brands, Inc.*, 431 F.2d 455 (5th Cir. 1970).

D. Remedies

963. The trial court's remedial powers in suits brought under Title VII and the ADA include the power to declare a practice unlawful, enjoin further discrimination, order reinstatement or instatement of the plaintiff together with full backpay and lost benefits. Backpay, characterized as 'make whole' relief, generally runs from the date of the unlawful occurrence until judgment is entered. Backpay liability, however, is reduced by any amount the plaintiff earned or could have earned with due diligence. In cases where reinstatement or instatement is impractical, the court also may award front pay in lieu of placing the plaintiff into the position from which (s)he was wrongfully excluded. A front pay award is the exception; reinstatement or instatement are the remedies usually awarded.

The remedies described above are considered equitable remedies and for years were the only ones available under Title VII. However, the 1991 Civil Rights Act amended Title VII (and the newly enacted ADA) to allow recovery of compensatory and punitive damages in cases involving malice or reckless indifference. These damages are capped, with the amounts recoverable dependent upon the size of the employer. Compensatory and punitive damages are limited to $50,000 for employers with 100 or fewer employees; $100,000 for those with 101 to 200 employees; $200,000 for those with 201–500 employees; and $300,000 for those with over 500 employees. These caps do not apply to the equitable remedies of backpay, front pay and lost benefits.[1042]

The Supreme Court has held the required showing of malice or reckless indifference is satisfied when the employer's conduct is with knowledge that it might be acting in violation of the law.[1043] However, an employer may be held vicariously liable for punitive damages only when a managerial employee is acting within the scope of his employment. And, even then, there is no vicarious liability if the employer made good faith efforts to comply with the statute.

Punitive damages, moreover, are not available under the ADA when the employer has made a good faith effort to reasonably accommodate an individual's disability, even if those efforts ultimately are found to be insufficient to avoid liability. Nor, under the ADA and Title VII, may punitive damages be recovered from a government employer. Finally, compensatory and punitive damages may not be recovered for race discrimination claims under Title VII if those damages are recoverable under section 1981. However, since section 1981 contains no caps on compensatory or punitive damages awards, the remedial structure for race discrimination claims under section 1981 is more favorable than that of Title VII.

964. Both Title VII and the ADA provide that a 'prevailing party' is entitled to recover attorneys' fees and costs. This is a departure from the usual US rule that attorneys' fees generally are not recoverable in civil litigation in the United States. The Supreme Court has held that if a plaintiff is the prevailing party, attorneys' fees should be awarded in all but special circumstances. However, a winning defendant

1042. *Pollard* v. *E.I. du Pont,* 532 US 843 (2001) (although the cap extends to 'future pecuniary' damages, Congress did not intend to include front pay in the cap).

1043. *Kolstad* v. *American Dental Association*, 527 US 526 (1999).

is entitled to recover its attorneys' fees only if the court finds the 'claim was frivolous, unreasonable, or groundless, or that the plaintiff continued to litigate after it clearly became so'.[1044]

E. Federal Sector Procedures under Title VII and the Rehabilitation Act

965. When first enacted, Title VII did not protect federal sector employees. As amended, however, it now protects most federal workers. Although the ADA does not reach the federal sector, federal employees are protected against disability discrimination by the Rehabilitation Act. The substantive protections basically mirror those available to private sector employees, but the procedures for perfecting a Title VII or Rehabilitation Act claim are different for federal employees. Section 717 of Title VII, which also governs federal employees' claims under the Rehabilitation Act, differs markedly from the procedures that govern private sector and state and local government employees.

To perfect their Title VII claim, employees or applicants who believe they have been victims of discrimination by a federal agency must contact that agency's Equal Employment Opportunity counselor within 45 days of the complained of act. The individual may participate in a counseling process or in an Alternative Dispute Resolution Process (ADR), typically mediation. If the counseling or ADR is unsuccessful, the individual may file a complaint with the agency which then investigates the complaint and the aggrieved party has the opportunity to request an adversarial hearing on the charge. If the agency has not made a decision on the charge within 180 days, the individual may file suit. Alternatively, the individual may allow the proceedings to run their course.

After the agency's determination is made, the individual has two options: a) file suit within 90 days of the agency's determination or b) appeal the agency's decision to the EEOC. If unhappy with the EEOC's decision, the claimant has 90 days to sue. Whichever route is followed, the suit is in district court and is litigated under the same rules as are used for other Title VII litigation and the trial is *de novo*.

V. Processing a Charge of Discrimination under the ADEA

A. Filing a Charge of Discrimination

966. In most ways, the procedures for bringing a claim under the ADEA are similar to those applicable to Title VII and to the ADA, as described in paragraphs 954–956, above. Differences do exist.

In states where no deferral agency exists, a charge must be filed with the EEOC within 180 days of the occurrence of the allegedly unlawful employment practice. In cases in which a 706 agency exists, a charge must be filed with the EEOC within 300 days of the act's occurrence or within 30 days after termination of state agency

1044. *Christiansburg Garment Co.* v. *EEOC*, 434 US 412 (1978).

proceedings, whichever is earlier. However, unlike Title VII, the ADEA does not require that a charge of discrimination first be filed with the state before the ADEA filing with the EEOC will be valid. If a charge with the appropriate state agency has not been filed before suit is brought, the court stays proceedings and allows that filing to be made, with the suit proceeding 60 days after the filing with the state agency or after the state agency terminates its proceedings, whichever is earlier.

A right to sue letter is not required to bring an ADEA suit. If the EEOC issues a right to sue letter, the charging party must bring suit within 90 days of its receipt. ADEA claims may be tried by a jury.

B. Remedies

967. The remedies available under Title VII (back pay, front pay, reinstatement, attorneys' fees, etc.) also are available under the ADEA, except that compensatory and punitive damages are not recoverable. Instead, upon a showing that the employer's violation of the ADEA was a willful, an award of double damages is made. A willful violation is one in which the employer acts knowing its conduct violates the ADEA or with reckless disregard as to whether its conduct was lawful.[1045]

VI. Alternative Dispute Resolution

968. The Federal Arbitration Act (FAA), which was adopted in 1925, makes an arbitration provision covering future disputes enforceable 'save upon such grounds as exist at law or in equity for the revocation of any contract' if the provision is contained 'in any maritime transaction or a contract evidencing a transaction involving commerce' provision in any maritime transaction or a contract evidencing a transaction involving commerce.[1046] At the time the Act was adopted, the Supreme Court's decisions construing the federal Constitution limited Congress' power to legislate respecting commerce to those situations which either directly involved the transportation of goods or persons between states or foreign countries, the operations of carriers conducting such transportation, or the equipment, by-ways, and other instrumentalities for carrying goods and people in such commerce. Thus, standards of employment and labor relations of those working on interstate railways, over-the-road carriage, and in seafaring were within the scope of Congress' power but not those of workers who manufactured goods being shipped to markets in other states or nations. Support for the Federal Arbitration Act came from those advocating the need to facilitate enforcement of commercial contracts involving interstate transactions. Operating in that context, Congress, in defining 'commerce' in the Federal Arbitration Act, stated at §1 'herein contained shall apply to contracts of employment of seamen, railroad employees, or any other class of workers engaged in foreign or interstate commerce'. Thus, on its face it appeared that the FAA would not be available to enforce an arbitration provision in an employment contract.

1045. *Hazen Paper Co.* v. *Biggins*, 507 US 604 (1993).
1046. 9 US Code §2.

Nevertheless, in *Circuit City Stores, Inc.* v. *Adams*, 532 US 105 (2001), the Supreme Court held, 5–4, that employment contract provisions for arbitration of future disputes are enforceable even when the dispute involves a statutory claim. That case arose when Adams, in seeking his job, signed an application that included a statement agreeing to settle 'any and all previously unasserted claims arising out of or relating to my application or candidacy for employment and/or cessation of employment … exclusively by final and binding *arbitration* before a neutral Arbitrator' (emphasis was in the original). By way of example the statement said it included 'claims under federal, state, and local statutory or common law.' Two years later Adams sued his employer in state court alleging that because of his sexual orientation he had been the victim of sexual discrimination and harassment in violation of state statutes and state tort law principles. In upholding a federal district court's grant of a stay of that suit on the ground that it had to be resolved by arbitration, the Supreme Court invoked the maxim *ejusdem generis* (when general words follow specific words, the general words are construed to embrace only objects similar in nature to those enumerated by the preceding specific words), as well as its conclusion that the §1 phrase 'engaged in commerce' is a term of art having a narrower meaning than 'involving commerce', the phrase used in FAA §2 which specifies the scope of the Act's coverage. Acknowledging that there are arguments based on statutory history that would support a different result, the Court declared that plain meaning of the text required it to conclude that 'section 1 exempts from the FAA only contracts of employment of transportation workers'.

The dissenting justices, observed that the legislative history amply demonstrated that the FAA was intended to cover commercial, as distinguished from employment, contracts; that the exclusionary language was designed to clarify that intent and thereby eliminate the Seamen's Union's opposition to the Act; and that canons of interpretation are a fallback that ought not be used when there are good reasons for not doing so. If a canon of interpretation was needed, the dissenters explained that *ex abundanti cautela* (abundance of caution) provides a more appropriate guide to understanding the role of the §1 exclusion. The dissenters additionally noted that when the Act was adopted in 1925, the enumerated types of employment were the only ones thought to be within the scope of Congress' legislative authority and that the 'engaged in commerce' language revealed Congress' intent to 'exclude to the limits of its power to cover employment contracts in the first place'.

969. The *Circuit City* decision leaves many unanswered questions. The FAA requires parties to arbitrate only if they have voluntarily contracted to submit their disputes to that process. 'Whether the parties have agreed to arbitrate is determined under ordinary state law contract principles'.[1047] In *Circuit City* the Court expressly did not address the question of whether the job application was an enforceable employment contract covered by the FAA. There are a variety of doctrines under which state courts refuse to enforce contracts. In addition to fraud, coercion and overreaching, state courts reject purported contracts that are illusory. For example, in one case, an appellate court refused to apply the *Circuit City* decision where, as a condition of employment the worker was required to entered into a contract with

1047. *Gibson* v. *Neighborhood Health Clinics, Inc.*, 121 F.3d 1126, 1130 (7th Cir. 1997).

an arbitration agency in which he agreed to submit all disputes with his employer to arbitration under that agency's rules. Because the appointing agency retained sole discretion to modify the procedural rules for the process, the court declared the agreement illusory and, therefore, unenforceable under state law.[1048]

Another question not answered in *Circuit City* was whether the FAA prevents the Equal Employment Opportunity Commission from suing to obtain a remedy for an employee who has executed an employment application containing an agreement to arbitrate all statutory or other disputes. The Supreme Court resolved that issue in *EEOC* v. *Waffle House, Inc.*, 534 US 279 (2002), where it ruled, 6–3, that the EEOC is the master of its own suit and, therefore, cannot be barred by an arbitration provision in an employment contract from seeking any available remedy for an employee whose rights under the Americans with Disabilities Act were violated.

An unresolved question under *Circuit City* is the definition of 'transportation workers', the one category of employees held by the Court to be excluded from the enforcement of employer imposed arbitration provisions. For example, assume that a payroll clerk for a trucking company has a statutory claim against her employer and was required to sign an arbitration provision of the sort used by *Circuit City, Inc.* Is she a transportation worker and, therefore, excluded from the FAA's coverage? On the other hand, if a worker whose employment contract requires arbitration of claims is in the transportation category excluded from FAA coverage, does that exclusion constitute federal preemption that precludes enforcement of the arbitration provision pursuant to a state arbitration statute that would require that her claim be decided by an arbitrator instead of by the state court?

Also to be resolved is what protections the arbitration process must extend to employees before a pre-dispute agreement to arbitrate statutory claims will be enforced. Among the questions raised, to which no bright line rules have yet emerged, are: the appropriate sources for panels of persons qualified to serve as an arbitrator of statutory claims, the respective roles of the employer and employee in selecting the impartial decision maker, the degree to which the employee can be compelled to bear the cost of retaining an arbitrator, the extent of discovery available in such proceedings, the remedies the arbitrator must be empowered to award, the necessity for a written explication of the arbitrator's findings of fact and reasoning, and the scope of judicial review of such awards.[1049]

Increasingly, as part of the mandatory arbitration provisions they require unrepresented employees to sign, employers include a waiver of the claimant's right to pursue the claim jointly or in a class or collective action with other employees. Because the prospective damages for an individual claimant most often are relatively small in comparison with the costs of obtaining legal counsel to pursue the claim, being barred from joining with similarly placed claimants poses a substantial barrier to pressing the claim. Such waivers, therefore, have been challenged and the NLRB has held that when an employer imposes such a waiver it is interfering with the employees' NLRA Section 7 right to engage in concerted activities for mutual

---

1048. *Penn* v. *Ryan's Family Steak Houses, Inc.*, 269 F.3d 753 (7th Cir. 2001).

1049. *See*, for example, *Cole* v. *Burns Int'l Security Services*, 105 F.3d 1465 (DC Cir. 1997) and *Penn* v. *Ryan's Family Steak Houses, Inc.*, above. *See generally*, W. Gould, 'Kissing Cousins: The Federal Arbitration Act and Modern Labor Arbitration', 55 *Emory L.J.* 609 (2006).

aid or protection, a right also guaranteed by the Norris-LaGuardia Act.[1050] Appellate courts are divided over the correctness of the Board's decision[1051] and, as of this writing, the issue has been argued but not yet decided by the US Supreme Court.

In 1995, a committee sponsored by the American Bar Association developed its *Due Process Protocol*, a recommended list of conditions for fair arbitration hearings in cases involving disputes based on statutory claims.[1052] In addition to endorsing the ABA recommendations, the National Academy of Arbitrators has developed and adopted its more comprehensive *Guidelines on Arbitration of Statutory Claims Under Employer-Promulgated Systems.*[1053] It remains to be seen what effect these recommendations will have on courts and legislatures in resolving the foregoing questions.

Still another issue is whether a union may waive bargaining unit employees' rights to a judicial forum for statutory claims. In a 5–4 decision, the Supreme Court held that the sole remedy for employee claims of age discrimination, prohibited by the Age Discrimination in Employment Act, is submission to arbitration if the employees are covered by a collectively bargained agreement that clearly and unmistakably requires employees to arbitrate such claims. *14 Penn Plaza LLC* v. *Pyett*, 556 US 247 (2009). Thus, a union's bargaining authority includes displacing the right of individual employees to elect whether to pursue their personal statutory remedies in the courts rather than through arbitration.

970. Unlike Title VII, the ADA or the ADEA, the Equal Pay Act (29 US Code §206(d)), which was incorporated into the FLSA, does not require individuals to pursue an administrative remedy before filing suit. Instead, claimants who believe they have been the victims of an Equal Pay Act violation are permitted to sue their employer (public or private) in state or federal court. Suit must be brought within two years (three years for willful violations) of the challenged action.

The EEOC also may bring suit to enforce the Equal Pay Act. Once the EEOC brings suit, the right to bring an individual action is lost if such a suit has not already been filed.[1054]

1050. 29 US Code §§ 102, 115, 157. *Murphy Oil* 361 NLRB No. 72 (2014); *D.R. Horton*, 357 NLRB 2277 (2012).

1051. Accord, *NLRB* v. *Alternative Entertainment,* 858 F.3d 393 (6th Cir. 2017); *Morris* v. *Ernst & Young, LLP,* 834 F.3d 975 (9th Cir. 2016); *Lewis* v. *Epic Sys. Corp.*, 823 F.3d 1147 (7th Cir. 2016). Contra, *D.R. Horton* v. *NLRB*, 737 F.3d 344 (5th Cir. 2013). Horton's waiver provision prohibited the arbitrator from consolidating claims or fashioning them as a class or collective action. The term 'class action' refers to a special type of procedure under the Federal Rules of Procedure and does not encompass joint claims of the sort brought under the FLSA, collective claims brought by an authorized agent, or the joining of common claims filed by various claimants. Nevertheless, the court rejected the NLRB's position because Supreme Court decisions treat arbitration as favored, the NLRA did not explicitly modify the older Federal Arbitration Act, and the federal class action rules did not exist when the NLRA and LMRA were enacted.

1052. ABA Task Force on Alternative Dispute Resolution in Employment, *A Due Process Protocol for Mediation and Arbitration of Statutory Disputes Arising Out of the Employment Relationship*. See naarb.org/due-process-protocol.

1053. The *Guidelines* can be found on-line at the web site of the National Academy of Arbitrators at: http:// naarb.org/employment-arbitration-policy-and-guidelines.

1054. H. Lewis and E. Norman, *Employment Discrimination Law and Practice*, 2d ed. §7.20 (2004).

Remedies available for Equal Pay Act violations include back pay, liquidated damages for willful violations, attorneys' fees and costs. Compensatory and punitive damages are not available, and injunctive relief is not available in an individual employee's action. When the EEOC brings suit under section 17 of the FLSA, it may obtain injunctive relief and recover unpaid wages but the EEOC is not awarded attorneys' fees or liquidated damages. The 'Paycheck Fairness Act of 2009' (Public Law 111-2) made provision for more aggressive enforcement of the Equal Pay Act, introduced incentives for compliance with the Act, reduced the scope of the 'bona-fide factor' defense, strengthened the no retaliation provision, and expanded the remedies available to victims of gender-based pay discrimination.

Chapter 12. Enforcement of the Worker Adjustment and Retraining Act

971. The Worker Adjustment and Retraining Act (WARN) (29 US Code §2101), also known as the federal Plant Closing Act, is enforced by a civil suit against the employer in federal district court. Employees can sue for wages and benefits owed as a result of the employer's failure to provide the required period of notification respecting a mass layoff or terminations. Similarly, if within three weeks of the layoff or termination the employer failed to pay affected employees the amount due them under the Act, suit can also be brought by a unit of local government to recover a civil fine of up to $500 for each day the employer failed to give that local government notice of the impending layoffs or terminations. In its discretion, the court may also award reasonable attorneys' fees to the prevailing party. (American courts normally do not award an attorney's fees as part of the recovery).

Chapter 13. Enforcement of the Family and Medical Leave Act (FMLA)

972. The Secretary of Labor is responsible for administration and enforcement of the FMLA (29 US Code §2601). The Department of Labor can use its investigative authority to examine employer records and to make inquiries in order to discover any violations of the Act. The affected employees can sue the employer in federal or state court within two years of a violation, or three years in the event of a willful violation, without prior recourse to any administrative procedures. An individual's right to bring an action is lost, however, if the Secretary of Labor sues on the individual's behalf or for injunctive relief.

Relief available under FMLA includes back pay and liquidated damages. An employer may avoid an award of liquidated damages by showing that it acted in good faith and with reasonable grounds for believing its conduct was lawful. Even if the FMLA violation did not result in any loss of pay, an employee may recover out-of-pocket expenses incurred because of the employer's FMLA violation, such as the cost of employing (for up to 12 weeks) a caregiver for a family member with a serious health condition. The prevailing employee (but not the Secretary of Labor) is also entitled to recover reasonable attorneys' fees, reasonable expert witness fees and other costs of bringing the action. (Such fees and costs normally are not allowed under American law.)

Part IV. Extraterritoriality (Choice of Law)

Chapter 1. Problems of Extraterritoriality among the States

973. Because the US is a federation of states with limited sovereign powers, legal issues arising in one state may involve claims of rights that are governed by the laws of another US state or by federal law. The Constitution of the United States addresses this possibility in the broadest terms where it provides in Article IV section 1: 'Full Faith and Credit shall be given in each State to the public Acts, Records, and judicial Proceedings of every other State.' Although the same provision gives Congress the power to regulate how such issues should be resolved, Congress has not legislatively adopted choice of law rules.

Under the Full Faith and Credit clause, however, Congress has adopted legislation requiring each state to give to the decisions of federal courts and courts of other states the same dignity it would give to its own courts in a like case and under similar circumstances.[1055] Thus, as a general rule, upon exhaustion of opportunities for appellate review, the decisions of one state's courts or administrative agencies must be treated as the law of the case (*res judicata*) by the courts of any other state presented with the same question involving the same parties. Therefore, unless fraudulently or corruptly obtained, the first jurisdiction's decision prevails with respect to the issues it decided even if the court to which the question is later presented believes that the court of the sister state was in error or that it did not have jurisdiction over the question.[1056] In addition, the Full Faith and Credit Clause does not compel a state to substitute the statutes of other states for its own statutes dealing with matters over which it has authority to legislate (jurisdiction).[1057]

A related, but different exception to the rule of finality of another state's judicial resolution arises when the state in which full faith and credit is sought is enforcing a program of benefits an employer is required to provide its employees. In that situation, the first state's decision respecting the extent of benefits owed by the employer does not prevent a sister state that has authority over the employment

1055. 28 US Code §§1738–1739.

1056. *Stoll* v. *Gottlieb*, 305 US 165 (1938); *University of Tennessee* v. *Elliott*, 478 US 788, 798–799 (1986). But *see* footnotes 1026 and 1027, below, and accompanying text.

1057. *Pacific Employers Ins. Co.* v. *Industrial Accident Comm'n*, 306 US 493, 501 (1939); *Franchise Tax Board of California* v. *Hyatt*, 538 US 488 (2003).

relationship from later deciding that under its own law the employer owes a more generous benefit.[1058]

State courts lack authority to control persons, activities, or property beyond their borders. Thus, in order for a state court to have jurisdiction (competence), there must be a legally significant contact between that state and the legal status of the defendant within the state or with the activities at issue. Hence, the state whose decision is asserted as controlling must have minimal contacts to impose its law on parties or events. Similarly, in order to lawfully bring parties into state court, that state must have minimal contacts with the parties or their activities, or receive the parties' consent to have their case tried by the court.[1059] If the first court acted without having authority over the persons or the subject matter, its decision is not entitled to full faith and credit by a sister state unless in the first court there was a full and fair opportunity to litigate the issue of whether it had jurisdiction and that challenge was not raised; that is, the objection was waived by the failure to assert it.[1060]

974. The generally accepted proposition is that a case is governed by the choice of law rules of the court in which the case is litigated. On the other hand, another generally accepted principle is that if the parties to a contract designate the jurisdiction whose law is to control the interpretation of that contract, the parties' choice will be honored unless that choice would alter the conflict of laws rules or the procedural rules of the court that hears the case.[1061] In addition, most courts do not enforce the rule of another jurisdiction if that rule violates a strong public policy of the state in which the contract is being enforced or if the transaction and the parties have no reasonable relationship to the state whose law was selected in the contract. Thus, on occasion courts refuse to abide by a contractual choice of law in cases involving a contractual restriction upon a former employee's competitive activity since protecting the competitive environment involves a strong public policy of the place in which competition is to be maintained.[1062]

1058. In *Thomas* v. *Washington Gas Light Co.*, 448 US 261 (1980), a decision in which a majority of Justices agreed upon the result but not the reasoning, Thomas worked for an employer headquartered in the District of Columbia and performed work there but, at times, also in two adjacent states. He was injured while working in an adjacent state and initially filed a workers' compensation claim in that state. He later filed a claim in the District of Columbia seeking more extensive disability benefits than those awarded by the state where the injury occurred. The Supreme Court rejected the employer's *res judicata* defense to the second claim. Some of the Justices who joined in allowing the second recovery indicated they would not have done so had the first state's law made it clear that the benefit awarded under its workers' compensation program was to be the sole workers' compensation recovery available to the claimant.

1059. E. Scoles, P. Hay, P. Borchers and S. Symeonides, *Conflict of Laws*, 3d ed., §§3.21–3.23, 8.4 (2000).

1060. *Durfee* v. *Duke*, 375 US 106 (1963).

1061. Scoles *et al.*, §§18.1–18.5 (2000); *Restatement, Conflict of Laws 2d*, §187; *Abf Capital Corporation* v. *Grove Properties Co.*, 23 Cal. Rptr. 3d 803 (Ct. App. 4th Dept., 2005).

1062. E. Scoles *et al.*, above, at §§18.4–18.8; *Blalock* v. *Perfect Subscription* Co., 599 F.2d 743 (5th Cir. 1979); *King* v. *PA Consulting Group, Inc.*, 485 F.3d 577 (10th Cir. 2007); G. Lester and E. Ryan, 'Choice of Law and Covenants Not to Compete: United States: Choice of Law and Employee Restrictive Covenants', *31 Comp. Lab. L. & Pol'y J. 389* (2010).

975. Initially, in the absence of a choice of law provision in the parties' contract, American courts applied the law of the place where the contract was made to determine whether the contract was enforceable and to interpret its meaning. In tort actions, American courts traditionally applied the law of the place where the injury occurred. Although a majority of states probably still adhere to these basic concepts, a significant number now use alternative approaches and some scholars contend that even where courts purport to apply the above traditional rules, they have recognized sufficient exceptions to constitute a substantial modification of those rules, especially in the torts area.[1063]

The principal alternative to the traditional rules is the 'most significant relationship' approach. Under this concept, the court applies the law of the jurisdiction that it finds had the most substantial contacts or interests respecting the transaction or events and the resulting dispute. Some suggest that in fact, under the guise of this analysis, and sometimes under the guise of more traditional analysis, judges seek the 'better' rule of law to apply to the circumstances of the particular case.[1064]

1063. F. Juenger, *Choice of Law and Multistate Justice*, pp. 116–118 (1993).

1064. F. Juenger, above, at pp. 169–170, 195–237; *Restatement, Conflict of Laws 2d*, §6 Comment to Subsection 2.

Chapter 2. The Law of Other Nations Applied in the US

976. The US Constitution does not automatically give decisions of the courts of other nations full faith and credit but, in the absence of applicable treaties or conventions, normally the federal and state courts recognize and enforce such decisions under the doctrine of comity.[1065] However, comity is not given to decisions of another jurisdiction whose exercise of jurisdiction over a person or activity is deemed unreasonable. In resolving that issue courts weigh whether the legal system in question would give reciprocal recognition to US judgments. In addition, comity is denied if the American court finds that the court issuing the decision does not adhere to fundamental rules of fair procedure.[1066]

Some treaties require that the decisions of the courts of the treaty partner be given full faith and credit. (Because both treaties and conventions have the authority of federal law, they have equal preemptive force on state courts.)[1067] Although this is required by some multilateral treaties, such as the Convention on the Recognition and Enforcement of Foreign Arbitral Awards, US bilateral treaties have avoided this subject.[1068]

Arbitration awards issued in other countries are enforceable in the US pursuant to its adoption of the Convention on the Recognition and Enforcement of Foreign Arbitral Awards (9 US Code §§201–208).

977. Choice of law rules when applied to the laws of other nations operate under the same principles as when applied to the law of sister states within the United States. These rules are discussed above in paragraphs 973–975. Moreover, courts in the US recognize the law of sister states without requiring that its specific contents be pleaded and proved and, under the Uniform Certification of Questions of Law Act, the high court in a majority of states will provide to another court a declaration of its law respecting unsettled matters. In contrast, although some states extend the same recognition to the law of other nations, in many instances the parties seeking recognition of foreign law must assist the court in understanding the foreign law by proof that includes testimony from expert witnesses.[1069]

1065. Scoles *et al.*, §24.6 (2000).
1066. Scoles *et al.*, §§24.33–24.37; *Restatement, Conflict of Laws 2d*, §403, Reporters Note 5.
1067. *Martin* v. *Hunter's Lessee*, 11 US 603 (1813); *United States* v. *Pink*, 315 US 203 (1942).
1068. Scoles *et al.*, above, §24.39.
1069. E. Scoles, P. Hay, P. Borchers and S. Symeonides, *Conflict of Laws*, 3d ed., §§3.47, 12.15, 12.17 (2000); *Restatement, Conflict of Laws 2d*, §474. *See also*, Hague Evidence Convention.

Chapter 3. Applying US Law beyond its Borders

978. Although an individual state of the United States cannot extend its legal authority beyond its borders, the Supreme Court has held that the law of the United States can control extraterritorial events. Moreover, some federal laws are specifically designed to regulate activity beyond US borders. For example, American corporations whose shares are publically traded are subject to federal criminal and civil sanctions if they, or persons or companies they control or substantially influence, directly or indirectly offer or give anything of value to officials or political candidates or political organizations of another country where the offer or gift is an effort to obtain or retain business, secure an improper commercial advantage, or cause such a person or entity to violate official duties unless such payment is lawful under the laws of that country (Foreign Corrupt Practices Act, 15 US Code §§78dd-1to 78hh-1).

On the other hand, the Supreme Court has held that it will find that Congress intended to give extraterritorial effect to its laws only if that intention is clearly expressed.[1070] Accordingly, in one case the Court held that even though a statute required that construction enterprises working under a contract with the federal government pay a 50 percent premium for work performed in excess of eight hours a day, the law did not expressly apply beyond US territory and, therefore, the Court ruled that it did not protect American workers employed by American companies doing such work in Iraq and Iran.[1071]

Consistent with the above proposition, in *EEOC* v. *Arabian American Oil Company*, 499 US 244 (1991), the majority of the Court concluded that the language of Title VII of the 1964 Civil Rights Act was not sufficiently clear in revealing a legislative intention to regulate the overseas employment of Americans by American corporations. A few months after this case was decided, Congress amended Title VII to expressly include US citizens employed in a foreign country as coming within the Act's definition of 'employee'. However, the amendment also stated that conduct otherwise prohibited by the Act is not unlawful 'with respect to an employee in a workplace in a foreign country if compliance … would cause such employer … to violate the law of the foreign country in which the workplace is located'.[1072] Similar language is found in the Age Discrimination in Employment Act. Demonstrating the limited nature of this extraterritorial protection, in applying the latter statute to the forced retirement at age 65 of an American working in Germany, the US Court of Appeals for the District of Columbia ruled that the employee could not sue its American employer for damages because the forced retirement had been ordered by the German Labor Court to avoid nationality discrimination in the application of the mandatory retirement rules established by the employer and its Works Council. The court explained that failure to force the worker's retirement would have violated German law and, therefore, could not be treated as age discrimination under the amended ADEA. It is unclear whether the court would have reached that

1070. *Benz* v. *Compania Naviera Hidalgo, S.A.*, 353 US 138 (1957); *RJR Nabisco* v. *EC*, 136 SCt 2090 (2016).
1071. *Foley Bros., Inc.* v. *Filardo*, 336 US 281 (1949).
1072. 42 US Code §2000e-1(b).

result if the worker had established that there were suitable transfer opportunities for him outside of Germany so that his continued employment would have ceased to affront the law of the host country.[1073]

The anti-discrimination laws allow for distinctions based on *bona fide* occupational qualifications even though qualifying characteristics, such as the requirement of advanced education, sometimes result in favoring particular groups. However, just as catering to local discriminatory customs is not sufficient to justify unlawful discrimination as a *bona fide* occupational qualification, it has been observed that the overseas legal compulsion defense must be based on law, not custom.[1074]

Extraterritorial effect was given to the NLRA in a case involving a representation proceeding initiated by an American union on behalf of American workers employed aboard an American owned dredge that was moved to Hong Kong harbor after the workers' representation petition had been filed. The dredge owner sought to enjoin the NLRB from conducting an election by mailed ballot on the ground that a portion of the dredge workers were required by Hong Kong law to be Hong Kong nationals employed under Hong Kong's employment regulations. The appellate court rejected the request for injunctive relief and held that the work fell within the jurisdiction of the NLRB because a ship is considered to be part of the territory of the territory where it is registered. On the ground of prematurity, the court expressly avoided reaching the question of whether it would be appropriate or even permissible to include Hong Kong nationals in the bargaining unit for which the election was to be held.[1075] On the other hand, a different federal appellate court ruled that because the NLRA does not expressly provide for extraterritorial application, the NLRB lacked authority to find an American employer guilty of an unfair labor practice when it terminated the employment of workers who, while on a temporary assignment in Canada, refused to continue to work unless their employer increased their per diem living allowance in an amount equal to amount the employer was saving on the original projected maximum it expected to pay for their daily lodgings.[1076]

Several courts have rejected efforts to obtain the extraterritorial protection of US labor laws when asserted by persons who were neither US citizens nor US residents.[1077] (However, *see* paragraph 984, below.) In one situation a Mexican national

---

1073. *Mahoney* v. *RFE/RL, Inc.*, 47 F.3d 447 (DC Cir.), *cert.* denied 516 US 866 (1995).

1074. Note, 'American Employees in the Arabian Gulf', 14 *N.Y.L. Sch. J. Int'l & Comp. L.* 317, 367–370 (1993).

1075. *NLRB* v. *Dredge Operators, Inc.*, 19 F.3d 206 (5th Cir. 1994).

1076. *Asplundh Tree Expert Company* v. *NLRB*, 365 F. 3d 168 (3d Cir. 2004). The NLRB has not accepted the Third Circuit's reasoning and continues to give remedies where the extraterritorial conduct affects labor-management relations within the United States. *California Gas Transport, Inc.*, 347 NLRB 1314 (2006), enforced without reaching this issue in *California Gas Transport, Inc.* v. *NLRB*, 507 F.3d 847 (5th Cir. 2007). See text in the last paragraph below for the tests of when a law is to be enforced even though some of the conduct in question was extraterritorial.

1077. *VanBlarion* v. *Burlington Northern R.R.*, 17 F.3d 1224 (9th Cir. 1994) (when US and Canadian railroads merged, Canadian citizens employed in Canada by a US owned railroad not protected by job security provisions imposed by US law); *Cruz* v. *Chesapeake Shipping, Inc.*, 932 F.2d 218 (3d Cir. 1991) (federal minimum wage and overtime laws not applicable to non-American seafarers on a US flagged ship that does not touch US ports and does not carry US cargo)(but see critique in *Dredge Operators*, above at footnote 54); *Carnero* v. *Boston Scientific Corp.*, 433 F.3d

applied at the Mexican office of an American company for work in the United States and was expressly rejected because he was over 40 years of age. Although the rejection for this reason clearly would have violated the Age Discrimination in Employment Act if he had applied for the job in the United States, an appellate court held that the Act was not intended to protect foreign nationals from age discrimination overseas and, therefore, did not protect the job applicant even though the work was to be performed in the US. The court justified its ruling on the ground that it was unwilling to bring a very large group of additional employees within the Act's protection unless Congress explicitly expressed such an intention.[1078]

The Court has also stated that even if a statute does not clearly indicate by language or context an extraterritorial purpose, if the conduct relevant to the statute's focus occurred in the United States, the statute can be enforced even if other conduct occurred abroad.[1079]

1 (1st Cir. 2006) (Argentinean working for an Argentine subsidiary of publically traded US corporation not given whistleblower protection under the Sarbanes–Oxley Act of 2002 when discharged for reporting that managers were defrauding shareholders by inflating sales figures. Although acknowledging that this result frustrates the Act's purpose of protecting US shareholders, it explained that the decision was necessitated by Congress' seeming failure to anticipate such cases with its resultant failure to designate a venue in which such suits can be brought.).

1078. *Reyes-Gaona* v. *North Carolina Growers Association, Inc.*, 250 F.3d 861 (4th Cir.), *cert.* denied 534 US 995 (2001).

1079. *RJR Nabisco* v. *EC*, 136 SCt 2090, 2101 (2016).

Chapter 4. Applying US Law to Foreign Nationals within US Borders

979. In an early decision, the Supreme Court declared that although the law of the United States is exclusive and absolute within its territorial boundaries, the nation can consent to limit the application of that law.[1080] Therefore, US law should be applied to foreign nationals employed or doing business in the territorial US unless by law or treaty Congress has exempted or excluded the foreign nationals or businesses from the particular laws. As discussed below, the Supreme Court often finds such exemptions or exclusions even though the statutory or regulatory rule in question does not expressly provide for that exception.

980. Most leading case decisions in this area involve merchant seafarers. For example, in *Benz* v. *Compania Naviera Hidalgo, S.A.*,[1081] a suit was brought under Oregon state law after workers refused to cross a picket line and, therefore, were unable to load cargo or repair a vessel docked in Portland, Oregon. The vessel was owned by a Panamanian corporation and operated under a Liberian flag with a crew from Germany and Britain. The union pickets supported the ship's striking crew which demanded improvements in their pay and work conditions. At the time, American ship owners often conducted their business under such foreign corporate and flagging arrangements (known as flags of convenience) to take advantage of resulting favorable tax and regulatory treatment. The union tried to have the suit dismissed on the ground that the state law and court were preempted by the LMRA. The Supreme Court, which did not discuss whether Americans owned or controlled the corporation that was seeking damages resulting from the union's activities, rejected the union's motion to dismiss. It reasoned that Congress did not fashion the LMRA to resolve labor disputes between foreign nationals and the master of a ship flying a foreign flag. Noting the diplomatic protests likely to result from imposing regulations on the operations of ships flying the flags of another nation, the Court concluded that it should not construe the US labor–management statute as intended to apply to such situations without that intention being clearly expressed by Congress.

The Court continues to follow the *Benz* decision's approach by applying a presumption against extending US labor laws to foreign vessels with foreign crews, even when the ship is in an American port carrying American cargo. Thus, in *McCulloch* v. *Sociedad Nacional de Marinaros de Honduras*,[1082] a case in which a labor organization was seeking an NLRB election to establish its status as the majority representative selected by the ships' crews, the Supreme Court held that even though the ships regularly carried cargo to US ports and were owned by an American corporation, the fact that the ships flew a foreign flag was enough to prevent

---

1080. *Schooner Exchange* v. *M'Fadden*, 11 US (7 Cranch) 116 (1812). See, too, *Garb* v. *Republic of Poland*, 440 F.3d 579, 585-86 (2d Cir. 2006) explaining the distinction drawn between extending sovereign immunity to the public acts of a foreign government but not to its private or commercial activities. *Also, see* discussion in paragraph 983, below.

1081. 353 US 138 (1957).

1082. 372 US 10 (1963).

their crews from obtaining the protection of the National Labor Relations Act. The Court also noted that the seafarers who were trying to invoke the NLRA were foreign nationals, not Americans. In a companion case,[1083] the Supreme Court upheld a state court injunction against picketing designed to organize the non-American crews of an Italian owned and operated ship which was registered in Liberia but which made regularly scheduled cruises out of New York. The Court explained that foreign-flag ships employing non-American crews are not covered by the regulations of the National Labor Relations Act because they are not engaged in 'commerce' within the meaning of that Act. Applying similar reasoning, the US Supreme Court has allowed a state court, applying state law, to enjoin peaceful picketing of a foreign-flag vessel where the picketing was designed to encourage a boycott of the vessel because its foreign crew worked for lower wages than American crews and thereby took jobs away from American seafarers. The majority of the Supreme Court explained that federal regulation of boycott activities did not preempt the state court from issuing an injunction because foreign-flag vessels with foreign crews do not engage in 'commerce' as that term is used in the NLRA.[1084] In a later, related case, by a 5–4 vote, the Court also rejected the argument that the state court injunction interfered with the picketers' freedom of expression. The Court majority noted that it long has treated picketing as combining conduct with expression and, therefore, has permitted states to impose reasonable restrictions on the conduct aspect of picketing when that conduct interferes with economic activity.[1085]

In contrast, the Court has protected the right of an American union to picket foreign-flag ships to protest substandard wages paid American longshore workers who load cargo onto the ships.[1086]

981. A 1953 Treaty between the United States and Japan provides that a company of one country is entitled to 'engage, within the territories of the other Party, accountants and other technical experts, executive personnel, attorneys, agents and other specialists of their choice'. Treaties with many other nations contain comparable or even broader language permitting foreign companies to favor their own nationals in staffing operations in the US.[1087] In *Sumitomo Shojio America, Inc.* v. *Avagliano*, 457 US 176 (1982), a corporation formed in the United States, but wholly owned by a Japanese company, tried to rely on the treaty in order to avoid having to answer charges that it discriminated against women in hiring and promoting workers to executive, managerial and sales positions. The Supreme Court rejected that defense on the ground that the treaty language, and the interpretation

---

1083. *Incres Steamship Co.* v. *International Maritime Workers Union*, 372 US 24 (1963). *See also*, *Lim* v. *Offshore Specialty Fabricators, Inc.*, 404 F.3d 898 (5th Cir.), *cert.* denied 546 US 826 (2005) (holding that a US court could not hear the Fair Labor Standards Act claim of Philippine residents employed by a US corporation aboard a foreign flag vessel operating in US waters since their employment contract, executed in the Philippines, established an arbitration tribunal and the Convention on the Recognition and Enforcement of Foreign Arbitral Awards made that provision enforceable).

1084. *Windward Shipping Ltd* v. *American Radio Association*, 415 US 104 (1974).

1085. *American Radio Association* v. *Mobile Steamship Association*, 419 US 215 (1974).

1086. *International Longshoremen's Association* v. *Ariadne Shipping Co.*, 397 US 195 (1970).

1087. *See*, for example, Article XII(4) of the 1954 Treaty of Friendship, Commerce and Navigation between the United States and Greece.

given to it by the diplomatic representatives of both countries, limits the term 'company' to those entities that are formed by the sovereign whose nationals are seeking to invoke treaty protection. Since the employing entity was formed in the United States, even though wholly owned by a Japanese company, the employing entity could not invoke the special privileges the treaty grants to Japanese companies. In reaching this decision, however, the Supreme Court left the door open to allowing a Japanese parent company to favor Japanese nationals in hiring or assigning employees to key managerial positions in its US subsidiary corporation. The Court noted that a *bona fide* qualification for some positions in a US operation of a Japanese parent company may require thorough knowledge not only of the Japanese language, but also of Japanese customs, culture, and business practices (a justification recognized by the antidiscrimination statute as a legitimate ground for nationality discrimination).[1088]

982. Federal appellate courts have permitted Japanese parent companies to give favored treatment to managers assigned to positions in the US when those Japanese nationals represent the parent company's interests in the operations of US subsidiaries. In reaching this result, the courts noted two considerations not discussed by the Supreme Court in *Sumitomo.*[1089] First, they emphasize that the discriminatory treatment at issue favored persons on temporary assignment to jobs involving oversight responsibility. The courts have suggested that such oversight is an exercise of what the appellate courts find to be a treaty protected privilege of the foreign parent company to direct its US operations even though those operations are carried out by a corporate entity chartered in the US.[1090] Secondly, the work forces in these cases included other persons of Japanese ancestry who were not given favored treatment.

983. Persons employed in the US by foreign embassies in household capacities are barred by the Vienna Convention on Diplomatic Relations, from bringing claims based on US labor protective statutes.[1091] On the other hand, under the Vienna Convention on Consular Relations, foreign consular personnel have a lower level of immunity from suits by their domestic servants.[1092]

Diplomatic immunity is a dimension of the broader customary convention of international law known as the doctrine of sovereign immunity. That doctrine has been codified in the US by the Foreign Sovereign Immunities Act (28 US Code §§1602–1611) which protects foreign governments and officials from suit in US courts when engaged in governmental activity. However, the statute expressly rejects the defense of sovereign immunity in suits arising out of the commercial activities of governments if those activities have a connection with US commerce

1088. 457 US at 189 n. 19.
1089. The *Sumitomo* case is described and cited in the previous paragraph.
1090. *Bennett* v. *Total Minatome Corp.*, 138 F.3d 1053, 1061 (5th Cir. Tex. 1998).
1091. *Tabion* v. *Mufti*, 73 F.3d 535 (4th Cir. 1996) (Philippine national employed in the US as a household servant of a Jordanian diplomat had no redress for claimed violations of minimum wage laws, breach of contract, and false imprisonment).
1092. *Park* v. *Shin,* 313 F.3d 1138 (9th Cir. 2002) (domestic cook could sue for FLSA violations where the Consul personally paid wages from own income and meal preparation for guests was only an occasional part of duties).

or have a direct affect on such commerce. The Act also rejects the sovereign immunity defense in maritime actions concerning commercial activity of vessels, or mortgage interests in vessels, suits respecting property taken in violation of international law, suits involving various types of property transfers where the property is located in the US, various types of suits for conduct causing injury to persons or property in the US, or enforcement of arbitration provisions in contracts with a foreign sovereign. Additionally, sovereign immunity cannot be asserted in a damages action against a sovereign or its officials resulting from heinous acts that violate the norms of international law.[1093]

1093. *Hilao* v. *Marcos*, 25 F.3d 1467 (9th Cir. 1994), *cert.* denied, 513 US 1126 (1995). *See also*, paragraph 984, below.

Chapter 5. US Court Application of the Law of Nations

984. Although the United States has been slow to adopt international conventions respecting employee rights and employment standards, the federal courts enforce established principles of international law. Thus, based on jurisdiction granted to federal courts by the Alien Tort Claims Act (28 US Code §1350), which was adopted in the late 18th century, American courts entertain suits against individuals or entities for conduct that violates the law of nations. However, the Supreme Court has stated that such claims must be grounded in the international norms that were recognized by the civilized world when the statute was adopted or are claims the civilized world presently recognizes which are 'defined with a specificity comparable to the features of' those recognized in the late 18th century.[1094]

Blackstone's Commentaries is the primary source of guidance used by lower federal courts in indentifying wrongs against the law of nations. *Blackstone's* specifically identifies offenses against ambassadors, violation of safe conducts, and piracy as wrongs against the law of nations. Nevertheless, lower courts have additionally listed claims based on state sponsored torture, genocide, slave trade, forced child labor, hijacking of aircraft, war crimes, and certain acts of terrorism as acts defined by international law with sufficient specificity and consensus to be wrongs covered by the Alien Tort Claims Act.[1095] In *Kiobel* v. *Royal Dutch Petro. Co.*, 569 US 108 (2013), the Supreme Court ruled that under the Alien Tort Claims Act relief is not available for conduct suffered by a non US citizen on the territory of another nation (as contrasted with on the high seas).

Another limitation on judicial enforcement of the law of nations is the US version of the acts of states doctrine which provides that if a claim is based on the improper governmental action of another nation, the dispute must be addressed by the political, not the judicial branch. Accordingly, under the acts of state doctrine the judiciary must stay its hand to avoid embarrassing the executive branch in international affairs. However, a suit against an official for personal conduct, as contrasted with authorized official conduct, falls outside of the acts of state defense. The defense also is not available if the foreign sovereign has indicated that it has no objection to the suit.[1096]

A related set of recent statutes, the Trafficking Victims Protection Act, provides criminal sanctions and civil remedies against perpetrators of human trafficking and involuntary servitude.[1097]

1094. *Sosa* v. *Alvarez-Machain*, 542 US 692, 725 (2004).

1095. *Aldana* v. *Del Monte Fresh Produce, NA, Inc.*, 416 F.3d 1242 (11th Cir. 2005); *Doe* v. *Exxon Mobile Corp.*, 654 F.3d 11 (DC Cir. 2011).

1096. *Hilao* v. *Marcos*, 25 F.3d 1467 (9th Cir. 1994), *cert.* denied, 513 US 1126 (1995).

1097. 18 US Code §§1589–1591, 1595. See, for example *US* v. *Kalu,* 791 F.3d 1194 (10th Cir. 2015)(applying the Act to impose prison term and restitution for victims where a recruiter of Philippine nurses used false promises regarding the level of work and compensation they would receive for the fees they paid, and when promises not fulfilled, coerced them to continue to pay fees or he would have them deported).

Selected Bibliography

TEXTS

R. Adams, *Industrial Relations Under Liberal Democracy*, 1995.

American Labor in the Era of World War II, 1995 (S. Miller and D. Cornford, eds.).

J. Atleson, *Labor & Wartime State: Labor Relations and Law during World War II*, 1998.

J. Atleson, *Values and Assumptions in American Labor Law*, 1983.

R. Bales, *Arbitration Law*, 2017 (with D. Nolan).

R. Bales, *ADR in the Workplace,* 2013 (with L. Cooper and D. Nolan)

R. Bales, *Understanding Employment Law 2d ed.*, 2013(with J. Hirsch and P. Secunda).

I. Bernstein, *The Lean Years: A History of the American Worker, 1920–1933*, 1960.

I. Bernstein, *Turbulent Years: A History of the American Worker 1933–1941*, 1969.

M. Bernstein and J. Bernstein, *Social Security: The System that Works*, 1987.

A. Blum, *A History of the American Labor Movement*, 1972.

D. Bok and J. Dunlop, *Labor and the American Community*, 1970.

D. Brody, *Labor Embattled*, 2005.

W. Bush, *The Family and Medical Leave Act*, 2d ed., 2017 (co-ed. with J. Paul).

R. Colker, *Federal Disability Law in a Nutshell,* 4th ed., 2010 (with A. Milani).

J. Conison, *Employee Benefit Plans in a Nutshell*, 3d ed., 2003.

R. Covington, *Employment Law in a Nutshell,* 4th ed., 2017 (with J. Seiner).

R. Craver, *Employment Law,* 4th ed., 2010 (with E. Shoben, E. Schroeder & M. Rothstein)

J. Dunlop, *The Management of Labor Unions*, 1989.

F. Elkouri and E. Elkouri, *How Arbitration Works*, 8th ed., 2016 (K. May, P. Sanders, M. Sullivan, eds.).

S. Estreicher, *Labor Law*, 2016 (with M. Bodie).

G. Fink, *Biographical Dictionary of American Labor*, 1984.

G. Fink, *Labor Unions*, 1977.

M. Finkin, *Cox and Bok on Labor Law,* 16th ed., 2016 (with R. Gorman & T. Glynn).

M. Finkin, *Privacy in Employment Law*, 4th ed., 2013.

R. Freeman and J. Rogers, *What Workers Want*, Ithaca, NY, 1999.

R. Freeman and J. Medoff, *What Unions Do*, New York, NY, 1984.

R. Freeman, *America Works: The Exceptional Labor Market*, 2007.

J. Getman, S. Goldberg and J. Herman, *Union Representation Elections: Law and Reality*, NY, 1976.

J. Getman, Pogrebin and Gregory, *Labor–Management Relations and the Law*, 1999.
J. Getman, *The Supreme Court on Unions: Why Labor Law is Failing American Workers,* 2016.
J. Getman, *Restoring the Power of Unions,* 2010.
R. Gorman and M. Finkin, *Labor Law Analysis and Advocacy*, 2013.
W. Gould, *A Primer on American Labor Law*, 2013 (5th ed.).
W. Gould, *Black Workers in White Unions*, 1977.
T. Haggard, *Understanding Employment Discrimination Law*, 2d ed., 2009.
J. Higgins, ed., *The Developing Labor Law,* 7th ed., 2 vols., 2017.
J. Hood, *Workers' Compensation and Employee Protections Laws in a Nutshell*, 65th ed., 2017 (with B. Hardy and L. Simpson).
J. Hutchinson, *The Imperfect Union: A History of Corruption in American Trade Unions*, NY, 1970.
J. Jacobs, *Mobsters, Unions, and Feds, NY, 2006.*
I. LeBeau, ed., *Employee Benefits Law*, 4th ed., 2017 (with J. Lewis and M. Rumeld, eds.)
R. Lee, *Eisenhower and Landrum-Griffin*, Lexington, KY, 1990.
R. Lee, *Truman and Taft-Hartley*, Lexington, KY, 1966.
D. Leslie, ed., *The Railway Labor Act,* 2d ed., Washington, DC, 2005.
B. Linderman, ed.., *Employment Discrimination Law*, 5th ed., 2013 (with P. Grossman and C. Weirich, eds.).
J. McClellan, *Crime Without Punishment*, NY, 1962.
F. McCulloch and T. Bornstein, *The National Labor Relations Board*, 1974.
H. Millis and E. Brown, *From the Wagner Act to Taft-Hartley*, Chicago, 1950.
D. Montgomery, *The Fall of the House of Labor*, 1987.
D. Nolan, *Labor and Employment Arbitration in a Nutshell*, 2d ed., St. Paul, MN, 2007.
W. Osborne, ed., *Labor Union Law and Regulation*, Washington, DC, 2003.
T. St. Antoine, ed., *The Common Law of the Workplace*, 2d ed., Washington, DC, 2005.
C. Summers and R. Rabin, *The Rights of Union Members*, 1979.
P. Taft, *Organized Labor in American History*, 1964.
P. Taft, *Rights of Union Members and the Government*, 1975.
D. Westman, *Whistleblowing: The Law of Retaliatory Discharge*, 3d ed., 2017 (with N. Modesitt).
A. Zack, *Public Sector Mediation*, Washington, DC, 1985.

GOVERNMENT PUBLICATIONS

M. Campbell and E. Brewer, eds., *The Railway Labor Act of 1926: Legislative History* (3 vols.).
NLRB, *Legislative History of the Labor–Management Relations Act, 1947* (2 vols.).
NLRB, *Legislative History of the Labor–Management Reporting and Disclosure Act, 1959* (2 vols.).
NLRB, *Legislative History of the National Labor Relations Act, 1949* (2 vols.).

US Dept of Labor, *Legislative History of the Labor–Management Reporting and Disclosure Act of 1959 – Titles I–VI.*

Selected Bibliography

Table of Cases

The numbers given refer to paragraphs.

Index

The numbers given refer to paragraphs.

Index

Index

www.ingramcontent.com/pod-product-compliance
Ingram Content Group UK Ltd.
Pitfield, Milton Keynes, MK11 3LW, UK
UKHW020129290926
15471UKWH00003B/380

9 789403 500133